On the Rails around The Alps

M000191549

THOMAS COOK

On 5 July 1841 Thomas Cook, a 33-year-old printer from Market Harborough, in Leicestershire, England, led a party of 570 temperance enthusiasts on a railway outing from Leicester to Loughborough which he had arranged down to the last detail. This proved to be the birth of the modern tourist industry. In the course of expanding his business Thomas Cook and his son John invented many of the features of organised travel which we now take for granted. Over the next 150 years the name Thomas Cook became synonymous with world travel.

Today the Thomas Cook Group employs over 10,000 people worldwide, with more than 1600 locations in over 100 countries. Its activities include travel retailing, tour operating and financial services – Thomas Cook is a world leader in traveller's cheques and foreign money services.

Thomas Cook believed in the value of the printed word as an accompaniment to travel. His publication *The Excursionist* was the equivalent of both a holiday brochure and a travel magazine. Today Thomas Cook Publishing continues to issue one of the world's oldest travel books, the *Thomas Cook European Timetable,* which has been in existence since 1873. Updated every month, it remains the only definitive compendium of European railway schedules.

The *Thomas Cook Touring Handbook* series, to which this volume belongs, is a range of comprehensive guides for travellers touring regions of the world by train, car and ship. Other titles include:

Touring by train

On the Rails around France (1995)
On the Rails around Britain and Ireland (1995)
On the Rails around Europe (Second Edition Published 1995)
On the Rails around Eastern Europe (1996)

Touring by car

On the Road around California (1994)
On the Road around Florida (1995)
On the Road around New England (1996)
On the Road around Normandy, Brittany and the Loire Valley (1996)

Touring by ship

Greek Island Hopping (1996)

For more details of these and other Thomas Cook publications, write to Passport Books at the address on the back of the title page.

ON THE RAILS AROUND

The Alps

A Comprehensive Guide to Travel by Train

Edited by Melissa Shales

PASSPORT BOOKS
a division of *NTC Publishing Group*

Published by Passport Books,
a division of NTC Publishing Group
4255 West Touhy Avenue,
Lincolnwood (Chicago),
Illinois 60646-1975 USA.

Text:
© 1996 The Thomas Cook Group Ltd
Maps and diagrams:
© 1996 The Thomas Cook Group Ltd

ISBN 0-8442-9993-6
Library of Congress Catalog Card
    Number: 95-71566

Published by Passport Books in conjunction
with The Thomas Cook Group Ltd.

Managing Editor: Stephen York
Project Editor: Deborah Parker
Map Editor: Bernard Horton
Additional maps: Caroline Horton

Cover illustration by Michael Bennallack–
    Hart
Text design by Darwell Holland
Text typeset in Bembo and Gill Sans using
    QuarkXPress
Maps and diagrams created using Aldus
    Freehand and GST Designworks
Printed in Great Britain by Silverscreen
    Print PLC, Newton Aycliffe, Co.
    Durham

Written and researched by
Kate Calvert
Paul Duncan
Robin Gauldie
Paul Murphy
Gillian Thomas and John Harrison

Series and Book Editor:
Melissa Shales

ABOUT THE AUTHORS

Melissa Shales is Series Editor, *Thomas Cook Touring Handbooks*. Former editor of *Traveller* magazine, she is the author of eight guides on destinations as far apart as India, Zimbabwe and France.

Kate Calvert started travelling at the age of two and has been going ever since. Her enthusiasm for farther flung cultures was fired by a classic round-the-world trip.

Paul Duncan corresponds regularly for a number of British and Italian publications, and has written a number of travel books on Italy.

Robin Gauldie is a freelance journalist specialising in travel and tourism. He is the author of a number of guidebooks, including several covering Greece.

Paul Murphy made his first grand tour of Europe at the age of 12. A full-time travel writer since 1989, he has written and contributed to many guidebooks.

Gillian Thomas and **John Harrison** are married and have three children. Both are freelance travel writers. John, who loves travelling anywhere by train, has spent many years with the BBC. Gillian worked for its News Office in Paris before she became a freelance journalist.

ACKNOWLEDGEMENTS

The writers and publishers wish to thank all the individuals and organisations who generously gave their time and expertise in the preparation of this book, and especially the following:

Austrian National Tourist Office, London; Austrian Railways; Berne Tourist Office; Dorint Hotels; Gruner Baum Hotel; Hotel Wilden Mann, Lucerne; InterCity Hotels; Interlaken Tourist Office; Jungfraujoch Railways; Klaus Kreher and Karin Rebbin, Deutsche Bahn, London; Anthony Lambert; Lauda Air; Evelyn Lafone, Swiss National Tourist Office, London; Lucerne Tourist Office; Lugano Tourist Office; Peter Mills and Christine Lagardère, French Railways, London; Carine Oberegger, Geneva Tourist Office; Niklas Ringel; Anne-Marguerite Raybaud, Chemin de Fer de Provence; Radisson Hotels; Heidi Reisz, Swiss National Tourist Office, London; Romantik Hotels; Jeanie Schaerer, Lausanne Tourist Office; Marie-Therésé Smith, French Government Tourist Office, London; Agatha Suess, German National Tourist Office, London; St Moritz Tourist Board; Swissair; Swiss Federal Railways; Marion Telsnig, Austrian National Tourist Office, London; Tourist Offices of Wels, Linz, Jenbach, Bludenz, Bad Ischl, Scladming, Spittal an der Drau, Villach, Klagenfurt, Melk and Graz; Zermatt Tourist Office; Zurich Tourist Board; the staff of all the Tourist Offices who provided assistance; and the editor and compilers of the *Thomas Cook European Timetable*.

Help us update

Thomas Cook Publishing are constantly updating this and their other rail travel titles in the *Thomas Cook Touring Handbooks* series. Prices, opening hours and other details are continually changing. Please do send us any corrections, updates or other contributions to the next edition. All will be acknowledged; those readers whose comments are most useful will be credited in the next edition, and will receive a free copy of the new edition (or any other guide in this series) with our thanks.

If you have any other comments or suggestions to improve future editions, please use the Reader Survey form at the back of this book. All replies will be acknowledged.

5

CONTENTS

ROUTES AND CITIES

*In alphabetical order. For indexing purposes, routes are listed in both directions – the reverse direction
to which it appears in the book is shown in italics.
See also the Route Map, pp. 8–9, for a diagrammatic presentation of all the routes in the book.
To look up towns and other places not listed here, see the Index, pp. 348–49.*

7

REFERENCE SECTION

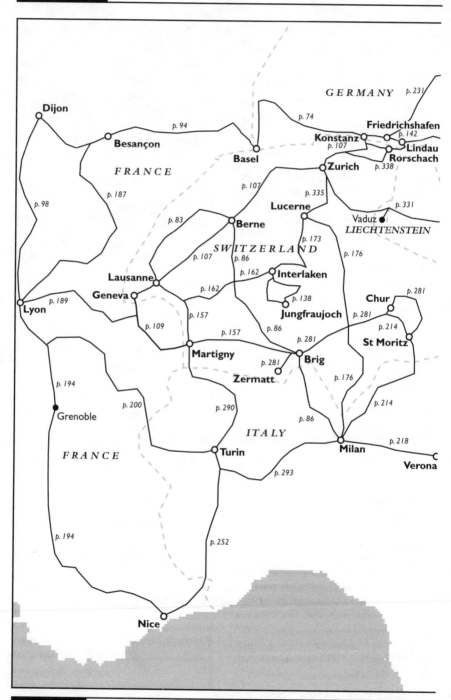

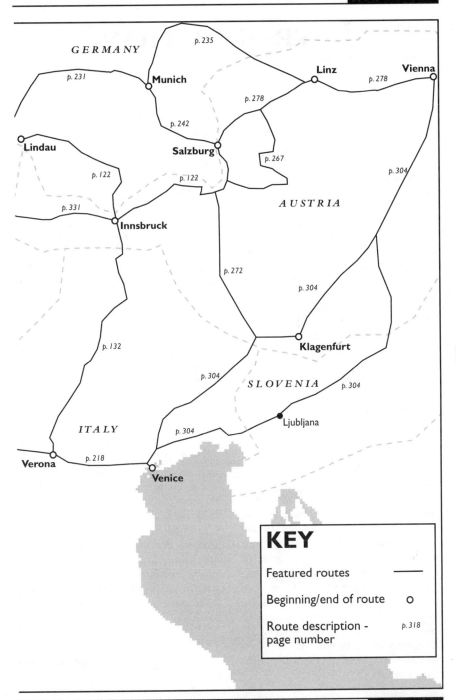

GERMANY

p. 231

Munich

p. 235

Linz

p. 278

Vienna

p. 242

p. 278

Lindau

Salzburg

p. 267

p. 122

p. 122

AUSTRIA

p. 304

p. 331

Innsbruck

p. 272

p. 304

p. 132

Klagenfurt

p. 304

SLOVENIA

p. 304

ITALY

p. 304

Ljubljana

Verona

p. 218

Venice

9

KEY

Featured routes	——————
Beginning/end of route	O
Route description - page number	*p. 318*

INTRODUCTION

Every Western child for the last 30 years has grown up with *The Sound of Music*. Astonishingly, this land of edelweiss, dirndl skirts, mountain lakes and snowy peaks is still alive and well, along with painted chalets, pretty as music boxes, emerald green meadows, cows with bells on, the music of Mozart, beer steins and cheese fondue.

The Alps are Europe's largest and youngest mountain range, stretching in a broad arc from the south of France through Switzerland, northern Italy, southern Germany, Slovenia, Liechtenstein and Austria. Altogether, they are over 965 km long and 200 km wide and cover more than 207,200 sq km. The highest peak in the range, and the high point of Europe, is Mont Blanc, on the French/Italian border, at 4807 m, but there are many mountains over 3050 m. The average height of the range is 1800–2400 m. With some 1200 glaciers, as well as many springs and, in early summer, gushing torrents of melting snow, this is also Europe's main watershed; both the Rhine and the Rhone start their lives here.

For thousands of years, these jagged mountains were a formidable barrier between the Germanic north and Roman south of Europe. But where armies fear to tread, money will always find a way and in the sheltered valleys grew wealthy trading cities such as Geneva and Zurich. The mountains themselves were virtually ignored until the 19th century introduced a new fashion for outdoor exercise. TB clinics sprouted in the clear mountain air, and hearty travellers began to stride across the passes or swing up cliff faces with crampons and ropes. Skiing, once a vital method of transport, became one of the world's most popular sports and a money-making machine for the Alpine regions.

Almost simultaneously, technology conquered the natural barrier. If engineers couldn't get over a mountain, they simply blasted a tunnel through it. To get people right up to the peaks, they developed funiculars and rack railways and a host of other ingenious forms of transport. Today, the Alps are a year-round holiday playground, particularly well-suited to travel by rail, with a wide network of lines, excellent trains and regular services to even some of the smallest villages, from where private railways power you up to the mountain heights.

This book covers all the major destinations – and a great many minor ones – accessible by train, together with an outer ring of cities, from Lyon and Milan to Venice and Vienna, which act as gateways as well as having world-class cultural importance. We have tried to be as accurate and as up to date as possible, but things do inevitably change; prices go up, restaurants close, and so on. We apologise in advance for any errors which may creep in over the life of this edition and would appreciate your help in keeping us up to date. Please do write in with any corrections, additions or suggestions, or simply with your experiences on the rails around the Alps.

Melissa Shales

HOW TO USE THIS BOOK

ROUTES AND CITIES

On the Rails around the Alps is formatted to reflect the way people actually travel by rail: not restricting themselves to one country but crossing borders (sometimes a bureaucratic process, but often hardly noticeable) and following where the international rail lines lead them.

Therefore, the book divides Alpine Europe (which covers Switzerland and Austria, as well as Alpine France, Germany, Italy and Slovenia) not into countries but into **recommended routes** – over thirty of them – chosen to make the most of the potential that rail offers for smooth connections between cities and nations (and often for sightseeing while travelling). For the most part each route begins and ends in a **key city**; these are major cultural and sightseeing centres or cities with important rail connections – thought they can be both. Every route and every key city has its own chapter in this book. Occasionally a route ends in a town not requiring a chapter to itself, so then the town description is placed in the route chapter, e.g. Martigny, covered at the end of the Turin–Martigny chapter.

The routes often cross borders; some of them can be travelled in a few hours, some would require a lot longer to complete without stopping. But stopping is the whole point; you can break your journey for a few hours or a few days, as you wish, at towns and cities along these routes, all of which are worth visiting in their own right. Many more **smaller cities, towns, attractions and points of interest** along each route are described in the order in which you will encounter them in the direction of the route. The direction in which the routes are laid out assumes that most readers will be beginning their travel at a 'gateway' city – Geneva, Lyon, Milan, Munich, Vienna, Venice, Zurich – and proceeding across the Alps. Bear in mind that, of course, every route we have suggested can be travelled in the opposite direction to the one we have given: for instance, the Basel–Konstanz route can also be travelled in the Konstanz–Basel direction.

The order of chapters is alphabetical: chapters on key cities are usually followed by one or more chapters describing routes beginning in those cities; e.g. the chapter on Berne is followed by routes from Berne to Geneva and to Milan.

The routes are designed to be used as a kind of menu from which you can plan an **itinerary**, combining a number of routes which take you to the places you most want to visit. By using the **Contents List** on pp. 6–7 (which list the routes in both directions) and the planning map on pp. 8–9, you can easily plan possible tours.

WITHIN EACH ROUTE

Each route chapter begins with a short introduction to the route, followed by a **route diagram** such as the one at the top of the next page. This summarises the route and shows the main intermediate stops, as well as intersecting routes and Side Tracks. The diagram is followed by a section on **Trains**, giving a good idea of frequency of service and other rail travel advice; it is often divided as follows:

11

Stops on the main route

Lausanne

Erlenbach

Zweisimmen

Château
d'Oex

Lenk

Montreux

Gstaad

Diablerets

Lausanne–Brig, p. 157

Side track
destinations

Intersecting route

FAST TRACK

This details the fastest rail service between the start and end cities, sometimes along a different line from the On Track.

ON TRACK

This is the full route, which takes in the towns along the way. Each point-to-point service is described separately. Journey times and frequencies can only be approximate, and you should use the local timetables (at the station) to verify exact departure times, etc.

You can pick and choose whether you visit all the suggested stops, or skip some of them.

SIDE TRACK

This heading is frequently used after a description of a place, to highlight departures from there, off the recommended route, that lead to places of interest; these may be described in full or indicated in a paragraph or two. In general, Side Tracks assume a detour longer than a simple half-day trip. The extent of the Side Track (before you rejoin the main route) is shown by the grey margins and the end-sign.

CITY DESCRIPTIONS

Whether a place is given a half-page description within a route chapter or is a key city with an entire chapter to itself, we have concentrated on practical details: local sources of **Tourist information**; **Getting around** in city centres (by public transport and on foot); **Accommodation** and **Food and drink**; post and phone **Communications**; **Entertainment** and **Shopping** opportunities; under **Sightseeing**, for reasons of space, we have often had to concentrate only on the highlights; tourist offices will provide you with plenty of extra information and ideas. The larger cities have all this detail; in smaller places some categories of information are less relevant and have been omitted or summarised. Where there is a something to say which would interrupt the flow of the main description, we have placed occasional **feature boxes**.

Although we mention good independently owned hotels in most places, we always also list the international hotel chains which have a property in the area, by means of code letters to save space, such as *BW* for Best Western. Such hotels are seldom found outside large cities in in this part of Europe. The codes are explained on pp. 342–43 along with the central booking numbers for the chains

MAPS

In addition to the diagram which accompanies each route, and the rail maps in colour at the end of the book, we provide maps of major cities (usually the central or historic area, or as far out as the main rail station where possible).

Symbols used on city maps

i	*Tourist Information*	🚌	*Bus Station*
✉	*Post Office*	M	*Metro Station*
†	*Church*	⚐	*Cathedral*

Abbreviations

To save space the following abbreviations have often been used in the text.

DM	Deutsche Mark	**km**	kilometres
FFr.	French Francs	**m**	metres
L.	Italian Lira	**min(s)**	minute(s)
ÖS	Austrian Schilling	**tel:**	telephone
SFr.	Swiss Francs	**Jan, Feb**	January, February etc
hr(s)	hour(s)	**Sun, Mon**	Sunday, Monday etc.

Addresses and Places

As well as the abbreviations, with their full versions and the English meanings, we also give the English equivalents of some unabbreviated words often found in place names and street signs. The obvious ones are not explained here (for instance, the word for 'museum' is recognisable in nearly all European languages. In this list, terms found in Germany also apply to Austria and German-speaking parts of Switzerland; words used in France and Italy will also be found in French and Italian regions of Switzerland.

Altstadt (Germany) Old Town

av. (France) Avenue

Bhf (Germany) Bahnhof; i.e. Rail Station

blvd (France) Boulevard

ch (France) chemin i.e. way

Dom (Germany) Cathedral

Gare (France) Station

Fussgängerzone (Germany) pedestrian area

Hbf (Germany) Hauptbahnhof; i.e. Main Rail Station

H

-kirche (Germany) Church

Landstr. (Germany) Landstrasse; i.e. Road

pl. (Germany) -platz (France) place i.e. Square

Pza (Italy) piazza; i.e. Square

r. (France) rue i.e. street

Rathaus (Germany) Town Hall

rte (France) route i.e. road

Schloss (Germany) Castle, Palace

See (Germany) Lake

-str. (Germany) -strasse, i.e. Street

V. (Italy) Via; i.e. Street

13

THE REST OF THE BOOK

Travel Essentials is an alphabetically arranged chapter of general advice for travellers in Alpine Europe. **Travelling by Train** takes a more detailed look at how the rail system operates, what tickets or passes you will need, sleeping cars, and so on. **Country by Country** is designed to provide a basic run-down of facts and advice on each of the nations covered in this book. Information common to many destinations within a particular country is given here and not repeated in each city description. **Sample Itineraries** gives advice about planning a trip and gives some themes and ready-made ideas for tours which you can use or adapt in your own planning.

At the end of the book, **Conversion** **Tables** provide a quick way of translating metric measures and Continental clothing sizes to their British and American equivalents, followed by two pages of **Hotel Central Booking Numbers and Codes**, decoding the abbreviations we use throughout the book for hotel chains, and providing information for remote booking of accommodation with them. **Through Routes** supplements our network of recommended routes with details of faster long-distance rail travel.

Finally, the **Index** is the quick way to look up any place or general subject. Use it to locate places, large and small, and topics of interest. And please help us by completing and returning the **Reader Survey** at the very end end of the book. Happy travelling!

TRAVEL ESSENTIALS

The following is an alphabetical listing of helpful tips for those planning an Alpine holiday by rail.

ACCOMMODATION

Europe offers an excellent choice of accommodation, from five-star hotels to room only. Your main problem may lie in finding something to suit your budget.

City tourist offices are almost always your best starting point if you haven't pre-booked. If they don't handle bookings themselves (there's usually a small charge), they will re-direct you to someone who does and/or supply you with the information to do it yourself – tell them your price horizons.

If you prefer to book hotels in advance, this can usually be done by Thomas Cook or another good travel agent at the same time as you make your travel arrangements.

This book indicates which of the major international or national chains are represented in each city, by means of initials under the 'Accommodation' heading: e.g. 'BW, Hn, Hd' means that Best Western, Hilton and Holiday Inn have branches there. Further details can be obtained from the chain's central reservations office (for phone numbers and decoded initials see pp. 342–343) or through a travel agent.

Hostelling International (HI)

For those on a tight budget, the best bet is to join **HI (Hostelling International)**. Membership of a national association will entitle you to use over 5000 HI hostels in 60 different countries and, besides camping, they often provide the cheapest accommodation. The norm is dormitory-style, but many hostels also have single and family rooms. Many offer excellent-value dining and many have self-catering and/or laundry facilities. Membership for those over/under 18 is currently: Australia A$44.50/22.30; Canada $25/12; England and Wales £9.30/3.20; Republic of Ireland £7.50/4; New Zealand NZ$30/11; Scotland £6/2.50; South Africa R.35 (free for those under 16); USA $25/10. Buy their directory *Hostelling International Europe* (£6.99 for the European edition), which lists hostel addresses, contact numbers, locations and facilities. Some are open 24 hours, but most have lock-out times and Reception's hours are usually very limited – so check what they are and advise them if you are arriving out of hours. It is not compulsory to reserve accommodation, but it is advisable – especially in summer, when many hostels fill well in advance and even those with space are likely to limit your stay to three nights if you just turn up. In winter (except around Christmas) bookings can be slow and it's worth asking if there are any special price deals available.

For information, to join, and to book accommodation in advance: Australia, *tel: (02) 565 1699*; Canada, *tel: (613) 237 7844*; England (and Wales), *tel: (01727) 855215*; Republic of Ireland, *tel: (01) 830 4555*; New Zealand, *tel: (03) 379 9970*; Scotland, *tel: (01786) 451181*; South Africa, *tel: (021) 419 1853*; USA, *tel: (0202) 783 6161*. Wherever we have given accommodation details, we have included hostels (represented by '**HI**').

15

In places where **rooms in private houses** are an option, local tourist offices can usually help by giving you a list – some will also help you find space. As well as being cheaper than hotels, this form of accommodation is a good way to meet local people, but you may be expected to stay for more than one night.

Camping

This is obviously the cheapest form of accommodation, if you are prepared to carry the equipment. There are campsites right across Alpine Europe, with facilities ranging from basic communal toilets and showers to luxury sites with dining-rooms, swimming pools and complexes of permanent tents, aimed at tourists with children. The drawback is that they are often miles from the city centres.

There is no really good pan-European guide to campsites, but most tourist offices can provide a directory for their country. Either contact them before you leave home or ensure you arrive in a new town early enough to get information from the local tourist office.

BICYCLES

Despite the Alpine hills, cycling is becoming more and more popular there. Indeed it is often the best way to explore locally. Mountain bikes with their fat tyres and multi-gearing are, after all, built for negotiating rough ground. However anyone who is new to this kind of terrain will probably find cycling steeply downhill almost as difficult as uphill because of having to keep the brakes on while still maintaining balance.

Bikes can be hired at stations throughout the Alps in Austria, Germany and Switzerland - often more cheaply than at a cycle-hire shop - and can be dropped off at another within the same country. In France, the only Alpine stations hiring out bikes are Annecy and Aix-les-Bains. None in Italy do so. Bikes can be carried on most local trains though there is an additional charge for this, except in France. On express services they usually have to be despatched separately as luggage and you may have to arrange this in advance. However French TGVs accept folding bikes in a special container free.

BORDERS

Land borders between the EU (European Union) countries are virtually non-existent and it's only if you arrive/leave by air or sea that you're likely to encounter any formalities. Checks between the EU and other West European countries are seldom more than perfunctory.

CHILDREN

Travelling by train with children is easier than you might think – as long as you have someone to help you haul bags and pushchairs up the steps. Most children find train travel a great novelty and thoroughly enjoy themselves. However, they can get bored on long journeys and become a menace to themselves, you and your fellow passengers, so make sure you are not short of ideas to keep them amused and have plenty of food and drink at hand.

If the children are old enough, ask them to keep a detailed travel diary. This will focus their attention on what they see and do, make them think about the whole experience (and remember it afterwards). Collecting and displaying anything from tickets and postcards to dried flowers can become a whole new game.

Most tourist destinations in Europe are reasonably well adapted for children and babysitters are not hard to find, if you ask at the local tourist office or church. Many hotels offer family rooms or provide a cot

Alpine Temperatures and Precipitation

This chart gives an idea of the average maximum and minimum temperatures and days of rainfall (and snowfall when the temperature is low enough) you are likely to encounter at various times of the year in sample destinations across the Alps.

	Lower Alps	Upper Alps	Munich	Venice	Vienna	Zurich
January						
Highest	5°C/41°F	-7°C/20°F	1°C/35°F	6°C/42°F	1°C/34°F	2°C/36°F
Lowest	-5°C/24°F	-11°C/13°F	-5°C/23°F	1°C/33°F	-4°C/25°F	-3°C/26°F
Rain days	9	16	16	6	15	14
April						
Highest	15°C/60°F	-2°C/29°F	14°C/56°F	17°C/62°F	15°C/58°F	15°C/59°F
Lowest	3°C/38°F	-6°C/20°F	3°C/38°F	10°C/49°F	6°C/42°F	4°C/40°F
Rain days	9	16	15	9	13	13
July						
Highest	26°C/79°F	8°C/47°F	23°C/74°F	27°C/81°F	25°C/76°F	25°C/76°F
Lowest	54°C/12°F	3°C/37°F	13°C/55°F	19°C/66°F	15°C/60°F	14°C/56°F
Rain days	7	18	16	7	13	14
October						
Highest	16°C/61°F	2°C/35°F	13°C/56°F	19°C/65°F	14°C/56°F	14°C/57°F
Lowest	5°C/42°F	-3°C/27°F	4°C/40°F	11°C/53°F	7°C/44°F	6°C/43°F
Rain days	9	13	13	7	13	12

in a normal double. If you can't find suitable restaurants, there is almost always a café or fast-food place with a children's menu or, at the very least, the sort of food they won't spit out. The biggest problem is keeping some sort of familiar routine going. Many sights and forms of transport accept babies for free, and children under 12 for half price.

For useful reading try: Maureen Wheeler, *Travel with Children*, (Lonely Planet, £5.95/US$10.95).

CLIMATE

The altitude of the Alps makes most places fresher in summer and snowier in winter than elsewhere in Western Europe. However temperatures are rarely extreme, though they can easily drop to minus 5° C

in winter depending how high you are in the mountains. Snow covers many towns and villages from January to March. The higher ski slopes, where the weather can be wonderfully crisp and sunny with the clear blue skies, usually remain open until well into April. Summers are pleasantly warm – around 23–27° C without any humidity – from June to September. The Mediterraean coast remains considerably milder throughout the winter and is several degrees hotter in summer. It is also the driest area. Elsewhere you can expect some rainy days – or snow in winter. May and June are the best months for Alpine flowers.

CLOTHING

As the Alps are predominantly a holiday

area, dress is mostly informal. You will rarely need dressy clothes except for dining at a classy restaurant or visiting a casino, but it pays to have some smart casual clothes for evening wear. Many places will bar those in jeans or trainers. Anyone wearing shorts or a sleeveless top may be excluded from some churches. You can encounter rain or cool weather at any time so at least one sweater and waterproof jacket are an essential part of your kit anywhere.

In addition, take at least two skirts or pairs of trousers; a pair of shorts; three to four shirts or blouses and three sets of underwear and non-synthetic socks (one on, one in the wash, one spare). For women, a huge t-shirt is useful for a beach cover-up and sleeping in, as well as during the day. Shoes should be comfortable, but light, and well broken-in before you set out, and a pair of flip-flops is useful for unhygienic showers and overnight travel. Other than that, look for comfortable, easily washable clothes that pack small and do not need ironing.

For hot weather, clothes should be kept loose and made of cotton or cotton-mix – the least sticky in summer. For changeable weather, it's practical to wear several layers. In midwinter, when trains can be less than cosy, you will need a warm coat or cold-weather jacket, a scarf, hat, gloves and sensible, non-slip footwear. However you can rely on bars, restaurants, hotel and guest houses being very warm indeed.

Pack a tube of Travel Wash (available from most chemists) and a piece of string to serve as a washing line, so you can wash clothes through as you travel and save on the expense and inconvenience of using a launderette.

If you plan to do some serious walking, or just take a cable car remeber that the highest mountains have snow all year.

Shops throughout the Alps are invariably well-stocked with outdoor gear, from boots to jackets and accessories. Prices may be higher than at home, but you can rely on good quality and plenty of choice.

Similarly for skiers, boots and equipment can be hired in every resort, either by the day or longer. Ski-wear is also on sale everywhere during the winter season. Though ski-shops are usually more expensive than department stores, they often have plenty of bargains on offer, including second-hand boots, at the end of the season. In general Alpine shops are strong on design and you can be sure of finding all the latest trends in clothes as well as ski and walking boots.

CONSULAR SERVICES

Most embassies/consulates/high commissions will lend a helping hand if their nationals have *real* problems – and charge a small fee for any services rendered. The Australian, Canadian, UK and US embassies produce free leaflets outlining their services. Help should be available if: a) your passport is stolen (or a replacement travel document to get you home); b) if there's a death or serious accident (advice on procedures, next of kin notified – probably also sympathetic help); c) if you go to jail (don't expect sympathy, or direct intervention, but they will explain your rights and tell you how to get a lawyer).

Should something happen to make the area dangerous (an act of God, local rebellion etc.) contact your embassy to register your presence and ask for advice.

In case of real financial trouble, embassies *may* agree to make a small loan or contact next of kin with a request for help, but they do not look kindly on people who have simply overspent.

Do *not* expect them to act as surrogate travel agents, banks, interpreters, etc. That is not their function. If your own country has no representation, contact one with which it has ties, e.g. Commonwealth citizens can try the British Embassy. They may help and you should at least get some advice about what to do next.

CURRENCY

The European Union countries and Switzerland place no limit on the import/export of currencies. That said, it is never advisable to carry more cash than necessary and it is sensible to take most of your money (but not all – some small-denomination local cash is essential) in the form of Eurocheques, travellers' cheques and credit cards. Don't rely too heavily on credit cards; fraud has made some people wary of them. There is no black market in currency in Western Europe.

The Thomas Cook offices listed throughout this book will cash any type of Eurocheque/travellers' cheque and will replace Thomas Cook travellers' cheques if yours are lost/stolen.

Always try to obtain a little local currency before you enter a new country. If you are unable to do so and arrive outside banking hours, the best bet (albeit an expensive option) is to ask the receptionist at a big hotel to change some for you.

Try to ensure you always carry one or two coins of each denomination, so that you don't get caught out by not having the right change for slot machines.

In border towns and on cross-border transport, you can almost always use either of the relevant currencies (a good way to dispose of excess coins), but you generally pay less if you choose the one in which prices are marked.

CUSTOMS

Importing narcotics and offensive weapons is banned throughout Europe – and penal-

ties for carrying them can be very severe; so do not be tempted, and do not carry things for anyone else, especially when you are crossing borders.

Professional crooks are very good at passing themselves off as harmless and in need of help, and some people are languishing in jail today because they believed a hard-luck story or did someone a 'small' favour. Pornography is also banned in many countries and, since it is notoriously difficult to define, it is better to avoid carrying anything that might offend. If you have to take a prescribed drug on a regular basis, carry something (such as a doctor's letter) that will prove it is legitimate.

Customs Allowances in the EU

European Union member states (Austria, France, Germany and Italy) have set the purchase of tobacco, alcohol and perfume at the same basic allowance for each country and these apply to anyone aged 17 or over. (For Liechtenstein, Switzerland and Slovenia see Country by Country).

To all intents and purposes, there are no restrictions between the EU countries for goods bought in ordinary shops and including local taxes, but you may be questioned if you have excessive amounts. Allowances are:

800 cigarettes, 200 cigars, 400 cigarillos and 1 kg tobacco

+ 90 litres wine (max. 60 litres sparkling)

+ 10 litres alcohol over 22% volume (e.g. most spirits)

+ 20 litres alcohol under 22% volume (e.g. port and sherry)

+ 110 litres beer.

The allowances for goods bought outside the EU and/or in EU duty-free shops are:

200 cigarettes or 50 cigars or 100 cigarillos or 250 g tobacco★

19

+ 2 litres still table wine
+ 1 litre spirits or 2 litres sparkling or fortified wine
+ 8 litres Luxembourg wine if imported
via the Luxembourg frontier
+ 50 g/60 ml perfume
+ 0.5 l/250 ml toilet water.

*Some EU countries have more generous
tobacco allowances for non-Europeans
arriving from outside Europe, so check in
the duty-free shop or with your carrier.

Allowances for those returning home:

Australia: goods to the value of Aust$400
(half for those under 18) plus 250 cigarettes or 250 g tobacco and 1 litre alcohol.
Canada: allowances apply to anyone aged
19 or more (a year younger if you are
entering AL, MN or QU). You are
allowed 50 cigars and 200 cigarettes and
400 g tobacco plus 1.1 litre alcohol or 24
x 355 ml bottles/tins beer, as well as gifts
not exceeding Can$60 each in value.
New Zealand: goods to the value of
NZ$700. Anyone over 17 may also take
200 cigarettes or 250 g tobacco or 50 cigars or a combination of tobacco products
not exceeding 250 g in all plus 4.5 litres of
beer or wine and 1.125 litres spirits.
South Africa: goods to a total value of
500 Rand. Those aged 18 or more are
allowed 400 cigarettes and 50 cigars and
250 g tobacco plus 2 litres wine and 1 litre
spirits plus 50 ml perfume and 250 ml toilet water.
Republic of Ireland and **UK:** standard
EU regulations apply (see foregoing notes
and above).
USA: goods to the value of US$400 as
long as you have been out of the country
for at least 48 hrs and only use your
allowance once every 30 days. Anyone
over 21 is also allowed 1 litre alcohol plus

100 (non-Cuban) cigars and 200 cigarettes
and a reasonable quantity of tobacco.

DISABLED TRAVELLERS

Europe, in theory, provides more facilities
for the disabled traveller than many other
parts of the world. In practice, however,
those facilities that do exist often fall short
of real needs and expectations, and there
may be a shortage of helpful bystanders.
Travel is feasible, but it will almost
inevitably be more expensive, as it is usually only the modern trains and more upmarket hotels that cater for the disabled
traveller. You will also have to throw out
any thought of spontaneity and make
meticulous plans, always writing and
phoning ahead to make sure you have a
reservation and that there is someone on
hand to help you. The amount of advance
warning required for trains varies. For
example, Austrian State Railways ask for
three days' notice, while the ever-efficient
Swiss need only one day.

There are two main problems to face
with the trains – how to get onto them,
and whether there is space for you once on
board. Although modern rolling-stock
tends not to have wide gaps between train
and platform, in many stations the platforms are quite low and passengers have to
climb steep steps to board trains. Once
aboard, only the more modern carriages
provide space for a wheelchair; otherwise,
space will be provided in the baggage car.
The new express services, such as the
French TGV, do provide proper facilities
for disabled travellers.

National rail offices may have leaflets
about rail travel for disabled travellers and
offer discount passes.

UK information: RADAR, *Unit 12,
City Forum, 250 City Rd, London EC1V
8AF; tel: (0171) 250 3222,* publish an
annual guide called *Holidays and Travel*

Abroad (£5 inc. postage), which contains useful addresses and gives details of facilities for the disabled in different countries, including their trains.

US information: SATH (Society for the Advancement of Travel for the Handicapped), *347 5th Ave, Suite 610, New York NY 10016; tel: (212) 447 7284.*

For useful reading try: Susan Abbott and Mary Ann Tyrrell's *The World Wheelchair Traveller* (AA Publishing, £3.95); and Alison Walsh's *Nothing Ventured: A Rough Guide Special* (Penguin, £7.99).

DISCOUNTS

In many countries reductions are available on public transport and on entrance fees for senior citizens, students and the young. Some proof of your eligibility is usually required, so always carry something that will provide evidence of your status, e.g. an official document that shows your age or a student card.

If you are a student, get an International Student Identity Card (ISIC) from your student union, as this is recognised everywhere and offers a wider range of discounts than national union cards.

Some destinations offer (for a small fee) a book of discount vouchers covering anything from museums to restaurants. Many discount passes for tourists, including some rail passes, must be purchased before you leave home as they are not available in the country itself. Contact the relevant tourist offices to ask about any such deals.

DRIVING

If you might want to hire a motor vehicle while you are away, check requirements with the AA/RAC, or your own national motoring organisation, well before you leave, so that you have time to get any

necessary documentation and additional insurance cover.

To hire a vehicle (except a moped), you usually have to be over 21, with two years' driving experience. In most European countries your national licence is valid for up to six months, but you may need a translation as well and it can be easier to get an international licence. Always check that the vehicle is in good condition before you set out, with especial attention to brakes, lights and tyres (including the spare).

Most road signs are standardised throughout Europe, but the quality of signposting varies dramatically, as do speed limits. Check for local peculiarities before you set out. Except in the British Isles, Europeans drive on the right.

ELECTRICITY

With a few exceptions, the European countries use 220V. The shape of plugs varies and, if you are taking any sort of electrical gadget, you should take a travel adaptor. It is unlikely that you will face power cuts, but a small torch (flashlight) is a useful back-up and essential if camping.

HEALTH

Before you go

Europe, as a whole, is reasonably hygienic and there are no compulsory vaccination requirements. However, it is always advisable to keep your tetanus and polio protection up to date and vaccination against typhoid and hepatitis A is also a good idea. You must be able to produce a certificate against yellow fever if you have been in a yellow fever endemic zone in the six days before entering Europe. It's always a good idea to visit your dentist for a check-up before you leave home.

If you are a UK citizen, you should fill

in Form E111 before you go (available from post offices). This (free) form entitles you to treatment under the reciprocal health arrangements that exist across most of Europe, but only on the same basis as citizens of the country. This means you may have to pay up-front and reclaim the cost when you return home – and/or some parts of your treatment may not be free. Therefore it may be better to take out an insurance policy that provides medical cover (see Insurance, p. 22). Procedures for each country are detailed in the booklet containing the form. It's worth visiting a pharmacy before consulting a doctor: European pharmacists tend to be well trained and may well save you medical bills by prescribing something that solves your problem.

Risks

Although most of Europe is temperate, there is a definite risk of sunburn in the south and in high mountain areas. Don't spend hours outdoors without using a sun protection cream. If you are skiing it needs to be a high-factor one as the sun is fiercer and burns more quickly when you are high up with dazzling snow all around.

Holiday romances are all very well, but don't get so carried away that you forget all about AIDS – and other unpleasant sexually-transmitted diseases. If casual sex is your scene, fine, but do take precautions – one glorious night is not worth a (short) lifetime of regret.

Rabies exists in Continental Europe and, while the risk is very small, you should be wary of stray and wild animals. Lyme disease – caught from ticks in undergrowth – is present in Central European forests. Wear long trousers and long-sleeved shirts to avoid picking up these insects. Symptoms are similar to arthritis and if they show up within 3

months of possible exposure ask your doctor for a blood test; early treatment is nearly always effective.

Food and water

Tap water in throughout the Alps is safe to drink. If in doubt, buy tinned or bottled drinks and water.

HITCHHIKING

If you are on a budget, you may want to try hitchhiking, rather than using public transport. This can be fun and is a good way to meet the locals, but it can also be dangerous. To avoid trouble, don't hitch alone, or take any ride when you are outnumbered or clearly physically weaker than the people in the car.

INFORMATION

Addresses of national tourist offices are given in the Country by Country section. Once in a new town, look for a sign displaying a lower case **i** (often black or white on a blue or green background), which is the usual symbol for information in Europe. It may indicate merely a noticeboard (or similar), but, with luck, may point you towards a tourist information office.

Even the smallest towns invariably have one - the Alps are a prime tourist destination - though, except in Germany, they are liable to close for one or two hours at lunchtime. Opening hours also tend to be shorter on Sundays. Try to get hold of a street map in advance so that you can at least find your way around if the office is closed when you arrive. To get your bearings, head early on for a highspot like a church tower for a bird's eye view of the local layout.

INSURANCE

Take out travel insurance that covers your

health as well as your belongings. It should also give cancellation cover and include an emergency flight home if something goes really wrong. The Thomas Cook Recommended Traveller Insurance package offers comprehensive medical insurance, including repatriation, as well as travel cover and is available from all Thomas Cook retail travel shops in the UK. If you are likely to do something that might be classified as risky (e.g. ski, drive a moped, paraglide), make sure your policy does not exclude that risk. Thomas Cook offers a ski insurance policy. Enquire at any Thomas Cook branch in the UK.

LANGUAGE

Arm yourself with a copy of the *Thomas Cook European Travel Phrasebook* (£4.95/US$7.95) if you are visiting countries where language is likely to be a problem. It contains over three hundred phrases, each translated (with phonetic spellings) into a number of European languages including French, German and Italian. Phrases cover the everyday needs of a rail traveller, from arriving in a station to booking accommodation, eating out, changing money and coping in an emergency.

Before you go, learn a few basic phrases, such as: 'Hello. I'm sorry, but I don't speak ... Does anyone here speak English?'.

Your chief asset, if you have no language in common with the people you meet, will be your willingness to use sign language. It's amazing what you can do without words, as long as you are prepared to have a go. If you want to know where the post office is, for example, showing someone an addressed envelope may get the message across. Smiles also go a long way towards breaking the ice and encouraging people to be helpful, but be careful that your friendliness is not misinterpreted.

Keep a pen and paper handy at all times, then you can ask people to write down such figures as times and prices. Similarly, if they don't understand your pronunciation, you can write down what you are trying to say and let them read it – or vice versa.

LUGGAGE

Always travel as light as possible. The amount of space available for storing luggage on trains varies considerably. Soft-sided bags may be less secure than hard suitcases, but are lighter and easier to squeeze into cramped spaces. Backpacks are the best option if you have a lot to carry; otherwise, go for a large, zippable canvas or plastic bag, with a shoulder strap to leave your hands free.

If you're buying a backpack for the first time, shop carefully and be prepared to spend a bit more than the minimum to ensure comfort and durability (the best brands have a lifetime guarantee). Essential features are a strong internal frame, padded shoulder straps and a hip strap, to lift the bulk of the weight away from your neck. Some frames are specially adapted for women. Don't be too ambitious about how much you can carry – 50 litres for women and 60 for men is about right.

Most stations (and other transport hubs) have baggage lockers. These are your best option unless your luggage is very bulky though security alerts occasionally result in them being taken temporarily out of service. Most stations also have manned luggage offices, though these often close for lunch and are unlikely to be open after mid-evening. Also they usually charge per item.

Many stations will forward your bags to your next destination, but check that the office there will be open when you arrive.

23

OPENING HOURS

A rough guide to opening hours is given in the Country by Country section, but there are many variations and you should not assume that, for example, every bank will be open during all the banking hours listed – while some may stay open longer. Sunday is the usual closing day for shops and businesses (and public transport tends to be sparse), while many tourist attractions remain open on Sun, but close on Mon or Tues. Timings are also subject to seasonal variations, with many places closing altogether in winter. The definition of summer and winter (especially in areas with a distinct seasonal difference) often changes every year and is determined by the weather in spring and autumn, so anyone travelling between the seasons should be prepared for changes to the advertised opening times.

PASSPORTS AND VISAS

EU citizens can travel to other EU countries with a National Identity Card in lieu of a full passport, but do ensure that any identity document is valid well beyond the end of your stay. British citizens need a full passport. The individual requirements for West European travellers are given in the Country by Country section. As for non-European travellers, this book concentrates on requirements for citizens of Australia, Canada, New Zealand, South Africa and the USA; others should check requirements with the relevant embassies in good time to get any necessary documents. *Anyone* planning to stay more than 90 days in a single country may need a visa and should check well before travelling.

Some countries will refuse entry to anyone who does not have an onward/return ticket and visible means of support. How this is defined can vary, but in essence it means having sufficient money to cover the cost of food, accommodation and other expenses during your stay. A credit card is a practical way of avoiding precise cash requirements.

In many cases visa requirements have more to do with residence than with nationality, e.g. the visa requirements for an Indian living in India and an Indian living in the UK may be different. People who live abroad should check which regulations apply to them.

Where a country is not mentioned specifically, nationals of that country should assume that they need both a full passport and a visa. Even if you can theoretically obtain a visa at the border, it is probably easier to get it in advance. Allow plenty of time, especially if you need to get several, as it can be a long process. Bear in mind that most visa departments have short, and often eccentric, opening hours. You will also need a whole stack of passport photos and will find that many countries ask you to pay in cash or by postal order and will not accept cheques or credit cards.

PUBLIC HOLIDAYS

These have been listed under the individual headings in the Country by Country section. Many are religious holidays, whose dates vary from year to year; these are given by name rather than date, in chronological order.

The principal ones are Good Friday and Easter Monday (March/April); May Day; Ascension Day (the 6th Thursday after Easter); Whitsun/Pentecost (on Monday, 11 days after Ascension); Corpus Christi (early June) and Christmas Day. If an official holiday falls on a weekend, the following Mon or Tues often becomes a holiday as well. Over Christmas most things close altogether; on most other public holidays a good rule of thumb is to assume that Sun hours/schedules will apply.

There are some local festivals (e.g. saints' days) which are celebrated only in one town but which can disrupt everything in the area. Some are noisy, colourful and great fun, others nothing more than an interruption to normal service. If time is important to you, check in advance to see if your visit will coincide with any sort of holiday and, if it does, bear in mind that all transport services are liable to be severely restricted. Always double-check schedules locally.

SALES TAX

Value Added Tax is automatically added to most goods in Western European countries. The level varies, but is usually 10–20% (in Switzerland it can be as low as 6% and in France as high as 23% on some items). It may, or may not, be shown separately on price tags.

In most places, non-residents can reclaim the tax on major spending. This often applies to receipts over £30, but every country sets a different limit. The refund is also intended to apply to only one article, but if you buy several things in the same shop on the same day, the authorities seldom argue.

In order to reclaim your Value Added Tax, ask the shop assistant to fill in a tax refund form for you. Show the form, the receipt and the goods to Customs on leaving the country and they will give you an official export certificate. This can sometimes be exchanged on the spot; alternatively, post the certificate back to the shop (within a month) and (in due course) they will send the refund. Many shops will send the goods directly to your home, but anything you save in paperwork at the time is likely to be offset by Customs formalities in your own country.

SECURITY

The best way to avoid becoming a victim of theft is to give the impression that you are not worth robbing (e.g. do not flash expensive jewellery or rolls of banknotes). Use a hidden money-belt for your valuables, travel documents and spare cash. Never carry a wallet in a back pocket or leave your handbag open and use a bag with a shoulder strap slung horizontally. In public places, take precautions with anything that is obviously worth stealing – wind the strap of your camera case round the arm of your chair and place your handbag firmly between your feet under the table while you eat. Never leave luggage unattended – apart from the risk of theft, many countries are very terrorist-conscious and chances are it will create a bomb scare. Use baggage lockers if you arrive at a place one morning and intend to leave the same day. When using computerised lockers, be careful that nobody sees your re-entry code.

When you're sleeping rough, in any sort of dormitory or on trains, the safest place for your small valuables is the centre your sleeping-bag – determined thieves have been known to slice off the bottom. In sleeping-cars, padlock your luggage to the seat and make sure the compartment door is locked at night. There is a tendency for backpackers to trust each other, but don't take this too far. Like other groups in society, some are the good guys; others are not. Be particularly safety-conscious in areas around travel terminals, especially in large cities.

Mugging is a problem in some areas, but not rife in European city centres, where pickpockets are usually the main threat. If you are attacked, let go of your bag (or anything else of obvious value) – you are more likely to be attacked physically if the thief meets with resistance. If

---

The Thomas Cook Worldwide Network Customer Promise

Customers who purchase their travel product from any Thomas Cook Worldwide Network office are entitled to the following services at any other Worldwide Network travel location, free of all standard agency service charges:

airline reservations
airline ticket reconfirmation, revalidation or re-routing
changes to travel arrangements
hotel reservations
car rental reservations
travel planning assistance
emergency assistance

These services are available at all Thomas Cook travel agency locations (not bureaux de change) mentioned in this book.

---

you do run into trouble, report the incident to the local police without delay, even if it is only to get a copy of their report for your insurance company.

Carry half a dozen passport photos (useful for all sorts of purposes) and photocopy the important pages and any relevant visa stamps in your passport. Store these safely, together with a note of the numbers of your travellers' cheques, insurance policy and credit cards (keep this away from the documents themselves). If you are unfortunate enough to be robbed, you will at least have some identification – and replacing the documents will be easier.

SMOKING

Smoking is now banned in many public places and, even where it is allowed, there may be a special area for smokers. In some countries, such as France and Italy, the prohibitions are often ignored by the locals, but play safe if in doubt and ask before lighting up.

TELEPHONES

You should have few problems finding a phone in European towns and everywhere is on direct-dial. Useful telephone numbers are provided throughout the book and in the Country by Country section you will find advice on how to make calls, together with emergency phone numbers.

TIME

There are several time zones within Europe but everywhere in the Alps uses Greenwich Mean Time + 1hr in winter and + 2hrs in summer.

TOILETS

Although not a universal concept, pictures representing a male and a female are commonly used in Europe. The term 'WC' is also quite widespread and if you see words beginning 'toilet' or 'lava' you are probably (though not necessarily) on the right track.

In some countries you may come across

places where both sexes use the same facilities, even if there are separate entrances, so don't assume automatically that you are in the wrong place. The quality varies considerably. Many are modern, clean and well-equipped, others are of the hole-in-the-ground variety or not very well maintained. So be prepared for anything. This includes always carrying some paper, as you will be very lucky if you never find it missing.

Unfortunately not all countries recognise the need for public facilities and they can be difficult to find, so make use of anything the station has to offer before you set out to explore. You can often get away with using the facilities in hotels if you look as if you might be staying there. If not, service stations or eating/drinking places are the best bet – but be prepared to buy something as, understandably, many reserve the use of their facilities for their clients.

USEFUL READING

Thomas Cook Publications

The *Thomas Cook European Timetable (ETT)*, published monthly at £8.40, has up-to-date details of most rail services and many shipping and ferry services throughout Europe. It is essential both for pre-planning and for making on-the-spot decisions about independent rail travel around Europe. A useful companion to it is the *Thomas Cook New Rail Map of Europe* (£5.65). Both of these publications are obtainable from some stations, any UK branch of Thomas Cook or by phoning *(01733) 268943*. In North America, contact the **Forsyth Travel Library Inc.** *1750 East 131st St, PO Box 480800, Kansas City, MO 6414; tel: (800) 367 7984* (toll-free).

Thomas Cook Travellers (£7.99), pub-lished in the USA as *Passport's Illustrated Travel Guides* ($12.95), cover the following major Alpine destinations: Munich and Bavaria, Provence, Venice and Vienna. These guides and the *Thomas Cook European Travel Phrasebook* (£4.95) are available from many book shops in the UK and the USA (publisher: Passport Books) and from UK branches of Thomas Cook.

Other useful books

The best series of guides are: *Lonely Planet* and *Rough Guides*, for budget travellers; the *Michelin Green Guides* or *Blue Guides* (A & C Black) for cultural sightseeing and the *AA Essential Guides* as excellent pocket guides for short stops. If you want to work for a while, buy *Work Your Way Around the World* (Vacation Work, £10.95). The *Travellers Handbook* is also extremely useful for pre-travel planning (WEXAS, £14.95).

WHAT TO TAKE

A few really useful things are: water-bottles, pocket knife, torch (flashlight), sewing kit, padlock and bicycle chain (for anchoring your luggage), small first-aid kit, safety matches, mug and cutlery, small towel, wash kit, string (for washing-line), travel adapter, universal plug, sunglasses, alarm clock, notepad and pen, pocket calculator (to convert money), a money-belt and a good book. For clothing, see the clothing section on p. 17–18. If you wear spectacles, take a spare pair and a copy of your prescription.

If you're not sure what you're doing about accommodation, take a lightweight sleeping-bag, a sheet liner, inflatable travel pillow, earplugs and eyemask. Strong plastic containers can come in handy and are safer (and lighter) than glass ones. Finally, pack some plastic bags – they weigh virtually nothing and are useful for all sorts of things.

TRAVELLING BY TRAIN

This chapter is packed with hints about organising an excursion around the Alps by rail.

INFORMATION AND BOOKING

In the UK
Sources of international rail tickets, passes and information include; **French Railways**, *179 Piccadilly, London W1V 0BA*, or contact their **Rail Shop**, *tel: (0990) 300003*. **International Rail Centre**, *Victoria Station, London SW1V 1JY; tel: (0171) 834 2345*. **Wasteels Travel**, *Victoria Station, London SW1V 1JY; tel: (0171) 834 7066*. **Campus Travel (Eurotrain)**, *52 Grosvenor Gardens, London SW1W 0AG; tel: (0171) 730 3402*. **German Rail**; *tel: (0891) 887755 or 0181 390 8833*.

In the USA
Sources of tickets, passes and information include: **Forsyth Travel Library Inc.**, *1750 East 131st Street, PO Box 80800, Kansas City, MO 64148; tel: (800) 367 7984* (toll-free). **Rail Europe Inc.**, *230 Westchester Ave, White Plains, NY 10604 and 2100 Central Ave, Suite 200, Boulder CO 80301; tel: (800) 4-EURAIL* (toll-free) or, for Eurostar, *tel: (800)-EUROSTAR* (toll-free). **DER Tours**, *tel: (800) 782 2424*.

Several national rail networks have offices in the USA; information is listed for individual countries in the Country by Country section (see pp. 37–62).

Elsewhere
International rail information and tickets in **Australia/Canada/New Zealand** are obtainable from Thomas Cook branches (and branches of Marlin Travel in Canada). To contact **Rail Europe** in Canada, *tel: (800) 361-RAIL* (toll-free). In **South Africa** from branches of Rennies Travel (Thomas Cook network member).

EUROPEAN RAIL PASSES

Many countries have rail passes valid only for domestic travel. Those most likely to be of interest are detailed in the Country by Country section and can usually be purchased from any branch of the national railway and its appointed agents. Your passport is required for identification, and one or two passport-size photos may be needed.

European-wide passes generally cover all the ordinary services of the national rail companies and can be used on most special services if you pay a supplement. However, if the pass has been purchased in North America there is no supplement to be paid. A few passes, such as Eurail, cover most supplements. Many passes also give free or discounted travel with privately owned rail companies (including steam and cog trains), buses and ferries. You get details of these and other extras when you buy the pass.

If you are planning a long journey, consider the following international passes, which are common to most of Europe.

Inter-Rail Passes
The **Inter-Rail Pass** has launched generations of young people into the travelling life. A well-established scheme, it provides a practical and ultra-cheap way of seeing

most of Europe by train. It can be bought by anyone who will be under 26 on the first day for which it is valid, if they have lived for at least six months in one of the European countries where the pass is valid (see list below), or are a national of that country and hold a valid passport. It can be purchased up to two months before travel begins. The current cost is £249 for a month and you can buy consecutive passes for longer journeys. You will not get free travel in the country where you buy the pass, but you may be eligible for some discount.

Inter-Rail provides unlimited second-class rail travel for a month on the national railways of: Austria, France, Germany, Italy and Switzerland as well as Belgium, Bulgaria, Croatia, the Czech Republic, Denmark, Finland, Greece, Hungary, the Republic of Ireland, Luxembourg, Morocco, the Netherlands, Norway, Poland, Portugal, Romania, Slovakia, Slovenia, Spain, Sweden and Turkey. It also includes a free crossing on the Hellenic Mediterranean/Adriatica di Navigazione shipping lines between Brindisi in Italy and Patras in Greece (you will have to pay port tax of approximately L.10,000 from Italy to Greece or Dr.1500 from Greece to Italy). There are free or discounted crossings on other ferries, so check.

In the UK, Inter-Rail provides a discount of 34% on rail travel (including Eurostar) and a discount on the rail portion of tickets between London and the Continental ports, as well as good discounts (up to 50%, depending on the company) on most ferries to Europe.

Zonal Inter-Rail Passes

These regional variations on the Inter-Rail Pass are for those under 26. The same rules about eligibility apply. For zonal passes, Europe has been divided into seven geographical zones:

1) United Kingdom and the Republic of Ireland.
2) Sweden, Norway and Finland.
3) Denmark, Switzerland, Germany and Austria.
4) Poland, the Czech Republic, Slovakia, Hungary, Bulgaria, Romania and Croatia.
5) France, Belgium, the Netherlands and Luxembourg.
6) Spain, Portugal and Morocco.
7) Italy, Slovenia, Greece, Turkey (including shipping lines between Brindisi and Patras).

Passes are available for 1 zone (15 days: £179); 2 zones (1 month: £209); and 3 zones (1 month: £229). If you have a definite route in mind, these can offer savings over the standard Europe-wide pass.

Inter-Rail 26+ Pass

This is the same as Inter-Rail, except that it is for people over 26 and excludes Belgium, France, Italy, Morocco, Portugal, Spain and Switzerland. The current cost is £269 for a month or £209 for 15 days.

Eurail Passes

These are available only to people living outside Europe and can be obtained from the agents listed (under 'In the USA' and 'Elsewhere') on p. 28. You can get the passes once you've arrived but at much higher prices. Since you can buy them up to six months in advance, there is no point in waiting until the last minute.

Eurail offers unlimited travel on the national railways of: Austria, Belgium, Denmark, Finland, France, Germany, Greece, Hungary, the Republic of Ireland, Italy, Luxembourg, the Netherlands,

Norway, Portugal, Spain, Sweden and Switzerland. They also cover most private railways and a few selected ferries. A complete list of bonuses is included on the complimentary map issued with your tickets.

The basic **Eurail Pass** has no age limit. It provides first-class travel on all services and even covers most of the supplements for travelling on express and de luxe trains. It also gives free or reduced travel on many lake steamers, ferries and buses. There are several versions, valid for 15 days, 21 days, 1 month, 2 months or 3 months. Current prices range from US$522 for 15 days to US$1468 for 3 months.

The **Eurail Youth Pass** is much the same, but cheaper, as it is designed for those under 26 and is based on second-class travel. There are versions valid for 15 days (US$418), 1 month (US$598) and 2 months (US$798).

The **Eurail Flexipass** is similar to the basic Eurail pass, but allows you to travel for any 10 days (US$616) or any 15 days (US$812) within a two-month period.

The **Eurail Youth Flexipass** allows second-class travel for those under 26 within a two-month period for 10 days (US$438) and 15 days (US$588).

The **Eurail Saverpass** is designed for groups of 3–5 people travelling together at all times (between 1 Oct and 31 Mar two people travelling together is allowable) and offers first-class rail travel over a 15-day period for US$452, 21 days for US$578 and 1 month for US$712.

EuroDomino Freedom Pass

This is a catch-all title for a whole series of passes allowing unlimited travel on the national railway of an individual country. They are not valid for travel in your own country. Conditions of use are the same everywhere and the options available are for any 3, 5 or 10 days within a period of one month. The passes can be purchased by non-Europeans. They cover many of the fast-train supplements.

There is no age limit, but the price depends on age. Those under 26 pay less but are restricted to second-class, while those over 26 can opt for either class. The price varies according to the size of the railway network in the country chosen. For France the price of the passes range from £85 (youth) for 3 days second-class travel to £310 for 10 days first-class travel. For Switzerland these cost £79 and £229 respectively, and in Austria the passes are priced between £79 and £279.

Passes can be purchased up to two months before travel begins. Countries currently offering them include: Austria, France, Germany, Italy, Slovenia and Switzerland.

In the UK, holders of any Euro-Domino Freedom pass can get up to 50% discount off the rail/ferry ticket from London to a Continental port. Other ferry discounts are also available.

Europass

Available in the USA only, Europass is valid for first-class rail travel for anything from 5 to 15 days in a 2-month period. The 5–7 day pass (US$316–400) allows you to visit three countries, 8–10 days (US$442–526) covers four countries and 11–15 days (US$568–736) covers five countries – but they must be adjacent. The basic cost covers France, Germany, Italy, Spain and Switzerland. For a supplement (from US$29 to US$90), you can add Austria, Belgium/Netherlands/Luxembourg, Greece and/or Portugal.

For those under 26 the EuroYouth Pass is available for second-class travel; for details contact the agents listed (under 'In the USA') on p. 28. Various bonuses are available and listed on the map which accompanies the rail pass.

Rail Europ Senior Card

This card is for those over 60. It offers a discount of 30% (sometimes more) off the cost of cross-border rail travel (excluding supplements) between the participating countries: Austria, Belgium, Croatia, the Czech Republic, Denmark, Finland, France, Germany, Greece, Hungary, the Republic of Ireland, Italy, Luxembourg, the Netherlands, Norway, Poland, Portugal, Romania, Slovakia, Slovenia, Spain, Sweden, Switzerland and the UK.

Most countries have a rail card for their senior citizens, which is needed to buy the Rail Europ Senior Card. In the UK the Senior Railcard is available to people over 60 (it costs £16 p.a.) The Rail Europ Senior Card, available from British Rail International, costs an extra £5. It becomes valid on the day of purchase and expires on the same date as the domestic card.

REGIONAL EUROPEAN RAIL PASSES

Central Europe Pass

This is available in the USA only and provides unlimited rail travel throughout the Czech Republic, Germany, Poland and Slovakia for any 5 days within a month. The pass is available for first-class travel only and costs US$296. There are no youth reductions.

Youth Passes

If you are under 26, there are many other discounted tickets and passes available. Some are to single destinations or for travel in single countries, others to whole groups of countries. Passes come under many different names, such as Euro-Youth, Explorer Pass and BIJ (Billets International de Jeunesse). If the Inter-Rail/Eurail passes are too general for your needs, contact an organisation that specialises in youth travel such as **Campus** or **Wasteels** (see p. 28).

TICKETS

Always buy your ticket before travelling, unless you board at an unstaffed station, or you could face heavy penalties or even criminal prosecution. Throughout Alpine Europe tickets are easily available from many travel agents as well as at stations.

Never buy a standard ticket without asking what discounts are available, especially if you are prepared to travel outside peak periods, such as rush hour and the weekend.

Most countries have discounts for children, but there is no set definition of what constitutes a child. They are generally classed as adults at 11/12 years, but the age at which they change from infants (who travel free) to children can range from 2 to 5 years inclusive. Generally the norm is for children to pay approx. 50% of the adult fare and for babies to travel free – but babies are not entitled to a seat in crowded trains.

Quite a few countries also offer domestic rail cards which give substantial discounts to the disabled, elderly or students – although, in most cases, the international passes already mentioned are better value.

ADVANCE RESERVATIONS

Seats on many trains cannot be booked but, when they can, it is usually worthwhile, especially in high season and around public holidays (such as Christmas and Easter), when popular routes can fill up a long way ahead and you could spend hours standing in a crowded corridor. In some cases, you may be refused permission to board at all if there are no seats available.

For a quiet journey, with a chance to sleep, choose a seat in a compartment. For a lively journey, with conversation and panoramic views all round, choose an open carriage. In both cases, window seats are less disturbed than corridor seats. Solo travellers (particularly women) should always stick with the crowds, for security. If you are travelling during the busy summer period and have no reservation, board your train as early as possible.

Some of the major express trains (usually marked in timetables by an 'R' in a box) are restricted to passengers with reservations and you can usually make a reservation about two months in advance. In all cases, booking is essential if you want sleeping accommodation. Bookings can usually be made by contacting the national railway representatives of the country through which you intend to travel. In the USA, advance reservations and sleeping-cars can be booked through **Forsyth Travel Library Inc**; *tel: (800) 367 7984* (toll-free).

SUPPLEMENTS

Rail pass holders are often exempt from the routine surcharges applied to travel on express trains, but not always. If you opt to travel by an express service, therefore, rather than a slower alternative (there almost always is one), you should ask about supplements before committing yourself. There will certainly be a supplement for special high-speed services (such as the French TGV, the German ICE and the Italian ETR 450 Pendolino), which have higher-than-normal fares for ordinary tickets.

Holders of a first-class Eurail Pass can use most of the special services without paying extra, but even they should check its validity if they want to use one of the new breed of luxury trains.

There's usually a fee for reserving seats but it is seldom large and is normally included in the supplementary payments for the faster trains. Sleeping accommodation (see p. 34) always attracts charges of some kind. Sort out the extras before you start your journey – and make sure you know exactly what you are paying for. You may be able to pay the supplements on the train, but it almost always costs more than doing it in advance.

TYPES OF TRAIN

Many of the best daytime international trains are now branded EuroCity (or **EC**). To qualify, trains have to be fast and offer a certain standard of service, such as food and drink during the journey. All have names, and the EuroCity network continues to expand.

Many overnight trains carry names as well as numbers; some, such as the *Schweiz* and *Train Bleu*, having long histories. Most are just ordinary trains, but there is a new breed of high-quality night service known as EuroNight (**EN**) with air-conditioned coaches and extras such as evening drinks and breakfast, which are available even to couchette passengers.

The **IC** or InterCity label is applied by many countries to the fast long-distance trains, although there are slight variations in what they provide. The **ICE** (InterCity Express) designation also crops up in several countries, but is mostly applied to the latest high-speed trains in Germany. **IR** is the classification for inter-regional express services which make more stops than InterCity services; it is used mainly in Germany (where it stands for 'Inter-Regio') and in Italy (where it's short for 'Interregionale'). These names are all used to distinguish the faster long-distance trains from local or stopping trains. Types of train unique to a specific country are described in the Country by Country section.

Most longer-distance trains in Europe offer both first- and second-class travel, but second class is the norm for local stopping services. Where overnight trains offer seating accommodation, this is usually second class only. As a rule, second class is perfectly OK for all but the most ardent comfort-seeker.

FINDING YOUR TRAIN

In small stations, you are faced with a limited choice of platforms and can usually

---

Jenbach station

For the railway connoisseur, the town of Jenbach near Innsbruck in Austria has a very special appeal. Its station has the distinction of being the only one in Europe served by trains with three different gauges.

Normal-size trains, including expresses to cities as far away as Hamburg and Rome, speed through it on the centre tracks.

The north side, beside the station building, is the bottom terminus of the **Achenseebahn**, a metre-gauge railway which climbs a twisting 5-mile track to the Achensee lake up in the mountains (see p. 127). On the flat stretches at either end, its strangely-tilted steam locomotive looks as if it is about to trip over. In fact it was deliberately built like that to keep the water in the boiler in a level position on the long slope.

The far side of the station is the bottom terminus of the Zillertalbahn whose 760-mm track runs for 20 miles up the pretty Ziller valley to the busy holiday resort of Mayrhofen. Two of the trains (daily in summer and at Christmas) are steam-hauled.

---

find a friendly soul to point you in the right direction.

Most large stations have electronic departure boards or large paper timetables (often yellow for departures and white for arrivals) which list the routes, the times of departure, the relevant platforms and the arrival times at larger places. They are usually kept reasonably up to date, but watch out for nasty surprises, such as the seemingly ideal train which only runs on the third Sunday in August. In some stations, the platforms are also labelled with details of regular trains or the next departure and may even give the location of special carriages and the facilities on board.

If a platform is long it is possible that two trains will be leaving it at the same time, going in opposite directions, so double-check that you are boarding in the correct place: the trains often have destination boards on each carriage. It is necessary to be a little careful even when there is only one train, because quite a few split *en route*, with only some carriages going the full distance. If you have a reservation, all you need do is board 'your' carriage (they are all numbered, usually on cards by the entrance). If you are not booked and the destination boards are unclear, ask an official for assistance: if officials speak no English, showing your ticket should be enough for them to put you in the right portion of the train.

First-class coaches usually have a yellow stripe along the top of the windows and large number '1's on the side of the coach, on the door or on the windows. No-smoking coaches (the majority) are distinguished by signs, usually of a cigarette with a red cross, or one red band, over it.

A sign near the compartment door often gives seat numbers and sometimes indicates which are reserved. In non-compartment trains, seats are usually numbered

33

individually (on the back or on the luggage rack) and reserved seats may have labels attached to their head-rests (or the luggage racks). In many countries, however, reserved seats are not marked – so be prepared to move if someone who has booked boards the train.

Station announcements are often unintelligible, even if they are in your own language, but are sometimes important. If you hear one that you don't understand shortly before your train is due to leave, ask someone nearby whether the announcement concerned your train. The ideal is to find an official, but other travellers are often helpful. If a lot of people near you start to move away hurriedly, there has probably been a change of platform and, if you ask enough of them, you might actually find the new platform before the train pulls out.

34

GETTING OFF

Some stations are very sparsely signed with their names. Indeed many country ones have just a single name-board half-way along the platform, usually on the station building. So as your destination approaches, unless it is a big town or the end of the line, it may be advisable to keep track of where you are on a map or the list of stations on the route's timetable, or by checking with other passengers.

OVERNIGHT TRAINS

A night on the train, being rocked to sleep by the clatter of the wheels, is not to be missed. Sleeping-cars can cost about the same as a hotel but have the advantage of covering large distances as you rest and you won't waste precious holiday time in transit. You can also save quite a bit of money, if you are prepared to use couchettes or to curl up on the ordinary seats. Don't do this too often without a

break, however, or you will end up totally exhausted. The chatter of other passengers, the coming and going at stations and even the regular checks to make sure you still have all your bags can lead to a disturbed night. Take earplugs and an eyemask and, as there are often no refreshment facilities, take plenty of water and a supply of biscuits with you. If you have a rail pass and the night train is due to reach your next destination too early in the morning, consider booking to a town an hour or so further along the line; you can then get some extra sleep and backtrack to the place you actually want to visit on an early train – but don't forget to check the timetables to ensure that there is a suitable early train back!

Within Alpine Europe, it's unlikely you'll notice the borders, even if you're awake, and it's highly unlikely you will be disturbed. Attendants will give you an alarm call if you tell them you are leaving the train before the final destination – specify the stop rather than the time, so you can sleep longer if the train runs late. If you want to go to sleep before other passengers have arrived, switch on their berth lights and switch off the main overhead light. Before boarding, sort out the things you will need for the night and put them somewhere easily accessible (preferably in a small separate bag), as busy compartments don't allow much room for searching through luggage.

Sleepers and couchettes can usually be reserved up to three months in advance; early booking is recommended as space is limited. If you don't have a booking, it's still worth asking the conductor once on board. Keep some local currency handy to pay him.

SLEEPING ACCOMMODATION

Sleeping-cars have bedroom-style compartments with limited washing facilities (usually just a wash-basin) and full bedding. WCs are located at one or both ends of the coach. An attendant travels with each car, or pair of cars, and there are sometimes facilities for drinks and/or breakfast – but be prepared to pay extra.

First-class sleeping compartments usually have one or two berths and second-class compartments have two or three berths. However, there are some special sleeping-cars (described as 'T2' in schedules) which have only one berth in first class and two in second class. Unless your group takes up all the berths, compartments are allocated to a single sex and small unaccompanied children are placed in female compartments. You should claim your berth within 15 mins of boarding the train or it may be reallocated.

Couchettes are more basic – and much cheaper. They consist of simple bunk beds with a sheet, blanket and pillow. They are converted from the ordinary seats at night and there are usually four berths in first class and six in second class, with washing facilities and WCs at the end of each coach. Males and females are booked into the same compartment and expected to sleep in their daytime clothes.

In a few cases (notably Italy), overnight trains have airline-style reclining seats, which are allocated automatically when you make a seat reservation. These are sometimes free if you have a rail pass.

WASHING

Showers are still rare in European trains, but a few of the luxury-class compartments include them.

The Germans and Austrians are introducing 'hotel' trains with showers in some compartments. A few rail stations have low-cost showers for public use.

EATING

Most long-distance trains in Europe have dining-cars serving full meals and/or buffet cars selling drinks and snacks. There is an increasing tendency for refreshments to be served aircraft-style from a trolley wheeled through the train. Dining-cars are sometimes red or indicated by a red band above the windows and doors. Quite a few services offer full meals only to first-class passengers, while others offer nothing but a full-scale, four-course production. Dining-cars often have set times for full meals.

Buffets are usually open to both classes and serve for longer periods, but even they may not be available for the whole journey.

Always take emergency rations, including a full water-bottle and a packet of biscuits. Food and drink are usually expensive on trains so, if you need to save money, take a picnic. Long stops may allow time to get out and buy food and drink. Check that you have the right currency and make sure you have enough time.

35

BAGGAGE

Lockers are invaluable if you want to look round a place without carrying heavy baggage and most stations (and other transport hubs) have them. The initial payment generally covers 24 hrs, but you are allowed to stay longer (usually up to a week, but check). The newest lockers have display panels and are automatic: you simply pay any excess when you return. With older lockers, you have to pay the excess to station staff (at the left-luggage office, if there is one). Baggage trolleys (where available) are usually free, but often supermarket-style: you need a coin to release them – which you get back when you return them to a stand.

How Mountain Railways Work

Mountain railways throughout the Alps use one of several rack-and-pinion systems which enable the trains to go safely up and down steep gradients. The idea dates back to 1811 when John Blenkinsop, manager of Middleton Colliery near Leeds in the north of England, concluded that a locomotive would never be able to pull coal wagons along smooth rails because the driving wheels would slip.

He therefore devised a rack and pinion system whereby a geared-down cog wheel (pinion) under the locomotive helped it move along by engaging with a flat toothed ladder (rack) laid along the centre of the track. It worked well but was soon abandoned when he realised that smooth rails did in fact provide sufficient grip. Also, it had limited the train's speed to about 5 mph. The idea was revived in 1863 by a Swiss engineer, Niklas Riggenbach, and by 1869 mountain railways were being built with gradients of betwenn 1 in 5 and 1 in 20, creating the risk of trains slipping uncontrollably. The first one in Switzerland was installed in 1871 on the line up the Rigi mountain from **Vitznau** (see p. 336).

In 1882 another Swiss engineer, Roman Abt, devised a refinement to make the connection between locomotive and track more powerful. He added a second rack alongside the first, staggering their teeth so that the tooth of one was opposite the jaw of the other. It made its debut on the Blankenburg-Tanne line in the Harz Mountains in Germany in 1885.

Today trains use racks to go up and down startlingly steep gradients throughout the Alps. They make climbs – and descents possible and safe up to 48 degrees. Sometimes three-rack ladders have been used in which each one's teeth are positioned one-third of the way along the jaws of the other two.

One of the best places to see the rack system in operation is at the Swiss end of the spectacular mountain line which runs through **Chamonix** from **St-Gervais-Le Fayet** in France (see p. 109–113). Just before the train begins its hair-raising 1-in-5 descent to the flat Rhône valley at Martigny, it slows to walking pace and you hear a clanking and grinding of metal as the pinion locks into the rack.

Another intriguing traction system is used in Lyon on the two funicular railways that climb through steep tunnels from the bank of the Saône to the heights of the Old Town. Whereas most funiculars have two straight tracks side-by-side, these have only single tracks apart from short passing sections half-way. To complicate matters further, the tracks include bends.

The principle used is the same as in all funiculars where (like cable cars) the weight of the carriage going up is largely counterbalanced by the weight of the one going down, but here the cables are kept in position from bend to bend by ingeniously-positioned horizontal pulley-wheels. You can get a good view of how they work by looking through the carriage's front and rear windows.

Altogether the variety of traction systems adds considerable interest to travelling around the Alps by train. Most main lines have overhead electric cables but many country routes remain diesel-hauled. Watch out too for third-rail systems where the locomotive's shoe brushes along the side of an electric rail which is covered by a wooden shelf to protect it from the worst winter weather.

Some of the most scenic rides on rack railways in the Alps include those on the **Montreux–Rochers de Naye** line (see p. 159), the **Gornergrat-Bahn** from Zermatt (see p. 284) and on the **Brienzer Rothorn rack railway** (p. 174).

COUNTRY BY COUNTRY

AUSTRIA

Capital: Vienna (**Wien**). **Language**: German; English is widely spoken in tourist areas. **Currency**: Schilling (ÖS75); 1 Schilling = 100 Groschen.

Passports and Visas

An EU National Identity is sufficient. Visas are not needed by nationals of the EU, Australia, Canada, New Zealand or the USA. Others should check.

Customs

EU nationals may import tax and duty paid items for personal use. Non-European residents arriving from outside Europe may bring 200 cigarettes or 50 cigars or 250g tobacco, 1 litre spirits and 2.25 litres wine or 3 litres beer and may bring other commodities duty-free to a value of ÖS2500.

Tourist Information

You will find a tourist information service of some sort in almost every town and even villages providing information on accommodation and local attractions. Staff almost invariably speak some English but bear in mind that opening times vary widely and are particularly restricted at weekends outside major centres and tourist resorts in high season. The tourist office sign to look out for is the international green 'i' though the official name varies from place to place. *Fremdenverkersbüro* is one of the most common.

Useful Addresses in Australia

Embassy, *12 Talbot Street, Forest, Canberra ACT 2603, PO Box 3375 Manuka,* *Canberra ACT 2603; tel: (62) 951376.* **National Tourist Office,** *1st Floor, 36 Carrington St, Sydney NSW 2000; tel: (2) 299 2621*

Useful Addresses in Canada

Embassy, *445 Wilbrod St, Ottawa Ontario KIN6M7; tel: 789 1444.* **National Tourist Office,** *2 Bloor St E/Suite 3330, Toronto, Ontario M4W1A8; tel: (416) 9673381*

Useful Addresses in Republic of Ireland

Embassy, *15 Ailsbury Court Appts, 93 Ailsbury Rd, Dublin 4; tel: (1) 2694577* **National Tourist Office,** *Marrion Hall, Strand Rd, Sandymount PO Box 2506, Dublin 4; tel: (1) 2830488*

Useful Addresses in South Africa

Embassy, *1109 Duncan St, Momentum Office Park, 0011 Brooklyn, Pretoria, PO Box 95572 0145 Watercloof, Pretoria; tel: (12) 463361.* **National Tourist Office,** *Private Bag X18 Parklands 2121, Johannesburg; tel: (11) 4427235*

Useful Addresses in the UK

Embassy, *18 Belgrave Mews West, London SW1X 8HU; tel: (0171) 235 3731.* **National Tourist Office and Railways**, *30 St George St, London W1R 0AL; tel: (0171) 629 0461*

Useful Addresses in the USA

Embassy, *3524 International Court NW, Washington DC 20008; tel: (202) 895 6700.* **National Tourist Office,** *500 Fifth Ave (Suite 2009-2022), New York,*

37

NY 10110; tel: (212) 944 6880; PO Box 1142 New York NY 10108-1142 or PO Box 491938 Los Angeles, CA 90049; tel: (310) 477 3332

STAYING IN AUSTRIA

Accommodation

The Austrian National Tourist Office can supply information about all types of accommodation, including camping. **Hotels** are graded on the usual five-star system, but even one-star establishments are pricey. *Gasthaus/Gasthof* indicates an inn and *Früstuckpension* a bed-and-breakfast place. The best value is usually a private room (*Privatzimmer* – look for *Zimmer frei* signs), but many require stays of several nights and some charge a supplement for short stays. *Jugendherberge* is the word for a **youth hostel.** In summer some universities let rooms and it's always worth asking when you're in a university town.

Camping is popular and there are lots of sites. The general standard is high, with cleanliness and efficiency the keynotes, and hot water available almost everywhere; the down-side is the high prices. For camping information *tel: (01222) 89121222.* Many sites open summer only, but some open year round. In Alpine areas there are numerous refuge huts, details available from the local Tourist Office. For all accommodation it is advisable to book ahead for July, Aug, Christmas and Easter.

Several resorts, indicated by **GC** next to tourist office details, issue a **guest card** to visitors, some only for a specified number of nights or for those in higher quality accommodation. The cards entitle holders to anything from free escorted mountain hikes to discounts for ferries and museums. The cards are generally issued by the Gasthofs or hotels.

Accommodation in Austria that is shown as **very expensive** is priced at over ÖS2000; **expensive** up to ÖS2000; **moderate** up to ÖS1000; and **budget** indicates prices up to ÖS400.

Addresses

A number of smaller centres, for example Strobl on the Wolfgangsee, do not have street names but just house numbers. The tourist office map is helpful but these places are usually small enough that locals will know wherever you are looking for.

Eating and Drinking

The Austrian pattern is: continental breakfast, lunch (1200–1400), coffee and pastries

---

A Few Useful Words

Altstadt – old town
Bauernmarkt – farmers' (food) market
Berg eg Muttersberg – mountain
Biedermeier – roughly equivalent to Victorian
Burg – town
Dom – cathedral
Hauptplatz – main square
Imbiss – serves snacks to standing customers
Jugenstil – art nouveau
Kapelle – chapel
Neustadt – new town
Obere – above/upper
Ort – village or town
Pfarrkirche – parish church
Rathaus – town hall
Schloss – castle
See eg Traunsee – lake
Stuben – eating place where people linger to talk
Tal eg Zillertal – valley
Turm – tower
Untere – below/lower
Wirt – inn

mid-afternoon, and dinner (1800–2200). Lunch is usually more expensive in cafés than in restaurants. Drinks in bars and clubs cost more than in eating places. A filling snack, sold by most butchers, is *Wurstsemmel* – slices of sausage with a bread roll. Tea and coffee are widely available. Beer is the most popular drink, but Austrian wine is good and *schnapps* comes in many varieties. A service charge of 10–15% is included in restaurant bills. It is the custom to leave a further 5% if happy with the service.

Opening Hours

Banks: in Vienna – Mon, Tues, Wed, Fri 0800–1230 and 1330–1500, Thur 0800–1230 and 1330–1730 (some do stay open through the lunch hour). Elsewhere, the norm is Mon–Fri 0800–1230 and 1430–1600. **Shops**: Mon–Fri 0800–1830 and Sat 0800–1300 (in larger towns some stay open until 1700 on the first Sat of the month). **Museums**: there is no real pattern to opening times and several of the smaller ones open only a few days a week, so check locally.

Postage

Post offices can be recognised by a golden trumpet symbol and are often located close to the station or main square. They all handle poste restante (*Postlagernde Briefe*). Nationwide hours are Mon–Fri 0800–1200 and 1400–1800, but offices in major towns tend to stay open during lunch and on Sat. The main post offices in cities frequently open 24 hours a day. Stamps (*briefmarke*) can also be purchased at *Tabak/Trafik* stands. Approximately 340 post offices will cash Eurocheques.

Public Holidays

1, 6 Jan; Easter Monday; 1 May; Ascension Day; Whit Monday; Corpus Christi; 1, 15 Aug; 26 Oct; 1 Nov; 8, 25, 26 Dec. Many people take unofficial holidays on Good Friday, Easter Sunday, Whit Sunday, 2 Nov, 24 Dec and 31 Dec.

Public Transport

The efficient Austrian **long-distance bus system** consists of orange **Bundesbahn buses**, run by **ÖBB** and generally based near rail stations, and yellow **Post-buses**, run by the postal system, which usually leave from beside post offices. Both serve mountainous areas and other places inaccessible to trains, rather than duplicating inter-city rail routes.

All cities have excellent **bus and/or tram systems**. It is possible to buy tickets on board, but is cheaper to get them in advance from *Tabak/Trafik* booths. They are validated in a little machine on board, often marked with an 'E' (*Entwerter*).

Taxis in larger cities charge by officially controlled metres. If fares have been changed, the additional payment is in the form of a supplement to the charge shown. There is an extra charge for luggage. In smaller towns there are fixed charges for certain destinations and fares for longer distances are agreed beforehand.

Telephones

The system is efficient and it is quite easy to use ordinary pay-phones. Most boxes have instructions in English and most of the international operators speak it. Even remote places have booths that will take telephone cards, *Wertkarten*, available from post offices, stations and some shops. Note that Austrian phones charge for use of line, not just connected calls. This means that you will need coins even when using international phone chargecards. It is easier to use the metered phones in post offices where payment is made afterwards. Note that whatever type of phone you

39

use, if using an account based telephone charge card you will still have to pay cash as well.

To call abroad from Austria: *tel: 00*. To call Austria: *tel: 43*. Note that other dialling codes are not yet uniform. Post office phone counters can give the correct ones to use from the area. To call international enquiries and operator: *tel: 08*. Long distance calls are approximately 35% cheaper between 1800 and 0800 and on public holidays.

To call national enquiries and operator: *tel: 16 11*. **Emergencies:** Police: *133*; Fire: *122*; Ambulance: *144*.

For loss or theft of Thomas Cook Travellers Cheques, *tel: 0660 6266* (local call charge payable).

RAIL TRAVEL WITHIN AUSTRIA

The national rail company is **Österreichische Bundesbahnen (ÖBB)**. Most lines are electrified and the railway system is fast and reliable, with *IC* trains every 1–2 hours and regional trains timed to connect with *IC* services. Other fast trains are: *D* (ordinary express trains often with second-class seating only); *E* (semi-fast or local trains which are usually second class); *EC*; and *EN*.

Major services have both first- and second-class seating and some overnight trains have sleeping-cars (up to three berths) and couchettes (four or six berths).

First-class fares are one rate only – no supplements are charged. There are two rates of second-class fares with second class travel on *EC* trains charged at a higher tariff (ÖS20–50 depending on the number of km travelled) than on ordinary trains. The difference between the fares can be paid on the train.

Reservations are usually possible and are recommended at peak times. They are free for first-class *EC* and *IC* travel, and second-class *EC* trains, if bought in advance. They can be made up to three months in advance for sleeping-cars and two months in advance for couchettes.

Stations

Almost every station offers left luggage facilities and a majority hold at least an accommodation leaflet and/or town map – useful if you arrive after tourist office hours.

Fares and Passes

The main domestic passes are: **Bundesnetzkarte**, valid for first- (ÖS5900) or second-class (ÖS4300) travel

---

Greenery

Austria vies with Germany as Europe's greenest country with 'green' and organic shops fairly common. Greenery extends further than specialist shops though. It is rare to find anything but recycled toilet paper and many hotels do their best to limit the environmental – and financial – costs of their business. That includes suggesting that if you rehang your towels they will not change them every day.

The ecological issues are now spreading to the landscape where the earnings from smallholdings are not enough to stop a drift to the cities. The disappearance of the small pastures, often so steep they defy machines, will change the country's appearance. This has led to the proposal of subsidies for 'landscape guardians' but many in the country object to what they consider would be a demotion. In any case, such a subsidy could prove difficult now that Austria has joined the EC. It seems likely that Austria will, in many places, return to its natural woods.

Trachten

Every town and certainly every village of standing in Austria has its own costume, worn until recently every Sunday and holiday. Modernisation has gradually eroded the custom, although travelling around you will see that some country ladies still follow it.

However, Austrians are traditionalists and they have not abandoned the habit entirely. Today there are numerous shops specialising in Trachten – clothes with something of the traditional style and made in high quality wool and heavy linen. They are, however, slightly different in cut – very tight in the bodice for example, not a realistic option for real farm workers – and in a range of colours from shocking pink to gentian blue as well as the more traditional soft greens and even black.

The modern Trachten are high quality – a good buy if you like the style – but they are expensive. As a result they are no longer an indicator of the wearer's village but of their financial and social standing – and therefore usually worn by those of a conservative outlook.

for one month on all OBB lines, including several private and mountain railways, and the **Österreich-Puzzles** (Austrian Puzzles) Ost, West, Nord and Sud, covering geographical boundaries and giving unlimited rail travel for any 4 days within a 10-day period (ÖS1740 first class, ÖS1090 second), for those under 26.

FRANCE

Capital: Paris. **Language:** French; many people can speak a little English, particularly in Paris. **Currency:** French Francs (FFr.); 1 Franc = 100 Centimes. There are 5, 10, 20 and 50 centime coins and FFr.1, 2, 5, 10 and 20 coins. Notes come in FFr.20, 50, 100, 200 and 500 denominations.

Passports and Visas
EU Nationals do not need visas for stays of less than three months; for longer visits a residence permit (*carte de séjour*) is required, either from the French consulate at home or from the *Service des Étrangers* at local *préfectures de police* in France. Visas are not needed by nationals of Canada, New Zealand or the USA except for stays of over 90 days. Australians and South Africans do need visas.

Customs
Standard EU regulations apply (see p. 19). There are restrictions on the importation of items such as recreational drugs, weapons and animals; for up-to-date regulations, contact the French consulate.

EU residents are liable to local sales taxes but there no extra duties for tax-paid goods for individual consumption. A sales tax is applied to most items, modest for staple ones but much higher for luxury goods. If you spend more than FFr.2,000 in a shop, ask for a TVA reclaim form which must be completed and stamped by the sales person. When you leave France you will need to present the form(s) at Customs for verification before reclaiming any refund. Non-EU residents should remember that they may be liable to customs duty when they import the goods into their own country.

Tourist Information
Information offices, known as *Syndicats d'Initiative* and *Offices de Tourisme*, are often marked with a large 'I' sign. They offer a wide range of tourist information including town-centre maps, accommodation lists and details of local attractions.

41

Besançon, Digne-les-Bains, Dijon, Grenoble and Lyons have *Accueil de France* tourist offices which means they will also make accommodation bookings (throughout France) for a small fee. Most tourist offices open Mon–Sat 0900–1200 and 1400–1800 and many also open on Sun in high season. There's a 24-hour leisure information line (in English); *tel: (1) 49 52 53 56.*

Useful Addresses in Australia
Embassy, *6 Perth Ave, Yarralumla, Canberra, ACT 2600; tel: (06) 270 5111.* **Tourist Office,** *BNP House, 12 Castlereagh St, Sydney, NSW 2000; tel: (02) 231 5244.* **SNCF:** *c/o Thomas Cook, 175 Pitt St, Sydney, NSW 2000; tel: (02) 229 6611.*

Useful Addresses in Canada
Embassy, *42 Promenade Sussex, Ottawa, Ontario Q1M 2C9; tel: (613) 789 1795.* **Tourist Office,** *30 St Patrick St (Suite 700), Toronto, Ont M5T 3A3; tel: (416) 593 6427.* **SNCF:** *c/o Rail Europe Inc, 2087 Dundas East (Suite 105), Mississauga, Ont L4X 1MZ; tel: (905) 602 4195.*

Useful Addresses in the Republic of Ireland
Embassy, *36 Ailesbury Rd, Ballsbridge, Dublin 4; tel: (01) 260 1666.* **Tourist Office,** *35 Lower Abbey St, Dublin 1; tel: (01) 703 4046.*

Useful Addresses in New Zealand
Embassy, *Robert Jones House, 1–3 Willeston St, Wellington; tel: (04) 472 0200.*

Useful Addresses in South Africa
Embassy, *807 George Ave, Arcadia, Pretoria 0083; tel: (012) 435 564.* **Tourist Office,** *Craighall, Johannesburg 2024; tel: (011) 880 8062.* **SNCF:** *c/o World Travel Agency, 8th Floor Everite House, 20 De Korte Bramfontein, 2001 Johannesburg; tel: (011) 403 2606.*

Useful Addresses in the UK
Embassy, *58 Knightsbridge, London SW1X 7JT; tel: (0171) 201 1000.* **French National Government Tourist Office (Maison de la France):** *178 Piccadilly, London W1V 0AL; tel: (0891) 244123;* calls cost £0.49 per min peak rate, £0.39 at other times. **French Railways (SNCF) and Rail Shop,** *179 Piccadilly, London W1V 0BA; tel: 0990 300003.*

Useful Addresses in the USA
Embassy, *4101 Reservoir Rd NW, Washington DC 20007; tel: (202) 944 6000.* **Tourist Office,** *444 Madison Ave (16th Flr), New York, NY 10020-2452; tel: (212) 838 7800.* **SNCF:** *c/o Rail Europe Inc, 225/230 Westchester Ave, White Plains, NY 10604; tel: (914) 682 2999.*

STAYING IN FRANCE

Accommodation
Accueil de France supply free lists of most types of local accommodation, but usually charge about FFr.10 to make bookings. Advance reservations are recommended for the larger towns and resort areas in summer. You can get lists of all types of accommodation from French tourist boards before you go, but be prepared to pay.

Hotels: Local authorities classify hotels on a five-grade scale according to their facilities. Those which are *'sans etoile'* – unstarred – may still be good value and the best advice is to look at a room before taking it. If a hotel is listed as 'IC' – *Instance de classement* – it means that it is waiting for its grade to be awarded. Hotel prices are invariably quoted for doubles – singles often cost the same – and may include Continental breakfast. By law, the tariff must be displayed at reception and in the rooms. As a guide, expect to pay between FFr.260 and 380 for a comfortable two-star double room.

Associations of independent hotels include:

Relais et Châteaux, *av. Marceau, 75116 Paris; tel: 47 23 41 42*, is a group of luxury manors and châteaux, some old and very stately, others more modern but with a grand atmosphere in special surroundings. They also pride themselves on their cuisine. French-English directory available free from **Relais et Chateaux**, *7 Cork Street, London W1X 2AB; tel 0171 287 0987*, or £5 by post. **Logis de France**, *83 av. d'Italie, 75013 Paris; tel: 45 84 70 00*, are family-run one- and two-star excellent-value hotels. Over 4000 are listed in their guide, available from bookshops (£12.95) or by post in the UK (£13.95) from *French Government Tourist Office, 178 Piccadilly, London W1V 0AL*. They are invariably good places to eat, often featuring regional specialities. Members display a distinctive yellow *cheminée* (fireplace) logo. **Fédération National des Gîtes Ruraux**, *35 r. Godot de Mauroy, 75009 Paris; tel: 47 42 20 20*, offers thousands of self-catering cottages in country locations, usually rented out by the week. 2000 are detailed in the English brochure available from **Gites de France Ltd**, *178 Piccadilly, London WV1V 9DB; tel: 0171 493 3480*. Local tourist offices supply lists of *chambres d'hôte* – private homes offering accommodation. Gîtes de France also publish 'French Country Welcome' which gives details of around 14,000 bed and breakfast establishments; £11.50 from Gites de France (by post £2.35 extra).

Youth hostels: Auberges de Jeunesse (AJ) are sometimes HI and sometimes purely French. Usually good quality and not necessarily cheaper than a budget hotel, they are open to all ages. Membership of a youth hostel association in your own country allows you to use any of the 200-plus hostels in France run by the **Fédération Unie des Auberges de Jeunesse (FUAJ)**, *27 r. Pajol, 75018 Paris; tel: 44 89 87 27*. You can usually buy a Hostelling International Card on the spot.

Camping is popular and sites are classified with one- to four stars depending on facilities. **Michelin** and **Fédération Française de Camping et Caravanning**, *78 r. de Rivoli, 75004 Paris; tel: 42 72 84 08*, produce guides. The cheapest sites with good facilities are usually *Camping Municipal*. Book in early, especially for July–Aug. Alternatively, local tourist offices have lists of farms with campsites (*camping à la ferme*) which are a simpler alternative. **Farmhouse** accommodation is often available too.

In mountain areas, a chain of refuge huts is run by **Club Alpin Français**, *24 av. de Laumière , 75019 Paris; tel: 42 02 68 64*.

Eating and Drinking

Breakfast normally consists of coffee, tea or hot chocolate and croissants or bread with butter and jam, but eggs, cold meats etc. can invariably be ordered as an extra. Lunch is served from midday to around 1400 and dinner from around 1900 – after 2100 you could have problems outside tourist centres. In cafés, drinks cost a little more if you sit at a table so to save money stand at the counter. In restaurants, eating à la carte is more expensive than choosing the *menu du jour* or *table d'hôte* which can be superb value and may even include a drink. Baguettes with a variety of fillings

43

from cafés and stalls are cheap – as are *crêpes* (sweet and savoury pancakes), pizzas and other fast food. The home-grown chain is **Quick**.

Restaurants must display priced menus outside, including all charges. Customers leave a tip if they are especially pleased with the service. Restaurants and cafés are supposed to provide a non-smoking area.

Maps

The **Institut Géographique National** (IGN) is the official cartographic body in France; the IGN Map 901, a general map of France (scale 1 cm = 10 km) is useful for planning countrywide routes. Specialist maps include Map 902 (1 cm = 10 km) which shows major historic sites, Map 903 (1 cm = 10km) tracing the national long distance footpaths and Map 906 (1cm = 1km) designed for cyclists. There are various Outdoor Activites maps (1cm = 1km) covering national parks and tourist areas.

The most useful regional maps are the Série Verte (Green Series), in 74 sheets (1 cm = 1 km). For walkers and cyclists, the Série Bleue (Blue Series) covers France in 2000 sheets with a detailed scale of 4cm = 1km.

Local maps and guides can usually be bought at tourist offices which invariably also have free town-centre maps.

Money

Most major banks, large rail stations and hotels, as well as the Thomas Cook offices listed throughout this book, exchange foreign currency and travellers' cheques. (Thomas Cook Travellers Cheques at Thomas Cook bureaux are encashed commission-free). With a pin number, cash can be withdrawn from cash dispensing machines bearing the appropriate symbol.

Credit and charge cards are widely accepted in shops, hotels and restaurants, particularly Carte Bleue/Visa/Barclaycard, MasterCard/Access/Eurocard, American Express and Diners Club. However French credit cards have a chip or *'puce'* which contains ID information, so cards with information on magnetic stips are not always easily read by French card machines. If you have a problem you will need to persuade the shop assistant/hotelier to confirm its validity with their *'centre de traitement'*.

In case of loss, cardholders should always carry a note of their bank's 24-hr contact number.

Price tags and receipts use a comma between the francs and the centimes rather than a decimal point.

Opening Hours

Banks: Mon–Fri or Tues–Sat 0900–1200 and 1400–1600/1700. They usually close early on the day preceding a public holiday. **Shops:** Tues–Sat 0900–1200 and 1430–1830. A few open Mon and through the midday break, especially food shops, which also frequently open Sun morning and stay open late.

Museums: 0900–1600 (with many variations and usually later in summer). Closed one day a week (usually Mon or Tues) and most close on public holidays. Many offer free or discounted entrance on Sun.

Postage

Most post offices (*PTT: Poste et Telecommunications*) open Mon–Fri 0800–1900; Sat 0800–1200. Look for yellow signs with *La Poste* in blue. To save time queuing at the counter, some have self-service franking machines which weigh letters and packages and then print franked stickers. Coin-operated stamp machines provide booklets of ten FFr.2.80 stamps. Postboxes are mustard yellow and fixed to walls. Stamps (*timbres*) can also be purchased from any café or shop with a *Tabac* sign, a long red triangle.

You can have post sent for collection c/o Poste Restante in every office (address letters to *Poste Centrale* for the main one in the town). Mail is held for a month and to collect it you have to show proof of identity and pay a small fee. Post information; *tel: 05 05 02 02*.

Public Holidays

1 Jan; Easter (Good Fri to Mon); 1 and 8 May; Ascension Day; Whit Sun and Mon; 14 July; 15 Aug; 1 and 11 Nov; 25 Dec. When they fall on Tues or Thur, the French like to '*faire le pont*' – extend the holiday by including the preceding Mon or following Fri.

Public Transport

Train and bus stations are usually close together, making access to town centres easy. Bus services shown as *Autocar* are run by SNCF and accept rail passes/tickets – so always ask if yours is valid. *Guide Régional des Transports* (from SNCF and bus stations: *gares routières*) is a free guide which provides information about train and bus services between main towns.

Bus services within towns are good during the day, but infrequent after around 2030 and on Sun. Public transport in rural areas is sparse.

Licensed **taxis** (avoid others) are metered, with white roof-lights if they are available, orange ones if they are not. You can pick them up at ranks (*stations de taxi*) – there is invariably one at the railway station – as well as on main streets. There are surcharges for luggage, extra passengers and animals. If your journey will take you out of town, check the price with the driver before starting. The usual tip is 10–15% of the fare.

Summer Time

Summer time begins on the last Sun in March, when clocks are put forward by one hour, and ends on the last Sun in September.

Telephones

The efficient system is run by **France Telecom** (logo: a digital dialling pad enclosed in an oval). All numbers have eight digits, but this will be increase to ten in Oct 1996. Phone boxes are plentiful in towns and villages throughout the Alps and most have instructions in English. Many post offices have metered phones where you pay when you have finished. Some phone booths take coins but the majority now take only credit cards or phonecards (*télécartes*). These are available from post offices and newsagents in units of 50 and 120. Domestic calls are 50% cheaper Mon–Fri 2230–0800, Sat after 1400 and Sun.

To call abroad from France; *tel: 19* followed by the country code. To call France; *tel: 33*. To call the Paris region from elsewhere in France use the prefix *161*; no prefix is needed for other French regions unless you are calling from Paris, in which case the prefix is *16*. Operator; *tel: 13* (national), *tel: 14* (international). Directory enquiries; *tel: 12*.

Emergencies: Police: *17*; Fire: *18*; Ambulance: *15*. From Oct 1996 *112* will cover all emergency services. Loss or theft of Thomas Cook Travellers Cheques, *tel: 05 90 8330* (toll free).

RAIL TRAVEL WITHIN FRANCE

The national rail company is **Société Nationale des Chemins de Fer Français (SNCF)** which operates a nationwide (premium–rate) number in most regions for information and bookings; *tel: 36 35 35 35*. Except in the Paris

45

region, the network of local lines is not very extensive. French trains are fast, reliable and comfortable, though not always frequent. The French are proud of the TGV (*Train à Grande-Vitesse*), one of the fastest in the world, with speeds of up to 300 kph. In late 1996 double-decker TGVs will come into service.

Overnight trains carry both sleeping-cars (*wagons-lits*) and couchettes (six berths and mixed sexes, so don't undress).

Dining-cars, as such, are disappearing and in first class you usually have a meal delivered to you on a tray. On most long-distance trains, there is either a buffet or a trolley service.

Fares and Passes

All tickets must be date-stamped before you board, by using the orange machines (*composteurs*) at the platform entrance. France has two fare periods on most routes (more on some); basically, blue is for quiet periods and white for peak. SNCF issues a (free) calendar detailing the periods. Reservations, for a small supplement, are compulsory for sleeping-cars and the TGV. They are recommended for international travel and during white periods. Most domestic passes entitle you to make bookings free, but the number of seats available to pass holders is limited, so book early. **Carrissimo** is for those aged 12–25 and gives four or eight journeys at 50% discount in blue periods or 20% discount in white periods: up to four people can travel together, but each person counts as one journey. **Carte Vermeil Quatre Temps** is for travellers over 60, providing a 50% discount on four single (or two return) journeys beginning in a blue period. **Carte Vermeil Plein Temps** is essentially the same as Rail Europ Senior (see p. 31). There is no age limit on the (free) **Carte Couple**, which allows a

couple (proof of co-habitation and a photograph required) to travel in blue periods at a 25% reduction. **Carte Kiwi** gives under-16s and up to four relatives or friends a 50% discount; one card covers four single journeys and another unlimited travel for one year.

GERMANY

Capital: Bonn/Berlin (the functions of the capital are gradually being transferred to Berlin). Germany is a federal republic, divided into states (*Länder*) whose governments have extensive powers independent of the federal government.

Language: German. English and French are widely spoken in cities, especially by young people. In rural areas of southern Germany, English is less widely spoken. In German it is customary to roll several words into one and the polysyllabic result can be daunting. You will find it less confusing if you split the words into their component parts. *Hauptbahnhof*, for example, is an amalgam of *haupt*/chief, *bahn*/railway and *hof*/yard. **Currency**: Deutsche Marks (DM). 1 Mark = 100 Pfennig.

Passports and Visas

EU National Identity Cards are acceptable as are ID cards for citizens of the Czech and Slovak Republics, Hungary, Iceland, Liechtenstein, Malta, Monaco, Poland, and Switzerland.

Visas are not needed by nationals of Australia, Canada, New Zealand or the USA. Others should check.

Tourist Information

There are helpful tourist information offices in virtually every town or resort, usually within a couple of hundred metres of the station. English is widely spoken and a wide range of English-language leaflets is available. Most offices offer a room-finding service.

Customs

Standard EU regulations apply, see p.19. Danes must spend at least 24 hrs in Germany before taking their allowances home.

Useful Addresses in Australia

Embassy, *119 Empire Circuit, Yarralumla, Canberra, ACT 2600; tel: (62) 701911.* **German National Tourist Office,** *Lufthansa House, 9th Floor, 143 Macquarie St, Sydney 2000; tel: (2) 367 3990.*

Useful Addresses in Canada

Embassy, *275 Slater St, 14th Floor, Ottawa K15 H9; tel: (613) 232 1101.* **German National Tourist Office,** *North Tower, Suite 604, 175 Bloor St E., Toronto, Ontario M4W 3R8; tel: (416) 968 1570.*

Useful Addresses in South Africa

Embassy, *16 Kapteijnstreet, Johannesburg; tel: (11) 725 1519.* **German National Tourist Office,** *22 Girton Road, Parktown, Johannesburg; tel: (11) 643 1615.*

Useful Addresses in the UK

Embassy, *23 Belgrave Square, London SW1X 8PZ; tel: (0171) 235 5033.* **German National Tourist Office (DZT),** *Nightingale House, 65 Curzon St, London W1Y 7PE; tel: (0171) 495 3990.* **German Rail,** *The Sanctuary, 23 Oakhill Grove, Surbiton, Surrey, KT6 6DU; tel: (0189) 887755 or (0181) 390 8833.*

Useful Addresses in the USA

Embassy, *Germany, 4645 Reservoir Road NW, Washington DC 20007-1998; tel: (202) 298 8140.* **German National Tourist Office,** *Chanin Building, 122 East 42nd Street (52nd Floor), New York, NY 10168-0072; tel: (212) 308 3300.* **German Federal Railroad (DB),** *747 Third av. (33rd Floor), New York, NY 10017; tel: (212) 371 2609.*

STAYING IN GERMANY

Accommodation

The general standard of accommodation is high. So are prices. You will be doing well if you find a room for less than DM30 in smaller towns and villages, remote areas, or DM70 in cities. All over Germany the prices vary enormously according to demand. In the Alpine resorts rooms are understandably at their most expensive during the peak ski season (Christmas to mid-March) and during the summer peak in July and August when the mountains attract vast numbers of visitors.

Germany is a year-round tourism and business destination, and in the cities there is no real low season for hotels. Avoid *Messen* (trade fairs) and other special events when prices are at their highest; the DZT publishes a twice-yearly events calendar. Some major business cities such as Frankfurt, which have little allure for tourists, can be a bit quieter and cheaper in August. By contrast, Munich is busy in summer and is at its most crowded and expensive during the annual Oktoberfest beer festival, which despite its name is sometimes held in September. Check with DZT or local tourist office for dates.

Hotels and **boarding houses** (*gasthof/gasthaus*) can be booked in advance through a department of DZT: **Allgemeine Deutsche Zimmerreservierung** (ADZ), *Corneliusstr. 34, Frankfurt/Main; tel: (069) 74 07 67.* Advance booking is essential in high season and always advisable. *Pensionen* or *Fremdenheime* are pensions and *Zimmer* means 'room' (generally in a private

47

home). These are usually cheap but some expect you to stay for at least two nights. Look for signs in the windows (*Zimmer frei* and *zu vermieten* indicate availability; *besetzt* means they are full) or book through the local tourist office. In some of the most popular Alpine resorts the local tourist office runs an accommodation service from a small office at or close to the rail station. These offices do not usually operate in winter. You must be prepared to pay for guesthouse accommodation in German cash, as credit cards and cheques are seldom accepted by small establishments.

Jugendherberge (DJH) are **youth hostels** and there are around 600 in Germany (mostly affiliated with the HI). In Bavaria there is an age limit of 27, elsewhere there is no limit but preference is usually given to the young. It is necessary to book well ahead in peak season. In Germany they really are youth hostels and often used by school parties, which has resulted in the introduction of a new category of accommodation, *Jugendgästehaus*, which is aimed more at young adults.

The medium-price InterCity Hotels chain has hotels conveniently located at next to stations in a number of major cities.

Camping is the cheapest form of accommodation and site facilities are generally excellent. Southern Germany's summer weather, even in the cooler mountain resorts, makes camping a pleasure. Relatively few sites are within easy walking distance of stations, but most suburban campsites are no more than a short bus ride from the city centre. **Deutscher Camping-Club** (DCC), *Mandlstr. 28, Munich*, publishes an annual list of 1600 sites (price DM34.80). DZT publishes a free list and map showing more than 600 of the best sites nationwide.

Eating and Drinking

Breakfast is any time from 0630 to 1000. Lunch is around 1200–1400 (from 1130 in rural areas) and dinner 1800–2130 (earlier in rural areas).

German cuisine is fairly rich and served in large portions, with pork and potatoes the staple ingredients, but it's easy to find lighter things, such as salads. Breakfast is often substantial (and is usually included in the price of a room), consisting of a variety of bread, cheese and cold meat. Germans eat their main meal at midday, with a light supper in the evening, but restaurants and pubs also offer light lunches and cooked evening meals. The cheapest way to eat is to patronise *Imbisse*: roadside stalls serving a variety of snacks but especially *Wurst* (sausage). For lunch, the best value is the daily menu (*Tageskarte*). There are simple restaurants (*Gaststätten* and *Gasthöfe*) which include regional dishes.

Bavaria is world-famous for its beer, which can come in huge steins holding a litre (sometimes more) but is more usually drunk by the half-litre. A visit to a Munich bierkeller is a 'must' and southern Germany also produces a range of fine wines, both red and white. Those of the Rhine valley vineyards are of course the best known, but there are a great many others to sample. Bavaria is also famed for its many varieties of bread and many kinds of sausage. Main meals are heavy on meat and low on vegetables. South German cooking often uses *Knödel* (dumplings) instead of potatoes and is heavy on the meat.

Vegetarian options include Käsespätzle, which are plump noodles served with melted cheese and crispy onions. The most widely-served types of beer include *helles* (pale) *dunkles* (dark) and dunkles *weissbier* (dark wheat-beer), which packs a powerful punch.

In authentic traditional beer-gardens (as opposed to those attached to tourist restaurants) budget conscious travellers can save money by bringing their own snacks. Those reckoned to go best with Bavarian beer include giant pretzels, salted mackerel, and a cheese and paprika spread called *Obatzda*. Another Bavarian speciality is *Weisswurst*, a white veal sausage which is boiled and served as a mid-morning snack with sweet mustard, large pretzels, and a glass of *Weissbier*.

Opening Hours

These vary from place to place and are not standard even within one city. As a rule of thumb: Banks: Mon–Fri 0830–1300 and 1430–1600 (until 1730 Thur). Hours have been shorter in the east, but are changing. Shops: Mon–Fri 0900–1830 (until 2030 Thur) and Sat 0900–1400. Shops next to stations are permitted to sell food and drink outside thse hours. Museums: Tues–Sun 0900–1700 (many until 2100 on Thur). Some open Monday and some close for an hour or more at lunch.

Postage

The usual post office hours are Mon–Sat 0800–1800 and the main post office in each town has a poste restante facility. Address letters to the *postlagernde*. All postal codes in Germany have been changed, so check that any you have are still current.

Public Holidays

1, 6 Jan; Good Friday; Easter Sunday–Monday; 1 May, Ascension Day; Whit Sunday–Monday; Corpus Christi★; 15 Aug★; 3 Oct; 1 Nov★; Day of Prayer (third Wednesday in November); 24, 25 Dec; 26 Dec (afternoon). The Munich Oktoberfest beer festival in 1996 takes place Sept 21 to Oct 6.
★Catholic feasts, celebrated only in south.

Public Transport

Most inter-city travel is by train, complemented by buses on smaller rural routes. Most of these are run by **Omnibus-Verkehrs Gemeinschaft Bahn-Post**, a joint post office and DB operation, so you can get information about them at the rail stations. Europabus also operates coaches on a number of tourist routes; information from **Deutsche Touring**, *Am Romerhof 17, D-60486 Frankfurt/Main*.

Many big cities have a **U-bahn** (U) underground railway and an **S-bahn** (S) urban rail service. City travel passes cover both, as well as other public transport. International passes usually cover the S, but not the U. Where ferries are an integral part of the city's transport, they are often included in the city transport pass.

A day card (*Tagesnetzkarte*) or multi-ride ticket (*Mehrfahrkarte*) usually pays its way if you take more than three rides. If there's no machine at the stop, get your ticket from the bus driver. The usual system is to get tickets from automatic machines and then validate them in little boxes at the station or on board the vehicle.

Several river-ferry and cruise lines operate on Germany's rivers; **KD Rhine Line** on the Rhine, Main, Elbe and Moselle and Berlin-based **White Fleet** on the Elbe, Saale and the Mecklenburg lakes. Book these through travel agents.

You can hire bicycles at 370 stations at DM7/DM9 per calendar day.

Telephones

Black telephone boxes have instructions in English and most operators speak it. **Kartentelefon** boxes take only cards, which you can buy at any post office, priced DM12 or DM50. To call abroad from Germany: *tel: 00*. There are a few exceptions, but the kiosks all give full

49

information. To call Germany: *tel: 49.* To call the international operator: *tel: 0010.* To call the national operator: tel: 010; international directory enquiries: *tel: 001188;* national directory enquiries: *tel: 01188.* Emergencies: Police: *110;* Fire: *112;* Ambulance: *112.*

RAIL TRAVEL WITHIN GERMANY

Deutsche Bahn (DB), the national railway network, is modernising rapidly, with a mixture of state-of-the-art and older rolling stock. There are also some privately owned railways. The main station in each town is the *Hauptbahnhof* (Hbf) and any sizeable station will be able to supply a computer print-out showing the connections along the route in which you are interested. Train tickets must be purchased before you board, unless you are prepared to pay a hefty supplement.

Long-distance trains are: *ICE* (an ultra-modern service which cruises at up to 174 mph), *IC* and *IR* plus *EC* and *EN.* The *RB* and *RSB* are modern, comfortable regional services linking up with the long-distance network. There are also reasonably fast *Eilzug (E)* and *D* trains. Ordinary commuter trains – *City-Bahn (CB), S-Bahn* and *Nahverkehrszug (N)* – are all slow services. Because of the nature of the terrain, rail travel in the German Alpine regions is usually much slower than in the rolling farmland of much of southern Germany.

Most German trains offer both first and second class, but some are second class only. Overnight services often have second-class seating and sleeping accommodation (sleeping-cars with up to three berths and/or couchettes with four or six berths). Seat reservations are possible for most fast trains, but not local trains.

All long-distance trains have dining-cars. If you are travelling with a bicycle

you need a *Fahrrad-Karte* allowing you to put your bike in the luggage van of *D, IR* and *E* trains (not on *ICE, EC* or *IC*). Available at any station or from German Rail offices, this costs DM5.40 to DM8.60 and on *IR* trains a reservation is strongly recommended and costs an extra DM3.50.

A new overnight luggage service allows your luggage to be picked up before 1800 for delivery to your next desintaion within Germany by 1000 in major cities and elsewhere. It costs DM28 for each case up to 30 kg. Properly packaged skis can also be sent ahead for DM46.

Passes

The **EuroDomino Pass** (sold in North America as the **GermanRail Pass**) buys unlimited travel for any three, five or ten days in a one month period and covers all scheduled services, *S-Bahn* airport connections and supplements for *IC, EC* and *ICE* trains. Seat, couchette and sleeper reservations extra.

German **Regional Passes** are sold only in the UK. There is no age limit and they are available for first- and second-class unlimited travel within one of 15 designated German regions for any 5 or 10 days in a 21-day period. They can be used on any *DB* trains (including *IC* and *EC*) and on the *S-Bahn,* but not on the *ICE* unless you are prepared to pay a supplement. **Tramper-Monats** tickets (available to anyone under 23 and to students under 27) give second-class travel for a month on all *DB* trains (except the *ICE,* for which a supplement is payable) as well as on railway-run buses (*Bahnbusse*) and the *S-Bahn.*

BahnCards give half-price travel on all trains for a full year. **EuroDomino** and other passes may or may not give you free or discounted travel on ferries plying the Bodensee. DB lakeside ticket offices, which sell ferry tickets, may tell you you do not have to pay, but this message does not seem to have reached the ticket officers on board the ferries, who at best grudgingly offer a 50% discount.

Deutsche Bahn also has a Web site offering timetable information on http://www.germany.net/gast/antrag.html (in German only) and offers an English-language booking service on Compu-Serve.

ITALY

Capital: Rome *(Roma)*. **Language:** Italian is the only official language but there are strong dialectal differences. In the cities and tourist areas many people speak some English, but it's seldom spoken at all off the beaten track. **Currency:** Lira (L.).

Passports and Visas
An EU National Identity Card is sufficient. Visas are not needed by Commonwealth citizens or nationals of the USA. Others should check.

Customs
Standard EU regulations apply (see p. 19).

Tourist Information
Most Italian towns, main railways stations and airports have a tourist information office. For information about a city, its hotels, sights and their opening hours, listings, maps, useful brochures and general advice, go to the **APT** *(Azienda Promozione Turistica)*. A big city will also have an **EPT** *(Ente Provinciale per il Turismo)* which is the provincial branch of the state organisation. It will provide information about the province, local festivals, hotels, give directions, and so on. Both the APT and the EPT are likely to be open from Mon to Sat from 0800 or 0900–1230 and 1600–1900. Sunday opening, if it occurs, will be from about

1000–1230 only. Neither will book hotels for you or arrange theatre tickets, but, if you ask specifically for it, they will provide a guide or direct you to an agency which will do the same (for a fee). A guide can be a great help in certain places – where many places are closed for reason other than that the custodian is having lunch, or can't be bothered to open up.

An **AAST** *(Azienda di Informazione e Accoglienza Turistica)* is generally a smaller, local office which may open infrequently, while a **Pro Loco**, which is found in villages attached to a large church or civic headquarters, may open only on demand. Be sure to look out for these. They often have more detailed local information than the APT.

On the whole Italy's tourist information offices are extremely helpful and provide a wide range of information. Only in major cities might you expect them to speak English. It is good idea to visit the **ENIT**, the Italian State Tourist Office, in your own country before you leave for Italy. It also has a huge range of information about most destinations in addition to hotel and campsite lists, prices, maps and so on.

Useful Addresses in Canada
Italian State Tourist Office (ENIT), *1 Placeville Marie, Suite 1914, Montreal, Quebec H3B 3MN; tel: (0514) 866 7667.*

Useful Addresses in Republic of Ireland
Italian State Tourist Office (ENIT), *47 Merrion Square, Dublin 2; tel: (01) 766 397.*

Useful Addresses in the UK
Consulate, *38 Eaton Place, London SW1X 8AN;* (Visa) *tel: (0171) 259 6322.* **Italian State Tourist Board,** *1 Princes St, London*

51

W1R 8AY; tel: (0171) 408 1254. **Italian Rail Travel, Wasteels,** *adjacent to Platform 2, Victoria Station, London SW1V 1JT; tel: (0171) 834 7066.*

Useful Addresses in the USA
Embassy, *1601 Fuller Street NW, Washington, DC 20009; tel: (202) 328 5500.* **Italian Government Travel Office (ENIT),** *630 Fifth Ave (Suite 1565), Rockefeller Center, New York, NY 10111; tel: (212) 245 4822 or 2324; 360 Post Street, Suite 801, San Francisco, CA 94108. Tel: (415) 392 6206.* **Italian Rail Travel, CIT Tours Corporation,** *594 Broadway (Suite 307), New York, NY 10012; tel: (212) 697-2100.*

STAYING IN ITALY

Accommodation
All **hotels** are classified according to a five-star system and inspectors set a maximum (seasonal) rate that must be displayed in each room. It does not necessarily include showers or breakfast, but extras must be listed separately, so complain (to the tourist office if all else fails) if your bill does not agree with the rates listed. You must, by law, obtain a receipt from all hotels.

Most establishments now term themselves hotel or *albergo,* but some are still called *pension* (one-, two-, or three-star) or *locande* (one-star). There are many *private rooms,* unofficial and otherwise. You can find the unofficial ones by looking for signs saying *affitta camere,* often in shop windows. It's worth trying to bargain, but you will usually pay about the same as for a one-star hotel. *Alberghi diurni,* near stations or in the centre, are essentially **day rooms:** you can have a wash without taking a room for the night.

There is no shortage of **youth hostels,** but relatively few belong to the **HI** and the standard varies considerably. It is often just as cheap and more convenient to stay at a one-star hotel.

Camping is popular and there are over 2000 sites (all tourist offices have information about their area), but they are often fairly expensive and/or difficult to reach without a car. There are few places where you can rough camp without asking permission. **Touring Club Italiano (TCI),** *Corso Italia 10, Milano; tel: (02) 85 261 or 852 6245,* publish an annual guide. Alternatively, you can get a list from **Federcampeggio,** *Casella Postale 23, 50041 Calenzano (Firenze); tel: (055) 88 215 918,* who can also make bookings. These two organisations produce a detailed directory of campsites, *Campeggi e Villagi Turistici in Italia,* available from bookshops in Italy (L.30,000).

Agriturismo, *Corso V Emanuele 101, 00186 Roma; tel: (06) 852 342,* has information about staying in rural cottages and farmhouses. **Club Alpino Italiano,** *Via Fonseca Pimental 7, 20122 Milano; tel: (02) 26 141 378,* can supply details of mountain refuge huts.

Eating and Drinking
In Italy eating and drinking is an enjoyable national pastime. Frequently, visiting a restaurant or walking to a café or bar to enjoy a drink or an ice cream is a form of entertainment akin to going to the movies. It involves dressing up, meeting friends, labouring over a single coffee or ice cream and mingling with the crowds of other people indulging in the same exercise.

In Italy, a *trattoria* is generally less expensive than a *ristorante.* In the former, you might find a homelier atmosphere, a smaller range of things on the menu, and mother, father, grandmother and all the sons busily running the place morning, noon and night. Informal, busy and noisy, jugs of local wine can be ordered for at a very small price. There may not be a menu; the waiter will simply tell you what they have that day so, if you don't understand, perhaps have a look into the kitchen. The *ristoranti* are more formal, with a wider variety of menu choices and a wine list. Be prepared to spend more. A *pizzeria* is exactly what it says it is – probably the best place to find pizza – and an *osteria* is basically an old-fashioned restaurant. Unless you have a specific recommendation for one of these, they are best avoided because they can be expensive.

At both lunch and dinner, there is a wide range of food available, wherever you are. Most interesting though are the regional variations of even simple pasta dishes. A full meal will consist of an *antipasto* (cold, preserved vegetables, salami, fried courgette flowers, mozzarella, and so on) followed by a first main course, *il primo,* and then a second, *il secondo. Il primo* might be either pasta, soup, *gnocchi* (little potato dumplings) – it is absolutely alright just to have this on its own. *Il secondo* is the meat or fish course and, as with the pasta course, this can be ordered as a meal in itself. As with fish, meats – roast or boiled – will come on their own so, if you want vegetables, *il contorni,* you must order them separately from whatever has been cooked that day. Meals are often rounded off with salad, *insalata,* cheese (you can just ask for a lump of *pecorino romano* or *parmigiano,* parmesan), fruit or *dolci* – something sweet. These vary considerably from place to place. *Cassata* is ice cream made from ricotta cheese. Elsewhere there may be *zabaglione, zuppa inglese,* literally, English soup, that is trifle.

Vegetarians will find a huge range of dishes to suit their tastes. Luckily Italian food is very versatile – though make sure

that the tomato sauce covering your pasta doesn't contain meat (*al pomodoro* is with tomato, *al ragu* is with meat).

When the bill comes, expect to find that you're paying a cover charge – referred to as *pane e coperto.* This is fairly standard wherever you are. On top of that you will be expected to provide a tip of around 10%.

If you want to avoid eating out, *alimentari* often prepare delicious sandwiches – simply point out what you want them to be filled with – and will provide wine (and open the bottle for you), beer and fruit juices. *Rosticcerie* are good for mouth-watering hunks of rosemary-flavoured chicken roasted on a spit, while *tavole calde* are cheap sit-down places. Smaller establishments rarely have menus: just ask for the dish of the day if you want something reasonably priced. Menus – and prices – are displayed by the entrance.

Coffee comes in many forms, from *espresso* to liqueur. *Un caffe* is a short, strong *espresso* while *un cappuccino* is a milky coffee. You might like a freshly-squeezed orange juice, in which case ask for a *spremuta d'arancia.* There are various types of Italian beer and many fine wines – many available in bars. Here too you will find particularly good breakfast or lunchtime snacks: *brioche* or *cornetto* (a jam or custard-filled croissant), *crespoline* (pancakes), *foccacia* (heavily salted, slightly oily, crusty bread), *tramezzini* (toasted sandwiches), *panini* (filled rolls), pastries, even a bowl of pasta. Bars are also the place to try the local 'fire waters' such as *grappa.* If you stand by the bar and eat you will be charged less than if you sit down and, if you want to use the lavatory, remember that you may have to buy something first.

Opening Hours
Banks: Mon–Fri 0830–1300 and usually

for an additional hour in the afternoon (exactly when varies). **Shops:** (usually) Mon–Sat 0830/0900–1230/1300 and 1530/1600–1900/1930. In July/Aug many close Mon morning or Sat afternoon. A few stay open all day, every day. **Museums:** national museums and archaeological sites usually open Tues–Sun 0930–1300/1400 and some re-open 1600–1900, but there is no real pattern. Although Mon is the usual closing day, it can be Sun or Tues or they may stay open all week. Most sites and museums refuse entry within an hour or two of closing.

Postage

Usual post office hours are Mon–Sat 0800–1830, but there's no Satur opening in many small places. The postal service is slow and it's worth paying for anything urgent to be sent express. Stamps *(francobolli)* are available from post offices, tobacconists *(tabacchi)* and some gift shops in resorts. Poste restante *(Fermo posta)* is possible at most post offices, but you have to pay a small amount when you collect.

Public Holidays

All over the country: 1, 6 Jan; Easter Mon; 1 May; 15 Aug (virtually nothing opens); 1 Nov; 8, 25, 26 Dec.

Regional saints' days include: 25 Apr in Venice; 24 June in Florence, Genoa and Turin; 7 Dec in Milan.

Public Transport

Buses are often crowded, but serve many areas inaccessible by rail and tend to be punctual. Services are drastically reduced at weekends and timetables do not always reflect this fact. Tickets for long-distance and local buses are usually obtained before boarding (some local ones are bought on board). Long-distance tickets are usually available from train stations or CIT offices, while local tickets are from machines, news-stands or tobacconists.

Taxis are metered, but can be expensive, with a substantial flat fare to start with and extra charges for baggage, journeys out of town and travel on holidays or late at night. You can hail taxis on the street, but steer clear of unofficial ones.

Telephones

The phone system is in a constant state of over-haul, with frequently changing numbers ranging from two to eight digits. Directories may list two numbers – try both. If they're of different lengths, the longer is likely to be the new one.

Most public phones have instructions in English and take coins, phonecards *(carte telefoniche/scheda)*, or both. Cards are available from automatic machines near the phones, tobacconists and news-stands. You can make international calls by using a phonecard, but in some small towns you must go to an office of the state phone company, **SIP**, or (occasionally) **ASST**. They often have branches in the stations; if not, you should find one near the main post office. You may also come across the old phones that take only tokens *(gettoni)*. If so, you should be able to get the tokens from whoever owns the phone, or find an automatic dispenser nearby. *Gettoni* are often accepted as small change, so don't be surprised if you are given some instead of small denomination coins.

Scatti phones are quite common – these are metered and you pay the operator/owner when you have finished, but they are normally in places like bars and the 'operator' may well add a service charge, so check before you commit yourself. Hotels invariably charge over the odds.

To call abroad from Italy: *tel: 00*. To call Italy: *39*. For English information and assistance for intercontinental calls: *170*. For English information on calling Europe and the Mediterranean area: *176*. For local operator assistance: *15*. For local directory enquiries: *12*. **Emergencies:** Fire: *115*; Police, Ambulance and other services: *113*. Loss or theft of Thomas Cook Travellers Cheques; *tel: 1678 72050* (local call charge payable).

RAIL TRAVEL WITHIN ITALY

The national rail company is **Ferrovie dello Stato (FS)**. The **Pendolino (ETR 450)** trains reach up to 155 mph. These are luxury express services between major cities. Reservations are necessary and there is the usual basic supplement to use the trains plus another (usually £10–£20) before you board (which, in first class, covers such extras as hostess service, newspapers and food).

Reservations are also obligatory for *IC* and *EC* services. *IR* trains are semi-fast expresses. The *espresso* are long-distance domestic trains, with both first and second class, which stop only at main stations. The *diretto* stop frequently and are very slow, while the *locale* stop almost everywhere. The rail network is extensive and the service reasonably punctual. Some long-distance trains won't carry passengers for short distances. Sleepers have single or double berths in first class, three berths (occasionally doubles) in second class; couchettes have four berths in first class and six in second class.

Most long-distance trains have refreshment facilities. Dining-cars offer a full service at meal times and snacks the rest of the day. Buffet cars are self-service, catering coaches or bar cars. Don't drink the tap water on trains. Queues at stations are often long and it's better to buy tickets and make reservations at travel agencies (look for the **FS** symbol).

Fares and Passes

Biglietto Chilometrico can be used by up to 5 people, but the allowance is divided by the number of travellers. It is valid for 3000 km, in the course of which you can have 19 different stops over a period of 2 months. The **Italian Flexicard** allows travel for any 4 days out of 9, any 8 days out of 21 or any 12 days out of 30. It should be purchased in the UK as it is available in very few other places. The **Travel-at-will** tickets allow non-Italian residents to travel on any Italian train for 8, 15, 21 or 30 days. All three domestic passes give a choice of first- or second-class travel. If you board without a ticket there is an automatic fine of up to 20% of the fare. Buy tickets for short journeys (up to 100 km) from any tobacconist.

SLOVENIA

Capital: Ljubljana. **Language:** Slovene. **Currency:** The *Tolar* (SLT) is divided into 100 *stotini*. Coins come in denominations of 50 *stotini*.

Passports and Visas

Citizens of Britain, Ireland, Australia, New Zealand, Canada and the USA need only a valid passport to enter Slovenia.

Customs

Goods purchased in Slovenia exceeding 9000 tolars are eligible for tax refunds.

Tourist Information

Look for signs that read 'Turist Biro'. The country's travel agencies have a reputation for being helpful to independent travellers. and one, Kompas, has offices abroad.

Useful Addresses in the UK

Embassy, *11–15 Wigmore Street, London W1H 9LA; tel: (0171) 495 7775.*

Slovenian Tourist Board, 2 Canfield Place, *London NW6 3BT; tel: (0171) 372 3767.*

Useful Addresses in the USA

Embassy, *1252 New Hampshire Ave NW, Washington, DC 20036; tel: (202) 667 5363.* **Tourist Office,** *122 E 42nd St, Suite 3006, New York, NY 10168 0072; tel:(212) 682 5896.*

STAYING IN SLOVENIA

Accommodation

The quality and standards of the accommodation in Slovenia is very high and is easily comparable with Italy. **Hotels** are classified not by stars but by letters. **L**, for example, signifies an establishment in the luxury class, and **A** the business class. **B** is a rung down (expect an private bathroom) and **C** at the bottom (expect to share a bathroom). **Guesthouses** *(gostilne)* are very popular indeed and are cheaper than hotels. Often they are located in out of the way places devoid of any hotels. **Private rooms** *(zasebne sobe)* are also available; ask for a list at the tourist office. That way you get a glimpse into the daily lives of the locals in rural or urban locations.

Eating and Drinking

Nothing symbolises Slovenia's geographic position as a crossroads between north and south and east and west more eloquently than the national cuisine. German and Italian, Slav and eastern Mediterranean – influences are all felt – and tasted – everywhere. There is also an ancient Slav culinary tradition, mostly deriving from Slovenia's peasant culture, but this is slowly being eroded as local cafés and eating places replace old-fashioned fare with dishes more suitable to international tastes.

Eating in a restaurant *(restavracija)* is generally more expensive than an inn *(gostilna),* while bars and snack bars *(okrepčevalnice)* and *kavana* (the indigenous version of an Viennese coffee house) are the places to find really inexpensive, filling snacks for breakfast or any other meal for that matter. The *kavana* are the places to have heart-stopping black coffee – *kava*. In addition to these, pavement kiosks serve delicious hot or cold take-aways which are useful for picnics or for meals eaten walking along. *Delikatesa,* delicatessen, are best for buying *salama* (salami) or sausages, preserved vegetables and *sir* (local cheese), though don't forget to investigate the supermarkets because, providing you stick to locally made ingredients, these can be a very inexpensive way of stocking up. For bread *(kruh),* go to the bakery *(pekarna),* and there are markets where fruit and vegetables are in plentiful supply.

Eating out, expect to find menus burgeoning with meat dishes – grilled meat, offal (particularly liver, *jetra,* and grilled or fried brains, *mozgani*) and schnitzel-type dishes (with pork, *svijina,* or veal, *teletina*). A strong stomach is needed for some of these, as is a hearty constitution since plates are heaped with food. Slovene frankfurters *(hrenovke)* are particularly delicious – try them in hotdogs from a snackbar – as are spicy sausages *(kranjska klobasa).* Wherever you go you'll find a version of goulasch *(golaz).* Slovenia's proximity to Italy is not forgotten: another popular dish is *zlikrofi* which, basically, is ravioli with a potato, onion and bacon filling. Coastal menus feature *školjke* and *kalamari,* squid.

Slovenian wines, both red *(crno)* and white *(belo)* are fairly well known outside the country – white Ljutomer, for example, is widely available throughout Europe. These, or beer, are drunk either with meals or in a *vinarna,* a wine cellar or a *pivnica,* a beer hall, as are a huge variety of local aperitifs – such as the brandy-like *sadjevec* or the gin-like *brinovec*.

Opening Hours

Banks: Mon–Fri 0700–1800 and Sat 0700–1100. In addition to this, you can expect at least one bank to be open in major centres on Sun morning for a few hours. Money exchanges (*menjalnica*) have more flexible hours. Expect to find prices of important goods and services quoted in a major foreign currency. This is due to the fact that Slovenia has rampant inflation. Major credit cards are fairly widely accepted – but don't depend on being able to use them, as are travellers' cheques. **Shops:** Most shops are open Mon–Fri 0900–1800 and Sat 0900–1300. Both shops and banks are closed on public holidays. **Museums:** while generally closed on Mondays, the opening times differ widely from place to place.

Public Holidays

Jan 1 and 2, Easter Monday, April 27, Aug 15, Dec 25.

Public Transport

Buses: the bus network in Slovenia is very comprehensive indeed – both within the cities and towns and out in the countryside. Almost every little village is linked to the network, though you may have to wait for your connection. One source of confusion however, if you're new to it, is the array of bus companies offering their services. One you've mastered who does what, you'll find that their services are well co-ordinated. Bigger cities have bus stations with information services and computerised booking which means that you can reserve a seat in advance of travelling – useful on public holidays and in the summer particularly on routes connecting the hinterland with the sea.

Postage

The post offices (*poşta* or *PTT*) are open Mon–Fri 0800–1800 and Sat 0800–1300. In some of the bigger cities, post offices are also open for a few hours on Sun. If they're not, buy stamps (*marke*) at a newsstand.

Telephones

Post offices also sell tokens (*ʒetoni*) for use in public call boxes, and telecards (*telekartice*) are also available – both can also be had from a news-stand. For greater convenience, if you need to make an overseas call, go to a post office and make it in one of the cabins provided there. It's often easier to pay after the call: simply watch the meter and stop when your limit is reached. The international dialling code for Slovenia is *38*. To call Slovenia: tel: *386*.

Emergencies: police: *92*; ambulance: *94*; fire: *93*.

Loss or theft of Thomas Cook Traveller's Cheques, *tel: 0044 1733 502995* (reverse charges).

RAIL TRAVEL WITHIN SLOVENIA

Unless you want to stop at every single station on your route, avoid the slow trains, the *potniski*. This service, while extremely comprehensive and generally faster than taking the bus, has its drawbacks.

The *IC* trains are the much faster intercity versions which generally cost more. For an express service, refer to the *IC* (InterCity) or *ZV* (*zeleni vlaki* – the green trains) entries on a timetable. Seats on these must be reserved in advance

Fares and Passes

Both **EuroDomino** and **InterRail** passes are valid for Slovenia.

SWITZERLAND

Capital: Berne. **Language**: German, French, Italian and Romansch are all official languages of Switzerland. Around 65% of the country speak German, 18 per cent French (mainly in the west), 10 per cent Italian (in Ticino) and only 1 per cent speak Romansch (confined to the Graubünden region). Most Swiss people are at least bilingual and knowledge of English is widespread. Swiss-German has many peculiar words and phrases terms which may be decipherable to German speakers, of which the most useful for the visitor is the general greeting 'Gruezi' (Hello). **Currency**: Swiss Francs (SFr.); 1 Franc = 100 Centimes.

Customs

The following allowances are for visitors aged 17 or over: 200 cigarettes or 50 cigars or 250g tobacco, 2 litres alcohol up to 15% volume, and 1 litre over 15% volume. People who live outside Europe are entitled to twice the tobacco allowance.

Passports and Visas

EU National Identity Cards are sufficient. All other travellers require a valid passport. Visas are not needed by nationals of Australia, Canada, New Zealand or the USA. Others should check.

Tourist Information

There is a tourist office (*verkehrsbüro/office du tourisme/ufficio turistico*) in almost any town or village where visitors may set foot and the standard of information and the level of help is invariably excellent. Thoughtfully, many offices leave leaflets with accommodation and other basic details in holders outside the office when they are shut. If that fails then ask at the railway station.

Useful Addresses in the UK

Embassy, *16/18 Montagu Place, London W1H 2BQ; tel: (0171) 723 0701*. **Swiss**

National Tourist Office (SNTO) and Railway Representatives, *Swiss Centre, Swiss Court, London W1V 8EE; tel: (0171) 734 1921.*

Useful Addresses in the USA

Embassy, *2900 Cathedral Ave NW, Washington, DC 20008-3499; tel: (202) 745 7900.* **Swiss National Tourist Office (SNTO)**, *Swiss Center, 608 Fifth Ave, New York, NY 10020; tel: (212) 757 5944.* **Railroad Representatives**, *Rail Europe Inc., 226/230 Westchester Ave, White Plains, NY 10604; tel: (800) 682 2999 (toll-free).*

STAYING IN SWITZERLAND

Accommodation

Hotels: Switzerland has been welcoming tourists for well over a century and leads the world in hospitality standards. Staff are usually very well trained and English is the lingua franca. Of course, with high standards (and the very high cost of Swiss living) come high prices and you'll be very lucky to get anything of reasonable quality for less than SFr.50 per single room or SFr.80 per double room. In rural areas it is often possible to get rooms in **private houses**, or even better on farms, but these are few and far between in cities. Budget travellers tend to rely on camping or on youth hostels (*Jugendherbergen/Auberge de Jeunesse/Alberghi Svizzeri per la Gioventu*). Ask the SNTO for a copy of their useful map brochure which gives details of all 79 HI-affiliated hostels, right down to a key which tells you which ones are classified as 'romantic'! It is essential that you book well ahead.

Every major town and major station has a hotel-finding service. The tourist office always offer accommodation details and often provide a booking service, sometimes free and seldom expensive. Direct telephone booking boards may also be found outside some stations, whereby you simply choose the hotel you like from the details posted in front of you, pick up the attached telephone and make a reservation. The usual one- to five-star system applies, with the term *garni* meaning bed and breakfast only. There is an additional U (for *unikat*/unique) classification, signifying that the particular establishment cannot (for various reasons) be graded. Apartments and aparthotels are not common in Switzerland.

If you don't want twin beds, you must ask for a 'matrimonial' or 'French' bed.

Once at your hotel enquire about a Visitor's Card which will entitle you to various discounts on tourist leisure activities (eating out, transport, shopping etc.), though do note, not all areas operate such a scheme.

The **Swiss National Tourist Office (SNTO)** can provide information on accommodation but do not make bookings. They also publish a *Swiss Hotel Guide for the Disabled*, which distinguishes between those places suitable for people with walking impediments and those suitable for wheelchairs. **The Swiss Hotel Association, Schweizer Hotelier Verein (SHV)**, *Monbijoustr. 130, Postfach, 3001 Bern; tel: (031) 370 41 11,* publish an annual hotel guide in four languages which includes information for disabled travellers. The SNTO also provide a useful leaflet, *Travel Tips for the Disabled*.

There are hundreds of **campsites** in Switzerland (most open summer only). They are graded on a one- to five-star system; guides are available from specialist bookshops or **Schweizer Camping und Caravanning Verband**, *Habsburgerstr.35, 6004 Luzern; tel: (041) 23 48 22* or **Verband Schweizer Campings**,

Seestr.119, 3800 Interlaken; tel: (036) 23 35 23. 'Rough' camping is not officially permitted, though it does happen.

Eating and Drinking

There is a wide range of both food and eating-places, though as the Swiss have no strong culinary traditions of their own they draw on the culture (French, German or Italian) that is most prevalent in that particular region.

The cheapest places to eat are supermarket or department store cafeterias, such as those housed in the ubiquitous **Migros** outlets. Look out too for **EPA, Co-op, Manora**, and in Ticino, **Inova**. These are all self-service buffet establishments and surroundings can vary enormously from functional canteen to full-blown restaurant. Another cheap option is the ubiquitous *Bahnhof Buffet* café-restaurant which can be found even at small stations.

At lunch time (and quite often in the evenings) most restaurants advertise a fixed-price dish-of-the-day menu (*tagesteller, plat du jour, piatto del giorno*) that is usually good value. Service is invariably god but tipping in Swiss restaurants is *not* the norm.

Start the day with *Birchermuesli*, a vastly superior creamy porridge-like version of the thin muesli cereal most people are familiar with. The rest of the breakfast buffet is standard international-European fare, comprising cereals, fruits, cold meats and cheeses. Coffee is the most popular hot drink, served milky and frothy (called *renversée* in French-Switzerland). If you want expresso in Ticino ask for a *ristretto*. Tea is common and is served black unless you specifically request milk.

Not surprisingly Swiss cheese is a ubiquitous ingredient in local dishes. The classic Swiss *fondue*, for instance, is bread dipped into a pot containing melted cheese (typically Emmental and Gruyère), garlic, wine and kirsch. Other popular types of fondue are: *fondue bourguignonne*, where chunks of meat are dipped into hot oil and served with a variety of dipping sauces; *fondue chinoise*, where thinly sliced meat is plunged into a simmering stock (which is then consumed after the meat). Fondues are often a social occasion and popular custom has it that should you drop your bread, or meat, the next round of drinks is on you – so be careful!

The other classic Swiss cheese dish is *raclette*, which is simply a slab of melted cheese (a suitable type of *raclette* cheese is chosen in order to avoid it becoming rubbery when it cools), served with bread, boiled potatoes, gherkins and silverskin onions. Few restaurants serve a selection of Swiss cheeses as a meal course (and those that do are the more expensive types) so if you want to sample them you will have to shop around and buy them for picnics.

The ubiquitous meal accompaniment in German-speaking areas (which is most of the country) is *rösti*, fried shredded potatoes and onions. Some restaurants offer a range of *rösti* dishes, adding sausage, ham, peppers and the like to make a filling and usually good value one-pot meal. A similar all-inclusive peasant meal is provided by *Bernerplatte*, comprising a medley of ham, sausage, bacon, potatoes, beans, sauerkraut or whatever else the chef cares to throw in.

Other local specialities (unfortunately often out of the price range of budget travellers), include: from Graubünden, *Bündnerfleisch* – air-dried beef, which is smoked and thinly sliced: local freshwater fish, usually from the lakes, most notably *egli/perche* (perch) and *forellen/truite* (trout). More affordable is the delicious Lucerne special, *Kügelipasteti* (a large vol-au-vent filled with meat and mushrooms in a

cream sauce) and *Schweingeschnetzeltes*, the pork version of the famous and widespread Zurich speciality, *Kalbsgeschnetzeltes/ Emincé zurichoise* (veal in cream sauce).

The Swiss are largely a carnivorous nation and vegetarian dishes, let alone restaurants, are a novelty.

Good quality European lagers and wines are always on hand to wash down your meal. Wine is usually ordered by the decilitre (dl) and is served in a glass flask. As a guide 1 dl is just under a standard wine glass measure. Two wines that you may not be familiar with are *fendent* and *dôle*. The former is a thin white wine, a favourite accompaniment to *fondue* and *raclette*, while the latter is a big fruity red, excellent with hearty meat dishes.

An American burger chain representative can always be found in the larger towns (and MacDonalds are even represented on some trains) but for local fast food look for stalls selling German-style sausage (*bratwurst, cervelat* etc.) which are usually served with a warm bread roll.

Opening Hours

Banks: Mon–Fri 0800–1200 and 1400–1700. **Shops**: Mon–Fri 0800–1200 and 1330–1830, Sat 0800–1200 and 1330–1600. Many close on Mon morning. **Money change** desks are also located at most railway stations. Rates are not much less than at the bank and these desks do open longer hours than banks. **Museums**: the usual closing day is Mon. Most museums also offer free admission on one day each week. Opening hours and free-admission days vary, so check locally.

Postage

Post office opening times are usually Mon–Fri 0730–1200 and 1345–1830; Sat 0730–1100. In cities however, major branches usually stay open for much longer. Poste restante (*Postlagernd*) facilities are available at most post offices.

Public Holidays

1 Jan; Good Friday; Easter Monday; Ascension Day; Whit Monday; 1 August; 25, 26 Dec. 2 Jan, 1 May and Corpus Christi are public holidays in some areas.

Public Transport

Swiss **buses**, both long-distance and local, are famously punctual. Bright yellow **Postbuses** fill gaps in the railway network and always stop at the railway station and post office. Free timetables are available from post offices and Swiss Pass (see p. 62) is valid for all services, but there is a surcharge (SFr.5) for some scenic routes (pay the driver or buy your ticket on the bus). If you don't have a Swiss Pass, it may be worth buying a regional 7-day pass (from any post office in that region). It's seldom worth buying a city transport pass as the best way to get around most compact Swiss city centres is on foot. Tickets for municipal buses must always be bought in advance, from machines by the bus stops. Once again, Swiss Pass covers the vast majority of municipal services.

Another popular way of getting around is by bicycle. The Swiss are avid cyclists so facilities are good. Over 200 railway stations have cycles for hire and operate a most convenient system whereby you may deposit your bike at any one of the other 200 stations in the country (prices start at SFr.15 per day). And don't forget that you can send your luggage ahead so you don't have to worry about carrying it with you!

Telephones

The national network is **PTT** and all their offices (usually, but not always, located in post offices) sell phonecards (*taxcard*). Phonecards are also available from most rail stations. In the PTT offices you can pay for international calls when you have finished. All telephone boxes have instructions in English and all telephone operators can speak English. The pink pages at the front of directories list local and international codes.

To call abroad from Switzerland: *tel: 00*. To call Switzerland: *tel: 41*. To call international enquiries and operators: *tel: 191*. To call national enquiries and operators: *tel: 111*. **Emergencies**: Police: *117;* Fire: *118;* Ambulance: *144*. Loss or theft of Thomas Cook Traveller's Cheques, *tel: 155 0130* (toll free).

RAIL TRAVEL WITHIN SWITZERLAND

The principal rail carrier is **Swiss Federal Railways (SBB)**, known in French as *CFF* and in Italian as *FFS*; but there are many other small, private lines. The train service is fast, clean and as punctual as one would expect in a country noted for producing high-quality clocks and watches. The fastest trains are the various types of *EC (Eurocity)* and *IC (Intercity)*. All express trains stop only at major cities. *Regionalzüge* are slow local trains which stop more frequently.

Some international trains have sleepers with three berths and/or couchettes for up to six people. Reservations are compulsory for the special observation/sightseeing cars of certain services (e.g. the *Glacier Express*), though it is also worth noting that many of these 'special' services are running along ordinary service lines and no booking is needed (see individual routes for details). Sleeping cars can be booked up to three months in advance, couchettes and seats up to two months ahead. If connecting by air, you can check in and book your luggage right through to its final destination from any station in the country, saving you the effort of lugging about.

Railway station telephone information is currently being centralised onto a single national numbers: *157 22 22,* (though many stations may still be contacted direct). You can dial *157 22 22* from anywhere in the country (though not from outside Switzerland) and be connected to an English-speaking operator who will answer queries on timetables, fares and the like. However this is a relatively expensive premium-rate line (SFr.1.19 per min.), so remember to collect timetables and other information personally from the station or try calling on the direct telephone numbers (where given) in the text.

One of the joys of the Swiss public transport system is the synchronisation of all major services, so you needn't worry about stepping off one platform to find your connecting service from the next platform departed two minutes ago. This general rule also applies to postbuses, funiculars and other means of transport.

Fares and Passes

European rail passes (see p. 28) are valid on some private railways in Switzerland. The two most useful discount tickets are the **Swiss Pass** (valid for 4, 8, 15 days or for 1 month) and the **Flexi Pass** (valid for any 3 days in a 15-day period). Both are available from the SNTO for first- or second-class travel on SBB services and also cover buses and regular boat services.

Liechtenstein

Although the Principality of Liechtenstein is technically a separate country it has no major distinguishing features from Switzerland. Most importantly, as far as visitors are concerned, it shares the same currency and has no entry formalities on the Swiss border. For full details see p. 58.

Panoramic coaches

Panoramic coaches (used on the MOB, the *Glacier Express*, and other lines) are specially designed to afford the maximum field of visibility, particularly useful when passing mountain scenery. The windows are not only much bigger, but the roof too is also mostly glass. The only snag is taking photographs, as it is impossible to open such windows!

Beware, however, that these will only entitle you to a discount, not free travel, on several mountain railways and famous private railway lines such as those run by the Montreux-Oberland-Bernois (MOB) and the Jungfraujoch companies. As these are the country's most scenic routes, which you certainly won't want to miss, you should allow for this extra expenditure when calculating your travel budget.

The **Tell Pass** covers travel by rail, ferry and bus in the Lake Lucerne area. The 15-day pass gives 5 days of free travel within a central zone, plus half-price travel on other specified routes for the duration of the pass. The 7 day version allows 2 days free travel. Details available from travel and tourist offices.

Two more passes that may be considered are: the **Half-Fare Travel Card**, simple and self-explanatory but only valid for one year or one month, therefore only useful if you intend to spend a month or more in Switzerland; the **Swiss Card**, which entitles you to travel free of charge from the border or airport station to your destination and back, plus the option of buying all other train, postbus and boat tickets at half-price. Finally there is also a **Family Card**, issued free of charge, which allows your own children (up to the age of 16) to ride free.

A train seat with a fine view, a yellow bus in a mountain village en route to the heart of the country, a gently rocking paddle steamer. The Swiss Pass, a timeless journey, the freedom of Switzerland.

The freedom of Switzerland can be yours for as little as £138 for 8 days with the Swiss Pass.

Journey unrestricted on the whole 16,000kms of the Swiss Travel System. On any train in the world's finest railway system, including the famous panoramic routes (with the exception of mountain summit railways, where major reductions are offered).

By paddle steamer and postbus throughout Switzerland. And by tram and bus services in 36 towns and cities.

And with the free Family Card, any of your children up to the age of 16 can travel with you free.

For information on the Swiss Pass, Flexi-Pass and Swiss Card call Switzerland Tourism on 0171 (011 44 171) 734 1921. Or fax us on 0171 (011 44 171) 437 4577. Or E-mail: switzerland@mail.bogo.co.uk

Holidays at long last. Switzerland is yours.

SAMPLE ITINERARIES

Half the fun of a journey lies in the planning and plotting, in the endless hours of day-dreaming before you set out. By dividing the region into recommended routes, this book is intended to make it easy and pleasurable to plan your ideal tour. For those who like a little help in making up their minds, or who like to follow a specific theme, we have put together a selection of sample itineraries, lasting from a few days to three weeks in length. You could use them as a blueprint for a trip but may well prefer to use them as a framework on which to hang your own personal adventure.

The itineraries below are all designed as circular routes, beginning and ending at one of the major international air gateways. Suggested overnight stops are in bold.

I. THE GRAND TOUR

28 days
The way to wring the most possible benefit from your rail card, with a whistle-stop tour round the major cities in the region.
Day 1: Arrive **Zurich** (p. 325); Day 2: in **Zurich**; Day 3: Zurich–**Lucerne** (route, p. 335); Day 4: in **Lucerne** (p. 168); Day 5: Lucerne–**Berne** (p. 79); Day 6: in **Berne**; Day 7: Berne–**Geneva** (route, p. 83); Day 8: in **Geneva** (p. 102); Day 9: Geneva–**Lyon** (route, p. 189); Day 10: in **Lyon** (p. 180); Day 11: Lyon–**Turin**

(route, p. 200); Day 12: in **Turin** (p. 286); Day 13: Turin–**Milan** (route, p. 293); Day 14: in **Milan** (p. 205); Day 15: Milan–**Venice** (route, p. 218); Days 16–17: in **Venice** (p. 296); Day 18: Venice–**Vienna** (route, p. 304); Days 19–20: in **Vienna** (p. 315); Day 21: Vienna–**Salzburg** (route, p. 278); Day 22: in **Salzburg** (p. 261); Day 23: Salzburg–**Munich** (route, p. 242); Day 24: in **Munich** (p. 224); Day 25: Munich–**Liechtenstein** (p. 165); Day 26: in **Liechtenstein**; Day 27: Liechtenstein–**Zurich**; Day 28: Fly home.

2. GREAT EASTERN LOOP

28 days
Cut the region in half to take in a little more of the great outdoors...
Day 1: Arrive **Zurich** (p. 325); Day 2: in **Zurich**; Day 3: Zurich–**Konstanz** (p. 142); Day 4: Touring Konstanz and the Bodensee (p. 142–146), overnight in **Lindau**; Day 5: Lindau–**Garmisch-Partenkirchen** (Innsbruck–Friedrichshafen route, p. 122); Day 6: Visit Zugspitze and Neuschwanstein, overnight in **Garmisch -Partenkirchen** or **Innsbruck**; Day 7: to/in **Innsbruck** (p. 118); Day 8: Innsbruck to **Salzburg** (p. 126); Day 9: in **Salzburg**;
Day 10: Salzburg–**Vienna** (p. 278); Days 11–12: in Vienna; Day 14: Vienna–**Ljubljana** (p. 304); Day 15: in **Ljubljana**; Day 16: Ljubljana–**Venice** (p. 304) ; Days 17–18: in **Venice**; Day 19: Venice–**Verona** (p. 218); Day 20: Verona–**Milan** (p. 218); Day 21: in

Planning Your Itinerary

There are a few golden rules to remember when planning a trip:

1. Work out train times with an up-to-date copy of the *Thomas Cook European Timetable* and the *Thomas Cook New Rail Map of Europe* (see p. 14). Do pay attention to footnotes as they may refer to changes in the usual timetable. Recheck the timings as you go - there may have been changes, and there may also be convenient local trains which the Thomas Cook timetable doesn't have the space to include. There are detailed leaflets available free at most rail stations. Ask the staff to double-check anything you do not understand, or just to reassure yourself.

2. Always check onward services to your next destination before leaving the station. You don't want to miss the last train for three days. Also make sure that you do not have to reserve a seat or couchette in advance and whether there will be any surcharge on your pass.

3. If the place you are planning to visit is very small and you have luggage with you, check beforehand if there is somewhere to leave your bags. You don't want to lug them around all day.

4. When deciding on your itinerary, check the opening times of any 'must see' sights. There is nothing worse that travelling hundreds of miles to see a chateau only to find that it is closed. Make sure you are in a suitable place over any public holidays. Remember that the sights may be quite a distance from the station, and build in enough time to get there, as well as for meal breaks.

5. Always prebook your first and last nights' accommodation, particularly if you are arriving in the evening or have an early morning flight out. This takes the pressure off and leaves you free to sort yourselves out at leisure.

6. Unless you have accommodation prebooked, plan to arrive at your overnight stop in plenty of time to find lodgings (usually by about 4pm). Make the tourist information office your first call.

7. Don't move towns or hotels every night. You get tired and also run out of clean clothes. Laundry breaks are essential on a touring holiday.

8. Don't try to be too ambitious or too organised. If you try and cram absolutely everything in to a split second timetable, you will end up frazzled and fractious and unable to enjoy anything. Rather, allow for a leisurely meander, with time to smell the flowers and sip the coffee. If you miss a few sights, or have to cover a smaller area, does it really matter? If it does, you can come back next year.

Milan: Day 22: Milan–**Stresa** for Lake Maggiore (Bernee–Milan route, p. 86); Day 23: Stresa–**Spiez** (Bernee– Milan route) or **Interlaken** (p. 135); Day 24:

Day trip up the Jungfraujoch (Interlaken–Jungfrau route, p. 138), overnight in **Interlaken**; Day 25: Interlaken–**Lucerne** (Lucerne–Interlaken route, p. 173); Day 26: in **Lucerne** (p. 168); Day 27: Tour of Lake Lucerne, Lucerne–**Zurich** (p. 335); Day 28: Fly home.

3. GREAT WESTERN LOOP

28 days
...*Or go west into France, for a taste of the beach as well as the snow.*
Day 1: Arrive **Zurich** (p. 325); Day 2: in **Zurich**; Day 3: Zurich–**Lucerne** (p. 335); Day 4: in **Lucerne**; Day 5: Lucerne–**Lugano** (Lucerne–Milan route, p. 176); Day 6: in **Lugano** and the Italian lakes; Day 7: Lugano–Milan; Day 8: in Milan; Day 9: Milan–Turin (p. 293); Day 10: in Turin; Day 11: Turin–**Menton** or **Monte Carlo** (Nice–Turin route, p. 252);

Days 12–13: Along the Riviera to **Nice** (p. 245); Day 14: in **Nice**; Day 15: Nice–**Digne** (Lyon–Nice route, p. 194); Day 16: Digne–**Grenoble**; Day 17: in **Grenoble** (p. 113); Day 18: Grenoble–**Lyon**; Day 19: in **Lyon** (p. 180); Day 20: Lyon–Annecy (Lyon–Geneva route, p. 189); Day 21: Annecy–**Geneva** (p. 102); Day 22: in **Geneva**; Day 23: Geneva–Berne (p. 83); Day 24: in **Berne** (p. 79); Day 25: Berne–**Interlaken** (p. 135);

Day 26: Day trip up the Jungfraujoch (Interlaken–Jungfrau route, p. 138), overnight in **Interlaken**; Day 27: Interlaken–**Zurich** (p. 325); Day 28: Fly home.

4. EDITED HIGHLIGHTS

14 days each
Several individual routes, with their attendant key cities, offer quite enough entertainment to keep travellers happy for two weeks.

A) GENEVA–KONSTANZ (P. 107)
This takes in all the major cities in Switzerland, with easy access to high mountains.

B) MILAN–VENICE (P. 218)
Follow the Shakespeare trail through Verona, Padua and Venice, to visit several of the most magnificent historic towns in northern Italy.

C) VENICE–VIENNA (P. 304)
There are two alternate routes offered for this long trek, which could easily be combined into a circular tour, with one route heading through the magnificent Italian Dolomites and the Austrian 'riviera' and the other stretching along the coast to Trieste before winding its way north through Slovenia.

THEMES

For those interested in specific subjects, we have put together lists of some of the best options on offer, to help you map a route.

Suggested sights under each theme are listed in alphabetical order, with a cross-reference to appropriate route and page.

5. TRANSPORTS OF DELIGHT

Easy access to the peaks, for those who aspire to ever greater heights. In addition to the list below, there are numerous small rack railways, cablecars and chairlifts operating in and around all ski resorts.

AUSTRIA

Bockstein, near Badgastein, an underground railway to a natural sauna (Salzburg–Klagenfurt, p. 272).
Hallstatt cablecar, to giant glacial ice caves (Salzburg Loop, p. 267).
Schafbergbahn rack railway, near St Wolfgang, outside Salzburg.

GERMANY

Zugspitzbahn cog railway, up Zugspitze, Germany's highest mountain, from Eibsee, near Garmisch-Partenkirchen (p. 123).

FRANCE

Chemin de Fer de la Mure, from St-Georges-de-Commiers, near Grenoble (p. 117)
Montenvers Railway, from Chamonix (Geneva–Martigny, p. 109)
Rive Bleue Express, along the southern shore of Lake Geneva (Geneva–Martigny, p. 109)
Téléphérique de l'Aiguille du Midi, Europe's first cableway, from Chamonix (Geneva–Martigny, p. 109).
Train des Pignes, private metre-gauge line from Nice to Digne (Lyon–Nice, p. 194).
Tramway de Mont Blanc, up the side of Europe's highest mountain (Geneva–Martigny, p. 109)

SWITZERLAND

Berneina Diavolezza, cable car up to a magnificent view over the Berneina Pass (Milan–Chur, p. 214).
Brienzer Rothorn, the world's last steam cog railway (Lucerne–Interlaken, p. 173).
Gornergrat–Bahn, funicular ride with views of the Matterhorn and onward cablecars (St Moritz–Zermatt, p. 281).
Jungfraujoch, an expensive, spectacular day trip by train up the Jungfrau, with associated lifts and cablecars. From Interlaken (p. 135).
Schilthorn, an interconnecting journey with a railway, cableway and funicular, between Interlaken and Lauterbrunnen (Interlaken–Jungfrau, p. 138).
Pilatus, the world's steepest cog railway up to the summer snows. At Alpnachstad, near Lucerne (Lucerne, p. 168).
Rigi, the world's oldest cog railway, from Weggis, near Lucerne.
Titlis, 45 mins up the mountain by cablecar, including the world's first revolving cabin, near Lucerne (Lucerne–Interlaken, p. 173).

6. ON THE PISTE

In a region thick with ski resorts, these are the great and the glorious.

AUSTRIA

Innsbruck (p. 118).
Kitzbühel (Innsbruck–Salzburg, p. 126).
Schladming (Salzburg loop, p. 267).
St Anton Am Arlberg, centre for a number of small but important resorts (Zurich–Innsbruck, p. 331).

FRANCE

Mont Blanc, centred around Chamonix and St-Gervais-Le Fayet (Geneva–Martigny, p. 109).
Chambéry, main centre for many of France's most famous ski resorts, including Méribel, Courchevel, La Plagne, Les Arcs and Val d'Isère (Lyon–Turin, p. 200).

GERMANY

Garmisch-Partenkirchen (Innsbruck–Friedrichshafen, p. 122).

ITALY

Bardonecchia (Lyon–Turin, p. 200).

Limone Piemonte (Nice–Turin, p. 252).

SWITZERLAND

SWITZERLAND

Andermatt (Lucerne–Milan, p. 176).
Chateau d'Oex (Lausanne–Interlaken, p. 162).
Crans–Montana, near Sion (Lausanne–Brig, p. 157).
Davos (St Moritz–Zermatt, p. 281).
Gstaad (Lausanne–Interlaken, p. 173).
Jungfrau, centred around Grindelwald, Wengen and Mürren (Interlaken–Jungfrau, p. 138).
Klosters (St Moritz–Zermatt, p. 281).
St Moritz (Milan–Chur, p. 214).
Verbiers (Turin–Martigny, p. 290).
Zermatt (St Moritz–Zermatt, p. 281).

7. MECHANICAL GENIUS

Switzerland is famous for its clocks, but it does not have the monopoly on mechanical wizardry.

68

Basel, Switzerland, for the Holbein and Tinguely fountains (p. 70).
Berne, Switzerland, for the Zytgloggeturm clock and the historic fountains in the Gerechtigkeitgasse (p. 79)
Besançon, France, for the Astrological Clock in the Cathédrale de St-Jean (Dijon–Basel, p. 94)
Geneva, Switzerland, for the Jet d'Eau, the Horloge Fleurie, the Musée de l'Horlogerie et de l'Emaillerie and for some serious shopping (p. 102).
La-Chaux-de-Fond, Switzerland, for the Musée International d'Horlogerie (Berne–Geneva, p. 83).
Salzburg, Austria, for the Glockenspiel and the castle barrel organ (p. 261).
Thun, Switzerland, for the Museum für Uhren und Mechanische Musikinstrumente at Oberhof (Berne– Milan, p. 86).

Vienna, Austria, (p. 315) for the art nouveau Anker Clock and the Uhrenmuseum.

8. BRICKS AND STONES

Almost every old town in Europe has, or had, a castle, palace or stately home, while they all had a variety of churches. Most are worth a quick visit – these must be seen.

AUSTRIA

Innsbruck, for the baroque Domkirche St Jacob and the rococo Basilika Wilten (p. 118).
Melk, for the abbey and Schloss Schallaburg (Salzburg–Vienna, p. 278).
Salzburg, for the Festung Hohensalzburg, the Dom, St Peterstift, Lustschloss Hellbrunn and numerous other buildings of note (p. 261).
Vienna, for Stephansdom, the Hofburg, Schloss Schönbrunn and much, much more (p. 315).

FRANCE

Annecy, for the château and the Palais de l'Ile (Lyon–Geneva, p. 189).
Cluny, for its massive medieval abbey, founding house of the Cistercian order (Dijon–Lyon, p. 98).
Entrevaux, for the fort and town ramparts (Lyon–Nice, p. 194).

GERMANY

Augsburg, for the Rathaus, the Schaezler–Palais, and access to the Romantic Road (Munich–Friedrichshafen, p. 231).
Garmisch-Partenkirchen, for access to Ludwig of Bavaria's magnificent trio of castles – Hohenschwangau, Neuschwanstein, and Linderhof (Innsbruck–Friedrichshafen, p. 122) .
Meerburg, on Lake Constance, for the Altes Schloss, the oldest inhabited castle

in Germany and its delightful baroque replacement, the Neues Schloss (Konstanz and the Bodensee, p. 142).
Munich, for the Liebfrauendom, Asamkirche, Schloss Nymphenburg and a great deal more (p. 224).
Passau, for Stephansdom (Munich–Linz, p. 235).
Regensburg, for the Domstadt, old town and Schloss Thurn und Taxis (Munich–Linz, p. 235).
Ulm, for the Munster and Memmingen (Munich–Friedrichshafen, p. 231).

ITALY

Bellinzona, for the Castelgrande, Castello di Montebello, the Castello di Sasso Corbaro and a host of charming churches (Lucerne–Milan, p. 176).
Como, for the Duomo, medieval San Fedele and Romanesque Sant'Abbondio (Lake Como, page 147).
Milan, for the Duomo Santa Maria Delle Grazie, the Castello Sforzesco and many other magnificent buildings and museums (p. 205).
Pavia, for the old town and the Certosa di Pavia (Turin–Milan, p. 293).
Tirano, for the Sanctuary of the Madonna di Tirano (Milan–Chur, p. 214).
Turin, for San Lorenzo, the Basilica di Superga and the Palazzina Mauriziana di Caccia (p. 286).
Venice, for everything, particularly the Piazza San Marco (p. 296).
Verona, for San Zeno Maggiore, the Roman Arena, and a range of other delightful buildings (Milan–Venice, p. 218).
Vicenza, for the Villa La Rotonda and many other works by Palladio (Milan–Venice, p. 218).

SWITZERLAND

Lausanne, for the medieval Cathédrale de Notre-Dame (p. 153).
Montreux, for the Château de Chillon (Lausanne–Brig, p. 157)
Sion, for the fortified medieval Collégiale (Lausanne–Brig, p. 157).
St Gallen, for the Cathedral, Collegiate Library and access to Appenzell (Zurich–Rorschach, p. 338).
Thun, for Schloss Thun and Schloss Oberhof (Berne–Milan, p. 86).

9. GREAT LAKES

The Alpine region contains some of Europe's most beautiful lakes. The following selection highlights some of the most impressive.
Aix-Les-Bains, for Lac du Bourget, the largest natural lake in France, with attendant hot springs (see Lyon–Geneva, p. 189).
Lake Como, the most beautiful of the Italian lakes and a popular resort for 2,000 years (p. 147).
Lake Constance, known locally as the Bodensee, on the borders of Switzerland, Germany and Austria (p. 142).
Lake Garda – dramatically beautiful resort area, accessible from Trento (Innsbruck–Verona, p. 132 and Milan–Venice, p. 218).
Lake Lucerne, chocolate box perfect lake, crowned by a wooden bridge (p. 138).
Lake Geneva, Europe's largest freshwater lake, known locally as the Lac Léman with Geneva (p.102), Lausanne (p. 153), Montreux (p. 159), Annemasse (p. 110) and Évian-Les-Bains (p. 110) encircling its shores.
Lake Maggiore, a charming Italian resort region, accessible from Stresa (Berne–Milan, p. 86)
Priensee, one of the Germany's prettiest lakes, complete with an island castle and steam railway, accessible from Prien Am Chiemsee (Munich–Salzburg, p. 242).

69

BASEL (BÂLE)

Basel borders both France and Germany, and is a major European rail hub. However, the approach to the city by train can be less than scenic. This is a city of two very different faces, as the view from Mittlere Brücke will show you. Look up river and you will see the very un-Swiss sight of a large industrial port, with major oil and pharmaceutical installations. Look back and you will be reassured to see the twin towers of the city's handsome red cathedral. Below them the old town is a charming maze of narrow streets converging on the splendid Marktplatz. Basel is also a cultural centre, home to some of the Switzerland's finest museums and galleries.

TOURIST INFORMATION

The main tourist office is at *Schifflände; tel: 261 50 50*, near the **Mittlere Brücke**, open Mon–Fri 0830–1800 and Sat 0830–1300. There is also an office at the SBB station, *tel: 271 36 84*, open Mon–Fri 0830–1800 and Sat 1830–1230 (longer hours in summer).

ARRIVING AND DEPARTING

Stations: The main station, **SBB (Schweizerische Bundesbahnen)**, *tel: 157 33 33*, is a 15-min walk south of the centre (tram nos 1/8) and handles Swiss and principal German services. The French part of the station, **Bahnhof SNCF**, *tel: 271 50 33*, handles services to France.

Badischer Bahnhof DB (Deutsche Bahn), *tel: 690 11 11*, (in Kleinbasel, but linked to SBB by rail) handles local German services.

GETTING AROUND

Most of the old centre is pedestrianised and all the main city sights are within walking distance. Elsewhere there's a frequent tram and bus service; information and tickets are available from machines at every stop. There's also a ferry service across the river.

STAYING IN BASEL

Accommodation

Most hotels in Basel are expensive and it's best to avoid the end of Oct and Mar when people in suits flock to the city (for major business fairs) gobbling up most of the accommodation.

Chain hotels in Basel include: *BW, GT, Hn, Mz, MO, RC, SL, Ss, Sw, Tp, WS*.

There are no outstanding cheap hotels in the old town. Among the cheaper options are **Stadthof**, *Gerbergasse 84; tel: 261 87 11*; **Klingental Garni**, *Klingental 20; tel: 681 62 48*; and **Badischer Hof Garni**, *Riehenring 75; tel: 691 77 80*. If you don't mind spending a little more, consider the characterful **Helvetia**, *Küchengasse 13; tel: 272 06 88*.

HI: *St Alban-Kirchrain 10; tel: 272 05 72*, a 15-min walk from the SBB station or tram no. 2, then a 5-min walk.

Camping: Camp Waldhort, *Heideweg 16, Reinach; tel: 711 64 29*, is the nearest site to town, 6 km south of the SBB station (tram no. 11 to Landhof).

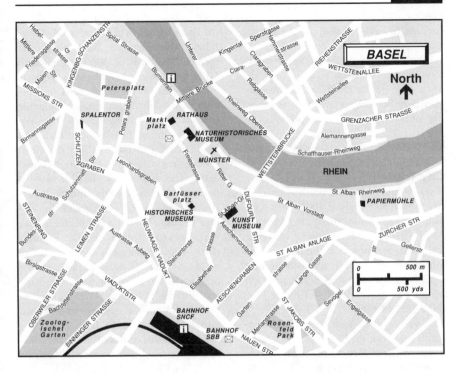

Eating and Drinking

You don't have to stray too far from *Marktpl.* for good local food. Just off here *Schneidergasse* is a popular street with some good cheapish eating houses, including **Hasenburg Château Lapin**, *tel: 261 32 58*, friendly and down-to-earth, with a good selection of *rösti* dishes. Try their *Schweingeschnetzeltes* (pork in a cream and wine sauce), a favourite local variation on the more expensive speciality *kalbgeschnetzeltes*, made with veal. One of the most interesting establishments in town (it's an hotel with a small arts complex attached) is the **Kunsthotel Teufelhof**, *Leonhardsgraben 47; tel: 261 10 10*. Its restaurant is for gourmets with fat wallets but the café serves affordable dishes.

There are various types of **food cruises** along the Rhine, including a Mexican night, the 'Captain's Dinner' (a five-course surprise menu), Sunday brunch and a Spaghetti cruise.

A good place for a picnic is *Peterspl.*, just west of *Marktpl.*, off *Petersgraben*. If you want a sandwich with a view, then climb up to the **Pfalz**, next to the Münster (see Sightseeing).

Communications

The main post office, **Hauptpost** is on *Kirschgartenstr.*, and opens Mon–Fri 0730–1830, Sat 0800–1100. For poste restante, the **Postzentrum** on *Gartenstr.*, is next to the SBB, open Mon–Fri 0600–2200, Sat 0600–2000, Sun 0900–1200 and 1500–2200.

The telephone code for Basel is *061*.

ENTERTAINMENT

Basel is a cultured town with regular productions of opera, theatre and classical concerts. See *Basel Live*, available from the tourist office, for what's on.

The Basel **Fasnacht** is Switzerland's most famous carnival. It takes over the town promptly at 0400 on the Monday after Ash Wednesday and lasts for three days of noisy colourful fancy dress fun.

SIGHTSEEING

City Tours

If you would like to see Basel by coach, a city tour departs daily at 1000, May–Oct, from the rail station SBB/Hotel Victoria. At SFr.20, it's quite expensive however, and the best way to see the centre is on foot. Much of it is pedestrianised anyway, is on foot. Walking tours depart from the Münster on Mon, Wed and Fri at 1500 (June–mid-Oct).

If you wish to look around independently however, the logical place to start is at the **Mittlere Brücke**. Not only is the tourist information office here, but of the six Basel bridges which across the River Rhine, this offers the best views. The medieval centre is on the south bank in **Grossbasel**, while **Kleinbasel** is the small modern area on the north bank, notable only for its nightlife and modern shopping facilities.

From Mittlere Brücke wend your way south, parallel to the river, to the 12th-century red sandstone **Münster** (Cathdral). The exterior is notable for its decorative twin towers and a lovely Romanesque portal, surrounded by elegant carvings. Within is the simple marble tomb of the Dutch scholar Erasmus (1466–1536), who spent the last years of his life in Basel. His dissatisfaction with the religious practices of his time paved the way for the Lutherans. Outside, admire the view from the adjacent tree-shaded square, known as the **Pfalz**.

Guided tours of the Münster are combined with lunchtime concerts at 1200 on Mon, Wed and Fri (June–mid-Oct.

The King's Head

Der *Lällenkönig* is the unofficial mascot of the city, erected by the citizens of Grossbasel ('Great Basel') as a mark of contempt for their working class neighbours. Look carefully high up on the corner of the building at the southern end of the Mittlere Brücke and you will see *Der Lällenkönig* – the head of a king sticking his tongue out towards Kleinbasel. The inhabitants of Kleinbasel ('Little Basel') have however worked out a suitably riposte to this insult. Once a year a character dressed as the legendary *Wilde Mann* ('wild man' or savage) performs a dance on the Mittlere Brücke, which culminates in him showing his backside to Grossbasel!

Museums and Galleries

Basel has been sponsoring artists for over three centuries and features around 30 major museums and galleries. The **Historisches Museum** has been housed in the Gothic **Barfüsserkirche**, on *Barfüsserpl.*, since 1894. It contains 13th- to 16th-century *objets d'art*, including Luther's chalice, among the Reformer's personal possessions, locally made tapestries, and the original *Lällenkönig* (see box, left). *Barfüsserpl.* is also a regular market venue. The 18th–19th-century sections of the museum collection are on display in the **Haus zum Kirschgarten**, *Elisabethenstr. 27*, about 300 m north of SBB. The **Antikenmuseum** (Museum of Ancient Art), *St-Alban-Graben 5*, goes back somewhat further, with some very fine ancient Greek artefacts.

The world-class **Kunstmuseum** (Fine Arts Museum), *St-Alban-Graben 16* (tram no. 2), was constructed in 1932–36, especially to house the art treasures the town had been accumulating since the 17th century. These include important works by Witz and the world's largest collection of works by the Holbein family, featuring Holbein the Younger's *Portrait of Erasmus*. Significant modern contributors include Van Gogh (*Daubigney's Garden*) Picasso, Braque and Dalí. Bang up to date is the permanent collection of the **Museum für Gegenwartskunst** (Museum of Contemporary Art), *St-Alban-Rheinweg 60*, which includes pieces by Stella, Warhol and Beuys.

For something rather different visit the **Basler Papiermühle**, *St-Alban-Tal 35–37*, a restored medieval papermill which offers a history of paper-making.

At *Augustinergasse 2* are two more museums: the **Naturhistorisches Museum**, which displays natural history exhibits ranging from dinosaur skeletons to minerals; and the **Museum für Völkerkunde**, an excellent global ethnographical collection.

Other Sights

The pride of Basel is the recently restored 16th-century **Rathaus** (Town Hall), which boasts an ornate and very picturesque red façade that includes an enormous clock. It towers over **Marktplatz**, the historic and modern heart of Basel, which hosts a colourful daily fruit and vegetable market.

Of the two main surviving medieval city gates, the one to see is the splendid 14th-century **Spalentor**, *Spalengraben*. Near here, on *Spalenvorstadt*, is the pick of the town's older fountains, the **Holbeinbrunnen**, based partly on a Holbein drawing and a Dürer engraving. By con-

---

Art for the People

The citizens of Basel take their art very seriously. In 1967 they voted by referendum to purchase two of Picasso's better know pictures: *L'Arelquin Assis* (Harlequin Seated) and *Les Deux Frères* (The Two Brothers). Picasso swas so delighted with this that he donated another four pictures, free of charge, to the museum.

---

trast the **Fasnacht-Brunnen/Tinguely-Brunnen,** *Theaterpl.*, is an extraordinary fountain that was built in 1977 by Jean Tinguely (see Geneva to Konstanz route, p. 108) and resembles a watery scrap-yard.

The **Zoologischer Garten**, *Binningerstr. 40*, west of SBB, has gained a reputation for breeding armoured rhinos, but is also known for its collections of pygmy hippos, gorillas and penguins. Elephants provide rides for children.

OUT OF TOWN

Augst is 20 mins by train (plus a 10-min walk) from SBB but if you have time take the enjoyable ferry ride from the dock at Schifflände (summer only, 1 hr 30 mins). The extensive ruins of an old Roman settlement, **Augusta Raurica**, have been completely rebuilt and the site takes some time to explore fully. Its magnificent and varied collection can now be seen in the **Römermuseum**, a reconstruction of an ordinary Roman home. A 2nd-century AD theatre is used for diverse summer performances.

It's quite easy to explore the **Black Forest** (see p. 74) from Basel. You can do it independently as trains run from Kleinbasel to Freiburg and Karlsruhe, or take an organised tour from the city.

BASEL–KONSTANZ

The cross-border route enters Germany just north of the Swiss capital and runs parallel to the Rhine and the French border. Several charming small towns lie along the route, which loops south-east from Offenburg, passing through the thickly-wooded southern part of the Black Forest, to arrive at Konstanz.

An alternative way to savour most of the southern route is by boat, as the stretch of the Rhine from Schaffhausen to Lake Konstanz (via Stein-am-Rhein) is one of the most picturesque, unspoiled parts of this great river. This is certainly the slow option, taking around 4 hrs 30 mins upstream from Schaffhausen and 3 hrs 45 min the other way. Aside from taking in the lovely scenery at a leisurely pace, it may also prevent you from overdosing on the architectural delights of Schaffhausen and Stein-am-Rhein, which are quite similar to each other.

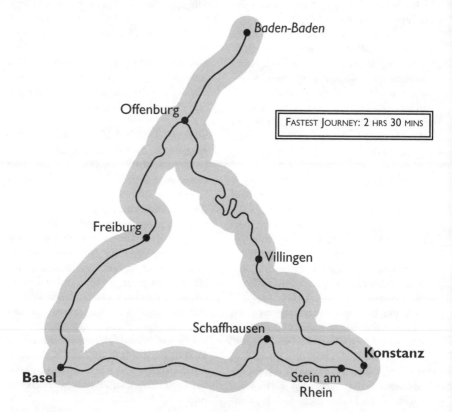

FASTEST JOURNEY: 2 HRS 30 MINS

TRAINS

ETT tables: 300, 305, 304, 730, 731, 734.

FAST TRACK

➡️ No through trains run between Basel and Konstanz, the quickest route involves changing at Zurich and Weinfelden, with a journey time of 2 hr 30 min.

ON TRACK

⇢ Basel–Freiburg–Offenburg

An hourly Inter City service links Basel SBB with Freiburg and Offenburg. Basel to Freiburg takes 41 mins, Freiburg to Offenburg 30 mins.

Offenburg–Villingen–Konstanz

Hourly trains link Offenburg, Villingen and Konstanz. Offenburg to Villingen takes 1 hr 15 mins, Villingen to Konstanz about the same.

Basel–Schaffhausen

Basel Badbahnhof to Schaffhausen takes around 1 hr 30 mins with trains at approximately two hourly intervals.

Schaffhausen–Stein am Rhein

A local journey of 25 min.

Stein am Rhein–Konstanz

A change of train at Kreuzlingen is needed on the journey of about 45 min. Trains are hourly throughout the day.

FREIBURG

Station: Hbf, *tel: (0761) 19419.*
Tourist Office: *Rotteckring 14, tel: (0761) 368 9090,* is two blocks from Hbf. Open Mon–Sat 0900–2130 and Sun 1000–1200.

ACCOMMODATION

Most cheaper accommodation is away from the centre. Cheaper guesthouses and bed and breakfast places can be booked through the tourist office for a small fee. **HI:** *Kartauserstr. 151; tel: (0761) 67656,* on the east side of town, (tram no.1 to *Hasemannstr.*). **Campsite**: **Hirzberg**, *Kartauserstr. 99; tel: (0761) 35054,* is nearby.

SIGHTSEEING

Freiburg, the first major German town on this route, is worth a stop for a look at its restored **Altstadt** (Old Town), about 10 mins walk from Hbf.

The best way to explore the town is on foot, but multiple-use tickets for the bus and trolley-bus system are sold at Hbf. The heart of the old town is the red sandstone **Münster** (cathedral), *Münsterpl.*, with a 116 m spire which is the town centre's main landmark. Outside, a carved frieze depicts Old Testament scenes. Stained-glass windows dating from the 13th–16th centuries shed coloured light on a Romanesque Gothic interior. *Münsterpl.* is also the location of Freiburg's daily market, where stalls sell everything from freshly picked fungi to cheap clothes and toys.

On one side of the square stands the **Historisches Kaufhaus**, the original city merchants hall, with an arcade surmounted by spires and statues. On either side of this stand the baroque **Erz-bischofliches Palais** (Archbishop's Palace) and the **Wenzingerhaus**. The other focus of historic buildings in the old city is *Rathauspl.*, where you will find the elegant Renaissance **Neues Rathaus**, the Gothic **Martinskirche** monastery church and the **Haus zum Walfisch** where the 16th-century theologian Erasmus lived for two years. The **Augustiner Museum**, *Salzstr.*, in a former monastery, houses a superb display of 13th–15th century religious art and traditional crafts from the Upper Rhine region.

75

OFFENBURG

Station: Hbf: *Hauptstr. 1, tel: (0781) 19419.*

Tourist Office: *Gartnerstr. 6, tel: (0781) 82253,* 10 mins walk from Hbf, open Mon–Sat 0900–2130 and Sun 1000–1200.

STAYING IN OFFENBURG

The **Hotel Sonne**, *Hauptstr. 94, tel: (0781) 71039,* dating from 1350, and rebuilt in 1689, and is Offenburg's oldest hotel. Chain hotels include *Do* and *BW*. **HI:** youth hostel **Schloss Ortenberg**, *tel: (0781) 31749.* Mid-priced hotels include **Hotel-garni Drei Konige**, *Klosterstr. 9, tel: (0781) 24390,* in the centre of the old town; **Hotel-garni Rheinischerhof**, *Haupstr. 52, tel: (0781) 24275,* midway between the Hbf and tourist office; **Gasthaus Badischerhof**, *Spitalstr. 6, tel: (0781) 24976,* next to the city museum. The tourist office will find cheaper accommodation in Offenburg and in the surrounding Black Forest region.

SIGHTSEEING

Much of Offenburg was destroyed by a great fire in 1689 and most of its historic buildings date from the 18th and 19th centuries, with a handful of earlier relics. Main sights cluster round the **Fischmarkt**, a picturesque square in the town centre, with a 16th-century fountain and an 18th century tollhouse, the **Salzhaus**. Next to it is the **Sankt Andreas Hospital**, founed for the care of the poor in 1300 but rebuilt in the early 18th century. The **Ritterhaus**, *Ritterstr. 10,* was built in 1784 as the mayor's residence and today houses the municipal museum. The **Judenbad**, *Mikwe,* is a rare survival from the 13th and 14th century when it was a religious and social centre for the city's Jewish community. The **Capuzinerkloster**, *Gymansiumstr.,* was built 1641–47 and is the only major building to survive the great fire of 1689 unscathed.

 **SIDE TRACK FROM OFFENBURG**

BADEN-BADEN

Station: Hbf: *tel: (07221) 19419,* is a long way north-west of the centre but buses are frequent. It is 20 min from Offenburg by frequent trains.

Tourist Office: *Haus des Kurgastes, Augustapl. 8, tel: (07221) 21 27 50,* open Mon–Sat 0900–2130 and Sun 1000–1200.

STAYING IN BADEN BADEN

Baden Baden is an expensive place to stay. If your budget will stretch, spoil yourself at the town's most elegant hotel, the **Brenners Park-Hotel**, *Lichtenthaler Allee,* set in parklands with its own thermal spa. Chain hotels include *BW, Ch, RC, Rk, SL.*

SIGHTSEEING

Baden Baden's mineral **spa** and natural hot baths have attracted visitors since Roman times, but the town came into its own as a resort for European high society in the 19th century, when the casino was built. The aristocrats have been succeeded by elderly Germans, whose health insurance pays for an annual therapeutic visit and thermal treatment, and the general ambience is a bit geriatric. However, the waters will do wonders to cure the aches and pains of too many hours on the rails. Take the two-hour 14-stage 'Roman-Irish' treatment at the old-world **Friedrichsbad**, *Römerpl.,* which will leave you feeling years younger. Nudity is mandatory here, and you pay extra for the surroundings; for a cheaper bath, visit the next-door **Caracalla-Therme,** also on *Römerpl.,* where you can wear your togs. Foundations of the **Roman baths** can be seen beneath *Römerpl..* Round off your trip with a visit to the **Kurhaus Casino,** *Kaiserallee 1,* with an ornate mid-19th century interior featuring frescos and chandeliers.

VILLINGEN-SCHWENNINGEN

Stations: Hbf, Villingen, *tel: (0764) 19419;* **Hbf Schwenningen,** *tel: (0731) 19419.* Bus 7281 runs between the two stations, which are 3 km apart, approximately hourly between 0445 and 2005. Journey time is 13 mins.
Tourist Office: Hbf Schwenningen, *tel: (01720) 821209,* open Mon–Fri 0900–1200, 1400–1700.

ACCOMMODATION AND FOOD

There is a town plan and list of hotels and guesthouses at the bus stop outside Villingen Hbf. The tourist office in Schwenningen will make bookings. Mid-priced hotels include **Hotel Baren,** *Barengasse 2, Villingen, tel: (07721) 55541;* **Hotel Ketterer,** *Brigachstr. 1, Villingen, tel: (07721) 22095;* **Gasthaus Schlachthof,** *Schlachthausstr. 11, Villingen tel: (07721) 22584.*

SIGHTSEEING

The twin towns of Villingen and Schwenningen are separated by 3 km of farmland and by the European watershed, the invisible line either side of which rivers either drain north into the North Sea like the Rhine, or south-east into the Black Sea like the Danube. Villingen is by far the more picturesque of the two communities. The old town centre is 1 km from Hbf, entered through the arched **St Ursula Tor,** *Bickenstr.,* and with a striking 12th-century Romanesque cathedral, the **Mün-**ster unser Lieben Frau,** and an interesting **museum** of local artefacts in the **Altes Rathaus,** both on *Munsterpl.*

SCHAFFHAUSEN

Station: *tel: 053 25 54 31.*
Tourist Office: *Fronwagturm; tel: 053 25 51 41.*

Schaffhausen is an historic town, guarded by a sturdy castle, and features many beautiful old buildings, Pick up a town trail leaflet from the tourist office and/or join one of the guided walks (SFr.10; English is spoken) which depart from here (May–Oct; Mon, Wed, Fri at 1415).

From the station cross Bahnhofst. into Löwengässchen then turn left onto **Vorstadt.** This is one of the pedestrianised old town's two principal streets and immediately on the right is the 17th-century **Zum Goldenen Ochsen** (the House of the Golden Ox), a splendid example of the type of house that the town is famous for with a superbly carved oriel window and mural-covered façade (this one depicts the main Trojan War protagonists). *Vorstadt* also boasts two notable 16th-century fountains, the **Mohrenbrunnen** (Moor's Fountain) and the **Metzgerbrunnen** (Butcher's Fountain). Behind the latter is the tourist office, occupying an 18th-century tower topped with a fine 16th-century astronomical clock.

Turn left into **Vordergasse** for more oriel windows and the unmissable **Haus Zum Ritter** (Knight's House), built in 1492, and rebuilt in 1566. It is adorned with what is claimed to be the most important Renaissance fresco north of the Alps, though the original fresco now resides in the town's **Museum zu Allerheiligen** (All Saints Museum) and what you see here is a copy. The Museum is just behind, along *Münstergasse,* in the complex

77

of buildings which surrounds the city's **Münster** (Minster). The Münster is a fine example of the Romanesque style, dating from the 12th-century; do look into the cloister – said to be the largest in Switzerland – and the museum which contains some superb religious and fine art treasures.

A short walk away is the castle, known as the **Munot**, built in the 16th century. It's a steep climb, up through a vineyard, to enter the perfectly circular outer walls. Once inside the sheer bulk of the suppoting pillars and thickness of the walls is quite startling. A spiral path, large enough to accommodate a horseman, leads to the battlements, from where you can enjoy a fine roofscape of old Schaffhausen.

From the castle, walk back along Vordergasse admiring the buildings that you missed by diverting for the Münster.

The mighty **Rheinfall** (Rhine Falls) lies 3 km from the town centre. From Bahnhofst. take bus no. 1 or 9 to Neuhausen then a 5–10-min walk. The Rheinfall is the biggest waterfall in Europe, measured not in terms of height (23 m), but in volume. To appreciate its full thunderous power – William Wordsworth called it 'a fearful thing whose nostrils breathe blasts of tempestuous smoke' – you must cross the river. From here you can also take a boat ride and climb the water-battered cliff right in the middle of the falls.

If you feel like splashing out for a night (SFr.145-190 for a double room) the turn-of-the-century **Park Villa**, *Parkst. 18; tel: 053 25 27 37,* oozes character and is close to the station. **HI**: *Randenst. 65; tel: 053 25 88 00,* (bus no. 3 to *Schützenhaus,* then 3-min walk).

STEIN AM RHEIN

Station: *tel: 157 22 22.*

Tourist Office: *Oberstadt 10; tel: 054 41 28 35.*

In any vote as to which is the most picturesque town in Switzerland Stein am Rhein would always figure prominently. The station. is on the south bank of the river and is a 10-min walk from the old centre on the north bank; once across the bridge you step straight into the heart of a living picture-postcard. The only drawback, inevitably, is the town's popularity, so try to visit early or late in the day, or slightly out of season, to avoid the crowds.

The centre of activity is **Rathausplatz** where magnificent frescos and superb oriels abound. The oldest, and newest frescos are the scenes above the **Hotel Restaurant Adler** and adjacent **Chäs Graf,** painted in 1520-5 and 1956 respectively. Opposite, the **House of The Red Ox** and the colourful knights statue make up the most-photographed composition in town.

If you would like to see behind the façade the **Museum Lindwurm**, on *Understadt,* is highly recommended. The construction of this splendid three-storey complex spans the 13th–19th century and is now devoted to everday life in the 19th century. There are an amazing variety of rooms, outhouses, and an atmospheric attic to explore and the interpretation is first-class (there's even a dressing-up area for kids). At the far end of *Understadt* is one of the handsome tower gates for which the town is also famous. There are several more small museums in the centre, the best of which is the local history collection in the **Kloster St George** (St George's Monastery), the superbly preserved former home of the Benedictine Monastery.

HI: *Niederfeld, Hemishoferst. 12,* 1.5 km from the centre, 5-mins walk from *Strandbad* – a bathing area and the nearest bus stop.

BERNE (BERN)

Alongside Zurich and Geneva the picturesque, medieval town of Berne seems tiny and almost provincial, yet – keep reminding yourself – this is the capital of Switzerland. The roots of its power and status go back to the 16th–18th centuries when Berne was a powerful city state, ruling great tracts of the country. Museum battle trophies are one legacy of this era, but the architecture of Berne, fit to grace any capital, is a more civilised reminder of its golden age. The old city in its present form was built with great harmony and purpose in the 16th and 17th centuries.

TOURIST INFORMATION

The **main office** is in the station complex; *tel: (031) 311 66 11.* Open daily 0900–2030 (June–Sept), Mon–Sat 0900–1830 and Sun 1000–1700 (Oct–May). In summer an information booth also opens by the bear pits (see p. 82).

ARRIVING AND DEPARTING

Station: Bahnhof (Bhf), *tel: (031) 21 11 11*, is a 5–10-min walk from the centre (tram no. 12).

GETTING AROUND

Berne sits on a horseshoe-shaped peninsula enclosed by the **River Aare**, which is crossed by three high-level bridges. The station lies to the western end of the old centre and from here the city's main thoroughfare runs due east through the town centre down to the Nydeggbrücke. En route it changes name four times – *Spitalgasse, Marktgasse, Kramgasse, Gerechtigkeitsgasse*. Walking from one end to the other (downhill) takes around 15 mins. Catch tram no. 12 back up. Almost everything of interest is on or just off this street. There's an excellent tram and bus network.

STAYING IN BERNE

Cheap accommodation is not plentiful, but at least there are some affordable options in the centre. Hotel chains include: *AC, BW, MO, Mv, RC, Sh, WS.*

Inside the old town are four reasonably priced two-star hotels: **Hospiz zur Heimat**, *Gerechtigkeitsgasse 50; tel: 311 04 36;* **Nydeck**, *Gerechtigkeitsgasse 1; tel: 311 86 86;* **Goldener Schlüssel**, *Rathausgasse 72; tel: 311 02 16;* plus the three-star **Goldener Adler**, *Gerechtigkeitsgasse 7, tel: 311 17 25* – the nicest rooms are on the top floor. There is another affordable two-star hotel, **The National**, *Hirschengraben 24; tel: 381 19 88*, just a short walk from Bhf, while the friendly one-star **Marthahaus-Garni**, *Wyttenbachstr. 22a; tel: 332 41 35*, is a short bus ride (no. 20) north.

HI: *Weihergasse 4; tel: 311 63 16*, a 10-min walk from Bhf, immediately below the Bundeshaus. **Campsites: Eichholz**, *Strandweg 49; tel: 961 26 02*, 3.5 km south-east of the centre (tram no. 9 to *Wabern* terminal). Bungalows: **Eymatt**, *Hinterkappelen; tel: 901 10 07*, 5 km north-west of the centre (bus nos 3 or 4 to *Eymatt*).

Eating and Drinking

The area around *Spitalgasse, Bärenplatz, Zeughausgasse* is good for menu browsing.

79

Probably the best value lunch in town is at the pleasant self-service restaurant of the **EPA department store** which straddles *Zeughausgasse* and *Marktgasse*. Two characterful (though not particularly cheap) establishments are to be found on *Gerechtigskeitgasse*. At *no. 62* is the **Klötzlikeller**, Berne's oldest wine cellar, dating from 1635, serving snacks and full meals; *tel: 311 74 56*. At *no. 18* the **Belle Époque** is a popular small daytime café purveying pastries and snacks in pleasing period surroundings; *tel: 311 43 36*. Along the street at *no. 51*, **Arlequin** offers national and local dishes at reasonable prices; *tel: 311 39 46*, while at *no. 7* the restaurant of the **Goldener Adler hotel**; *tel: 311 17 25*, is affordably priced. Vegetarians should try **Menuetto**, *Herrengasse 22; tel 311 14 48*. For a picnic with a view, cross the Nydeggbrücke and walk up to the lovely **Rose Garden** or cross the Lorrainebrücke to the **Botanical Gardens**. The best place to buy your provisions is at the market on *Bärenpl.* (see Sightseeing, p. 81).

Communications

The main **post office**, *Shanzenstr.*, is open Mon–Fri 0730–1830, Sat 0730–1100. An express counter opens Mon–Fri 0600–0730, 1830–2000, Sat 0600–0730, 1100–1800, Sun 1000–1200 and 1600–2200. The area telephone code is *031*.

Embassies

Australia: *Alpenstr. 29; tel: 351 01 43*.
Canada: *Kirchenfeldstr. 88; tel: 352 63 81*, (**Consulate:** *Belpstr. 11; tel: 311 22 61*).
Ireland: *Kirchenfeldstr. 68; tel: 352 14 42*.
UK: *Thunstr. 50; tel: 352 50 21*.
USA: *Jubiläumsstr. 93; tel: 357 70 11*.

ENTERTAINMENT

Berne does not enjoy the cultural riches of Geneva or Zurich but it does have a municipal **theatre** on *Kornhauspl.*, and its own symphony orchestra. The city also has a reputation for fringe events. Ask at the tourist office or pick up the local papers to see what's on. The annual music highlight is the **International Jazz Festival**, late April–early May.

The main event in the Berne social calendar is the **Zibelmärit** (Onion Market), held on the 4th Mon in Nov. This is a street festival which goes back many centuries and is a much livelier and more general carnival than its name suggests.

SIGHTSEEING

Strangely, for such a pedestrian-friendly city, there are no official guided walking tours. Ignore the expensive guided coach tour and do your own walking tour. Good maps and detailed pamphlets are available free from the tourist office. The long central street from **Spitalgasse** to **Gerechtigkeitsgasse**, with its almost continuous arcades and ancient façades is a sight in itself, particularly on special occasions and holidays when it is decked with large heraldic flags and banners, and yet more glorious in summer when the geraniums are in bloom in hundreds of window boxes. It is enhanced further by a clutch of historic *Brunnen* (fountains), all erected in the 16th century.

From the station, the first of these fountains is the **Pfeiferbrunnen**, on *Spitalgasse*, a flamboyant and enigmatic bagpiper figure with technicolour carvings and flowers around the base. Continue on to *Bärenpl.* and directly ahead the 13th-century **Käfigturm** (prison tower) marks the old western boundary of the town. It now houses an audio–visual show on the city. The **Bundeshaus** (parliament building) to the right, is a reminder of the city's capital status and is open to visitors. With its grand domes, frescos and stained-glass

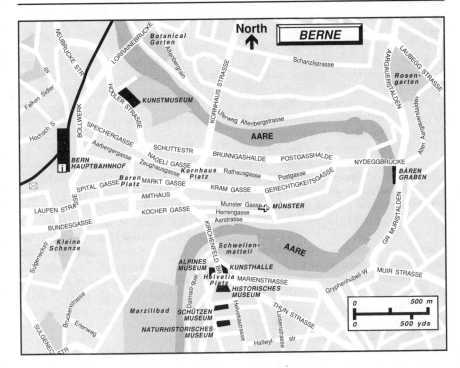

windows, it's well worth a look (free tours daily Sun–Fri except during parliamentary sessions). A lookout point around the back of the building provides great views.

Straight ahead is the country's most famous clock tower, the Zytgloggeturm, which was the original western gate, first built in the 12th century. Before passing under here, make a short detour to the left to the city's most famous fountain, the **Kindlifresserbrunnen**, depicting a macabre child-eating ogre. If you come here on Tues or Sat, the pavements will be covered with fruit, vegetable, flower and general merchandise traders, their stalls stretching all the way from *Bundespl.* to *Waisenhauspl..* There is also a daily summer market (May–Oct) on *Bärenpl.*

The **Zytgloggeturm** has always been a significant monument: every other city clock once took the official time from here; all distances and milestones were measured from here; the official linear measures for a metre and the ancient double-meter can still be seen inside its archway. In the 16th century an astronomical clock was added to its Kramgasse face and a figure play was also introduced. At four minutes to each hour exactly a mechanical jester summons a lion, a rooster, a knight and a procession of bears. If you'd like to examine the 16th-century clockwork from the inside there are guided tours daily at 1630, May–Oct.

Ahead is the bizarre **Zähringenbrunnen** depicting a bear in a suit of armour. The legend behind this is that Berne was founded in 1191 by Berchtold V, Duke of Zähringen, who declared he would name his new city after the first creature he killed while hunting. The poor victim, a bear (*Bär* in the local tongue, also pronounced bear) thus became the town's ubiquitous symbol and *Bär* eventually became Berne.

A few yards further along on the right is the **Einstein-Haus**, a small museum housed in the apartment where the physicist lived in 1905 while working on his theory of relativity. From brains to brawn, straight ahead is the **Samsonbrunnen**.

Duck through one of the alleyways to the right or go right around the block to *Münsterpl.* Construction on the Gothic **Münster** (cathedral), began in 1421 and building continued through the Reformation. Although many decorative touches were removed during this period, it retains a magnificent polychrome depiction of the Last Judgment above the main entrance, plus elaborate carvings on the pews and choir stalls and some superb 15th-century stained glass. The 100-m high steeple (Switzerland's tallest) was topped off only in 1893. You can ascend its 344 steps for a marvellous 360-degree view. If you're not feeling up to the climb, you can still enjoy a good view over the river and across to the Alps, from the leafy *Münsterpl.* behind the cathedral.

Before returning to the main street keep straight on to admire the **Rathaus** (town hall), rebuilt 1939–42. Next to it is another 16th-century fountain. Back on the main street, (now *Gerechtigkeitsgasse*), ahead is arguably the finest of all the fountains, the **Gerechtigkeitsbrunnen**, where the blindfolded Goddess of Justice stands over the severed heads of a pope, an emperor, a sultan and a mayor.

Cross the river by the 15th-century **Nydeggbrücke** and to the right are the 500-year-old **Bärengraben** (bear pits), the rather forlorn-looking home of Berne's mascots. The plump brown beasts are generally eager to accept food (on sale) and may even perform tricks. At least they breed happily in their concrete bunker and

the cubs usually make their first public appearance at Easter.

It's a steep 10–15-min climb up the hill facing you but at the top is the **Rosengarten** (rose garden) with an outdoor café and the classic picture-postcard view across the city.

The Museums

The city's prime art collection, the **Kunstmuseum** (Fine Art Museum), *Hodlerstr.8–12*, near the Lorrainebrücke, north of the station, stands apart from the main museum grouping. It has a fine display of works by Ferdinand Hodler and is home to the world's largest collection of Paul Klee paintings. Look too for exhibits by such diverse artists as Fra Angelico, Matisse, Kandinsky, Cézanne and Picasso.

All the other major museums are around *Helvetiapl.*, south of the River Aare, across the Kirchenfeldbrücke (tram nos. 3/5). The **Kunsthalle**, *Helvetiapl. 1*, hosts exhibitions of contemporary art. Opposite, the **Schweizerisches Alpines Museum** contains items connected with the history of mountaineering. The **Bernisches Historisches Museum,** on the south side of *Helvetiapl.*, is the country's second largest historical museum. The highlights are its superb Flemish tapestries, souvenirs of the once-powerful city state's Burgundian conquests, and its church treasures, but there is much else to see.

The **Schweizerisches Schützenmuseum**, *Bernastr. 5*, is devoted to firearms and the country's shooting tradition. Nearby, the **Naturhistorisches Museum** (*no. 15*) features African animals, the inevitable brown bears and Barry, the St Bernard dog who rescued over 40 people. Philatelists should not miss one of the world's largest collections of postage stamps, in the **Schweizerisches PTT Museum**, *Helvetiastr.16*.

BERNE–GENEVA

This green and pleasant journey through the bucolic Vaud (Lake Geneva) region has the bonus of long stretches of lakeside to enjoy. Sit on the right-hand side of the carriage ,when travelling from Berne, for fine views of Lakes Geneva, Neuchâtel and Ligerz. The towns of Biel/Bienne, Neuchâtel and Yverdon-les-Bains all enjoy a lake setting and provide relaxed undemanding breaks.

FASTEST JOURNEY: 1 HR 45 MINS

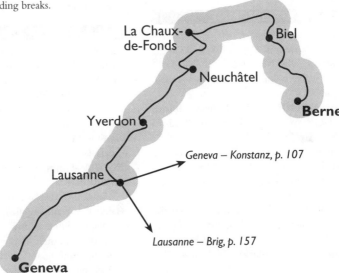

83

TRAINS

ETT tables: 260, 250, 255, 260.

FAST TRACK

➤ The through trains between Berne and Geneva take around 1hr 45 mins with an hourly frequency and buffet facilities. The direct route is much shorter than the scenic On Track route.

ON TRACK

Berne (Bern)–Biel
Trains run every 30 mins on the 30-min journey between Bern and Biel.

Biel–La Chaux-de-Fonds
An hourly service taking around 45 mins.

La Chaux-de-Fonds–Neuchâtel
Thirty-five min journey time with trains every hour.

Neuchâtel–Yverdon-les-Bains
Trains take 23 mins and run every 30 mins.

Yverdon-les-Bains–Lausanne
A frequent service taking 24 mins.

Lausanne–Geneva (Genève)
At least 3 trains an hour link Lausanne with Geneva, taking about 40 mins for the journey.

BIEL/BIENNE

Station: *Hauptbahnhof; tel: 157 22 22.* The old town is a 10-min walk along *Bahnhofstr.* via *Nidaugasse;* the lake is a 5-min walk, behind the station, via *Badhausstr.*

Tourist Office: **Verkehrsverband**, *Veresiusstr.* (next to HB); *tel: (032) 22 75 75.*

German-speaking inhabitants call the town Biel, the French call it Bienne, and this is the only town in Switzerland where French and German share equal billing. Sightseeing is divided largely between the lake and the old town. The latter is a small area, based around the two squares of the **Ring** and **Burgplatz** which feature a notable collection of 16th-century structures. On *Burgpl.* is the step-gabled **Town Hall** and the old **Arsenal** (now the Municipal Theatre), while the Ring features the **Forester's Guildhouse**, two fine **fountains** and a 15th-century **church**. Off *Burgpl.* is the **Burg** (castle) itself (not open to the public).

Lake Biel (*Bielersee* or *lac de Bienne*) is famous for **St Peter's Island**, a charming, peaceful protected nature reserve where the only development has been the old monastery, beautifully renovated as the **Restaurant-Hotel St Petersinsel**; *tel: (032) 88 11 14.* After the Swiss-born French philosopher, Jean-Jacques Rousseau, pronounced that the two months he spent here in 1765 was 'the happiest time of his life' the popularity of St Peter's Island was guaranteed. Rousseau's room is preserved as an exhibit and the hotel is still the most atmospheric place to eat and sleep in Biel/Bienne, costing SFr.170-200 per double room with shower. Eating here is also recommended, with the option of a picnic area, complete with barbecue grills. It's a 50-min boat journey from Schifflände, behind Biel HB.

LA CHAUX-DE-FONDS

Station: **Gare**; *tel:157 22 22.*
Tourist Office: **Office du Tourisme**, *Espacité 1; tel: (039) 28 13* 13. It has accommodation listings.

The only real reason to visit this modern uninspiring town is the award-winning **Musée International d'Horlogerie** (a 5-min walk from the station). La Chaux-de-Fonds is a principal centre for Swiss watch and clock manufacture and the museum displays over 3000 time-related items ranging from the sundial to the atomic clock. Many of the pieces are works of art in their own right and the displays and lighting are excellent.

Adjacent are two lesser collections, the **Musée d'Histoire Naturelle** and the **Musée de Beaux Arts.** The latter includes work by the famous architect, Le Corbusier, born in La Chaux-de-Fonds in 1887.

Keen horologists with time on their hands should also consider the 7-min side trip to **Le Locle**, where there is another fine museum of timepieces.

HI: the youth hostel is at *r. de Doubs 34; tel: (39) 28 25 18.*

NEUCHÂTEL

Station: Gare; *tel: (038) 24 45 15,* located 1 km north of the town centre (bus no. 6 to *pl. Pury*).
Tourist Office: Office du Tourisme, *r. de la Place-d'Armes 7; tel: (038) 25 42 42.*

ACCOMMODATION

There is a good **HI Youth Hostel,** *r. du Suchiez 35; tel: (038) 31 31 90,* two km from town, (no. 1 bus from *pl. Pury* to *Vauseyon,* then 3-min walk).

SIGHTSEEING

Neuchâtel, the cantonal capital, is a pleasant blend of old and new, set on the lake of the same name. **Place Pury** is the main square and adjacent is **Place des Halles** where markets are held. Its handsome late 16th-century **Maison des Halles** (Market Halls) building now functions as a restaurant, worth visiting for the food and the architecture.

The **Château de Neuchâtel** is a short steep walk away. Built between the 12th and 16th centuries the castle is an imposing sight from the outside and now functions as the cantonal office. Free guided tours take you inside though little of historical interest remains. The **chemin de ronde** (walkway) offers fine views over the town. The adjacent **Collegiate Church** (late 12th-century) is included in the tour and features a splendid 14th-century monument to the Counts of Neuchâtel. Across the road is the **Tour des Prisons** (prison tower) with more views and historical town models.

Neuchâtel boasts four museums; the **Musée d'Ethnographie,** the **Musée d'Histoire Naturelle,** the **Musée d'Archéologie,** and biggest and best of all the **Musée d'Art et d'Histoire,** on the lake front. Its tour de force is the **Automates**

Jaquet-Droz, three automatons made by watchmaker Jaquet Droz between 1764 and 1774. They may be rudimentary by the standard of today's audio-animatronics, but in their day they were one of the wonders of Europe and were paraded before royalty. Nowadays they only perform on the first Sun of each month (1400, 1500, 1600). At other times a film (in English) explains their story.

Le Lac de Neuchâtel joins the town to Yverdon-les-Bains (see below), **St Peter's Island** (see above) and the beautiful old town of **Morat** (Murten).

YVERDON-LES-BAINS

Station: Gare ; *tel: 157 22 22.* The old town is a 5-min walk away.
Tourist Office: Office du Tourisme, *pl. Pestalozzi; tel: (024) 23 62 90.*

ACCOMMODATION AND FOOD

There are a handful of hotels in the town, covering the range from one- to four-stars. The **HI** youth hostel is at *r. du Parc 14, tel: (024) 21 12 33.*

The **Buffet de la Gare,** *av. de la Gare; tel: (024) 21 49 95,* offers a choice of three restaurants, a large terrace and a shady garden.

SIGHTSEEING

Set on the southern shore of Lac Neuchâtel, Yverdon-les-Bains is a spa resort where, for centuries, visitors have taken the waters (presently at the **Centre Thermal,** just off *av. des Bains*). The centre of town, **Place Pestalozzi,** is marked by a 13th-century castle which is home to the **municipal museum** – a varied collection ranging from local memorabilia to Egyptian mummies. Opposite, the **Maison d'Ailleurs** (literally, the 'House of Elsewhere') is a science-fiction museum.

85

BERNE–MILAN

Berne and Milan may both be European capitals but there the similarity ends. One is sleepy, quaint and old fashioned, the other is frenetic, vivacious and desparately fashionable. En route there is glorious mountain scenery, particularly between Spiez and Kandersteg, as the route literally cuts through the majestic Bernese Oberland, and lovely lakes and castles to explore.

Berne

Thun

Spiez

Mülenen

Brig

St Moritz – Zermatt, p. 281

St Moritz – Zermatt, p. 281

Stresa

Milan

86

FASTEST JOURNEY: 4 HRS

TRAINS

ETT tables: 82, 280, 365.

FAST TRACK

Five through trains run between Berne and Milano Centrale with journey times of around 4 hrs. Many more journeys are possible by changing trains at Brig. A new Pendolino train service is due to be introduced for 1997 with much quicker journey times.

ON TRACK

Berne (Bern)–Thun–Spiez
A frequent local service supplements the InterCity trains taking around 30 mins

to link Bern with Thun, and 15 mins Thun with Spiez.

Spiez–Brig

An hourly service operates through the Simplon Tunnel linking Spiez to Brig. The spectacular journey takes around 65 mins with most trains offering refreshment cars.

Brig–Stresa

Trains operate every 2 hours on this route between Switzerland and Italy. The trains taking just over 1 hr.

Stresa–Milan (Milano)

Around 12 trains a day link Stresa and Milano Centrale. Other services are available to Milano Porta Garibaldi. Journey times are about 1 hr.

THUN

Station: Bahnhof (Bhf); *tel: 157 22 22*. A 5-min walk from the centre of town via *Bahnhofstr.* and *Bahnhofbrücke.*
Tourist Office: Verkehrsbüro, in the station, *tel: (033) 54 72 56.*

ACCOMMODATION AND FOOD

The 19th-century **Hotel Emmental**, *Bernstr. 2; tel: (033) 22 01 20*, has just been smartly renovated and costs around SFr.150 per couple. The bar-food is good here too.

For daytime eating in town try **Le Pavillon**, *Aare Zentrum, Aarestr.*, for an excellent value self-service buffet.

SIGHTSEEING

Thun (pronounced Toohn) is a delightful old town, straddling the **River Aare**, with several of its buildings on an island in the middle of the river. The Aare pours into **Lake Thun** (Thunersee), one of Switzerland's most attractive lakes.

Thun's main shopping street, **Hauptgasse**, is a charming split-level street where you walk along the roofs of the lower tier of shops to see the upper tier. Between numbers *55* and *57 Obere Hauptgasse* a narrow stairway takes you up to the castle. Perched high above the town, **Schloss Thun** (Thun Castle), built in 1186, is a fairy-tale fantasy. Its Romanesque tower with a great red central sloping roof section and four slim corner turrets, topped with red spires, is the town's trademark. Directly behind it the snow-capped Stockhorn provides a picture-postcard backdrop. The castle is great fun to explore, with a lively Historical Museum now filling its huge rooms. Bang up to date is the **Kunstmuseum Thun** (Museum of Fine Arts) featuring a good collection of Swiss Pop Art and other 20th-century Swiss contributions. It's housed in the old **Grand-Hôtel Thunerhof**, *Hofstettenstr.*

Down on the lakefront (turn right from Bhf and walk for 10-mins) is another museum in a grand setting, the **Schweizerisches Gastronomie Museum** housed in the 150-year old Schloss Schadau. Appropriately there's a gourmet restaurant here, but for cheaper eats the adjacent Schadau Park is a perfect picnic site. The castle park also features a pavilion housing **Wocher's Panorama of Thun 1810**. This large painting in the round is said to be the oldest of its kind in the world.

Just a little way along the lake shore the **Strandbad Thun** is a beautifully located outdoor swimming pool complex, also excellent for alfresco snacking.

OUT OF TOWN

Ferries ply the lake to various destinations. **Oberhofen** is a favourite destination (if possible take the romantic 1906-built *Blümlisalp* steamer) on account of the

87

splendid **Schloss Oberhofen** which boasts a Turkish smoking room, a Napoleon III drawing room, a medieval chapel and many artefacts from the Museum of Berne collection. Nearby at the **Zentrum Wichterheer** are two more collections. The **Im Obersteg Sammlung** is one of the country's most important private art collections, including works by Picasso and Chagall. Also within the estate is the **Museum für Uhren und mechanische Musikinstrumente** (Museum of Timepieces and Mechanical Musical Instruments) containing over 2000 items spanning seven centuries.

The same boat service also links Thun to Spiez (see below) and Interlaken (see p. 135). Steam fans should note that a brand new museum, **Vaporama**, celebrating the steam engine, and particularly steam-powered boats, is currently under construction in Thun.

Note: although there is no formal museum pass for the Thunersee region, just show your last museum ticket to get a discount on your next visit.

SPIEZ

Station: Bahnhof, *tel: 157 22 22*. The station is high on the hill with a marvellous view of the castle and lake. It's a 10-min walk straight down.

Tourist Office: Verkehrsbüro, next to the station; *tel: (033) 54 21 38*.

Like Thun, Spiez (pronounced Shpeetz) enjoys a classic lake-and-mountain setting with a romantic Romanesque castle at its heart. Unlike Thun, however, that's almost all there is to Spiez.

Schloss Spiez, erected as a medieval fortress, evolved into a 17th–18th-century residence, and rooms have been arranged into different periods to reflect the castle's long history. The picturesque 10th-century church in the grounds is also open

to visitors. A short walk from the castle lies the **Heimat– und Rebbaumuseum** (Heritage and Wine-making Museum), It's housed in a beautiful archetypal Swiss chalet, built in 1728, and has a charming slice-of-rural-life collection (open Wed, Sat and Sun pm.).

> **SIDE TRACK**
> **FROM SPIEZ**
>
> For a marvellous view over the whole of the Thunersee area take the regional train south for the short 7-min journey to **Mülenen** (this is on the main Berne-Milan line but Inter-City trains do not stop here). A funicular then makes the ascent up the 2362-m high **Mt Niesen.**

BRIG

For details, see p. 284.

LAKE MAGGIORE

Station: Stresa, 300 m south-west of Lake Maggiore.

Tourist Office: *Via Principe Tomasa 70, Stresa; tel: (0323) 30150.* Open Mon–Sat 0830–1230 and 1500–1815, Sun 0900–1200. Enquire about programmes for the international classical music festival held here late in Aug, early in Sept.

The Simplon Tunnel

This route cuts and dives through dramatic terrain straddling the borders of both Switzerland and Italy. The most dramatic feature of this route is, however, manmade: the Simplon Tunnel. A staggering 19.9 km in length, it is the longest in the Alps. Entering the tunnel south of Brig in Switzerland, the train emerges in Italy to the north of Domodossola, before heading on to Stresa.

ACCOMMODATION

There is a wide range of accommodation in Stresa, most of it blessed with coveted lakeside views and much of it very expensive. In the lower price bracket, there are fewer options and what there is tends to be modern. **Arona**, to the south, is a better option for camping and for the cheapest hotels. **Camping**: **Lido**, on the lake shore, very close to the station, *tel: (0322) 243 383.*

SIGHTSEEING

Stresa is situated on the west bank of Lake Maggiore, Italy's second largest lake after Garda. It is the first major halt on the Italian part of this route after Domodossola.

One of the most charming towns on Lake Maggiore, Stresa has been a much-visited holiday resort since the 19th century. It is an elegant, low-key place famous for its views and for its proximity to the magical **Borromean Islands**.

There are four islands – **Isola dei Pescatori**, **San Giovanni**, **Isola Bella** and **Isola Madre** – which poke up out of the water in the western spur of the lake, just to the north-east of Stresa. Frequent ferry services link the islands to Stresa. Isola Bella is probably the most celebrated. In the 17th century, Count Carlo Borromeo III commissioned Angelo Crivelli to lay out a garden in a series of ten formal terraces, an extravagant gift designed to indicate his devotion to his wife Isabella. Exotic plants, statuary, fountains, peacocks and a sumptuously decorated villa completed the picture. Beautiful it might be, but it has succumbed to the ravages of tourism.

Isola Madre is much gentler; it too has a famous garden and a small palace of the Borromeo family. More peaceful than both, but no less picturesque, is Isola dei Pescatori whose tiny fishing village is the focus of many afternoon outings. San Giovanni is private.

Stresa is an excellent base from which to explore the lake. Getting about is easy: slow ferries and faster hydrofoils zig-zag from shore to shore. Contact **Navigazione Sul Lago Maggiore**; *tel: (0322) 46551/2/3/4.*

Arona, to the south, is chiefly known as the birthplace of St Charles Borromeo (1538–84) – a Church reformer and an instigator of the Council of Trent. A huge bronze statue of him towers above old Arona and the castle in which he was born. **Pallanza**, on the opposite (northern) shore from Stresa and **Baveno**, west of Stresa, are both popular resorts, particularly in peak season. Queen Victoria holidayed here in 1879 and, ever since, Bavena has been favoured by the British. Pallanza's main attraction is the **Villa Taranto** whose 50-acre gardens were planted in the Thirties with some 20,000 different kinds of plants – including giant Amazonian water lilies – by a Scotsman anxious to take advantage of the area's excessively mild climate. Moving up the lake beyond Pallanza, **Ghiffa** and **Cannero Riviera** are pretty stone-built villages with wonderful lake views while **Cannobio**, the last major halt before Swiss Lake Maggiore, has one interesting site: the Bramante-inspired **Santuario della Pietà** which St Carlo Borromeo had built at the location of a miracle.

On the south-east side of the lake, **Angera** is dominated by a castle built by the Visconti family, the **Rocca di Angera**. Opposite Stresa, on the east side of Lake Maggiore, **Laveno** is a popular centre for ceramics and the place from which to catch the cable car up to the **Sassa del Ferro** (1062 m). From the top there are magnificent views out over the lake to the Alps beyond.

89

DIJON

Dijon in the heartland of France, was capital of the Dukes of Burgundy from 1364–1477. The city is famed for its riches, its medieval architecture, but perhaps most of all as the home of Dijon mustard. Many of the buildings date from the 14th–15th centuries but others include some of the finest examples of Renaissance architecture in France. In spite of this, the city centre, one of the first in the country to be pedestrianised, is no museum piece, but a lively place to shop in attractive surroundings. Architecture aside, the wines and gastronomy of Burgundy are reason enough to spend time in Dijon – a meal and bottle of wine at one of the local restaurants will be a memory to cherish.

TOURIST INFORMATION

Tourist Office: *pl. Darcy, 21000 Dijon; tel: 80 44 11 44*. Near the station and on edge of pedestrian centre. Helpful, multilingual information; accommodation booking service, FFr.15. Currency exchange. Open 0900–2100 summer, 0900–1200, 1400–1900 winter. **Branch Office** including administration: *34 r. des Forges*; in a 15th-century mansion in the centre.

CIJB (Centre Information Jeunesse de Bourgogne); *22 r. Audra; tel: 80 30 35 56*, for student and youth information.

ARRIVING AND DEPARTING

Station
Gare Ville *av. du Mar. Foch; tel: 36 35 35 35*. The station is a 5-min walk from the city centre along *av. Foch*. Café/bar: just outside station. 24-hr Accueil to welcome travellers; left luggage lockers. **SOS Voyageurs**: for help *tel: 80 43 16 34*. Open Mon–Sat 0830–1800. Trains to Beaune every 20 mins.

Buses
Gare Routière de Dijon, *av. Mar. Foch* (behind train station) *tel: 80 42 11 00* for information. Information office open Mon–Sat 0730–1230, 1345–1830, Sun 0730–1230. Provides services to local villages but they are slow.

GETTING AROUND

Dijon is made for walking. Most of the streets and buildings were built when feet were the main form of transport and the whole of the old centre is traffic-free. It's no more than 15 min walk from *pl. darcy* along the main shopping street, *r. de la Liberté*, to the Ducal Palace in the centre at *pl. de la Libération*. Bus services are highly efficient but are likely to be useful only for getting further afield such as to Lac Kir. Take line 18 from *pl. Darcy* – **STRD** information booth at *pl. Grangier; tel: 80 30 60 90*. Tickets FFr.5, day-pass FFr.15, 12-trip card FFr.39.

Main **taxi** ranks are at the station, *pl. Grangier* and *pl.de la Libération; tel: 80 41 41 12*.

STAYING IN DIJON

Accommodation
There is no shortage of hotels, but many are geared towards the business

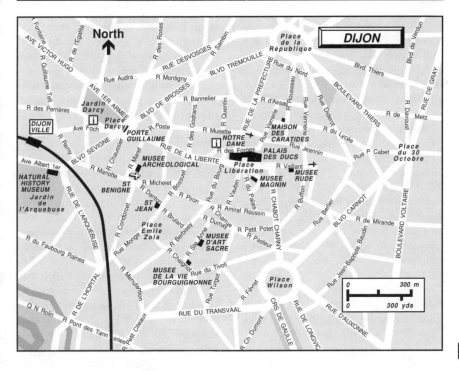

traveller, and accommodation can be tight in summer season. Most are in the two-star category. Chain hotels include *BW, CI, Hd, Ib* and *Mc.* **Ibis Central**, *3 pl. Grangier, 21000 Dijon; tel: 80 30 44 00,* is well positioned on the edge of the old town and its Grill Rotisserie has a good reputation. Lower-priced hotels are dotted around the old town; try *r. Monge.*

HI: Centres de Rencontres Internationales, *1 blvd Champollion; tel: 80 72 95 20.* Four km from the station. Take bus no. 5 from outside the post office just east of *pl. Darcy.*

Eating and Drinking

The citizens of Burgundy are renowned for their love of food and drink. *Kir*, an apéritif of white wine and *crème de cassis* – blackcurrant liqueur – was invented here (see p. 93). The town is, of course, also famous for its mustard which is made with white wine rather than vinegar. *Pain d'épice* – a spicy bread – is another speciality. *Hors d'oeuvres* include *jambon persillé* (jellied ham) and snails – the latter basted in garlic butter. Classic main courses are *coq au vin* (chicken in red wine) and *boeuf bourguignonne* (beef in red wine).

Restaurant prices can be high but there is plenty of choice, particularly around the market hall and also around *pl. Émile Zola* where everyone eats out of doors when the weather is warm. Try **Moules Zola**; *tel; 80 58 93 26* for mussels (reserve a table or be prepared to wait) or **Le Germinal**, *r. Monge* alongside *pl. Émile Zola; tel: 80 58 93 26*, where specialities include smoked salmon salad in a bowl and frogs legs with rice.

To save money, feast on ready-made *pâtés*, pies and salads with mayonnaise from a *charcuterie* or one of the stalls in the 19th-century market hall, a striking cast-iron edifice with blue pillars, open Tues, Fri and Sat mornings. The stalls also have an array of cheese, fruit and vegetables. Outside in r. *Odebert*, **Aux Delices d'Italie** makes the best ice-cream in town.

Burgundy wine is of course up there with the best in the world. To sample it at an actual vineyard, take a train to Nuits St George or to Beaune (20 mins, see p. 99). The **Côte de Nuits** area is the home of famous white wines like *Musigny, Clos de Vougeot* and *Chambertin*. The **Côte de Beaune** region produces the more delicate reds and whites like *Corton, Beaune* and *Pommard*.

Communications

Post Office: *pl. Grangier; tel: 80 50 62 19*. Poste restante, telephones; open 0800–1900 Mon–Fri, 0800–1200 Sat.

ENTERTAINMENT

Dijon is a student town with a cultural scene to match.

Theatre is strong, the best performances being at the **Théâtre du Pavis Saint-Jean**, r. *Danton; tel: 80 30 12 12*, situated in a converted church. Opera and classical music grace the **Théâtre de Dijon**; *pl. du Théâtre; tel: 80 67 23 23*.(seats FFr.75–250, student tickets available 30 mins before performances, FFr.50).

Those in search of more frenetic nightlife should look for the discos and clubs around *pl. de la République* and in the station area.

Events

Each June **Été Musical** is a summer festival of classical music, with top symphony orchestras, choirs and bands; *tel 80 30 61 00*. During mid-June and Aug the **Estivade** festival of music, dance and theatre

takes over the streets and courtyards; reservations *40 r. des Forges; tel: 80 30 31 00*. At the end of Aug, 400 folk groups gather in Dijon and the towns around it for the **Folkloriades Internationales** which features parades and street performances; *tel: 80 30 37 95*.

SIGHTSEEING

The small central part of old Dijon has been traffic-free for over 20 years and, not least because one of its mayors was also Minister of the Environment, the fine old buildings have been painstakingly renovated, making it a pleasure to explore. Outstanding examples of architecture from all periods remain, from medieval to art nouveau. A walking tour leaflet from the tourist office covers all the main sights, and is best used in conjunction with a museum day-pass at FFr.17 (available from any museum). The **Clé de la Ville passport** at FFr.50 includes admission to seven museums and a guided tour or audio cassette commentary.

Dijon's most impressive building, at its geographical and administrative heart, is the extravagant **Palais des Ducs de Bourgogne**. In their time (1364–1477) the dukes of Burgundy rivalled the kings of France for control of eastern France. The 15th-century **Tour Philippe le Bon**, the oldest part, soars above the palace, most of which was built 200 years later, designed by Le Vau, the architect of Versailles.

Part of the palace is now used as the City Hall but the east wing houses the **Musée des Beaux Arts**, *Cour de Bar; tel: 80 74 52 70*, open 1000–1800, closed Tues. This is one of the oldest museums in France with outstanding collections of European paintings from the 14th–18th century as well as works by 19th- and 20th-century masters including Picasso,

Dufy and Bonnard. The **Salle des Gardes** houses a magnificent marble and alabaster monument to the dukes. Near the entrance is the spacious former ducal kitchen with six fireplaces, now a bookshop.

From the palace, head around the corner to the quaint narrow streets in the oldest part of the town. Many of the half-timbered 17th-century houses in *r. Vannerie* are now antique shops. In *r. Chaudronnerie*, look out for the **Maison des Cariatides** and in *r. de la Chouette* the elegant 300-year old **Hotel de Vogue** which has a glazed tile roof. And peep into the courtyard of the **Hotel de Bouhier** to see its beautifully-carved gateway. Nearby the 500-year-old **Maison Millière**, with its decorative roof, was a shop in medieval times. Also in *r. de la Chouette*, a tiny brass owl – hence the street's name – is set in one of the side buttresses of **Église de Notre Dame** (Church of Our Lady), *pl. Notre Dame*. Rub it with your left hand for good luck. The façade of the church is decorated with rows of gargoyles which stick out dramatically – the best view is from underneath. Above them the 14th-century **Horloge de Jacquemart** has life-size figures that chime quarter hours.

Fine-art and fine furniture combine at the **Musée Magnin, 4** *r. des Bons Enfants*; *tel: 80 67 11 10*, in a former mansion house, open 1000–1800 summer, 1000–1200, 1400–1800 winter, closed Mon.

Dijon was the birthplace of the sculptor François Rude, famous for the *Arc de Triomphe* in Paris. The **Musée Rude, 8** *r. Vaillant; tel: 80 74 52 70*. open 1000–1200 and 1400–1745 closed Tues, is devoted to his work.

On the south side of the old town, the former **convent** of the Bernardines now houses two museums, **Musée de la Vie Bourguignonne et d'Art Sacré**, *15-17*

r. Sainte-Anne; tel: 80 44 12 69. open 0900–1200 and 1400–1800 closed Tues. One is devoted to sacred art, the other to life in old Burgundy including original shops rebuilt in full-scale street scenes. Near the station in the **Jardin de l'Arquebuse** are the **Natural History Museum** and **Botanical Gardens**, *1 r. Albert 1er; tel: 80 76 82 84*, museum open 0900–1200 and 1400–1800 closed Mon and gardens 0730–2000 summer, 0730–1800 winter. The Amora mustard company has a small **museum** on its history, *48 Quai Nicolas Rolin; tel: 80 44 44 52*, open by arrangement Tues and Sat pm.

Kir

The now-famous aperitif called **Kir** is officially only 35 years old but the drink has existed for centuries. For 600 years blackcurrants have been grown on the mountain ridges above the Burgundy vineyards, first by monks for medicinal purposes and then by farmers who hit on the idea of adding the juice to *marc* – the local brandy.

Rajafia, as the farmers called it, became popular in the last century when it was first produced commercially as *Crème de Cassis*. To popularise it, local cafés offered free samples and the workmen who went in for a drink after a hard day's work used it to sweeten cheap white wine.

In 1960 the mayor of Dijon, Canon Kir, decided he could help promote the town and the local wine if he declared that the *Blanc-Cassis* mixture should be given an official name. What better than his own!

The official recipe is one-third *Cassis* and two-thirds *Aligoté*, the local white Burgundy wine. Sparkling white *Crémant* turns it into *Kir Royal* and red *Burgundy* into *Kir Cardinal*. The perfect accompaniment is said to be *gougères* – cheese puffs.

93

DIJON–BASEL

The scenery soon begins to change once you leave the flat countryside around Dijon. Farmland with fields of corn and sunflowers gives way to woods as the line runs south-east, crossing the Norge, Tille and Saône rivers and then entering the green foothills of the Jura mountains around Dôle. There it swings north-east and the views become more and more Alpine as it runs alongside the River Doubs. On the way to Besançon, which is set in a bowl of forests, the hills get steeper on either side. Beyond it, they really close in and the line has to twist and turn beside the river. Watch out for the imposing castle at Montbeliard. Nearing Belfort the countryside flattens out once more. Distant tower-blocks herald the town's approach and you get a quick glimpse of its formidable Citadelle on the right.

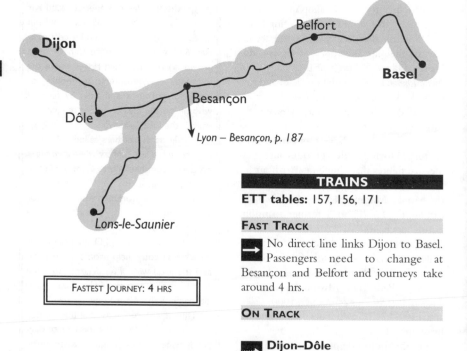

Lyon – Besançon, p. 187

FASTEST JOURNEY: 4 HRS

TRAINS

ETT tables: 157, 156, 171.

FAST TRACK

No direct line links Dijon to Basel. Passengers need to change at Besançon and Belfort and journeys take around 4 hrs.

ON TRACK

Dijon–Dôle

A frequent if not very regular service operates on this route with journeys of around 30 mins. Some trains are TGV's, which require passengers to pay a supplementary fare.

Dôle–Besançon
Around 15 trains a day link these towns but, again, the service is not regular and you will need to consult the timetable to avoid those periods when no trains operate. The journey takes 35 mins.

Besançon–Belfort
Ten to 15 trains a day, a combination of local stopping trains and expresses, provide the service between Besançon Viotte and Belfort. The journey takes just under 1 hr 30 mins.

Belfort–Basel
Between 7 and 9 services are available each day, with some requiring a change of train in Mulhouse. The journey takes between 1 hr and 1 hr 30 mins.

DÔLE
Station: *pl. de la gare; tel: 84 72 81 23.*
Tourist Office: *6 pl. Grévy, 39100 Dôle; tel: 84 72 11 22.* Open Mon–Fri 0830–1200 and 1400–1800 (except Mon am), Sat 0900–1200.

ACCOMMODATION AND FOOD
The town has a good selection of hotels. For budget accommodation, try around the station. **HI**: *pl. Jean XXIII, tel: 84 82 36 74.*

The old town is the best place for interesting restaurants where you can sample regional Jura dishes such as smoked sausages and fondues.

SIGHTSEEING
This is a busy town at the junction of the **River Doubs** and the **Rhine-Rhône canal**. It was once the capital of the fiercely independent Comté region which

succeeded in keeping its independence under the counts of Burgundy and as part of the Holy Roman Empire. After a long siege in 1674 it was eventually subdued and brought under the umbrella of Louis XIV's France. The old town is charming, full of winding alleys, fountains and 15th-century houses. Head for *pl. aux Fleurs* for the best view. The huge **Notre-Dame**, with soaring vaulted roof and square bell tower, dates from the 16th century and houses a fine 250-year-old de Riepp organ.

The town's more recent claim to fame is as the home of the scientist **Louis Pasteur** who was born in 1822 at *43 r. Pasteur.* Now a museum, *tel: 84 72 20 61,* it contains a reconstruction of the workroom his father used as a tanner. Open Mon–Sat 1000–1200 and 1400–1800; closed Tues. There are several interesting old houses in the street, including a 17th-century hospital (*Hôtel-Dieu*) whose beautiful courtyard has two floors of arched arcades. The old tanners' quarter alongside the canal is also worth a wander.

95

BESANÇON
Station: Besançon Viotte, *av. de la Paix; tel: 36 35 35 35,* about 1 km north-west of the town centre, 15 mins on foot or take a bus.
Tourist Office: *2 pl. de la 1ère Armée Française, 25000 Besançon; tel: 81 80 92 55.* Open Mon 1000–1900, Tues–Sat 0900–1900 (Apr–Sept); Mon 1000–1800, Tues–Sat 0900–1800 (Oct–May), Sun 1000–1200, 1500–1700 (mid-June–mid-Sept), 1000–1200 (mid-Sept–mid-June).

GETTING AROUND
Besançon's **Vieille Ville** (old town) is surrounded on three sides by a noose-shaped meander of the River Doubs. To reach the tourist office from the rail station, walk down the steep *av. Mar. Foche* then turn

left along the river. Bus nos 4 and 8 run frequently into the town from the far side of the station car-park. Bus map and timetable at the entrance. Throughout the town, bus services run every 10 mins Mon–Sat 0600–2000, every 15 mins 2000–0000 and Sun. Buy tickets on the bus; FFr.5.50 or 10 for FFr.49. A little road 'train' does a 40-min circuit of the town April–May and Sept 1100–1800, June–Aug 1000–1800. For 24-hr taxis, *tel: 81 88 80 80*. Boat trips from *Pont de la République*.

ACOMMODATION AND FOOD

Finding somewhere to stay is relatively easy as there are plenty of mid-priced hotels, especially around the rail station. International hotel chains include *Ca, Ib, Mc* and *Nv*. **HI: Foyer Mixte de Jeunes Travailleurs Les Oiseaux**, *48 r. des Cras; tel: 81 88 43 11*. **Centre International de Séjour,** *19 r. Martin du Gard; tel: 81 50 07 54*.

The best selections of restaurants are in *r. Bersot* and *r. Mégevand*.

SIGHTSEEING

Besançon, a busy university town, commands an impressive setting amid the foothills of the Jura mountains. There are glimpses of the town with wooded hills around it from the front of the station. In the old town, grand stone buildings line the narrow streets with shops between them. The **Porte Noire**, *r. de la Convention*, is a reminder that its history dates back to Roman times.

The Citadel, built in the 17th century by the military architect Vauban, stands high above the town guarding the top of the noose formed by the river. Inside, the **Musée de la Résistance et la Déportation**, *tel: 81 65 07 51*, gives a compelling view of the role of the Vichy Government during World War II. Open 0945–1645 winter, 0915–1815 summer. Admission FFr.30. **Musée des Beaux Arts**, *1 pl. de la Révolution, tel: 81 81 44 47*, is one of the oldest museums in France with an impressive collection of Renaissance paintings. Open 0930–1200, 1400–1800. Closed Tues. Admission FFr.20, free Wed and Sun.

A curiosity is the 56-dial **Astrological Clock** in **St Jean Cathedral** which has a cast–iron frame and moving figures. It was built in 1858 when the town had a thriving clock and watch-making industry. Visits to see it strike the hour, beginning 10 mins beforehand, from 0950 to 1750 (not 1250). Closed Tues. Admission FFr.14. The **Clef de la Ville** passport available from the tourist office covers entrance to the Musée des Beaux Arts, Citadel and Astrological Clock as well as a walking tour with audio-cassette. FFr.78.

> ### SIDE TRACK
> ### FROM BESANÇON
>
> It takes just over an hour to reach Lons-le-Saunier from Besançon, with 5 or 6 trains each day.

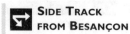

LONS-LE-SAUNIER

Station: Boulevard Gambetta; *tel: 84 24 01 25*.
Tourist Office: *1 r. Pasteur, 39000 Lons-le-Saunier; tel: 84 24 65 01*. Open Mon–Sat 0830–1200, 1400–1800 (Sat until); also Sun 1400–1800 in summer.

This picturesque town, capital of the Jura area, is in the middle of the 50-mile **Route des Vins** du Jura. Vineyards on the rich limestone and red clay soil stretch south from Arbois to Beaufort and several of the towns are accessible by train. Wine festivals are held on various dates. Check details at the tourist office. ▲

BELFORT

Station: *av. Wilson; tel: 36 35 35 35*; on edge of the pedestrianised shopping area. **Tourist Office**: *2 r. Clémenceau, 90000 Belfort; tel: 84 28 12 23*. Open Mon–Sat 0900–1230 and 1330–1900, Sun 1000–1330 in summer; Mon–Sat 0900–1230 and 1330–1800 in winter. To reach the new **Congress Centre**, turn left out of station and bear right on *Faubourg de France* and cross the river; 15 mins walk.

ACCOMMODATION AND FOOD.

Rooms in middle-range hotels are usually easy to find. The grandest – and oldest – is the family-owned **Grand Hôtel du Tonneau d'Or**, *r. Reiset; tel: 84 58 57 56*. Hotel chains include *BW, Cl, F1, Nv*.

HI: Foyer de Jeunes Travailleurs, Residence Madrid, *6 r. de Madrid; tel: 84 21 39 16*. **Camping: Les Promenades d'Essert**, *av. Gén. Leclerc; tel: 84 21 03 30*.

The most interesting restaurants are in the old town; try **Au Pied du Lion**, *pl. de la Grande Fontaine, tel: 84 54 06 95*.

GETTING AROUND.

Bus services are frequent but the town centre is manageable on foot. A little road 'train' takes a circular 45-min route from *pl. d'Armes* and *Fontaine de Rougemont* via the old town and **Citadelle** high on a rocky outcrop high above it. Daily May–Sept 1000–1900 and July–Aug 0800–2200. Tickets FFr.30. Frequent bus services run from the rail station to the **Vosges Mountains** including **Ballon d'Alsace**, 30 mins away.

EVENTS

Whitsun is the liveliest time in Belfort when **F.I.M.U.**, an international festival of university music, takes place with classical, rock and jazz concerts, all free. Annual **Euro-Rock festival** in July and hot-air balloon championships in Sept.

SIGHTSEEING

The tower blocks which greet the visitor arriving by train are a reminder that Belfort is a working, rather than tourist, town. TGV and Eurostar trains are made there and can often be seen 'parked' in the station's extensive sidings. But the town has historic gems too, particularly a 22 m-long lion carved in the local red sandstone which sits at the bottom of the high Citadelle walls. Erected by August Bartholdi (who also designed New York's Statue of Liberty), it commemorates the town's 103-day seige during the Franco-Prussian war in 1870. The lion looks its most spectacular at night when floodlit. The **Citadelle**, built by the military architect Vauban in the 17th century, housed 50,000 troops during the Franco-Prussian war and now contains a military museum; *tel: 84 28 12 23*. Open May–Sept 1000–1900, Oct–Apr 1000–1200 and 1400–1700, closed Tues; FFr.11. In the **pl. d'Armes**, the centre of the old town, are the 18th-century red sandstone **Cathédrale de St-Christophe**, notable for its organ, and the **Town Hall**.

Vosges Mountains

The **Ballon d'Alsace** is the highest spot, at 1247 m, on the so-called *Route des Crètes* – the road of the peaks – which runs north/south along the backbone of the Vosges. Three long-distance paths meet there so it an admirable setting-off point for walking in the forests and sunny mountain pastures – *chaumes* – of the **Parc Naturel Régional des Ballons des Vosges**. At the summit itself a short nature trail is laid out.

DIJON–LYON

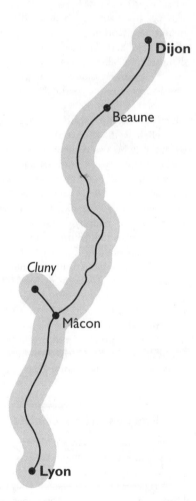

Dijon

Beaune

98

Cluny

Mâcon

Lyon

FASTEST JOURNEY: 1 HR 30 MINS

Through the gastronomic heart of France, this route takes you south from Dijon, capital of Burgundy, past the great vineyards of Beaune. A detour off the main line at Chalon-sur-Saône goes to the city of Cluny with its dramatic abbey, model for many of the cathedrals of Europe. The journey is gentle, past rolling fields of corn and sunflowers. Cows graze in green pastures – in many ways this is the utopian picture of rural France. Miles of vineyards stretch into the distance framed to the west by the misty ridges of the Mont du Charola.

South of Mâcon, the line takes you through the Beaujolais region, following the banks of the River Saône. All is calm, almost monotonous, until the sudden appearance of the suburbs of France's second city, the frenetic metropolis of Lyon (see p. 180).

TRAINS

ETT table: 149.

FAST TRACK

A dozen trains a day run between between Dijon Ville and Lyon Part-Dieu. The journey takes between 1 hr 30 mins and 2 hrs 15 mins.

ON TRACK

Dijon–Beaune
A frequent service links Dijon Ville

and Beaune each day. Journey time is 30 mins.

Beaune–Mâcon

Eight trains a day link the two towns, the journey taking just under an hour.

Mâcon–Lyon

Frequent trains run between Mâcon Ville and Lyon Part-Dieu or Perrache. The journey takes around 50 mins.

BEAUNE

Station: *av. 8 Septembre*; *tel: 80 44 50 50*, for information. Luggage lockers; station closed 2400–0500.
Tourist Office: *r. de l'Hôtel Dieu, 21200 Beaune*; *tel: 80 26 21 30*. Open Mon–Sat 0900–2100, Sun until 1900 in summer, 0900–1800 in winter. It has an accommodation service, lists and maps of vineyards and suggested tours. Currency exchange. Free guided tours of the town (in French) July–Aug at 1500.

GETTING AROUND

The town is small and easily accessible on foot. Most of the sights are contained within the old ramparts.
Bus Station: **Transco**: *tel: 80 42 11 00* (based in Dijon). Many buses follow wine routes through the *Côte d'Or* region.

ACCOMMODATION AND FOOD

Popular with foreign tourists, Beaune fills up quickly in summer and reservations are a good idea. Hotel chains include *Ct, Ib, Mc* and *Nv*. There are no youth hostels (better to base yourself in Dijon, under 30 mins by train). Look for budget hotels in the streets around the station.
Camping: Les Cent Vignes; *10 r. Auguste Dubois*; *tel: 80 22 03 91*. A walk of 20 mins from the centre, north on *r. Lorraine* from *pl. Monge*. Open Mar–15 Oct.

In Beaune drinking comes before eating, but this is still Burgundy and the dedication to the stomach persists. There are plenty of good value restaurants, serving local dishes such as snails, paté and distinct cheeses. Try the streets around *pl. Madeleine.*

ENTERTAINMENT

Wine! This is the centre of the **Côtes de Beaune** vineyards, some of the finest in Burgundy. The tourist office has lists of local wineries offering *dégustations* (tastings). Although their prices tend to be higher than in supermarkets the whole experience of wine-tasting is definitely worth the investment. Welcoming cellars include: **Marché aux Vins**, *5 r. Nicolas Rolin*; *tel: 80 22 27 69*, in a 15th-century church just behind the *Hôtel Dieu*. Tastings of 40 Burgundy vintages. Open 0930–1130, 1430–1800, admission FFr.40.
   Maison Calvet, *6 blvd Perpreuil*; *tel: 80 22 06 32*. In buildings dating from the 14th century with endless tunnelled cellars and fine wines, for FFr.25 a tour. Open 0900–1330, 1400–1700, closed Tues.
   Halles Aux Vins, 28 r. Sylvestre Chauvelot; *tel: 80 22 18 34*, in a 13th-century crypt, with 18 wines on offer, right down to the oldest *grands crus*. FFr.40, open 1000–1200 and 1400–1800.

EVENTS

Anim'été, a summer-long street festival, including organ recitals and carillon concerts is held during Aug. **Baroque music festival** at weekends during July and **international folk festival** on first weekend in Sept. **Wine festival** held in Nov.

SIGHTSEEING

Beaune was once home to the dukes of Burgundy. The 15th-century ramparts still impress today, protecting a charming old

99

town of cobbled streets and fine mansions. Much of the wealth gained from taxing both wine-growers and river traffic on the Saône went into fine buildings. But not all the town's sights are obvious. Underground, Beaune is riddled with the vaulted cellars where the *'négociants'* – wine merchants – store their supplies until they reach maturity.

With its multi-coloured tiled roofs and intricate spires, the **Hôtel Dieu**, *r. de L'Hotel-Dieu, tel: 80 24 45 00*, is one of the most outstanding buildings, notable for its exquisite courtyards. It was built in 1443 as a hospice by a wealthy tax collector, Nicholas Rolin, who was chancellor of Burgundy. Today it is a museum with tours of the medieval hospital wards. Open 0900–1130 and 1400–1730 in winter, 0900–1800 Easter–Nov.

The dukes of Burgundy left behind a grandiose palace when they departed for bigger and brassier Dijon. The palace now houses a museum dedicated to wine, the **Musée du Vin**, *r. d'Enfer; tel: 80 22 08 19.* displaying antique wine-pressing machines and casks, as well as thousands of bottles (empty). Open 0930–1800. Closed Tues Dec–Mar.

MÂCON

Stations: Mâcon-Ville, *r. Victor Hugo.* For information (0900–1900, closed for lunch), *tel: 85 38 44 48*; for reservations, *tel: 36 35 35 35.* For the town centre and river head down *r. Gambetta* and turn left along *r. Carnot*, an easy 10-min walk. **Gare TGV** on the main Paris-Lyon line is 5 km east of the town centre; *tel: 85 32 90 50* for reservations, *tel: 36 35 35 35* for information.

Tourist Office: *187 r. Carnot, 71000 Mâcon; tel: 85 39 71 37.* Smart modern office with a waterfall down the outside of the windows. Comprehensive information

Mâconnais-Beaujolais Wine Road

Mâcon makes a good base for tours of the **Burgundy vineyards**. The most practical way of doing one is to hire a car at the rail station as buses are infrequent and slow. The tourist office has a free 112-page booklet detailing 12 circuits (in French, English and German) which take in 65 villages where the famous vintages are produced, as well as sightseeing 'musts' like Romanesque churches, castles and caves.

Among the most famous names, **Pouilly-Fuisse** is the pride of the Grand White Burgundy wines, reaching its peak after two or three years. With a delicate hazelnut aroma, it is particularly suitable for drinking with trout, snails, Bresse chicken, lobster and foie gras. The less expensive **Pouilly-Loche** is best drunk young but **Pouilly-Vinzelles** should ideally be left to mature for between 5 and 12 years. **Mâcon** wine comes in a light fruity red – which must be drunk young – and a dry white, excellent with fish. Red **Beaujolais-Villages** can be drunk young or old, depending on its origins. There is also the little-known white **Beaujolais**.

Red and white **Burgundy** which come from Chardonnay grapes are among the region's best-known wines. **Bourgogne Aligoté** is the wine which should be used to make Kir (see p. 93) and the sparkling **Cremant de Bourgogne**, produced by the strictly controlled *methode champenoise*, comes as brut, dry or semi-dry.

on the town and the area's vineyards. Accommodation service. Open Mon–Sat 1000–1200 Oct–May, 1000–1900 June–Sept, Sun 1400–1800.

ACCOMMODATION

Try along the riverside for hotels from budget to up-market. Mâcon's **campsite**, *1 r. des Grandes-Varennes, tel: 85 38 54 08,* (no reservations) is one of the biggest in the region with 200 pitches. 3 km out of the town, it is particularly handy for the **Maison du Vin** where wine producers sell direct to the public.

EVENTS

L'Été Frappé – Crazy Summer – takes place June–Aug, offering a free happening every evening, from music and street theatre to sports and processions. Details from the tourist office.

SIGHTSEEING

On the banks of the broad river Saône, Mâcon is an attractive little town in the heart of wine country. The old quarter, around pedestrianised *r. Carnot* and *pl. de la Baille*, has several unusual little gems. Stop for a drink at the old **Maison de Bois** – wooden house – on the corner of *pl. aux Herbes* and take a close look at its saucy carved decorations. Climb **St-Vincent** tower which partly dates back to the 6th century, including the rough stone slope at the start of the spiral way up, unchanged in 1100 years. And pause at the **Musée des Ursulines**, first a nunnery, then a boarding school, prison and barracks, but now housing an eclectic mix of archaeology and 17th-century art; *r. des Ursulines.* **Pl. aux Herbes** has a daily market and there is a big Sat morning along the *Promenade Lamartine* beside the river. Incidentally there are no boat trips.

 **SIDE TRACK FROM MÂCON**

SCETA Voyageurs runs buses from Mâcon to Cluny three times a day. The buses are en route to Chalon-sur-Saône, which is about 20 mins south of Beaune by rail, and therefore an alternative starting point for this side track. The journey to Cluny takes 45 mins–1½ hrs; rail passes accepted; *tel: 85 93 50 50.*

CLUNY

Rail shop (no station): *9 r. de la République; tel: 85 59 07 72.*
Tourist Office: *6 r. Mercière, 71250 Cluny; tel: 85 59 05 34.* Organises tours of the abbey in summer. Open 1000–1900 summer, 1000–1200, 1430–1830 winter. Currency exchange.

ACCOMMODATION

Accommodation can be tight in Cluny, especially at Easter and in high season. The best bet for budget rooms is **Cluny Séjour**; *r. Porte de Pans; tel: 85 59 08 83.* **Camping: Camping Municipal St-Vital**; *r. des Griottins; tel: 85 59 08 34,* near bus station. Open June–Sept.

SIGHTSEEING

Cluny is quiet, pretty and welcoming – an ideal stop-over on the journey south. For over 1000 years it has been revered for the huge **Ancienne Abbaye St-Pierre et St-Paul**, *tel: 85 59 12 79,* which was founded in 910 and grew to control Cistercian monasteries from Portugal to Russia. Its abbots were as powerful as kings and popes. Sadly greed and revolution tore down much of it, though the ruined towers give an idea of its former magnificence. Open daily. Treasures collected by the monks are displayed in the **Musée Ochier** in the former Bishop's palace, where tours of the abbey begin every hour during summer. Concerts take place in the abbey and Notre-Dame church during Aug.

101

GENEVA (GENÈVE)

Geneva is Switzerland's most famous city – home to the International Red Cross, the European section of the United Nations and the birthplace of the Geneva Convention. It also has a world-famous landmark, the Jet d'Eau water fountain, spouting high above the lake which bears the city's name. It is ironic then that Geneva is the least typically Swiss of all the country's large cities. This is mainly because of its international status (a third of Geneva's inhabitants are non-Swiss) and also partly because of its proximity to France. Besides its handsome lakeside setting, the city has a fine old town, over 20 top-class museums and a busy cultural scene to enjoy.

TOURIST INFORMATION

The main office is in **Gare de Cornavin**; *tel: 738 52 00*. Open Mon–Fri 0800–2000, Sat–Sun 0800–1800 (mid-June to mid-Sept); Mon–Sat 0900–1800 (mid-Sept to mid-June). There is a smaller central office at *pl. du Moulard 4; tel: 311 99 70*, open Mon 1230-1830, Tue–Fri 0900–1830, Sat 1030–1630. **Infor Jeune**, *r. Verdaine 13, tel: 311 44 22*, is an information office specifically for young travellers, open Mon–Fri 1000–1800.

ARRIVING AND DEPARTING

Airport: Genève-Aéroport (Cointrin); *tel: 799 31 11*, is a fully equipped international airport, 5 km from the city centre. There is a rail link to Gare de Cornavin

which departs every 10 mins with a journey time of 6 mins. Bus no. 10 also connects the airport to the city centre.
Stations: Gare de Cornavin, *tel: (022) 731 64 50*, is the main terminal, 10-mins walk north of the centre (bus nos. 5/6/9). **Gare Genève Eaux-Vives**, *tel: (022) 736 16 20*, on the eastern edge of the city, is the terminal for SNCF services from Annecy and St Gervais (bus no. 12).

GETTING AROUND

Geneva is split by the River Rhône into two distinct sections. The international area is on the **Rive Droite** (north bank) while the old town and main lakeside promenade lies on the **Rive Gauche** (south bank). The main sights divide between these two areas and a bit of route-planning is worthwhile. There's a good network of buses and trams to get you between the two.

STAYING IN GENEVA

Accommodation

Because of the prestigious international nature of the city, most hotels are expensive, but there are plenty of hostels and private rooms. Ask at the tourist office or the Infor-Jeune office for a copy of *Info-Jeunes*, which lists cheap accommodation and places to eat plus other information useful to budget travellers.

Hotel chains in Geneva include: *BW, Ch, EG, Ex, Hd, Hn, Fm, IC, IE, Mz, MO, Mv, P, Pu, Rd, Tp, WS*.

Info-Jeunes lists at least a dozen very cheap hotels, all within walking distance of the centre. A little more expensive but still

102

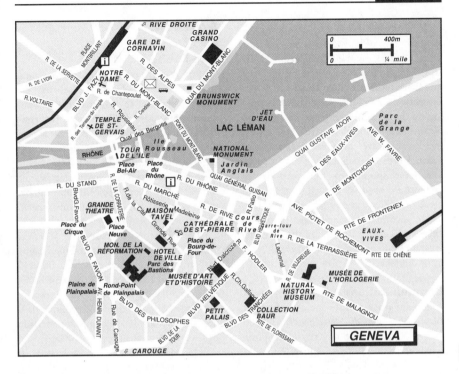

GENEVA

cheap by Geneva standards is the **St Gervais**, *Corps-Saints 20; tel: 732 45 72*, a short walk from the Gare Cornavin.

Geneva offers many lodgings in university and religious institutions (see *Info-Jeunes* for a full list). Those enjoying the most attractive and central location are the *logements universitaires, r. de Candolle 4; tel: (022) 705 77 20*, set in the beautiful Parc des Bastions (see Sightseeing), adjacent to the old town.

HI: *r. Rothschild 30; tel: (022) 732 62 60*, 15 mins from Cornavin (bus no. 1).

Campsites: Camping Sylvabelle, *chemin de Conches 10; tel: 347 06 03*, 3 km south-east (bus no. 8/88), also offers bungalows; **Camping de l'Abarc**, *rte. de Vernier 151; tel: 796 21 01*, 6 km west (bus no. 6); **Camping Pointe-à-la-Bise**, *Vésenaz; tel: 752 12 96*, 7 km north-east, close to the shore of Lac Léman (bus E).

Eating and Drinking

Because of its French influence and cosmopolitan nature, Geneva claims to be the culinary centre of Switzerland. The majority of such places, however, cater for international business people. A good place to look for reasonably priced restaurants is the *r. de Lausanne* (turn left out of the Gare de Cornavin). Look too around *pl. du Cirque (blvd Georges-Favon)*. Here the **Cave Valaisanne et Chalet Suisse** is a long-time favourite for all things Swiss; *tel: 328 12 36*. Nearby the simple café-style **Grappe Dorée**, *blvd Georges-Favon 14; tel: 29 77 98*, offers local cheese specialities. For a special occasion and the very best Swiss cuisine, try **Les Armures**, *1 r. du Puits-St-Pierre; tel: 310 34 42* (next to the old arsenal and the *Hôtel de Ville* in the centre of the Old Town); its prices are surprisingly reasonable.

Consult *Info-Jeunes* (see Accommodation) for a list of University restaurants; the most central is the **Cafétéria UNI-Bastion** at *Pl. de l'Université* by the Parc des Bastions. **Parc des Bastions** is also the perfect central picnic spot. For picnicing by the lake there is plenty of greenery by the Jardin Anglais but the best spot is the lovely **Parc la Grange/Parc des Eaux Vives** (see Sightseeing).

Cheese specials to look out for in Geneva are *steack au fromage* (a steak-sized piece of melted cheese, battered and deep fried), *malakoff* and *croûte*, two kinds of cheese and pastry dishes. By the lakeside, several restaurants offer *perche* (perch), fresh from the lake.

Communications
The main **post offices** are at *r. du Mont Blanc, 18*, and *r. du Stand 55*, 0730–1200 (Sat 1100), 1345–1800. If sending poste restante, do specify which office. The telephone code for Geneva is *022*.

Consulates
Australia: *r. de Moillebeau 56-8, tel: 734 62 00.*
Canada: *Pré de la Bichette 1, tel: 733 90 00.*
New Zealand: *ch. du Petit Saconnex, tel: 734 95 30.*
UK: *r. de Vermont 37-9, tel: 734 38 00.* Also for citizens of Republic of Ireland.
USA: *ave. de la Paix 1-3, tel: 738 76 13.*

Geneva is a cultured city with no shortage of wealthy patrons and clients to produce and to enjoy its highbrow arts. Pick up a free copy of *Genève Agenda*, the city entertainment guide, listing theatre, dance, classical music, rock and jazz venues. **Carouge** is popular for its nightlife and **Au Chat Noir** here is one of the city's principal jazz venues.

Rive Droite
To the north of the centre (bus nos. 5/8/14/F/Z) is **pl. des Nations**, the focus of most of the international organisations are grouped. The **Musée International de la Croix-Rouge**, *av. de la Paix 17*, is a stern building with acclaimed high-tech, multi-media exhibits tracing the history of the Red Cross and its Islamic offshoot, the Red Crescent. Profoundly moving, it covers man's inhumanity to man as well as natural disasters.

The **Palais des Nations**, *av. de la Paix 14*, was built 1929–37 to house the League of Nations, which was dissolved in 1940 and replaced by the UN European headquarters in 1945. There are guided tours of this huge complex, though thankfully they don't cover all 1632 rooms: open daily Apr–Oct, Mon–Fri only Nov–Mar.

The **Musée Ariana**, *av. de la Paix 10* (next to the UN building), houses some 18,000 objects covering seven centuries of international glassware and ceramics.

Between here and the lake is the lovely **Jardin Botanique**, a perfect place for a peaceful stroll (once you are a little distance from the main road). It includes a deer and llama park and an aviary.

Rive Gauche
The **Jardin Anglais**, on the waterfront, is famous for its **Horloge Fleurie** (floral clock). Several pleasure craft make lake excursions from here. A popular jaunt is the 40-min **Croisière des Parcs et Résidences**, though the lake shores and scenery are rather sedate around Geneva and become more interesting further east. The city's trade mark, the fountain known as the **Jet d'Eau**, spouts from a nearby pier, though only between Mar and mid-Oct. From the gardens, on a clear day, you

can see Mont Blanc, the highest mountain in the Alps at 4807 m. In the foreground is the flat-topped massif of Mont Salève (see p. 106). Continue walking along the lakeshore to the **Parc La Grange**, a lovely park with a rose garden, an 18th-century mansion, an old farm building, and an orangery where summer theatre is held. Adjacent is the **Parc Eaux Vives**. *Mouettes* (water taxis) cross the lake at this point to the Jardin Botanique (see above) on the opposite shore.

You can take an organised walking tour of the **old town** (*la vieille ville*) with **Mincar**, *tel: 318 54 54*, but it's cheaper doing it yourself with a Walkman and a map, available from the tourist office (SFr.10 plus SFr.50 deposit). The official tour starts at the landmark **Tour de l'Ile**, at the entrance to the old town. This sturdy, 13th-century tower is a remnant of the old city walls fortifications. The main gathering place in the old town is the lively **Place du Bourg-de-Four**, Geneva's

oldest square, surrounded by handsome 16th–18th-century houses, and the site of the ancient Roman forum. From here *r. de l'Hôtel de Ville* leads to the 15th-century **Hôtel de Ville** (town hall) where the first Geneva Convention was signed in 1864. Note the unusual ramped tower, designed for access by horsemen. Adjacent is the old arsenal plus the oldest house in the city, the 12th-century **Maison Tavel**. It's now an excellent museum, with several period rooms and exhibits covering the 14th–19th centuries. Nearby the original 12th–13th-century Gothic façade of the **Cathédrale de St-Pierre** has some incongruous 18th-century additions, including a controversial classical portal. Most interior decorations were stripped out in the Reformation, but there are some fine frescos in the neo-Gothic **Chapelle des Maccabées**. Calvin preached here and his chair has been saved for posterity. The north tower, reached by a 157-step spiral staircase, offers a great view of the old town. Beneath the cathedral is the **Site Archéologique**, where catwalks allow you to see the result of excavations, including a 5th-century mosaic floor.

Immediately south west of the old town, the **Parc des Bastions** is a glorious green space which used to be the city's botanical gardens. It now houses the university (founded by Calvin in 1599) and the vast **Monument de la Réformation**, erected in 1917. This is a 90-m long wall featuring four central characters: Farel, who introduced the Reformation to Geneva; Calvin, who preached it with such fervour that the city became known as the Protestant Rome; Bèze, who succeeded Calvin in Geneva; and Knox, who spread the Reformation through Scotland. Each figure stands a massive 4.5m high.

A short walk north-west is the vast marble **Musée d'Art et d'Histoire**, *r.*

105

Eau la la

Far from being conceived as a mere aesthetic landmark or tourist attraction, the **Jet d'Eau** was invented as a technical necessity. In the 18th and 19th centures high pressure water was distributed under the city streets to power waterpumps in the workshops of Geneva. However, when the workshops closed for the weekend, it was impossible to stop the flow of water quickly, so causing a dangerous overload to the system. The Jet d'Eau was therefore born as a vital safety valve and in its current form dates from 1891. The present jet (the third on the site, installed 1947) has a capacity of 500 litres per second, reaches a height of around 140m and is the tallest fountain in Europe.

Charles-Galland 2, with several rooms in period style, Hodler landscapes and the famous painting, *La Pêche Miraculeuse* by Witz, which portrays Christ walking on the water – of Lake Geneva. There are also large sections on such diverse subjects as arms and porcelain. Nearby are two other major collections. The 19th-century **Petit Palais**, *terrasse St-Victor 2*, has an impressive array of modern art and includes works by Cézanne, Renoir and the Surrealists; the **Collection Baur**, *r. Munier-Romilly 8*, contains some lovely Japanese and Chinese *objets d'art*, ranging from Samurai swords to jade and delicate porcelain. Finally, in this area, don't miss the amazing assortment of time-pieces in the **Musée de l'Horlogerie et de l'Emaillerie**, *rte de Malagnou 15*. It's an experience to be there when they sound the hour.

West of the centre, next to Geneva Airport Railway Station, is the city's latest collection, the **International Motor Car Museum**, *Genève Palexpo, Voie-des-Traz 40; tel: 788 84 84*. It features hundreds of vehicles plus driving simulators and games. **Carouge**, south of the River Arve (20 mins by tram no.12), is a baroque suburb with fine 18th-century architecture. Centred on the plane-shaded *pl. du Marché* is a picturesque, bohemian area of Italian-style arcaded buildings. Many of these have recently been restored and are now home to small shops and a thriving community of craftsmen. The **Musée de Carouge**, *pl. de Sardaigne 2*, is housed in an old watchmaker's home and features locally produced ceramics and paintings. To see Carouge in full swing come on Wed or Sat morning when the **market** is held. Geneva's other notable market venue is **Plainpalais** which hosts a flea market (*marché aux puces*) all day on both Wed and Sat and fruit and vegetable stalls on Tues and Thur mornings.

OUT OF TOWN

A favourite outing for local families is a trip up **Mt Salève** (1100m). Catch bus no. 8 across the French border (take your passport) then walk to the *télépherique* (cable car). From here Mt Blanc looms large, there are great views of Geneva and the lake, and in the winter skiing is possible. For all-year round skiing and some wonderful scenery, organised trips are available to **Chamonix** and **Mt Blanc** (both in France, see p.112) while, due east, the 3000-m altitude glacier of **Les Diablerets** (p. 164) includes the option of riding on a 'snow bus', a coach on caterpillar tracks. The quickest route to Mt Blanc is due south via Annemasse on SNCF. If you want to use your Swiss Pass it's a long way north around the lake and you will have to change to French railways via Le Châtelard or Vallorcine (see p. 114). There is no direct public transport route to Les Diablerets which would allow a day trip.

From May–Sept **Compagnie Générale de Navigation (CGN)** operate regular scheduled lake ferries from quai du Mt-Blanc and Jardin Anglais; *tel: 311 25 21* (Swiss Pass is valid). The charming medieval village of **Yvoire** (90 mins) is a popular excursion. The same service also calls at Thonon-les-Bains (1 hr 55 mins) and **Evian-les-Bains** (2 hrs 30 mins), p. 110, before continuing east to Lausanne-Ouchy (3 hrs 15 mins). **Lausanne** is only 35-40 mins away from Geneva by express train and **Montreux/Château de Chillon** a further 20-mins west (see p.159). A closer *château* option is **Château de Coppet**, 20 mins by rail from Geneva; it's more of a stately home than a medieval knight's castle but it is still quite impressive (open Mar to Oct, closed Mon). Combine it with a visit to the adjacent town of **Nyon** where there is also a castle and three museums.

GENEVA–KONSTANZ

This whistle-stop cross-country journey takes in the very best Swiss cities and four of the finest lakes. By Swiss standards this is mostly a lowlands trip, though the mountains are always close, particularly so around Lucerne. If you want to 'do' Switzerland in two weeks then this itinerary may be for you.

> FASTEST JOURNEY: 4 HRS 40 MINS

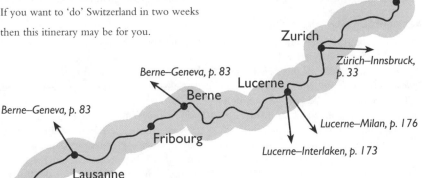

TRAINS

ETT tables: 250, 260, 265, 295, 299, 305, 304.

FAST TRACK

Quickest route is direct to Zurich and then change trains at Weinfelden with journey times of about 4 hr 40 mins.

ON TRACK

Geneva (Genève)–Lausanne
At least 3 trains an hour link Geneva with Lausanne, taking about 40 mins for the journey.

Lausanne–Fribourg–Berne (Bern)
An hourly service links Lausanne with Bern, all trains calling at Fribourg en route. Lausanne to Fribourg takes 45 mins, Fribourg to Bern 23 mins.

Berne–Lucerne (Luzern)
At least one train every hour taking 1 hr 15 mins.

Lucerne–Zurich
A 49-min journey each hour.

Zurich–Konstanz
A change of train is neccesary at Weinfelden. Journeys take just over 1 hr 30 mins.

LAUSANNE

(See p. 153.) Enjoy the magnificent water-side setting of **Ouchy** and visit the **Musée**

Olympique. Put the **Cathedral** and the **Collection de l'Art Brut** on your short-list and, if time allows, see the **Château de Chillon** at Montreux (see p. 159).

FRIBOURG

Station: **Gare;** *tel: 157 22 22.* The old town is a 5–10-min walk away via *av. de la Gare, r. de Lausanne* and *Grand-Rue.*
Tourist Office: *av. de la Gare,* next to the station; *tel: 037 81 31 75.*

ACCOMMODATION AND FOOD

There are relatively few cheap hotels in Fribourg. Try the **Central**, *r. N.-de Praroman 2; tel: 22 21 19* (near *pl. Georges Python*). **HI**: *r. Hôpital,2; tel: 23 19 40.*

The picturesque old inn, **Au Soleil Blanc**, *r. Samaritaine 29; tel: 22 15 63*, is a good choice for fondues and it's right in the heart of the old town.

SIGHTSEEING

Fribourg is a beautiful ancient town with some superb architecture and a lovely setting. On *Grand-Rue* is the 16th-century **Hôtel de la Ville** (town hall), nearby on *r. Bougers* is the beautiful **Cathedral of St Nicholas**, constructed 1283–1490. The tower (open mid-June–Sept) gives a great view over the town. Go back uphill a short way along *r. de Morat* to find the **Église des Cordeliers**, (the Franciscan Church) with a magnificent High Altar.

Continue along *r. de Morat* to the **Museum of Art and History** where you can see many of the original Fribourg street fountains and some fine religious statuary. By contrast, the modern sculptures by Jean Tinguely are a startling combination of animal skulls and rusty bits of machinery. Go back downhill all the way to the charming square, **Place du Petit-St-Jean**. From the small stone bridge, **Pont du Milieu**, is the classic picture-

---

Jean Tinguely

The biggest collection of works of the acclaimed, and often controversial, artist and sculptor, Jean Tinguely (1925–91) may be seen in Fribourg (his birthplace). He is most famous for his bizarre fountains which are far removed from traditional Swiss fountains. Constructed from scrap metal, they writhe and turn and propel jets of water in all sorts of curious ways. The best example is in Berne (see pp. 79–82) but look too in *Grand-Place*, Fribourg. The next time someone tells you the Swiss are a dour staid people, tell them about Tinguely.

---

postcard view of the town hanging spectacularly above the **River Saane** (Sarine). For an equally picturesque scene, go back through the square to the covered 13th century wooden bridge, **Pont de Berne**.

BERN

The capital (see p. 79) is a charming small town, famous for its cobbled arcaded main street and fountains. Skip the museums and simply savour the old-world atmosphere.

LUCERNE

Lucerne (p. 168) is the quintessential picturesque small Swiss city. Within the town are many fine sights and attractions, adjacent is the beautiful lake with some famous peaks to climb.

ZURICH

Zurich (see p. 325) is only a big city in Swiss terms and despite a rather dour image abroad, its old quarter is just as interesting as any major Swiss old town. You'll find the best museums in the country in Zurich and plenty of nightlife too.

GENEVA–MARTIGNY

For soaring alpine scenery, ice-blue lakes and vertigo, the route from Geneva into the French Alps and back into Switzerland is difficult to surpass. The route offers a side trip to the elegant lakeside spa of Évian-les-Bains. Later as it climbs steadily upwards, there are side trips on narrow-gauge railways that go right up into the mountains. Beyond St-Gervais the route is on the metre-gauge line that crosses into Switzerland, with a change from French to Swiss train near the border. In winter this can be the coldest train in the Alps, so wrap up warmly. Wheels screeching, it twists and turns through steep valleys and along narrow ledges cut high on mountainsides before making its final dramatic descent down a hair-raising one-in-five gradient to Martigny.

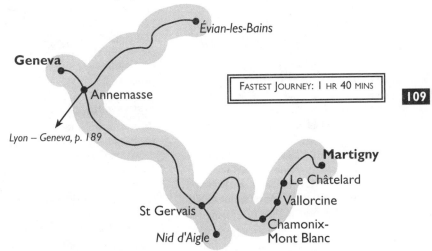

FASTEST JOURNEY: 1 HR 40 MINS

Lyon – Geneva, p. 189

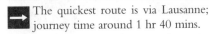

TRAINS

ETT tables: 250, 270, 167a, 167, 268.

FAST TRACK

The quickest route is via Lausanne; journey time around 1 hr 40 mins.

ON TRACK

Geneva(Genève)–Annemasse
This is a 10 min local journey .

Annemasse–St Gervais
A change of trains is required at La Roche-sur-Foron. The through journey takes between 1 hr 30 mins and 2 hrs.

St-Gervais–Chamonix–Vallorcine–Le Châtelard–Martigny
Eight or nine trains run each day on the

narrow-gauge rack-railway between St-Gervais and Martigny.

A change of train is required at Le Châtelard or Vallorcine. St-Gervais to Chamonix takes 35 mins, Chamonix to Vallorcine 35 mins, Vallorcine to Le Châtelard 6 mins, and Le Châtelard to Martigny 50 mins.

ANNEMASSE

Station: *pl. de la Gare; tel: 50 37 00 72;* left luggage lockers.
Tourist Information: Hôtel de Ville, *r. de la Gare, 74100 Annemasse; tel: 50 92 53 03*. Open Mon–Fri 0900–1200, Sat 1400–1800. Turn right from station along *r. de la Gare*, about 8 mins walk.

Shopping is one good reason for stopping at Annemasse – a large market is held on *pl. de la Libération* on Fri and a smaller one (food only) on Tues. The other is to take the cable-car (15 mins by bus no. 5 from the tourist office, FFr.6.50) that goes to the top of the **Salève** mountain (1375 m) for a view over **Lake Geneva** and its famous 150 m-high fountain to the north, and towards **Mt Blanc** to the east; FFr.57 return; every 12 mins Mon–Fri 0930–2000, Sat–Sun 0900–2300 (May–Sept), Tues–Sun 0930–1800 (Apr, Oct), Sat–Sun 0930–1730 (Christmas–Mar).

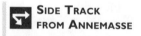

SIDE TRACK
FROM ANNEMASSE

ÉVIAN-LES-BAINS

Station: *av. des Bocquies; tel: 50 66 50 50*. For town centre and lake, turn right out of station and then left down *av. de Larringes*; a 20 min walk. Buses are very infrequent. Taxi: *tel: 50 75 03 17*.
Tourist Office: *pl. d'Allinges, 74502 Évian, tel: 21 51 26 95*. Open 0800–1200, 1400–1830, closed Sat–Sun Oct–Apr.

ACCOMMODATION AND FOOD

This genteel lakeside spa has hotels grand enough for royalty who, over a century ago, began flocking to it to take the waters. Indeed the majestic white **Hôtel Royal,** on a commanding hillside position overlooking the town, was built in 1905 with King Edward VII in mind. However there are also less exhalted places to stay, including apartments for rent.

HI: *C.I.S., av. de Neuvecell; tel: 50 75 35 87*. **Camping: Le Clos Savoyard**: *tel 50 75 25 84*; Open Apr–Oct.

Eating places range from town-centre restaurants to lake and mountainside cafes, but watch the prices. Try lake fish and *Savoyard* and **Swiss specialities.** If you strike lucky at the casino, its **La Toque Royale** restaurant serves a gourmet menu for a mere FFr.340; *tel: 50 75 23 32*.

SIGHTSEEING

With its 3 km-long promenade adjoining the town centre, Lake Geneva is as good a reason as any to visit Évian, an unashamedly relaxing place laced with colourful gardens and parks. Gambling at the **Casino Royal Évian**, in the elegant **Château de Blonay** which faces the lake, is the main attraction for some; *tel: 50 75 23 32*. Open 1500–0300 (0200 weekdays in winter); jacket and passport required, no jeans or trainers; admission FFr.65, minimum stake at the tables, FFr.20. Or you can feed the fruit machines with single francs from 1000, admission free. Others come to Évian to take its famous waters. The thermal spa, **L'Espace Thermal Évian**, has a large indoor pool and offers a wide variety of massages and beauty treatments; *tel: 50 75 02 30*. A free supply of the famous

Évian Water comes from a tap beside the company's exhibition hall in *r. Nationale*. The ornate Renaissance-style town hall began its existence as the holiday home of the Lumière family of cinema fame who lived in Lyon.

A musical fountain 'performs' a 30-min concert beside the lake, daily at 1700 and 2200 Apr–mid-Oct. Évian Music Festival conducted by Rostropovich, two weeks from end-May; *tel: 44 35 26 91*. Concerts at the spa held daily during July and Aug.

Boat trips go around the lake and across to Lausanne in Switzerland. The Rive Bleue Express runs eastwards along the scenic south shore of the lake on the narrow strip of land between the water and the Chablais mountains, across the border to le Bouveret 22 km away. A 1893 steam train makes the 65-min journey on Sun, diesels on Tues and Fri, and the return can be by boat. FFr.100 or FFr.200 with boat trip. Reservations, *tel: 25 81 43 12*.

ST-GERVAIS-LE FAYET

Station: St-Gervais-Le Fayet, *tel: 50 66 50 50*. This small station is actually in Le Fayet, from where a twisting 4 km road leads up to the attractive little town of St-Gervais. You can get there by bus (though services are infrequent), taxi (expensive) or on the Tramway de Mont Blanc (10 min journey, FFr.30 return).

Tourist Office: Le Fayet: *49 r. de la Poste, 74190 Le Fayet; tel: 50 78 00 23* (turn right off *r. de la Gare*). Open Mon–Fri 0830–1200 and 1330–1800 (to 1700 Sat). St Gervais: *115, av. du Mont Paccard, 74170 St Gervais, tel: 50 47 76 08*. Open 0900–1200, 1430–1915.

ACCOMMODATION AND FOOD

A ski resort in winter and walking centre

in summer, St Gervais has a range of small hotels and guesthouses. Hôtel Edelweiss, *225 Chemin du Vorassay, tel: 50 93 44 48*, can provide quiet rooms with Alpine views. Central reservations, *tel: 50 93 53 63*. Camping: Les Dômes de Miage, *tel: 50 93 45 96*.

Restaurants offer traditional Alpine fare including *Fondue Savoyarde*, *Pierre Chaude* and *Tartiflette* (a casserole of potatoes, onion and bacon topped with *Reblochon* cheese). Try them at Le Troubadour, *60 r. de la Vignette, tel 50 47 76 41*.

ACTIVITIES

In winter, skiers take the Tramway to the pistes above the town. There is also extensive off-piste skiing with guides. To ski further afield, the 2–13 day Mont-Blanc Skipass covers 25 different areas, a few linked by lifts, others a bus or train ride away. In summer, visitors come to walk and climb. Mountain Guides, *tel: 50 47 76 55*. You can also go fishing, canyoning, rafting, skating and swimming.

SIDE TRACK
FROM ST-GERVAIS-LE FAYET

TRAMWAY DU MONT BLANC

After leaving St-Gervais–Le Fayet, St Gervais itself is the first station on this famous metre-guage railway whose three electric trains, *Anne*, *Jeanne* and *Marie*, pull passengers through forests and around crags high into the mountains. The top terminus, Nid d'Aigle, at 2372 m, offers glorious Alpine views all around. The 12.4 km trip takes 1½ hrs; FFr.122 each way. For reservations, *tel: 50 47 51 83*. Wear walking shoes and, even in summer, warm clothes.

The snowy Bionnassay Glacier is just a 15-min stroll away, but experienced walkers could take the **Route Royale** all the way to **Mt Blanc**, a 10-hr climb. In winter this is a prime skiing region with access to some of the same pistes as Chamonix.

When the Tramway was first conceived at the turn of the century the grandiose plan was to take it to the 'Roof of Europe', the **Aiguille du Goûter** at 3863 m, linking up with a tunnel and lift to the summit of Mont Blanc! Engineers began the construction in 1905 but the line had only reached Nid d'Aigle when the World War I put a stop to further progress. Steam trains were replaced by electric ones in 1955, halving journey-times.

The Tramway runs throughout the year, with hourly services in summer, departing from Le Fayet from 0715 to 1710. In winter three services run each day, terminating three-quarters of the way up at Bellevue. ⛷

CHAMONIX MONT BLANC

Station: *av. de la Gare; tel: 50 53 00 44.* Information office open 0900–1200 and 1400–1715. Left luggage. Five min walk to town centre and tourist office along *av. Michel Crozand.*

Tourist Office: *45, pl. du Triangle de l'Amitié, 74400 Chamonix Mont-Blanc; tel: 50 53 00 24.* It has computerised information and accommodation service, and also sells hiking maps. Currency exchange. Open 0830–1930 in summer; 0830–1230, 1400–1900 in winter. **Compagnie des Guides**; *tel: 50 53 00 88.* **The Maison de la Montagne**; *pl. de l'Église; tel: 50 53 22 08,* provides information on hiking routes and weather conditions. Open similar hours to tourist office.

GETTING AROUND

Chamonix Bus, *pl. de l'Église; tel: 50 53*

05 55. During the ski season, buses depart every 20 mins up and down the 20 km valley from **Les Chavands** at one end to **Le Tour** at the other, free with a ski pass. Similar services in summer; tickets FFr.7.

ACCOMMODATION AND FOOD

There is wide selection of places to stay, from the sumptuous **Majestic hotel** to countless *gîtes*, hostels and apartments. Central reservations *tel: 50 53 23 33.*

HI: *127 montée Jacques Balmat; tel: 50 53 14 52,* in *les Pélerins,* (10 mins by bus from *pl. de l'Église*).

Restaurants abound, although those in the pedestrian zone of the town are very touristy. Small family restaurants can be found further afield, serving local specialities like *fondue, raclette* and fresh pasta.

ENTERTAINMENT

In winter the numerous bars and clubs are après-ski ghettos which get into their swing around 0100. Later the atmosphere can become raucous. Summer entertainment is more cultural, with concerts and films. A highlight is the **Fête des Guides** in Aug with processions and displays.

SPORTS

The town has a golf course, Olympic-size outdoor pool, two indoor pools, indoor Olympic ice-rink and a sports centre with tennis and squash courts, In summer, hiking is excellent. The many high mountain trails offer routes of varying lengths for every grade of ability and fitness. Mountaineering with a guide is also possible. Paragliding is increasingly popular with courses available for beginners – **École Parapente de Chamonix**; *79 r. Whymper; tel: 50 53 50 14.* In winter Chamonix is a ski centre of world repute, attracting both professionals and holidaymakers. The French national school for ski

Montenvers Railway

You don't have to be a skier, or even a walker, to reach the 7 km long **Mer de Glace**, Europe's biggest glacier. The red electric trains on the **Montenvers rack railway** make the 20 min journey up from a small station near Chamonix's main SNCF one. The 5-km long metre-gauge line, (opened in 1908 with steam trains – electrification came in 1954), climbs to a height of 1913 m, where you look down on the wide glacier which spills out like a giant tongue between steep mountain ridges. Round trip FFr.82; to check timetable, particularly in winter, *tel: 50 53 12 54*. As the train winds up the mountainside through tunnels and woods, past waterfalls and meadows, the views down over Chamonix and the wide River Arve valley get more and more enthralling, with glimpses of Mt Blanc peeping round the trees. From the top you can take a 'bubble' lift down to the edge of the wide glacier – or walk down.

Blanc, Chamonix boasts some of the world's best mountain views. The **Téléphérique de l'Aiguille du Midi** opened in 1955; when the first part was completed in 1924, it was Europe's first cableway. It ascends over thick forests to a 3842 m high needle-like summit beneath Mt Blanc. The two-stage journey takes 20 mins. Open 0700–1700 winter, 0800–1700 summer. FFr.180 return (allow at least 2 hrs for the full round-trip; reservations recommended Feb–May and July–Aug, *tel: 50 53 40 00*).

In summer the mid-way stage, **Plan de l'Aiguille**, is a starting point for several walks, including the 2-hour one back to the bottom. At the top, another cable car continues on to the **Helbronner** peak (Mar to Sept when weather conditions permit). This in turn connects with yet another down to **Le Palud** over the border in Italy near Courmayeur.

VALLORCINE

Station: *pl. de la Gare, 74660 Vallorcine; tel: 50 54 60 28.*
Tourist Office: a small wooden hut outside the station; *pl. de la Gare, 74660 Vallorcine; tel: 50 54 60 71.* Open 0900–1200 and 1430–1830 in summer, 0900–1200 and 1500–1730 in winter.

At this tiny French border village, 1260 m high (or sometimes at the following Swiss one of Le Chatelard-Fre), passengers change from the orange-pale grey French railcars to sleeker red-grey single-class Swiss ones, grandly known as the **Mont Blanc Express**.

For the next part of the journey, most of the best views are on the right, but you need a good head for heights. Near its summit (1370 m), shortly before Vallorcine, the line goes through a tunnel which in severe weather is used by road traffic too.

instructors is based there. However, the ten ski areas are very spread out, being stretched all along the Arve valley. At Argentière, the **Grands Montets** pistes are among the most challenging in the world.

A unique attraction for skiers is a day's excursion down the **Vallée Blanche** – white valley – beneath Mt Blanc. This is one of the longest ski descents in the world, an awesome trip down the Glacier du Géant and Mer de Glace. It starts at the top of the Aiguille du Midi cable-car and has to be done with a guide in groups of up to eight.

SIGHTSEEING

Overlooked by the snowy peak of Mt

GRENOBLE

This historic city, home to the great writer Stendhal, has moved with the times. Today its three 'powers' are said to be are 'university, research and industry'. The university, with 48,000 students, is one of the most famous in Europe for science and engineering. Many high-tech industries have settled in the area. Tourism is the other important activity, surrounded as the city is by the Alps. Indeed the tourist office, which opened in 1889, was the first in France. Now it concerns itself not only with Grenoble but with the Dauphine valley area where thousands enjoy skiing in winter and activities from walking to paragliding in summer.

TOURIST INFORMATION

Tourist Office: *14 r. de la République, 38000 Grenoble; tel: 76 42 41 41*, in a modern glass building, with excellent maps and the free glossy *Grenoble Magazine*. Accommodation booking service and guided tours of the old town June–Sept at 1700 daily except Sun, FFr.30, students, FFr.20. Open daily 0900–1230, 1330–1900 (June–Sept), Mon–Sat 0900–1230 and 1330–1800, Sun 1000–1200 (Oct–May).

Centre Informations Montagnes et Sentiers (CIMES): *Maison de la Randonnée, 7 r. Voltaire; tel: 76 42 45 90*, has information on hiking, biking and cross-country skiing.

Centre Régional d'Information

Jeunesse; *8 r. Voltaire; tel: 76 54 70 38*, provides student and youth information.

ARRIVING AND DEPARTING

Station

Gare S.N.C.F.: *pl. de la Gare; tel: 76 47 50 50*. Information office open Mon–Fri 0830–1830, Sat 0900–1800. Luggage lockers. For the town centre take *av. Félix Viallet* to the *Jardin de Ville* and turn right onto *r. de la République* (about 10 mins walk). Otherwise catch a tram (lines A and B outside the station).

Buses and Trams

TAG (Grenoble transport company): **Station de Tramway Grand' Place**, *av. Gén. de Gaulle*. Open Mon-Fri 0730–1830, Sat and school holidays 0930–1200, 1400–1800. Information *tel: 76 20 66 66*. **Gare Routière** (next to the station), *tel: 76 87 90 31* or *76 47 77 77*.

Taxis

Taxi Grenoble, 24-hr call service tel: *76 54 42 54*.

GETTING AROUND

It is possible to cover Grenoble on foot, but tram and bus services are very efficient (maps and information from the office in *pl. de la Gare*).

Bus/tram tickets are valid for one hour including stops and changes. FFr.7 one journey, 10-journey *carnet* FFr.49, *Visitag* day pass FFr 22. Single tickets can be bought on buses (not on trams), others at kiosks and machines, and must be validated on board.

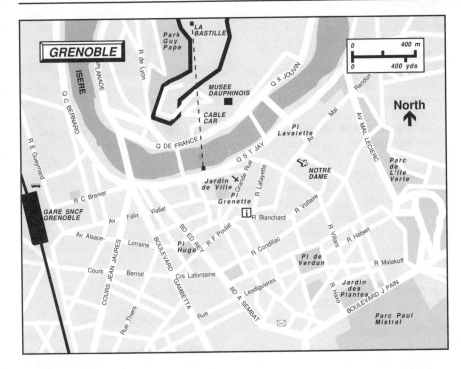

The **Bastille** fortifications on a hill across the river are served by a cable car from *quai Stéphane Jay, tel: 76 44 33 65,* a 3-min ride. 0900–2400 Apr–Oct (Mon from 1100), 1000–1800 Nov–Mar. FFr.32 return, students FFr.17.

STAYING IN GRENOBLE

Accommodation

Accommodation is plentiful, from large business hotels to budget establishments. Hotel chains in Grenoble include *F1, Ib,* and *Mv.*

Handy for the station are the **Hotel Terminus**, *10 pl. de la Gare; tel: 76 87 24 33,* and the less expensive one-star **Hotel Alize**, *1 pl. de la Gare; tel: 76 43 12 91.* The one-star **Hotel Victoria**, *17 r. Theirs; tel: 76 46 06 36,* is more centrally placed.

HI: *18 av. du Grésivaudan; tel: 76 09 33*

52. Four km from Grenoble. From the rail station walk to *cours Jean Jaurès* along *av. Alsace Lorraine.* Turn right onto the cours, bus stop no. 8 (direction *La Quinzaine*).

Camping: Les 3 Pucelles, *Seyssins; tel: 76 96 45 73.* South-west of the centre, near the youth hostel. Bus no. 8, as to HI.

Eating and Drinking

Grenoble offers food from all over the world – regional cuisine, including alpine specialities, North African, Italian, Indian and Vietnamese. The town's most famous dish is *gratin dauphinois* – sliced potatoes baked in a cream sauce. In cake shops look out for *gâteaux aux nois de Grenoble* – nut cake.

Try the streets around the **Jardin de Ville** for regional food, with North African cuisine a little further east in the old town. Vietnamese places are found around the station. Cafés and bars abound between *pl. St-André* and *pl. Notre Dame*.

Le Couscous, *19 r. de la Poste; tel: 76 47 92 93*, has North African specialities such as couscous and kebabs, while **La Qantara**, *2 r. Lazare-Carnot, tel: 76 47 42 60*, features Egyptian cuisine.

Le Saphir, *19 r. de Turenne; tel: 76 87 30 02*, serves Middle Eastern food.

Communications

Post Office, *7 blvd Mar. Lyautey; tel: 76 43 53 31*. Facilities include poste restante and currency exchange. Open Mon 0800–1800, Tues-Fri 0800–1830, Sat 0800–1200.

Money

Comptoir de Change, *r. Philis de la Charce*, near the tourist office.

ENTERTAINMENT

Grenoble is proud of its cultural heritage and there is no shortage of music, theatre and art. To find out what's on, pick up a free copy of *Contact* from the tourist office or bookshops.

Plays, opera and dance take place at the **Théâtre de Grenoble**, *2 r. Hector Berlioz; tel: 76 54 03 08*.

The **Companie Renata Scant** performs at *8 r. Pierre Duclot; tel: 76 44 60 92*, including a Festival of European Theatre in July. Concerts take place at **Summum**, *Grand'Place, tel: 76 39 63 00*.

There is no shortage of clubs and discos – remember this is a university town. Buy *Guide DAHU*, written by Grenoble students, for what's new and improved (FFr.15 from the tourist office).

SHOPPING

The main shops line a traffic-free route from *pl. de la Gare* along *av. Alsace Lorraine* and *r. Felix Poulat*. Several markets are held

every day except Mon, plus flea markets on Sun mornings.

SIGHTSEEING

At the heart of the city is the **old town** on the south bank of the river, the so-called *Village St-Hughes* with an impressive 13th-century cathedral, **Notre Dame**, and tall 17th- and 18th-century mansions which overshadow the narrow pedestrianised streets. Small shops and restaurants crowds along them too.

On the edge of the old town, the **Jardin de Ville** is a finely manicured garden, perfect for picnics. Excavations in the old *Saint-Laurent* church, now **Musée Archéologique**, *pl. Saint-Laurent, tel: 76 44 78 68*, show the origins of Christianity in the area during the 4th century; open 0900–1200, 1400–1800 closed Tues, admission FFr.15, students FFr.10.

In the former *Hotel de Ville*, the **Musée Stendhal**, *1 r. Hector Berlioz, tel: 76 54 44 14* is devoted to Grenoble's most famous son, writer and Napoleon-admirer Henri Beyle, better known as Stendhal; open 1400–1800, closed Mon. The apartment where he stayed as a child with his grandfather at **Maison Stendhal**, *20 Grande Rue, tel: 76 42 02 62*, stages exhibitions; open 1000–1200 and 1400–1800, closed Mon. A leaflet from the tourist office lists all the local Stendhal connections.

Also on the south bank beyond the old town, the new building which houses the **Musée de Grenoble** combines medieval ramparts with 21st-century glass, *5 pl. Lavalette, tel: 76 63 44 44*. This is one of the biggest museums in Europe, founded during the Revolution, with vast collections of 18th–19th-century art, including paintings by Rubens, Delacroix, Picasso, Matisse, Miró and Ernst; also a collection of Egyptian antiquity; open daily 1100–1900, Wed 1100–2200, closed Tues.

Ultra-modern art is found in **Le Magasin**, *155 cours Berriat; tel: 76 21 95 84*, a national art centre and museum converted from a warehouse designed by Gustave Eiffel of tower fame; open Tues–Sun 1200–1900. Admission to special exhibitions, FFr.15.connections.

The new **Musée de la Résistance et de la Déportation**, *14 r. Hébert; tel: 76 42 38 53*, depicts through sights and sounds the heroic exploits of 30 resistance groups which operated in the area during World War II; open 0900–1200, 1400–1800, closed Tues; admission FFr.15.

A trip up to the stark rock which looms over the old town from across the River Isère and its even starker fortress, **La Bastille**, is the highlight of Grenoble's sightseeing. A 'bubble' cable car whisks you dramatically up across the river. At the top, there is a restaurant and terraces to enjoy the view which extends to the the Alps.

Half-way down the hill again (or 250 steps up from *St Laurent* bridge) is the **Musée Dauphinois**, *30 r. Maurice Gignoux; tel: 76 85 19 00*, which traces the history and culture of the region from prehistoric times. The building itself is a listed monument, formerly a convent built in the 17th century. The top floor is now devoted to an exciting new exhibition on skiing, the only one of its kind in France. Decorated appropriately in crisp white, it traces 4000 years of conquest and adventure on the mountains in wintertime. Part of the first ever ski-lift, built in America's Sun Valley in 1937, is on show together with 400 pairs of skis, sticks and boots. These include the earliest skis from the 1880s to the latest models by Rossignol.

Chemin de Fer de la Mure

This metre-gauge line, which closed in 1988 after exactly 100 years, now operates special services with a commentary between April and October, providing 20 miles of breathtaking Alpine views. It was the first line in the world to be electrified, with high voltage DC current, in 1903, and the carriages date from between 1915 and 1932.

Twisting and climbing between **St-Georges-de-Commiers** (10 miles south of Grenoble on the line to Veynes) and **La Mure**, it is reputed to be the most spectacular line in France. After clinging to the sides of the River Drac gorge it passes beside the lake of Monteynard and below the dramatic cliffs of the Vercors. Trains make brief stops, usually on one of the 12 viaducts. There are also 18 tunnels.

The trains run weekends mid-Apr–mid-Oct, daily June–Sept; *tel: 76 72 57 11*. Return fare Ffr.95.

117

Old engravings, photographs and posters trace the full history of skiing from world champions to ski fashions. Open 0900–1200 and 1400–1800, closed Tues; admission FFr.15.

Excursions into the high mountains are possible in all directions from Grenoble. Due north, for example, is the beautiful Chartreuse are where monks of the **Grande Chartreuse** monastery first concocted the world-famous herb liqueur 400 years ago. The cellars and distillery – where the same secret recipe is still used – are down the valley in Voiron. Open daily, except weekends in winter.

INNSBRUCK

Innsbruck – Bridge over the Inn – is a bustling town. Capital of the Tyrol, with more than 100,000 inhabitants it is, along with Grenoble and Bolzano, one of the three largest towns in the Alpine range. The main street, Maria Theresiastrasse, was once a thoroughfare for travellers from the Brenner Pass and Italy to the south, and from Germany to the north

Innsbruck came under Habsburg rule in the 14th century, and Maximilian I presided over the town's period of greatest cultural and political importance at the end of the 15th century. The Alstadt, the medieval quarter founded in 1180, was beautifed with Maximilian's Goldenes Dachl. There was a second flowering at the end of the 18th century under Empress Maria Theresia, who graced the city with the Hofburg. Since then, thanks in recent years to the care of town planners, the city has changed little, its human scale framed by the grandeur of surrounding snow-capped peaks.

TOURIST INFORMATION

Tourist Office: *Burggraben 3; tel: (0512) 5356*, on the edge of *Altstadt*, 0800–1900, Sun 0900–1800; *Hbf: tel: (0512) 583766*, 0900–2200; offer free map with information on all tourist attractions, leaflet on walks in the area, accommodation listings and will book rooms ahead for ÖS30. It will also book concert tickets and sell ski/cable car passes and all public trans-

port tickets. The free Innsbrucker Summer/Winter brochure lists entertainment. Guest Card (GC) allows easy hikes in the surrounding area, daily June–early Oct, free including equipment hire, Tues evening free 'Lantern' hikes by night, discounts on cable cars and museums.

For information on the wider region see **Tirol-Info**, *Wilhelm-Greilstr. 17, tel: (0512) 5320* Mon–Fri 0830–1800, Sat 0900–1200.

ARRIVING AND DEPARTING

Airport: *tel: (0512) 22525*, is 5 km west reached by bus F from the *Hbf* in 15 mins, or 10 mins by taxi from *Maria Theresiastr.* (ÖS100). Served by **Tyrolean Airways**, *tel: (0512) 222277*, **Austrian Airlines/ Swissair**, *tel: (0512) 582985*, **KLM**, *tel: (0512) 588413*, **Lufthansa**, *tel: (0512) 59800*, **Air UK**, *tel: (0512) 2222*. **Station:** *(Hbf)*, *tel: (0512) 1717*. Trams 1, 3 and 6 connect with the *Altstadt*, a 10-min walk ahead down *Salurnerstr.* and right down *Maria-Theresiastr.*

GETTING AROUND

Innsbruck compact, and most sights are easily walkable from the *Altstadt*, but there is an excellent tram and bus system (ÖS28 for one day or four single tickets ÖS50, ÖS40 for students). Bikes can be hired from the station but mountain bikes only in *Igls* from **Sport Kaserer**, *Bilgiristr. 18*.

STAYING IN INNSBRUCK

Accommodation

The **Hotel Goldener Adler**, *Herzog-Friedrichstr. 6; tel: (0512) 58 63 34* (very

118

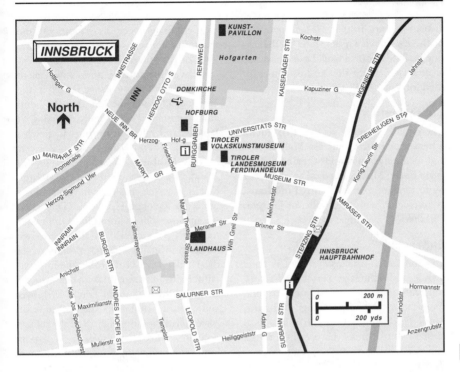

expensive) has seen guests from Goethe to Duke Albert of Bavaria but is rather touristy. An alternative is the **Schwarzer Adler**, *Kaiserjägerstr. 2; tel: (0512) 58 71 09*, (expensive) an inn since the 17th century expanding into part of the next door monastery. Hotel chains with property in the city include *BW*, *Rk*, *Sc* and *Sn*. **Pension Paula**, *Weiherburgg. 15; tel: (0512) 29 22 62* (budget) is below the Alpenzoo (transport as for youth hostel).

Budget rooms are scarce in June but 'summer hotels' usually open in university accommodation July and Aug. A relatively central hostel is **(HI) St Nikolaus**, *Innstr. 95; tel: (0512) 28 65 15*, the opposite side of the river from the *Altstadt* (bus K from *Hbf* to *St Nikolaus* then walk up hill). **MK Jugendzentrum**, *Sillg. 8a; tel: (0512) 571311* open Jul–Sept, is a short walk from the *Hbf*. **Camping Innsbruck**

Kranebitten, *Kranebitter Allee 214; tel: (0512) 284180*, is west of town (bus O).

Eating and Drinking

Food in the *Fussgangerzone* (pedestrian zone) is generally expensive though **Restaurant Weinhaus Ottoburg**, *Herzog-Friedrichstr. 1*, is a pleasant traditional *Weinkeller* and restaurant. For outdoor and indoor eating there is the *Fischerhaüsl*, *Herreng. 8*, open to 0100. Alternatives include the **Schwarzer Adler**, with traditional meals like venison ham and dumplings or the **Stieglbrau Restaurant**, *W Greilstr. 25*, offering beer and matching food. For more of a snack there's **Hortnagel Pronto**, *Maria-Theresiastr. 5*.

Communications and Money

The **Main Post Office** (with impressive

turn-of-century hall) is *Maximilianstr. 24*, or there's *Südtirolerplatz*, next to the station. Outside normal bank hours, places to change money are the Tourist Office or the Hbf, open 0730–2000.

ENTERTAINMENT

There are concerts in the **Provincial Theatre** and the **Congress Hall** weekly and in summer in the **Hofgarten**. There is an **Early Music Festival** in Aug. For more modern events try the **Treibhaus,** *Angerzellg. 8,* with live music, or **Utopia,** *Tschamlerstr. 3,* with jazz and rock.

SHOPPING

Heimatwerk, *Meranerstr. 24,* offers good Tyrolean clothing at reasonable prices. Innsbruck is also a good place to find sports gear. Try **Sporthaus Witting,** *Maria-Theresiastr. 39.* **Swarovski,** local crystal manufacturers, have a shop at the end of *Herzog-Friedrichstr.* closest to *Maria-Theresiastr.*

Brakmayer, *Leopoldstr.,* corner of *Grossmayerstr.,* en route to the *Wiltenstift,* offers a vast range of traditional and modern pewter objects.

SIGHTSEEING

The Tourist Office books daily city tours ÖS150 though the major sights are easily located. The **Altstadt** centres on the city's emblem, the 15th-century **Goldenes Dachl** ('Golden Roof') with 2657 gilded copper tiles. It was erected by Emperor Maximilian and depicts him with his two wives. The building was used as the royal lodge during popular festivals and tournaments, but it currently houses the **Olympiamuseum**; *tel: (0512) 5360575,* which celebrates Innsbruck's hosting of the Winter Olympics (1964 and 1976).

The old town has a number of splendid 15th- and 16th-century buildings, some with elaborate stucco decorations plus the traditional convex windows to catch extra light on the narrow streets. The nearby city tower, **Stadtturm**, offers an excellent view. Behind the *Goldenes Dachl* is the baroque **Domkirche St Jakob,** with amazing *trompe l'oeil* ceiling (depicting St James) and altar featuring Cranach's Intercession of the Virgin

The **Hofburg**, *Rennweg; tel: (0512) 587186,* was built on the site of a large building which has grown ever larger under the Tyrolean Habsburgs. The palace has an enormous ballroom lined with portraits of the Empress's children and other relatives, several once resident here, while the 16th-century **Hofkirche**, the imperial church, is crammed with enormous bronze statues of more family members and most notably the Emperor Maximilian's tomb which 28 of the statues decorate. This is considered the most important example of German Renaissance sculpture. The Emperor certainly saw it as glorifying his reign. Rather more attractive is the **Silberne Kapelle** (the Silver Chapel), finished at the end of the 16th century. It was built by a Tyrolean Archduke so that he could be buried with his commoner wife. The chapel takes its name from a large embossed silver madonna.

The neighbouring **Tiroler Volkskunstmuseum,** *Universitätsstr. 2; tel: (0512) 584302,* concentrates on Tyrolean culture, featuring wood-panelled rooms in period styles, traditional costumes and the like. The **Tiroler Landesmuseum Ferdinandeum,** *Museumstr. 15; tel: (0512) 59489.* is more diverse, with exhibits including beautiful old stained glass, medieval altars and works by Cranach and Rembrandt, as well as Tyrolean paintings.

The **Triumphforte**, *Leopoldstr.,* is an

18th-century triumphal arch. It was originally planned to celebrate the dynastic marriage of Leopold, Grand Duke of Tuscany with the Infanta of Spain. However, as the Emperor Franz died suddenly, half the decorations were then devoted to funeral trappings. The arch is not far from the **Landhaus**, built in 18th-century baroque style for local government.

Still walking distance, but almost twice as far again, are the beautiful rococo **Basilika Wilten** in cream and white-grey, full of light and generous windows, culminating in four marble columns and a giant crown over Our Lady. The baroque **Stiftskirche Wilten** across the road is rather heavier with lots of black and gold.

At *Maria-Theresiastr. 38* is the **Palais-Trapp-Wolken-Stein** (bearing the Von Trapp family's coat of arms), with a pleasant café in the inner courtyard.

On the opposite side of the river the **Alpenzoo** is the only European zoo at this altitude, housing 800 animals of 140 Alpine species – most extinct or almost in the wild. Cross the **River Inn** by the covered bridge and follow the signs or take bus Z or tram 1 and Hungerburgbahn funicular – free if you buy a zoo ticket before boarding. The funicular continues beyond to a plateau from where a succession of cable-cars take you almost to the summit of **Nordkette**, the peak which dominates Innsbruck.

Just out of town (trams 3 and 6) is **Schloss Ambras**, a medieval castle rebuilt in Renaissance style, containing paintings and weapons belonging to Archduke Ferdinand, displayed much as they were in his day.

Outdoors

Innsbruck is a perfect base for Alpine walking, with 400 different routes on offer, for example from the top of the Nordkette, plus outdoor pursuits from paragliding to rafting and of course skiing using the 150-plus cable cars and chair-lifts. Details from the tourist office.

SIDE TRACKS FROM INNSBRUCK

Igls is a pretty ski-resort village on the outskirts of town (bus J or tram 6), the site of the 1976 Winter Olympics. The **Tourist Office** is above the Innsbruck one, *Burggraben 3; tel: (0512) 598 50*, Mon–Fri 0800–1900. It dispenses free brochures and maps, plus a list of *Privatzimmer*. Accommodation booking is free. There are cable car and chair lift connections to the mountain top. It's another good base for summer hiking. There are regular summer concerts in summer, Tyrolean evenings (featuring music and yodelling) in winter. A hotel chain with property here is *RC*.

Another small village worth a visit is **Fulpmes**, if only for the pleasure of the **Stubaitalbahn** tram, which has been trundling up the Stubai valley since 1904. It passes a few small villages but mostly green fields and forest full of wildlife. The **Tourist Office** *tel: (05225) 62235*, turn left out of the station, follow road slightly down and ahead to the T-junction, is in the modern building directly ahead. Mon–Fri 0800–1200, 1500–1800, July–Sept plus Sat 0900–1200, 1600–1800, mid Dec–mid Apr, plus Sun 0900–1100, has accommodation listings, walking information and changes money. GC free and reduced rates for swimming, skiing, concerts etc. Most of the attractions are outdoors with various walking routes and cablecars serving them plus an Alpine and Ski School (glacier skiing in summer) but there is also a Blacksmith's Museum open Weds.

INNSBRUCK–FRIEDRICHSHAFEN

This spectacular route from Austria to Germany passes through dizzying Alpine passes, entering Germany just before the village of Mittenwald. The train crosses and recrosses the border, passing close to Bavaria's fairytale castles, before leaving the Alps behind to descend into the wooded hills of the Allgäu region and the enchanting lakeside town of Lindau, at the east end of the Bodensee.

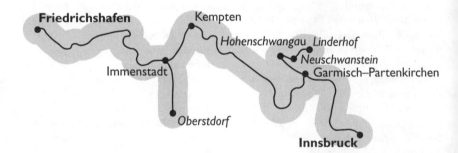

FASTEST JOURNEY: 3 HRS 25 MINS

TRAINS

ETT tables: 800, 800a, 761, 767, 765.

FAST TRACK

The fastest route is through the Austrian Arlberg changing trains at Lindau and/or Bregenz. The journey takes 3 hr 25 mins and operates every 2 hours.

ON TRACK

Innsbruck–Garmisch-Partenkirchen

An hour and 25 mins is needed to reach the twin towns of Garmisch-Partenkirchen in Germany from Austrian Innsbruck; trains operate every 2 hrs.

Garmisch-Partenkirchen–Kempten

An irregular service with a change of train at Pfronten-Steinach links these two towns. The journey takes nearly 2 hr 30 mins.

Kempten–Friedrichshafen

A change of train is needed at Lindau. The journey takes 2 hrs.

GARMISCH-PARTENKIRCHEN

Station: Hbf; *tel (08221) 19419.*
Tourist Office: *Richard Strauss Platz, tel: (08221) 18022.* Mon–Sat 0800–1800 and Sun 1000–1200.

STAYING IN GARMISCH-PARTENKIRCHEN

In winter, accommodation is tight as the resort is packed with skiers, especially at weekends.

A tourist **office accommodation booth at Hbf** is open daily from 0800 until the arrival of the last train from Munich at 1923. There is a large supply of affordable rooms in private homes. When the office is closed, a touch-screen display of accommodation and a courtesy phone are available. **HI: Youth Hostel**, *Jochstr. 10, tel: (08221) 2980,* 4 km from town, in Burgrain, bus nos. 3/4 from Hbf. **Camping**: *Zugspitze, tel: (08821) 3180.* Hotel chains include *Ra, Rk.*

A US military base is located in the village and has its own hotel, the **General Patton Hotel**, technically for US and NATO military and their families but with affordable rooms sometimes available. Mid-priced guesthouses include the **Buchweiser**, *Olympiastr. 17*; **Hotel Schell**, *Partnachauenstr. 3, tel: (08821) 2989*; cheap rooms include **Fremdenzimmer Maurer**, *Torlenstr. 5, tel: (08821) 2924.*

The biggest concentration of restaurants is around *Marienplatz*, about 5 mins walk from Hbf. The smartest is the terrace restaurant and beergarden of the **Romantik Posthotel Clausen**. Opposite, the **Bistro Mukkefuck Cafe**, *Zugspitzstr. 6*, is bright and affordable.

SIGHTSEEING

Once two quiet Bavarian villages at the foot of Germany's highest mountain, the **Zugspitze** (2966 m), Garmisch and Partenkirchen were merged to host the 1936 Winter Olympics. Now Germany's most popular ski resort, the town is surrounded by 68 miles of alpine runs and 93 miles of cross-country trails. In summer, the village is a good base for mountain walking and climbing, with cable cars and a cog railway running all year. The **Olympic Ice Stadium** is open year from July to Easter. The **Heimatmuseum**, *Ludwigstr. 47*, is a fun place that displays local crafts, carnival masks and historic mountaineering photos.

Most visitors want to ascend the Zugspitze, for which the base is **Eibsee**, a mountain lake reached by the **Zugspitzbahn** cog railway. Once at Eibsee, you can take the **Eibseebahn** cable car to the summit or continue by rack railway through a winding tunnel to the **Hotel Schneefernhaus** (2650 m) from where the **Gipfelbahn** cable car goes to the summit. You can walk to the Customs border post at **Zugspitzkamm** (2805 m) and take the Tiroler Zugspitzbahn cable car to **Ehrwald** in Austria. Whichever route you take, the views are fantastic and many people go up one way and down another. Eurail passes give discounts on the cog railway and cable cars.

Other local peaks accessible by cable car are **Osterfelderkopf** (2050 m), **Wank** (1780 m), **Kreuzeck** (1650 m), **Eckbauer** (1238 m) and **Hausberg** (1330 m). The last is the base for exploring the spectacular **Partnachklamm Gorge**. There is no cable car up Alpspitze, but the ascent is popular with fit walkers.

123

◣ SIDE TRACKS FROM GARMISCH-PARTENKIRCHEN

From Garmisch Hbf buses run to Hohenschwangau, Neuschwanstein and Linderhof, the three Bavarian

Royal Castles built in the 19th century by Maximilian II and his son 'Mad' King Ludwig II. **Hohenschwangau** is the oldest of the three, but Neuschwanstein, towering on a rocky outcrop above it, is by far the most famous and the most stunning. Hohenschwangau was originally a seat of the Schwangau dynasty, one of the most powerful medieval aristocratic familes in southern Germany. Their line died out, and the castle fell into disrepair before being restored by the Imperial councillor Hans von Paumgartner. As a boy, Prince Ludwig spent many summers there, and the castle's paintings of scenes from the romantic German sagas, episodes of Bavarian chivalry and the knightly rulers of Schwangau fired his imagination. On becoming king, he set out to build Neuschwanstein, a dream castle of his own, laying the foundation stone on Sept 5 1869, hiring the finest artists and craftsmen to bring it to life. Ludwig spared no expense in building his fairy-tale fantasy. The site was long associated with the legendary Knights of the Swan, and Ludwig's sumptuous apartments and halls are decorated with romanticised medieval scenes inspired by the opera's of Ludwig's protégé Wagner. **Neuschwanstein** marks the high point of 19th-century Romanticism and a visit is mandatory if you are passing this way. The 30-min climb up to the castle is steep, but buses and – more romantically – horse-carriages, are available. **Linderhof**, some 20 km east, was envisioned by Ludwig as a miniature Versailles. The charming small château in landscaped gardens contained such ingenious gimmicks as a dining-room table which could be raised and lowered through the floor

with each course, so Ludwig could dine undisturbed by servants.

Neuschwanstein is open April 1–Sept 30 0830-1730, Oct 1–March 31 1000-1600; Linderhof is open April 1–Sept 30 0900–1730, October 1–March 31 1000–1600. Orange and green RVO buses leave Garmisch-Partenkirchen Hbf three times daily in summer, once daily in winter, and take 2 hrs 25 mins. Details from the tourist office.

Tourist Information: *Münchnerstr 2, Schwangau; tel: (08362) 81980.*

OBERAMMERGAU

The other side track from Garmisch-Partenkirchen is to Oberammergau, the pretty village which is famed for its Passion Play, performed by local people every ten years since 1634 in thanks for their deliverance from the Black Death in 1633 (next performance of the play: 2000). RVO buses leave from Garmisch-Partenkirchen three times daily. Visit the Pilatushaus workshop, where you can watch the famed local woodcarvers at work (June to Oct only). Cable cars run to the **Laber** and **Kolben** summits, immediately above the town, from where there are spectacular views south to the Alps.

GARMISCH TO KEMPTEN

From Garmisch-Partenkirchen the line to Pfronten and Kempten doubles back into Austria, puttering through fertile valleys dotted with little log haybarns and surrounded by looming crags. Get off at **Erwald Zugspitzbahn**, about 25 km from Garmisch-Partenkirchen, for the cog railway to the Zugspitze summit. There is a magnificent view of the lower slopes to the left as the train pulls out of the station. Just after passing through **Pfronten**, the

The Passion Play

As the opening date of the Oberammergau Passion Play draws near, the number of local men sporting a beard increases dramatically. Around 1500 local people are involved in the production, and facial hair is a prerequisite for most male characters. The play re-enacts the last days of Christ in a 5½ hr, 16-act epic which begins with the Last Supper and ends with the Resurrection. The Passion Play attracts at least half a million visitorsto each decade's performance.

ruins of **Schloss Eisenberg**, a 13th-century castle, appear on a crag some 3 km to the right of the line. By the time the train reaches Kempten the Alps are far behind, though the countryside is still hilly

KEMPTEN

Stations: *Hbf; tel: (0831)*. Ostbahnhof, the town's oldest and smaller station, is used only for a few trains daily from Pfronten. Hbf is 2 km from city centre. Take any bus from Hbf to *Residenzplatz* or *Hofgarten* in the city centre.
Tourist Office: In the *Rathaus, Rathauspl.* Open Mon–Fri 0800–1200 and 1330–1700, Sat 1000–1300.

ACCOMMODATION AND FOOD

HI Youth Hostel, *Saarlandstr 1; tel: (0831) 73663*. Mid-priced hotels include **Bahnhof Hotel**, *Mozartstr 2; tel: (0831) 73420*. Cheaper lodgings include **Gasthof Goldene Traube**, *Memmingerstr. 7; tel: (0831) 22187*; **Hotel Pension Berg Cafe**, *Hohenweg 6; tel: (0831) 73296*.

Most of Kempten's eating-places are located on *Fischerstr.*, a pedestrianised extension of *Bahnhofstr.*

SIGHTSEEING

Known in Roman times as Cambodunum, Kempten's past is revealed in the **Archäologischer Park**, immediately across the river from the medieval *Altstadt*, the remains revealing where the Roman town once stood. The **Residenz**, (the Ecclesiastical Residence) *Residenzplatz*, is an ultra-elaborate baroque-Rococo confection, and the **St Lorenz Basilica**, also on *Residenzplatz*, is worth looking at. The **Rathaus**, on *Rathausplatz*, is an elegant 18th century complex of buildings. Museums include the **Allgäuer Heimatsmuseum**, *Kornhausplatz*, which concentrates on folk arts and crafts from the Allgäu region; and the **Römisches Museum**, *Zumsteinhaus*, which focuses on Kempten's Roman past.

IMMENSTADT

SIDE TRACK FROM IMMENSTADT

The small town of **Immenstadt**, some 10 km south of Kempten, has little to offer except for a large swimming and boating lake, the Alpsee, 3 km from the town centre, but is the gateway to the Allgäuer Alps.

From Immenstadt Bf trains run several times daily through increasingly mountainous scenery to the small picture-postcard resort of **Oberstdorf**, the best base for exploring the region, and onwards to Einödsbach, the end of the line. Towering above this tiny village and straddling the German-Austrian border is the 2657 m peak of the **Krottenkopf**, which can be ascended by cable-car.

FRIEDRICHSHAFEN

For details see Munich–Friedrichshafen route, p. 231.

INNSBRUCK–SALZBURG

The soft green fields lining the valley bottoms between the two major cities of west Austria almost look like lawns. This route takes in some of the world's best-known ski resorts.

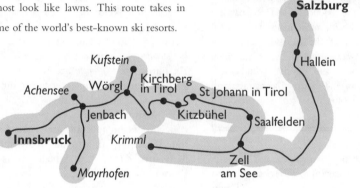

TRAINS

ETT tables: 800, 810.

FAST TRACK

The fast trains operate every two hours on a route that cuts the corner between Innsbruck and Salzburg by travelling through Germany. These *Korridor-Zugs* do not stop in Germany and no border formalities are required. The journey takes 2 hrs.

ON TRACK

Innsbruck–Jenbach

Expresses and local trains give a service of up to 3 trains an hour taking around 30 mins.

Jenbach–Kirchberg–Kitzbühel–St Johann –Saalfelden–Zell am See

An hourly express service from Innsbruck link these ski-resorts. Jenbach to Kirchberg in Tirol takes 38 mins, Kirchberg in Tirol to Kitzbühel takes 15 mins, Kitzbühel to St Johann in Tirol 10 mins, St Johann in Tirol to Saalfelden 35 mins, and Saalfelden to Zell am See 10 mins.

Zell am See–Hallein

A change of train at Bischofshofen is usually required on this 1 hr 30 mins journey.

Hallein–Salzburg

At least 1 train every hour links Hallein with Salzburg in 20 mins.

JENBACH

Station: *tel: (05244) 2425.* Rents bikes and changes money to 2000.

Tourist Office: *Achenseestr. 37; tel: (05244) 3901,* Mon–Fri 0900–1230, 0130–1800, Sat 0900–1200, left out of station following road to join the main road uphill. The Tourist Office is on the right and offers free maps and accommodation list and will book accommodation for the same day. Accommodation is easier to come by and slightly cheaper in Jenbach than in the nearby mountain resorts so it makes a convenient base. The best hotel is the **Gasthof Jenbacherhof**, *Postg. 22/3; tel: (05244) 2442* (moderate) at the top of the town. Cheaper are private rooms (*Privatzimmer*) listed by the Tourist Office. Eating is also cheaper. **Gasthof Neuwart**, *Achenseestr. 38*, serves local food. **Baguette, Achenseestr. 36**, offers more international snacks. **Vinzez Leitner**, *Tratzburgstr. 3*, an award-winning sausage and ham producer, offers a Tyrolean evening Tues.

⤴ SIDE TRACKS FROM JENBACH

The **Achenseebahn railway** from the main station chugs up to the limpid **Achensee** at little over double walking speed. Ferries connect with the trains (May–Oct) or you can walk round the path at the water's edge. Sailing and windsurfing are the major attractions.

In the opposite direction the *Zillertalbahn* leaves the main station (with some services by steam).for Mayrhofen at the end of the line.

MAYRHOFEN

Station: *tel: (05285) 2362*
Tourist Office: Europahaus; *tel: (05285) 2305,* crossing main road parallel to railway downhill, right and straight towards the large modern building. It opens Mon–Fri 0800–1800, Sat 0800–1200, 1500–1800, Sun 0900–1200, offers free map with accommodation list and sells walking maps and booklets. It also offers almost daily free walks July and Aug. Guest Card (GC) reductions on cable cars and entertainments. These include concerts and tea dances year-round, and folk festivals in July and Aug. The more ath-

letic can try hang gliding, fishing, canoeing, archery, cycling and summer skiing on the **Hintertux glacier** at the top of the Tuxertal. Another big attraction is the nearby 372 sq km **Zillertaler National Park**. Buses from the station serve the Hintertux glacier and ice caves. The local mountain guides will design a personal route from around ÖS500.

Alpenhotel Kramerwirt, *Am Marienbrunnen 346; tel: (05285) 2615,* built 1674, right by the church (expensive). **Campingplatz Kröll**, *Laubichl 127; tel: (05285) 2580,* is nearby. **Konditorei Kostner**, *Hauptstr. 414*, is the place for coffee, cakes and relaxing. **Wirtshaus zum Griena**, *Dorfhaus 768*, is known for Tyrolean dishes. **Die Gute Stube**, *Elisabeth Hotel, Einfahrt Mitte 432*, is the top restaurant.

The train stop before Mayrhofen is **Zell am Ziller**, known for its Gauderfest (first Sun in May), the oldest festival in Tyrol. Events include wrestling, ram fights and ringing bells to the grass to wake it up. Evening entertainment is singing, dancing and zither playing. The rest of the time the **Tourist Office**, *Dorfpl. 3a; tel: (05282) 2281,* offers free help booking rooms. GC discounts include ice skating, curling, swimming, and free guided hikes (June–Sept).

WÖRGL

⤴ SIDE TRACK FROM WÖRGL

Trains run from Wörgl to Munich (p. 224), stopping en route at Kufstein.

KUFSTEIN

Station: *tel: (05372) 6921.*
Tourist Office: *Münchnerstr. 2; tel:*

128

(05372) 62207, directly out of station on the left before the bridge Mon–Fri 0830–1230, 1330–1730, Sat 0900–1200 (July–end Sept), Mon–Fri 0830–1230, 1400–1700, Sat 0900–1200 (Oct–June), it offers free map and will book accommodation. GC free biking and hiking tours.

On the river is **Hotel Auracher Löchl**, *Römerhofg. 3–5*; *tel: (05372) 62138* (moderate). **Gerl**, *Gilmstr. 30*; *tel: (05372) 61069* (budget) is in the centre. **Camping Kufstein**, *Salurner-str. 36*; *tel: (05372) 63689*, is on the river, approx 15 mins on foot. A hotel chain with property here is *BW*. Try the richly decorated **Batzenhausl Weinhaus**, *Römerhofg. 1*, specialising in local dishes.

SIGHTSEEING

At the foot of a rocky outcrop below a Teutonic fortress, Kufstein is a town rebuilt after an 18th-century commander razed it to give a clear view of an attacking Bavarian army. There is a lift Easter–mid Oct to the **Schloss** and **Emperor's Tower** from the riverside. Alternatively steep, covered steps from the top of the main square lead through the 7–8 m thick walls to the central courtyard and café under trees. The **Heimatmuseum** of local furniture, wildlife and weaponry, housed here, is open to guided tours. Below the fortress is the **Heroes' Organ**, the largest instrument of its kind in the world with 4307 pipes with 46 registers and can be heard for miles on still days. At the foot of the Schloss steps is a **Planetarium**, and continuing straight ahead from the town square in *Kinkstr.* is a monument to Josef Madersperger, reputedly the inventor of the sewing machine, who was born here. The

Festival of the Fortress includes a season of concerts June–Oct.

KIRCHBERG IN TIROL

Station: *tel: (05357) 22430*.
Tourist Office: *Hauptstr. 8*; *tel: (05357) 2309*, turn left out of station, right at main road and continue to find on left. Open Mon–Fri, 0800–1800, Sat 0800–1300, Sun 1000–1200, (main summer and winter seasons; shorter hours outside these), it offers a free map with the accommodation list. There is an electronic 24-hr booking board outside and cash machine.

A small town known largely for winter sports, a number of pleasant cafés plus a few shops make it a pleasant place to use as a base for mountain excursions.

KITZBÜHEL

Station: **Hbf**, *tel: (05356) 4055 1385* is the main stop. Rents bikes. Hahnenkamm on the opposite side of town is closer (and downhill) to the centre.
Tourist Office: *Hinterstadt 18*, *tel: (053546) 21552272*. From Hbf head left, and right across the main road to the edge of town, up steps ahead to the right and left into *Fussgängerzone*, then first right leading to the tourist office. Open Mon–Fri 0830–1830, Sat 0830–1200, 1600–1800, Sun 1000–1200, 1600–1800, (June 20–Oct 2 and Christmas–Easter; shorter hours outside these seasons). The office changes money in the ski and summer seasons, offers free town and hiking maps and will report accommodation availability. GC mountain hikes daily June to mid-Oct departing 0900 and tours of the town Mon–Fri.

ACCOMMODATION AND FOOD

An electronic accommodation board outside the tourist office is operational 0600–2200. In town **Neuhaus**, *Franz-*

Reischstr. 23; *tel: (05356) 2200* (budget) is the cheapest hotel. Cheaper are *Privatzimmer*, listed by the Tourist Office, or bed and breakfast establishments such as **Arnika**, *St Johannerstr. 32*; *tel: (05356) 2775* (budget) or **Hörl**, *Josef-Pirchlstr. 60*; *tel: (05356) 3144* (budget). **Camping Schwarzsee**, *Reitherstr. 24*; *tel: (05356) 2806*, is reached by train to the Schwarzsee stop or a half-hour-plus walk from town. Hotel chains with properties here include *BW*, *Rk*, and *RC*.

The restaurant of the **Romantikhotel Tennerhof**, *Griesenauweg 26*, slightly out of the centre, is rated as one of Austria's best. Good value is **Florianstube**, *Gasthof Eggerwirt* - a typical Tyrolean *stube*. Or try **Gasthof Huberbräu**, *Voderstadt 18*. The **Bauernmarkt** is held Weds and Fri all day, Sat to noon.

ENTERTAINMENT

The ski elite arrive Jan for the **Hahnenkamm Ski Competition**, a World Cup leg held on one of the world's trickiest ski runs. Spectator tickets are available at the gate. In July and Aug there are free open-air concerts.

SIGHTSEEING

The **Heimatmuseum** on *Hinterstadt* looks at pre-historic European mining, inspired by the town's own history with copper and silver since the 16th-century. At the top of the *Hahnenkammbahn* is the small **Bergbahn Museum** on the history of 100 years of skiing, which has videoclips of past races and a larger than life skier for visitors to climb in and experience racing almost first hand. The **Hornbahn** lift goes to the **Alpenblumengarten** with around 200 Alpine flowers in their natural environment, late May to mid-Oct. Nearby **Schwarzsee** heats up to a suitable temperature for summer swimming. In winter

the **Kitzbühel Ski Circus** makes it possible to ski downhill for 50 miles. There is also curling, toboganning and some hiking. A network of hiking tracks can be reached by buses from outside the main station plus cable cars. There is a three-day summer cable-car pass for ÖS320.

ST JOHANN IN TIROL

Station: *tel: (05352) 62305-385.*
Tourist Office: *Poststr. 2*; *tel: (05352) 63335*, (straight out of the station and left at the junction. At the square turn left and first right to find the office on the right). Open Mon–Fri 0800–1200, 1400–1800, Sat 0830–1200, 1600–1800, Sun 1000–1200 (July, Aug, end Dec–end March), the office offers a free map with accommodation list, and in July and Aug organises free cycling, hiking and village tours.

ACCOMMODATION AND FOOD

There's a wide choice of hotels and *Privatzimmer* and the Tourist Office will make bookings in advance. **Gasthof Post**, *Speckbacherstr. 1*; *tel: (05352) 62230* (moderate) in the centre of town was first built 1224. Two possible pensions are **Aloisia**, *Schwimmbadweg 8*; *tel: (05352) 62419* (moderate) or **Haselmaier**, *Wieshoferstr. 10*; *tel: (05252) 62267* (budget).

ENTERTAINMENT

Tyrolean Music Evenings are held two or three times a week July–mid-Sept plus other concerts held year-round. At the end of Sept cows are decorated to be brought down from the summer pastures in a traditional festival, but the surrounding mountains are the main attraction.

SAALFELDEN

Station: *tel: (06582) 23440.*
Tourist Office: *Bahnhofstr. 10*; *tel: (06582) 72513*, (out of the station to the

129

path almost immediately opposite, following it for about 15 mins into the town. From there take a right and the office is left on the first square). Open Mon–Fri 0800–1200, 1400–1800 Sat 0900–1200, offers a free map with accommodation list, free walking tours Fri half day, Wed/Thurs full, and biking tours Tues.

ACCOMMODATION AND FOOD

The Tourist Office will book accommodation. The **Hindenburg**, *Bahnhofstr. 6*; *tel: (06582) 2303* (moderate–expensive) offers a pleasant outdoor restaurant. **Gasthof Saliterwirt**, *Uttenhofen 5*; *tel: (06582) 3381*, out of town approx 15 mins from station, classifies itself as a youth hostel. Slightly closer is **Pension Zur Schmiede**, *Thor 11*; *tel: (06582) 2454* (budget). For atmosphere with your food there's **Schloss Stüberl**, *Dorfheimerstr. 25*, in one of the town's castles.

SIGHTSEEING

The biggest sight is the 16th-century **Ritzen Schloss**, with local history material and items like a peasant's room of the 1700s. Mainly a summer resort, the big attraction in Saalfelden is the limestone plateau, the **Steinernen Meer** (stone sea) a nature reserve reached by bus no. 1 to Pabing and then a 1–2-hr climb. There are a number of huts on the Meer.

ZELL AM SEE

Station: *tel: (06542) 3214357.*
Tourist Office: *Brucker Bundestr. 1*; *tel: (06542) 26000*, Mon–Fri 0800–1200, 1400–1800, Sat 0800–1200 (May–early July, Nov–Christmas, early Jan, early March-end April), Mon–Fri 0800–1800, Sat 0800–1200, 1600–1800, Sun 1000–1200 (July and Aug, Christmas–early Jan, Feb–early March); right from the station and left at the pedestrian crossing

then right at the main road. The Tourist Office is on the right. Offers free town maps, biking maps and useful walking material. Will book accommodation for a deposit of 20% of weekly price. There is an electronic booking board 0800–2400. GC reduction on lifts, boats, bike hire etc.

ACCOMMODATION AND FOOD

Hotel Salzburger Hof, *Auerspergstr. 11*; *tel: (06542) 28280*, (very expensive), is a five-star chalet-style property near the lake, or there's the **Grand Hotel**, *Esplanade 4*; *tel: (06542) 2388* (very expensive) in a Victorian building. Cheaper is **Hotel St Hubertushof**, *Seeuferstr. 7*; *tel: (06542) 3166* (moderate–expensive). (**HI**) **Haus der Jugend**, *Seespitzstr. 13*; *tel: (06542) 57184*, is on the lakefront with quality rooms. **Seecamp Prielau**, *Thumersbacherstr. 34*; *tel: (06542) 2115*, is also on the lakefront on the eastern edge, reachable by ferry.

The *Fussgängerzone* is the place to find eateries. The smart place for coffee and cakes is **Konditorei Cafe Mosshammer**, *Stadtpl.* Cheaper places include self-service **Prima**, *Loferer Budesstr. 5*, or the **Sennstub'n**, *Schlosspl. 1*, for grilled food. For a meal in a garden try **Hotel Feinschmeck**, *Dreifaligkeitg.*

There are two Summer Festivals, one mid July with swimming and rowing competitions and another at the beginning of Aug with brass band, costume parades, fireworks, dancing and food stalls in the park. In Jan there is ice sculpting and in Feb international husky racing.

SIGHTSEEING AND ENTERTAINMENT

The town hinges round a tiny **Altstadt** with the Church still partly romanesque, and the **Bogturm** (Baliff's Tower) containing a **Heimatmuseum**. However, the main attraction here is the **Zeller See**, which mirrors the surrounding rocks, snows and meadows and warms fast in summer. In summer the area above nearby Kaprun can offer glacier skiing and the valley itself is worth exploring mid-May–late Oct (bus no. 3430 from the post office and station or in winter a ski bus). In summer four cable cars offer an opportunity to ride up the neighbouring mountains.

SIDE TRACKS FROM ZELL AM SEE

The **Krimml** railway out of Zell am See station ends 3 km from Krimml village, buses meeting the trains. The attraction is three large waterfalls at the edge of the **Hohe Tauern Park** where you can see up to 57 sq m of water per second. Unfortunately the place is often crowded. Zell am See is also a starting point for the **Grossglockner Highway**, a spectacular mountain road through the Hohe Tauern Park and past the **Grossglockner**, Austria's highest mountain at 3798 metres. ⛷

HALLEIN

Station: tel: (06245) 802760.
Tourist Office: *Untere Markt 1*; tel: *(06245) 85394*, straight out the station up Bahnhofstr. curving left at the top and at next junction turning right across the bridge and straight ahead. Open Mon–Fri 0800–1630, it offers information leaflets including accommodation list, GC reductions to tourist sights and chairlift.

ACCOMMODATION AND FOOD

Gasthof Brückenwirt, *Rifer Hauptstr 3*; tel: *(06245) 76194* (moderate) or **Hotel Bockwirt**, *Thunstr. 12*; tel: *(06245) 80623* (moderate) are two options. **(HI) Jugendherberger Schloss Wispach**, *Wispachstr. 7*; tel: *(06245) 80397*, is in a castle about 20 mins from the station (Apr–Sept) with giant medieval rooms. The more central of the two campsites is **Camping AU**, *Budestr. Nord 24*; tel: *(06245) 80417*. Alternative cheap accommodation is *Privatzimmer* in Hallein or more in Bad Dürrnberg, the nearby hill with salt water spas. In Hallein itself the good value places to eat tend to be around the *Oberer* and *Untere Markts* and in alleys near the *Kornsteinpl.* **Gasthaus Stadtkrug**, *Bayrhamerpl. 10*, is one possibility. One of the top restaurants is **Gasthof Löwenbräu**, *Schöndorferpl. 3*, opposite the Rathaus.

SIGHTSEEING

Hallein's name is based on the Celtic word for salt which made the area rich as long as 2500 years ago. The **Keltenmuseum**, *Pflegerpl. 5*; tel: *(06245) 80783*, has some priceless pieces of Celtic workmanship. The **Salt Mines** themselves in Bad Dürrnberg can also be visited, tel: *(06245) 8528515*. These are entered by electric train before moving through on foot in traditional miners' clothes, sliding from level to level. A cable car connects Hallein to the mines from *Zatloukalstr*. There is also a reconstructed **Celtic Village** above Hallein, tel: *(06245) 8528522*.

Though Hallein is industrial, the centre is medieval and almost untouched. Specific attractions include the home of Franz Xaver Gruber, composer of Silent Night, and **Brennerei Gugelhof**, *Davisstr. 11*; tel: *(06245) 80621*, a family-run distillery where you can see how the Schnapps is made and sample fruit and grain varieties. Late June and early July is the **Halleiner Stadtfest**, with music and street theatre. During the Salzburger Festspiele one opera is performed at the Hallein Pernerinsel. For tickets see Salzburg pp.261–266. There is also an International Folk Festival in Sept.

131

INNSBRUCK–VERONA

One of the most popular points of entry into Italy from the north is the Brenner Pass which, at only 1375 m, is the lowest of all the Alpine passes. Once it brought conquerors. Now, heading into the wealthy, mountainous, part German-speaking, part Italian-speaking autonomous Trentino-Alto Adige region, it is a route frequented by travellers.

> FASTEST JOURNEY: 3 HRS 40 MINS

TRAINS

ETT tables: 70, 380.

FAST TRACK

A train operates every two hours through the Brenner pass between Innsbruck in Austria and Verona in Italy, taking 3 hrs 40 mins.

ON TRACK

Innsbruck–Steinach in Tirol
A roughly hourly local service links these towns with journey times of 25 mins.

Steinach in Tirol–Bolzano
A change of train is neccesary at the border at Brennero. The journey takes around 2 hrs.

Bolzano–Trento
A frequent service operates on this route taking 45 mins.

Trento–Verona
Up to 3 trains an hour take just over 1 hr.

STEINACH

Station: *tel: (05272) 6203.*
Tourist Office: *tel: (05272) 6270,* Mon–Fri 0830–1200, 1400–1800; turn left out of station, right after 50 m to the main road then right to the Rathaus. It offers a free map and accommodation list, free guided mountain tours Tues, Wed, Thurs in July and Aug, Wed rest of year,

walking maps ÖS25 or 58. Guest Card (GC) discounts on sports facilities, items from the tourist office and cable cars. The office will book accommodation.

The best option is the four-star **Hotel Steinacherhof**, *Bahnhofstr. 168; tel: (05272) 6241* (moderate) or there is **Hotel Post**, *Brennerstr. 45; tel: (05272) 6239* (moderate), right in the centre, or a range of *Privatzimmer*.

Steinach, on the Brenner Pass route, had become a health resort by the last century, taking advantage of a location at the junction of several mountain valleys. Founded in the Middle Ages it also enjoys its past, boasting **St Erasmus Pfarrkirche** with impressive baroque choir. Traditional town band and choir and folk dance group performances alternate in summer once a week.

BOLZANO

Station: *Piazza Stazione, tel: (0471) 974 292*. Close by is the bus station – *Via Garibaldi; tel: (0471) 971 259* – which serves the inaccessible towns and villages of the region.

Tourist Office: *Piazza Walther 8, tel: (0471) 970 660*. Mon–Fri 0830–1800, Sat 0900–1230. For information about the region, there is an information office at *Piazza Parrochia 11/12, tel: (0471) 993 808*.

For mountaineering information, the **Club Alpino Italiano (CAI)** is at *Piazza dell'Erbe, tel: (0471) 971 694*.

ACCOMMODATION

There is a fairly wide range of accommodation available from the hugely expensive to the moderately affordable. For accommodation up in the nearby Colle/Kolhern, take the cableway from *Via Campiglio*. **Camping**: the **Moosbauer** campsite is situated on the main Bolzano-

Merano road, just outside the city, *tel: (0471) 918 492*.

SIGHTSEEING

Is this Austria or Italy? Situated at the junction of the Rivers Talvera and Isarco, and ideal as a base from which to explore the region, Bolzano (Bozen if you speak German) was, from the 14th–19th centuries, mostly in the possesion of Austria. Street names may be in Italian, but dishes on menus are distinctly German, as is the architecture.

The focus of Bolzano's outdoor life is the **Piazza Walther** where open-air cafés compete for custom in the shadow of a statue of the troubadour, Walther von der Vogelweide. To one side of the square is the **Duomo**, a 14th- and 15th-century building which became a cathedral only in 1964. Gothic in style, it has a colourful mosaic roof and an ornate spire.

Better than the Duomo, however, is the **Chiesa dei Francescani**, the Franciscan church on *Via dei Francescani*. Built in the 14th century, it has a wonderful Gothic cloister. Inside, the altarpiece by Hans Klocher is worth making an effort to see. The **Chiesa dei Domeniciani**, the Dominican monastery in *Via Capuccini*, is now the Conservatory of Music. Worth seeing are the 15th-century frescos in its cloister and, in its **Cappella di San Giovanni**, frescos of the School of Giotto.

The **Museo Civico** (*Via Museo*) houses a collection of Germanic-looking folk craft and a selection of Gothic and baroque art. In the suburb of Gries (to the north-west) are the baroque **Abbey** of the Benedettini and the ancient parish **church** of Gries.

TRENTO

Station: *Via Pozzo, tel: (0461) 234 545*. A second station, **Trento-Male** station at

133

Via Seconda da Trento 7, gives access to the Val di Non and Cles. *Tel: (0461) 822 725*. **Tourist Office**: *Via Alfieri 4, tel: (0461) 983 880,* provides information on the city itself. Sept–July, Mon–Fri 0900–1200, Sat 0900–1200 also Sun, 1000–1200 July–Aug. Ask for *Viva Trento*, the local listings magazine for details of the many festivals and events held in and around the city.

ACCOMMODATION

There are some comfortable, expensive hotels in the city but a dearth of cheaper ones. **HI** Youth Hostel: **Giovane Europa**, *Via Manzone 17, tel: (0461) 234 567*. **Campsite**: take bus no. 2 from the station to a riverside location at *Via Lung'Adige Braille 1, tel: (0461) 823 562*.

SIGHTSEEING

Although always a fairly strategic location, Trento, known to the Romans as Tridentum, only became an important market town in the 16th century. It enters history as the focus of the Council of Trent, three meetings of which were held here between 1545 and 1563 – in the **Duomo** (cathedral). This building, in *Piazza Duomo*, begun in the 13th century, is an interesting place to visit. Not only can the medieval crypt and the foundations of the early Christian basilica be seen, but over the altar is a baldacchino (canopy) modelled on Bernini's in St Peter's in Rome. Next to the Duomo is the battlemented **Palazzo Pretorio** with its medieval tower, the **Torre Civica**. This group of buildings houses the **Museo Diocesano Tridentino** which contains a magnificent collection of items from the Duomo's Treasury – paintings, reliquaries and a series of 15th-century Flemish tapestries by Peter van Aelst.

In *Via Bernardo Clesio* is the **Castello di Buonconsiglio**, a vast and stately residence of the former powerful bishop-princes of Trento. Formed from an amalgam of the 13th-century Castelvecchio and the 16th-century Magno Palazzo, it houses in part the **Museo Provinciale d'Arte** which contains a remarkable fresco cycle depicting the daily labours of 15th-century peasants and their noble counterparts. This, the *Cycle of the Months* contains an early depiction of Trento itself.

> ## SIDE TRACK TO LAKE GARDA
>
> Lake Garda is the most dramatic of all the Italian lakes – and it has the cleanest water. It is also the least affected by the ravages of tourism. Its beauty and surroundings have inspired writers for centuries – Virgil left us his thoughts, so did D H Lawrence.
>
> Of the places dotted about its shores, those worth visiting are, on the southern shore, **Desenzano del Garda**, a busy resort (tourist office: *Porta Vecchio 27, tel: (030) 914 510*), **Sirmione** (tourist office: *Viale Marconi 2, tel: (030) 916 114*), with its dramatic castle of the Scaligera family, the **Rocca Scaligera**.
>
> On the western shore, **Gardone Riviera** is the location of writer Gabriele D'Annunzio's eccentric villa, **Il Vittoriale**. **Limone sul Garda** (*Piazzale A De Gaspari, tel: (0365) 954781*) is a pretty village tumbling into the lake, while **Riva del Garda** (tourist office: *Giardini di Porta Orientale 8, tel: (0464) 554 444*) is a busy, sophisticated resort with plenty of hotels. **Torbole** and **Malcesine**, both on the eastern shore, are the places to windsurf. 🛶

INTERLAKEN

Interlaken began life in 1130, as a village surrounding an Augustinian monastery. The monks have long gone but the 35-acre meadow in the centre of the town, which was once part of the monastic grounds, has been deliberately left undeveloped so that the view of the Jungfrau (4158 m) and the surrounding peaks is undisturbed. Interlaken's main attraction is as a base for exploring these spectacular mountains, so the view is not only an aesthetic delight for the locals, but a giant living advertisement to its visitors.

TOURIST INFORMATION

Tourist Information: *Höheweg 37; tel: (036) 22 21 21*. Sept–June: Mon–Fri 0800–1200. July–Aug: Mon–Fri 0800–1830 Sat 0800–1700; Sun 1700–1900.

To save wasting time and money on a journey when clouds will obscure the view, close circuit televisions relay pictures of the peaks to booking offices.

ARRIVING AND DEPARTING

Stations: Ostbahnhof, *tel: (036) 22 27 92*, is on Lake Brienz, (*Brienzer See*) and is a 10–15-min walk from the centre. **Westbahnhof,** *tel: (036) 26 47 50*, by Lake Thun (*Thuner See*) is central, The two stations are 15 mins apart on foot, 5 mins by rail.

Ferries: There are two landing stations for services on Lake Thun and Lake Brienz. Each is directly behind the train station. Services are operated by the **Navigation Co. of Lakes Thun and Brienz,** *tel: (033) 36 02 59*.

GETTING AROUND

The town centre lies between Ostbhf and Westbhf, which are joined together by *Bahnhofstr./Höheweg*. You don't need transport to get around but hiring a bike for exploring the adjacent lakesides might be fun. Horse and carriage rides trot around town but these are quite expensive – bargain if you want to take one.

STAYING IN INTERLAKEN

Accommodation

There's no shortage of hotels, many catering largely for tour operators, but private rooms are better value. Register early in the height of both the summer and winter seasons.

Hotel chains in Interlaken include: *BW, EG, IE, MO, Sn, WS.* The three-star **Hotel Weisses Kreuz,** *Höheweg; tel: (036) 22 59 51*, is very central and offers comfortable simple rooms at competitive rates. There's also an excellent private hostel: **Balmer's Herberge,** *Hauptstr. 23; tel: (036) 22 19 61*, 15 mins walk from both stations, in the suburb of Matten (bus nos. 5/15). **HI:** *Aareweg 21; tel: (036) 22 43 53*, 20 mins walk east from Ostbahnhof, in the village of Böningen on Lake Brienz (bus no. 1). Seven **campsites** are close to the centre of Interlaken, so ask the tourist office for details.

Eating and Drinking

Interlaken doesn't offer a wide choice of interesting cheap eats. The **Bernerhof,**

Bahnhofstr. tel: (036) 23 16 10, is reasonably priced, conveniently central and nicely relaxed with a comprehensive Swiss menu. For Italian food try the **Trattoria Toscana**, *Jungfraustrasse 19; tel: (036) 23 30 33*. Vegetarians should try the brasserie-style **Vegetaris**, *Hotel Weisses Kreuz, Höheweg; tel: (036) 22 59 51*. The **Riverside Bar** at the *Hotel Belle Vue, Marktgasse 59, tel: (036) 22 44 31*, with a pleasant riverside terrace, is a popular place for food and live music (as is the adjacent **Anker** pub/restaurant, *Marktgasse 57*). If you want to splash out in Interlaken then **La Terrasse** at the **Grand Hotel Victoria-Jungfrau Hotel** is recommended, *Höheweg 41; tel: (036) 27 11 11*.

The old monastic meadows on the Höheweg are the obvious place for a picnic. However, you will find opportunities for even more scenic snacking on the walking trails in the area.

ENTERTAINMENT AND EVENTS

Interlaken nightlife is restrained and centres on the **Kursaal** (Casino), though high rollers should note that the ceiling for bets is only SFr.5. It also stages regular concerts and folklore evenings. If their particular brand of packaged Switzerland is not to your taste try the **Anker** or **Riverside Bar** (see above). The town's main cultural attraction is the **Tell Open-Air Theatre** (performances end June–early Sept) which has been producing its version of Schiller's famous legend since 1912, in the Rugen woods close to the town centre. The performance is in German but an English synopsis is available. Tickets are available from the Tell Office, *Bahnhofstr.*

Sporty types should pick up the *Adventure World* brochure from the tourist office. Activities covered include river rafting, canyoning (traversing gorges and rapids), paragliding and bungee jumping.

SIGHTSEEING

The mountains are the main attraction and the **Jungfrau** is the holy grail for most travellers, with the **Schilthorn** also very popular (see pp. 139–140). There are however many other worthwhile, and much cheaper, mountain excursions in the near vicinity. It's also worth remembering that Interlaken's two **lakes**, Thun and Brienz, also offer a wealth of sporting and sightseeing opportunities.

There is not a great deal to see within the town of Interlaken. Next to Westbhf station is the **Modelleisenbahn-Treff** (model railway exhibition) but this is recommended only for harassed parents or die-hard mini-train spotters. Instead, turn left out of the station, walk along *Bahnhofstr.* for a hundred metres or so, turn left onto *Marktgasse* and cross the River Aare to the old part of town known as **Unterseen**. Here, gathered around the attractive *Marktpl.* square, are the oldest buildings in the region; a 17th-century town hall, a 14th-century church with an unusually shaped tower and, accommodated in one of the square's many old houses, a small **Touristik Museum**. This deals with the history of tourism on the surrounding peaks but won't occupy you for very long. The riverside area of Interlaken is the most pleasant part of town and there are footpaths along the river, though no obvious walking circuits.

Return back along *Marktgasse* and directly opposite is *Centralstr. 3*, where between mid–May to Sept on Wed and Thur you can watch cheese being made at the **Chäs-Dörfli**.

Return to *Bahnhofstr.*, (which becomes *Höheweg* at this point) and continue along here. To your right is the *Höhematte*, the wide open meadows of the Höheweg, an idyllic scene often complete with grazing cows. Look on the left-hand side for the

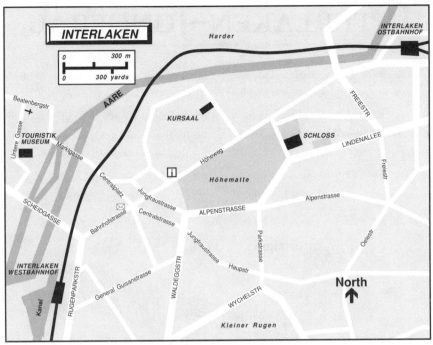

distinctive 19th-century **Kursaal** building (see Entertainment and Events).

For those for whom the Jungfrau and the Schilthorn are just too expensive, there are two much cheaper funicular rides close to town. **Harder Kulm** (1320 m), access from *Brienzstr.*, near Ostbahnhof, offers excellent views of the Bernese Alps and the town's two lakes. There's also a small alpine **wildlife park** at the base, featuring ibex and marmots. If the weather is good consider an evening trip (Fri only, mid-June–mid-Sept) to see the sun setting on the Eiger, Mönch and Jungfrau. You can also enjoy a meal with musical entertainment at the Harder Kulm restaurant. **Heimwehfluh** (669 m), access from the end of *Rugenparkstr.* (a short walk west along *Bahnhofstr.* from Westbhf) is much less elevated but enjoys a good panorama of Interlaken. There's also a model railway, a mechanical 300-m bob-sled run

and a children's playground. Walking trails continue from both Heimwehfluh and Harder Kulm.

Two other mini-mountain excursions for walkers, quite close to town on the shore of Lake Thun, are the **Niederhorn** and the **Beatenberg**, both rising over 1200 m. Just below these peaks are the **Beatushöhlen** (the caves of St Beatus) where you can journey 1000 m into the side of the mountain amid impressive stalagmites and stalactites (buses from both railway stations). Serious walkers should also note the spectacular paths from **Schynige Platte** (1967 m) to the north west of Interlaken. Access is by cog-wheel train from **Wilderswil** (bus 5 from Westbhf) and the views and hiking trails from here – to Faulhorn, Lake Bachalp (Bachalpsee) First and Grindelwald (see pp. 138–140) – are magnificent. There's also an alpine garden to enjoy.

INTERLAKEN–JUNGFRAU

The excursion to the Jungfraujoch is not only Europe's highest railway journey; it is the most heavily hyped, the most expensive (over SFr.150 standard fare) and the most over-subscribed trip in the country. It is one of the very few times when a Swiss train may be uncomfortably crowded and (horror of horrors) services may even run late. Is it all worthwhile? For most visitors the answer is a resounding yes. There's an awful lot more to the Jungfrau region than a one-day rail journey however, so try to take some out time en route to the top.

138

TRAINS

ETT tables: 288, 287.

ON TRACK

Interlaken–Grindelwald
Hourly service taking 36 mins from Interlaken Ost, with extra trains at peak periods.

Grindelwald–Kleine Scheidegg
Hourly service taking 35 mins, with extra trains at peak periods.

Kleine Scheidegg–Jungfraujoch
Hourly service taking 51 mins, with extra trains at peak periods.

Kleine Scheidegg–Wengen
Hourly service taking 30 mins, with extra trains at peak periods.

Wengen–Lauterbrunnen
Hourly service taking 17 mins, with extra trains at peak periods.

Lauterbrunnen–Interlaken
Hourly service taking 22 mins to Interlaken Ost, with extra trains at peak periods.

GRINDELWALD

Station: **Bahnhof**; *tel: 157 22 22.*
Tourist Office: Verkehrsbüro, *Sportszentrum; tel: 036 53 12 12.*

ACCOMMODATION AND FOOD

The **HI Hostel**, *Terrassenweg; tel: 036 53 10 09*, a 15-min walk, or bus no. 4 (to *Gaggi*) from Bhf, is in a fine old wooden house and enjoys geat views. Cheap accommodation can also be found at the **Mounty E&G**, a simple, comfortable 'Alpenpub' designed for younger travellers; *tel: 036 511 05*. For details of Grindelwald's four campsites, enquire at the tourist office.

For hearty local food try the **Hotel Fiescherblick**; *tel: 036 53 44 53.*

SIGTHSEEING

At an altitude of 1034 m this classic alpine village lies in the shadow of the Eiger and is a great base for winter sports, summer walking and, of course, climbing. It was patronised by British ski-tourists as long ago as the late 19th century and has remained a firm favourite with them ever since. In summer you can visit the two natural attractions of the **Blaue Eisgrotte** (Blue Ice Grotto), a 15-min walk from the Hotel Wetterhorn, and the **Gletscherschlucht** (Glacier Gorge), a 30-min walk

from the centre. There's also a folk museum in Grindelwald.

> #### ⤵ SIDE TRACK FROM GRINDELWALD
>
> The **First** region, with over 90 km of well-marked walking paths is marvellous hiking territory, particularly around the scenic **Bachalpsee** (Bachalp lake). A gondola lift makes the 5-km journey from Grindelwald to First at 2168 m. The **Pfingstegg** cable car is another popular ascent with great views and the usual well-marked walking trails to follow. See also Wengen, p. 141.

KLEINE SCHEIDEGG

All Jungfraujoch trains stop here, with the option (going down) of changing to either the west branch of the line (Wengen and Lauterbrunnen), or the east branch (Grindelwald). Kleine Scheidegg is nothing more than a single hotel and a few other buildings which congregate around the station but its setting, 2061 m high, at the foot of the north face of the Eiger, is breathtaking. If you want to move up closer to the great mountain take the 1-hour hike to **Eigergletscher** (2320 m), where there is a restaurant.

139

The eyes in the sky

It would be a terrible waste of money and time to visit the Jungfrau and the Schilthorn in poor weather when the views are completely masked by cloud. In order to ease the dilemma for visitors, cable television has been installed on both mountain tops and pictures are relayed to the booking offices in Interlaken.

Wrap up warm for both peaks, even in summer. Thin layers are best so you can peel off a little at a time if the sun is fierce.

JUNGFRAUJOCH

Station: *tel: 036 55 24 05.*
Information office: inside complex or in advance **Jungfraubahnen**, *Harderstr. 14, Interlaken; tel: 036 22 45 85.*

Before the holy grail is reached, the train makes two brief stops inside the tunnel, at **Eigerwand** (2865 m), and at **Eismeer** (3160 m), so that legs can be stretched and views can be enjoyed through purpose-cut windows. It was originally planned to take the tunnel to the very peak of the Jungfrau but this proved unfeasible so instead a saddle (or coll) in the mountain (*joch* in German) as near to the top as possible was chosen for the station site.

At the underground station, gloomy tunnels lead to a gleaming visitor centre which gives access to the icy world at an altitude of 3454 m. Make straight for the **Sphinx observatory** as here is where queues are longest. A lift takes you up another 119 m to an observation deck (at 3573 m the highest in Europe) offering marvellous views. Only mountaineers or helicopter pilots can get any higher. There is another observation point, called **The Plateau**, literally a finger of rock, fenced off to stop visitors slipping into oblivion, where the giants of the **Mönch** (4099 m) and the **Jungfrau** (4158 m) tower to right and left respectively. The **Eiger** (3970 m) is just visible behind the Mönch.

Below the Plateau the **Aletsch Glacier** sweeps smoothly past and from another exit it is possible to walk right alongside here. Husky dogs offer sleigh rides (in high season), a ski-school operates and helicopter rides are also available. Back inside the complex is the **Eispalast** (Ice Palace), a perma-frost grotto of ingenious ice carvings.

The Jungfraubahn

In case you were wondering as to the purpose of building a railway so high, in such difficult conditions, just look at the milling crowds.

It was built purely for tourism, begun in 1896 by the railway pioneer, Adolf Guyer-Zeller. His application to the Swiss Parliament was also helped considerably by the fact that he offered to spend SFr.100,000 of his own money equipping a meteorological station on the summit (meteorological data is still collected here and there is a High Alpine Research Institute on site).

Guyer-Zeller estimated that the cost would be around SFr.10 million and that it would take 7 years to build. However, despite round-the-clock work it took 16 years and cost some SFr.15 million. Nonetheless, it made a profit during its first full year and has done so every year (bar one) throughout its 100 years.

WENGEN

Station: Bahnhof; *tel: 036 55 15 43.*
Tourist Office: Verkehrsbüro; *Bahnhofpl. 12; tel: 036 55 14 14.*

Like Grindelwald, Wengen is a picturesque village at the foot of the imposing mountains, offering tremendous wintersport and summer hiking opportunities. (A favourite round-trip is by rail to Kleine Scheidegg, then walking back to Wengen.) As this is a car-free village, it is even quieter than its counterpart to the east. Also like Grindelwald (and Mürren) Wengen owes its early patronage to the British, which accounts for the English-style pubs and the English church here.

The **Bergheim YMCA**; *tel: 036 55 27 55* is probably the best cheap-sleep deal here.

⏩ SIDE TRACK FROM WENGEN

At 2230 m **Männlichen** sits on the top of the ridge that divides the two branches of the Jungfraubahn and can be reached from both Wengen, and on the other side of the mountain – via Europe's longest gondola lift journey (6.2 km) – from Grindelwald. This is also wonderful walking territory with 360-degree views from the top of the ridge. A favourite round-trip is a walk along the ridge to Kleine Scheidegg (around 75 mins) then the railway back to Wengen (or Grindelwald). ⏪

LAUTERBRUNNEN

This is the lowest of the Jungfrau resorts at a mere 796 m and is better known as a jumping-off point (see Side Track below). Not surprisingly, given its position, Lauterbrunnen is awash with waterfalls (around 72 of them) and the two most famous are the **Staubbach Falls** and the **Trümmelbach Falls**. The latter can actually be viewed from a special area inside the mountain and lies a short bus journey from Lauterbrunnen. The Staubbach Falls on the edge of the village carry a lesser volume of water and crash into a fine spray, but were still sufficiently impressive to inspire Goethe to laud them in his *Song of the Spirits over the Water*.

⏩ SIDE TRACKS FROM LAUTERBRUNNEN

The second most popular excursion in this area (after the Jungfrau itself) is to the **Schilthorn** (2970 m), which not only provides the perfect family-shot of the famous trio of Jungfrau, Mönch and Eiger, but offers views as far as Mont Blanc and the Black Forest. Spend 60 mins looking out the window of the revolving restaurant here and you will see the whole of the 360-degree panorama without the need to turn your head. The fame of the Schilthorn has most recently been guaranteed by the James Bond film, *On Her Majesty's Secret Service*, which filmed cable-car and ski-chase sequences here. The Schilthorn railway company has capitalised on this and today the mountain is almost as well known by its film name, *Piz Gloria*. Although this excursion is not quite as injurious to your wallet as the Jungfraujoch, at around SFr.100 (standard fare from Interlaken Ost) it is the country's second most expensive ascent. The longest aerial cableway in the Bernese Alps (30 mins) links the mountain top with **Stechelberg**, 2123 m below, though most visitors come by way of Mürren.

The popular car-free village of **Mürren**, perched at an altitude of (1634 m), is reached from Lauterbrunnen by funicular railway (around 30 mins). The only other access is by cable car from Stechelberg on the opposite side of the Lauterbrunnental valley. It's a picturesque place with narrow streets adorned with picture-book chalets and enjoys marvellous views. Boasting excellent snow conditions, Mürren is an important wintersports resort and one of the birthplaces of Alpine skiing. In summer it is a fine walking centre. If you want to stay cheaply overnight in Mürren there are a few *pensions,* enquire at the tourist information office in the sports centre; *tel: 036 55 16 16.*

An enjoyable excursion (Swiss Pass valid) can be made by mountain railway and aerial cableway between Lauterbrunnen, Grütschalp, Mürren and Stechelberg, returning to Lauterbrunnen by postbus. ⏪

KONSTANZ AND THE BODENSEE

Lake Constance, known to German speakers as the Bodensee, is a true inland freshwater sea bordered by Switzerland, Germany and Austria. Rail lines run around the shore of the lake, with three ferry fleets giving you the option of going part of the way by water. The railway line west of Friedrichshafen loops inland, meeting the lake shore again near Uberlingen, so if you don't want to miss the very attractive lakeside town of Meersburg a ferry ride is a must.

GETTING AROUND

A circular tour around the Bodensee is possible, with frequent services (at least one an hour on all lines), but you will have to change train. Konstanz to Radolfzell takes 15 mins; change for Friedrichshafen (55 mins). From there Lindau is 30 mins, then 10 mins to Bregenz in Austria. Head into Switzerland via St Margrethen (15 mins), then onto Rorschach (11 mins) and along the lakeside to Kreuzlinger (1 hr). From there a 3-min ride takes you back into Germany to Konstanz.

However, the best way to see the lake is by boat. Services are frequent in high summer but patchy at other times. Ferries connect all the towns mentioned below.

KONSTANZ

Station: Hbf, *tel: (07531) 19491.*
Ferries: DB ferries cross the lake to Mainau and Meersburg. DB and **SBB ferries** operate to the Swiss shore.
DB Bodensee Schiffsbetriebe, *Hafenstr.*

6, tel: (07531) 281389. The ferry harbour is about 300 m walk from Hbf.
Tourist Office: *Bahnhofpl.13, D-78462 Konstanz, tel: (07531) 900376.* Mon–Fri 0900–1200, 1400–1800 (Jan–Apr); Mon–Fri 0900–1800, Sat 0900–1300 (May–Sept); Mon–Fri 0900–1300 (Oct–Dec).

ACCOMMODATION

The tourist Office makes a DM5 charge for finding a room. Chain hotels in Konstanz include *Rm.*

The poshest place in town is the lovely **Steigenberger Inselhotel Konstanz**, overlooking the lake, *Auf der Insel 1, tel: (07531) 1250.* **Hotel Barbarossa**, *Obermarkt 8–12, tel: (07531) 22021,* is housed in a 12th-century building. Mid-range properties include **Hotel Garni Hirschen**, *Bodanpl. 9, tel: (07531) 22238,* and **Hotel Bayrischerhof**, *Rosgartenstr. 30, tel: (07531) 22075.* Near the station are **MagoHotel Garni**, *Bahnhofpl. 4, tel: (07531) 27001,* and **Bahnhofhotel**, *Bahnhofstr 10, tel: (07531) 24635.*

SIGHTSEEING

Konstanz stands on a narrow isthmus which separates the main body of the Bodensee from a y-shaped inner lake, the **Untersee,** connected to the outer lake by the channel of the Rhine. The Swiss border is less than 500 m south of the Hbf and harbour, and all the sights are within a 500m radius of the Hbf.

The grand 14th-century **Konzilge-baude** (Council Building) faces the **Gondelhafen** (Gondola Harbour). Built

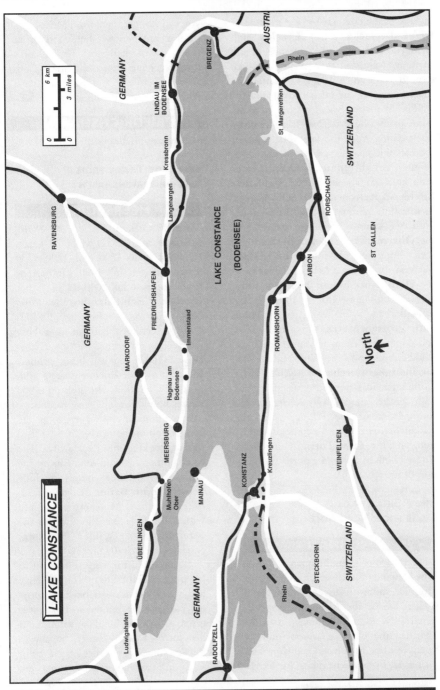

LAKE CONSTANCE

6 km
3 miles
0

GERMANY

AUSTRIA

BREGENZ

LINDAU IM BODENSEE

Rhein

St Margerethen

SWITZERLAND

Kressbronn

Langenargen

RAVENSBURG

LAKE CONSTANCE (BODENSEE)

RORSCHACH

ST GALLEN

ARBON

FRIEDRICHSHAFEN

GERMANY

ROMANSHORN

North

143

MARKDORF

Immenstaad

Hagnau am Bodensee

MEERSBURG

WEINFELDEN

Muhlhofen Ober

MAINAU

KONSTANZ

Kreuzlingen

ÜBERLINGEN

GERMANY

SWITZERLAND

Ludwigshafen

RADOLFZELL

Rhein

STECKBORN

in 1388 as the city granary, it is now a festival and conference hall. The 9-m high **Imperia statue**, at the entrance to the harbour, was cast in 1993; the goddess-like figure holds two clowns, one wearing the imperial crown, the other the papal tiara.

The **Münster**, *Munsterpl.* is a Romanesque basilica built 1052–8. It has an older crypt dating from the late 10th century, Gothic side-chapels added in the 14th century, a 17th-century nave and a spire built in 1865. The nearby **St Stephanskirche** is a Romanesque church, enlarged in the 15th century in late Gothic style, with 18th-century ceiling paintings. On the **Obermarkt**, a complex of three historic buildings includes **Hotel Barbarossa**, an inn since 1419, and flanking it the **Haus zum hohen Hafen**, a 15th-century building with a 19th-century painted façade by Haberlin, and the **Haus zum grossen Mertz**, dating from 1368 and containing elements dating from the Middle Ages up to the 17th century. The **Dreifaltigkeitskirche**, *Rosgartenstr.*, has a Gothic basilica, fine baroque altars and 15th-century frescos. On *Rheinsteig,* the south bank of the Rhine, stand the **Rheintorturm**, a 12th-century fortification, and the **PulveTurm** (Gunpowder Tower) built in 321 as the north-west bastion of the city walls.

SIDE TRACK FROM KONSTANZ

MAINAU

The Bodensee's unique microclimate – the waters of the lake store heat, keeping its shores relatively warm even when the nearby Alps are snow-covered – is ideal for flower growing. Mainau, the 'island of flowers', midway between Friedrichshafen and Konstanz, is served by frequent trans-lake ferries;

you can also get there from Meersburg, from where there is a shuttle ferry from the western harbour. The island's flower gardens attract enthusiasts from all over Germany, and the season starts with tulips and daffodils at Easter.

FRIEDRICHSHAFEN

See Munich–Friedrichshafen, p. 234

SIDE TRACK FROM FRIEDRICHSHAFEN

MEERSBURG

Tourist Office: *Kirchstr. 4, 88709 Meersburg, tel: (07532) 43 11 10.* Open Mon–Fri 0900–1200 and 1400–1730 (Oct–Apr open only 1430–1700); Apr–Sept also open Sun 1000–1400.

Ferries: Schiffslandestelle, *Am Hafen, 88709 Meersburg, tel: (07532) 6033.* Meersburg harbour is a busy intersection for ferries.

Buses: RAB regional buses connect Meersburg with Friedrichshafen Hbf, *tel: (07541) 22077.* The bus stop is 800 metres uphill from the ferry harbour.

Accommodation, especially at the budget end of the market, can be hard to find; booking ahead is advisable. The tourist office can find rooms in private homes. Mid-range hotels include **Gasthof Zum Baren**, *Marktpl. 11, tel: (07532) 43220.* More expensive, but with a lovely lakeside location, is the **Strandhotel Wilder Mann**, *Seepromenade, tel: (07532) 9011.*

Be prepared for a steep hike up to Meerburg's historic heart from the ferry harbour, which is overlooked by splendid old baroque buildings. The lower town, many of its buildings dating from the turn of the century, is almost Riviera-like in summer, with palm trees and pavement cafés along the lake-front. The upper town is the jewel of the Bodensee region. Half-timbered buildings, their woodwork painted bright red and green, cluster on steep cobbled streets around the pink and white baroque palace and the tall stone walls of the old castle. Meersburg was founded in 1088 and its buildings are outstandingly well-preserved. The **Altes Schloss** (Old Castle) **Burgmuseum**, housed in the oldest inhabited castle in Germany, has a magnificent collection spanning several centuries, and it takes the better part of a morning to do justice to its 28 rooms, cluttered with weapons and suits of armour, paintings and elegant furniture. The **Neues Schloss** (New Palace), *Schlosspl.*, opposite, is a pink and white baroque confection built during the 18th century for Johann VIII, prince-bishop of Stauffenberg, whose florid coat of arms adorns the portico. The building is lavishly decorated with frescos and stucco ceilings, while allegorical statues stand in every corner. ⬛

LINDAU

Station: Hbf: *tel: (08382) 19419.*
Ferries: DB Erlebnis-Flotte, *Am Hafen, 88131 Lindau, tel: (08382) 6099.* The ferry harbour is across the street from Hbf. Ferries sail to Friedrichshafen, Meersburg, Mainau island and Konstanz, plus Bregenz and Rorschach.
Tourist Office: Opposite Hbf on *Bahnhofpl., tel: (08382) 260026.* There are guided walks around the town every Mon at 1000 in summer.

ACCOMMODATION

Tourist Office has a 24-hour accommodation information line, *tel: (08382) 19412,* and can find rooms. Accommodation can be very hard to find in summer. Cheaper

rooms can be found in Lindau-Aeschach, on the mainland opposite Lindau island, about 2 km away across the causeway. **Campsite: Camping Lindau-Zech,** *Frauenhoferstr.,* on the lake 6 km from the island (bus no. 4 from Hbf to *Zech*). In the mid-range, the **Alte Post** inn at *Fischergasse 108* is excellent value. At around the same price, **Hotel Vis a Vis,** *Bahnhofpl.4, 8990 Lindau tel: (08382) 3965,* is across the road from Hbf. There are a number of elegantly old-fashioned 19th-century luxury hotels, including **Hotel Bayerischer Hof, Hotel Reutemann** and **Hotel Seegarten,** all under the same management and within 250 m of the Hbf at *Seepromenade, tel: (08382) 5055.*

SIGHTSEEING

The breathtakingly pretty medieval town of Lindau stands on an island in the Bodensee, connected to the mainland by a causeway. On the opposite shore, the Swiss and Austrian Alps rise above the lake. The ferry harbour is on the south shore, separated from a pretty yacht harbour by a small peninsula, the **Romerschanze**. The town became a fashionable spa resort in the 19th century. Landmarks on the harbour include the massive stone **Lion of Bavaria**, dating from 1856, and the **Mangturm**, a massive stone lighthouse with a gay red and yellow tiled spire. The harbour was built from the old stones of the former city wall, demolished in the 19th century when Lindau lost its status as a free city. Inland from the harbour are streets lined with higgledy-piggedy old houses with overhanging balconies, window boxes and a wealth of decorative detail. The **Altes Rathaus** (*Reichspl.*) dates from 1436 but its striking painted façade – depicting the nobles of the free cities of Germany in 1496 – dates from 1882, when it was rebuilt. In front of the Rathaus the **Lindavia fountain** represents the patron goddess of the town, but no longer holds its original golden linden bough, which was stolen so often the town refused to replace it. The **Rathaus** occupies the block between *Reichspl.* and *Maximilianstr.*, the main street of the old town, and its *Maximilianstr.* façade has a striking, brightly painted ten-stepped gable. *Maximilianstr.* is a glorious cluster of four- and five-storey medieval buildings with stucco and timber façades. Lindau's oldest **church,** St Peter's, at the corner of *Zeppelinstr.* and *Schrannenpl.*, is decorated with faded murals which were discovered earlier this century – when the church was in use as a hay barn – to have been painted by Hans Holbein the Older. They were restored in the 1960s.

BREGENZ

For details see p. 331.

RORSCHACH

For details see p. 340.

ARBON

Station: Bahnhof; *tel; (071) 46 58 88,* the centre is a 5–10 min walk.
Tourist Office: *Bahnhofstr. 40; tel: (071) 46 33 37.*

Arbon is the most attractive of the Swiss Bodensee settlements with a small old town behind its popular marina. Just before the town centre are lakeside cafés and gardens with the picturesque backdrop of church and castle. The Church of St Martin has recently been renovated. Next door the **Schloss Arbon**, a typical 16th-century Swiss castle, now holds a historical museum with a comprehensive collection of local artefacts ranging from the Stone Age (Arbon is one of the oldest Bodensee settlements) to the 19th century. Step off *Hauptstr.* to either side to find some fine

half-timbered 18th-century buildings. Look out for the **Rotes Haus** (opposite the church), the **Rathaus/Polizeiposten** (*Promenadenstr.*), **Zum Storchen** (*Walhallstr.*) and adjacent to the latter, the houses on *Schmiedgasse*. Behind the Rathaus is the old **Fischmarktplatz**, home to more picturesque houses, a witty modern fishwife statue and the Fri market.

For refreshments in ancient surroundings continue along *Hauptstr.* **Wirtschaft Zum Römerhof**, *tel: (071) 46 17 08,* offers top-quality local dishes at moderate–expensive prices. Further along is the **Gasthof/Brauerei Frohsinn**; *tel: (071) 46 10 46.* The food is varied and good (including a vegetarian selection) at cheap–moderate prices; beer is brewed on the premises; there is a *kegelbahn* (skittles alley) and you can sleep off any excesses at around SFr.160 per double room.

ROMANSHORN

There's little to detain travellers in this industrial town. It is only a 30-min diversion to the charming town of Frauenfeld.

SIDE TRACK FROM ROMANSHORN

FRAUENFELD

This is home to two of the cantonal museums of Thurgau. The **Kantonal Historisches Museum** (History Museum) is located in the **Schloss** (castle), which has a huge 13th-century keep with a red-and-white timbered top storey. The most interesting part of the museum is the reconstructed interiors of local houses. Nearby is the **Kantonal Naturmuseum** (Natural History Museum). Most of the the charming Old Town was rebuilt after two disastrous fires and now dates from the late 17th century.

LAKE COMO

Lake Como has always been the most revered of Italy's lakes. In antiquity its beauty was much lauded by both Pliny the Elder and Pliny the Younger – and none of it has diminished over the last 2000 years or so. In fact Lake Como and its many lovely lakeside resorts – Bellagio and Menaggio among them – are more popular than ever.

It's a region of thick waterside woodland, dramatic mountain backdrops, luscious gardens and handsome lakeside villas which has always been popular with the English (particularly the Shelleys and Wordsworths) though nowadays they're outnumbered by weekending Germans and wealthy Milanese.

As the lakeside road threads its way in and out of tunnels as it heads north up the lakes's western edge, there are magnificent views out over the water to the Orobi Alps over in the east.

Lake Como has two southern arms. Como commands the western one, and Lecco (see page 215) the eastern one. The former is infinitely more beautiful than the latter and, unsurprisingly, far more popular, with a Belle Époque appeal that never seems to have evaporated.

In between the two, in a region called La Brianza, is a series of five small lakes set in gentle wine-growing country.

COMO

Station: There are several stations in Como. **San Giovanni** deals with the main line from Chiasso to Milan. Frequent local trains from Milan Nord, Saronno, Varese Nord and Novara Nord run to **Como Nord Lago** on a private railway service.

Tourist Office: *Piazza Cavour 17; tel: (031) 262091.* There is another in San Giovanni Railway Station; tel: *(031) 26721424.* Ask for a copy of *Turismo Proposte,* the listings publication for venue around Lake Como.

Como lies on the Lucerne–Milan route, see p. 176.

GETTING AROUND

The boat service on Lake Como links Como with the main towns mentioned in this chapter (see ETT table 364). It operates seasonally with up to a dozen sailings on some routes in high summer but few sailings in midwinter.

The boat service is supplemented by a fast hydrofoil service; for details contact **Navigazione Lago di Como**; *tel: (031) 27 33 24.*

The **Navigazione Lago di Como**, *Piazza Cavour; tel: (031) 304060,* runs the lake's **steamers** and **hydrofoils**. There are frequent services all around the lake, to Tremezzo, Menaggio, Bellagio, Varenna and Colico and a less frequent service to Lecco.

There are also **car ferries** that operate between Como and Bellagio, Varenna and Cadenabbia - a particularly useful service because the winding lakeside roads mean that traffic moves very slowly indeed.

ACCOMMODATION

Accommodation in Como is very varied. At the upper end of the scale it is immensely luxurious, at the other the best comment is that there is a meticulous attention to cleanliness. Some of the cheapest accommodation in town is along *Via Borgo Vico* – conveniently close to San Giovanni station. There is a **Youth hostel**, **Villa Olmo**, *Via Bellinzona 2; tel: (031) 573 800*. Open Mar–Nov only. Take bus nos. 1 or 6 from San Giovanni station. Younger women might consider staying at the **Ostello per la Protezione della Giovane**, *Via Borgo Vico 182; tel: (031) 573 540*.

SIGHTSEEING

Como, located at the southern tip of the lake, commands a stretch of water 50 km long and, at its widest point, 4.4 km across. It features in the annals of Roman history as the birthplace of both Pliny the Elder and the Younger and it has a niche in Italy's textile and fashion world as the leading silk city in the country. It's an elegant, well-bred city whose ancient heart follows the street pattern imposed on it by the Romans. There isn't an awful lot to do here, though it is an extremely good base from which to explore the lake. It is also the main port of call for steamers and hydrofoils operating on the lake. There are good public beaches at Como.

Como's centre of gravity is **Piazza Cavour** which, by the side of the lake, is the hub of the town's cafe life. Nearby (just to the west), the **public gardens** focus on the **Museo Volta** which is devoted to the doings of Alessandro Volta, a pioneer of electricity and man who gave us the electric volt. He was born in Como. Not far away, the **Duomo** (cathedral), in *Piazza Duomo*, straddles the stylistic change from the Gothic to the

Renaissance and although it was begun in the 14th century, it wasn't finished until the 18th – at the hand of Northern Italy's master of the baroque, Juvarra (his is the cupola). All over the building the Gothic and the Renaissance are sparring partners: there is a magnificent rose window and pinnacles which contrast sharply with the Renaissance entrance portal and, within, choir and transept. There is also a set of 16th-century tapestries and paintings by two followers of Leonardo da Vinci, Luini (an *Adoration of the Magi* and a *Madonna*) and Ferrari *(Flight into Egypt)*. Still in *Piazza Duomo*, the town hall, the 13th-century **Broletto** is difficult to miss: its facade is striped white, pink and grey. Here too is the 13th-century **Torre del Comune**.

Elsewhere in town, 12th-century **San Fedele** *(Via Vittorio Emanuele)* has some lovely medieval carvings – see the north east doorway. This was once the town's cathedral. Eleventh-century **Sant' Abbondio** *(Via Sant'Abbondio)*, Como's loveliest Romanesque monument dedicated to the third bishop of Como, has two campanili, and interesting 14th-century frescos in the apse. The church of **Santa Cecilia**, whose façade incorporates fragments of Roman columns, is very close to the **Porta Vittoria**, an ancient gate topped by a 12th-century tower.

The **Museo Civico** *(Piazza Medaglie d'Oro Comasche)* houses a huge array of artifacts detailing the entire history of the city from the Neolithic period to the present. The display includes Roman urns, sculpture and sarcophagi, medieval pieces from various local churches, and a fairly comprehensive collection of items relating to the Risorgimento and World Wars I and II. At *Via Diaz 84*, the **Pinacoteca** contains, amongst other things, a small collection of medieval paintings from the

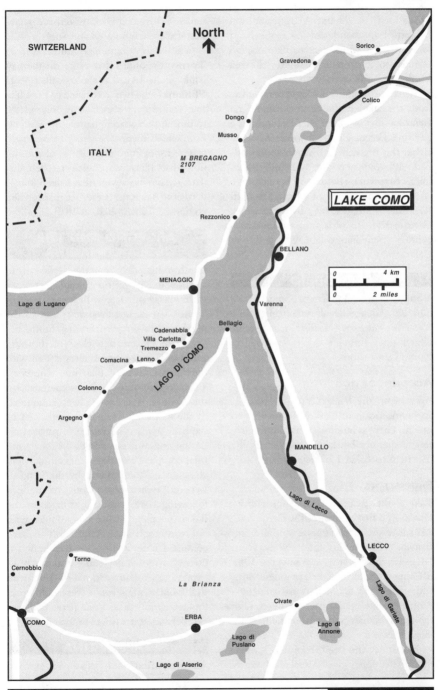

North

SWITZERLAND

Sorico

Gravedona

ITALY

Colico

Dongo

Musso

M BREGAGNO
2107

LAKE COMO

Rezzonico

BELLANO

0   4 km

0   2 miles

MENAGGIO

Lago di Lugano

Varenna

Bellagio

Cadenabbia
Villa Carlotta
Tremezzo
Comacina   Lenno

LAGO DI COMO

Colonno

Argegno

MANDELLO

Lago di Lecco

LECCO

Torno

Cernobbio

La Brianza

Lago di Garlate

Civate

COMO

ERBA

Lago di
Annone

Lago di
Puslano

Lago di Alserio

149

Monastery of Santa Margherita del Broletto.For wonderful lake views, a funicular goes (from next to Como Lago Station) to the top of **Brunate**, the hill overlooking the city.

An excursion from Como, and away from the lake, is the route into the **La Brianza** region which lies between the city and Lecco. Centred on the town of **Erba,** this is a wine-growing region studded with country houses and well-known for its **furniture-making.** There are five lakes here, the biggest of which, **Lago di Annone**, is presided over by the town of **Civate**, the site of a once-famous 8th-century Benedictine abbey called San Calocero.

CERNOBBIO

Tourist Office: *Via Regina 33b; tel: (031) 510198.* Ask for details and maps of the 130-km walk, the *Via dei Monti Lariani* which goes through the mountains on Como's west shore.

ACCOMMODATION

Apart from the Villa d'Este (see below), accommodation in Cernobbio isn't up to much. There is little that is in the moderate-inexpensive bracket. However, try the **Terzo Crotto**, at *Via Volta 21.*

SIGHTSEEING

Taking the steamer going north from Como, the first port of call is Cernobbio, a small resort made famous by the errant British queen, Caroline, who, from 1816–17, took over what is now the **Villa d'Este** – one of the lake's grandest villas, and since 1873 a hotel. A palatial 16th-century building, its gardens filled with fountains, statues and clipped hedges are magnificent.

For those who need to be near Como, this is extremely well situated if costly refuge. There is a good waterfront **market** at Cernobbio (Wed and Sun).

The villa theme predominates: at **Torno**, opposite Cernobbio, on the east bank of the lake, has the so-called **Villa Pliniana** which is associated with Pliny the Younger. However, it is only related to him in that it occupies the site of a villa near which there is a spring from which water gushes intermittently – a phenomenon that Pliny was quick to describe. These days, however, the Villa Pliniana derives its fame from the fact that Rossini composed *Tancredi* here in 1813.

ARGEGNO AND THE ISOLA COMACINA

Continuing on up the lake from Cernobbio, **Argegno** (about 20km), a small village of ancient, tottering wooden houses, has tremendous views out to the north and to the east. Further north, the village of **Colonno** is close to the little island of **Comacina** which is dotted with the ruins of no less than nine churches. This was one of the earliest settlements on the lake and, after having been conquered by the Romans, its history is marked by its status as a place of refuge – particularly during the warring Middle Ages – and then complete abandonment until its purchase after World War I by the King of Belgium (who subsequently returned it following a great deal of fuss made by the Italian people). Today it is popular with not very good artists who seem to have colonised it for themselves – although it does also sport one of the region's most expensive restaurants, the **Locanda dell'Isola**. Unless you're very rich, enter this establishment at your peril; the very excellent food has prices to match.

TREMEZZINA

Accommodation: in this area it tends to

be rather expensive. Tremezzo has an inexpensive hotel, the **Darsena**. Proceeding further north (about 15 km), **Tremezzo** is a lovely resort particularly popular with the English. It is only one of the towns of a district called Tremezzina – from which Lake Como's reputation as an idyllic flower-filled haven derives.

It has a fairly mild climate, which may account for the proliferation of camellias, the rhododendrons and the magnolias. Brightly painted villas and palaces adorn the town which is a good place to eat in or to dawdle in a café. **Tourist office:** *Piazza Fabio Filzi 2; tel: (0344) 40493.*

Between Tremezzo and Cadenabbia is the **Villa Carlotta**, an 18th-century villa lived in by a Prussian princess who was responsible for the magnificent gardens. A visit will give the chance of viewing an important work of sculpture, Antonio Canova's *Cupid and Psyche.*

Other Tremezzina towns to visit are **Lenno**, south of Tremezzo, which is the site of another villa built by Pliny the Younger who, in his *Comedia* explains that he was able to fish from its windows.

The Two Plinys

Pliny the Elder, Gaius Plinius Secundus (c.23–79AD), was a Roman scientist, best known for his one surviving work, a fascinating encyclopaedia of Natural History, published in 77AD. He died two years later during the eruption of Mount Vesuvius. His nephew, Gaius Plinius Caecilius Secundus (Pliny the Younger: c.61–c.112AD) served as a Roman senator, consul and governor of Bithynia, but is also most famous for his writings, with ten books of correspondence with Emperor Trajan showing a vivid and invaluable account of life in the Roman Empire.

Mezzagra is not so blessed with charm: here Mussolini and his mistress Clara Petacci met their end.

MENAGGIO

Tourist Office: *Via Lusardi 8; tel: (0344) 32924.*

ACCOMMODATION

The range of accommodation here is varied. Most of it is hugely expensive. However, there is a good **youth hostel** here: **Ostello La Primula**, *Via 1V Novembre 38; tel: (0344) 32356.* Open Mar–Oct. Otherwise, there is a campsite, the Lido; *tel: (0344) 31 150.* Open May–Sept.

SIGHTSEEING

The reason to come to Menaggio, apart from admiring the view across the water to the little town of Varenna on the east bank, is that it is an excellent base from which to start a number of walks in the surrounding mountains. The best of all is that which climbs up to **Monte Bregagno** from which there are tremendous views out over the lake. There is a good public **beach** at the Lido at Menaggio, which also has a large swimming pool. Menaggio is also a good base from which to do some cycling.

North of Menaggio (about 35 km), the village of **Rezzonico** has an interesting castle. The place gave its name to the Rezzonico family one of whose members was to become Pope Clement XIII (1758–1769). About 12 km further on, **Musso** is overlooked by the **Rocca di Musso** from which the pirate, Giacomo de'Medici (nicknamed *Il Medeghino*), terrorised the lake with a fleet of ships, exacting a toll from anybody using it and the surrounding valleys. Still further on are **Dongo, Gravedona** and **Sorico**.

151

DONGO, GRAVEDONA AND SONNO

Accommodation: around Gravedona the lakeside is fairly flat and therefore good for **camping**. The **Serenella**, along with a small, simple hotel of the same name, is open Apr-Sept; t*el: (0344) 80060*. Otherwise, there is a variety of inexpensive hotels at **Domaso**, just to the north of Gravedona. **Dongo**, **Gravedona** and **Sonno** are all worth a quick look. Once part of an medieval independent republic whose chief claim to fame was that its inhabitants doubted that the Pope was Christ's representative on earth. Peter of Verona, a particularly vicious inquisitor, was sent to put them back on the straight and narrow and, in the process, sent hundreds of locals to be burned at the stake. However, once they'd had enough of him and his ways, they turned on him and chopped him up – so the Pope had him canonised. Of the three 'parishes', Gravedona is the most important. Apart from the fact that its coastline is sheltered enough for **windsurfing** and **sailing,** there are one or two interesting buildings to be seen here. Sixteenth-century **Palazzo Gallio** with its four corner towers is one, and the little 12th-century church of **Santa Maria del Tiglio** is another. Inside the latter a carving depicts a centaur pursuing a deer – poignantly symbolic of the Church under persecution. Before leaving, be sure to visit the little church of **San Vicenzo** nearby. It has an interesting 5th-century crypt.

BELLAGIO

Tourist Office: *Lungolago A Manzoni 1;* tel: (031) 950204.

ACCOMMODATION

Bellagio's accommodation is of exceptionally high quality – with prices to match. At the lower end of the scale, try the **Metropole**, *Piazza Mazzini 1; tel: (031) 950409,* and the **La Spiaggia**, *Via Paolo Carcano 21; tel: (031) 950313.*

GETTING THERE

Bellagio is served by **steamer and hydrofoil** from Como.

SIGHTSEEING

Bellagio is one of the loveliest spots on the lake. However, because of its location on a headland tightly surrounded by mountains, it is extremely difficult to get to. However, once there, it is the place to swim – the water is very clean here – and it is a good base from which to explore the little villages and hamlets in the mountains surrounding it. This place is the epitome of *fin de siecle* melancholy, and it is worth every effort made getting there.

Directly across the water is one of Lake Como's most lovely resorts, **Bellagio**. Although its charm is somewhat beleaguered by the amount of tourism it sustains, and which is quite out of proportion to its scale, its position on a headland facing down the body of the lake is incomparable. From Bellagio, Lake Como resembles the sea, and indeed when the early morning mists obscure the opposite banks, the expanse of water seems infinite. This is the Capri of Como: there are expensive boutiques with outrageous prices, cafés and narrow, cobbled lanes compete with villas and gardens to walk in. Of the gardens, the **Villa Melzi** and **Villa Serbelloni** are the most interesting. Villa Melzi houses a small museum of Egyptian sculpture while Villa Serbelloni is supposed to occupy the site of Pliny the Younger's other lakeside villa, *Tragedia.* Both are situated just outside Bellagio. In the town (*Via Garibaldi*) is the 12th-century church of **San Giacomo**.

LAUSANNE

Lausanne, the prosperous, handsome capital of the Vaud region, basks on a hillside enjoying wonderful views of Lake Geneva and the Savoy Alps. It is very much a split personality city. Above is the old town, crowned by a stern cathedral. Below, the Mediterranean-like gardens and promenades of Ouchy reflect in the calm lake waters, stirred but never shaken, by pedaloes, yachts, windsurfers and passenger steamers. In 1915, Baron Pierre de Coubertin, founder of the modern Olympics, chose Lausanne as the headquarters of the International Olympic Committee. The city has never hosted the Games but remains at the heart of the movement.

TOURIST INFORMATION

The **main tourist office** is at *av. de Rhodanie 2, Ouchy; tel: 617 14 27.* Mon–Sat 0800–1900, Sun 0900–1200 and 1300–1800 April–Sept. Mon–Fri 0800–1800, Sat 0800–1200 and 1300–1700 mid-Oct–March. Pick up a free copy of the comprehensive booklet *Lausanne Useful Information.* There is another tourist office at the station (open July–Sept 1000–2100, Oct–June afternoons only) but the service here is limited.

GETTING AROUND

The **station, Gare CFF**; *tel: (021) 320 80 71,* lies between the centre and Ouchy, joined to both by the Metro. The old town is perched 130 m above the lake and the two are linked by the **Métro** (actually a funicular). It takes less than 5 mins between the old town, the station (below it) and Ouchy (the waterfront). The old town is relatively small and, despite its hills, best explored on foot (much of it is pedestrianised). Elsewhere, there is an excellent network of buses and trams.
Ferries: CGN (Compagnie Générale de Navigation sur le Lac Léman), *17 av. de Rhodanie; tel: 617 06 66,* run regular boat service to neighbouring towns, villages and just across the lake, France.

STAYING IN LAUSANNE

Accommodation

Ask the tourist office for their lists and brochures dealing specifically with family guesthouses and low-cost accommodation. Budget accommodation can most easily be found in the upper part of Lausanne, whereas the more popular Ouchy is generally quite expensive. Adjacent to Ouchy, the pleasant waterside suburb of Vidy is a good alternative.

Hotel chains include: *BW, Ib, IE, Mz, MO, Mv, Nv, Rd, RC, Tp, WS.*

The popular new **Jeunotel**, *ch. du Bois-de-Vaux 36, Vidy; tel: 626 02 26,* lies on the lakeside just west of Ouchy. It's a hi-tech monochrome building that resembles a modern art gallery and offers simple but comfortable modern rooms and dormitories. If you prefer to be in the thick of things and don't mind paying in the region of SFr.150 per double room per night, then the **Hotel Angleterre**, *Place du Port 9,* offers two-star facilities, good atmosphere and literary cachet (Byron wrote *The Prisoner of Chillon* here).

153

HI: *ch. de Muguet 1; tel: 616 57 82,* near Ouchy, by the lakeside. Campsite: **Camping de Vidy**, *ch. du Camping 3; tel: 624 20 31*, offers bungalows as well as canvas, has a fine situation and a very good reputation.

Eating and Drinking

Most of the interesting and/or affordable refreshment places are away from Ouchy. The tourist office produce a useful brochure *Restaurants Night-Clubs* which details several eating options and includes price guidelines.

In the heart of the old town try **Manora**, *17 pl. Ste-François*, a good-value self-service buffet restaurant. Nearby, fashion victims flock to **Le Tinguely**, *Lausanne Palace, Grand-Chêne 7-9; tel: 312 37 18*, a restaurant bar created by artist Jean Tinguely where French food mingles with his famous scrapyard art.

Immediately on the Ouchy waterfront is the popular self-service **Buvette d'Ouchy** with superior quality, Swiss-style fast food. A stone's throw away is the rather more expensive **Hotel Angleterre** (see above), which specialises in fish. One of Ouchy's most memorable eating experiences is at the fashionable **Caféteria du Museé Olympique**; *tel: 621 67 08*, serving excellent international cuisine on a large outdoor terrace with marvellous views. Lausanne's speciality is *perche* (perch), fresh from the lake. Try it at **La Vaudaire**, *ch. du Camping 7; tel: 625 40 46*, which enjoys a verdant lakeside setting. Another place serving fish in delightful surroundings is the **Auberge du Lac de Sauvabelin**, *Pinte à Fromage; tel: (021) 647 39 29*, a haven of rural tranquility on a small lake in the forest, 5-mins from the city centre (bus no. 16). Close by is the rustic **Chalet Suisse**, *Signal de Suvabelin; tel: (021) 312 23 12*, where you can over-

look Lake Geneva and the Alps while dining on fondue and other typical Swiss cheese dishes. The flower gardens of Ouchy are a glorious spot for snacking.

Communications

The main **post office** is at *pl. St-François 15*, open Mon–Fri 0800–1830, Sat 0730–1100. There is also a post office near the station, *43 bis, av. de la Gare*. The telephone code for Lausanne is *021*.

Lausanne has a reasonable range of night-time entertainment venues, most of them in the upper part of town. Pick up the tourist boards *Restaurants Night-Clubs* brochure for a list of cabaret style clubs and look in their *Useful Information* brochure for other venues. The centre for highbrow performing arts is the **(Palais de) Beaulieu**, *10 Av. de Bergières; tel: (021) 643 21 11*. **Lac Léman (Lake Geneva)** is a magnet for watersports fans. Windsurfing, waterskiing and, for the less daring, pedaloes are all available at Ouchy or Vidy. The lake is the biggest freshwater expanse in Europe (measuring 225 sq miles) and with unpredictable local winds, it's even a challenge to experienced yachtsmen. Craft of various size are for hire at both Vidy and Ouchy marinas.

Lausanne has been a cultural centre for centuries and the medieval town surrounding the cathedral has been carefully restored. Walking tours depart from the town hall, Mon–Sat 1000 and 1500 May–Sept.

The Centre

The upper Metro terminal is at 'Sainfe', *pl. St-François*, dominated by the 15th-century steeple of the medieval **Église St-**

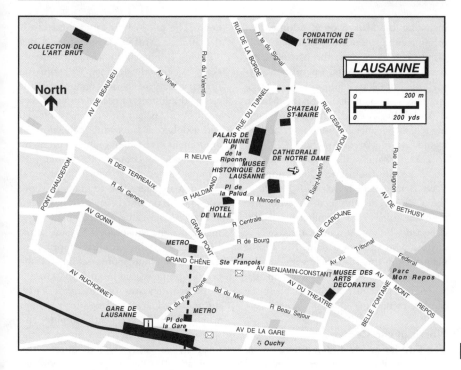

COLLECTION DE
L'ART BRUT

FONDATION DE
L'HERMITAGE

LAUSANNE

North

AV DE BEAULIEU

Av Vinet

Rue du Valentin

RUE DE LA BORDE

R te du Signal

RUE DU TUNNEL

0   200 m
0   200 yds

CHATEAU
ST-MAIRE

RUE CESAR ROUX

PALAIS DE
RUMINE
Pl
de la
Riponne

R NEUVE

MUSEE
HISTORIQUE DE
LAUSANNE

CATHEDRALE
DE NOTRE DAME

Rue du Bignon

PONT CHAUDERON

R DES TERREAUX

R du Geneve

R HALDIMAND

Pl de
la Palud

R Mercerie

R Saint-Martin

AV DE BETHUSY

AV GONIN

HOTEL
DE VILLE

R Centrale

RUE CAROLINE

AV RUCHONNET

METRO

GRAND PONT

GRAND CHÊNE

R de Bourg

Pl
Ste François

Av du Tribunal

Federal

AV BENJAMIN-CONSTANT

MUSEE DES
ARTS
DECORATIFS

Av

Parc
Mon Repos

AV DU THEATRE

BELLE FONTAINE

MONT

REPOS

GARE DE
LAUSANNE

R du Petit Chêne

METRO

Bd du Midi

R Beau Sejour

Pl de
la Gare

AV DE LA GARE

Ouchy

155

François (St Francis' Church).

Looming above all in the old town is the magnificent **Cathédrale de Notre-Dame**, consecrated in 1215. Italian, Flemish and French craftsmen all had a hand in its construction and it is accepted as a perfect example of Gothic architecture. Most of the interior decorations were destroyed during the Reformation in 1536, but the basic structure was unchanged and there are glorious rose windows, intricately carved choir stalls and a few surviving frescos. Following a tradition that has died out elsewhere, the watch is still called from the steeple every hour from 2000 to 0200. The **Musée Historique de Lausanne**, *pl. de la Cathédrale 4*, is housed in the **Ancien-Evêché**, which was the bishops' palace until the early 15th century. Among the exhibits is a remarkable large-scale model

of 17th-century Lausanne. Also by the cathedral is another fortified bishops' residence (dating from the 15th–16th centuries), the **Château St-Maire**, now the seat of the cantonal government (part open to the public).

The **Escaliers-du-Marché**, a wooden-roofed medieval staircase, links the cathedral square to *pl. de la Palud*, an ancient square, which stages a market every Wed and Sat morning. Look for the monumental 18th-century **Fontaine de la Justice** and a clock with moving figures that spring to life every hour. Also on the square are the arcades of the restored 15th–17th-century **Hôtel de Ville** (town hall). West of the cathedral, the splendid Florentine-style **Palais de Rumine**, *pl. de la Riponne,* was built by a Russian family at the turn of the century. It now houses the university, as well as several museums, including: the **Musée de Zoologie**, featuring a complete mammoth skeleton and a busy colony of ants; the **Musée cantonal des Beaux-Arts**, a permanent display of 18th–20th-century French-Swiss art, plus temporary exhibits; the **Musée d'Archéologie et d'Histoire**, containing relics from ancient times, most notably a gold bust of Marcus Aurelius.

Take a 10-min walk north-west (or bus no. 2) to the fascinating **Collection de l'Art Brut**, *av. des Bergières 11,* housed in the Château de Beaulieu. This bizarre post-war gallery was founded by a local collector who sought remarkable works of anyone who was not a trained or formal painter, from amateur dabblers and simple-minded recluses to the criminally insane. It's not a particularly comfortable place but it is compelling.

North of the Centre

The **Fondation de l'Hermitage**, *rte du Signal 2*, is an early 19th-century villa full of period fixtures and fittings, which hosts top-quality touring exhibitions of contemporary art. The view from the villa gardens, over the city and the lake to the Alps, is magnificent. For more great lake views take bus no. 16 to the **Forêt de Sauvabelin** which lies 150 m above the city centre. This 140-acre beech forest offers a choice of walking paths and encompasses a deer reserve around a small lake (a natural skating rink in winter). Paths lead to the **Vivarium**, *ch. de Boissonnet*, a reptile zoo.

Ouchy

The **quai de Belgique/quai d'Ouchy** is a shady, flower-lined, waterside promenade, with great views across Lake Geneva to the Savoy Alps. Ouchy's most prominent waterside landmark, the 13th-century keep of **Château d'Ouchy** is now a smart

hotel. The pride of the city's museums is the unique **Musée Olympique**, *quai d'Ouchy 1*, housed in a state-of-the-art complex, cleverly designed to retain the natural beauty of its surrounding park. It covers the history of the Olympic movement from Ancient Greece to Atlanta '96 and exhibits a fascinating collection of equipment and memorabilia used by famous athletes from both winter and summer games. Audio-visual displays and the latest in interactive technology allow you to focus on whichever sport or chosen year takes your fancy. Directly behind the museum is the **Musée de l'Elyseé,** *av. de l'Elysée 18*, the country's principal museum of photography, set in a 17th-century house within beautiful parkland.

Immediately east of Ouchy is **Vidy**, distinguished by its lakeside parkland where there is excellent camping and sporting facilities. It is also home to the Château de Vidy which houses the International Olympic Committee, and the remains of the Roman port of *Lousonna*. The adjacent **Musée romain de Lausanne-Vidy**, *ch. du Bois-de-Veaux 24*, will tell you more about Lausanne's Roman period.

Frequent trains link Lausanne with the waterfront towns of Vevey and Montreux (see pp. 158–160), but unless you're in a hurry take the boat. Ferries from Ouchy (see Ferries, above) also go to **Geneva** (at the western end of the lake, see p. 102) and **Evian-les-Bains** (in France, just 35-min away on the southern shore).

Two nearby places also worth a visit are Pully (bus nos. 4, 8, 9, train or boat) for its restored roman villa, and **St-Sulpice**, (regional train or boat in summer), a picturesque village with a famous 11th-century Romanesque church.

LAUSANNE–BRIG

The sophisticated lakeside resorts of Montreux and Vevey, known collectively as 'The Pearl of the Swiss Riviera', form a sharp contrast to the simple pleasures and towns of the Valais region. Once away from Lake Geneva this route largely follows the floor of the Valais so it is important to take the spectacular side-tracks to Rochers-de-Naye, Gruyères and the Grand Dixence Dam to get the most out of this trip. Sion is by far the most interesting of the Valais towns and makes a good overnight stop before continuing east.

FASTEST JOURNEY: 85 MINS

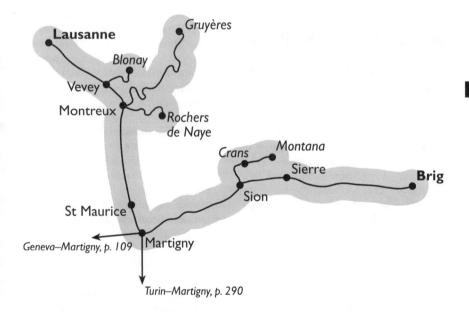

Geneva–Martigny, p. 109

Turin–Martigny, p. 290

157

TRAINS

ETT tables: 270.

FAST TRACK

One to two trains an hour operate between Lausanne and Brig taking between 85 and 115 mins for the journey.

ON TRACK

Lausanne–Vevey–Montreux
Two to three trains an hour operate

between Lausanne and Montreaux calling at Vevey en route. Lausanne to Vevey takes 20 mins, Vevey to Montreaux 8 mins.

Montreux–St-Maurice–Martigny–Sion

One to three trains an hour operate between Montreaux and Sion, most call at St-Maurice and Martigny. Montreaux to St-Maurice takes 20 mins, St-Maurice to Martigny 12 mins, Martigny to Sion 30 mins.

Sion–Sierre–Brig

An hourly service links Sion, Sierre and Brig. Sion to Sierre takes 11 mins, Sierre to Brig 35 mins.

VEVEY

Station: *Gare, tel: 921 29 16*, a 3-min walk north of *Grande Place*.

Tourist Office: *Grennette-Grande Place 29; tel: 921 48 25.*

Although Vevey has a lower profile than its glamorous lakeside neighbour, Montreux, it is at least as attractive and offers more sightseeing opportunities. The most scenic route from Lausanne is by boat (from Ouchy), disembarking at Vevey-Marché on the corner of **Grande Place** – the huge square which is the hub of the town and features the large colonnaded **La Grennette** (the Corn Exchange), built 1808. A large folklore market is held here each Sat from July through Aug. To find old Vevey explore the streets east of *Grande Place*.

Despite its modest size Vevey counts five museums, the most central being the **Swiss Camera Museum**, just off *Grande Place*. The most cultured collection is at the **Musée Jenisch** of Fine Art and Prints, *av. de la Gare 2*, including woodcuts engravings and etchings by Dürer,

Canaletto and Rembrandt. Perhaps the most popular museum is the hands-on child-friendly **Musée de l'Alimentarium** (Food Museum) on the waterfront next to Vevey-Plan landing stage. This is a Nestlé Foundation project (the group headquarters is also here), continuing a long tradition of chocolate-making in this area. The town's interesting **Musée Historique** deals with local history and in particularly its winemaking tradition, which is based on the renowned Lavaux wine country. The **Lavaux vineyards** a few miles to the east of Lausanne are famous throughout Switzerland. Organised tours are available or you can visit the vineyards and their *caveaux* (winegrower's cellars) by yourself. Enquire at the tourist information office in Lausanne.

The **Musée Suisse du Jeu** (Swiss Games Museum) is a lively collection of games through the ages, housed in the delightful Château de la Tour-de-Peilz (trolley bus 1).

⤵ SIDE TRACKS FROM VEVEY

Steam buffs should note that on a summer weekend you can take the funicular from Vevey to Blonay for a ride on a vintage steam train at the **Blonay-Chamby Railway Museum.** The line continues up to the spectacular belvédère of **Les Pléiades** (1360 m).

Literary and film buffs may already associate Vevey with Charlie Chaplin and Graham Greene. Greene died in Vevey in 1991 but is buried in the cemetery at **Corsier**, a short bus ride from Vevey. Chaplin, who died in 1977, is honoured by a memorial statue in Vevey (on *Quai Perdonnet*) though he lived in Corsier for 25 years and also lies in the Corsier Cemetery alongside his wife.

The bus to Corsier stops by the Funiculaire du **Mont Pèlerin**. which at an altitude of 1080 m is also a worthwhile excursion with fine views.

MONTREUX

Station: *Gare tel: 963 45 15*
Tourist Office: *pl. du Débarcadère; tel: 963 12 12*

ACCOMMODATION AND FOOD

Hotels are plentiful. At the top of the range are the five-star **Le Montreux Palace**, *Grand-rue 100; tel: (021) 962 12 12*, and **Royal Plaza Inter-Continental**, *Grand-rue 97; tel: (021) 963 51 31*, but there are mnay less expensive establishments, full details of which can be found at the Tourist Office.

A good budget place to eat is **Restaurant City**, *av. des Alpes, 37*, almost opposite the station. There's a good selection of self-service food and a balcony with an excellent lake view.

SIGHTSEEING

Montreux has long been renowned for its mild micro-climate and as the home of Switzerland's finest castle. During the 19th century many famous visiting writers and artists gave the town their seal of approval and with the construction of its casino in 1881 (the first in the country) Montreux launched itself as the 'Swiss Monte Carlo' celebrity-resort that it still is today.

The six-mile long **lake promenade**, beautifully landscaped with exotic trees and colourful flowers, is the place to be seen and many expensive hotels lie along here. Above, just behind the station, is the quiet old town – far removed from the money and bustle below. Between the station and the old town is the **Musée du Vieux-Montreux**.

The **Montreux Golden Rose TV**

Festival (June) and the **Montreux Jazz Festival** (July) are the two most famous of many events and conventions which bring fame and wealth to the town. If you intend staying in Montreux when either of these are on book well ahead. And for the low-down on everything that is happening in the Montreux-Vevey area pick up a copy of the excellent *Tourist Info Pass* from the tourist office.

For everyday sightseeing Montreux's big attraction is the **Château de Chillon**. This actually lies just outside Montreux, at Veytaux; take the boat, the bus (no. 1) or a 45-min waterfront stroll. It's a magnificent thoroughly medieval 13th-century fortress, quite compact, set on a rock at the water's edge, straight out of a fairy-tale. There are many rooms to explore, some are beautifully decorated and all exude an ancient atmosphere. The most famous part of the castle is the dark vaulted hall, formerly the dungeon, where the Reformation preacher, Bonivard, is said to have been chained to a pillar for four years. In 1816 Lord Byron visited the castle, heard the story of Bonivard, and wrote of his plight in the poem *The Prisoner of Chillon*. Even if you have never read the poem (which in its day put the Château on the map) you can still see Byron's name, carved by himself on Bonivard's pillar.

SIDE TRACKS FROM MONTREUX

For a magnificent view over Montreux and the eastern end of Lake Geneva board the funicular for **Rochers de Naye** (2042 m). It's an alarmingly steep 55-min climb and if you have a Swiss Pass the journey as far as Caux (1050 m) is free and very worthwhile. The summit is snow-clad for most of the year, but in summer a garden blooms with almost one thousand species of alpine

159

plants and flowers. An old-fashioned steam train makes the ascent from Caux to the summit on summer weekends and Tues–Sun in July and Aug.

One of the most popular Swiss excursion for all visitors is **Gruyères**, approximately 75 mins from Montreux (via Montbovon) or direct on one of the *Supertrain de Chocolate* or *Superpanoramic Express* specials (enquire at Montreux station). It's a compact picture-book site, set within whitewashed city walls on a green hill, below Mount Moléson (2002 m). The 13th-century Savoyard **Château de Gruyères** dominates the small traffic-free village-town and is surrounded by many fine houses dating from the 15th–17th centuries. The castle boasts fine views, a 14th-century chapel and a museum with some intersting historical treasures. Near the station is a **dairy** where you can see the world-famous local cheese being made

ST-MAURICE

Station: *Gare Care;* a 5-min walk from the Abbey.
Tourist Office: *Agaune Voyages, Grande-Rue, 48; tel: 025 65 27 77*

St-Maurice is a small town wedged between the mountains and a huge cliff, and is famous for its **Abbey Treasury**. The town has been a place of pilgrimage since the 4th century when Saint Maurice and his Theban legion were massacred for their Christian beliefs. The Treasury is a repository of 1700 years worth of pious offerings. Posted summer opening hours are 1030, 1500 and 1630 (also 0930 and 1430 July, Aug); winter 1500, 1630 only, but *tel: 025 65 11 81* to confirm. Aside from the 17th-century Augustinian Abbey itself, there is a Military Museum in the town castle and a **Grotte aux Fées** ('Fairy

Grotto') complete with underground lake and waterfall.

SION

Station: *Gare; tel: 157 33 33,* the old town is a 5–10 min walk along *av. de la Gare/r. de Lausanne.*
Tourist Office: *pl. de la Planta: tel: 022 85 86.*

ACCOMMODATION AND FOOD

There's a **HI hostel**, *r. de l'Industrie, tel: 027 23 74 38* just behind the station. For a little more comfort but still within the low–budget price range try the two-star **Hôtel de la Matze**; *tel: 027 22 36 67, r. de Lausanne* (new town section), or the one-star **Hôtel La Chane**, *Porte Neuve 9; tel: 027 22 32 71,* right in the old town. The restaurant of the latter is noted for its Valais cuisine.

SIGHTSEEING

Sion, the capital of the Valais, is a picturesque and lively small town, harmoniously blending old and new. Its most striking visual feature is its two castles, perched on adjacent hillocks, which rise like two sore thumbs from the Valais floor. Orientation is simple with the new town to either side of *av. de la Gare*, which leads from the station to the main city square, *pl. de la Planta*. From here *r. de Lausanne* runs into the old town.

Sion has a colourful history of powerful bishops who ruled the Valais as a separate state and the **Musée de l'Eveche/Trésor de la Cathédrale** (Bishop's Museum/ Cathedral Treasury), on the corner of *pl. de la Planta*, displays some of their past wealth. Off *r. de Lausanne*, hidden away in a narrow arcade leading to *r. de Conthey*, is the **Maison Supersaxo**, built in 1505 by George Supersaxo, a scheming State Chancellor (who adopted his curious name from Latin). Only the staircase and two rooms are open but it's worth a visit (free entry) for its opulent ceiling alone. A few yards away is the landmark 17th-century **Hôtel de la Ville** (town hall), brightly painted and topped with a fine astronomical clock. Its front doors are superbly carved and there's more intricate workmanship to admire inside.

To either side of the town hall narrow alleys lead to *r. des Châteaux*, which leads uphill to the town's castles, passing en route the **Musée Cantonal des Beaux-Arts** (Fine Arts Museum) and the **Musée d'Archéologie**. The former is housed in La Majorie, the old bishops' palace.

The highest of the two castles, the **Château de Tourbillon**, built in the 13th century, burned down in 1788 and is now a mere shell. It's a tiring climb but arguably worth it for the views. The lower castle, the **Collégiale (Église fortifiée) de Valère** is actually a picturesque fortified church complex. The 12th-century Gothic church, in need of some repair, is very atmospheric, with an unusual organ loft, jutting high from the wall looking just like a ship's stern. The organ dates from the 14th century and is said to be the oldest playable one in the world. There are also 15th-century frescos, superb capitals and fine 17th-century choir stalls to admire. Above the church is a colourful museum including Roman antiquities and medieval religious pieces.

Back in the old town wander round the cobbled streets and alleyways and visit the **Notre-Dame-du-Glarier Cathedral** which dates from the 15th century, notable for the tombs of many bishops, its altar and carved choir stalls. The unusual stone tower a few yards away rejoices in the name **Tour des Sorciers** (the Sorceror's Tower) and is a relic of the 12th-century city walls.

SIDE TRACKS FROM SION

The Sion area is famous for winter sports with its most famous resort, **Crans-Montana**, 40 min away by postbus. This is actually two resorts in one, of which Crans-sur-Sierre, set around a number of small lakes, and renowned for its golf courses, is the most attractive. Montana lies 1.5 km east, connected to Sierre (see below) by funicular and postbus.

If you would like to see one of the country's greatest civil engineering projects, take the postbus from the station to Dixence to witness the **Grand Dixence Dam**. The favourite statistic is that the dam is twice the height and twice the volume of the Great Pyramid in Egypt. Fly up above the lake on the Dixence–Lac-des-Dix cable car for marvellous views of the dam and the surrounding Hérémence valley.

SIERRE

Tourist Office: *pl. de la Gare, 10; tel: 027 55 85 35*

Sierre, also known by its German name Siders, is a relatively quiet, small town. Its main street *r. du Bourg* boasts several fine 16th-and 17th-century houses and one of these, the **Hôtel Château-Bellerive** is open to the public, housing a museum dedicated to the Austro-German poet Rainer Maria Rilke (1875–1926).

The area's sunny climate and chalky slopes produce some of the country's best wines. You can learn about them at the **Musée de la Vigne et du Vin**, in the 16th-century Château de Villa, on *r. Manoir*.

LAUSANNE–INTERLAKEN

The burgeoning ski playground of Gstaad, which stretches as far as Château d'Oex (20 km to the west) and Zweisimmen (25 km to the northwest), is the dominant feature of this route. Don't let the expensive image put you off, however, as the magnificent snowy countryside is one of the joys of Switzerland.

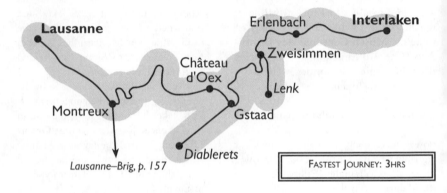

Lausanne–Brig, p. 157

FASTEST JOURNEY: 3HRS

TRAINS

ETT tables: 260, 280, 270, 275, 276

FAST TRACK

The fastest and simplest way is via Bern where a change of train is needed. Overall journey time is around 3 hrs.

ON TRACK

Lausanne–Montreux
A 30-min run at least once each hour.

Montreux–Château d'Oex–Gstaad
A roughly hourly service throughout the day operates between Montreux and Gstaad. All trains call at Château d'Oex.

Montreux to Château d'Oex takes around 1 hr, Château d'Oex to Gstaad 20 mins.

Gstaad–Zweisimmen
The 30-min journey operates once or twice each hour.

Zweisimmen–Erlenbach
An hourly service taking 30 mins.

Erlenbach–Interlaken
A change of train at Spiez is required Overall journey time is 35 mins.

MONTREUX

For the description of Montreux see the Lausanne–Brig route, p. 157.

Scenic Travel

For the best possible views along this very scenic journey change at Montreux and board the **Crystal Panoramic Express** (operated by the Montreux-Oberland-Bernois MOB railway) with its specially designed maximum visibility carriages. This stops at Château d'Oex, Gstaad and Zweisimmen. This service only runs at certain times so consult your timetable or call MOB; *tel: 021 963 5125* for details. As this is a private company Swiss Pass is not valid for free travel but holders will qualify for a discount.

CHÂTEAU D'OEX

Station: *tel: 157 33 33.*
Tourist Office: *tel: 029 4 77 88.*

Chateau d'Oex (pronounced 'day') is a ski resort famous for its **International Hot-Air Ballooning Week**, which takes place every Jan. This is the world's premier mountain ballooning event and is held here on account of its special microclimate. It is a specially magical sight to watch 80 giant multi-coloured balloons (entry is by invitation only) rise almost silently and effortlessly against a Christmas-card backdrop, but if you can't make it then, Châteaux D'Oex is still worth a visit as balloons are frequently in the sky here (a flight costs around SFr.325). If you plan to stay in Château d'Oex during that week do book well ahead. In the summer there are many other sporting activities on offer, including rafting, kayaking, canyoning and hiking in the surrounding Enhaut countryside.

For non-sporting types the **Musée du Vieux Pays-D'Enhaut** features bygones and room reconstructions, and the local industry of cheesemaking is demonstrated to tourists at the **Le Chalet** *fromagerie*. The end product is a variety known as *Etivaz*, named after a neighbouring village.

Despite its upmarket image there is a reasonable range of cheap accommodation in the village; **HI: Les Riaux**; *tel: 029 4 64 04*, is a 10-min walk from the station. The one-star **La Pritanière**; *tel: 029 4 61 13*, is simple and friendly, while the two-star **Des Bouquetins**; *tel: 029 4 57 04*, costs little more and is surrounded by meadows.

GSTAAD

Station: *tel: 157 33 33*
Tourist Office: *tel: 030 4 71 71*

Gstaad has been a celebrity resort for some many years and attracts winter sports followers on account of its excellent facilities and its scenic **Weisse Hochland** ('the White Highlands') skiing area.

The original village has been overtaken by tourism but at least retains its pretty chalet character. Sitting comfortably high above the village is the famous **Gstaad Palace Hotel**, built in 1812 in neo-baroque castle style. If you have to ask the price, it's too expensive!

In summer, cableways transport walkers and mountaineers, and sports such as golf, horse riding and tennis (the Swiss International Tennis Open is held here) replace snowboarding, telemark and cross-country skiing. Sports aside, there is little to see in Gstaad though culture vultures do beat a path to the annual **Yehudi Menuhin Festival** of classical music concerts (held in Aug). The prime venue is the beautiful 15th-century **Church of St-Maurice** in the adjacent pretty village of **Saanen**, a 5-min train journey from Gstaad.

Also in Saanen is the **HI: Chalet Rüblihorn**; *tel: 030 4 13 43* and a range of more affordable accommodation.

163

↱ **SIDE TRACK
FROM GSTAAD**

The formidable glacier of **Les Diablerets** is a popular mountain excursion with visitors to the Vaud region. From the village of Les Diablerets (1150 m) a bus runs to Col du Pillon, then cable cars ascend via Pierre Pointes and Cabane des Diablerets to the top station of **Scex** (pronounced Say) **Rouge** at an altitude of 3000 m.

The views are wonderful and for the more active there is all-year skiing. A specially designed 'snowbus' on caterpillar tracks explores the immediate surrounds. ⛷

ZWEISIMMEN

Often overlooked by visitors, this is the capital of the Simmental region and functions not only as a holiday overspill for Gstaad, but as an agricultural and market centre. It's a pretty village with many chalets in the elaborate picturesque style for which the Simmental is famed. The 15th-century **Church of St Maria** also boasts some fine woodwork in its lovely ceiling and there are frescos to enjoy too, featuring St George and the Dragon. A museum of local Simmental history occupies the old schoolhouse in the village.

↱ **SIDE TRACK
FROM ZWEISIMMEN**

Lenk is a skiing, mountaineering and health resort, once famous for its sulphur springs. If you're not in a sporting mood or don't wish to take the waters, it's still worth a trip to see the town's waterfalls. From the village a 10-min postbus ride will take you to the powerful **Simmenfälle** which roar down the side of the Wildstrubel mountain (3243 m). Also worth seeing are the

Iffigenfälle (3 km south of the village, no public transport) with a spectacular drop of some 130 m. ⛷

ERLENBACH

Station: *tel: 157 33 33*

The most distinctive feature of this unspoiled place is the saddleback roofs and coloured façades of its houses, most of which date from the 18th century. It's worth the walk uphill to the **parish church** (take the covered wooden stairs off *Dorfstr.*) to discover its excellent 15th-century murals. Intrepid types might like to note that white water rafting is available in Erlenbach. From the station it's a 15-min walk to the cable car which ascends the **Stockhorn** (2190 m) and offers marvellous views across the mountains and the lakes of Interlaken.

'*Winter Madness*'

Before 1850 it would have been regarded as eccentric to spend a holiday in Switzerland in the winter, among howling winds, biting cold and avalanches. Sensible people wintered on the French Riviera. However, when Dr Spengler cured two patients of tuberculosis at his Davos clinic, the word spread that Alpine air was good for the health. Then Johannes Badrutt of St Moritz bet two of his English summertime guests that they would enjoy a winter visit – if they didn't, he would refund the cost. They did, and Swiss hotels and resorts became fashionable for winter holidays, providing creature comforts, sleigh-rides, skating competitions, and the like. In the 1880s skiing reached Switzerland, imported from Scandinavia, largely by British sportsmen. This made Switzerland no. 1 in winter sports destinations, a position which it has never lost.

LIECHTENSTEIN

This tiny hidden piece of Europe, wedged between Switzerland (from whom it has been independent since 1719) and Austria, covers just 158 sq km. The Principality is green, mountainous, certainly attractive, yet little visited and little known. For travellers, as opposed to mere tourists, such characteristics may prove an irresistible draw.

TOURIST INFORMATION

Liechtenstein National Tourist Office/Verkehrsbüro: *Städtle 37, Vaduz; tel: (075) 232 14 43.* Open Mon–Fri 0800–1200, 1300–1700. This is by far the best office in Liechtenstein so make good use of it. The staff may be busy stamping passports (see below) but once available they can be very helpful, suggesting routes, offering guide services, booking accommodation and generally pointing you in the right direction. Do pick up a copy of the invaluable *Liechtenstein Tourist Guide.*

ARRIVING, DEPARTING, GETTING AROUND

The railway passes through Liechtenstein linking the Swiss town of Buchs (see p. xxx) with the Austrian town of Feldkirch (see p. xxx). En route it stops at Schaan, Nendeln and Schaanwald (Swiss Pass valid), though only Nendeln boasts station facilities. However, as Vaduz is by far the most sensible first port of call, the best way into the principality is by postbus. The nearest stations on the Swiss side are at Sargans (17 km from Vaduz) and Buchs (7

km from Vaduz). From here regular post-buses cross the border, which is signposted but easily missed. There are no formalities on the Swiss frontier; the same regulations apply on the Austrian side as for entering Switzerland.

All buses go to the capital Vaduz, stopping conveniently almost right outside the tourist office on the main street, *Städtle.* The postbus departure rank, from where routes service most of the country, is opposite. Fares up to 13 km cost SFr.2, over 13 km is SFr.3. Swiss Pass holders ride free.

VADUZ

Tourist office: see above.

The two-street town of Vaduz is certainly one of the smallest European capitals but when the tour buses come into town there's no lack of activity. The first mad scramble is for the tourist office, not to glean information, but to get passports stamped! This is not mandatory, merely a novelty which the tourist office happily promote. It costs SFr.2 and, judging from the queues, is one of the Principality's top revenue sources. If you're unlucky enough to arrive requiring information at the same time, it's best to come back later. After a coffee and souvenir shopping, it's back on the coach for a whistle stop tour of the rest of Liechtenstein, or back to the country of origin.

STAYING IN VADUZ

Accommodation
The two best affordable hotels are the **Landhaus Prasch**, *Zollstr. 16; tel: (075) 232 31 40*, and the **Hotel Engel**, *Städtle*

165

13; tel: (075) 232 03 13. Both are three-star and charge SFr.120–150 per double room per night.

Rooms in private homes may also be available, though in the 1995 official guide only one in Vaduz is listed; **Romy Nigg**, *Austr. 21; tel: (075) 232 29 94.*

Eating and Drinking

The two finest places to eat and drink in Vaduz, albeit at a price, are the **Gasthof Löwen**; *Herrengasse 35; tel: (075) 232 00 66,* and **Restaurant Torkel**; *Hintergasse, tel: (075) 232 44 10.* Both are a 3–5-min walk from the centre. The Torkel is situated right in the Prince's own vineyards and is therefore an excellent choice for wine lovers. The 600-year-old Löwen is also set in a vineyard with a delightful outdoor eating area. Goethe ate here, probably admiring the 16th-century fresco in

the dining room. The food at both establishments is French influenced.

More affordable choices include the **Hotel Engel**, *Städtle 13; tel: (075) 232 03 13,* or the cheap-and-cheerful, English pub-like **Old Castle Inn**, *Äulerstr.*,

The best spot for a picnic is the small **Haberfeld park**, a short walk from the centre (pick up a map from the tourist office).

The main historical sight in the capital is **Schloss Vaduz** (Vaduz Castle). Most of it dates from the 16th century, though parts go back some 800 years. This is still very much the home of the Prince and his family and unfortunately for visitors is not open to the public. The castle is perched high above the main street and only a determined effort to look upwards will spot it – indeed many visitors must leave completely oblivious to its existence. It's a steep walk via *Backagässli* (by the Burg Brasserie) and *Haldenweg* but it's well worthwhile for the view and the chance to peer through the gates.

Next to the tourist office is the state's major cultural attraction, the **Staatliche Kunstsammlung** (State Art Collection). This gallery, with revolving exhibitions, draws from the private collection of the Prince and contains some first-class works;. Recent exhibitions have featured Picasso, Old Italian Masters, German Expressionism plus Klee, Kandinsky, Klimt and Macke.

On the other side of the tourist office is the **Postage Stamp Museum**, a one-room treat for philatelists who don't mind sliding out trays to reveal rare and unusual issues, but of limited general appeal.

Another specialist museum, the **Ski-Museum**, Bangarten 10, presents a century of European skiing.

Behind the Scenery

Though you would never guess so from the pastoral and mountain landscape, Liechtenstein is one of the most highly industrialised nation in the world in relation to its size: chemical, pharmaceutical, metal and food industries providing work and wealth for its 30,000 inhabitants. The per-capita income for the Principality is also one of the world's highest. Tourism is a major contributor and philately also brings in significant revenue. Liechtenstein stamps are highly collectable, reflected not only by the Postal Museum but by the size of the Vaduz post office/philatelic centre, from where stamps are mailed to all corners of the world.

The state's advantageous banking and tax laws mean that many foreign companies are officially based (however tenuously) in Liechtenstein.

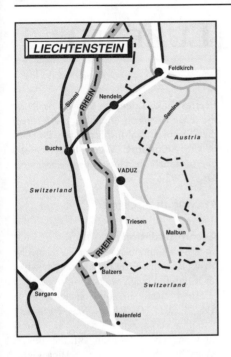

(The Liechtenstein National Museum is presently closed, awaiting a new home.)

Walking back along *Städtle* in the direction of Buchs is the Parish Church. This is of no special interest but the adjoining area contains the **Tombs of the Princes** of Liechtenstein. Enquire at the tourist office for details of access.

OUTSIDE VADUZ

There are only 46 hotels in the whole of Liechtenstein so it's best to book as early as possible. Vaduz can be used as a base for anywhere in the principality but beware, the postbus service finishes quite early in the evening. Prices are comparable with Swiss rural areas.

The only **HI** hostel is the **Youth Hostel Schaan-Vaduz**, *untere Rütigasse, 6, tel: (075) 232 50 22*, located between Schaan and Vaduz; (bus no. 5 from Schaan railway halt, then 5-min walk).

Campsites: **Mittagspitze**, *Triesen; tel: (075) 392 26 86*. **Bendern**; *tel: (075) 373 12 11* Ask the tourist office for details of rooms in private houses (numbers are usually very limited).

Balzers

You'll have a good opportunity to see impressive **Schloss Gutenburg**, atop the village, as the postbus does a 360-degree circuit of Balzers. There's a picturesque church and the whole scene is set against the snowcapped mountains. (Note: the castle has been closed for major refurbishment so may not be open to the public.)

Malbun

Tourist Office: *tel: (075) 263 65 77*.

At an altitude of 1600 m Malbun is the principality's winter sports centre with reasonable, relatively inexpensive facilities for beginners and intermediate skiers, albeit on a small scale.

Nendeln

If you are taking the train to Feldkirch and have time to kill at Nendeln, this is the home of **Schaedler Keramik**, the principality's oldest ceramic works, established in 1836. You can watch pottery being made and painted (weekdays only, closed 1200–1330).

Triesenberg

Tourist Office: *Dorfzentrum; tel: (075) 262 19 26*.

This is the prettiest village in Liechtenstein, beautifully set on the mountain side above Vaduz featuring many old Valaisian style houses. The **Walser Heimatmuseum** (open afternoons only) explains how Triesenberg was settled by people from the Swiss Valais region in the 13th century and exhibits other aspects of village history.

167

LUCERNE (LUZERN)

Lucerne is the quintessential Swiss picture-postcard city; narrow pedestrianised streets leading to medieval squares covered with picturesque frescos; a rushing river criss-crossed with ancient, covered wooden bridges; a skyline crowded with ancient towers and spires and the whole set on a glorious lake amid mighty mountains. No wonder then that tourists have been coming here since the mid-19th century, encouraged by luminaries such as Alexander Dumas, Mark Twain and Richard Wagner who have all waxed lyrical about the town. And despite some signs of modern commercialism, in essence Lucerne has changed little since their day.

TOURIST INFORMATION

Tourist Information: *Frankenstr. 1; tel: 51 71 71* (by station). Open Mon–Fri 0830–1800; Sat 0900–1700; Sun 0900–1300. In winter it closes Mon–Fri 1200–1400; Sat 1300 and all day Sun.

ARRIVING AND DEPARTING

Station: Lucerne **Bahnhof** lies on the south bank of the River Reuss, where it meets the lake; *tel: 157 33 33.* It is less than 5-mins walk from the old centre.

GETTING AROUND

The old town centre is small and mainly pedestrianised. Most of the town's attractions are within or immediately adjacent to this area.

Ferries: **Lake Lucerne,** known locally as the *Vierwaldstättersee* (literally, the lake of the four forest cantons) is plied by 20 craft of the **Schiffahrt Vierwaldstättersee**, five of which are vintage paddlesteamers, *tel: 367 67 67.*

STAYING IN LUCERNE

Accommodation

Lucerne is so popular and such a relatively small place, that early booking is advisable for its limited range of cheap options.

Hotel chains in town include: *AC, BW, IE, MO, Tp, Rk* and *SL.*

For a room with a view in a picturesque central location on the River Reuss, try the busy one-star **Pickwick**, *Rathausquai 6; tel: 51 59 27*, where all bedrooms overlook Lake Lucerne. There is a popular bar here so you shouldn't want for company. In the same budget-price band are the **Tourist Hotel**, *St Karliquai 12; tel: 51 24 74*, set in a quiet location by the river and the city walls, and the **Schlüssel**, *Franziskanerpl. 12; tel: 23 10 61.*

HI: *Sedelstr. 12, Am Rotsee; tel: 36 88 00*, is a large modern facility by a lake just north-west of town (bus no. 18 to *Gopplismoos*; after 1930, tram no. 1: *Schlossberg* plus 10–15-min walk). It's a 30-min walk from Bhf but from the town centre you can halve this time if you have a good map. **Campsite:** *Lidostr. 8; tel: 31 21 46* (bus no. 2: *Verkehrshaus*), is in an enviable position just behind the Lido and beach, a 30-min walk east of town.

Eating and Drinking

Competition for visitors' francs tends to

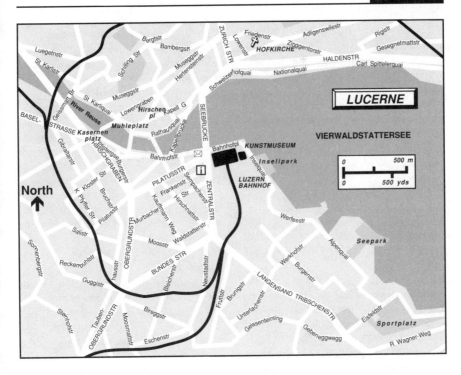

keep prices reasonable, even in the restaurants and cafés dotted around Lucerne's prettiest squares, so shop around. For a good selection of different *rösti* or cheese dishes in a friendly rustic setting, try **Walliser Spycher**, *Eisengasse; tel: 52 85 29*. In a similar vein, but more upmarket, is the **Walliser Kanne**, *Burgerstr. 3; tel: 23 07 47*. **Café Hug**, *Mühlepl.* (by the Spreuerbrücke), enjoys a conservatory by the river and is a busy daytime place serving affordable snacks and full meals.

Gourmets with fat wallets should ask at the tourist office for a *City Highlights* brochure. On the 'Culinary Delights' page special restaurant menus are highlighted. Top of the pile is **Le Trianon** in the **Grand Hotel**, opened in 1870 by César Ritz and Auguste Escoffier.

The best place for a picnic is by the lake, behind the station, either at the **Inselipark** or (further along) the **Seepark**.

Lucerne's speciality is *Kügelipasteti*, a large vol-au-vent case filled with meat and mushrooms in a rich sauce. Fish from the lake also features in posher restaurants.

Communications

The main **post office** is on the corner of *Bahnhofstr.* and *Bahnhofpl.* Open Mon–Fri 0730–1830, Sat 0800–1100. The telephone area code is *041*.

ENTERTAINMENT

Given its popularity Lucerne has surprisingly little organised nightlife. Only lovers of kitsch should be tempted to the folklore night at the **Stadtkeller**, while the seedy nightspots on *Eisengasse* should be given a very wide berth. For a laid-back blues-and-jazz atmosphere with occasional live music, moderately priced French cuisine and snacks, visit **Bistro du Theatre**, *Theaterstr. 5; tel: 210 12 74.* Nearby you can get a panorama of Lucerne by night from the **Penthouse Bar** (with penthouse prices) on top of the Hotel Astoria, *Pilatusstr. 22.* The main event in the city's social calendar is the **International Music Festival** featuring world-class classical music performances, running from mid-Aug through the first week in Sept.

SIGHTSEEING

Old Town

Walking tours are conducted daily at 0930 and 1400 mid-April–Oct; Wed and Sat during the rest of the year. Tours last 2 hrs and the price, including a drink, is SFr.15. From mid-May–Oct on Sat, 'Tower Power' walks are also given along the city walls. Meet at the tourist office.

Lucerne's trademark is its picturesque 14th-century **Kapellbrücke**, a wooden-roofed pedestrian bridge that straggles crookedly across the **River Reuss**. Unfortunately a large section of this burned down in 1993 and the new lighter coloured replacement wood can clearly be distinguished from the ancient boards. From the roof beams are suspended a famous series of 17th-century triangular-shaped paintings of historical scenes. Some of these also perished in the fire but you would be hard pressed to distinguish originals from expert copies. Halfway across the bridge is a sturdy 13th-century octagonal **Water Tower** which has undergone several changes of function over the centuries, including use as a gaol (not open to the public).

Near the Kapellbrücke on the south side of the river is the **Jesuit Church**, plain from the outside, but with a gorgeous pink-and-white baroque interior dating from 1677. Behind it is another fine

church, the **Franziskanerkirche**, (the Franciscan Church) originally built in the 13th century. A short distance further along the river is another medieval roofed bridge, the **Spreuerbrücke**, also with 17th-century paintings – here depicting the macabre Dance of Death. The paintings on this bridge and on the Kapellbrücke are illuminated by night, though arachnophobes should note that this also brings to light huge spiders in the eaves!

Standing to either side of the bridge on the south bank are two of Lucerne's less-visited museums. The **Historisches Museum**, *Pfistergasse 24*, is housed in the old 16th-century arsenal. The **Natur-Museum**, *Kasernenpl. 6*, dedicated to natural history, won a European Museum of the Year award in 1987 and features live animals .

Cross the river to **Weinmarkt** and admire the fine wall frescos – those on the **Hotel Des Balances** are notable. The adjacent square of **Kornmarkt** features more murals: look for those on the **Zunfthaus zu Pfistern**, formerly a guild-hall, now a restaurant. An odd bulbous roof, built to a weatherproof Berne farm-house design, and a handsome blue-and-red clock face, top the landmark 17th-century **Rathaus** (town hall). Its arcades are filled by market stalls on Tues and Sat. Adjacent to the Rathaus is **Am Rhyn Haus**, *Furrengasse 21*, which contains a small collection of works executed by Picasso towards the end of his life. Of equal if not greater interest however, is the collection of some 200 photographs by David Douglas Duncan, showing Picasso at work and relaxing. Two blocks north of here, **Hirschenpl.** is adorned with yet more murals but the prize for outdoor art must surely go to the two giant wall paintings on tiny **Sternenpl.**, which are spectacularly illuminated by night.

Löwenpl. square, to the east end of the old town is home to a cluster of attractions. King of them all is the **Löwendenkmal** (Lion Memorial), a massive and touching portrayal of a dying lion, carved out of a cliff, 'the saddest and most moving piece of stone in the world', according to Mark Twain. It commemorates the Swiss Guards massacred in Paris during the French Revolution, and is almost as much a city symbol as the Kapellbrücke. Adjacent is the **Gletschergarten** (Glacier Garden), *Denkmalstr. 4*, an interesting natural phenomenon created by movements of the Reuss glacier millions of years ago. You'll need a guide to make sense of it however. There's also an ingenious Victorian mirror-maze here of which you will struggle to make sense!

The **Alpineum**, *Denkmalstr. 11*, features five dioramas of famous Swiss mountain scenes. Unless this is your particular cup of tea however, ignore it and cross the square to the **Bourbaki Panorama**, *Löwenstr. 18*, an unusual, huge and very impressive 360-degree, late 19th-century painting depicting the retreat into Switzerland from a Franco-German battle. It's a lot more interesting than it sounds.

For an excellent view, ascend the hill, starting due west from *Löwenpl.*, to the **Museggmauer**, well-preserved remnants of the old city's 14th-century fortifications. You can follow this all the way and climb three of its nine surviving towers, as it curves westwards to finish close to the northern end of Spreuerbrücke at the fortified gate of **Nolliturm**.

Lakeside

The major landmark immediately east of the old town is the graceful twin-spired **Hofkirche** (Cathedral), which features an organ with 4950 pipes plus a 10-ton bell.

The main lakeside attraction is the **Verkehrshaus** (Transport Museum), *Lidostr. 5*, 2 km east of town (near the campsite), which can be reached by a pleasant 30-min lakeside walk, by bus no. 2, or by boat. This is the biggest transport museum in Europe and is also the country's most visited museum (free to InterRailers). Exhibits span the ages and the whole transport spectrum from penny-farthings to space rockets. There is a 360-degree cinema, a planetarium, a train cabin-simulator and lots of interactive exhibits. Allow at least half a day here, then repair to the adjacent **Lido** swimming pool which also boasts a small sandy beach.

On the opposite side of the lake, 1.5 km south-east of the centre (bus nos 6, 7 or 8; boat to Tribschen; 30-min walk from the station) lies the **Richard Wagner Museum**, *Tribschen, Wagnerweg 27*. During Wagner's six years here he composed *Siegfried* and the *Meistersinger*.

The **Kunstmuseum** (Museum of Fine Art), *Robert-Zünd-str.*, next to the railway station is only worth a visit if you fancy the current touring exhibition, as the permanent collection is surprisingly small.

OUT OF TOWN

Mountains

A trip to **Mt Pilatus** (2132 m) is one of the favourite days out from Lucerne, not only for the views but for the variety of transport that may be taken en route. You could take the train to **Alpnachstad** (journey time 20 mins) but the lake ferries are much more inviting, and just when it seems that you have gone right past the mighty mountain, the base station for the cog railway heaves into view. This little red railway is the steepest of its kind in the world, at its most inclined crawling up the mountain at a vertiginous 48-degree angle. A cable car makes the long descent on the other side of the mountain to **Kriens,** from where a short walk will take you to the no. 1 bus stop and return to Lucerne.

Just as popular is a trip up the 'Queen of Mountains', **Mt Rigi** (1798 m); see p. 336. Take the boat to **Vitznau** (Swiss Pass valid), then the railway and finally the cable car to **RigiKulm** which is within a 5-min walk of the summit. On a clear day the view is magnificent. You can come back via **Weggis** (change at Rigi Kaltbad).

Other good mountain excursions include the **Stanserhorn** (via Stans, 20 min by train from Lucerne), the **Klewenalp** (via Beckenried, on the lake), and **Titlis**, see p. 173.

Lake Lucerne

There are many sights to see from the boat en route to Flüelen, part of the *William Tell Express* excursion (see also p. 176). Three are particularly important, and all

are in the beautiful fjord-like southern part of the lake known as the **Urnersee** (Lake Uri). As the boat leaves Brunnen you will see a 26-m high obelisk-shaped rock protuding from the lake. This crag is known as the **Schillerstein**, a tribute to Friedrich Schiller, who wrote the play *Wilhelm Tell* in 1859. **Rütli**, the next stop, is where in 1307 the 'Oath of Eternal Alliance' was declared by the cantons of Uri, Schwyz and Nidwalden with the intent of driving the hated Austrian Habsburgs from the country. Although the oath is not connected to William Tell, he was part of the struggle against the Austrians. There's no need to disembark as you can see the **Rütli Meadow**, where the meeting happened, from the boat.

Two stops after Rütli is Tellsplatte where **Tellskapelle** (Tell Chapel) is covered in murals which relate how our hero escaped from his captors at this spot.

LUCERNE–INTERLAKEN

This relatively short journey is particularly enjoyable for its lakeside scenery. Lake Lucerne may only be glimpsed fleetingly but the Sarnersee and the Lungernsee are appetisers for the beautiful Brienzersee (Lake Brienz). Brienz, with its excursions, is worth at least a day in its own right and another pleasurable option is to take the boat from here to Interlaken.

FASTEST JOURNEY: 2 HRS

Lucerne

Hergiswil

Alpnachstad

Brienz

Interlaken

Meiringen

Mt Titlis

173

TRAINS

ETT table: 285.

FAST TRACK

 An hourly service taking nearly 2 hrs to reach Interlaken Ost

ON TRACK

 Lucerne (Luzern)–Hergiswil–Alpnachstad–Meiringen–Brienz–Interlaken

The hourly service calls at all these stations. Luzern to Hergiswil takes 12 mins, Hergiswil to Alpnachstad 5 mins, Alpnachstad to Meiringen 1 hr 14 mins, Meiringen to Brienz 13 mins and Brienz to Interlaken Ost 21 mins.

HERGISWIL

Hergiswil serves as the starting point for a side track to Mt Titlis.

SIDE TRACK FROM HERGISWIL

Highest of all the peaks in this spectacular region is **Mt Titlis**, perched at 3020 m directly above the village of **Engelberg** (an hour from Lucerne). Do visit Engleberg's huge **Benedictine monastery** (tours Mon–Sat) and baroque monastery church. From the village centre it's a 45-min three-part cable-car ride to the summit of Mt Titlis, with the last section of the ascent made in the huge **Rotair**, the first revolving cable car in the world. The marvellous views en route change from the grassy valley floor to icy glacier crevasses. From the peak observation area you can see from the Bernese Alps to the Jura. On the snow-covered summit there's an ice palace and glacier walks. 🏔

ALPNACHSTAD

See Lucerne chapter, p. 171.

MEIRINGEN

Station: Bahnhof; *tel: 157 22 22.*
Tourist Office: Verkehrsbüro, *Bahnhofstr. 22; tel: (036) 71 43 22.*

Meiringen is a pleasant, largely modern, small town with two strange claims to fame. In the late 18th century it is said that the meringue was born here (hence its name) and a hundred years later this is where the great Sherlock Holmes met his end, along with the arch-villain Moriarty. Well, not actually in Meiringen, but at the **Reichenbach Falls** a 10–15-min walk from town. Before heading off there, visit the small **Sherlock Holmes Museum**, located in the basement of the English church, which features a thorough interpretation of the great detective's fictional dwelling at 221b Baker Street, London. Continue the pilgrimage by following the signposts to the funicular railway which ascends to the Reichenbach Falls. These are best seen in full flood in summer; in winter water is diverted from them for hydro-electric purposes.

The 17th-century **church** of St Michael is one of the few old buildings to have survived fires which devastated the town in the last century.

BRIENZ

Station: Bahnhof; *tel: 157 22 22.*
Tourist Office: Verkehrsbüro, *Hauptstr. 143; tel: (036) 51 32 42.*

Brienz is a pleasant quiet alternative base away from the high-season crowds of Lucerne and Interlaken. There are two campsites, **Camping Aaregg**; *tel: (036) 51 18 43* by the lake, a 15-min walk east of the centre and almost adjacent, **Camping Seegärtli**, *tel: (036) 51 13 51*, next to a small beach. There's a handful of reasonably-priced hotels. **HI:** *Strandweg 10; tel: (036) 51 11 52.*

Wood carving is the hallmark of Brienz. Most of the picturesque chalets in this small village-town advertise the skills of the local craftsmen and there's no shortage of wooden souvenirs. The **Schnitzlerschule**, *Schleegasse*, (wood-carving museum) and its violin-making school are open to visitors' gaze (most Wed afternoons). The town's charm also lies in its lakeside setting. Take the short walk along the front to the lovely **church** which boasts some fine exterior paintings.

Brienz also has two excellent short excursions to offer. Opposite the station, the **Brienzer Rothorn rack railway** is the last steam-powered cog railway in Switzerland. It's a wonderful sight, puffing its way up to the summit of the **Rothorn** height (2350 m). Beware, however, that electric trains also make the ascent so enquire at the Rothorn Bahn station; *tel: (036) 51 12 32*, to ensure a steam ride. Also from here, buses run to the celebrated **Ballenberg Freilichtmuseum** (Open-Air Museum). Here, over 70 picturesque farmhouses and buildings, demonstrating a whole variety of regional styles, have been moved in their entirety, in order to create a new 'living museum' village. Traditional crafts and industry, including wood-turning and roof-making are demonstrated, and there are special events days (craft fairs, sheep shearing) too. It's a big site, so allow at least half a day and consider taking your own food, as picnic or barbeque facilities are provided. Local foods, such as Ballenberg sausages smoked on site, are a tempting picnic treat.

BRÜNIG PANORAMIC EXPRESS

Reserve now!

Luzern
Pilatus
Sarnen
Brienzer Rothorn
Brienz
Brünig
Interlaken
Meiringen
Jungfrau-Region

Contact (UK):
Switzerland Tourism
Swiss Federal Railways
Swiss Centre, Swiss Court
London W1V 8EE
Telefon: (0171) 734 19 21
Telefax: (0171) 437 45 77

Contact (CH):
Incoming Services
Schweizerische
Bundesbahnen
CH-8058 Zürich Flughafen
Telefon: 0041 1 814 18 03
Telefax: 0041 1 813 03 30

SBB Brünig

LUCERNE–MILAN

Lucerne

Flüelen

Altdorf

Locarno

Bellinzona

Lugano

Como

Milan

FASTEST JOURNEY: 4 HRS 15 MINS

This picturesque journey includes some of the finest lake scenery in both Switzerland and Italy and traverses historic passes between the two countries. Once through the Gotthard tunnel the scenery changes dramatically from snowy peaks and wooden chalets to an emerald green valley dotted with rustic granite houses and tall campaniles.

The first part of the journey runs through William Tell country, and a special 'William Tell Express' (by boat and train) runs along the route between Lucerne and Lugano; for details contact the Lucerne tourist office; *tel: 041 51 18 91.* See also the Lucerne chapter, p. 172.

TRAINS

ETT tables: 84, 290.

FAST TRACK

One train every two hours runs between Lucerne and Milano Centrale. The journey takes 4 hrs 15 mins.

ON TRACK

Lucerne (Luzern)–Flüelen
One train every two hours takes 1 hr. An alternative to rail is the *William Tell Express,* (see p. 172) which covers this part of the journey by boat.

Flüelen–Bellinzona
An hourly service takes 37 mins.

Bellinzona–Lugano

Two or three trains an hour taking around 30 mins.

Lugano–Como

An hourly service, taking 40 mins.

Como–Milan (Milano)

A roughly hourly service links Como with Milano Centrale. The journey takes 40 mins.

FLÜELEN

This village serves as the starting point for a side track deeper into William Tell country.

SIDE TRACK FROM FLÜELEN

A bus service links Flüelen with Aldorf, which lies just to the south of the village. The journey takes 7 mins.

ALTDORF

Tourist Office: next to Tell Memorial, *Rathauspl. 7; tel: (044) 2 28 88.*

This is the scene of the most famous incident in the William Tell legend – the shooting of the apple off his son's head. A handsome statue of Wilhelm, with the unscathed Tell junior, stands in the compact picturesque main square, backed by a colourfully painted 13th-century tower.

BELLINZONA

Station: *tel: (092) 24 72 42.* Turn left out of the station and walk for 5 mins along *Viale Stazione* to the centre.
Tourist Office: *tel: (092) 825 21 31.*

Although Bellinzona is much smaller than Lugano and is much less famous than Locarno, it is the capital of the Ticino region, largely on account of its historical role as defender of the Alpine Passes. This is immediately evident in its huge castle,

William Tell

Whisper it carefully north of the Gotthard, but it's probable that William Tell only ever existed in legend. Tell, like Robin Hood, is a folk-symbol of the heroic resistance of the patriotic, honest countryman against tyrannical overlords. Just as Robin Hood fought the Sherrif of Nottingham, the evil agent of wicked King John, so William Tell fought (and killed) Gessler, the bailiff of the hated Habsburgs who oppressed Switzerland in the Middle Ages. If you want to learn more about the man with the unerring aim, visit the **Tell Museum** in the village of Bürglen (3 km south-east of Altdorf), where he was supposedly born.

the aptly-named **Castelgrande**, rising above the centre of town on a giant glacial rock base. Built between the 13th and 15th centuries, this formidable stronghold now houses a lively museum which traces the history of the castle and the site before that. To emphasise Bellinzona's medieval importance there are two more castles. Both are above the town and command superb views. The 14th-century **Castello di Montebello** is the nearest, a short walk uphill. It is basically a smaller version of Castelgrande and holds an archaeological and historical museum. A long steep hike will bring you to the 15th-century **Castello di Sasso Corbaro**, the smallest of the three, with a museum of art and Ticino traditions. A wall once linked all three of these castles, effectively spanning the whole navigable valley and sections of this can still be seen throughout the town.

The centre of Bellinzona is compact and comprises a series of piazzas interlinked with Lombardian arches where modern architecture, pastel-washed houses, stylish shops and fine old churches intermingle happily. The baroque interior of the early 16th-century **Church of SS Pietro and Stefano** is particularly notable. Behind the tourist office in the handsome **Palazzo Civico** (town hall) there are also fine wall paintings to enjoy. A 5-min walk along *Via Lugano*, (a continuation of *Viale Stazione* through the centre of town) is the **Santa Maria delle Grazie Church**, which boasts a superb 15th-century fresco of the Crucifixion. Also along here is Bellinzona's principal art gallery, the **Villa dei Cedri**.

↰ SIDE TRACK FROM BELLINZONA

LOCARNO

Station: *tel: (093) 33 65 64.*
Tourist Office: *Largo Zarzi 1; tel: (093) 31 03 33.*

Locarno (around 20 mins by train), situated on Lake Maggiore, is an important resort town. Its mellow climate and exotic lakeside flora give it a very Mediterranean atmosphere, and behind the handsome, sprawling **Piazza Grande** there's a warren of old streets to explore. Start at the top and take the funicular (a short walk from the main station) to the **Sanctuary of Madonna del Sasso**. This has been a place of pilgrimage for centuries and the complex contains some fine ancient religious objects and paintings. It's also well worth a trip for its superb views.

The atmospheric 15th-century **Castello Visconti**, just off Piazza Grande, is now home to the **Museo Civico e Archeologico**, featuring some fine Roman glass. By contrast, the town's other cultural landmark is the ultra-modern **Pinacoteca Casa Rusca** (Museum of Contemporary Art) with a large section on the works of Jean Arp (a former resident). ↰

LUGANO

Station: *tel: 157 22 22* (SFr.1.19 per min). A short funicular ride links the station to the centre of town.
Tourist Information: *Riva Albertoli 5; tel: (091) 21 46 64.*

ACCOMMODATION AND FOOD

Lugano is a wealthy town, patronised by wealthy holidaymakers, and so good budget accommodation is scarce.

There's a pleasant **HI youth hostel** at *Savosa, Via Cantonale 13; tel: (091) 56 27 28* (bus no. 5 to *Crocifisso* then 5-min walk) with its own swimming pool.

Away from the centre of town are two beautifully situated one-star hotels at the charming lakeside village of Gandria; the **Locanda Gandriese**, *Sotto alla Chiesa; tel: (091) 51 41 81*, and **Miralgol**; *tel: (091) 51 43 61*. Facilities are basic, but at around SFr.90 the picturesque position and the lake views are a bargain. Not much more expensive is the two-star **Zurigo Garni**, *Corso Pestalozzi 13; tel: (091) 23 43 43*, right in Lugano city centre.

The self-service **Ristorante Inova** (part of the Inovations Department Store) on *Piazza Cioccaro* offers a wide range of high quality, excellent value meals in very pleasant surroundings, well above the average department store standard. It also opens late. The **Parco Civico** is the best place for a picnic; stock up at **Gabbani Charcuterie** – a tourist sight in its own right, with its tempting window display featuring gigantic hanging salamis. It's just off *Piazza Cioccaro* and there's a colourful fruit and vegetable shop opposite.

SIGHTSEEING

Every Tues morning at 0930 (Apr–Oct) a

free guided walking tour departs from the Church of Santa Maria degli Angioli (see below) on *Piazza Luini*. Book the day before with the tourist office.

Lugano is the biggest and most rewarding town in Ticino with a magnificent setting on **Lake Lugano** which has earned it the nickname, the 'Rio de Janeiro of the Old World'. The town sits in a bay of the lake with twin mountains, cloaked in lush sub-Alpine vegetation, to either side. The lake, which flows into Italy, is very beautiful with picturesque settlements descending the emerald slopes to dip their feet into the water. The Swiss Pass is valid on the regular scheduled boat service which takes in Castagnola, Campione d'Italia, San Rocco and Caprino and you should definitely break your tour at the charming village of **Gandria**. There are also many excursions on offer (ferry operators: **Società Navigazione del Lago di Lugano**; *tel: (091) 51 52 23*).

The best place to view the full extent of Lago Lugano is from the sugar loaf-like **Monte San Salvatore** (912 m), though **Monte Brè** (933 m) gives a much better view of the town of Lugano. Funiculars run to both peaks.

Like Locarno the **lakeside promenade**, including the Parco Civico, is a delight, with many Mediterranean species of flora and outdoor art works which reflect the town's strong artistic and cultural heritage.

The station is perched above the lake and halfway down the hill is the **Cathedral of San Lorenzo**. It's worth a visit for the view alone. The centre of town revolves around the **Piazza della Riforma** where Lugano café-society is at its most prominent. Off here is a delightful maze of Lombardian arches and architecture, interconnecting with several smaller piazzas, many of which are traffic free.

Designer boutiques and expensive jewellery shops underline the local wealth.

On the busy front is the small **Church of Santa Maria degli Angioli**, quite unprepossessing from the outside, but housing marvellous Renaissance frescos.

Pre-eminent among the town's many museums and galleries is the world-famous **Fondazione Thyssen-Bornemisza**. The Old Masters may have gone (in 1992 to Spain) but the permanent collection of around 150 19th- and 20th-century paintings and watercolours remain (note limited opening hours; Fri–Sun 1000–1700). The gallery enjoys a beautiful setting in the **Villa Favorita**, Castagnola (bus no. 1 or boat). A 5-min walk from the Villa Favorita is another excellent collection, the **Museo delle Culture Extraeuropee**, based in the **Villa Heleneum**. There's more modern art to see in the **Villa Malpensata**, (on the front) and in **Museo Cantonale d'Arte**, *via Canova*, (off the *Piazza della Riforma*). The latter features a collection of 19th- and 20th-century works, mostly by local artists, and also hosts international exhibitions. In the **Parco Civico** is yet another art gallery, the **Villa Ciani** which houses the town's fine art collection (currently closed for restoration). Also in the park is the Cantonal Natural History collection.

It is worth crossing the lake for the **Museo Doganale** (Swiss Customs Museum) at Cantine di Gandria (don't confuse this with Gandria on the opposite side of the lake). This is a lively exhibition showing not only the history of smuggling in these parts, but also the often-dangerous work of the modern customs officer (boat from Lugano Giardino, museum open afternoons only, free entry).

179

COMO

For details, see p. 147.

LYON

France's second biggest city has long been forgotten by the powers-that-be in Paris. Lyonnais, the people of the city, are reputed by their fellow citizens to be the unfriendliest in France. Fog and pollution are said to reign supreme. For many French people, Lyon is just somewhere to get through on their way south.

But once they take a closer look, they invariably want to return. For this great metropolis at the junction of two of Europe's greatest rivers – the Saône and the Rhône – is very inviting. The people are hard-working and proud (this was the centre of the French Resistance during World War II), but also courteous and sociable.

Lyon has been a crossroads since early Roman occupation in 43 BC and is used to greeting strangers. The bustling city has much to offer the visitor – in particular its cuisine, served in traditional 'bouchons', or inns. Many consider the city to be the capital of gastronomy, and restaurants abound, from three Michelin stars to simple one-room family establishments.

Lyon can also offer you the largest Renaissance quarter in France, museums galore, and a thriving student-oriented nightlife.

TOURIST INFORMATION

Tourist Office: *pl. Bellecour, 69000 Lyon* (east of Lyon-Perrache rail station); *tel: 78* 42 25 75. It provides free guides and maps to the city. Open Mon–Fri 0900–1900, Sat 0900–1800 in summer; Mon–Fri 0900–1800, Sat 0900–1700 in winter. Multi-lingual guides can be booked for tours.

Branch offices: *pl. St-Jean, av. Adolphe Max; tel: 78 42 25 75.* Just across the Saône from *pl. Bellecour.* Open Mon–Sat 1030–1930, Sun 1000–1800 in summer. Mon–Fr 0900–1300 and 1400–1800, Sat 0900–1700 and Sun 1000–1700 in winter.

Also at Perrache rail station, **Centre d'Échanges**, with accommodation service, maps etc. Open Mon–Fri 0900–1800, Sat 0900–1700 in summer. Mon–Fri 0900–1300 and 1400–1800, Sat 0900–1700 in winter. Also in summer a tourist office opens on the *Fourvière Esplanade.*

Centre Régional d'Information Jeunesse: *9 quai des Célestins; tel: 72 77 00 66.* Open Mon 1200–1900, Tues–Fri 1000–1900, Sat (Sept–June) 1000–1700. Closed from 31 July to 15 Aug. For student and youth information including jobs, accommodation, transport.

ARRIVING AND DEPARTING

Airport
Aéroport Lyon-Satolas: *32 km east of Lyon; tel: 72 22 72 21.* Facilities include restaurants, exchange office and tourist information.

From the airport a regular bus service runs every 20 mins (30 mins on Sun) between 0600 and 2300 to and from Perrache rail station (via Part-Dieu rail station), FFr.50.

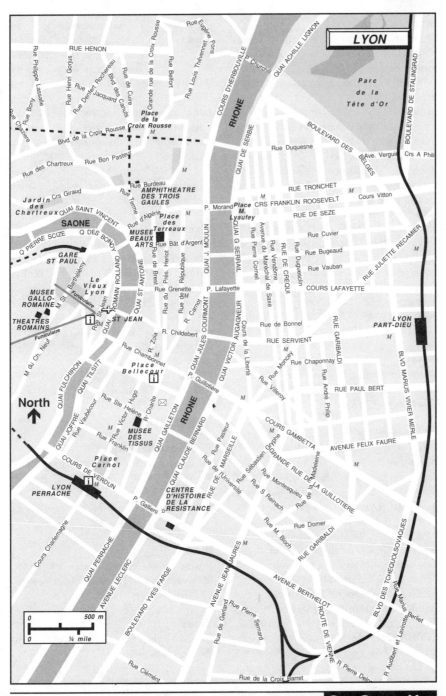

LYON

Parc de la Tête d'Or

RUE HENON
Rue Eugène Pons
Rue Louis Thévenet
Rue Philippe Lassalle
Rue Bony
Rue Henri Gorjus
Rue Denfert Rochereau
Blvd des Canuts
Rue de Cuire
Grande rue de la Croix Rousse
Rue Bellort
Rue Chazière
QUAI D'HERBOUVILLE
P. Churchill
QUAI ACHILLE LIGNON
BOULEVARD DE STALINGRAD
Place de la Croix Rousse
Blvd. de la Croix Rousse
Rue Bon Pasteur
Rue des Chartreux
Crs Giraud
Rue Burdeau
Rue Terme
AMPHITHEATRE DES TROIS GAULES
RHONE
QUAI DE SERBIE
Rue Duquesne
BOULEVARD DES BELGES
B.Ave. Verguin
Crs A Phili
Jardin des Chartreux
QUAI SAINT VINCENT
Rue d'Algérie
Place des Terreaux
P. Morand
Place M. Lyaufey
RUE TRONCHET
CRS FRANKLIN ROOSEVELT
Cours Vitton
SAONE
Q DES BONDY
MUSEE BEAUX ARTS
Rue Bât d'Argent
RUE DE SEZE
Q PIERRE SCIZE
QUAI ROMAIN ROLLAND
Rue du Prés. Heriot
Rue de la République
QUAI J. MOULIN
QUAI G. SERRAIL
Avenue du Maréchal de Saxe
Rue Pierre Corneil
Rue Vendôme
RUE DE CREQUI
Rue Cuvier
Rue Bugeaud
Rue Vauban
Rue Duguesclin
RUE JULIETTE RECAMIER
GARE ST PAUL
Barthélémy
Le Vieux Lyon
Funiculaire
Rue St Jean
QUAI ST ANTOINE
Rue Grenette
Rue du Bœuf
P. Lafayette
COURS LAFAYETTE
MUSEE GALLO-ROMAINE
M St.
ST JEAN
R. Carnot
R. Childebert
QUAI JULES COURMONT
QUAI VICTOR AUGAGNEUR
Rue de Bonnel
RUE SERVIENT
RUE GARIBALDI
LYON PART-DIEU
THEATRES ROMAINS
Funiculaire
M du Ch. Neuf
R. Zola
Rue Chambonnet
Rue Morcey
Rue Chaponnay
Rue André Philip
BLVD MARIUS VIVIER MERLE
181
North
QUAI FULCHIRON
QUAI TILSITT
QUAI JOFFRE
Rue Vaubecour
Rue Ste Helène
Rue Victor Hugo
Place Bellecour
P. Guillotière
Cours de la Liberté
Rue Villeroy
RUE PAUL BERT
R. Charle
Rue Franklin
MUSEE DES TISSUS
RHONE
QUAI GAILLETON
COURS GAMBETTA
AVENUE FELIX FAURE
Place Carnot
COURS DE VERDUN
LYON PERRACHE
P. Gallieni
QUAI CLAUDE BERNARD
CENTRE D'HISTOIRE DE LA RESISTANCE
Rue Pasteur
Rue de MARSEILLE
Rue de l'Université
Rue Sébastien
Rue Montesquieu
Rue S. Reinach
GRANDE RUE DE LA GUILLOTIERE
Rue de la Madeleine
Rue Domer
Rue M. Bloch
RUE GARIBALDI
Cours Charlemagne
QUAI PERRACHE
AVENUE LECLERC
BOULEVARD YVES FARGE
Rue de Gerland
AVENUE JEAN JAURES
Rue Pierre Semard
AVENUE BERTHELOT
ROUTE DE VIENNE
BLVD DES TCHEQUOSLOVAQUES
Rue Marius Berliet
R Pierre Delc
R Audibert et Lavirotte
Rue Clément
Rue de la Croix Barret

0   500 m
0   ¼ mile

Stations

There are two mainline stations in Lyon. Many trains stop at both so check on your final destination.

Lyon-Perrache is the more central, *tel: 78 92 50 50.* It provides tourist information and money exchange offices, luggage lockers, a restaurant and bar as well as **SOS Voyageurs** – an information and practical assistance service for passengers *(tel: 78 37 03 31)* open 0800–2000. The station is closed 2400–0500. For the town centre, head north from *pl. Carnot*, then it's a 5-min walk along *av. Victor Hugo* to *pl. Bellecour.*

Lyon-Part-Dieu is on the east bank of the Rhône and serves the business district (same telephone number as Lyon-Perrache for information). It has a restaurant and luggage lockers. **SOS Voyageurs** open 0800–2200, *tel: 72 34 12 16.* Station closed 0130–0445.

Buses

Perrache Station: services to Vienne, Annecy and Grenoble. *tel: 78 71 70 00.* Open 0630–1700.

Lyon is big (population 1.5 million). Nature, in the form of the two rivers, the Saône and the Rhône, has divided the city into thirds. On the west bank of the Saône is **Vieux Lyon** (Old Lyon), with its attractive Renaissance streets. On the east bank of the Rhône is the **business centre**, the Part-Dieu rail station and shopping centre, and many of Lyon's high-rise offices and apartment blocks. In between, bordered by the Saône and Rhône, is the mainly **pedestrianised centre** of the city, from *pl. Bellecour* and Perrache rail station, to the **Hôtel de Ville** and the ancient quarter of **Les Terreaux**.

The central area between Perrache and the *Hôtel de Ville*, and across the Saône to **Vieux Lyon**, is manageable on foot. To go further afield, take a bus, funicular *(funiculaires)* or subway train *(métro)*, run by **TCL** *(Transports en commun lyonnais)*; *tel: 78 71 70 70.* Information booths can be found everywhere, including the rail stations and the main metro stops. Get the *plan de réseau* from the tourist office or any TCL branch.

Lyon is a relatively safe city. Wander anywhere during the day. At night some care is needed around the Perrache station.

Tickets

Tickets last 1 hr, good for buses and trolleys, and metro FFr.7.50; a carnet of ten is FFr.65, students FFr.54. A **Ticket Liberté**, FFr.23, covers unlimited travel for one-day on all TCL services, available from tourist offices, TCL booths or automatic vending machines (which take coins and credit cards).

Metro

The metro is modern, clean and safe. There are four lines, A, B, C and D which criss-cross the city. It operates 0500–2400.

Funicular Railway

Funiculaires depart every 10 mins from Vieux Lyon metro station. to the Roman theatre at St-Just (0545–2400) and the **Fourvière Esplanade** high above the city (0600-2200).

Buses

Buses cover every corner of Lyon, 0500–2400 with a limited night bus service. Same ticket price as above.

Taxis

For 24-hr taxis *tel: 78 28 23 23.* Fare to the airport is about FFr.250.

Accommodation

Lyon is a business town and filled during the week with briefcases and expense-accounts. The central hotels are often booked out Mon–Thur but this is a big city and you can always find a room. Try around the Perrache rail station or north in **Le Terreaux** (take metro line A north from the rail station to *Hôtel de Ville*). **Hotel Plaza Republique**, *5, r. Stella 69002 Lyon; tel: 78 37 50 50*, is a smart small hotel with friendly efficient service and centrally-situated near *pl. Bellecour*.

Chain hotels include *Ca, Ct, Hd, Ib, Mc, Nv, Pu* and *Sf*. Budget accommodation abounds – try *cours de Verdun, r. Victor Hugo* near the Perrache rail station; *pl. Croix-Paquet* in Les Terreaux, near the Hôtel de Ville; and *r. Lainerie* in Vieux Lyon.

HI: *51 r. Roger Salengro, 69200 Vénissieux; tel: 78 76 39 23*. Just outside the city – take bus no. 35 (last bus at 2100) from *pl. Bellecour* to stop: *George-Lévy* (30-min journey).

Centre International de Séjour: *46 r. du Commandant Pegoud; tel: 78 01 23 45*. Take bus no. 53 from Perrache, direction *St-Priest*, to stop: *États-Unis Beauvisage*.

Camping: Dardilly; *Ecully-Dardilly; tel: 78 35 64 55*. Take bus no. 19 from the Hôtel de Ville, direction *Ecully-Dardilly* to *Parc d'affaires*. Open year-round.

Eating and Drinking

Some visitors come just for the food. Lyon boasts more famous chefs than almost any other city in Europe and some of the best restaurants in France. Food is serious business here but not just for the wealthy, even on a tight budget you can eat very well. Countless small cafés exist, often serving an imaginative local *plat du jour*, the chef's

whim of the day.

The most traditional of Lyonnais restaurants are the *bouchons*, travellers' inns, mainly in **Les Terreaux** and **Vieux Lyon**. Twenty or so survive, serving hearty meals based on tripe, pork and sausages washed down with local Beaujolais wines. The oldest is **Le Soleil**, *2 r. St-Georges* in Vieux Lyon.

Lyonnais cuisine is very much based on meat dishes, particularly pork, Bresse chicken, plump sausages (*andouillettes*), tripe and potatoes baked in a creamy sauce (*gratinées*). The food is undeniably rich and full of flavour. Though the cooking is never fancy, it is always performed with great attention to detail. Apart from a great array of sausages, expect to find hot pâtés and sea-food, invariably with accompanying sauces and lots of fresh vegetables.

For good eateries in **Vieux Lyon** head for *pl. Neuve St Jean* and *pl. de la Baleine*. Try **L'Amphitryon**, *33 r. St Jean; tel: 78 37 23 68*, for inexpensive menus and a view of the passing strollers. Away from this busy tourist area, the *r. des Marroniers* just to the east of *pl. Bellecour* off *pl. Antonin Poncet* is a good bet. **Les Trois Tonneaux**, *3 r. des Marroniers; tel: 78 37 34 72*, includes traditional Lyonnaises dishes in its menus. Or try the streets around the **Cordeliers** metro including *r. Mercière* which is exclusively devoted to restaurants.

To discover where all the wonderful fresh produce comes from, wander round Lyon's great markets, open daily except Mon. The largest and most animated are at *quai St Antoine* on the Saône, west of metro Cordeliers, and along *blvd de la Croix-Rousse*, north of Les Terreaux. The covered market at **Les Halles** is more grandiose and expensive, but more varied, with meat joining the fruit and vegetables at *cours Lafayette*.

Do not miss the **Renée et Renée** cheese shop in the market there – it's one of the best in France; *tel: 78 62 30 78.*

Communications

Post Office: *pl. Antonin Poncet; tel: 72 40 65 22,* next to *pl. Bellecour.* Facilities include poste restante, photocopying, telephones and currency exchange. Open Mon–Fri 0800–1900, Sat 0800–1200.

Money

There are **Thomas Cook** bureaux de change at both Lyon-Part-Dieu and Lyon-Perrache stations. The bureaux at Part-Dieu is open Mon–Sat 0800–1900, Sun 1030–1900 (winter). **AOC** money exchange is at the St Jean tourist office, *av Adolphe Max.*

Consulates

Canada: *74 r. de Bonnel; tel: 72 61 15 25,* near to Part-Dieu. Open Mon–Fri 1000–1200.
UK: *24 r. Childebert; tel: 78 37 59 67.* Follow *r. de la République* to metro: *Bellecour.* Open Mon–Fri 1000–1230 and 1400–1730.

ENTERTAINMENT

Theatre, a resident opera company, film, ballet and dancing late into the night – Lyon has all the big-city attractions. A weekly publication *Lyon Poche* lists the week's events (FFr.7 from news-stands).

Cinemas

Lyon was birthplace of the cinema. The brothers Lumière invented moving pictures while working with their father who was a local photographer. Their legacy is numerous cinemas as well as the **Institut Lumière**, *r. du Premier Film; tel: 78 78 18 95,* south-east of the centre in *Montplaisir* (metro: *Montplaisir-Lumière*). It shows films

free on Tues and Thurs during the summer on the square outside.

Clubs

Lyon is a student city and naturally clubs and discos abound. The best areas are near the Hôtel de Ville in *r. Algérie* and *pl. des Terreaux* or along *Quai Pierre Scize* on the Vieux Lyon side of the Saône. These do not get going until after midnight – head to a bar first. Most discos/clubs charge entry, up to FFr.100 at weekends (including your first drink).

Dance and Opera

Maison de la Danse; *Théâtre du 8ème, 8 av. Jean Mermoz; tel: 78 75 88 88,* has modern dance, Latin and African, as well as classical ballet.

The 1200-seat **Lyon Opera House** soars up to 18 different seating levels. Under the orchestral direction of Kent Nagano the company is now one of Europe's finest. The opera house is at *9 quai Jean Moulin,* just east of the Hôtel de Ville. Reservations *tel: 72 00 45 45,* from 1100–1900. Seats cost between FFr.70–360.

Puppets

Lyon was birthplace of **Guignol**, the French equivalent of 'Mr Punch', who proceeds through a series of stock adventures, beating fellow puppets on the head as he goes. The **Guignol de Lyon** theatre, *2 r. Louis Carrand* in the old town, *tel: 78 28 92 57,* puts on classical performances for kids and adults alike.

Theatre

The Lyonnais love their theatre and boast 15 different stages throughout the city. The most illustrious is the Italianate **Théâtre des Célestins** at *4 r. Charles Dullin; tel: 78 37 50 51,* just north-west of

Films and Puppets

The famous cinema pioneers Auguste and Louis Lumière grew up in Lyon. Their photographer father, Auguste, moved the family there in 1870 when they were small children. After living first in *rue de l'Hotel de Ville*, he had a small château built in the Monplaisir district. Today it house the Institut Lumière. The brothers attended La Martinière technical lycée, where Louis developed the Etiquette Bleue, a dry photographic plate which the family's small factory at Monplaisir started to manufacture. Further experiments led to the first moving pictures, when they used a hand-operated camera to film the factory's workers coming out on a bright sunny day in 1895. *Sortie des Usines Lumière* only lasted 41 seconds but caused a sensation when it was premiered at a national photography congress in Lyon shortly afterwards.

Lyon's famous puppet character Guignol was created by Laurent Mourguet, who was born into a family of silk workers in the St Georges district in 1768. Fascinated by puppets from childhood, he gave shows both outdoors and in a theatre in *rue Lainerie*. There he invented a glove puppet activated by three fingers. Being easier to operate than a string one, it enabled him to create a cast of larger-than-life characters, the most famous of which was the witty Guignol, who constantly poked fun at the authorities and at the failings of his friends.

pl. Bellecour. Tickets run from FFr.70–250. Cheapest tickets are on sale the evening of the performance.

Events

May: **Biennale Theatre Jeune Public**; *tel: 78 64 14 24*, an international festival of improvisation.

May/June: **Festival Estival du Vieux Lyon**; *tel: 78 42 39 04;* chamber music. May–Sept: **Summer festival of music and theatre**; *tel: 72 10 30 30.* Sept: **Chamber Music Festival 'Les Musicades'**; *tel: 78 39 28 41* and **Biennale de la Dance**; *tel: 72 40 26 26* (alternates with modern art).

Oct: **Grand Prix de Tennis**, *Palais des Sports; tel: 78 23 45 45.*

Nov: **Festival de Musique du Vieux Lyon**: *tel: 78 42 39 04.* Sacred music takes over the churches with Gregorian chanting and organ recitals.

Dec: **Illuminations on 8 Dec**, when every window contains a lit candle. For information *tel: 78 27 71 31.*

SHOPPING

The poshest shops, for haute couture, jewellery and china, are grouped along *r. Emile Zola, r. Gasparin* and *r. Président Herriot* between *pl. Bellecour* and *pl. des Jacobins.* For less exhalted purchases take a short detour east along *r. de la République* for department stores like **Printemps, Prisunic-Grand Bazar** and **Galeries Lafayette.** Antique shops are gathered along *r. Auguste Comte* beyond Perrache station. 260 shops are housed on four levels in the Part-Dieu station complex, one of the largest shopping centres in Europe.

SIGHTSEEING

Guided tours are available on Saturdays from the Tourist Office, *pl. Bellecour,* departing 1430, cost FFr.50. A general tour of the city by bus runs from Apr–Oct – useful if you have little time for sightseeing. Contact **Cars Philibert**, *tel: 78 98 56 00.*

One of the most pleasant ways to see Lyon is from the river, especially after dark when over 100 buildings are floodlit. Boat trips run from Apr–Oct, departing hourly 1400–1700 from *quai des Célestins; tel: 78 42 96 81,* and also at 1800 May–mid-July and 2130 July and Aug. Trips lasts 1–1¼ hrs, FFr.42 round trip. Also lunch and dinner cruises.

To see more than one museum, a 3-day **'Key to Lyon'** chequebook is available from the tourist offices, FFr.90. It includes a conducted or audio-guided city tour, admission to 6 museums and one-day travel pass.

Like Paris, the best way to see Lyon is to stroll it. Start at the tourist office in *pl. Bellecour* and head north. *Pl. des Terreaux* is a bustling landmark including the best of Lyon's museums – **Musée des Beaux Arts**, *pl. des Terreaux; tel: 72 10 17 40,* France's second-largest fine arts museum. It contains collections of Italian Renaissance, 19th- and 20th-century French masters, sculpture and tapestry (Open 1030–1800, closed Mon, Tues; admission FFr.20). The **Musée d'Art Contemporain** in the Cite Internationale, *Quai de Gén. de Gaulle; tel: 78 30 50 66,* contains works post-1960 (open 1200–1800, closed Mon, Tues).

South of *pl. Bellecour* is a monument to Lyon's textile history, and its role as Europe's silk capital – **Musée des Tissus**; *34 r. de la Charité; tel: 78 37 15 05.* Open 1000–1730, closed Mon, admission FFr.26. Silk made Lyon one of Europe's wealthiest cities in the 18th century, with 28,000 looms run by *canuts* or silk-weavers. Old looms are still in use at **Maison de Canuts**, *10-12 r. d'Ivry; tel: 78 28 62 04.* Open Mon–Fri 0830–1200 and 1400–1830. Sat 0900–1200 and 1400–1800, admission FFr.6.

Just across **Pont Gallieni** from the tourist office is the most poignant museum in Lyon – **Le Centre d'Histoire de la Résistance et de la Déportation**, *14 av. Berthelot; tel: 78 72 23 11,* marking the history of Lyon during the German occupation in World War II. Open 0900–1730, closed Mon, Tues, admission FFr.20.

The best preserved Renaissance district in France leads back from the river. Renovated Renaissance mansions abound in **St Jean, St Paul** and **St Georges** quarters. The **Cathédrale St-Jean**, started in 1180, contains a unique mixture of building styles and a 14th-century astronomical clock.

Julius Caesar was responsible for developing the Roman town of *Lugdunum,* centred on the hillside of **Fourvière** above the old town. The funicular from Vieux Lyon metro station takes you up the hill to the **Esplanade** for a fine view of the city. The **Musée Gallo–Romain** at *17 r. Cléberg; tel: 78 25 94 68,* has an impressive collection of mosaics, coins and swords (open 0930–1200 and 1400–1800, closed Mon, Tues, admission FFr.20), but the most interesting sight is the **Théâtre Romain**, *8 r. de l'Antiquaille,* the oldest in France, just down the hill from the museum, with seating intact, and remains of gigantic columns (open 0900 to dusk, admission free). North of *pl. des Terreaux* is another vestige of the city's Roman past – **L'Amphithéâtre des Trois Gaules** in Croix-Rousse; *Jardin des Plantes* (open dawn–dusk, admission free). This was the site of an altar built to Rome and Emperor Augustus, the founder of Lyon.

East of the Rhône is modern, with the older university area to the south and a new campus, the **Cité Internationale**, north of the **Parc de la Tête d'Or**, which houses Interpol's Headquarters. In between is the city's commercial centre around the new Part-Dieu development.

LYON–BESANÇON

This route heads through the heart of the Jura, a beautiful region of forests, lakes and gentle hills. In summer it is an area in which to go walking, riding, boating and fishing. In winter the small towns are transformed by snow into resorts that offer some of the best cross-country skiing in France.

At Bourg-en-Bresse the route turns east off the main line to follow a wriggling course through the mountains.

Besançon

Arc-et-Senans

Morez

St-Claude

Bourg-en-Bresse

Lyon

FASTEST JOURNEY: 2 HRS 30 MINS

187

ON TRACK

Lyon–Bourg-en-Bresse
A frequent service runs from Lyon Part-Dieu and Lyon Perrache to Bourg-en-Bresse taking just over 1 hr.

Bourg-en-Bresse–St-Claude
Only 3 or 4 trains a day run from Bourg-en-Bresse to St-Claude. The journey takes nearly 2 hrs.

TRAINS

ETT tables: 156, 170a, 157.

FAST TRACK

Six or 7 trains a day make the 2 hr 30 mins to 3 hr journey.

St-Claude–Morez
This 27-min journey is made by 5 or 6 trains a day.

Morez–Arc et Senans–Besançon
The journey from Morez to Besançon requires a change of train at Mouchard and takes nearly 3 hrs. Very few trains make the 6-min journey between Mouchard and Arc et Senans, so check the timetables carefully before travelling.

BOURG-EN-BRESSE
Station: *pl. de la Gare; tel: 74 21 13 31.*
Tourist Office: *Centre Albert Camus, 6 av. Alsace-Lorraine; 01000 Bourg-en-Bresse; tel: 74 22 49 40.*

A busy market town dotted with nicely restored half-timbered buildings, it is famous for *poulet de Bresse,* its tasty free-range chickens raised on maize, and for the church and **monastery of Brou,** *63 blvd de Brou, tel: 74 22 26 55,* on the south-east edge of the town. The flamboyant Gothic church has beautiful stained-glass windows and finely carved oak choir stalls and rood screen. It houses the intricate marble tombs of Philibert, Duke of Savoy, and his wife, Margaret of Austria, who had the church built after his death in 1504. Open 1000–1200 and 1400–1630 in winter, 0830–1200 and 1400–1830 in summer. A museum of **local history,** *tel: 74 22 22 31,* is in the cloisters. Open 0900–1200 and 1400–1700 in winter, 0900–1230 and 1400–1900 in summer.

Among the hotels with restaurants in the town is **Hôtel le Mail,** *46 av. du Mail, tel: 74 21 00 26.*

ST CLAUDE-SUR-BIENNE
Station: *av. de la Gare; tel: 84 45 03 05.*
Tourist Office: *1 av. de Belfort, 39200 St Claude-sur-Bienne; tel: 84 45 34 24.*

The setting of this small town is superb – on a ridge above the rushing Bienne and Tacon rivers and surrounded by mountain peaks. Not surprisingly it is an excellent walking base; with three hours to spare, the **Queue de Cheval** – horse's tail – waterfall is worth seeing.

MOREZ
Station: *17 av. du Gén. de Gaulle; tel: 84 33 00 95.*
Tourist Office: *75 pl. Jean Jaurès, 39400 Morez; tel: 84 33 08 73.*

This small holiday resort, popular particularly for cross-country skiing, lies along a single street at the bottom of narrow gorge of the River Bienne. The reward for climbing to the **Rocher au Dade** cliffs above – a two-hour walk there and back – is a panoramic view over the Bienne valley.

ARC-ET-SENANS
Station (no booking office): for information, *tel: 84 37 87 76.*
Tourist Information: apply to **Doubs Département Office,** *7 av. de la Gare d'Eau, 25031 Besançon; tel: 81 65 10 00.*

In its time the village's **Royal Saltworks** was a model factory, designed by the visionary architect Claude Nicolas Ledoux as part of a grandiose plan to produce salt from water piped from Salins-les-Bains using fuel from the Chaux forest. Production ceased in 1895 but the buildings, laid out in a semi-circle, have been converted into a museum, *tel: 81 54 45 00,* with models of Ledoux's remarkable designs. Open 0900–1200 and 1400–1800; admission FFr.29.

BESANÇON
For information on Besançon, see Dijon–Basel route, p. 95.

LYON–GENEVA

From Lyon this route first heads north-east to Ambérieu-en-Bugey, crossing the River Ain. From there it twists and turns south-east between wooded mountains to Culoz and, after crossing the Rhône and running down the east side of Lac de Bourget, comes to two of France's most beautiful towns – the historic spa of Aix-les-Bains and the 'Venice of the Alps', the canal-riddled town of Annecy. From Aix-les-Bains the route runs north through Annecy to La Roche-sur-Foron.

Here – most unusually – the line first goes straight past the town before doing a complete U-turn back into it, an indication of the hilly terrain and the lack of funds that engineers building it had to contend with. Soon the countryside flattens out though there are still mountains in the distance on the final stretch through Annemasse to Geneva.

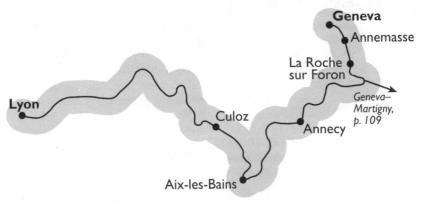

```
FASTEST JOURNEY: 2 HRS
```

TRAINS

ETT tables: 159, 167, 167a.

FAST TRACK

Six trains a day link Lyon Part-Dieu and Geneva taking just over 2 hrs.

ON TRACK

Lyon–Culoz
Around 6 trains a day make this journey, taking just over 1 hr.

Culoz–Aix-les-Bains
Just 4 trains a day call at Culoz and Aix-les-Bains, taking 20 mins for the journey.

Aix-les-Bains–Annecy

Frequent trains make the 35 min journey. Note that travelling on any of the TGV services that make this trip requires the payment of a supplementary fare.

Annecy–La Roche sur Foron

Ten trains a day make the 40 min journey between Annecy and La Roche sur Foron.

La Roche sur Foron–Annemasse

This is a 17 min journey, with up to 9 trains a day.

Annemasse–Geneva (Genève)

A frequent local service runs from Annemasse to Genève Eaux-Vives station, taking 10 mins for the journey.

CULOZ

Station: *Gare SNCF; tel: 79 87 00 28.*
Tourist Information: *6 r. de la Mairie, 01350 Culoz; tel: 79 87 00 30.* Open 0900–1200 and 1400–1700. Closed Sat afternoon.

The town centre is a short walk down *av. de la Gare.*

ACCOMMODATION

Try **L'Hôtel Restaurant du Commerce**, *av. de la Gare; tel: 79 87 00 03.*

SIGHTSEEING

One-time border town between France and Switzerland, Culoz developed greatly during the 19th century. In its heyday it attracted such literary people as Paul Bourget and Gertrude Stein – who rented an attractive mansion, **Clos Poncet**, by the park for visits in the 1840s.

The town is a gateway to the **Marais de Lavours** national park, a beautiful area of marshland for walking. The **Association des amis du marais de Lavours** organises guided walks to see the wildlife in summertime (programme available from the tourist office).

High above the town on the *rte de Béon* is the **Château de Montvéran**, open by arrangement for guided tours – by the count himself, *tel: 79 87 01 33.* It was built on the ruins of a medieval castle, some of which can still be seen. The impressive view inspired the great pianist Sergei Prokofiev, who used to stay here.

AIX-LES-BAINS

Station: Gare SNCF, *pl. de la Gare; tel: 36 35 35 35.* Information open Mon–Sat 0830–1200, 1400–1830. Lockers available. For the tourist office cross *blvd Wilson,* head down *av. de Gaulle,* cross the square and the office is on the left around the corner. For the lake, head left out of the station to *av. du Grand Port.*
Tourist Office: *pl. Maurice Mollard, 73100 Aix-les-Bains; tel: 79 35 05 92.* Housed in a national monument, which was once a Roman temple. Excellent information service, free map and guide to town in English. Open Mon–Sat 0845–1200, 1400–1830; also Sun 0915–1215, 1400–1800 in summer.

GETTING AROUND

Central sights are easily accessible by foot – the *Thermes Nationaux* (central baths), *L'Arc de Campanus* (Roman funeral arch), *Musée Faure* and *Casino.* For the lake and aquarium, it is best to take a bus (bus no. 2 from the centre except Sun, direction *Aix-Plage*); to walk there takes about 30 mins.

The bus service is highly efficient: an inclusive map is available from the tourist office (FFr.10). A single journey costs FFr.7. For taxis, *tel: 79 35 08 05.*

ACCOMMODATION AND FOOD

Despite its reputation as a deluxe spa town, Aix boasts a pleasant selection of budget hotels. Easter and high summer season are crowded periods. Budget accommodation is plentiful along *blvd Wilson* and *av. du Tresserve* (to the east of the station).

HI: *promenade de Sierroz; tel: 79 88 32 88*. Bus no. 2 towards the lake, get off at Camping. Reservations necessary, as it fills up with groups. Reception open 0700–1000 and 1800–2200.

Camping Municipal Sierroz, *promenade de Sierroz; tel; 79 61 21 43*. Open Mar 15–Nov 15. Reservations imperative July–Aug.

Aix has a wide range of eateries, although more in the upper price range, and the town centre contains numerous smaller restaurants and places to buy sandwiches. Picnics are popular, down at the lakeside.

Bars are expensive. For an introduction to local wines, the tourist office runs tours of the vineyards.

COMMUNICATIONS AND MONEY

Post Office: *av. Victoria; tel: 79 33 15 15*. Open Mon–Fri 0800–1900, Sat 0800–1200. Poste restante facilities available just round the corner at *av. Marie de Solms*. Banks with currency exchange facilities can be found on *pl. Carnot*.

ENTERTAINMENT

Aix Poche gives details of cultural and other events in Aix, available free from the tourist office.

In July, opera takes place at the **Casino** (*tel: 79 88 09 99* for information). Classical music takes place throughout the summer at the **Théâtre de Verdure**, with larger concerts at the **Palais du Congrès**. In autumn, a Berlioz concert opens the **Festival des Nuits Romantiques**, while winter sees theatre and music continue at the Palais du Congrès and Casino.

The pink and white **Casino**, *18 r. du*

Casino; tel: 79 35 16 16, is open to over-18s. Clubs and bars in Aix are expensive, congregating around the Casino and *pl. du Revard*.

SIGHTSEEING

Water is the essence of Aix-les-Bains – the Romans first built thermal baths here 2000 years ago. The rich and famous from all over the world patronised them right up to the start of World War II. A bust of **Queen Victoria** in *pl. du Revard* commemorates her three visits to Aix in the 1880s. In recent years the baths have attracted a wide French clientele as some treatments are covered by the French national health service.

Aix is also a lakeside town, on the edge of **Lac du Bourget**, the largest natural lake in France (16 km long). With wooded hills rising steeply on the far side, it has been an inspiration for centuries to poets, monks and fishermen.

Organised tours of the city, bath complexes and local wine country run from **Kiosque No. 4** outside the *Thermes Nationaux; tel: 79 88 09 99*; open Mon–Fri 0930–1900, Sat 1000–1800, Sun 1000–1500 in summer, Mon–Sat 0930–1200 and 1400–1900 in winter.

The **Thermes Nationaux** are the birthplace of the city – tours run Tues–Sat at 1500, cost FFr.15. Inaugurated in 1784, the baths have continued a tradition of welcoming royalty, begun in Roman days. Lesser baths include **Les Thermes d'Aix-Marlioz** to the east of the centre.

Musée Faure, *blvd des Côtes; tel: 76 61 06 57*, on a small hill to the west of the centre, contains Rodin statues and an impressive array of Impressionist art, including works by Cézanne, Sisley, Degas, Bonnard and Renoir.

If you wonder what lives in the lake, look no further than **L'Aquarium d'Aix**

191

beside it, where 42 fish species are on display (*Le Petit Port; tel: 79 61 08 22*, admission FFr.20, open 1000–1800, closed Mon).

No trip to Aix is complete without an excursion to **L'Abbaye d'Hautecombe**, a boat ride across the lake to a mystical monastery on the west shore (Open Mon and Wed–Sat 1000–1130 and 1400–1700, Sun 1400–1700). Inspiration for the poet Lamartine, this haunting building houses the tombs of the Dukes of Savoy. Catch an early morning boat from **le Grand Port**, departures morning and afternoon, 1–2 hrs, free at the monastery, FFr.50 return.

Other boat tours are available, contact **Bateaux du Lac du Bourget**; *Le Grand Port, Les Belles Rives; tel: 79 63 45 00*.

ANNECY

Station: *pl. de la Gare; tel: 36 35 35 35*. Most sights and amenities are towards the lake. Take *r. Sommeiller* to *r. Président Favre*, turn right to the Bonlieu shopping centre at *pl. de la Libération*. Information open 0900–1200, 1400–1900. Lockers available. **Tourist Office:** *1 r. Jean Jaurès, 74000 Annecy*, at *pl. de la Libération; tel: 50 45 00 33*. Situated in the **Bonlieu** shopping centre, with a big team of staff, this office has lots of good information, including the useful *Guide Pratique d'Annecy*. Open 0900–1200, 1345–1830; 0900–1830 (July–Aug); Sun 1500–1800 (Oct–May).

GETTING AROUND

Annecy town centre and its **old town** are easily visited on foot. For the lakeside beaches, take a bus from *r. de la Préfecture*. Bus information at the kiosk on *r. de la Préfecture; tel: 50 51 70 33*.

Boats serve the towns around *Lac d'Annecy*. Departures from 1030 at *pl. des Bois*, near the château. Open Apr–Oct. **Compagnie des Bateaux du Lac d'Annecy**, *tel: 50 51 08 40*. Also round-trips and lunch and dinner cruises.

ACCOMMODATION AND FOOD

Annecy lives up to its nickname of 'Venice of the Alps' in more ways than one. Accommodation can be over-subscribed and expensive. **Hotel Bonlieu**, *5 r. Bonlieu, tel: 50 45 17 16*, is a moderately-priced no-frills new hotel near the lake. Hotel chains include; *Ca, IH, Me, Nv*. Cheaper options can be found in the area just north of the station – try *r. de Narvik* and *r. Fabien-Calloud*. There are several hostels with large four-bed or dormitory rooms.

HI: *La Grande Jeanne, 16 rte de Semnoz; tel: 50 45 33 19*. Bus no. 19 from the Hôtel de Ville (direction *Semnoz*, last bus 1900, fare in FFr.7). **Camping**: *rte de Semnoz; tel: 50 45 48 30*. Open Jan–Oct, very popular.

Like elsewhere in Savoie, Annecy cooks up a good *fondue*. Restaurants can be expensive, so picnics might be the best option. There are markets around *pl. Ste-Claire* near the château, on Tues, Fri and Sun. For less expensive restaurants head into the old town and towards the canal. While catering for tourists, a number of small family-run restaurants serve good-value fare like *fondue savoyarde* and *raclette*.

COMMUNICATIONS

Post Office: *4 r. des Glières; tel: 50 33 68 20*. Facilities include currency exchange, photocopying and poste restante. Open 0800–1900, Sat 0800–1200.

EVENTS

The first fortnight in July sees the **Festival de la Vieille Ville** – the old town festival, with music, eating and dancing and traditional costumes. On the first Sat in Aug the **Fête du Lac** is the biggest bash of the year, with fireworks, decorated boats and music on the lake.

SIGHTSEEING

Convinced of its reputation as the prettiest town in France, Annecy greets myriads of tourists every summer. The canal runs through the heart of the town, hence the nickname 'Venice of the Alps'. Tours run at 1500 daily in summer from the tourist office.

Divide your time between the lakeside and the old town. The lakeside promenades and gardens are a must and offer ample picnic opportunities. Boats can be rented in the park at *Champ du Mars*. The nearest public beach is found at *r. des Marquisats*.

The pleasure of the Old Town lies in wandering. From the tourist office, start along *r. Royale*, then cut down to the canal. The Quays along the canal are supremely picturesque. Cross the canal to the **Palais de l'Île**, *tel: 50 33 87 31*, a triangular 12th-century building which juts picturesquely into the water. Not surprisingly it's reputed to be the most photographed building in France. Formerly a royal residence, courthouse and prison, it is now a museum with displays on the town as it used to be. Open 1000–1200, 1400–1800 and 1000–1800 June–Sept, closed Tues. Admission FFr.20.

Annecy's main attraction is the **château**, *tel: 50 33 87 31*. Its terrace offers a fine view over the town. Inside it houses excellent exhibitions ranging from ones on the history, archaeology and folklore of the lake to modern painting. Open 1000–1200, 1400–1800, closed Tues; July–Aug daily and also open 1200–1400 in Aug; admission FFr.30,

OUT OF TOWN

Ten km west of Annecy are the famous **Gorges du Fier**, one of the most amazing sights in the Alps, where waterfalls crash over a series of narrow gorges. *Tel: 50 46 23 07*, open mid-March–mid-Oct 0900–1800, in summer 0900–1900. Admission for the walk up to the waterfalls is FFr.23.

Nearby the **Château de Montrottier**, *tel: 50 46 23 02*, is a medieval castle containing an interesting collection of furniture, china, lace and weapons. Open Mar–Oct 0930–1130 and 1400–1750, closed Tues except in summer. Admission/tour FFr.25. Bus excursions are available from **Voyages Crolard**; *tel: 50 45 09 12*, adjacent to Annecy's rail station and the Bonlieu centre.

LA ROCHE SUR FORON

Station: *1 pl. de la Gare; tel: 50 25 94 74*. **Tourist office**: *pl. Andrevetan, 74800 La Roche sur Foron; tel: 50 03 36 68*; open Mon–Fri, 0900–1200 and 1400–1830, Sat 0900–1200 and (mid-Apr–mid-Sept) 1400–1730. From the station take the first right, *blvd St Bernard*, five mins walk.

This charming little medieval town is the gateway to the high Alps, where ridges of grey rock tower above the forests and meadows of the wide River Arve valley. From the 11th–13th centuries it was the seat of the **Counts of Geneva** and the ruined white tower perched on a rock was part of their castle, *tel: 50 25 82 29*. From the top, you get a splendid panoramic view of **Lake Geneva** and the chain of mountains bordering the Arve valley. Guided tours of the tower leave from the tourist office between 19 June and 17 Sept and cost FFr.10. There are also tours of the town which still has its 12th-century gates and two small castles, FFr.25.

ANNEMASSE

See Geneva–Martigny route, p. 110.

LYON-NICE

Running towards the mountains south-east from Lyon, this route soon links up with River Bourbre to follow its curving course towards Grenoble, high-tech city of the Alps. Then it uses three more river valleys – in turn the Gresse, Lunnel and Buëch – to lead it south through the mountains to St-Auban.

Even so, it has to follow a tortuous route, twisting and turning almost the whole way, offering ever-changing views of rivers and mountains.

Sadly no trains have run on the line from St-Auban to Digne since 1990, though the SNCF still maintains full booking offices at both stations. Instead it provides a bus service. From Digne a 1-metre gauge line – *Train des Pignes* – runs down from the foothills of the Alps. After following the flat bed of the Var, with views up to medieval villages perched on hillsides, it finally reaches the palm trees and crowds of the Côte d'Azur.

Lyon

Grenoble

Briançon

Veynes

Digne   Annot

St Auban   Puget-Théniers

Entrevaux   Touët-sur-Var

Villars-sur-Var

Nice

FASTEST JOURNEY: 6 HRS

TRAINS

ETT tables: 151, 164, 154, 158, 166, 151d.

FAST TRACK

Six trains a day take the fast route down the Rhône valley and along the coast. The journey takes around 6 hrs with most trains having buffets.

ON TRACK

Lyon–Grenoble

A frequent service throughout the day taking between 1 hr 30 mins and 2 hrs.

Grenoble–Veynes

There are 4 trains each day, taking 2 hrs for the journey.

Veynes–St Auban

Four trains a day take an hour for this trip.

St Auban–Digne-les-Bains

A bus service connects with all trains and takes 35 mins.

Digne-les-Bains–Annot–Entrevaux–Puget-Théniers–Touët-sur-Var–Villars-sur-Var–Nice

Four trains a day run between Dignes and Nice Gare du Sud. Digne to Annot takes 1 hr 30 mins, Annot to Entrevaux 17 mins, Entrevaux to Puget-Théniers 8 mins, Puget-Théniers to Touët 12 mins, Touët to Villars 10 mins and Villars to Nice 1 hr.

GRENOBLE

For details, see p. 114.

VEYNES

Station: *pl. de la Gare; tel: 92 51 50 50.*
Tourist Office: *2 blvd Gambetta, 05400 Veynes; tel: 92 57 27 43.*

Veynes serves as the starting point for this scenic side track up the Durace valley.

⤵ SIDE TRACK FROM VEYNES

The rewards for adding adding an extra 1½–2 hrs travelling each way for this side track are considerable. The line climbs through increasingly rugged and remote mountain scenery along the Durance valley. Approaching Embrun, it runs beside the **Lac de Serre-Ponçon**, Europe's largest man-made lake (in summer an hourly shuttle-bus, FFr.5 each way, runs from the station to the lakeside beaches). Briançon, at the end of the line, is Europe's highest town.

BRIANÇON

Station: *av. du Gén. de Gaulle, tel: 92 51 50 50.* A 20-min walk to the centre of the old town (at first flat but then a steep haul up). Buses run to the centre every 30 min from outside the station, Mon–Sat 0640–1840, Sun 0900–1140.
Tourist Office: *Maison des Templiers, Vielle Ville pl. du Temple, 05100 Briançon, tel: 92 21 08 50.* Free accommodation service, central reservations; *tel: 92 21 01 01.* Open 1000–1200 and 1430–1800. Closed Sun Oct–5 Dec and 10 May–15 June.

ACCOMMODATION AND FOOD

The most interesting hotels and restaurants are in the old buildings on the narrow streets of the **Vielle Ville** (old town). Try the **Hôtel du Centre**, *3 pl. du Temple tel: 22 21 10 55,* or the **Pension des Remparts**, *14 av. Vauban, tel: 92 21 08 73,* for a bedroom oozing with character. The more modern hotels are situated outside the ramparts, including four large **Résidences de Tourisme** for self-catering. These are particularly popular during the ski season when accommodation throughout the area is at a premium.

Camping: Le Champ de Blanc, *Pramorel, 05100 Briançon, tel: 92 21 07 71,* is 3½ km west of the town.

Six restaurants in the old town serve 15th-century dishes based on recipes found in Paris libraries. Their waiters dress in suitable costumes to serve these *Menus Vauban,* particularly on Fri. But beware: hearty appetites were common then and with delicacies like fillets of salmon filled with prawns followed by stuffed game, the four-course menus are definitely not for anyone wanting a light meal. Just outside the old town walls is the family-run **Le Panicant**, *4 Chemin Vieux, tel: 92 21 10 48,* for grills and other Alpine dishes. *Tourton,* a cheese and meat-filled doughnut sold by bakeries, makes a tasty snack.

EVENTS AND ACTIVITIES

During July and Aug a daily entertainment programme includes concerts, plays and children's activities. A multi-activity card provides discounts of up to 30% on sports facilities and entertainment (on sale at the tourist office).

SIGHTSEEING

At 1329 m, Briançon is the highest town in Europe – a ski centre in winter, thanks to a cable car which links it to the slopes of **Serre Chevalier**, and in summer a place for walking, climbing, rafting and paragliding. Since Roman times it has guarded the road to the **Col de Montgenèvre**, one of the oldest and most important passes into Italy. The old town, **Cité Vauban**, on a rocky hill high above its modern sprawl, is very special, being completely enclosed by ramparts and entered through massive gates. Its network of steep narrow streets lined by tall period houses (which are being lovingly restored) converges on the narrow *Grande Rue* which runs straight up the centre with an open gulley down the middle of it. Interesting small shops now occupy the ground floors. Though some of the buildings are older, like the **Maison des Templiers** and the **Cordeliers church**, the fortified town was planned in the early 18th century by Louis XIV's military architect Vauban.

Paths lead on up from the ramparts through tunnel ruins to Vauban's citadel which crowns it all and commands magnificent Alpine views. ⛏

ST-AUBAN

The isolated station at St-Auban, surrounded by chemical works and gigantic oil refineries, is on the main line from Grenoble to Marseille. SNCF runs three buses a day linking it to Digne station. The last train to make the journey was in 1990.

DIGNE-LES-BAINS

Station: Gare de Digne, *tel: 51 50 50 50.* The town centre is 10 mins walk from the station – turn left at the main road. The station is shared – with separate booking offices – between SNCF and the privately-run **Chemins de Fer de la Provence**, *40 r. Clément Roassal, 06007 Nice, tel: 93 88 34 72,* which runs four trains a day to Nice throughout the year plus special day excursions, including steam trains between Puget-Théniers and Annot in summer and ski-specials in conjunction with the Val d'Allos resorts in winter.

Tourist Office: *le Rond-Point, pl. du*

Tampinet, 04000 Digne; tel: 92 31 42 73, (on the way into town from the station). Money exchange facilities. Open Mon-Sat 0845–1800.

ACCOMMODATION AND FOOD

Accommodation may be a problem in Digne in high season, so reserve in advance – the hotels are clustered around the main street, *blvd Gassendi*. The best restaurants are attached to the hotels, but fast food can be found on *pl. de Gaulle*.

SIGHTSEEING

Digne, on the River Bleone, is the 'capital' of the sparsely populated **Alpes-de–Haute–Provence** département. Surrounded by a necklace of mountains, it nevertheless has a feel of the Midi with plane trees shading the bustling pavements along its long straight main street, *blvd Gassendi*. It is a typical provincial town, unassuming and quiet, renowned for the purity of its air and a place which enjoys its isolation.

The sights can easily be covered in an afternoon's wandering. From the tourist office, *blvd Gassendi* leads to the main square, *pl. de Gaulle*, with its glitzy **Hôtel de Ville**. From here, steps climb up to the old town with its narrow cobbled streets. At the top, the **Cathédrale de St-**

Train des Pignes

The metre-gauge line from Digne to Nice CFP (*4 bis, r. Alfred Binet*) is operated by **Chemins de Fer de la Provence (CP)**, one of France's few regular private rail services. The first section, from Digne to Mézek, opened in 1891 but the full line took another 20 years to complete. As the little railcars lurch and jolt around lonely hillsides and across deserted pastures, over rushing rivers and finally down the broad built-up valley of the Var, there are beautiful views from pine forests to deep gorges. On the green hillsides above, white rocks peep through the trees.

Several sections of the track, including a viaduct over the River Var, were washed away in the disastrous floods of November 1994. This put a major question-mark over the whole line as it had never been financially secure and the Department of Transport was unwilling to pay for repairs. Permanent closure seemed to be inevitable. However the public outcry was fierce, not least because the train provides reliable year-round transport for 30 small isolated communites. It also forms part of Nice's busy suburban network. *Nice-Matin* newspaper launched a campaign to save the line and the 80 million francs required for repairs were subsequently provided by a combination of local, regional and national funding. During the repair work, passengers were transported by road between the undamaged sections. The line has now been fully reopened to trains.

On their 151 km scenic journey, the trains pass through 25 tunnels – the longest, at La Colle-St-Michel is 3457 m – and cross 31 bridges and viaducts. The highest point, 1022 m, is half-way between Thorame-Haute station and the tunnel through La Colle-St-Michel. The carriages are small with only 50 seats and room for 24 standing passengers. As there is only one class and no reservations, it pays to arrive early during July and Aug. Air conditioning and a drinks service are among refinements planned for the near future.

Special excursions with steam trains run between Digne and Entrevaux at weekends during summer, details from **CP**, *40 r. Clément-Roassal, 06007 Nice; tel: 93 88 34 72 or (information): 93 82 10 17*. Booklets on the line and walking routes are on sale at stations.

Jérome dates from the 15th century, but recent excavations have revealed foundations of a 6th-century church. At the far end of *blvd Gassendi*, a curiosity is the **Grande Fontaine**, a fountain where water flows from a huge mossy face.

Another intriguing attraction is the **Fondation Alexandra David Néel**, dedicated to the life of one of the world's greatest travellers, Alexandra David Néel. She was a Frenchwoman who set out for India in 1891, at the age of 23, and walked across Tibet. Later a friend of Gandhi and the Dalai Lama, she returned to France at the age of 80 and set up home in Digne, her 'Himalayas in miniature'. She was visited by the Dalai Lama before her death in 1969 at the age of 101. Guided tours of the Foundation, including its **Tibetan shop**, *rte de Nice, 27 av. du Maréchal Juin; tel: 92 31 32 38*, daily at 1030, 1400 and 1600 Oct–June and 1030. 1400. 1530 and 1700 July–Sept.

If you have more time to spare, Digne's **thermal baths**, one mile along *rte des Thermes, tel: 92 32 32 92*, offer relaxing mud baths, inhalation and water massage. Guided visits Wed 1400 Apr–Oct. Also on the edge of the town is the **Reserve Naturelle de la Haute-Provence**, Europe's largest geological park, where fossils – millions of years old – are clearly preserved in slabs of calcium. The **Geology Centre** there, *Quartier Saint-Benoît, tel: 92 31 51 31* (take bus no. 2) is open daily 0900–1200 and 1400–1730, closes at 1630 Fri and is closed Sat–Sun Nov–Apr.

ANNOT

Station: *tel: 92 93 20 26*.
Tourist Office: *Mairie d'Annot; tel: 92 83 23 03*. Accommodation service. **Centre de Montagne**, *Colle Basse; tel: 92 83 28 14*.

Annot has gone through several transformations in its turbulent history. At the end of the 14th century it was a strategic market town, on the border of Provence, Piedmont and the County of Nice. In the 18th century it became an industrial centre. Nut oil distilleries, lavender processing and tile manufacture brought wealth and prosperity. With the demise of nut oil the town went into decline, until the advent of tourism. Today, the altitude (705 m) and mild climate have made it a highly popular summer mountain resort offering pursuits like walking, tennis, golf and horse-riding. Yet it still retains a Provençal charm, with shady plane trees and ancient tortuous streets. It also has some fine restaurants serving inexpensive local delicacies. Head into the old village and admire its 16th-century stone, fortified church and vaulted passageways. Take the picturesque *r. Craponne* to *pl. des Platanes* where the bridge on the **Vaïre** dates back to Roman times. The rocky outcrops which surround the town have been moulded by erosion into weird and wonderful shapes making for some spectacular walks. The caves of the **Chambre du Roi** above the station are particularly remarkable, having once served as a retreat in times of invasion. The highlight of the town's year is the Whitsun festival of **St Fortunat** which includes a procession commemorating the end of the Napoleonic Wars. Grenadiers dressed in red and white uniforms march through the town.

ENTREVAUX

Station: *tel: 93 05 41 38*.
Tourist Office: *Tour du Pontlevis; tel: 93 05 46 73*.

Clinging to a hillside, Entrevaux is in many ways the most dramatic sight in the whole region. Indeed many passengers ride on the train just to get there. It has been a place of strategic importance for centuries – a fort in Roman times and then in the Middle Ages on the border between the kingdom of France and the estates of the Dukes of Savoy. The present lofty **fort**, reached by a long series of steps which zig-zag up the steep rocky hillside, was built by Louis XIV's illustrious engineer Vauban at the beginning of the 17th century. A 10-franc coin gets you through the turnstiles at the drawbridge (which still works). The climb is strenuous – 30 mins up, 10 down – but the reward is a magnificent view over the **Var valley**.

The town also has ramparts and 17 of its ancient fortified gates are still intact. Variety is provided by the Luciani family's **motorcycle exhibition** showing models from 1904 up the present day; *tel: 93 71 99 65*. Open daily July–Aug 0900–1200, 1400–1900 or by arrangement.

PUGET-THÉNIERS

Station: *tel: 93 05 00 46*.
Tourist Office: **Syndicat d'Initiative**; *tel: 93 05 02 81*.

Puget comes as a shock – a sizeable town with plenty of tourist facilities (pool, tennis, fishing, canoeing) in the midst of the imposing mountains. Seven hundred years ago it was the headquarters of the **Templar Knights** and many of the houses date back to this time, still bearing the insignia of respective lords and knights. One street, *r. Gisclette*, contains the rings used to thread the chains which barred the road each night. The local church was built by the Templars and restored in the 17th century. The local people are very attached to the bronze statue, the **Naked Lady of Maillol**, which now commands pride of place in the main square. It was dedicated to the memory of **Auguste Blanqui**, a local 'agitateur' born in 1805,

who spent 40 years behind bars for campaigning for the rights of workers. The clergy were scandalised when the statue was put up in 1911 near the church, so it was hastily moved. Hidden for safety in the local abattoir and later in Nice during World War II, the locals insisted on having it back after the liberation in 1945. A copy stands in the Tuileries gardens in Paris.

TOUËT-SUR-VAR

Station: unstaffed.
Tourist Office: *Hôtel de Ville; tel: 93 05 75 57*.

This small medieval village clings tenaciously to a sheer cliff like a 380 m high fortress. Narrow alleyways and steep steps lead between terraces of quaint old houses whose balconies brim with flowers. **St Martin's church**, restored in 1986, straddles a waterfall on huge stone pillars. The newer, less interesting part of the town is down around the main road and old-fashioned station. For four days in the middle of Aug each year the local **Lou Festin** festival takes over the town.

VILLARS-SUR-VAR

Station: unstaffed.
Tourist Office: *Hôtel de Ville; tel: 93 05 70 04*.

Two km from the station on the Savel plateau, this little town has the distinction of its own *Appellation Controlée* wine, **Côtes de Provence**. The vineyards were first planted in the Middle Ages, at the same time as the streets were designed – motor vehicles are banned from the village. The **parish church** is the only real 'sight', containing a couple of paintings dating from the early 1500s. On 24 June visitors can join the annual procession along mountain tracks to **St Jean du Désert** for a festive picnic.

199

LYON–TURIN

Heading east from Lyon, the countryside is relatively flat but glimpses of distant mountains soon hint at the dramatic scenery to come. Shortly after Chambéry the line links up with the River Isère which it follows north-east to St-Pierre d'Albigny. From there the side-trip to Bourg St-Maurice stays with the river all the way. Meanwhile the main route links up with the River Arc at St Pierre d'Albigny to follow it east to Modane before diving into the mountains through the famous Fréjus Tunnel. All the way the train's progress is punctuated by bends, tunnels and viaducts – and the scenery is awe-inspiring as the peaks get higher and snowier. If you're a skier or walker you certainly won't want to rush to Turin, but rather pause at the mountain resorts for this route is the gateway to some of the best high-altitude areas in France – the Trois Vallées, La Plagne and Val d'Isère.

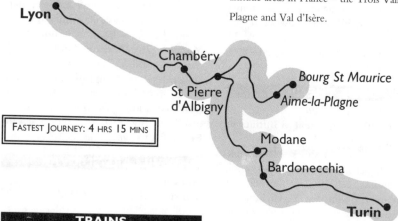

200

FASTEST JOURNEY: 4 HRS 15 MINS

TRAINS

ETT tables: 45, 152, 352.

FAST TRACK

At the moment three trains a day make the 4 hrs 15 mins journey. A new faster service is expected to begin in Winter 1996/7.

ON TRACK

Lyon–Chambéry
Ten trains a day run from Lyon Part-Dieu or Perrache to Chambéry, with journey times of about 1 hr 30 mins.

Chambéry–St-Pierre d'Albigny
The 20 mins journey is run 8 times a day.

St-Pierre d'Albigny–Modane
Four or five trains a day taking 1 hr 15 mins.

Modane–Bardonecchia

Ten trains a day run between French Modane and Italian Bardonecchia taking 17 mins.

Bardonecchia–Turin (Torino)

A frequent service with trains taking 1 hr 30 mins.

CHAMBÉRY

Station: Chambéry-Challes les Eaux: *pl. de la Gare; tel: 79 85 50 50*. The town centre is 5 mins walk down *r. Sommeiller*. **Tourist Office**: *24 blvd de la Colonne, 73000 Chambéry; tel: 79 33 42 47*. English-speaking staff provide walking tour maps. In the same building the **Agence Touristique Départementale de Savoie**; *tel: 79 85 12 45*, has information on ski resorts and summer hiking. Both open 0900–1200 and 1330–1800 Mon–Sat.

CIDJ: Youth information, *4 pl. de la Gare; tel: 79 62 66 87*.

ACCOMMODATION AND FOOD

Chambéry is never as crowded as its neighbour Aix (see p. 189) and has a good selection of attractive hotels. Chain hotels include: *Ca, Ib, IH, Mc, Nv*.

Hotels in the central area are surprisingly affordable; the area around the château is a good bet – *pl. St-Léger* and *pl. Hôtel de Ville*.

There are no campsites in the area.

The heartland of Savoie, Chambéry offers fine regional cuisine at affordable prices. Salamis, hams and various other salted meats are specialities and cheese is the basis of many dishes, particularly the sociable *fondue Savoyarde* eaten from a communal pot. **Thones** on Lake Annecy is the centre for making the rich *Reblochon* cheese which gets is name from 'reblocher', a local word meaning to milk a cow for the second time. Soft and creamy, it goes perfectly with the refined white wines of Savoy. There are numerous low-priced restaurants throughout Chambéry's **old town** – try *pl. Monge, pl. Hôtel de Ville* and *r. Croix d'Or*. **La Chaumière**, *14 r. Denfert-Rochereau; tel: 79 33 16 26*, is a cosy restaurant offering traditional dishes at an affordable price.

Communications

Post office: *pl. Paul Vidal; tel: 79 69 92 10*. Poste restante, telephones and currency exchange facilities.

SIGHTSEEING

Ancient capital of Savoie, Chambéry is the epitome of an Alpine town. With a distictly Italianate feel, it is quiet compared to the tourist meccas of Annecy and Aix and makes a good base for exploring the higher Alps. Most of the main sights are within the central area which is easily walkable; part of the centre is pedestrianised. Excellent guided tours of the château and the old town, daily in summer, weekends Oct–Apr. Chambéry's role as home to the Dukes of Savoy brought the town great riches. The old town abounds with magnificent mansions, especially along *r. Croix d'Or*.

The **Château des Ducs de Savoie**, *pl. du Château*, is the highlight. It was built in the 15th century and updated in the 19th. Now most of it is occcupied by the préfecture of police, but a small part can be visited including the attractive **Sainte Chapelle**. Outside the tourist office stands the town's most famous monument, the **Fontaine des Éléphants**, erected in honour of Général de Boigne who presented his home town with some of the fortune he made in India. Two museums are worth seeing: **Musée des Beaux Arts**, *pl. du Palais de Justice; tel: 79 33 75 03*, has the best collection of Italian paintings in France outside the Louvre, and **Musée Savoisien**, *blvd du Théâtre; tel: 79 33 44 48*, in a former convent, covers local history. Both open 1000–1200, 1400–1800, closed Tues.

Two km outside town along a marked trail, the **Sentier Jean-Jacques Rousseau**, is **Musée Rousseau**, *Chemin des Charmettes, tel: 79 33 39 44*, in the beautiful 17th-century country house where this famous French philosopher lived. Plenty of his memorabilia are on show, but the real attraction is his botanic garden. Open Apr–Sept 1000–1200, 1400–1800 summer, closed at 1630 winter. Closed Tues, admission FFr.20.

ST-PIERRE D'ALBIGNY

Station: *pl. de la Gare. Information; tel: 36 35 35 35.*
Tourist Office: (Wed mornings only), *Immeuble Le Savoie, 73250 St-Pierre d'Albigny; tel: 79 71 44 07.*

SIDE TRACKS FROM ST-PIERRE D'ALBIGNY

From St-Pierre (and Chambéry) a line runs as far as **Bourg St-Maurice**, through the heart of the Alps. This serves some of the best skiing and hiking areas in the Alps. Train stations serving the resorts are **Moûtiers** (for Méribel and Courchevel), **Aime-la-Plagne** (for La Plagne) and **Bourg-St-Maurice** (for Les Arcs, Tignes and Val d'Isère). The service from St-Pierre d'Albigny to Bourg St-Maurice (a journey of about 90 min) consists of about six trains a day, beginning with the overnight train direct from Paris.

MÉRIBEL/COURCHEVEL

Station: Gare SNCF Moûtiers; *tel: 79 85 50 50* for information; *79 62 40*

60 for reservations. Regular bus services run to Méribel (journey time 40 mins) and Courchevel (55 mins). **Bus: Trans Savoie**; *tel: 79 24 03 31.*
Tourist Office: Méribel: *73550 Méribel; tel: 79 08 60 01.* **Courchevel**: *73120 Courchevel; tel: 79 08 00 29.*

ACCOMMODATION

The best selection in the region in a wide range of prices – everything from first-class hotels to self-catering chalet apartments. Central booking; *tel: 79 00 50 00.*

SIGHTSEEING

In winter the **Trois Vallées** ski area, with **Meribel** in the centre linked by cable car to **Courchevel** over the Saulire mountain ridge on one side, and by chairlift over the Col de la Chambre to **Val Thorens** on the other, is one of the largest in the world. Meribel has a distinctly British atmosphere – indeed it was developed after World War II by a Scotsman, Colonel Peter Lindsay, who insisted on traditional Alpine chalet-style buildings. Courchevel is much more French and snooty.

Good walking trails criss-cross the area when the snow melts away in summer. Other sports are on offer too including paragliding, skating and golf – the 18-hole course is the best in the Alps; *tel: 79 08 52 33.* Meribel also has an ice-rink and a planetarium.

LA PLAGNE

Station: Gare SNCF Aime-la-Plagne; *tel: 79 09 77 04.* Regular bus service to La Plagne Centre (30–40 mins). **Bus: Voyages Bérard**; *tel: 79 09 73 45.*
Tourist Information: *Le Chalet, BP 62, 73211 Aime; tel: 79 09 79 79.*

ACCOMMODATION

A large range of self-catering chalet residences plus a few one to three-star hotels catering for winter and summer visitors. Central booking; *tel: 79 09 79 79.*

SIGHTSEEING

Purpose-built for skiing in the 1960s, La Plagne has six different resort areas, each like a village – **Plage Centre, 1800, Bellcôte, Belle Plagne, Villages** and **Aime** – all linked and offering varied skiing for all abilities, including challenging off-piste when the snow is good. Distant views of **Mont Blanc** and the **Matterhorn** add enchantment to the thrills. The resorts are also linked by chairlifts to four villages in the neighbouring valleys, **Montchavin, Les Coches, Champagny** and **Montalbert**. Over-16s can hurtle down the **Olympic bobsleigh run** (built for the 1992 Olympics); *tel: 79 09 12 73,* open Dec–Mar FFr.170, or in a competition bobsleigh, FFr.460 per go. In summer, skiing is possible on the 3000 m **Glacier de la Chiaupe** but most visitors then come to walk. White-water rafting, paragliding and mountain-biking are also on offer. Each of the resorts also organises children's activities which include everything from swimming to mountain-biking, rafting to archery. Children can join by the day or for the week.

LES ARCS

Station: Gare SNCF Bourg-St-Maurice; *tel: 79 85 50 50.* 5-min funicular railway to Arc 1800.
Tourist Office: *Maison des Arcs, 73700 Bourg-St-Maurice; tel: 79 07 12 57.*
Accommodation is plentiful and rea-sonably priced. Central booking; *tel: 79 07 26 00.*

Particularly popular with the young crowd, the skiing covers 200 km of pistes, the highest at 3200 m, with incredible views up to **Mt Blanc**. In summer **Bourg-St-Maurice** itself is the Alpine capital of water-sports, from rafting and jet-skiing to canoe-kayaking.

VAL D'ISÈRE/TIGNES

Station: Gare SNCF Bourg-St-Maurice; *tel: 79 85 50 50.* Regular buses to Tignes and Val d'Isère (50-min journey). **Bus: Autobus Martin**; *tel: 79 07 04 49.*
Tourist Information: *73150 Val d'Isère; tel: 79 06 06 60*; Tignes; *tel: 79 06 15.*
Accommodation is not inexpensive, but plenty of choice, particularly apartments. Central booking; Val d'Isère; *tel: 79 06 18 90*; Tignes; *tel: 79 06 35 60.*
The winter season stretches from Nov to May, offering some of the best skiing in Europe over the two linked ski areas. In summer there are miles of walking trails; also mountain-biking and extensive glacier skiing.

MODANE

Station: *1 pl. Sommeille; tel: 79 20 13 00.*
Tourist Office: *pl. du Replaton, 73500 Modane; tel: 79 05 22 35.*

ACCOMMODATION

The best selection is in the purpose-built ski resort of **Valfréjus**, a 7 km drive up from above Modane. Shuttle buses services during the ski season. **Bus: Transavoie Autocars**; *tel: 79 05 01 32.*
Camping: Le Camping Caravaning des Combes, *rte de Bardonnèche; tel: 79 05 00 23.*

203

SIGHTSEEING

Although Italy is a mountain range away, Modane in the river Arc valley has been very much a border town ever since the **Fréjus rail tunnel** was completed 1871 just after the arrival of the railway there. Modane's second tunnel (for road traffic), 12,870 m long, opened in 1980, having taken six years to build.

An exhibition in an old railway carriage at its **Monumental Entrance** on the road to Replat provides an fascinating insight into its construction, both the politics and technicalities involved. A nearby curiosity is the **Slanted Blockhouse** which protected the entrance and was blown up by retreating German troops in 1944 leaving it on the tilt – and distinctly unbalancing when you go inside. The **St-Gobain Fort** on the road to Aussois was part of the **Maginot Line** fortifications, built before World War II and capable of supporting 150 soldiers for a three-month siege (visits by arrangement). All three are now in the care of **l'Association du Musée de la Traversée des Alpes**; *tel: 79 05 01 50.*

Modane itself was badly bombed in 1943 – hence all the high-rise rebuilding. Its oldest and most attractive part clusters around the ancient **Chapelle Saint-Jacques**, which has recently been restored.

Being surrounded by mountains, the town is a popular walking and mountaineering centre in summer, but in winter most visitors come to ski. The Alpine hamlet of **Le Charmaix,** 7 km away, perched 1550 m high on a wooded hillside above the town has been transformed into a purpose-built ski resort and renamed **Valfréjus** with 52 km of pistes served by two cable cars. (**Tourist information**: *Résidence les Mélezets, 73500 Valfréjus; tel: 79 05 33 83*).

Fréjus Tunnel

The French call it the **Tunnel du Fréjus,** the Italians the **Mont Cenis Tunnel**. Completed in 1871, this is the first of the great Transalpine tunnels and it improved immeasurably communications between the eastern Mediterranean and Northern Europe. Its opening caused Brindisi to boom but for Marseille it was bad news.

It is 12.8 km long and took 15 years to build. A plaque commemorates Germain Sommeiller, a local engineer who developed the technology of tunnelling with compressed air. Sadly he died shortly before it was completed.

BARDONECCHIA

Tourist Office: *Via della Vittoria 44; tel: (0122) 99032.*

ACCOMMODATION

Accommodation here is fiercely competitive and there are more expensive hotels than there are cheaper ones. However, if you don't mind paying a litle bit more, you're almost guaranteed a view – they are almost universally tremendous.

SIGHTSEEING

Bardonecchia, the first halt in Italy after the tunnel, is a ski resort with an excellent reputation. Hugely popular with the Torinese as well as the French, it has a wide range of facilities. Well developed – although the old stone town centre is still intact – it also offers possibilities for walking, riding and skating. Historic sights are scarce although the **Museo Civico** (*Piazza Vittorio Veneto*) contains artefacts of local folkloric interest.

MILAN (MILANO)

Milan is the commercial hub of Italy, a city, packed with banks and financial institutions, which boasts a standard of living high even for the wealthy north of the country. It, and its industrial and commercial acumen, were chiefly responsible for the strength and assertiveness of the Italian post-war miracle. Today it is deeply style-conscious, as befits one of Europe's top fashion centres. Be prepared for inflated prices when shopping for clothes, modern furniture and antiques and when eating in drop-dead chic restaurants.

A Celtic and Roman settlement, Milan gained importance during the Middle Ages, under the authority of a series of influential bishops, and, even then, was known for its money changers. The Visconti and Sforza families ruled Milan during most of the 13th to 16th centuries. The Viscontis started construction on the Duomo, while the Sforzas built the castle and brought to Milan many of the top artists and thinkers of the time, including Leonardo da Vinci – whose Last Supper is the city's greatest treasure.

Modern Milan is one of Italy's great cities. Undervisited by dawdling tourists, partly because at first glance it is not as becoming as Florence, Rome or Venice. The city centre is filled with huge 19th- and 20th-century apartment blocks and quaint corners are hard to find. Nonetheless, they do exist: there are pretty brick-built Lombard Romanesque churches, tree-filled squares dominated by statues and, best of all, a vast early Renaissance castle as the city's focus.

This city is hugely cosmopolitan; Milan is Italy's Manhattan. It has the best clubs in Italy and is a shopper's paradise. But here too are some of the country's great artistic treasures – key paintings of the Italian Renaissance, magnificent churches in whose design Bramante had a hand. It also the scene of Europe's most important modern furniture fair. Here, too, good traditional cooking is highly sought after – as is more up-to-date cuisine which uses the best, well-tried Mediterranean ingredients.

TOURIST INFORMATION

Main APT office: *Palazzo del Turismo, 1 Via Marconi; tel: (02) 809 662*, to the right of the Duomo. Free maps and guides to Milan in English. Open Mon–Sat 0800–2000, Sun 0900–1200 and 1330–1700. **Branch**: **Stazione Centrale**; *tel: (02) 669 0532.*

ARRIVING AND DEPARTING

Airports
Malpensa, about 50 km north-west of Milan, serves intercontinental and charter flights. **Linate**, 7 km from Milan, handles domestic and European flights. Buses to and from both airports depart from the **bus terminal**: *Piazza Luigi di Savoia; tel:*

(02) 6698 4509, right beside Stazione Centrale. For information on flights from either airport, *tel: (02) 7485 2200*.

Stations

The vast majority of trains serve the monumental and fully-equipped **Stazione Centrale**, *Piazza Duca d'Aosta; tel: (02) 675 001* (metro lines 2/3). Some trains stop instead at **Stazione Porta Garibaldi**; *tel: (02) 655 2078* or **Stazione Lambrate**; *tel: (02) 675 001*, both served by metro line 2. Milan's prime position in the heart of northern Italy always helped its trade; now the city acts as the key node in Italy's railway system.

GETTING AROUND

Metro, Buses and Trams

The same tickets are used for all public transport. Single tickets (L.1200) are good for one journey on the metro or 1 hr 15 mins travel on the buses. Tickets are available from machines in metro stations or from tobacconists (*tabacchi*) and newspaper kiosks. A day pass (L.3800) and two-day pass (L.6600) are available from underground stations.

The metro, **Metropolitana Milano (MM)**, is clean, efficient and easy to use. There are three colour-coded lines. Cancel tickets in the gates at station entrances.

The **bus** and **tram** systems are more comprehensive and consequently more complicated, but stops have details of each route serving them. Buy tickets in advance and validate them in the machines on board.

Taxis

Milan's taxis are yellow and can be expensive. There's a substantial flat fare to start with and extra charges are applied for bag-

gage and travel on holidays or late at night. There are large ranks at Stazione Centrale and *Piazza Duomo* and cabs can also be booked by phone or hailed on the street. Avoid touts offering unofficial taxis.

STAYING IN MILAN

Accommodation

Accommodation in Milan does not escape the inflated prices of the rest of the city, but there are plenty of *pensions* around the station and the town centre. Major hotel groups are well represented and include *Ch, Ex, HI, Hn, Ib, Nv* and *Rm*. The tourist office will provide a full list of accommodation. Alternatively, the **Hotel Reservation Milan** service, *24 Via Palestro; tel: (02) 7600 7978*, can help find a room.

HI: **Youth Hostels**; *2 Via Martino Bassi; tel: (02) 3926 7095*, (metro line 1 to QT8 station). **Camping**: *Via G Airaghi; tel: (02) 4820 0134*. Open all year.

Eating and Drinking

The Milanese take their food seriously and are prepared to pay substantial sums for their meals. Unsurprisingly, restaurants can be very expensive. Better value eateries include the lunch spots catering for office workers, with many reasonable self-service restaurants around the town centre. Away from the city centre, as with any Italian city, there are family-run *trattorie* and a variety of other inexpensive places. At lunch-time, customers often eat standing up. *Pizzerie* and Chinese restaurants offer reasonably priced evening meals. Bars tend to serve more coffee than alcohol, along with *panini* – rolls with a multitude of fillings.

Regional specialities include *cotoletta alla milanese*, an Italian version of Wiener schnitzel, *risotto alla milanese* (rice dish) and

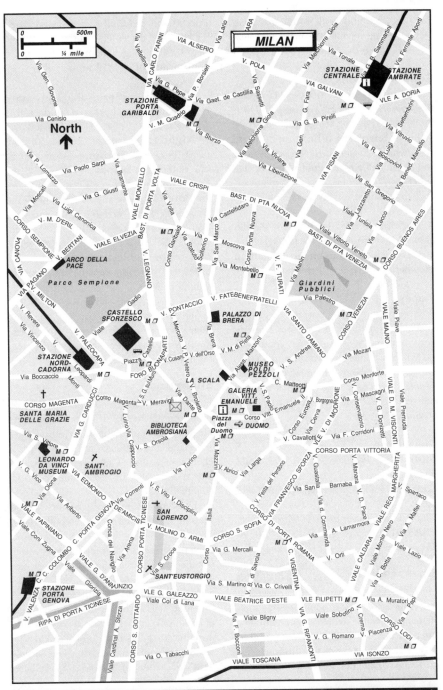

the vegetable and pork soup *minestrone*. Despite being inland, Milan has excellent fish, fresh from the coast.

Communications

The **central post office**, *1 Piazza Cordusio; tel: (02) 869 2069*, is open 24 hrs for telexes, faxes and telegrams.

Public **telephone offices** can be found at *Galleria V Emanuele II, 4 Via Cordusio*, and Stazione Centrale. Public phones take either coins or phonecards, the latter available from automatic cash dispensers and kiosks.

The dialling code for Milan is *02*. To phone Milan from abroad: *tel: 39 (Italy) + 2 (Milan) + number*; to phone Milan from elsewhere in Italy: *tel: 02 + number*.

Money

There is no shortage of bureaux de change in Milan; sometimes it seems as if every third building is a bank. At weekends, exchange facilities are available in *Piazza Duomo* and Stazione Centrale and in both airports. Automatic machines that convert cash are located in the town centre and in Stazione Centrale.

Consulates

Australia: *2 Via Borgogna; tel: (02) 7601 3330.*
Canada: *19 Via Vittor Pisani; tel: (02) 669 7451.*
UK: *7 Via S. Paolo; tel: (02) 869 3442.*
USA: *2 Via Principe Amadeo; tel: (02) 290 351.*

Milan's daily newspapers, *La Repubblica* and *Corriere della Sera* produce weekly supplements detailing Milan's entertainment and nightlife.

The city's most famous institution is the grand **La Scala** opera house. Donizetti,

Puccini and Verdi all staged operas here. Tickets are extremely elusive, but you may be able to get them on Mon, for a performance of classical music rather than opera.

The **Conservatorio** also hosts concerts. Cinemas cluster around *Corso Vittorio Emanuele*, near *Piazza Duomo*.

Nightclubs tend to close around 0200–0300. **Le Scimmie** (Monkeys) is one of the most famous.

Two of the more trendy areas of town are **Porta Ticinese** and **Brera**. The Porta Ticinese and the Navigli (canals) district is home to a high concentration of bars and venues (the actual Porta Ticinese is a remnant of the 14th-century city ramparts). Cafés and bars also dot the small streets around Brera.

Via Brera is the showcase of Milan's fashion industry. The Milanese care about their clothes and smart dress is the norm for almost all nightlife throughout the city, even informal promenading.

SHOPPING

For Italians - and foreigners - Milan is shopping Heaven. It's an expensive Heaven, particularly if it's clothes (also shoes and furs), modern furniture or jewellery you're after. The variety is astonishing and usually of exceptionally good quality.

The Milanese are very serious about dressing up. You rarely see anybody badly dressed, shabby or down-at-heel. Governing the façade they present to the outside world, regardless of wealth or indeed poverty, is the concept of *bella figura* (in basic translation this means 'looking good'). Thus by far the biggest range of fashion magazines on sale at news-stands turn out to be fashion bibles, each one avidly read out of necessity. The 'drop-dead' chic shop in *Via della Spiga*; here most of the designer labels (**Versace, Krizia**) have their shop windows. Neighbouring *Via S Andrea* (**Armani, Moschino**), *Via Montenapoleone* (**Gucci, Ferragamo**) and *Via Borgospesso* mop up the overspill. Those with smaller bank accounts should visit the shops in *Via Torino* and department stores **La Rinascente** and **Coin**.

In the centre of the city there is a concentration of furniture showrooms and shops. **Artemide**, one of the best, is at *Corso Monforte 19*. The longest, busiest, and possibly the densest shopping street in Milan is *Corso Buenos Aires* where it is possible to buy almost anything. Otherwise, the *Viale Papiano* market (Sat) in the **Navigli** district is good for cheap clothes and a variety of other bargains. The **Brera** district is worth visiting. Here there is a Mon market (*Piazza Mirabello*), while Naviglio Grande is the scene of a monthly **Antiques Fair** (last Sun of the month).

SIGHTSEEING

Piazza del Duomo

If a city can have such a thing as a 'signature building', then Milan's is undoubtedly the **Duomo** (Cathedral), *Piazza Duomo* (metro: *Duomo*). Extravagantly adorned with pinnacles, tracery and buttresses, it is rather an oddity in a country not noted for the Gothic style of its cathedrals. Milan's cathedral has a fight on its hands as it competes with surrounding neon signs, department stores and copious numbers of defecating pigeons, for the attentions of passing tourists in a rather down-at-heel, shabby square. As architecture goes, it is both magnificent and strangely ugly in equal measure. Napoleon liked it though: he was crowned King of Italy here in 1805. Work started in 1386, at the behest of Gian Galeazzo Visconti. Wanting a son,

and finding his prayers granted, he built this remarkable edifice as a tribute to the Virgin Mary. However it was not until 1958 that the last pinnacles were finished in a pale marble from the Candoglia quarry – from which the building is still furnished during repairs.

The Duomo is a magical and extravagant Gothic structure. Gothic artisans from the north were responsible for producing it and, although attempts were made to refashion it in prevailing Renaissance and baroque styles, it has survived as something of a misnomer in the annals of Italian architecure. Both longer and wider than St Paul's in London, it is overflowing with belfries, statues and pinnacles in white marble. It shimmers in the sunlight and glows in the winter fog. The comparatively stark interior is dimmed by vast quantities of fine stained glass and there are works of art which predate the cathedral's construction.

Stairs lead up to, over and around the extensive roof system, from which there are fine views out over the city to the Alps. It also provides the opportunity to examine close-up some of the adornments to the cathedral's exterior – not to mention the 15th-century dome whose spire is topped by a gilt statue of the Madonna. The **Cathedral Museum** (in the Royal Palace just by the Duomo) houses sculptures, carvings, stained glass, tapestries and other treasures removed for safekeeping from the Cathedral.

On the north side of *Piazza Duomo* is the **Galleria Vittorio Emanuele II**, a monumental 19th-century iron and glass shopping arcade known as the **Salon de Milan**. Here there are elegant cafés in which to shelter from the city's interminable winter drizzle. The Galleria leads through to *Piazza della Scala*, home of **La Scala** (more properly the Teatro alla

209

Scala), probably the most famous opera house in the world. For such a famous place, the scale and proportions of the theatre are remarkably sober, even insignificant – even though it can seat 2800 spectators. **La Scala Theatre Museum**, in the building, exhibits a huge array of opera memorabilia – scores, costumes, portraits and set designs. It also provides the opportunity to see into the opera house itself.

Nearby (*Piazza Belgioioso*) is the **Museo Manzoniano**, dedicated to the Italian novelist Alessandro Manzoni whose classic, *I Promessi Sposi*, profoundly shaped the Italian public's sense of literature and language. When it was written, only 4% of the population could speak Italian – the rest spoke in regional dialects. Its re-edition in 1841 marked an attempt to move from linguistic regionalism to nationalism – and Italian high school students have cursed Manzoni ever since. It is the mainstay of their literary eduction.

Piazza di Brera

The **Accademia del Brera**, *28 Via Brera*, is Milan's finest art gallery. Situated in a rare surviving quarter of old streets and alleys, it was founded by Napoleon and opened in 1809, housing many artefacts looted from across Italy's Northern Italian region. The collection concentrates on Italian artists of the 14th–19th centuries, although foreign schools of the 17th–18th centuries are also represented. There are some outstanding works here - notable among them Raphael's *Marriage of the Virgin* and Mantegna's *Dead Christ*. There are also works by Piero della Francesca, Bramante, Carpaccio, Bellini, Caravaggio, Veronese, Rembrandt, El Greco and Van Dyck. A wing houses the 20th-century collection which contains, amongst others, works by the Futurist painters Severini and

Balla. The gallery is housed in part of the **Palazzo di Brera**; in the courtyard stands a statue of Napoleon I which dates from 1809.

Piazza Pio XI

Further priceless art works are displayed in the **Ambriosiana Gallery**, *2 Piazza Pio XI* (metro: *Duomo* or *Cordusio*). The collection was begun by Cardinal Federico Borromeo early in the 17th century, and over the centuries judicious additions have been made so that today it is one of Italy's finest collections of paintings. Works by Leonardo da Vinci include the portrait of the musician Caffurio. Here too is Caravaggio's *Basket of Fruit* and Raphael's cartoons for the School of Athens fresco in the Vatican Palace in Rome. There are works by Pinturicchio, Jan Brueghal the Younger, Giorgione and Titian. An eccentric collection of artefacts includes the glove Napoleon wore at Waterloo.

The Ambrosiana also houses the **Biblioteca Ambrosiana**, a library founded by Borromeo at the same time. One of the greatest libraries in 17th-century Italy, it still houses a Virgil manuscript, a 5th-century version of the Iliad, early editions of Danté's *Divine Comedy* and a host of drawings by da Vinci. In all, there are over 30,000 manuscripts (closed for restoration).

Churches and Monasteries

Milan's single most famous painting, Leonardo da Vinci's *Last Supper* (1495–1497), dominates the old Dominican monastery refectory next to **Santa Maria Delle Grazie** (metro: *Cadorna*). The Last Supper, depicting Jesus saying 'One of you will betray me', attracts large crowds and a hefty entrance fee. Heavily restored after years of deterioration – practically since the artist finished

210

working on it – and following drastic wartime bomb damage, it nonetheless survives and can seen. It is one of the great paintings of the Renaissance. The church itself, a Renaissance building designed by Solari, and worked on later by Bramante, is also worth a look. Bramante was responsible for the tribune (1492), the choir, sacristy as well as the **Chiostrino**, the cloister. The external appearance of the church exemplifies the typical Lombard Romanesque brick and terracotta style of architecture.

Not far from Santa Maria Maggiore is the **Monastero Maggiore** (*Via Luini*) whose little 16th-century church of **San Maurizio** houses frescos by Bernardino Luini, an avid follower of Leonardo da Vinci. The monastery itself contains the **Museo Civico Archeologico**, Milan's archaeological museum, whose comprehensive collection of artefacts includes Greek and Roman ceramics, Roman glass, Etruscan objects and a collection of finds from the Holy Land.

The **Basilica of Sant'Ambrogio** (metro: *Sant'Ambrogio*) was built in the late 4th century by St Ambrose, patron saint of the city and former Bishop of Milan – a man so eloquent and smooth in speech that his name was given to a honey liqueur. Most of what is standing today dates from the 12th century, although the smaller campanile, 300 years older, is one of the most ancient in the region. The complex, and the basilica in particular, was the prototype for Lombardy's Romanesque basilicas. You enter through a huge porticoed atrium dominated by two towers, the left-hand Canon's Campanile (built 1144) and the right-hand Monks Campanile (built in the 9th century). In the church itself is some particularly fine Romanesque sculpture, including the pulpit. There are 10th–11th-century mosaics

in the apse and even older ones (5th century) in the little **Sacello di San Vittore in Ciel d'Oro**, at the end of the south aisle. In the crypt are housed the remains of St Ambrose. Bramante was here too: his is the **Portico della Canonica** (enter from the left aisle). The upper level of the Portico houses the **Museo della Basilica di Sant'Ambrogio** which contains a variety of items including illuminated manuscripts and architectural fragments relating to the building's earliest history.

Where *Via Spadari* meets *Via Torino*, is the church of **San Satiro**. Rebuilt by Bramante in 1476, it acquired a new façade in the 19th century. Don't be deterred by that however – or by the busy commercial surroundings. This is one of Milan's finest churches. Also by Bramante is the little **Baptistery** situated at the edge of the right aisle. Here too is the **Cappella della Pietà**, a rare surviving example of Carolingian architecture (9th century).

The **Basilica of San Lorenzo**, *39 Corso di Porta Ticinese*, has a similar history to Sant'Ambrogio, having been built around AD 500 and reconstructed some 700 years later. A notable portico of 16 columns from a Roman temple stands in front.

Museums and Galleries

The **Castello Sforzesco**, the castle of the Sforzas, in *Piazza Castello* at the end of *Via Dante* (metro: *Cairoli*), is a distinctive, seemingly indescructible fortress whose walls are nearly 12 ft thick in places. The present building was constructed by Francesco Sforza in the second half of the fifteenth century on top of an earlier Visconti fortress. It has been much knocked about throughout subsequent centuries, and during the last war it suffered extensive damage during air raids, following which parts of it were rebuilt –

211

including its towers which now contain cisterns. The castle now has a rather more benign role than in the past. Today it houses an encyclopaedic collection of galleries and museums, displaying everything from arms to furniture, from Egyptian art to musical instruments.

The pick of the bunch is probably the art gallery, the **Museum of Antique Art** and the **Pinacoteca.** The first contains Renaissance sculpture (its most magnificent piece is Michelangelo's *Rondanini Pietà*), furnishings and decorative arts. The seconds displays the works of a variety of Italian painters including Bellini, Mantegna and Lippi.

The **Cortile della Rocchetta**, a courtyard designed by Bramante and Filarete, gives access to the **Museum of Musical Instruments** which contains a spinet on which Mozart played. Here too are the **Egyptian Collection** and the **Prehistoric Collection.** Behind the castle is **Sempione Park**, the largest green space in central Milan. At the far end is the **Arco Della Pace** (Arch of Peace), which has seen many wars in its 150-year lifetime.

The **Poldi-Pezzoli Museum**, *12 Via Manzoni* (metro: *Montenapoleone*), was originally assembled by Gian Giacomo Poldi-Pezzoli, a well-to-do Milanese collector and donated to the city in 1879. It is yet another of the city's great collections and well deserves a visit.

The museum includes an excellent collection of Renaissance paintings including works by Botticelli, Pollaiuolo, Bellini, Lotto, Raphael and Mantegna.

There is also a collection of Renaissance armour and bronzes and a diverse and eclectic array of tapestries, glass and rugs.

Twentieth-century Italian art is displayed at the **Contemporary Art Museum**, *9 Palazzo Reale, Piazza Duomo*. It has an excellent collection of works by a range of Italian artists of the this century – including De Chirico and Mogdiliani. The **Civic Gallery of Modern Art**, on the edge of the Public Gardens (metro: *Palestro*) contains works by a variety of French Impressionists and their Italian contemporaries.

The gardens themselves, the **Giardini Publici**, were laid out in 1782 and they provide welcome respite from the unrelenting urban quality of this vast, busy, traffic-filled metropolis. Children can play here – there is a zoo and a playground – and here too is the **Natural History Museum** which contains an awesome stuffed white rhino.

The **Leonardo da Vinci National Museum of Science and Industry,** 21 *Via San Vittore* (metro: *Sant'Ambrogio*), is not just an attempt to capitalise on the great man's name.

In addition to the displays relating to Leonardo's own ideas, including a model of his famous air-screw, (precursor of the helicopter), there are exhibits relating the evolution of science. There are collections of musical instruments and radios, clocks and computers, and there is a collection of trains.

Two fairly new museums have been established in the chic *Via della Spiga* district (see 'Shopping'): the **Museo Civico di Milano** and the **Museo Civico di Storia Contemporanea**, both in the 18th-century *Palazzo Morando Bolognini* (*Via S Andrea*).

The first documents the history of Milan – essential viewing if you are trying to understand why Milan looks like it does.

The second museum documents Milan's history during the interwar years – and Mussolini is a much-featured item.

Other sights

Not far away (intersection of *Via della Spiga* and *Via Manzoni*), the **Archi di Porta Nuova**, the arches of the old city gate (the *Porta Nuova*), is a rare surviving feature of the city's 12th-century walls.

In the south east, the **Porta Romana** is one of Milan's original Renaissance gates (*Piazza Medaglie d'Oro*). It dates from 1598. Not far away is the church of **San Nazaro Maggiore** (*Corso Porta Romana*). Although begun in the 4th century, it has been rebuilt on several occasions and now presents a largely Romanesque face to the world. Its best feature is the **Cappella Trivulzio**, designed by Bramantino. Sixteenth century **Santa Maria presso San Celso**, *Corso Italia* typifies the Lombard Renaissance style. Its interior has paintings by, amongst others, Paris Bordone. Nearby is little **San Celso**, a 10th-century church much restored in the 19th century.

In the Western suburbs stands a modern structure as distinctive and monumental as either the Duomo or Sforza Castle. The **San Siro Stadium**, a futuristic construction of steel lattices and huge concrete cylinders, is visible for miles in all directions.

A different kind of Milan can be seen in the **Navigli** district (metro: *Porta Genova*). Once a working district of workshops, warehouses and bars catering for the needs of sailors focussed on two navigable canals – the Naviglio Grande and the Naviglio Pavese – this part of the city still has the flavour of a seaport and today is Milan's up-and-coming answer to London's Covent Garden or New York's Greenwich Village. Trendy, full of art galleries and funky shops, bars, clubs and restaurants, this is a haven from the often oppressively bourgeois flavour of the rest of the city.

 SIDE TRACKS FROM MILAN

There are frequent services from Milano Porta Garibaldi to **Bergamo** and the journey takes just over an hour.

Bergamo is a small, self-contained city looking out over the Lombard plain. Prosperous and sophisticated, its highlights in the **Citta Alta** (Upper Town) are the **Piazza Vecchia** with its 16th-century **Biblioteca Civica**, the **Torre Civica** and the **Palazzo della Ragione**, both of which date from the 12th century. But the real treasure of this city is the **Cappella Colleoni**, *Piazza del Duomo*, built (1476) to house the tomb of the illustrious *condottiere*, Bartolomeo Colleoni. The 14th-century **Baptistry** and the 12th-century **Basilica di Santa Maria Maggiore** are interesting neighbours for this extraordinary sculpture-festooned building, while the neo-classical **Duomo**, by contrast, is rather dull.

Bergamo has four museums. In *Via Colleoni*, the ancient **Cittadella** fortress houses the **Natural History Museum** and the **Archaeological Museum** and in *Via Arena* the **Museo Donizettiano** is associated with the musician Donizetti (who is buried in Santa Maria Maggiore). The **Pinacoteca Carrara**, *Piazza dell'Accademia*, contains an important collection of works by masters of the Renaissance.

Tourist Office: in the Citta Bassa, *Viale Giovanni XX111 106, tel: (035) 242 226*, and in the Citta Alta, *Vicolo Aquila Nera 3, tel: (035) 232 730*. **Cremona** is less visited but, as in Bergamo, a tour is easily accomplished in a day – enough time to see around the **Museo Stradivariano**, *Via Palestro 17*, the museum of the city's chief export to the world, the violin.

213

MILAN–CHUR

This route from the Italian lakes to Switzerland, which has no speedy direct service, skirts the eastern banks of the so-called Lago di Lecco, the righthand leg of the Lago di Como. The scenery becomes increasingly dramatic as the route proceeds north, darting in and out of tunnels deep in the rugged mountains which fall steeply down into the water. At Colico the line branches east and continues on through the Valtellina and in the shadow of the Orobi Alps before continuing on to Tirano. The latter section of this journey, from Tirano to Chur, is one of the most scenic in all Switzerland and is covered by the special Bernina Express service. The Bernina Pass itself (2253 m) is the figurative and literal highlight with marvellous panoramic views. After the Val Bernina are yet more wonderful scenic valleys, most notably the Engadine, which also hosts the super-resort of St Moritz.

Chur

St Moritz • **Bernina Diavolezza**

• **Poschiavo**

FASTEST JOURNEY: 7 HRS 30MINS

• **Tirano**

Sondrio

Lecco

Milan

TRAINS

ETT Tables: 362, 328, 330

ON TRACK

Milano–Lecco
A train runs in most hours from Milano Centrale to Lecco. The journey takes 40 mins.

Lecco–Sondrio
A roughly hourly service operates taking around 1 hr 30 mins.

Sondrio–Tirano

The frequent service takes around 40 mins.

Tirano–Poschiavo

50 mins is required for this journey with frequent trains.

Poschiavo–Bernina Diavolezza

The frequent service takes around 1 hr.

Bernina Diavolezza–St Moritz

The roughly hourly service takes 36 mins.

St Moritz–Chur

The hourly service takes just over 2 hrs with buffets on most trains.

There are many spectacular high-level bridges and viaducts on this route. Look out in particular for the famous Kreisviadukt, (Circular Viaduct) at Brúsio; the Landwasser Viaduct, 130 m long and 65 m high (between Tiefencastel and Filisur); the Soliser Viadukt (between Tiefencastel and Thusis), the Rhaetian Railway's highest at 89 m.

LECCO

Tourist Office: *Via Nazario Sauro 6; tel: (0341) 362 360.* Open Mon–Sat 0900–1230 and 1430–1800.

ACCOMMODATION

Lecco is a convenient place to stay – convenience and practicality come at the expense of beauty. However, the hotels are very reasonably priced particularly the **Alberi**, *Lungolago Isonzo 4; tel: (0341) 363 440.* It looks directly onto the lake. Just outside the town – about 1 km away at Malgrate – the more expensive **Il Griso**; *via Statale 29; tel: (0341) 202040* has wonderful views.

SIGHTSEEING

The first stop of any importance is Lecco, a small town which is a good focus for excursions into the surrounding countryside. Partly industrial, nonetheless its dramatic backdrop is worth the effort – but be prepared for early morning mists.

The **Villa Manzoni**, *Via Amendola* is Lecco's chief attraction. Birthplace of Alessandro Manzoni (1785–1873), writer of Italian literature's classic *I Promessi Sposi* it is now a museum. The **Basilica** in the town is also worth a visit: inside it is a set of Giottesque, 14th-century frescos.

Lecco is a very good base for excursions into the neighbouring **Grigna Mountains** and to **Mount Resegone** which dominates the town. The point of departure is **Mandello del Lario,** a very short train ride away to the north. A particularly good hike, one which involves scaling an iron arrangement of ladders and ropes (take walking boots and proper maps) begins at **Piani Resinelli** (take a bus from outside the station).

SONDRIO

Tourist Office: *Via C Battisti 12; tel: (0342) 512 500.*

ACCOMMODATION

There isn't a lot of choice here, though the town's old staging post hotel, **Bella Posta**, in *Piazza Garibaldi 19; tel: (0342) 510 404*, isn't too pricey.

SIGHTSEEING

The provincial capital, Sondrio, dominated by the **Castello Masegra**, is a fairly modern-looking town – although the last vestiges of former days struggle valiantly on.

Palazzo Quadrio houses the **Museo Valtellinese**, a museum of local traditions and folklore. It also has an archaeological

215

collection. This museum is a focal point for obtaining an overview of the area's enthnographic make-up.

Sondrio is situated in a region famous for its **wine** – in fact some of Italy's most renowned wines come from here (Sassella and Grumello, for example). While the vines can be seen growing carefully trained up and around frames on the steep surrounding hillsides, the wines can be tasted in the Palazzo Quadrio.

TIRANO

The Valtellina is curiously uneventful when it comes to listing the sites of real international interest. However, Tirano, the railway terminus at the bottom of the northern stretch of the Valtellina has one of the region's most significant attractions: the **Sanctuary of the Madonna di Tirano** (situated about 1 km from the city). This small building is a Renaissance masterpiece (begun 1505), having been built in the style of Bramante.

Of particular interest is the ornate stuccoed interior which contains a richly decorated wood organ (1617). In the town itself there is a series of small, **historic palaces** (left bank of the River Adda) built for, amongst others, the Pallavicini and Visconti families.

POSCHIAVO

Station: *tel: 157 22 22.*
Tourist Office: *Piazza Communale; tel: 082 5 05 71.*

Tucked just inside the Swiss-Italian border, Poschiavo is much more southern than northern influenced with a lovely central **piazza** surrounded by fine Italianate houses. Also on or just off the piazza is the 17th-century **town hall**, the Lombardian-style Gothic **Church of San Vittore** and the 17th–18th-century **Church of Santa Maria Presentata** fea-

Engadine Architecture

The villages of the Engadine region are characterised by large, sturdy, stone houses (designed also to accomodate the stable) adorned with *sgraffito*. This is a technique of mural decoration whereby a layer of plaster is cut or scratched to reveal different layers below. This is usually in just two-colours (top and base layers) and features geometric designs, arabesques and scrolls. Excellent examples of the art are to be found in Celerina, Samedan, and particularly **Zuoz**, the best preserved village in the Engadine with several superb 16th-century patrician buildings (from St Moritz to Samedan, 8 min; change for Zuoz 16–18-min).

turing a glorious ceiling. Look too for the colourful houses in the **Spaniola Quarter**, settled by Spanish emigrants in the 19th century.

BERNINA DIAVOLEZZA

Station: *tel: 157 22 22.*

If you only alight from the train once during this spectacular journey, then the **Diavolezza** (2973 m), reached by cablecar, gives probably the finest viewpoint over the whole Bernina Pass. This is a very popular skiing (and walking) area with the 10-km descent on the glacier from Diavolezza to Morteratsch a particularly famous run. (There's another famous viewpoint two stops later at Morteratsch. From here a 30-min walk will bring you to the **Chunetta belvedere** offering marvellous views over the glacier.)

ST MORITZ

Station: *tel: 082 3 31 34.*
Tourist Office: *Via Maistra 12; tel: 082 3 31 47.*

ACCOMMODATION AND FOOD

Accommodation and food are generally less expensive in St Moritz-Bad.

HI: *Via Surpunt 60; tel: 082 3 39 69.* This is an excellent place to stay; do book early.

(Note: St Moritz effectively closes down during May, early June and Nov.)

SIGHTSEEING

'Top of the World' shouts the latest St Moritz slogan and no matter that Verbiers, Gstaad, Zermatt, Davos and Klosters may all claim equal celebrity status, St Moritz still leads the way. Its location is superb scenically and with an average 322 days of sunshine per year St Moritz is officially the sunniest place in Switzerland.

Legend has it Swiss winter tourism first began here in 1864 when an enterprising St Moritz hotel pioneer offered four English summer visitors an all-expenses paid return winter visit. The English accepted, came at Christmas, loved it, stayed until Easter and spread the word (note the splendid posters for sale in the tourist office, depicting winter holidays in the 1890s).

In 1928 and 1948 St Moritz was Switzerland's only Winter Olympic host village and has subsequently flown the flag in many international ski and bobsleigh meeting. Novelty winter sports introduced to the world include *skijoring*, (where a horse pulls a skiier along by the reins) and latterly international golf, polo, cricket and other sporting tournaments have all been played on the town's frozen lake. International horse-racing on ice ('white-turf'), which usually takes place in Feb, is one of the great events in the St Moritz calendar.

The town is not resting on its laurels however, hosting the Polo World Championships (on grass!) in summer 1995 and the Bobsled World Championships in winter 1997. Before the century is out a casino and a cultural centre/regional museum are also planned.

St Moritz divides into Dorf (village) on the hill, and Bad (spa) 2 km downhill around the lake. St Moritz-Dorf is where the major hotels, shopping and the town's two museums lies.

The **Engadine Museum** is a regional collection of folklore and local artefacts while the **Segantini Museum** spotlights the work of the acclaimed local 19th-century artist, after whom it is named.

The centre for downhill skiing is **Corviglia** (2486 m) but even if you're not skiing it's worth the 2-km funicular trip for the fine views and a glimpse of the beautiful people at play.

To enjoy the rest of St Moritz you really need to participate in one of its myriad sports; walking is the most (perhaps only) affordable pursuit for travellers on a budget.

217

The Cresta Run

The famed Cresta Run was the world's first purpose-built bob-sleigh (bobsled) run and is still one of the world's scariest sporting pursuits.

To make the point as forcefully as possible the British club instructor briefs first-timers using an anatomical skeleton to point out just how many bones riders are likely to break if they don't follow procedures rigorously.

The course stretches over 1.4 km and ends near Celerina. A slightly safer ride is the 2- or 4-man Bob Run along the Olympic course, which visitors may ride alongside experienced 'pilots' for around SFr.180. For more details call the Cresta Run club; *tel: 082 3 41 10.*

MILAN–VENICE

The scenery is the least remarkable aspect of this route, though the halts, and the side tracks from them, more than make up for this. The route skirts the edge of high ground which ascends gradually to the north towards the Alps. To the south, the vast Lombard plain sweeps on towards the River Po beyond which are the rugged Apennines.

En route you will encounter some of Italy's most historic cities, graced with architecture ranging from the grandeur of the Roman era to the neo-classical elegance of the late Renaissance.

At Verona you can switch routes to Innsbruck–Verona (p. 132) if you wish to head north into the Austrian Tyrol.

Innsbruck–Verona, p. 132

Milan

Desenzano del Garda

Verona

Vicenza

Padua

Venice

FASTEST JOURNEY: 2 HRS 30 MINS

ROUTES

ETT Table: 350

FAST TRACK

A mostly hourly Inter City service is the fastest connection on this route with journey times of around 2 hr 30 mins. Most trains have refreshment services available. An additional hourly Interegionale (IR) service takes 3 hr 15 mins.

ON TRACK

Milan–Desenzano del Garda–Verona–Vicenza–Padua–Venice

The hourly services call at all these stations (IR trains only at Desenzano). Milan to Desenzano takes 1 hr 30 mins, Desenzano to Verona 17 mins, Verona to Vicenza 30 mins, Vicenza to Padova 18 mins and Padova to Venice St Lucia 20 mins.

TRAINS

DESENZANO DEL GARDA

Tourist Office: *Porto Vecchio 27; tel: (030) 9141510.* The tourist office at nearby Sirmione is at *Viale Marconi 2; tel: (030) 916 114.*

ACCOMMODATION

Accommodation is varied in Desenzano del Garda, none of it remarkable. Sirmione is a better option if you don't mind travelling between the two towns (about 10 km). Many of the hotels are pricey – and generally full particularly in July and Aug. For a cheaper option, try the **Hotel Grifone**, *Via delle Bisse 5; tel: (030) 916014.* The tourist office can supply a list of rooms and there is a **campsite** on *Via Colombara*, about 15-mins walk from the centre (in the direction of the mainland) – **Sirmioncino**, *tel: (030) 919 045.*

SIGHTSEEING

Desenzano del Garda is a good place to begin a tour of Lake Garda. A regular hydrofoil service connects it with Riva del Garda in the north, and with other ports up either side of the lake. Situated at the southern tip of Lake Garda, it is a small port-cum-resort which has seen better days. However it has been a popular holiday venue ever since the Romans discovered the health-giving properties of the thermal waters spouting from the lake at Sirmione (see below).

Desenzano del Garda is a town of cafés, lakeside restaurants and sweeping lake views. Its chief attraction is the excavated ruin of a 4th-century **Roman villa**, *Via Crocefisso*, which can be visited along with a small museum devoted to finds from the site.

It is just a few kilometres to **Sirmione**, a small resort straddling the narrow Sirmione peninsula poking out into the lake just to the east of Desenzano del Garda. More lovely than its neighbour, it is dominated by the dramatic **Castello Scaligero** (13th century) from which Mastino I della Scala of Verona terrorised the lake in the Middle Ages.

The **ruins** of the Roman spa can be visited (by the Lido). Called the **Grotte di Catullo**, it was long believed that this was the site of the lakeside villa of the Roman poet Catullus, who had much to say about the beauty of Sirmio in his verse. There's not much to see, although the waters are still frequented by those who want to take a cure. This is a charming spot, with a beach, wonderful views and a small museum housing miscellaneous fragments from the site.

> ### SIDE TRACK
> ### FROM DESENZANO
> From here you can side track north to the resorts around Lake Garda before continuing your journey eastwards or westwards. For more details of these places, see the Innsbruck–Verona route, pp. 132–134.

VERONA

Station: *tel: (045) 590 688,* 15–20 mins walk south of the centre (bus nos 1/8/51/58).

Tourist Office: *Via Leoncino 61; tel: (045) 592 828.* **Branch:** *Piazza delle Erbe 38; tel: (045) 803 0086.* Both open Sat 0800–1900/2000 and Sun 0900–1400. *Verona For You* lists entertainments.

ACCOMMODATION

There is plenty of cheap hotels and student accommodation (booking is essential for the opera season: July–Aug). Hotel chains with property in the town include: **HI:** *Salita Fontana del Ferro 15; tel: (045) 590 360,* 3 km from the station, across *Ponte Nuovo* (bus nos 2/20/32/59); permits

219

camping in the grounds. **Campsite:** *Via Castel San Pietro 2; tel: (045) 592 027,* mid-June–mid-Sept, walkable from centre (bus no. 3).

SIGHTSEEING

Walking is undoubtedly the best way to explore the centre, which is remarkably traffic-free by Italian standards. Get buses to travel further afield.

Verona was important ancient Roman city. Situated at the foot of the Alps on a navigable river (the Adige), it was of immense strategic value. At the time of its colonisation by the Romans (89 BC), it produced three important citizens – the poet Catullus (see 'Sirmione' above), Vitruvius, the most prominent architect and engineer under Emperor Augustus, and Pliny the Elder, the writer responsible for recording the eruption of Vesuvius as he watched.

In the Middle Ages Verona was smitten by internal warfare between rival local notables – providing Shakespeare with the inspiration for *Romeo and Juliet* – but during the Renaissance the city blossomed. Since then it's had a colourful history, having been linked to the fortunes of Venice and Austria. Badly bombed during the war, it nonetheless has much to recommend it.

Verona was at its peak in the 13th century, when ruled by the della Scala (Scaligeri) family, great art lovers. They commissioned works which impart considerable charm to the modern town. With lots of romantic rose-coloured marble, Verona is a good setting for *Romeo and Juliet*, but Juliet's house, *Via Cappello*, isn't worth the entrance fee. Her 'tomb', *Via del Pontiere*, is a restful spot.

The most significant of the many Roman remains is the **Arena,** *Piazza Bra*, which seats 20,000: one of the world's largest amphitheatres. After the Colosseum, this is one of the best-preserved antique amphitheatres in the Mediterranean world. The inner complex is virtually intact, complete with its 44 tiers of pink marble. It holds an annual opera and ballet festival which always includes a spectacular production of *Aida* (well worth attending, but hire a cushion).

Across the river, the **Museo Archeologico** displays Greek, Roman and Etruscan artefacts. There are good views from the terraces and the grounds contain the **Teatro Romano**, another ancient entertainment centre still used for performances, some of which are free. These include Shakespeare (in Italian), jazz and ballet. Above, the **Castel San Pietro** is a 19th-century fortification which obscures earlier constructions of the Roman and early Renaissance eras. Go up here for the most magnificent views out over Verona.

Other Roman remains include several monumental arches and parts of excavated streets. **Piazza delle Erbe**, originally the Roman forum and now the site of a colourful flea market, is the heart of the city and surrounded by Renaissance palaces. The **Arco della Costa** leads to *Piazza dei Signori*, also surrounded by impressive old buildings, including the **Palazzo degli Scaligeri** and graceful 15th-century **Loggia del Consiglio.**

Near the square, by the Romanesque church of **Santa Maria Antica,** are the extraordinarily ornate Gothic tombs of the dynasty, **Arche Scaligeri**. An equestrian statue that once topped one of them now stands outside **Castelvecchio Museum,** *Corso Cavour*, which houses weapons, jewellery and some notable religious paintings. The excellent works by little-known medieval artists rival those of the acknowledged masters, also displayed.

220

Just north-west of the centre is church of **San Zeno Maggiore,** a superb example of the Romanesque style which contains a notable Madonna altarpiece by Mantegna and magnificent 11th–12th-century bronze doors which created a nationwide demand for similar portals.

Sant'Anastasia is a mainly Gothic church with 14th-century exterior carvings. Inside, Pisanello's *St George and the Princess* is of particular interest. *Via Duomo* leads to the striped red and white marble **Duomo** (cathedral), a blend of Romanesque and Gothic that contains an *Assumption* by Titian and a choir by Sansovino.

SIDE TRACK
FROM VERONA

MANTUA (MANTOVA)

Tourist Office: *tel: (0376) 350 681.*

Mantua is a melancholy city, set in flat, damp landscape by the River Mincio. Its original claim to fame was as the birthplace of Vergil, the greatest of Roman poets. In the Middle Ages and the Renaissance it became powerful and extremely prosperous under its Gonzaga rulers. Any student of the Renaissance would be foolish to pass it by.

One of its most important monuments is the **Palazzo Ducale** whose principal treasures are Mantegna's frescos in the *Camera degli Sposi.* At the bottom of *Via Acerbi,* the **Palazzo Te** was designed and decorated by Giulio Romano – as was the interior of the **Duomo** *(Piazza Sordello). Piazza Mantegna* is dominated by the façade of Alberti's church, **Sant'Andrea,** one of the seminal works of Renaissance architecture, while **San Sebastiano** *(Via Acerbi),* also by Alberti, is the first

Renaissance church to be built on a central Greek cross plan.

VICENZA

Station: *tel: (0444) 325 045,* 10 mins walk south of the centre (bus nos 1/7). **Tourist Office:** *Piazza Matteotti 12; tel: (0444) 320 854.* Mon–Sat 0900–1230 and 1500–1800; Sun 0900–1230.

ACCOMMODATION

The cheapest hotels are away from the centre or in noisy locations, so it's worth considering two-star places. Book ahead for summer and autumn. **Camping:** *Campeggio Vicenza, Strada Pelosa 241; tel: (0444) 582 311,* 20 mins by bus (no. 1) from the station.

SIGHTSEEING

Most places of interest are in the old centre, and easily walkable; there is a good bus network.

A prosperous provincial city with a well-preserved medieval centre, Vicenza was largely rebuilt in the 16th century, to designs by Andrea di Pietro della Gondola, better known as **Palladio.** He gave his name to the Palladian style: an elegant form of architecture that applied Renaissance concepts to classical forms. Architectural pilgrims flock to the city, as do businessmen involved in the electronics industry, for Vicenza is situated in what might be called 'Italy's Silicon Valley'. Here, Federico Faggin, inventor of the silicon chip, was born.

Porta Castello (all that remains of the medieval castle), marks the start of *Corso Palladio,* which is the old town's main road and lined with imposing palaces, and *Contrà Porti* is another street with several fine buildings. The Gothic **Duomo,** about a block from Porta Castello, is a post-war reconstruction.

Palladio

The influence of Andrea Palladio (1508–1580) on the architecture not only of northern Italy but of the world cannot be overstated. His greatest works, such as the Villa La Rotonda (see below) and San Giorgio Maggiore and other buildings in Venice (see pp. 296–303), together with his *Four Books of Architecture*, inspired the revival of ancient Greco-Roman forms and principles of architecture throughout Europe and ultimately led to the elegance of the English Georgian and American Colonial styles of the 18th century.

The **Piazza dei Signori** was the Roman forum and is still the hub of the city. It is noted for the magnificent **Basilica**, a medieval palace which was once in severe danger of collapsing. Palladio's first public project was to shore it up using Ionic and Doric columns, saving it and establishing his reputation. The roof is concealed behind a statue-lined pediment, one of the hallmarks of his later work.

Still in *Piazza della Signoria*, there is the strange tower, the **Torre di Piazza** (12th–15th century), and another Palladio building, the unfinished **Loggia del Capitaniato** (1571), built in celebration of the Victory of the Battle of Lepanto.

Palazzo Chiericati, *Piazza Matteotti*, also by Palladio, houses the well-stocked **Museo Civico**, containing paintings by such masters as Tintoretto, Brueghal, Bassano, Veronese, Van Dyck and Memling.

The entrance ticket also covers **Teatro Olimpico,** the oldest indoor theatre in Europe, opened in 1585 and still in use during the summer months. Based on the theatres of Roman antiquity, this was Palladio's last work, and possibly his finest. It has excellent acoustics and a set (by Palladio and Scamozzi) designed in wood and stucco, destined as the backdrop for the theatre's first-ever production – Sophocles' *Oedipus Rex*. Also in the square, the 13th-century Dominican church of **Santa Corona** has two great paintings: Bellini's *Baptism of Christ* and Veronese's *Adoration of the Magi*. A third masterpiece, Vecchio's *Madonna and Child*, is in nearby **Santo Stefano**.

About 1.5 km south-east of the centre (bus nos 8/13) are two notable villas: **Villa Valmarana dei Nani**, an 18th-century country house with marvellous Tiepolo frescos; and **Villa La Rotonda**, Palladio's most famous creation, which inspired a number of great buildings including Chiswick House in London. Go on Wednesday, so you can see inside. Built not to live it but as a setting for occasional entertainments, the geometry of its design is flawless: a circular cupola atop a cube flanked by four symmetrical porches.

PADUA (PADOVA)

Station: Stazione Ferroviaria, *tel: (049) 875 1800*, at the northern edge of town.
Tourist Office: **APT,** in the station; *tel: (049) 27767*. Mon–Sat 0900–1800 and Sun 0900–1200. *Padova Welcome* is a very informative booklet about the town and area.

ACCOMMODATION

Plenty of choice (try around P*iazza del Santo)* but booking is advisable. University rooms may be available in summer, *tel: (049) 828 3111*. **HI:** *Via Aleardi 30; tel: (049) 28369* (bus nos 3/8/11). **Camping:** *Montegrotto Terme, Strada Romana Apponese; tel: (049) 793 400* (15 mins by train). It has a pool and thermal baths.

SIGHTSEEING

Padua, extensively damaged in World War II, has a history dating from 45 BC. Somewhat overshadowed by its more illustrious neighbour, Venice, it is often perceived as the poor relation. And yet Padua has an illustrious artistic inheritance. Giotto worked here, his frescos in the Cappella degli Scrovegni being the focal point of the earliest years of the Renaissance. Both Mantegna and Donatello worked here too, while the city's university (1222), one of Italy's most celebrated, is associated with Galileo, Dante and Petrarch.

Giotto's work is simply one compelling reason to visit Padua. In the **Cappella degli Scrovegni** in *Corso Garibaldi*, it is a glorious three-tier depiction of scenes from the New Testament. Its 36 panels were begun in 1304 and are still in near perfect condition today. This is possibly Giotto's masterpiece; it is here that he experimented with the depiction of three-dimensional volume in space – a departure from contemporary tradition so revolutionary that it ultimately changed the entire course of western European painting.

The adjacent **Museo Civico** holds a variety of mainly 14th–18th-century paintings (Giotto, Bellini, Titian, Veronese), and a collection of ancient Greek and Roman coins. The neighbouring **Eremitani** church, severely damaged in World War II air raids, once contained exceptionally important frescos by Mantegna (in the Ovetari Chapel). Much of it was restored from fragments - see in particular the Martyrdom of *St Christopher and St James*. The Eremetani also boasts a beautifully carved wooden ceiling.

Padua's other major attraction is 'Il Santo' – **the Basilica di Sant'Antonio,** *Piazza del Santo*. This is a mixture of archi-tectural styles (its oriental flavour is not unlike St Marks' in Venice) and a major pilgrimage centre, miraculous powers being attributed to relics of St Anthony whose tongue and jaw are housed here in a head-shaped reliquary. His chapel (on the left hand side) contains 16th-century panels depicting scenes from his life, but more notable are the sculpted panels lining the walls. These are by Sansovino and Lombardo. The basilica's high altar, with its bronze statues of the *Madonna* and the *Six Patron Saints of Padua* are by Donatello, as are the relief panels depicting the *Miracles of St Anthony*.

Donatello's magnificent **equestrian statue of Gattamelata** is the central point of the *Piazza del Santo*. This is one of the most important works of the Renaissance – it was the first major bronze of the period and the largest to be cast since antiquity. Gattamelata ('Honey Cat') was the nickname of Erasmo da Narni, one of the most formidable *condottieri* or mercenary leaders of Renaissance Italy.

Still in the piazza, the **Oratorio di San Giorgio** is adorned with frescos by followers of Giotto, while the works in the nearby 15th-century **Scuola del Santo** include early Titians. Just to the south is the **Orto Botanico**, Europe's oldest botanical gardens. Established in 1545, it was originally the university's herb garden and has changed little since.

There are some attractive 15th–16th-century buildings on **Piazza dei Signori.** Just to the south of this is the Duomo, a much-altered and not very interesting cathedral adjacent to the Romanesque **Baptistery**, lined with lovely 14th-century frescos. The 16th-century **University Building**, *Via VIII Febbraio*, where Galileo lectured, is worth a visit just to see the old anatomy theatre.

MUNICH (MÜNCHEN)

With a population of only 1.3 million, Munich, state capital of Bavaria, is big enough to be exciting, yet small enough to be approachable. The cliché view of Bavaria is beer, sausages, and a laid-back approach to life – although it is equally famous for its conservative politics. However, its capital city offers plenty to see and do and is far from lacking in cultural and historic attractions. It also has plenty of exciting nightlife. Allow at least two days. Munich is an ideal gateway for exploring the German Alps or travelling onward to Austria or Switzerland.

TOURIST INFORMATION

Fremdenverkehrsamt der Landeshauptstadt München (Munich Tourist Board), *Postfach 80313 München; tel: (089) 2 39 11* (0900–1500, Fri 0900–1230), has information centres at Hauptbahnhof (main railway station), *Bayerstr.* entrance; *tel: (089) 2391 256/257*, open Mon–Sat 0800–2200, Sun 1100–1900; at Munich Franz-Josef Strauss Airport, Central Building; *tel: (089) 97 59 28 15*, open Mon–Sat 0830–2200, Sun and hols 1300–2100; and in the city centre at *Rindermarkt/Pettenbeckstr.*, open Mon–Fri 0930–1800. A good city map is available free from all information centres. The tourist board also has two English-language information lines; for information on museums and exhibitions *tel: (089) 2391-62*, on excursions to Bavarian castles *tel: (089) 2391 72*. Youth information: try

Jugendinformation, Paul-Heyse-Str. 22; *tel: (089) 51410660*.

Thomas Cook, *Kaiserstr. 45*, offers a full range of services to visitors, including hotel reservations, car rental and bookings for sightseeing and excursions, as well as the services covered by the Thomas Cook Worldwide Customer Promise.

ARRIVING AND DEPARTING

Airport
Munich's **Franz Josef Strauss Airport** is Germany's second international hub (after Frankfurt). Flight information; *tel: (089) 97 52 13 13*.

S-Bahn line S8 runs every 20 mins from Hbf via the city centre to the airport between 0333 and 1153. First service from the airport is at 0355, last service at 0055. For the city centre, get off at *Marienpl.* Journey time is 36 mins. Buses run every 20 mins between 0310 and 2130 connecting the airport with the Hbf, journey time about 45 mins.

Stations
Hauptbahnhof München (Hbf), *Bahnhofpl.* (about 1.5 km from *Marienpl.*) is Munich's main railway station, and southern Germany's most important rail junction. Timetable information: *tel: (089) 19419*; fare information: *tel: (089) 55414*; ticket reser-vations: *tel: (089) 128 5857*; seat, sleeper and couchette reservations: *tel: (089) 1223 2333*; recorded information: *tel: (089) 11531 35*.

GETTING AROUND
You can get around the 3–4 sq km of the

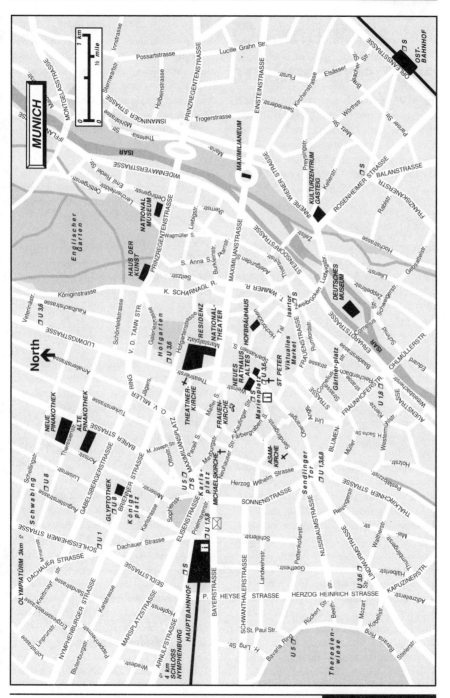

compact city centre easily on foot, and Munich rewards walkers more than most German cities, with its wide boulevards, gracious neo-classical buildings and neatly laid-out parks. For trips further afield, use the **MVV** public transport system, which combines buses, trams, S-Bahn (overground) and U-Bahn (underground) trains. You can get information on S-Bahn routes, tickets and timetables from **Deutsche Bahn** (German Federal Railways), *tel: (089) 557 575.*

Tickets

Buy them at stations, newsagents, hotel desks and campsites. A 12-strip **Streifenkarte** costs DM15; each strip is good for a four-stop trip. A **Tageskarte** (day trip ticket offering unlimited use of the system) costs DM10 for inner Munich, DM20 for the whole city, and is extra good value for night owls as it is valid from 0900 until 0400 the following day. For longer stays, save a lot of money with a personal ID card (**Stammkarte**) and weekly innerzone pass for DM34 from the Hbf MVV office. You'll need your passport and two passport-sized photos. MVV works on an honour system, which means they trust you to buy a ticket and validate it in the little blue box as you board your train, bus or tram. Plain clothes inspectors patrol; if you get caught without a validated ticket, you will be fined DM60 on the spot. Tickets cost DM8 (inner zone only) or DM16 and are valid 0900–0200. Tickets are valid for all forms of transport. A ticket good for all trains and buses and valid for the length of your stay is sold as part of the **Münchner Schlüssel** (Key to Munich) discount package offered by the tourist board (see Sightseeing).

Buses, trams and U-Bahn

Munich's public transport system is superb, with nowhere more than half a block's walk away from a stop or station. Everything runs 0430–0200. Get network map, timetables, and further information about tickets and discounts from the municipal transport authority, **München Verkehrs und Tarifverband (MVV)**, *Thiersch-str. 2, 80538 München; tel: (089) 23 80 30.*

Taxis

Official taxis are cream-coloured, plentiful and reliable. Fare per km is roughly equivalent to two single MVV tickets.

STAYING IN MUNICH

Accommodation

Finding accommodation is rarely a problem except during the city's biggest tourist attractions, the annual Oktoberfest beer festival and Fasching, the Bacchanalian carnival which precedes Ash Wednesday. You can book rooms at all prices through the tourist board offices at the airport, in the station, and in the city centre, but they do not take bookings by telephone.

International chains with properties in the city include *Ch, BW, Hn, Ke, Ma, Mc, Nv, Rm.*Mid-range hotels (Under DM100 single/DM150 double) near the Hbf include the **Hotel Pension Am Karlstor**, *Neuhauserstr. 47; tel: (089) 59 35 96*; **Hotel Haberstock**, *Schillerstr. 4; tel: (089) 55 78 55*; **Hotel Senefelder**, *Senefelderstr. 4; tel: (089) 55 15 40.* Other moderately priced hotels include **Hotel Andi**, *Landwehrstr. 33; tel: (089) 59 60 67*; **Hotel Arosa**, *Hotterstr. 2-4; tel: (089) 26 70 87*; **Hotel Brunnenhof**, *Schillerstr. 36, 80336; tel (089) 55 49 21*; **Hotel Herzog**, *Haberlstr. 9; tel: (089) 53 04 95*; **Hotel Präsident**, *Lindwurmstr. 13; tel: (089) 26 30 11.*

Discount rates are available at certain

times of year (including Nov–Dec and Jul–late Aug) through the tourist board's *Munich Key* voucher scheme; rates can be as low as DM183 double for a two-night stay.

The seasonal boom in visitors to the beer festival means Munich has a better-than-average supply of budget accommodation for younger travellers. There are two large **HI hostels: Jugendherberge Munchen**, *Wendl-Dietrich-Str; tel: (089) 13 11 56* with 509 beds and **Jugendherberge**, W-8000, Munich 70 JGH, *tel: (089) 723 65 50* with 344 beds. Other budget hostel accommodation is available in **DJH-Gastehaus**, *Miesingstr. 4; tel: (089) 723 65 60*; a last resort in summer is the **Jugendlager Kapuzinerholzl**, also called 'The Tent', *Franz Schankstr; tel: (089) 1414 300*, a marquee in the Botanischer Garten where DM13 gets you a foam pad, blankets, floor space, shower and breakfast. Further information on youth hostels in the region from **Deutsches Jugendherbergswerk**, Postfach 14 55, 4930 Detmold, *tel: 05231 7 40 10*. Tourist board offices also provide a hotel list which includes almost 2000 beds in hostels and dormitories run by other organisations in the city, but these cannot be booked through the tourist office.

Munich's warm summers encourage camping, and there are are three campsites in the suburbs: **München Langwieder See**, *Eschenriederstr. 119*, München 60, *tel: (089) 814 15 66*; **München Thalkirchen**, *Zentrallandstr. 49*, Munich 70, *tel: (089) 723 17 07*; and **München Obermenzing**, *Lochhausener Str. 59*, München 60, *tel: (089) 811 22 35*.

Eating and Drinking

Munich is preoccupied with food and drink, perhaps more than anywhere else in a country not noted for asceticism. The city's favourite snack is the *Weisswurst*, a white sausage flavoured with herbs and spices. Other typical dishes include *Schweinhaxen*, roast pork hocks, and *Leberkäse*, a liver-based meatloaf. If you are on a budget a bowl of *Gulaschsuppe* – originally a Hungarian import, now popular all over Germany – will fill you up nourishingly and make your marks go further. The best place for cheap eats is the **Viktualienmarkt**, the produce market where a score of traditional taverns sell beer, *schnapps*, sausage and soup. It also has a popular beer garden.

Munich is famous, too, for its many kinds of bread, but still more famous for its **beers**, from refreshing pilsner-type 'steins' to the extra-strong *Starkbiere*. Each brewery maintains its own beer-hall, including the legendary **Hofbraühaus**. There are beer gardens all over the city, some (mostly attached to restaurants) very touristy, others more traditional. In the latter, you can bring your own food; traditional snacks to accompany litres of beer include salted mackerel, giant pretzels, and cheese spreads. A favourite meeting place is the beer garden by the **Chinesische Turm** (pagoda) in the *Englisher Garten*.

Branches of the **Eduscho** and **Tchibo** stand-up coffee counter chains are good for cheap breakfasts; buy your pastries at the neartest bakery to eat with your coffee. Students can eat at any of the city's university 'mensa' cafeterias: Munich University, *Leopoldstr. 15*; Munich Technical University, *Arcisstr. 17*; and the Olympic Village, *Helene-Mayer-Ring 9*.

Inexpensive **vegetarian** restaurants in Munich include **Jahreszeiten**, *Sebastianpl. 9* (near the Viktualienmarkt); **Prinz Myshkin**, *Hackenstr. 2*; **Mango**, *Rosental 3-4* (both near *Marienpl.*); and the new **Das Gollier**, *Gollierstr. 83*.

Traditional **bierkellers**, with hearty

227

food, strong beer and oompah bands, include the **Augustiner Gross-gaststätten**, *Neuhauserstr. 16*, home of Munich's oldest brewery, which offers cut-priced snacks as part of the Munich Key programme; a slab of meatloaf, a huge pretzel and half a litre of beer for DM13.50. Other affordable restaurants include **Bayerische Donisl**, *Weinstr. 1 am Marienpl.* and **Zirbelstube**, in the *Eden-Hotel-Wolff, Arnulfstr. 4-8*. **Berni's Nudelbrett**, *Peterspl. 8 (Am Alten Peter, s. Marienpl.)* specialises in pasta, steak and seafood with a cheap three-course menu. Other inexpensive pasta joints include **Ciao Italia**, *Leopoldstr. 42*, and **Da Gino**, *Klenzestr. 99*. **Dimitri's**, *Hohenzollernstr. 13*, is a cheap and cheerful Greek restaurant. **Papas**, *Schlessheimerstr. 48*, is an inexpensive restaurant specialising in potatoes in every shape and form.

Communications

Postamt 32, *Bahnhofpl. 1; tel: (089) 53 88 27 30/27 33*, is the post office closest to the railway station, open 24 hrs for telephone calls, poste restante, and cheque and currency exchange. All mail addressed via poste restante is held here. Munich's telephone area code is 089 (89 from abroad)

Consulates

Canada: *Am Thal 29; tel: (089) 222 661.*
UK: *Amalienstr. 62; tel: (089) 394 015.*
USA: *Koniginstr. 5; tel: (089) 230 11.*

Money

Thomas Cook, *Petersplatz 10* in the centre of the city, will change all kinds of traveller's cheques and Eurocheques, as well as foreign currency. They also sell phonecards, and can provide emergency assistance if you have lost your Mastercard card or Thomas Cook traveller's cheques. Major credit cards are widely accepted in Munich.

Munich offers a full gamut of high and low culture, from a summer opera festival to the brass band rhythms of the **Oktoberfest** and other popular occasions. There are also plenty of rock, jazz and blues bars providing a venue for home-grown and visiting bands.

The Munich tourist office publishes a monthly programme, *Monatsprogramm*, available free or very cheaply from the information offices, news-stands, bookshops and in many hotels and pensions. It lists all kinds of events, from live music to museum and art gallery exhibitions. An English-language magazine, *Munich Found*, published monthly (DM4) contains up-to-date news on entertainment, events, nightlife and restaurants.

Theatres, Cinemas and Concerts

The **Nationaltheater** (Bavarian State Opera House) is the venue for opera, ballet and classical concerts (also performed in the **Gasteig Kulturzentrum** and in the **Staastheater** and *Gärtnerpl.*). Free lunchtime concerts are given daily at the Gasteig Kulturzentrum by students of the Richard Strauss Conservatorium. Check at the tourist office for details of other free concerts, which are frequent. Munich has several **cinemas**, some showing English-language movies which are subtitled in German rather than dubbed.

Music and Dancing

Backstage, *Helholzstr. 18; tel: (089) 18 33 30*, and **Substanz**, *Ruppertsr. 25; tel: (089) 21 27 49* are leading grunge metal, independent and hip-hop venues. **Park Café**, *Sophienstr. 7; tel: (089) 59 83 13*, plays anything from trance to acid jazz, as does **Pulverturm**, *Schleissheimerstr. 393; tel: (089) 351 99 99*. **Unterfahrt**, *Kirchnstr. 96; tel: (089) 129 85 18*, plays serious jazz for a more mature audience. **Rattlesnake Saloon**, *Schneeglockerstr. 91; tel: (089) 150 40 35*, plays live country and bluegrass.

Events

The main events on Munich's calendar are the annual **Oktoberfest**, which actually begins in mid-Sept and ends on the first Sunday in Oct, originally commemorating a royal marriage but now a mammoth beer festival; **Fasching**, the carnival season, which starts on January 7 and continues until Shrove Tuesday with costume balls and fancy-dress parades (high points are Fasching Sunday and Shrove Tuesday, with open-air events at the Viktualienmarkt and the central pedestrian streets around the cathedral); and **Christkindlmarkt**, the Christmas market held on the *Marienpl.* from the end of Nov to Christmas Eve. Candle-lit stalls sell mulled wine, snacks, and gifts and best buys include traditional Bavarian Christmas decorations.

SHOPPING

The **Karlsplatz** shopping mall mingles department stores, supermarkets and fashion stores, while the city's most elegant designer showrooms are along *Theatinerstr.* and *Maximilian-str.* There are expensive antique stores in the *Briennerstr.* and *Ottostr.* area, cheaper ones along *Türkenstr.* in Schwabing, traditionally the city's bohemian quarter and still a good place to look for the off-beat. Head for the Viktualienmarkt to stock up on wonderful bread, cheese and sausage for your next train journey or for a picnic.

SIGHTSEEING

The tourist board operates a scheme called *Münchner Schlüssel* (Munich Key), based on a book of coupons which allows reduced entrance charges to museums, theatres and special attractions, suggestions to help you plan your visit and a public transport ticket valid for the duration of your stay.

Munich's sights include the 15th-century **Frauenkirche** (Church of Our Lady) on *Frauenpl.*, with its twin onion domes. The **Altes Rathaus** (Old Town Hall) dating from the middle ages and now housing a delightful toy museum, and the 19th-century **Neues Rathaus**, both on the *Marienpl.*, the city's central square. Be there at 1100 or 2100, when the **Glockenspiel**, an ornate musical clock, strikes the hour. Its carillon commemorates two notable events in Munich's history, the end of the plague in 1517 and the wedding of Duke Wilhelm V and Renate of Lorraine in 1568. In the centre of *Marienpl.* stands a column topped by a gilt figure of the Virgin Mary, erected by the Prince Elector Maximilian I in gratitude for Munich's narrow escape from the rav-

History

Munich was founded in the 12th century, by Henry the Lion, Duke of Bavaria, to take control of the lucrative salt trade across the River Isar. By 1255 it was capital of Bavaria. Little remains of the Munich of that time. Though a few of the city's sights date from the later medieval era, Munich owes the most striking elements of its artistic and architectural heritage to the rulers of the Wittelsbach dynasty. Bavaria became an independent kingdom in 1805, with Munich as the royal residence. Bavaria retained its independence until 1870, when it joined the North German Confederation. The following year it was absorbed into the German Empire. In the intervening years, King Ludwig I endowed the the city with a wealth of classical public buildings and the city took on its modern outline.

ages of the Thirty Years' War (1618–1648). It is reckoned to be the city's central point. Also worth seeing are the ornate rococo **Asamkirche**, *Sendlinger Str. 61/2*, and the open-air produce market, the *Viktualienmarkt*. Along the Ludwigstr. are some of the city's finest 18th- and 19th-century buildings. The **Residenz**, *Max-Joseph-Pl. 3*, the baroque palace of the city's Wittelsbach princes, houses several museums (including paintings, tapestries, sculpture and furniture) and overlooks the manicured lawns and flowerbeds of the **Hofgarten**, the city's most imposing park. Chief among Munich's museums is the **Alte Pinakothek**, *Barerstr. 27*, with canvases by some of the greatest old masters. Reckoned to be among the six greatest collections of painting in the world, its treasures include 65 paintings by Rubens, a small but priceless gallery of Italian painting, and an unrivalled array of great German masters. The collection was begun by Duke Wilhelm IV of Bavaria (1508–1550) who commissioned a cycle of heroic paintings from antiquity. The museum building itself was commissioned by King Ludwig I, who reigned from 1825–1848, and was formally opened in 1836. It was severely damaged during World War II and reopened in 1957.

A tour of the museum begins with the works of older Dutch masters, including Roger van der Weyden, Hans Memling and Dirk Bouts, and continues through rooms of German masterpieces including a number of superb works by Albrecht Dürer. Two great altar paintings by Tiepolo, a *Madonna and Child* by Leonardo da Vinci, Filippo Lippi's *Annunciation* and three Madonnas by Raphael are among the gems of the Italian collection, which also includes works by Titian and Tintoretto. Even these, however, are outshone by the 17th century Flemish collection, dominated by Rubens, Rembrandt, Frans Hals and others. An entire hall is devoted to the jewel-like paintings of Jan Breughel. French painters of the 17th century are represented by Poussin, Lorrain and others. The museum's Spanish collection includes masterpieces by Velazquez, Murillo and El Greco. All in all, the Alte Pinakothek ranks with museums like the Louvre, the Uffizi and the Prado; it is worth coming to Munich if only to see its glories. Not to be missed, either, is the **Neue Pinakothek**, *Barerstr. 29*, with a fine collection of 19th-century European artists including David, Goya, Gainsborough and Turner through to the German and French Impressionists, Cezanne, Van Gogh, Gauguin and representatives of Symbolism and art nouveau from all over the world. **Schloss Nymphenburg**, summer palace of the Wittelsbachs, is worth visiting for its gardens, interiors and portrait gallery (U-Bahn: *Rotkreuzpl.*, then tram no. 12).

It's also possible to tour the film studios, **Bavaria Filmstadt**, *Bavariafilmpl. 7*, or visit the **BMW Museum**, *Petuelring 130*. Munich's most popular museum, however, and one of the best of its kind in the world, is the the museum of technology, the **Deutsches Museum** (German Museum), *Museuminsel 1*. Whether you want to play with hundreds of hands-on exhibits or to study a real U-boat at close quarters, it's easy top spend a whole day here – ideal for kids.

View of Munich

An unparalleled view is offered from the 290m-high **Olympiaturm** (Olympic Tower), in the Olympic park north of the city centre, which has three viewing platforms at the 190 m level, with a revolving restaurant. (Open 0900–2400, last ascent 2330; U-Bahn 3 to *Olympiazentrum*).

MUNICH–FRIEDRICHSHAFEN

This route to the shores of the Bodensee (Lake Constance) and the foothills of the Alps runs from Bavaria's capital through rolling farmland dotted with the characteristic onion-domed churches of southern Germany. On the way it passes through two of the regions larger industrial and commercial cities, each of which has an interesting historic core, with a chance to detour to the wonderful castles and countryside of the aptly-named Romantic Road.

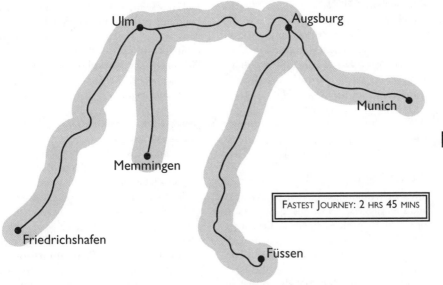

FASTEST JOURNEY: 2 HRS 45 MINS

231

TRAINS

ETT tables: 765, 761.

FAST TRACK

The quickest service is via Lindau. Trains run every 2 hours from München to Lindau and connect with trains for Friedrichshafen. The overall journey takes between 2 hr 45 mins and 3 hr 45 mins.

ON TRACK

Munich (München)–Augsburg
A very frequent service taking around 30 mins.

Augsburg–Ulm
Two trains an hour taking 40 mins.

Ulm–Friedrichshafen
One train an hour taking 1 hr 15 mins.

AUGSBURG

Station: Hbf, *tel: (0821) 19419*, 1 km west of Altstadt.

Tourist Office: *Bahnhofstr. 7; tel: (0821) 50 20 70*, 500m from Hbf. Open Mon–Fri 0900–1800, Sat 1000–1600, Sun 1000–1500.

GETTING AROUND

Take tram 2 from Hbf to the *Altstadt*. Everything of interest is within 500–750 m of the *Rathauspl*.

ACCOMMODATION

Hotel chains in Augsburg include *BW, Ib, Tp*. Mid-priced hotels close to the station include **Hotel Post**, *Fuggerstr. 5 and 7; tel: (0821) 36044*; **Hotel Iris**, *Gartenstr. 4; tel: (0821) 510981*; **Hotel Lenzhalde**, *Thelottstr. 2; tel: (0821) 520745*.

HI: *Beim Pfaffenkeller 3; tel (0821) 33909*; tram 2 to *Stadwerke*. **Campingplatz Augusta**; *tel: (0821) 707575* (bus to *Autobahnsee*) open year-round.

SIGHTSEEING

Two rich banking dynasties, the Welsers and the Fuggers, helped make Augsburg one of the wealthiest towns in Europe in the 15th century and endowed it with some of its finest buildings. The **Fuggerei**, a few blocks east of the Rathaus, was founded by Jakob Fugger in 1519 and its ivy-walled houses are still, as he intended, used as Catholic almshouses. Jakob Fugger's magnificent **town house** at *Maximilianstr. 36/38* was the scene of fierce religious debates between reformer Martin Luther and his opponents in 1518.

Augsburg's main Renaissance landmark is the onion-domed **Rathaus**, painstakingly restored after World War II. Its **Goldener Saal** (Golden Room) with marble floor, painted cedar ceiling and pillars adorned with gold leaf, is especially sumptuous. First built in 1615–20, it is considered to be the finest secular Renaissance building north of the Alps. The adjoining 70 m tower, **Perlachturm**, offers a fine view of the city. The **St Anna Kirche**, *Annastr.*, also bears the mark of the Fuggers in the shape of its Renaissance **Annaskapelle**. The **Maximilian Museum**, *Philippine-Welserstr. 24*, displays a fine colection of arts and crafts from the middle ages, south German sculpture, and gold and silverware. The **Schaezler-Palais**, *Maximilianstr. 46*, built in 1765–1770, is Ausgburg's finest rococo building, with an art gallery which contains works by Holbein and Dürer. In front of the place stands a figure of Hercules – the **Herkulesbrunnen** – one of three bronze Renaissance statues which adorn *Maximilianstr*.

⚡ SIDE TRACK FROM AUGSBURG

Augsburg is midway along the **Romantic Road**, which runs through some of Germany's prettiest countryside via a chain of picturesque towns, villages and castles. Northwards, the road leads to the jewels of the Romantic Road, **Nördlingen**, **Dinkelsbuhl** and **Rothenburg-ob-der-Tauber**, a completely restored 14th-century town, ringed by unbelievably picturesque town walls. South of Augsburg, the route follows the Lech Valley, to end at **Füssen**, a pretty town which is also a handy base for visiting the three nearby Bavarian Royal Castles. (Innsbruck–Friedrichshafen, see p. 122). Europabus services, on which Eurail and Euro Domino passes are valid, run in both directions from Augsburg Hbf.

Full information on the Romantic Road is available from the **Romantic**

Road Tourist Association, *Marktpl.,*
91550 Dinkelsbühl; tel: (09851) 90271,
fax (09851) 90279. 🖂

ULM

Station: Hbf; *tel: (0731) 91419.*
Tourist Office: *Munsterplatz; tel: (0731)*
64161. Open Mon–Fri 0900–1800 and
Sat 0900–1230.

GETTING AROUND

Ulm's handful of sights are within easy
walking distance of Hbf and each other.

ACCOMMODATION

The tourist office can find you a reasonably priced room fairly close to Hbf and
the centre. There are cheap **pensions** in
the suburb of **Pfuhl**, east of the centre.
HI: *Grimmelfingerweg 45; tel: (0731) 38 44*
55, 4 km south-west of the centre (bus no.
9 from Hbf or bus no. 4 from Rathaus,
both to *Schulzentrum*, then walk round the
stadium).

SIGHTSEEING

Ulm is divided into two cities by the
Danube. The newer part, **Neu Ulm**, on
the south bank, is a municipality in its own
right with little to interest the casual
visitor.

The original city centre has been wiped
out by war and industrial and commercial
development, but a few sights remain,
including the magnificent late-Gothic
Münster, on *Münsterpl.*, which survived
World War II bombing almost unscathed.
It has five impressive portals and the
Gothic west spire, at 161 m, is the tallest in
the world. The foundations were laid in
1377, but the spire was designed in the
15th century and not completed until
1890. A 768-step staircase leads to a view-
ing-point 143 m up with a superb view of
the Danube, the Black Forest and, on a

clear day, the Alps far to the south. The
graceful Gothic/Renaissance **Rathaus**,
Neuestr., is a photogenic complex of buildings restored in 16th-century style. The
exterior is covered by religious frescos and
statues, and there is an intricate astronomical clock on the west front. Immediately
behind the Rathaus is a renaissance mansion housing the **Ulmer Museum**, which
covers art and culture from prehistory to
modern times and is noted for works by
early masters from Ulm.

The **Metzgerturm**, *Donaustr.*, was
built as a prison in 1345 and, leaning 2 m
off the vertical, is predictably called the
Leaning Tower of Ulm. The **Fischer-
viertel**, the 16th-century fishermen's
quarter, is a picturesque area of half-
timbered houses where the small River
Blau flows into the Danube. Where the
two meet, the **Schiefe Haus**, built in
1500, leans precariously over the water.

233

⤴ SIDE TRACK
FROM ULM

The historic Imperial city of
Memmingen lies 55 km south of
Ulm. There are frequent trains from
Ulm Hbf, and from Memmingen you
can travel onward by rail to Kempten
(Innsbruck–Friedrichshafen, p. 125).

MEMMINGEN

Hbf: *tel: (08331) 2653.*
Tourist Office: *Ulmerstr. 9; tel:*
(08331) 850172.

ACCOMMODATION

HI: *Kempterstr. 42; tel: (08331)*
850396. **Campsite**: *Camping am See,*
Buxheim, 2 km from town centre; *tel:*
(08331) 71800. (Bus no. 3 to
Buxheimersee.) Medium-priced hotels
include **Hotel Adler**, *Maximilianstr. 3;*
tel: (08331) 87015.

SIGHTSEEING

Hbf is just outside the medieval centre, on the east side; follow *Maximilianstr.* for 500 m into the heart of town.

Founded in 1150 AD, Memmingen is a charming old market town with a treasury of pretty historic buildings within its medieval centre. Highlights include the fairytale Renaissance **Rathaus**, *Rathausplatz*, with its white curved gables and green domes; the graceful **Parishaus**, *Ulmerstr. 9*, a Rococo confection in pink and white built in 1736, which now houses the tourist office; the **Hermansbau**, *Hermansg.*, a baroque baronial residence built in 1766; the 16th-century **St Martinskirche**, with its octagonal bell-tower; the **city gates**, three of which have been meticulously restored; and an array of other fine buildings. ⬛

FRIEDRICHSHAFEN

Stations: Hbf: *Bahnhofpl.; tel: (07541)*
Hafenbf: *Seestr.; tel: (07541).*
Ferries: *Bodenseeverkehrsdienst, Seestr. 23; tel: (07541) 201389.*

Hbf is in the centre of the city, overlooking the yacht harbour. For ferries across the lake, continue to Hafenbahnhof, at the ferry harbour, or walk 1 km east from *Bahnhofpl.* along *Friedrichstr.*, turning right on *Buchhornpl.* to the harbour. Ferries operated by DB, SBB and OBB sail from Friedrichshafen to points east and west on the north shore of the Bodensee. Disembark at Lindau (see p. 145) for trains to Munich and at Bregenz in Austria, at the east end of the lake, for connections to Innsbruck (Innsbruck–Friedrichshafen see p. 122). Ferries also ply between Friedrichshafen and Romanshorn, on the Swiss southern side of the lake. Boats leave from the quay 50 m from Hafenbf; turn right on leaving the station.

Tourist Information: *Bahnhofpl. 2; tel: (07541) 30010.*

ACCOMMODATION

Chain hotels include *BW*. The most picturesque hotel is the first-class **Hotel Buchhorner Hof**, *Friedrichstr. 33; tel: (07541) 2050.* Slightly less expensive, the **Hotel Goldenes Rad**, *Karlstr. 43*, is handy for the harbour. Most accommodation is quite expensive. Cheaper places to stay include **Pension Wurster**, *Georgstr. 14; tel: (07541) 72694*; **Gasthof Dorkkrug**, *Konig Wilhelm Platz 2; tel: (07541) 55154.*

SIGHTSEEING

Friedrichshafen is a mainly modern town, with a handful of historic buildings which include the **Schloss**, dating from 1654 but expanded as a summer residence in the reign of Kaiser Wilhelm I – 1824–1918. It stands in its own grounds on a headland just west of the harbour, about 500 m from Hbf – turn right along *Friedrichstr.* and left on *Klosterstr.* The adjoining **Schlosskirche**, with its 54.9 m tower, is also worth a look. Opposite, the **Schulmuseum Friedrichshafen am Bodensee**, *Friedrichstr. 14*, is devoted to the history of education in Germany. Friedrichshafen is also the home of the **Zeppelins**, the giant airships named after their inventor, Ferdinand Graf Zeppelin. Used to bomb London during World War I and to carry passengers across the Atlantic in the 1930s, the Zeppelins fell from favour after the greatest of them, the *Hindenburg*, was destroyed by fire. A **Zeppelin Museum** is set to open in the Hafenbf building in 1996, featuring a 40 m scale model of the *Hindenburg*.

For details of **ferry excursions** from Friedrichshafen, see Konstanz and the Bodensee chapter, pp. 142–146.

MUNICH–LINZ

This route between Germany and Austria follows the River Danube (Donau) much of the way and incorporates two of Germany's most attractive old towns. It runs through flat farmland until some 20 mins south of Plattling where the Danube valley narrows to wooded hills. In Austria the countryside is idyllic rolling green with tiny settlements, interrupted only by comfortable towns.

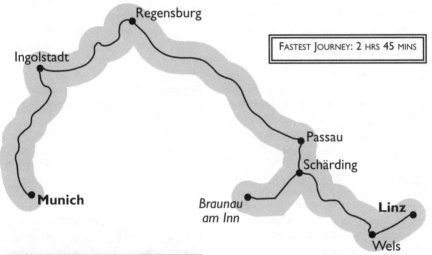

FASTEST JOURNEY: 2 HRS 45 MINS

235

TRAINS

ETT tables: 750, 755, 740.

FAST TRACK

 The fastest route is via Salzburg. The three through EuroCity trains take 2 hrs 45 mins; changing in Salzburg on the hourly service takes 3 hrs 30 mins.

ON TRACK

Munich (München)–Ingolstadt
Frequent trains take around 45 mins.

Ingolstadt–Regensburg
Ten trains a day link Ingolstadt with Regensburg taking 1 hr.

Regensburg–Passau
A frequent service taking between 1 hr and 1 hr 30 mins.

Passau–Schärding
A frequent but irregular service with trains taking 14 mins.

Schärding–Wels
A frequent service taking 1 hr.

Wels–Linz
A very frequent service taking 20 mins.

INGOLSTADT

Station: Hbf: 2 km south of the *Altstadt; tel: (0841) 7991.*
Tourist Office: *Hallstr. 5; tel: (0841) 305415,* Mon–Fri 0800–1200, 1300–1700.

ACCOMMODATION:

The **HI** is at *Friedhofstr. 4; tel: (0841) 34177.* The **campsite** is on the edge of town at *Auwaldsee; tel: (0841) 6 89 11.*

SIGHTSEEING

Ingolstadt is one of Bavaria's oldest cities, but it takes a second glance to detect its 13th-century origins and the remnants of its baroque heritage.

In the 13th century Ingolstadt was guarded by the **Herzogskasten fortress**, in the south-east corner of the old town. Now housing the city library, it displays richly-decorated gables, an addition made in the 14th century. From 1392 to 1447 Ingolstadt was one of two duchies which later merged to form Bavaria. Its ruler, Duke Ludwig the Bearded, endowed the city with many of its most striking sights, including the **Liebfrauenmünster**, begun in 1425 and completed more than a century later. A crescent of medieval walls, studded with turrets and bastions, surrounds the old town, pierced by three picturesque gates: the **Taschenturmtor** ('Pocket Tower' Gate), the **Kreuztor** (Cross Gate) and the **Feldkirchnertor**. Ludwig the Bearded also ordered the building of the **Neues Schloss** (New Castle) in 1418.

REGENSBURG

Station: Hbf; *tel: (0941) 19419,* is some 10 mins walk from the picturesque *Altstadt.*
Tourist Office: *Altes Rathaus; tel: (0941) 507 4410.* Mon–Fri 0830–1800, Sat 0900–1600 and Sun 0900–1200.

ACCOMMODATION AND FOOD

The only major chain hotels are *Ra* and *Ib.* Less expensive hotels and *pensions* include **Apollo**, *Neuprull 17; tel: (0941) 9150;* **Bischofshof Braustuben**, *Dechbettenerstr. 50; tel: (0941) 21473;* **Dozesancentrum Obermünster**, *Obermünsterpl. 7; tel: (0941) 5681 249;* **Schildbrau**, *Stadamhof 24; tel: (0941) 85724;* **Spitalgarten**, *St Kataherinenpl. 1; tel: (0941) 84774.* There are some cheaper central hotels, but you need to book in summer. Alternatively, you can pay for the tourist office to find you a room in a private home. **HI**: *Wohrdstr. 60; tel: (0941) 57402,* on an island in the Danube, 5-mins walk from the centre (bus no. 5: *Weissenburgstr.*). **Campsite**: *Am Weinweg 40; tel: (0941) 270025.*

Italische Eis Salon, *Dompl.*, has a shady terrace, where coffee, beer and ice cream are sold, opposite the Dom. **Picasso**, *7 Weiss Hahnen Gasse*, close to the river, is a good place for breakfast, brunch, snacks and coffee. **Hotel-Gaststatte Bishofshof**, just off *Dompl.*, has a pleasant courtyard-restaurant. **Historische Wurstküche**, *Weisselammgasse 3*, is Germany's oldest sausage house and sells nothing else. It's tiny and touristy, but part of the scene. You eat at rows of benches and tables on the cobbled Danube quay.

Across the Danube, **Alte Linde Biergarten**, *Mullerstr. 1*, on Sorat island is a lovely beer garden overlooking the river and the old town. Also on the island, **Pizzeria-Eiscafe Flair**, *13–15 zum Bruckenbazar*, is a cheap place for pizza, Greek gyros kebabs, ices and drinks.

GETTING AROUND

Everything of interest centres on **Altstadt**, a small area and easy to cover on foot. This is a place where legend and fact are almost

236

inextricably interwoven and incorporated into much of the architecture. Some background knowledge greatly enhances your enjoyment and a little homework with a specialised guide will pay dividends. There is a very efficient bus service; timetables are available from *Ernst-Reuter-pl. 2.* Danube Ferries depart from *Donaumarkt,* on the south bank of the river, between the Eiserne and Steinerne bridges.

SIGHTSEEING

The picturesque **Altstadt** stands on the south bank of the Danube and was little damaged in the war. Many of the buildings date from a time when there were strong trading links with Venice and show a distinctly Italian influence, painted in cool, pretty ice-cream colours – pastel pink, yellow and green. The 12th-century **Steinernebrücke** gives the best view of the medieval spires, towers and battlements along the waterfront. When it was built the bridge represented the only safe crossing on the Danube and gave Regensburg tremendous strategic importance.

Immediately to the south, the **Domstadt** is an ecclesiastical complex centred on a magnificent cathedral. The **Dom** was started in the 13th century, while its 105 m spires were completed 500 years later. Its attractions range from 14th-century stained-glass windows to a fine boys' choir (Domspatzen). In the Domschatz (Treasury) are some mouth-watering jewels and gold. During a Sept festival, the nearby goose fountain spouts beer instead of water (sold for charity).

The exterior of the **Alte Kapelle** belies the wealth of rococo decorations inside, including a marble altar and rich frescos. The **Porta Praetoria** is part of the 2nd-century Roman defences and recent excavations have revealed Roman remains beneath the *Niedermünster.*

The **Stadtmuseum**, *Dachau-pl.*, has over 100 rooms of exhibits on the town's cultural and artistic history.

Scattered around the town are some twenty towers in the style of Italian fortified palaces. There were sixty originally, but they were never defensive, just status symbols – the higher the tower, the more important the owner. Most striking is the largest and most elaborate, the **Baumburger Turm**, *Watmarkt;* the highest is the nine-storey **Goldener Turm**, *Wahlenstr.*, with a wine bar at the top.

The **Altes Rathaus**, *Kohlenmarkt*, is a Gothic structure, more interesting inside than out, so it's worth taking the **Reichstagsmuseum** tour. It also houses the city Tourist Office. **Haidplatz** is dominated by the **Haus zum Goldenen Kreuz**, another place with a fascinating history. If you can spot the small stone mouse on the right-hand corner, rub it – to ensure your purse will never be empty.

The **Johannes-Kepler-Gedächtnishaus**, *Keplerstr. 5*, is dedicated to the scientist/astrologer (1571–1630) who made several significant contributions to our knowledge of both planetary movements and optics.

The south-western part of town was formerly a monastic quarter and many of the old buildings survive. **St Jakob**, just off *Bismarck-platz*, was marked by splendid sandstone figures. These have been eroded over the centuries, but you can still see that the main (Romanesque) portal is a mixture of pagan and Christian images.

At the extreme southern end of the old city is the former Benedictine **monastery** of St Emmeran, once a great centre of learning. The Romanesque interior has been somewhat spoiled by over-ornamentation, but the 11th-century double portal survives and the crypt dates back to the 8th century. There are several superb sculptures on the monuments to historical figures.

At the **Schloss Thurn und Taxis,** several Benedictine buildings were turned into luxurious residences in Napoleonic times. The Thurn und Taxis dynasty pioneered Europe's postal service in the 15th century and retained the monopoly until 1867. They now own much of Bavaria and the state rooms are open to the public when the family is not in residence.

PASSAU

Station: Hbf; tel: (0851) 19419, west of the centre. Turn right and follow the Jugendherberge signs to the Rathaus or (Mon–Fri 0630–1830) take the City-Bus.
Tourist Offices: Main office: Rathauspl. 3; tel: (0851) 33421. Mon–Fri 0830–1200 and 1300–1700, Sat–Sun 0900–1300. They dispense a free monthly listing called Aktuell. **Branch:** Near Hbf: turn left and follow signs. Open Mon–Fri 0900–1700 and Sat–Sun 0900–1300 Apr–Oct.

GETTING AROUND

With the exception of the palace-castle, everything of interest is easily walkable. However, most cheaper accommodation is in the suburbs, easily reached by an efficient bus system. Ferries leave from the docks along Fritz-Schäffer-Promenade, in front of the Rathaus. There is a 'Three Rivers Round Trip' tour of the city, which runs (Mar–Oct) when sufficient people have turned up.

ACCOMMODATION

Chain hotels include Hd. **Hotel Herdegen**, Bahnhofstr. 5; tel: (0851) 955160, is reasonably priced and close to Hbf. **Hotel Wilder Mann**, Am Rathauspl.; tel: (0851) 35071/75, is also moderately priced and central. Cheaper guesthouses in the suburbs include

Pension Zur Brucke Gasthof, Landrichterstr. 13; tel: (0851) 43475; **Gasthof Zum Streiblwirt**, Rittsteigerstr. 87; tel: (0851) 81382; **Pension Vilsmeier**, Lindental 28a; tel: (0851) 36313; **Pension Gabriele**, Adalbert Stifterstr. 12; tel: (0851) 6446; **Gasthof Rosencafe**, Donaustr. 23; tel: (0851) 428 11.

The **HI** is housed in the palace-castle; tel: (0851) 41351, across the Danube. Cross the bridge by the docks and be prepared for a steep climb, or take the bus from Rathauspl. right to the door. Early booking is essential during school holidays. **Campsite**: Halserstr. 34; tel: (0851) 41457, by the River Ilz.

SIGHTSEEING

Passau is set on two peninsulas. The palace-castle is on the peninsula between the Danube and the Ilz, and the **Altstadt** between the Danube and the Inn.

Veste Oberhaus was the former palace of the bishops and now contains the magnificent **Cultural History Museum** with 54 rooms of art and artefacts spanning two millenia. It has a marvellous view .

On the other peninsula, the lofty **Stephansdom** with its green cupolas is a superb example of Italian baroque architecture, with hundreds of cherubs on the ceiling and the world's largest church organ (over 17,000 pipes), which is used for noon concerts on weekdays. Behind the Dom is the cobbled **Residenzplatz**, lined with Renaissance dwellings including the Domschatz (Treasury), housed in the **Residenz**, which contains a marvellous collection of gold items and tapestries. Also on Residenzpl. is the small **Spielzeugmuseum**, a collection of 19th-century toys.

SCHÄRDING

Station: tel: (07712) 30530.

Tourist Office: *Unterestadtpl. 11; tel: (07712) 4300*, 15 mins from the station, left to the path crossing open fields to reach the road, cross the river to the slope to the *Baumgartner* brewery, (founded 1609), following the road round to the town gate. The Tourist Office at the opposite side of the square, open Mon–Fri 0900–1800, Sat 0900–1200, offers a free map with suggested town walk and history notes in English. Will phone to check accommodation availability for visitors.

SIGHTSEEING

Brunnenthaler Konzertsommer, June–Aug includes concerts in Schärding. **Fishing** is popular, particularly with residents of the **Forstingers Wirtshaus Romantik Hotel** which owns fishing rights. Others need permits from **Günther Winroither,** *Passauerstr. 135.*

The town was first mentioned in the ninth century and still boasts a watergate on the river. The remains of the **Schloss,** *tel: (07712) 4300,* house the **Heimatmuseum** (local history museum) and there is a charming multi-coloured **main square,** originally 15th century but completely rebuilt after World War II bombing, giving it a faintly Disneyesque look.

SIDE TRACK FROM SCHÄRDING

Braunau am Inn is a pretty, Gothic town based round a generous main square. From Schärding, it takes around 40 mins to reach Ried am Innkreis by rail, and from there a connection to Braunau takes another 40 mins.

The **station,** *tel: (07722) 320934,* rents bikes. The **Tourist Office,** *Stadtpl. 9; tel: (07722) 2644* (left out of the station, left again at the main road, continuing straight ahead), offers accommodation lists and information

leaflet plus electronic information and left luggage lockers in *Theaterg.*

Hitler spent his first two years in a house in Salzburger Vorstadt but the main point of being here is to enjoy the relaxed atmosphere.

WELS

Station: *tel: (07242) 240 303.* Rents bikes and houses a cash machine.

Tourist Office: *Stadtpl. 55; tel: (07242) 434950* (straight out of the station, first right and third left to *Kaiser Josefpl.*, continuing ahead to the *Stadtpl.* with Tourist Office at the far end). Mon–Fri 0900–1900, Sat 0900–1200 (July and Aug), Mon–Fri 0900–1800 (Sept–June), has free maps, will enquire about room availability, and organises guided tours Weds 1900 or Walkman tours (ÖS20).

ACCOMMODATION AND FOOD

Hotel Hauser, *Bäckerg.; 7 tel: (07242) 454090* (moderate) in the *Fussgängerzone* offers excellent accommodation and a 10% 'green' discount for all arriving by train. **Gasthof Kaiserkrone,** *Bahnhofstr. 66; tel: (07242) 47365* (moderate) is right by the station. **Gasthof Augustin,** *Traung. 8; tel: (07242) 46305* (budget) is very central. The **HI: Jugendherberge,** *Dragonerstr. 22; tel: (07242) 67284* is 20 mins from the station (bus no.2 Mon–Sat). Hotel chains with property here include *BW* and *Sn.*

The area for food is around the *Stadtpl.* A wine bar is **Brüder Neumayr,** *Haferg. 9,* or you can enjoy beer brewed on site plus good traditional dishes in the **Gerstl Bräu,** *Freiung 9–11,* in the new central development. For coffee and cakes there's **Cafe-Konditorei Urbann,** *Schmidtg. 20.*

ENTERTAINMENT

There are regular **concerts** at the castle (free Thurs May–Aug; Wed tickets available *Stadtpl. 55*). The **Welser Volksfest** carnival is linked to the agricultural fair held in even years (Aug–Sept). There is also an April–May **Spring Fair**. Mid-July **Russian Portraitists** arrive to work in the *Stadtpl.* 1000–dusk from ÖS500. Every Sat morning is a **flea market** and Fri 1400–1700 a **Bauernmarkt**.

SIGHTSEEING

A site occupied by Romans and Celts, prosperity was based above all on the Baltic to Italy trade route. The **Stadtplatz** is lined by charming façades, most dating from the 16th to 18th century, though the structure of many buildings behind is medieval. The **Ledererturm** (Leather-workers' Tower), is all that remains of the city wall towers. The **Stadtpfarrkirche** at the opposite end of the square dates from the 14th century with an 18th-century tower.

Opposite the church is **Salome Althaus**, inhabited in retirement by the mistress of Salzburg's Archbishop Dietrich (of Schloss Mirabell fame, see p. 265). The **Castle** just behind has been turned into a museum, *tel: (07242) 235696*, with exhibits of local rural traditions and history plus a bread museum with over 1000 different types of bread and pastry.

Out of town is the **Vogelpark Schmiding,** *Schmiding 19, Krenglbach; tel: (07429) 46272*, (buses four times weekdays from the station, direction *Krenglbach, Gallspach, Grieskirchen* or *Haag)* with a bird park and excellent ethnic museum.

LINZ

Station: *tel: (0732) 6909.*
Tourist Office: *Hauptpl. 5; tel: (0732) 70 70 1777*, Mon–Fri 0700–1900, Sat and Sun 0800–1130 and 1230–1900 (tram 3 to *Hauptpl.* or 15 min walk) or there is a tele-phone connection from the small office in

the station (right at main concourse) 0800–1900. Staff will help find accommodation and provide plentiful information including a free map.

The main attractions can easily be toured on foot. Tickets for buses and trams are ÖS10 for short, ÖS18 for longer trips, ÖS35 for a full day.

ACCOMMODATION AND FOOD

There is a wide range of accommodation. Considered the best is **Hotel Schillerpark**, *Rainerstr. 2–4; tel: (0732) 6950* (very expensive). **Hotel Muhlvier-tlerhof**, *Graben 24–5; tel: (0732) 772268* (moderate) is in an 18th-century town-house. Just behind the *Hauptpl.* is **Goldener Anker**, *Hofg. 5; tel: (0732) 771088* (moderate). Hotel chains with property here include *BW, Ib, Nv, Rm*. **HI Jugendherberge Linz**, *Kapuzinerstr. 14; tel: (0732) 782720* offers airy rooms round a courtyard. The nearest camping is **Campingplatz Pleschingersee**, next to restaurant Kolmer; *tel: (0732) 247870* (tram 3 from Hbf to *Rudolfstr.* across the river, then bus 32).

The *Fussgängerzone* around *Hofg.* is the place for nightlife with plenty of cheap eating places. Elsewhere, try the smart **Restaurant Café Ursulinenhof**, *Landstr. 33*, or **Klosterhof**, *Landstr. 30*, with the biggest beer garden in Austria, or the **Wachauer Weinstube**, *Pfarrg. 29*. For the traditional *Linzertortes* (nut pastry topped with fruit jam) try **Jindrak Konditorei** with a branch at *Herrenstr. 22*. **Café Traximayr**, *Promenade 16*, is styl-ishly turn-of-the-century, offering hot dishes and foreign newspapers.

ENTERTAINMENT

The **Brucknerfest** in Sept includes three weeks of performances of concerts featuring works by local composer Anton

Bruckner in the striking, wedge-shaped *Brucknerhaus* on the riverside, which is also used year-round. **Ars Electronica** in June treats technology as art with shows for example on virtual reality and techno music. There are various **church** and **Landhaus concerts** in July and Aug. A **Street Artist Festival** lines the *Hauptpl.* and *Landstr.* in late July.

SIGHTSEEING

Austria's third city, Linz's prosperity is based on its position as a Danube port. The **Hauptplatz**, just off the river, is the old marketplace, now a large square of baroque and rococo façades. The 18th-century **Alter Dom**, *Domg.*, is simple outside but tastefully baroque within. The **Landhaus**, *Klosterstr. 7; tel: (0732) 7720*, is where Johann Kepler, astronomer and mathematician, developed the third law of planetary motion. A planet fountain depicts the solar system 1582 style.

Linzer Schloss, *Tummelpl. 10; tel: (0732) 774419*, was rebuilt after a fire in the last century and exhibits local artefacts from prehistory onwards. Nearby is **Martinskirche**, *Römerstr.*, the oldest church in the country, little changed since it was built in the 700s. Later additions include a 15th-century Gothic choir. The **Minoritenkirche**, *Klosterstr.*, was built in the 13th century but was later 'baroquised'. It contains an Annunciation by Bartolomeo Altomonte, considered the best work of art in the city. The **Botanical Garden**, *Roseggerstr. 20; tel: (0732) 2393*, has one of the biggest cacti collections in the world. Across the river is the **Postlingberg**, served by the world's steepest adhesion tram from *Landgutstr. 19; tel: (0732) 7801 7545.*

241

MUNICH–SALZBURG

This route passes through rolling farmland, dotted with the farming villages, well-kept market towns, and the typical onion-domes of Bavarian churches, to cross the River Inn at Rosenheim and run along the south shore of one of Bavaria's largest lakes, the Chiemsee, skirting the northern foothills of the Alps to cross the Austrian border just after Freilassing. This otherwise undistinguished small town is also the gateway to the high alpine resorts of Bad Reichenhall and Berchtesgaden.

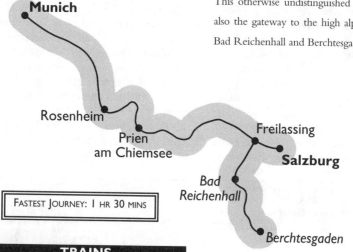

FASTEST JOURNEY: 1 HR 30 MINS

TRAINS

ETT tables: 790.

FAST TRACK

One or two trains each hour taking between 1 hr 30 mins and 1 hr 45 mins.

ON TRACK

München–Rosenheim–Prien am Chiemsee–Freilassing–Salzburg

An hourly *IR* service stops at these stations. Munich to Rosenheim takes 37 mins, Rosenheim to Prien 17 mins, Prien to Freilassing 37 mins and Freilassing to Salzburg 8 mins.

ROSENHEIM

Station: Hbf; *tel: (089) 19419.*
Tourist Office: *Kufsteinerstr. 4 (corner of Munchenerstr. and Salingarten), tel: (08031) 37080.* Open Mon–Fri 1000–1300, 1400–1700, Sat 1000–1200.

STAYING IN ROSENHEIM

Rooms can be booked through tourist office. Budget accommodation includes **Pension Seiffert**, *Munchener Str. 68, tel: (08031) 13986;* **Pension Alpenblick,** *Heilig Blut, Zugspitzstr. 6, tel: (08031) 66146;* **Pension Hess,** *Hochgernstr. 9, tel:*

(08031) 44555. Mid-range hotels include **Hotel Alpina**, *Heilig Blut, Transjochweg 12, tel: (08031) 62909;* **Parkhotel Crombach**, *Kufsteinerstr. 2, tel: (08031) 12082;* **Hotel Tyrol**, *Kufsteinerstr. 5, tel (08031) 31001.*

SIGHTSEEING

In Roman times Rosenheim was a military post guarding the crossing of the Inn. In the Middle Ages it became an important mercantile centre where the trade routes betwen Munich and Salzburg and between Regensburg and Innsbruck met. Today, it is a pleasant but unexciting town with a handful of tall pink, yellow and green traditional buildings around **Max-Josefs- Platz,** an open-air market since medieval times. The **Heimatmuseum**, *Ludwigspl. 26,* with a collection of furniture, artworks and documents relating to the city's past, is housed in a lovely 19th-century building embellished with onion-domes. The **Inn-Museum**, *Innstr. 74,* stands by the bridge across the river and is packed with paraphernalia about navigation on the river.

PRIEN AM CHIEMSEE

Station: Hbf; *tel: (089) 19419.*
Tourist Office: *Rathauspl. 11, tel (08051) 2280,* open Mon–Fri 0900–1200, 1400–1800, Sat 0900–1200.

SIGHTSEEING

The small town of Prien is the jumping-off point for the **Priensee.** Nicknamed the 'Bavarian Sea', this is one of Germany's loveliest lakes, with a spectacular alpine backdrop. The main attraction is King Ludwig II's **castle** on **Herreninsel** an island in the lake. In Prien itself, the **Galerie im Alten Rathaus**, *Rathauspl.,* displays a collection of 18th- and 19th-century landscapes from the region.

⤴ SIDE TRACKS FROM PRIEN

Ludwig II bought **Herreninsel,** largest of three islands in the lake, in 1875 and – inspired by his admiration for Louis XIV of France set out to built a second Versailles. The most striking sections of the building are the royal bedroom and the **Mirrored Gallery**, which was lit by more than 2000 candles. Open Apr–Sept 0900–1700 daily, Oct–Mar 1000–1600 daily. Information from Chiemsee Tourist Office (see above) and **Staaliche Verwaltung**, *Altes Schloss 3, Herrenchiemsee, tel: (08051) 3069.* Boats to the island leave from Prien/Stock, Prien's harbour suburb.

The **Chiemsee railway**, built 1887, runs around the shore of the lake for 22 km and connects with the main DB line at Prien. Steam trains operate year round; the return trip takes about 1 hr. **Chiemsee Schifffahrt Ludwig Fehler,** *Prien/Stock, tel: (08051) 6090.* ⬛

FREILASSING

Freilassing, local capital of the Rupertiwinkel region (St Rupert passed this way in the 7th century), is of interest only as a junction for the side track to Bad Reichenhall and Berchtesgaden.
Tourist Office: (for Rupertiwinkel region): *Postfach 2119, B3384 Freilassing, tel: (08654) 2312.* Open Mon–Fri 0900–1200, 1400–1800, Sat 0900–1200.

⤴ SIDE TRACKS FROM FREILASSING

BAD REICHENHALL

Station: Hbf: *tel: (089) 19419.*
Tourist Office: *Wittelsbachstr. 15; tel (08651) 3003.*

Bad Reichenhall stands in the centre

of a fertile valley protected and surrounded by alpine peaks, including the region's highest summit, the 1613 m **Predigstuhl,** which can be reached by cable car. There are more than 150 km of walking trails, ranging from easy walks through woods and pastureland to mountain hikes. The most striking building in the old town is the **Alte Saline**, the salt-works built in the reign of King Ludwig I, now containing the **Salzmuseum,** a fascinating exhibition focusing on salt, the 'white gold' which was for centuries the region's livelihood. The **Stadtisches Heimatmuseum,** *Getreidegasse 4,* includes exhibits highlighting the history of the town and the region. The **Faschingsorden-museum,** *Heilingbrunnerstr. 3,* contains the world's largest collection of carnival decorations. Historic buildings include the **St Zeno Münster,** a Romanesque basilica with a cloister housing reliefs dating from the reign of Emperor Frederick Barbarossa. For the finest view of the valley and its surroundings take the **Predigstuhlbahn** cable car, *Sudtirolerpl. 1,* to the peak.

BERCHTESGADEN

Station: *tel: (089) 19419.*
Buses: From outside Hbf, bus 9541 goes to Konigsee and to Bad Reichenhall in the opposite direction.
Tourist Office: *Konigseestr. 2, tel (08652) 9670,* open 0900–1200, 1400–1800, Sat 0900–1200.

There is an automatic toll-free phone booth and a list of more than 60 places to stay immediately outside the tourist office, which is 200 m from the station, across the bridge.

Two rivers join in the middle of Berchtesgaden, immediately opposite Hbf – one a milky blue colour, the other clear. There is a powerful mineral reek in the air from the dissolved mineral salts which made the town's fortunes, then turned it into a health resort. The scenery is unbelievably grand, with soaring peaks seemingly close enough to touch. Above the village, the **Kehlsteinhaus** or Eagle's Nest was built as a 50th birthday present for Berchtesgaden's most infamous resident, Adolf Hitler. Atop the 1834 m Kehlstein, it is now a restaurant with panoramic views, reached by a road and a series of tunnels which are a feat of mountain engineering. In the centre of the **Berchtesgaden National Park,** the emerald-green **Konigsee** is surrounded by mighty cliff walls and plummeting waterfalls, and can be explored on a fleet of electrically-powered, pollution-free cruise boats. Another mighty peak, the **Jenner,** stands above the Konigsee and in winter is the hub of Berchtesgaden's main ski area, connected to the village by a cable car. The ride takes 20 mins and is well worth it even in summer for the superb views. In Berchtesgaden itself, the **Royal palace** dates back to the 12th century and was originally a monastery, taken over by the Bavarian royal family as a summer residence. It is now a museum with a fine collection of period furniture and works of art. The **Heimatmuseum** exhibits the skilled woodcarvings for which the region became known in the 19th century. The most interesting man-made attraction in the area is the **Salzbergwek** (salt mine) begun 450 years ago. A 5-min trolley ride takes visitors some 700 m into the side of the salt mountain, from which you slide (alarmingly quickly) 40m down to the next level. ◢

NICE

Nice has been Queen of the Riviera ever since Russian princes and British aristocracy began to grace its opulent hotels in the middle of the last century. Today it is as vibrant as ever, attracting 3 million visitors a year who come to enjoy its long hours of sunshine. Second only to Paris as a tourist centre in France, it sees a covergence of backpackers of the world on the long beach throughout the summer months, joining those who can afford to holiday in its stylish hotels or cruise into the port. Out of season it is, not surprisingly, a popular venue for conferences.

But Nice is a place that people live and work in too. It is France's fifth most important city and has a burgeoning research industry, university and advanced technology centre. Buzzing with traffic and rapidly expanding into the hills around, it has a thriving life beyond tourism.

TOURIST INFORMATION

Tourist Offices: *av. Thiers, 06000 Nice* (on the left just outside the station); *tel: 93 87 07 07*, 0800–1900 in winter, 0800–2000 in summer. Also *2 r. Massenet* (off *promenade des Anglais*), *tel: 93 87 60 60*, and in *promenade des Anglais* near the airport, *tel 93 83 32 64*; both open Mon–Sat 0800-2000, Sun 0800–1200 (summer); Mon–Sat 0800-1900 (winter). Free hotel reservations and ample brochures on Nice and other towns and attractions in the area.

ARRIVING AND DEPARTING

Airport
Nice Côte d'Azur: *promenade des Anglais*. Airport information: *tel: 93 21 30 12*. Terminal One handles international flights, Air Littoral and TAT; Terminal Two handles domestic flights.

Airport to City: 6 km. Taxis to the centre cost about FFr.150. Airport buses run along *promenade des Anglais* to the *Gare Routière* (bus station) every 20 mins; the 20 min journey costs FFr.21. Bus no. 23 to Gare SNCF takes 20 mins, costs FFr.8.

Heli-Inter offers helicopter transits every 20 mins to Monte Carlo (15 mins) and seven flights a day to St Tropez during the summer.

Car hire companies at the airport include Avis, Budget, Citer, Eurodollar, Europcar and Hertz.

Station
Nice-Ville, *av. Thiers; tel: 36 35 35 35*. Information open Mon–Sat 0830-1830 (be sure to take a queuing ticket at the entrance), Sun 0830-1115, 1400-1700. Frequent services to all resorts along the Cote d'Azur. Station closed: 0130–0530. Left luggage open 0715–2200; baths and showers 0800–1900 in the basement. For the town centre, turn left from station to *av. Jean Médecin*, the main thoroughfare, turn right down to *pl. Masséna* (300 m), right again to the sea, a 15-min walk. Bus to the airport from outside the station, every 30 mins (FFr.20).

There are **Thomas Cook** bureaux de change next to and opposite the station (:see 'Money' below for details).

245

Buses

Gare Routière (bus station): *promenade de Peillon; tel: 93 85 61 81*. At *pl. Masséna* head north 300 m up *blvd Jean Jaurés*.

Ferries

SNCM, *Quai du Commerce* (on the east side of the port) *tel: 93 13 66 96*. Regular crossings to Corsica (from FFr. 229 one way, students from FFr.181) from the *Quai du Commerce*.

GETTING AROUND

Nice is a big, sprawling city. Broad avenues stretch back from the sea which is lined by the 5-km *promenade des Anglais* and shorter *Quai des États-Unis*. The **Old Town** quarter is manageable on foot but to get between the various museums and sights requires transport. Bus services are good including four night services until 0110.

Renting a car or motor bike is a popular option but the traffic is hectic and parking difficult. **Car and motor-bike hire: Nicea**, *9 av. Thiers* near the railway station; *tel: 93 82 42 71*.

Buses

Most services radiate from *pl. Masséna*. Buy tickets on board; FFr.8. A *carnet* of 5 costs FFr.32.50 or one, five and seven-day passes are available. Information *10 r. Félix Faure; tel: 93 16 52 10*.

Taxis

Taxis are expensive. Expect to pay FFr.50 for even the shortest trip. A journey to the airport from downtown can cost as much as FFr.200; *tel: 93 80 70 70*.

STAYING IN NICE

Accommodation

As Nice is one of Europe's most popular destinations it offers a wide range of accommodation. Hotel chains include *Bw, Ca, Ho, Ib, Md, Me, Nv, and Sf*. One of the best-placed medium-price hotels with sea views is the **Mercure**, *2 r.Halévy* (on the corner of *promenade des Anglais*) near *pl. Masséna; tel: 93 82 30 88*. It is advisable to book in advance even out of season because of the many congresses which take place. Early Feb is busy too during the carnival.

One of the world's most prestigious hotels is the **Negresco**, *37 promenade des Anglais; tel: 93 88 39 51*, a white and pink palace built for a former Romanian gypsy violinist, Henri Negresco. The same architect designed the Moulin Rouge and Folies Bergères in Paris and it abounds with extravagant furnishing and works of art. Those who cannot afford a room (at around FFr.1630 per night) should at least see the **Salon Royal**, adorned with a Baccarat chandelier made for a Tsar.

For the budget-conscious, good value accommodation is available near the station – *r. de Suisse, av. Durante, r. d'Alsace-Lorraine* – or in Old Nice, around *pl. St François*.

HI: Nice has three youth hostels, all far from the centre. **Mt-Alban**: *rte de Mont-Alban; tel: 93 89 23 64*, 4 km out of town uphill! (bus no. 5 from the station to *blvd Jean Jaurès*, then no. 14 to hostel). No reservations, open from 1000. Good view over the city.

Clairvallon Youth Hostel: *av. Scudéri; tel: 93 81 27 63*, is up in Cimiez to the north of the centre (bus nos 15 or 22, stop at *Scudéri*). Located in a park with pool.

Magnan: *31 r. Louis-de-Coppet* near the airport; tel: *93 86 28 75*. Take bus no. 23 from the station or 9, 10 and 12 from *pl. Grimaldi*.

Camping: The nearest campsites are at

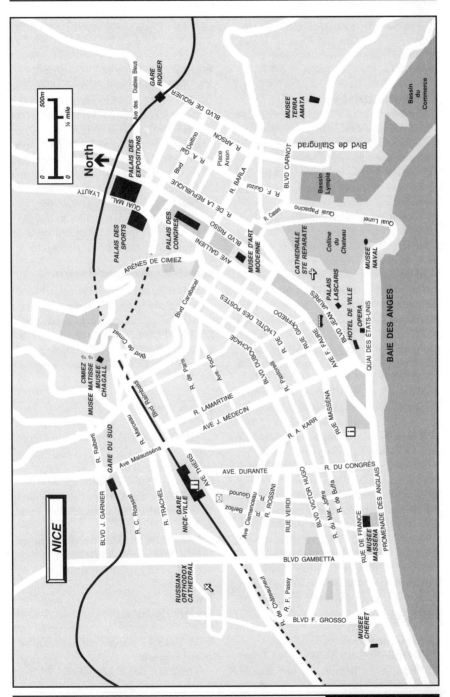

Cagnes-sur-Mer to the west, 15 mins by train. Sleeping on the beach is not allowed. Those who try can expect a hosing down in the early hours.

Eating and Drinking

A culinary paradise, Nice is influenced both by its neighbour, Italy, and Provencal cooking which combines local vegetables with delicately-flavoured herbs. Hence the popularity of *farcis* – stuffed vegetables, and *ratatouille* – stewed peppers, courgettes, tomatoes and onions.

Pissaladière – Niçois onion tart garnished with anchovies and olives is served with aperitifs. *Socca* is a traditional lunchtime snack often sold in markets from special carts – it's an enormous pancake made from crushed chick peas, served piping hot. And of course *Salade Niçoise* – the genuine article contains hard-boiled eggs, tomatoes, anchovies, cucumber, spring onions, broad beans and artichoke. *Pan Bagnat* is a large bun stuffed with *salad niçoise* and doused in olive oil - best eaten on the beach where the drips don't matter. Look out too for *estocaficada* – a tomato stew based on smoked haddock.

Vieux Nice (the old town) is the best area for eating – particularly *Cours Saleya*, which is covered with open-air tables in summer, and *r. Ste Répararte* and the other narrow side-streets around the cathedral. Prices tend to be high in these spots. For really good value, try **P'as de Pot?**, *2 r. Barillerie, tel: 93 85 79 32*. North of the old town, *pl. Garibaldi* boasts the best shellfish, notably at the inexpensive **Café de Turin**, and good *socca*. The *Zone Piétonne*, around *Av. Jean Médecin*, is the place for pizzas.

Communications

Post Office: *23 av. Thiers; tel: 93 82 65 00*. It has poste restante, money transfer and fax. Open 0800–1900, 0800–1200 Sat.

Money

Thomas Cook bureaux de change are at the station *12 av. Thiers; tel: 93 82 13 00*, open 0700–2200 and *13 av. Thiers, tel 93 88 59 99*, open 0800-2230. and *2 pl. Magenta; tel: 93 88 49 88*, open 0900–2300. In addition to changing all kinds of traveller's cheques, Eurocheques and foreign currency, and selling the *Thomas Cook European Timetable*, they also can offer emergency assistance to travellers who have lost their MasterCard cards or Thomas Cook traveller's cheques.

ENTERTAINMENT AND EVENTS

Nice is regarded as the cultural and social capital of the South of France, offering a choice of opera, concerts and plays. **FNAC** (*Fédération Nationale d'Achats des Cadres*) in the Nice Etoile shopping mall, *av. Jean Médecin*. supplies tickets; tel: *93 21 00 00*.

Opera and Music

Nice Opéra, *4 r. St-Françis-de-Paule; tel: 93 85 67 31*, is one of the best in France, staging opera and concerts. Chamber and sacred music concerts are staged at **Cathédrale Ste-Réparate**, *pl. Rossetti*.

CEDAC de Cimiez, *49 av. de la Marne; tel: 93 81 09 09*, is a major venue for jazz.

In summer the **Théâtre de Verdure**, *Jardin Albert I; tel: 93 82 38 68*, stages rock, jazz and other concerts in a marquee.

Theatre

Théâtre de Nice, *promenade des Arts; tel: 93 80 52 60*, in the huge Acropolis, part of the *Palais des Congrès*, stages opera, ballet and concerts.

Théâtre de l'Alphabet, *10 blvd*

Carabacel; tel: 93 13 08 88. More classical theatre productions.

Bars and Nightlife
In summer Nice grinds on long after midnight thanks to its many piano bars, discos and small clubs with live music, though it lacks sophisticated nightclubs with cabarets. The young generation like to gravitate to the beach. Gamblers head for **Casino Ruhl**, *1 Promenade des Anglais; tel: 93 87 95 87*. But for many it is entertainment enough simply to stroll along the *Promenade des Anglais* or sit on the *Cours Saleya* and watch the world go by.

Events
In Feb the **Nice Carnival** and **Battles of the Flowers** involve parades of dozens of giant floats throughout the day and night with bands and dancing, fireworks and the burning of the Carnival King. Around 1500 people take part and there's a different theme each year.

The Carnival

Occupying the two weeks before Lent, the Carnival, or Mardi Gras, is a tradition which has surprisingly authentic origins for an event which seems tailor-made to attract tourists. It is at least as old as the 14th century, and may be very much older if, as is thought, it derives from pagan springtime rites. The burning of the Carnival King may even be an echo of the human sacrifice which was associated with such rituals in other parts of pre-Christian Europe.

By the beginning of the 19th century it had fallen into decline, but was revived by the Russian community in the middle of the century. Its owes much to the painter Alexis Massa, who established its modern format in 1873.

In July international stars perform in the **Jazz Festival** in the Roman amphitheatre and gardens at **Cimiez** (tickets are available, usually up to the event, from FNAC and tourist offices).

SHOPPING
Shopping can be surprisingly good value. The outdoor markets and little shops in **Vieux Nice** are one of the best places to shop for art, cheap clothes and glorious food. In *Cours Saleya*, the food and flower market (0600–1730 except Sun afternoon and Mon) is replaced by a flea market on Mon (0800–1700). Craft stalls arrive on summer evenings.

For clothes and gift shops, head for the pedestrian area behind *pl. Masséna*. The **Galeries Lafayette** store and **Nice Etoile** shopping mall are in *av. Jean Médecin*.

SIGHTSEEING
With its tall shuttered buildings amd ornate balconies, **Vieux Nice** seems almost more Italian than French (indeed it was handed over to the King of Sicily in 1713 and only reunited with the rest of France in 1860). Wander the narrow streets to **Palais Lascaris**, *15 r. Droite; tel: 93 62 05 54*, a 17th-century palace/museum (open 0930–1200, 1430–1800, closed Mon and all Nov). Beyond, steps lead up to the château – though little remains of it – and a colourful park, small naval museum and breathtaking views.

At sunset, stroll the **promenade des Anglais** as the lights begin to shimmer and the **Negresco** hotel lights up like an elaborate wedding cake.

At the far west end of the *promenade des Anglais*, Nice's newest attractions are the **Parc des Miniatures**, *blvd Impératrice Eugénie; tel: 93 44 67 74*, featuring models of Riviera landmarks, and the tropical conservatories of the **Parc Phoenix**, *405 promenade des Anglais; tel: 93 18 03 33.*

Museums

Nice boasts some of the best museums and art galleries in France, 18 in all, reflecting the city's long history and its connections with great artists like Matisse, Chagall and Dufy. Admission is free except to the state-run **Musée Marc Chagall** and most are easily accessible by local bus.

Best of the bunch is the newly refurbished **Musée Matisse**, *164 av. des Arènes de Cimiez; tel: 93 81 08 08*, in a 17th-century Genoese-style villa amongst the Roman ruins of Cimiez – Matisse's personal collection of paintings and sculptures in a beautiful setting (bus nos 15, 17, 20, 22 from *pl. Masséna*); open 1100–1900 summer, 1000–1700 Oct–Apr, closed Tues. Admission charge for special exhibitions. Next door the **Musée Archéologique**, *160 av. des Arènes de Cimiez; tel: 93 81 59 57*, exhibits the copious finds dug up while excavating the Roman arenas at Cimiez (bus nos 15, 17, 20, 22 to *Arènes*); open 1000–1200, 1400–1800 (till 1700 in winter), closed Sun morning and Mon and all Nov. Matisse and fellow artist Raoul Dufy are buried in the neighbouring **Couvent des Frères Mineurs**, with a fine view across Nice to the sea. Also in Cimiez, the **Musée Marc Chagall**, *av. du Dr. Ménard; tel: 93 81 75 75*, is a graceful temple to Chagall's genius – beautifully lit to display the 17 huge canvases he painted on Biblical themes between 1954 and 1967 plus stained-glass windows, engravings, sculptures and ceramics (bus no. 15, open 1000–1900 summer, 1000–1230, 1400–1730 Oct–June, closed Tues). Admission FFr.27 winter, FFr.35 summer.

In the centre of town, the **Musée d'Art Moderne et d'Art Contemporain**, *promenade des Arts; tel: 93 62 61 62,* is unmistakable: a white marble cliff rising above the street, and filled with striking pop art including exhibits like squashed cars, with sculptures in the gardens and terraces outside; open 1100–1800, 1100–2200 Fri, closed Tues. The **Musée d'Art et d'Histoire** in *Palais Masséna, 65 r. de France, tel: 93 88 11 34*, a splendid old Italianate villa adorned with antiques, traditional artefacts and decorated with paintings by Renoir and local artists; open 1000–1200, 1500–1800 summer; 1000–1200, 1400–1700 winter, closed Mon.

East of the port, **Musée Terra Amata**, *25 blvd Carnot; tel: 93 55 59 93*, has displays of the prehistoric inhabitants of Nice from 400,000 years ago. On the same site where the ancient hunters' encampment was found (bus nos 1, 2, 7, 9, 10, 20); open 0900–1200, 1400–1800, closed Mon. The **Musée Naval**, in the historic *Bellanda Tower* in *Parc du Chateau; tel: 93 80 47 61*, overlooking the port, displays weapons, ships models and instruments. Hector Berlioz lived there for a short time; open 1000–1200 and 1400–1700, closed Mon and Tues.

Churches

Nice has two cathedrals, each in its own way tracing the cosmopolitan history of this Riviera resort.

The Italian influence in Nice can be seen in the **Cathédrale de Ste-Réparate**; *pl. Rossetti*, in *Vieux Nice*, a dimly impressive Catholic masterpiece built with Italian money in the 17th century to the town's patron saint.

To the west of the station, the **Cathédrale Orthodoxe Russe St-Nicolas**, *17 blvd du Tzarévitch; tel: 93 96 88 02*, is a mighty five-domed Russian Orthodox church built on the site of a villa where the young Tsarevich Nicholas died.

It was completed just five years before the Russian Revolution with royal roubles and remains a symbol of the aristocratic opulence that characterises the Riviera; open 0930–1200, 1430–1800 summer, 0930–1200, 1430–1700, closed Sun morning.

Beaches

The beaches of Nice are pebbly - there is no sand east of Antibes as far as the Italian border. This does not deter the sun-worshippers from crowding onto the long *Baie des Anges* beaches below the *Promenade des Anglais* all summer long. It's free to sit on most of the beach but private beach clubs cover some of the central section, charging around FFr.90 for a day's hire of lounger and umbrella, Hotels make special arrangements for their guests to use the facilities.

For less hectic sunworshipping, seek out the long stretch of beach between **Cagnes-sur-Mer** and **Antibes** to the west. However the prettiest bays are to the east at **Villefranche** (young, lively crowd), **Beaulieu** (old, sedate crowd) and **St-Jean Cap Ferrat** (well-heeled, laidback crowd). For more about these resorts, see the next chapter, the Nice–Turin route.

OUT OF TOWN

Renoir spent the last years of his life in **Cagnes sur Mer**, buying an isolated house in an olive grove overlooking the sea. Today this is the **Musée Renoir**, *chemin les Colettes; tel: 93 20 61 07*; open 1000–1200, 1400–1700, closed Tues, admission FFr.20; a delightful tour around the artist's life, with rooms as he kept them eighty years ago (from the rail station, take the bus to *Beal-Les Colettes*). Above the coast, the château of the medieval citadel is now a museum; **Montée de la Bourgade**; *Haut-de-Cagnes*, entrance *pl. Grimaldi; tel: 93 20 85 57*, open 1000–1200, 1430–1700 summer, 0900–1200, 1500–1700 Oct–Apr, closed Tues, admission FFr.20.

There are hourly buses from Nice bus station to **St Paul-de-Vence**, one of the coast's most picturesque *villages perchés*, home to artists and tourists. Wander through the narrow medieval streets and sip coffee while watching the *boulistes* argue another round. One of the most interesting modern art museums in France is here, **Fondation Maeght**, built by the Maeght family who were friends of Matisse; *tel: 93 32 81 63*, open 1000–1230, 1420–1800 winter, 1000–1900 July and Aug, admission FFr.25. The garden is a quirky sculpture park, designed by Miró.

Three km further up the valley is **Vence**, another delightful little town which seems far-removed from the glitzy coast. Here Matisse was nursed by local nuns and repaid them by designing and building a simple yet breathtakingly beautiful chapel – **La Chapelle du Rosaire**, *av. Henri Matisse; tel 93 58 03 26*; open Tues and Thurs, 1000–1130, 1430–1700. Matisse considered it his masterpiece.

Grasse is the centre of the world's perfume industry, producing essential oils and training the most famous 'noses' to create unique smells from a mixture of ingredients. There's a heady scent from the flowers grown all around, notably mimosa, lavender and roses. **Musée International de la Parfumerie**, *8 pl. du Cours; tel: 93 36 80 20*, has exhibits on the history of perfume and its production; open 1000–1900 June–Sept, 1000–1200 and 1400–1700 Oct–May except Mon and Tues and all Nov; admission Ffr.15.

NICE–TURIN

The corniche between Nice and the Italian border is one of the most beautiful coastlines in the world, with the tail-end of the Alps plunging into the Mediterranean, avenues of palm trees decorating small villages, and millionaires' palaces overlooking the sea. The railway hugs the coast, most of the way offering stunning views of the Côte d'Azur's red cliffs, glittering marinas and wealthy resorts. There is no real 'Fast Track' here – the point of the route is to enjoy the coastline before heading up into the Alps. At Ventimiglia the route leaves the coast to climb north through the mountains on its way to Turin. Four times, to gain height, it uses the ingenious expedient of disappearing into the mountainside and doing a complete spiral before emerging higher up.

252

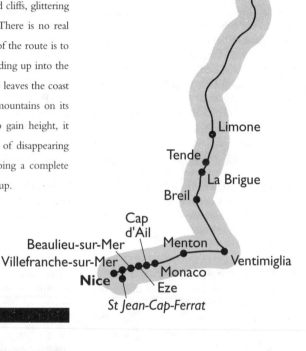

TRAINS

ETT Tables 354, 357.

ON TRACK

Nice–Villefranche-sur-Mer– Beaulieu-sur-Mer–Eze–Cap d'Ail–Monte Carlo–Ventimiglia

A frequent service operates along the Riviera. Nice to Villefranche takes 8 mins, Villefranche to Beaulieu 4 mins, Beaulieu to Eze 4 mins, Eze to Cap d'Ail 4 mins, Cap d'Ail to Monte Carlo 3 mins, Monte Carlo to Ventimiglia around 25 mins.

Ventimiglia–Briel–La Brigue–Tende–Limone

Eight trains a day run between Ventimiglia and Limone, all call at Breil and most at Tende and La Brigue. The journey from Ventimiglia to Breil takes 25 mins, Breil to La Brigue 35 mins, La Brigue to Tende 6 mins and Tende to Limone takes 20 mins.

Limone–Turin (Torino)

Four or 5 trains a day make this journey, taking around 1 hr 40 mins. Other services are available by changing trains at Cuneo and/or Fossano.

VILLEFRANCHE-SUR-MER

Station: *tel: 93 87 50 50* for information. **Tourist Office**: *Jardin François Binon, 06230 Villefranche*, near the *Basse Corniche; tel: 93 01 73 68*.

With one of the deepest ports on the Mediterranean, Villefranche is home to cruise ships and the occasional American aircraft carrier. The bay boasts the liveliest beach in the region, situated just below the rail station. When you tire of lying in the sun, stroll along the Italianesque **waterfront** and maze of old narrow streets where small restaurants abound.

Artist Jean Cocteau decorated the **Chapelle Saint-Pierre** on the *Quai Courbet; tel: 93 76 90 70*. Open 0930–1200 and 1400–1800, admission FFr.12.

SIDE TRACK FROM VILLEFRANCHE

ST-JEAN-CAP-FERRAT

Tourist Office: *59 av. Denis Séméria, 06230 St-Jean Cap-Ferrat; tel: 93 76 08 90*.

St-Jean Cap-Ferrat is a walk up from Villefranche beach, or a bus ride from Nice bus station. This peninsula contains the prettiest beaches in the region and some of the world's most expensive homes. Liz Taylor, Joan Collins and Mick Jagger are rumoured to have places here. The port is lined with restaurants, tranquil even in high season, and surprisingly inexpensive. A footpath leads around the peninsula, through pine woods, giving splendid views back along the coast. On the hump of the hill joining the mainland is one of the Riviera's most attractive museums, **Musée Ephrussi de Rothschild**; *tel: 93 01 33 09*, a villa once owned by Béatrice de Rothschild. The house is stunning, but the gardens are even more impressive – an eclectic masterpiece of exotic plants with views down to Villefranche and Beaulieu. Not to be missed (open 1000–1800 winter, 1000–1900 summer, admission FFr.34)

BEAULIEU-SUR-MER

Station: *tel: 93 87 50 50* for information. **Tourist Office**: *pl. Clémenceau, 06310 Beaulieu* (right outside the station), *tel: 93 01 02 21*.

Beaulieu was christened 'beautiful place' by Napoleon. Its mild climate has attracted retirees from all over Europe, giving the village a relaxed, if not comatose, air. The beach is pretty, offering views of Cap-Ferrat. **Villa Kerylos**, *tel: 93 01 01 44*, a replica of the house of a wealthy Athenian, circa 5th-century BC, was built by a rich archaeologist at the turn of the century. Marbles, ivories, bronzes, mosaics fill the villa and the Mediterranean laps at the doorstep. Open daily 1030–1230 and 1400–1800 winter, 1000–1900 summer; closed Nov. Admission FFr.30.

EZE

Station: *tel: 93 87 50 50*, for information.
Tourist Office: *pl. du Gén. de Gaulle, 06360 Eze; tel: 93 41 26 00.*

Perched 427 m above the Mediterranean, the medieval eagle's nest of Eze commands spectacular views. The rail station is by the sea, with steep tortuous steps climbing up the cliff to the village, once trodden by philosopher Friedrich Nietzsche. Once at the top you are greeted by narrow streets, arty boutiques and a **Jardin Exotique** filled with rare cacti (*tel: 93 41 10 30*, open 0900–1200 and 1400–1900, summer 0800–2000, admission FFr.10). Yet the real attraction (apart from the shopping in charming but overpriced shops) is the view – the best on the Riviera. On clear days you can see as far as St-Tropez, 100 km away.

CAP D'AIL

Station: *tel: 93 87 50 50* for information. Cap d'Ail (the 'Peninsula of Garlic') is a popular beach stop. The swimming is excellent, even though off pebbles. Cap d'Ail also boasts one of the coast's best youth hostels, perched above the Mediterranean; **Relais International de la Jeunesse**, *av. R. Gramaglia; tel: 93 78 18 58*. The maximum stay is three nights, since most people want to stay for a lifetime.

MONACO

Station: *pl. de la Gare, av. Prince-Pierre; tel: 93 87 50 50*, information 0900–1845. Station and luggage lockers are closed 0100–0530.

For the **Royal Palace,** head straight down to *pl. d'Armes*, continue towards the Port and a footpath leads up onto the palace rock. For the **Casino**, turn left at the port along *blvd Albert 1er*, and up the hill along *av. d'Ostende* (500 m). Otherwise take bus no. 4 from the station.
Tourist Office: *2a blvd des Moulins, 98000 Monaco*, near the Casino; *tel: 92 16 61 16* open Mon–Sat 0900–1900, Sun 0900–1200. Hotel reservations.

GETTING AROUND

Monaco is not big but very hilly. All sights are walkable from the rail station or there are buses. Strategically-placed lifts and escalators whisk people free between the different street levels. Taxis tend to be expensive.

STAYING IN MONACO

Accommodation

Half the hotels are in the top luxury category and budget accommodation is scarce, although not impossible to find. **Hôtel de Paris** next to the Casino, is one of Europe's most extravagant hotels. A drink in the bar costs almost as much as a normal hotel room, but is worth it for the glittering surroundings. Just round the corner on *Square Beaumarchais* is its *Belle Époque* rival, **L'Hermitage**, whose bar-terrace provides spectacular views down over the port. For less ruinously-priced places to stay, try *r. de la Turbie* near the station.

The **Centre de la Jeunesse** youth hostel, *24 av. Prince-Pierre; tel: 93 50 83 20,* is 100 m from the station. This excellent hostel (for 16–26 year olds and students up to 31), is a godsend, although it fills up rapidly in summer months – arrive after 0900 and you may not get a bed.

Eating and Drinking

You can eat like a prince in Monaco, at a price. But there is a wide range of restaurants, from very *haute cuisine* to simple Italian trattorie. If you come up lucky at the casino, head across the road to

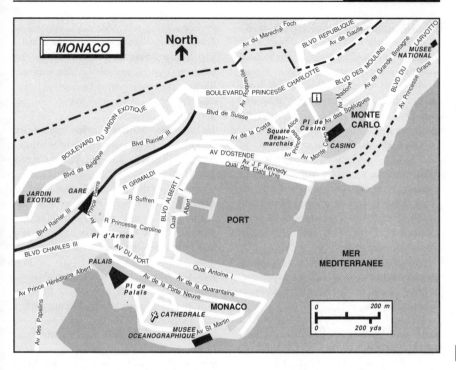

Map of Monaco, Monte Carlo and surrounding area, showing the Port, Casino, Palais, and Musée Océanographique.

Restaurant Louis XV at the **Hôtel de Paris**. Here, one of the world's top chefs, Alain Ducasse, masterminds menus fit for royalty. This was the favourite dining room of Edward VII when he was Prince of Wales, and present-day patrons include Pavarotti and Sting, not to mention Monaco's own princesses, Stephanie and Caroline. Yet eating with royalty is not the preserve of the wealthy. In *r. Suffren* up from the port, **Le Texan**, a Tex-Mex restaurant and bar with the cheapest beers in the Principality, offers good food and the possibility of brushing shoulders with the likes of Prince Albert and Boris Becker.

Inexpensive food is not that hard to come by, especially pizzas thanks to the proximity of the Italian border – again *r. de la Turbie* beckons. For lunch in the sun, head for the terrace bars along *quai Albert 1er*. Up on the rock in the **old town**, numerous small restaurants also offer inexpensive set menus.

Communications
Post Office: *pl. Beaumarchais; tel: 93 50 69 87*, sells both Monégasque and French stamps. Open 0800–1900, 0800–1200 Sat.

Money
Compagnie Monégasque de Change: *av. La Quarantaine; tel: 93 25 02 50* and numerous banks.

ENTERTAINMENT
Monaco is synonymous with gambling. There are five casinos but you have to be over 21 (take your passport) and smartly dressed. The most famous casino in the world, **Casino de Monte Carlo** in *pl.du Casino, tel: 92 16 23 00*, commands centre stage, adorned with flags and gold leaf.

You pay FFr.50 for the pleasure of walking into its hallowed halls (open from 1200 until the last gambler goes home to bed) and FFr.50 more to enter the Private Rooms and English Club, the holy of holies where serious money is won and lost. But to pop a few coins into slot machines in the entrance lobby is free.

The **Café de Paris** next door, *tel: 92 16 23 00*, has no entrance fee but is definitely more tacky; open from 1000. **Sun Casino** in *av. des Spélugues, tel: 92 16 23 00*, is glossy and modern, open from 1700, Sat and Sun 1600. The adjoining **Loews Casino**, *tel: 93 50 65 00*, specialises in slot machines, open from 1100.

Monaco is an enjoyable wandering ground at night. Bars can be expensive, but try the side streets off *r. Grimaldi* behind the port.

To catch a glitzy cabaret, head for **La Salle des Etoiles** at the **Monte-Carlo Sporting Club**, *av. Princesse Grace, tel: 92 16 22 44*, though do not expect to come back with a heavy wallet. Monaco's number one club is **Jimmy Z's**, *26 av. Princesse Grace; tel: 92 16 22 77*, with a strict dress code but free entry. Open 2330–dawn. Expect to pay about FFr.100 each for drinks.

Culturally, Monaco gets the best of the lot. In the **Salle Garnier**, *tel: 93 50 76 54*, part of the **Casino de Paris**, the world's opera stars join the resident **Ballet Russe de Monte Carlo**. This opulent theatre was built by Charles Garnier, who was responsible for the opera house in Paris. In their day Picasso and Cocteau designed the sets. Tickets are surprisingly affordable, from FFr.75 for students.

In summer, open-air cinema attracts large crowds at the **Cinema d'Été**, *av. Princesse Grace, tel: 93 25 86 80*, showing a different film in its original language each evening from 15 May–30 Sept.

For football fans, Monaco boasts one of Europe's top clubs at the futuristic 40,000-seat **Stade Louis II**, *Fontvielle* where the pitch is two storeys above the ground. Tickets are easy to come by.

Events

In Jan the **Monte-Carlo car rally** includes exciting stages in the hills behind Monaco. Feb sees the international **Circus Festival**.

End Apr the **Monte-Carlo Tennis Open** features top ATP players from the around the world, while end May the **Formula One Grand Prix** motor racing takes place on a circuit around the streets.

SIGHTSEEING

Flash, fast and finely manicured, Monaco will live up to expectations. Do not expect any bargains, but it costs little to stroll, admire the views and brush with opulence. In particular, wander the narrow streets of the **old town** on a headland above the port.

The Principality became an independent state in 1308, when the Grimaldi family bought the 194-hectare site from the city of Genoa. It grew rich from taxes levied on the lemons and olives of Menton, until the Mentonnais revolted in 1848. Faced with bankruptcy, Prince Charles III decided to open a casino, and the rest is history. So much money poured in that state taxes were abolished, and the grateful citizens renamed the hill by the Casino as Monte-Carlo (Mount Charles). Today the glitter has not worn off, and you are still likely to catch a glimpse of royalty in the street.

The **Casino** is the heart of Monte-Carlo. Its gilded opulence is definitely worth a look whether or not you are gambler.

High up on the Rock, the dazzling

white **Royal Palace** is small but regal. Be there punctually to see the changing of the guard as it takes place at 1155 precisely. The **State Apartments**, *tel: 93 25 18 31,* are sumptuous, open June–Sept 09300–1830, Oct 100–1700. Admission FFr.30.

Musée National, *17 av. Princesse Grace, tel 93 30 91 26,* is full of dolls and working models which are demonstrated regularly. Open 1000–1830 in summer and 1000–1215, 1430–1830 in winter. Admission FFr.26.

On the southern edge of the Rock, Monaco's most stimulating attraction is the **Musée Océanographique**, *av. St-Martin; tel: 93 15 36 00,* one of the world's great aquariums, developed by Jacques Cousteau. Open 0930–2000 summer, 0930–1900 Sept–June; admission FFr.60.

The **Cathédrale de Monaco**; *4 r. Colonel Bellando de Castro; tel: 93 30 88 13,* contains the tomb of Princess Grace.

Above the skyscrapers at the back of the town, Monaco's botanical garden, the **Jardin Exotique**, *tel: 93 30 33 65,* (take bus no. 2), sprouts 7000 different types of cactus. Open 0900–1800 (to 1900 in summer); admission FFr.34.

MENTON

Station: *pl. de La Gare; tel: 36 35 35 35.*

For the sea, head down *r. Edouard VII from pl. des Victoires.*

Tourist Office: *Palais de l'Europe, av. Boyer, 06500 Menton; tel: 93 57 57 00* (left from station then right). Open Mon–Sat 0830–1800 in winter, Mon–Sat 0830–1930 and Sun 0830–1230 in summer.

GETTING AROUND

Menton is very walkable, with the main town and sights concentrated at the eastern end of the long pebbly bay. To visit the dramatic perched villages, buses run regularly from the *esplanade du Carei* bus station.

STAYING IN MENTON

Accommodation

Sadly, the palatial hotels where royalty once stayed, including Queen Victoria in 1882, are now mostly retirement homes. Current acommodation is nothing special but includes a high proprotion of apartments, popular with families. For lower budget hotels try around the station, including *r. Albert 1er.*

HI: *plateau St-Michel, rte des Ciappes de Castellar; tel: 93 35 93 14.* Open Feb–Nov. **Camping**: **Camping Municipal du Plateau St-Michel**; *rte des*

257

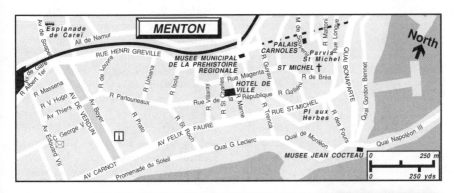

Ciappes de Castellar; tel: 93 35 81 23. Campsite next to the youth hostel, with a superb sea view.

Eating and Drinking

For dining, Italian-influenced places in the old town around **r. St-Michel** are best. For picnics the daily market in *pl. aux Herbes* (opposite the *Hôtel de Ville*) is one of the best on the Riviera, especially lively at weekends. The surrounding hill villages offer small family-run restaurants specialising in local country cuisine. Try Ste-Agnès.

Communications

Post Office, *cours Georges V; tel: 93 28 64 84*, has poste restante, currency exchange. Open 0800-1830 (1800 Thurs), Sat 0800-1200.

ENTERTAINMENT

The **Lemon Festival** in Feb is the highlight of the year, including concerts and theatre as well as parades of floats covered in lemons, fireworks and general jollifications. Otherwise nightlife is rather quiet, revolving round the bars and cafés which line the bay, with open-air events in summer.

SIGHTSEEING

Menton is synonymous with lemons and oranges.

Head along the sea wall around the small port and look back to the pastel façades of the **old town**. Also take the steps up to the **Parvis St-Michel** for views down over the sea. In the town centre, the narrow streets and some of the houses were constructed by the **Grimaldis** (the family of the Princes of Monaco) in the 15th century. **Église St-Michel**, built in 1640, is particularly impressive.

To the west the **Palais Carnolès**, *3 av. de la Madone, tel: 93 35 49 71*, houses an interesting art collection featuring Impressionist and modern paintings; open 1000–1200, 1500–1900 (1800 Sept–Jun), closed Tues.

The artist Jean Cocteau, who lived in the area, decorated the **Salle des Mariages** in the **Hôtel de Ville**, *pl. Ardoino, tel: 92 10 50 29*. Open 0830–1230, 1330–1700, closed weekends, admission FFr.5. **Musée Jean Cocteau**, *bastion du Vieux-Port, quai Napoleon III, tel: 93 57 72 30*, displays his mosaics, pastels and pottery. Open 1000–1200, 1500–1800, closed Tues.

VENTIMIGLIA

Station: 100 m from the old town.
Tourist Office: *Via Cavour 61, tel: (0184) 351 183.*

ACCOMMODATION

There are plenty of inexpensive hotels at and around Ventimiglia both in the vicinity of the station and along the seafront.

SIGHTSEEING

Old Ventimiglia, which is very small, is far more interseting than the modern town. The 11th–12th-century **Cathedral** with its **Baptistery** are both built in a version of the Lombard Romanesque. The former is fronted by an interesting portal (1222). Of the same period, **San Michele** has holy water stoups made from Roman milestones.

Vestiges of the Roman city survive: the ruins of Albintimilium can be seen to the west (1 km) - in particular the **theatre** (2nd century AD). The **Museo Archeologico** houses the finds from the site. At **Mortola Inferiore** (5 km) are the **Giardini Hanbury**, gardens laid out in the 19th century by Sir Thomas Hanbury and home to a wide variety of exotic and rare plants. At **Grimaldi** (10 km) remains of Neanderthal man were discovered at **Balzi Rossi**. Finds from this important site are on display in the **Museo Preistorico**.

BREIL

Station: *tel: 93 04 40 15.*
Tourist Office: *pl. Brancherie, 06540 Breil-sur-Roya, tel: 93 04 99 76* or, in winter, call the *Mairie, tel: 93 04 99 99.*

The grand orange-pink stone station and its row of arches seem incongruously large and ornate for such a small village. Like the others along this section of the line, it was built in the 1930s by **Mussolini** (whose family came from the area) to encourage the villagers' loyalty to Italy. When border changes were discussed after the World War II, the local people voted to become part of France instead. The date of the referendum – 16 Sept 1947 – is commemorated in street names in several of the villages.

With tall buildings towering over its single narrow main street, Breil still feels Italian. It is an excellent walking base, with the River Roya in the valley below, and surrounded by hills. The **Ecomusée du Haut Pays** in an old SNCF depot, *tel: 93 04 99 76*, brings the history of the valley to life, particularly its railways. It has an old steam locomotive, railcars, carriages and a model layout showing how tunnels on the lines to Nice and Ventimiglia twice cross each other inside the mountains. Open Sat–Sun 1000–1200 and 1530–1830 Oct–May, also Mon and Wed–Fri June–Sept.

LA BRIGUE

Station: *tel: 36 35 35 35.*
Tourist Office: *Pl. de Nice* (summer only); *tel: 93 04 61 01* at the *Mairie, pl. St-Martin, 06430 La Brigue.*

This attractive little Alpine town beside the River Roya has narrow streets lined with houses built in the local green stone. 800 m high and surrounded by wooded hillsides, it was a thriving cattle and wool centre in the Middle Ages. **St Martin's church**, dating from the 13th century, is crowned by a fine Italianate belfry. But the real gem is **Notre-Dame-des-Fontaines**, a tiny 13th-century chapel built at the source of a 'miraculous' spring in woods, 5 km away; key available at the *Auberge St Martin, pl. de l'Eglise.* The spring was thought to be miraculous because it flows intermittently. This is now known to depend on the rainfall and a syphon system in the rocks below. The chapel's interior is completely covered in a series of colourful square murals depicting the life of Saint Mary and the Passion of Christ.

TENDE

Station: *tel: 93 04 65 60.*
Tourist Office: *av. du 16th Septembre, 06430 Tende, tel: 93 04 73 71.*

This small town of tall medieval slate-roofed houses is built in tiers on the mountainside below the ruined castle of the **Counts of Lascarris**. The church of **Notre Dame-de-l'Assomption**, dating back to the 15th-century, is on the main street which slopes down from the rail station.

LIMONE PIEMONTE

Tourist Office: *Piazza Municipio, Limone Piemonte, tel: (0171) 92101.*

This is one of the best winter sports centres in the area. The skiing is excellent though the walking too, in the summer, around the edge of the **Parco Naturale dell'Argentara** has much to recommend it. Accommodation in Limone Piemonte is varied; the older hotels tend to be the

---

Mercantour National Park

A re they doodles made by bored shepherds or the religious symbols of pagan worship-pers? There are all sorts of theories about the ancient rock markings in the **Vallée des Merveilles** – Valley of Marvels – part of the **Mercantour National Park**, on France's border with Italy, west of la Brigue and Tende (nearest station: St Dalmas de Tende).

Altogether over 40,000 ancient rock engravings have been found, thought to date back to at least 1800 BC. Though originally discovered in the 15th century, it was an English priest and botanist, Clarence Bignell, who first brought them to public attention. He was on a week's study tour in the area, in particular looking for the rare saxifrage, a rock plant which only flow-ers every 10 years and then dies. But he became so fascinated by the primitive outlines he dis-covered etched on the rocks, each about six inches high, that he decided to move to Casterino nearby and lived there until he died in 1918.

The markings have intrigued archaeologists ever since but no one has been able to say for sure why they are there or what they depict. Many are similar, perhaps a horn, a spear or a man. Once you know what you are looking for, they are not difficult to spot on the boulders which cover this awe-inspiring rocky valley surrounded by smooth sand-coloured ridges of granite and dotted with pine trees. The colours of the rocks are remarkable too – shades of grey streaked with browns, purples and turquoise, and often covered with patches of vivid green lichens. In between, giant thistles sprout from the tufty grass.

You can go on a jeep tour with a guide as far the mountain refuge **des Merveilles** at 2111 m or on foot if you make the 2½-hour climb from the **Lac des Mesces**. The refuge has room for 64 people to stay overnight (advance booking essential in summer, tel: 93 04 64 64). Camping is also allowed, but for one night only. **Park office**, av. du 16 Septembre 1947, 06430 Tende, tel: 93 04 67 00.

---

more expensive than the modern ones which are generally featureless, if practical. However, at **Valle di Pesio** the monks take in paying guests at their Certosa di Pesio, *tel: (0171) 738 123.*
Tourist Office: *Corso Nizza 17, tel: (0171) 66615.* Ask for details of the Nov Piedmontese cheese exhibition.

ACCOMMODATION

There is a limited choice of accommoda-tion here here, though there are one or two inexpensive hotels in the old quarter.

SIGHTSEEING

Cuneo is primarily a centre from which to explore the valleys and peaks of the sur-rounding area. The provincial capital, it is situated at the confluence of the **Gesso** and **Stura** rivers and is famous nowadays chiefly for the huge Tues market held in *Piazza Galimberti.*

SALZBURG

Next to Vienna, Salzburg is Austria's biggest tourist draw and with good reason. As well as music – with both Mozart and Sound of Music connections – the town's Prince Archbishop rulers bequeathed it a fine castle, palaces, churches and an attractive *Altstadt*.

TOURIST INFORMATION

Tourist Offices: The main ones are: *Mozartpl. 5, Altstadt tel: (0662) 847568,* Mon–Sat 0900–1800 (Nov–March; open longer hours and Suns, Easter and summer); and *Hbf, platform 2; tel: (0662) 871712,* 0845–1930, 0815–2130 (July and Aug). The offices provide free city maps and information leaflets.

ARRIVING AND DEPARTING

Airport

4 km west of the city. Bus no. 77 every 15–30 mins 0554–2311 connects the *Hbf* with the airport – Walserfeld direction from the station, Hbf from airport – journey time approx 15 min. Taxis to the city centre, *tel: (0662) 8111,* around ÖS120 + ÖS25 at night. **Airport information** *tel: (0662) 8580251;*

Station

Hbf; *tel: (0662) 1717,* on the northern edge of the new town, 15–20 mins walk from the old centre (bus nos 1/5/6/51 to *Staatsbrücke,* the main bridge).

GETTING AROUND

Most of the centre is pedestrianised and most sights close enough for walking.

However, the bus and trolley-bus network is excellent and routes are indicated on all maps. Tickets ÖS14 from *Tabak/Trafik* kiosks, ÖS17 from vending machines, ÖS21 on the bus. Day passes are ÖS30. Horse-drawn *fiakers* are available in *Residenzpl.*

STAYING IN SALZBURG

Accommodation

Tourist Offices will book accommodation for the same day ,ÖS50 deposit, ÖS30 fee but ideally book ahead, especially during festivals, calling to warn of late arrival. If you can't find space, try the **Kasern Berg**, outside the area covered by the tourist office. It is reached by any northbound train to the first stop – *Maria Plain* – and walking up the hill. Alternatively there's **Hallein** (20 mins by train – see p. 131) or cross to **Berchtesgaden** (see p. 244).

The hotel patronised by visiting stars is the **Goldener Hirsch**, *Getreideg. 37; tel: (0662) 848511* (very expensive), in four medieval townhouses. **Hotel Blaue Gans**, *Getreideg. 43; tel: (0662) 841317* (expensive) is also probably 700 years old, as is **Hotel Elefant**, *Sigmund-Haffnerg. 4; tel: (0662) 843397* (expensive). **Pension Wolf**, *Kaig. 7; tel: (0662) 8434530* (expensive) is in a 15th-century building. Hotel chains with property in the area include: *BW, Hd, Mc, Nv, Rd, Rm, RC, Rk, Sh, SL, Sn* and *Tp.*

Avoid the pension proprietors touting at the *Hbf* who usually charge over the odds. In town, **Pension Junger Fuchs**, *Linzerg. 54; tel: (0662) 875496* (budget) just 10 mins from the sights can be noisy but is convenient. **Haus Kernstock**, *Karolingerstr. 29; tel: (0662) 82 74 69* (moderate) offers large rooms with balconies 12 mins from the station. More basic is **Hotel Merian**, *Merianstr. 40; tel: (0662) 820611* (budget) right behind the *Hbf*, open to travellers July–Sept.

Most convenient hostels are: **HI:** *Glockeng. 8; tel: (0662) 876241*, on the northern edge of Kapuzinerberg, open Apr–Oct (bus no. 29); **HI:** *Haunspergstr. 27; tel: (0662) 875030*, two blocks west of *Hbf*, but only open July–Aug; and **HI:** *Josef-Preis-Allee 18; tel: (0662) 8426700*, open year-round a little south-east of the *Altstadt* (bus nos 5/55). **Campsites** include: **Stadtblick**, *Rauchen-Bichlerstr. 21; tel: (0662) 50652* end Mar–end Oct, north of the town with views (bus no. 51); and **Camping Salzburg Nord Sam**, *Samstr. 22; tel: (0662) 660494*, in same direction but more convenient for transport (bus no. 33).

Eating and Drinking

Top of the range options include the elegant **Altstadt Radisson**, *Rudolfskai 28/Judeng. 8*, offering international and traditional food with river views, or the more purely traditional **Alt-Salzburg**, *Bürgerspitalg. 2*. Serious gastronomes might try **Gasthof Auerhahn**, *Bahnhofstr. 15*, with a garden and much-lauded proprietor cook. More moderately priced in the Altstadt is **s'Herzl**, *Getreideg. 37*, or on the other side of the river **Mundenhamer Brau**, *Rainerstr. 2*, near the *Hbf*. More budget is **Der Wilde Mann**, *Getreideg. 20*, with extremely generous *Wiener Schnitzel*. **Café Tomaselli**, *Alter Markt 9*, is the place the elegant have taken coffee for the last two centuries. *Beisl* in Salzburg also serve coffee, as well as tea and beer at different times of day. Beer gardens, however, are probably more typical. Worth a

visit is the **Augustiner Bräu**, *Augustinerg. 4*, where local beer is brewed by the monastery and served in giant steins from the traditional wooden kegs. The garden seats 1500. To reach it take bus nos 27, 49, 60, 80 or 95 to Barenwirt. Or walk along the river from the *Altstadt* in the direction of the current or through the woods on the *Mönchsberg*. The **K&K Stieglkeller**, *Festungsg. 10*, off *Kapitelpl.* near the *Festungsbahn*, has sold local Stiegl beer since 1838. **Sternbräu**. *Rudolfskai 22*, in the *Altstadt* has two gardens, restaurant and snack bars.

Communications and Money

The **Main Post Office** is right next to the train station, open 24 hours. There is a branch office at *Residenzpl. 9* open Mon–Fri 0700–1900, Sat 0800–1000, 26 July–21 Aug Sat 0700–1200. In addition to banks currency exchange is available at the *Hbf* daily 0700–2100.

Prices are high. An affordable purchase might be *Mozartkugeln* – balls of pistachio marzipan and nougat covered in chocolate. Those wrapped in red and gold are inferior to the ones the locals buy, from **Fürst**, *Brodg. 13*, handmade and wrapped in blue and silver.

The big one is the **Salzburger Festspiele**, founded in 1920, held late July–end Aug. For major events tickets have to be booked months ahead from **Kartenbüro der Salzburger Festspiele**, *A-5010 Salzburg, Postfach 140, fax: (0662) 846682*. Operas cost ÖS400–4200, orchestra concerts ÖS400–2000 though modern concerts drop to ÖS100. Last-minute standing tickets may be available in the *Kleinefestspielhaus*. Events connected to

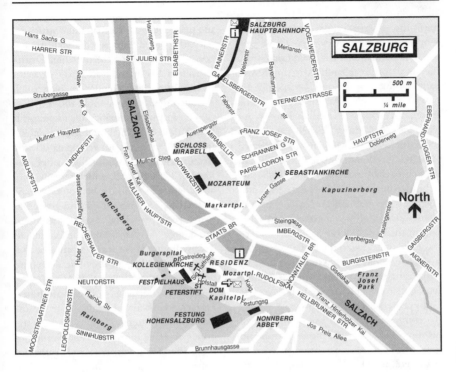

the festival include an opening *Fackeltanz* (torchdance) in the *Residenzpl.* and performances of *Jedermann* (Everyman), standing tickets only sold at the *Dompl.* door one hour before. Other events include the **Mozart Week** end Jan, and an **Easter Music Festival**.

In addition there are concerts every day of the year somewhere in the city. The Tourist Office has full details. Concerts by the **Mozarteum** music school are held at *Schwarzstr. 26; tel: (0662) 88 90 8*, usually free, and there are **Mozartserenaden** (chamber music) in the *Gotischer Saal* at the end of the *Getreideg.* **Festungskonzerte** are held in the *Hohensalzburg* and **Schlosskonzerte** in the *Schloss Mirabell* or the *Residenz*. The **Salzburger Marionettentheater**, *Schwarzstr. 24; tel: (0662) 872406* offers puppet performances to original festival opera recordings.

In Sept there are fairs for **Rupertitag** around the cathedral to celebrate the city's patron saint. Dec 3 and 4 there are **Krampuslaufe** – costumed and masked people running through the *Altstadt*, and Nov–Dec 24 there are **Christmas Markets** in *Mirabellpl.* and *Dompl.*

SIGHTSEEING

The city's wealth was founded on a salt industry dating back to the Iron Age, but tourism is now the main source of income. Much of the city's present appearance is due to the influence of the 16th-century Prince-Archbishop Wolf Dietrich, but Mozart is the dominant theme. Reminders of him are ubiquitous.

Above the *Altstadt* looms the formidable **Festung Hohensalzburg**, *Mönchsberg 34; tel: (0662) 80242123*. Construction of the castle began in 1077 and continued until the 17th century. The complex, which has fine city views, is almost perfectly preserved and has everything from medieval torture chambers to impressive early Gothic state rooms (seen only on guided tours) plus Austria's only barrel organ, a 200-pipe affair that booms out after the 7th-century 35-bell carillon of the **Glockenspiel**, *Mozartpl.*, has pealed (at 0700, 1100 and 1800). The castle can be approached on foot from *Festungsg.* behind the *Dom*, or take the lift. Alternatively the *Mönchsberglift* operates from *Gstatteng.* (by *Museumpl.*) and takes you to the *Café Winkler* lookout, whence there are trails east to the castle.

Narrow **Getreidegasse** is bordered by 17th–18th-century houses with decorative wrought-iron signs. At no. 9 is **Mozarts Geburtshaus**; *tel: (0662) 844313*, where the composer was born and spent most of his first 17 years. It's now a museum spreading beyond the original Mozart apartment, the exhibits including stage sets for his operas and an undersized violin he used when a boy. For pilgrims **Mozarts Wohnhaus**, *Makartpl. 8*, is where he lived 1773–1787 and houses objects relating to him as well as period instruments. The **Mozarteum**, *Schwarzstr. 26-8; (0662) 84 43 13*, holds the Mozart Archives and in the grounds is the wooden shack known as the *Zauberflötenhäuschen* where the composer reputedly composed the *Magic Flute*.

The restrained **Residenzplatz** is dominated by the **Residenz**; *24; tel: (0662) 80 42 26 90*, Dietrich's palace, built after the need for fortification had passed. Mozart conducted in the rooms designed to impress. Tours are hourly. ·

The **Dom**, in the adjacent *Dompl.*, considered the finest early baroque cathedral north of the Alps, is a magnificent light-filled building where for once the style is tastefully in proportion in a build-

ing that replaced a Romanesque structure. Mozart worked here as *Konzertmeister* and court organist. The connecting **Dommuseum** has an odd selection of items treasured by the Renaissance rulers, such as conch shells and a whale's tooth.

The **Franziskanerkirche**, *Hofstallg.*, is a mishmash of architectural styles combining more baroque with remnants of early frescos. More successful is the **Kollegienkirche**, *Universitätspl.*, which remains cool and collected within the baroque ethic. **St Peterstift**, *St Peter Bezirk*, on the other hand, rivals wedding cakes in its pastel mouldings; the organ takes decoration to its very limits. There is also an ancient and, when uncrowded, atmospheric cemetery, with catacombs dating to 250AD.

The enormous **Festspielhaus**, *Hofstallg.*, built into the side of the mountain on the western side of *Altstadt*, is the principal venue for the festival. North-east is the **Pferdeschwemme**, a 17th-century horse trough with an equine motif.

Across the river the wooded **Kapuzinerberg** is named after the simple Capuchin monastery on its summit. It offers views of the city and into Germany. North west is *Linzergasse*, a charming medieval street, leading to **Sebastiankirche**, where the graveyard contains the tiled mausoleum of Archbishop Dietrich and the tomb of Paracelsus, the 16th-century medic. *Makartpl.* is home to **Dreifaltigkeitskirche** (Holy Trinity), designed by Fischer von Erlach and noted for its elegant curving exterior as well as rather dark Rottmayr frescos.

Nearby is **Schloss Mirabell**, *Mirabellpl; tel: (0662) 84 85 86*, built in the 17th century for Dietrich's mistress, who managed to bear him 15 children. It was rebuilt in the early 18th century and further reconstructed after a fire in the 19th. It now houses public offices and the

Marmorsaal, an ornate white and gold venue for chamber music concerts. The style spills out on to the incredible **Angel Staircase**, with its mass of marble cherubs, visible to passers by at the entrance.

If you want to relive the **Sound of Music** story there's a choice of English-language tours approx ÖS300 lasting 3–4 hrs, most touted in the *Residenzpl.* You can save your money and avoid being rushed by doing it yourself. **Nonnberg Abbey** near the *Festung* is where Maria von Trapp was a teacher and parts of the film were shot. *Schloss Hellbrunn* grounds (see side tracks) was the venue for Liesl and Rolf's first kiss. **Schloss Leopoldskron** behind the Mönchberg played parts of the von Trapp house and there are various locations in the *Altstadt*, for example the *Petersfriedhof Cemetery,* where the family hid, and the *Festspielhaus*, venue for their last performance. **Mondsee** (hourly buses from *Hbf*) was substituted in the film for the von Trapp wedding which actually took place at the *Nonnberg Abbey*.

The **Baroque Museum**, *Mirabellgarten Orangerie; tel: (0662) 877432*, covers 17th- and 18th-century painting. The **Museum Carolino Augusteum**, *Museumpl. 6; tel: (0662) 84 11 34 24*, contains a selection of artworks from paintings to reconstructed fine period rooms, plus other changing exhibitions. The **Residenzgalerie**, *Residenzpl. 1; tel: (0662) 84 04 51*, has a selection of international Old Masters.

⏁ SIDE TRACKS FROM SALZBURG

Just south of town (5 km) is the 17th-century **Lustschloss Hellbrunn**; *Morzgerstr., Hellbrunn; tel: (0662) 820 372* (half-hourly bus no. 55 direction Grödig from *Hbf* or *Mirabellpl.*). This Italian-designed pleasure-palace is noted for elaborate water-based

booby-traps designed to catch the unwary. One is housed in stone table and chairs, meant to catch out drunken guests. The adjacent **Tiergarten** (zoo), keeps animals in natural surroundings, and in Apr–Oct there's the open air **Monatsschlössl** folk museum nearby.

The **Fuschlsee** is where Salzburgers take off for the beach and swimming but midweek is calm, even in the height of summer. Buses leave from *Hbf* and *Mirabellpl.* approx hourly, stopping at **Fuschl am See**. The **Tourist Office:** *tel: (06226) 250*, Mon–Fri 0830–1200, 1430–1700 (Oct–May; open later in summer and on Sats Jul–Aug), offers a free town plan with accommodation list and will book rooms for the same day. It also offers an events listing, for example, of the concerts each week May–Sept, and a free leaflet in English with ideas for walks and sells maps of the locality (ÖS10 with Guest Card). GC reductions on cable cars, maps, etc. There is a free beach (turn left down the side of the *Schnützenhof Hotel*), and one pay-for (ÖS35 day) back-tracking from bus stop. There is little in the way of sightseeing, though Thurs and Fri the renovated **Ruming-Mühle** demonstrates milling and baking in the traditional oven.

The best hotel, facing the lake, is **Ebners Waldhof mit Vitalschlössl**, *Seepromenade; tel: (06226) 264* (expensive). Just 50 m from the lake is **Alpenrose**, *Fuschl am See 58; tel: (06226) 207* (moderate). There is also **Camping Seeholz**, *Ilse Willstorfer; tel: (06226) 310* on the lake.

The **Wolfgangsee** is served by the buses between Salzburg and Bad Ischl and plied by ferries. First stop, at the northern end of the lake, is **St Gilgen** with a slightly purpose-built feel to it with beach, windsurfing and sailing school, **Tourist Office:** *Rathaus, Mozartpl.; tel: (06227) 348.* Open Mon–Fri 0900–1200, 1400–1700 (Oct–May; open later and at weekends in summer) will book accommodation. It also offers information and half- and full-day guided hikes once a week. Gentle skiing is available in winter. GC discounts on Wolfgangsee ferries.

Right in the centre is **Gasthof zur Post**, *Mozartpl. 8; tel: (06227) 7510* (moderate) or a touch more peaceful **Frühstückpensionen Helene**, *Brunnleitweg 20; tel: (06227) 310* (moderate). There is also a wide selection of *Privatzimmer*. The youth hostel is **HI:** *Mondseerstr. 7–11; tel: (06227) 365.* There is little in the way of specific sights but a plaque marks the house where Mozart's mother was born.

The main resort is the pretty **St Wolfgang. Tourist Office**, *Pilgerstr. 28; tel: (06138) 2239,* open Mon–Fri 0800–1800, Sat 0800–1200, offering free map, accommodation lists (though bookings must be made direct) and information everything from walking routes to evening entertainment. GC discounts on shopping and tourist attractions.

The town has a long history of visitors, starting in the 16th century when the **Pfarrkirche** was a pilgrimage centre, believed built where St Wolfgang built a hermitage. The 15th-century **altarpiece** is a particularly fine piece of Gothic art but perhaps more atmospheric are the pews, burnt by generations of candles.

Im Weissen Rössl, the White Horse Inn of operetta fame, *Im Stöckl 74; tel: (06138) 2306* (expensive) is the town's best known hotel. **Hotel Post**, *Am Marktpl. 87; tel: (06138) 2346* (very

expensive) is an alternative. Cheaper but still central options include **Gasthof Alpenrose**, *Im Stöckl 85; tel: (06138) 2481* (moderate) or **Pension Haus Kurz**, *Stern-Allee 172; tel: (06138) 2449* (moderate) 5 mins out of the centre. There are also numerous *Privatzimmer*. There are three **campsites** along the water of which **Camping Appesbach**; *tel: (06138) 2206*, is the closest to the centre, open May–Oct.

Just outside St Wolfgang is the **Schafbergbahn** rack railway; *tel: (06138) 22 32 0*, offering the pleasure of views over several of the *Salzkammergut's* 13 lakes and as far as the *Berchtesgaden Alps* on a fine day. There are hourly services with a further 30 mins walk to the top. Austrian Rail Passes are valid but holders must still queue for a colour-coded ticket entitling them to travel at a specified time.

At the southern end of the lake is **Strobl. Tourist Office:** *tel: (06137) 255*, Mon–Fri 0900–1200, 1400–1700, Sat 0900–1200 (Sept–June; open longer in summer). Strobl is a sleepy summer resort largely focused on the lake and surrounded by green fields, but with the attraction of a summer toboggan run. Smarter accommodation options include four-star **Villa Brandauer**, *Strobl 73; tel: (06137) 205* (very expensive) or relatively central three-star **Gasthof Kirchenwirt**, *Strobl 18; tel: (06137) 207-0* (moderate). There are campsites out of the centre but convenient from the ferry; **Camping Schönblick**, *Gschwendt 33; tel: (06138) 2471*, **Camping Zierlerbauer**;, *Gschwendt 31; tel: (06138) 2715*, and **Camping Weidingerbauer**;, *Gschwendt 41; tel: (06138) 2728*, all open June–Sept. 🔼

SALZBURG LOOP

Running past the glimmering lakes of Traunsee and Hallstattersee, and the narrow, wooded valley between them, this route opens out into the wider spaces south of the forbidding Dachstein Massif before looping back up past some of the sheerest rock face in Austria and into Salzburg.

TRAINS

ETT tables: 800, 815, 810.

ON TRACK

Salzburg–Gmunden
A change of train at Attnang Puchheim is required. Journey time 1 hr 20 mins.

Gmunden–Altmünster am Traunsee–Traunkirchen–Ebensee Landungsplatz–Bad Ischl–Hallstatt–Obertraun Dachsteinhöhlen–Bad Ausee
A frequent service calls at all these stations. Gmunden to Altmünster takes 5 mins, Altmünster to Traunkirchen takes 5 mins, Traunkirchen to Ebensee 8 mins, Ebensee to Bad Ischl 24 mins, Bad Ischl to Hallstatt 25 mins, Hallstatt to Obertraun 4 mins, Obertraun to Bad Aussee 12 mins.

Bad Ausee–Schladming
The through journey requires a change of train at Stainach Irdning, 1 hr 30 mins.

Schladming–Radstadt
A frequent service taking 20 mins.

Radstadt–Hallein
Change at Bischofshofen. Journey takes 1 hr 30 mins.

Hallein–Salzburg
Frequent service taking 25 mins.

TRAUNSEE

Gmunden is the first stop on this pretty lake, plied by ferries, notably July and Aug the **Gisela**, one of the oldest operating steamboats in the world. The **station:** *tel: (07612) 4207-34*, connects by 19th-century tram to the lakeside. The **Tourist Office:** *Am Graben 2; tel: (07612) 4305*, beyond and left from the last stop, open Mon–Fri 0800–1800, plus Sat and Sun 1000–1800 (July and Aug), offers free map, accommodation list and walks leaflet.

The office can book accommodation. Among four-stars is **Seehotel Schwan**, *Rathauspl. 8; tel: (07612) 33910* on the main square. Cheaper and fairly central is **Kurhaus Pichler**, *Kösslmülg. 7; tel: (07612) 2211* (moderate). There is a *BW*.

The most lauded restaurant is **Restaurant Marienbrücke**, *An der Marienbrücke 5*. For regional food there's **Hotel-Gasthof Steinmaurer**, *Traunsteinstr. 23*, especially for lake fish. Tues is a *Bauernmarkt*. There are **concerts** held Sun May–Sept and Sat July and Aug; a **Summer Carnival**, July ; the **Gmunder Festwoche** end Aug with concert, the **Lichterfest** with fireworks mid-Aug and a **Mountain Marathon** early July.

The **Esplanade** along the lake leads from the **Renaissance Rathaus** and its **Ceramic Glockenspiel** to the **Orth Schloss**, an island castle linked by a breakwater. The central **Heimatmuseum** contains items of local interest. **Schloss Weyer**, *Freyg. 27; tel: (07612) 50180*, holds a collection of Meissen porcelain.

The next stop is **Altmünster**. The **station**; *tel: (07612) 87190* hires bikes. The **Tourist Office**: *Markstr. 23; tel: (07612) 87181*, downhill and first left, continuing parallel to the lake and downhill at *Marktstr.* (20 mins), Mon–Fri 0800–1200, 1400–1800, Sat 0800–1200 (mid-May–mid-Sept), offers a free map in the accommodation list and events booklet, plus walking maps (ÖS15 or 80). This is a more relaxed location with **Gasthof Reisenberger**, *Maria-Theresiastr. 3; tel: (07612) 87216* (moderate) or **Gasthof Zur Post**, *Ebenzweierstr. 10; tel: (07612) 87166* (moderate). There's also **Campingplatz Altmünster**, *Seepromenade Hautstr. 17; tel: (07612) 87276*. The next village is **Traunkirchen** with *Traunkirchen Ort*, the station is unmanned but closer to the heart. Straight downhill is the main road and square with **Tourist Office**: *tel: (07617) 2234*, Mon–Fri 0800–1200, 1400–1700, Sat 1000–1200 . Places to stay include the **Frühstückpension Reithner**, *Traunkirchen 37; tel: (07617) 2371* (budget) on the way down from the station, or right on the water **Seepension Zimmermann**, *Traunkirchen 23; tel: 07617) 2371* (moderate). There is also **Strand-Camping**, *Viechtau 38; tel: (07617) 2281* (get off at the *Traunkirchen* stop and walk north).

At the bottom end of the lake is **Ebensee**, most convenient **Station** *Ebensee Landungspl.; tel: (06133) 542234*, right next to the **Tourist Office**: *tel: (06133) 8016*. Open Mon–Sat 0800–1200, 1400–1900 (July and Aug), Mon–Fri 0800–1200, 1300–1700 (Sept–

June). Events include the **Maypole Festival** (end May), the **Corpus Christi Procession** to the lake (mid-June), a **Fire Night** on the Feuerkogel mountain (June), the **Market Festival** (beginning of July) and **Folk Festival** (end July and Sept). In Jan is the **Glöcklerlauf** with giant and complex paper lanterns carried through the town to scare evil spirits. It's also an easy skiing spot. The **Heimatmuseum** looks at traditional woodworking and carnival traditions.

The Tourist Office will book rooms. **Hotel Post**, *Hauptstr. 19; tel: (06133) 5208* (budget) is recommended for food and has rooms. Cheaper is **Gasthof Kofler**, *Bergg. 1; tel: (06133) 5342* (budget). There is **HI: Jugendherberge Rindbach**, *Rindbachstr. 15; tel: (06133) 66981* approx 20 mins from the station, close to lake and free beach.

BAD ISCHL

Station: *tel: (06132) 24407-386.* Rents bikes.

Tourist Office: *Kurdirektion, Bahnhofstr. 6; tel: (06132) 235 2000*; Mon–Fri 0800–1800, Sat 0900–1600, Sun 0900–1130, 2 mins walk straight out of the train station and left on the main road.

ACCOMMODATION AND FOOD

The best hotel is probably **Hotel Goldenes Schiff**, *Adalbert-Stifter-Kai 3; tel: (06132) 24241* (expensive). An excellent option right by the station is **Sonnhof**, *Bahnhofstr. 4; tel: (06132) 23078.* **HI: Jugendherberge**, *Am Richenstag 5; tel: (06132) 26577* is in the town centre. **Konditorei Zauner**, *Pfarrg. 7*, founded for the rich, and still all cream and gold, is *the* place for pastries. There's a second branch on the river Esplanade. **KuK Hofbeisl**, *Wirerstr. 4* is a kind of brasserie.

SIGHTSEEING

Emperor Franz-Josef turned Bad Ischl into a holiday resort in the last century. The main attraction is the impressive period **Kaiservilla**; *tel: (06132) 23241*, and its park. Still owned by the Habsburgs and open only by guided tour.

The **Marmorschlossel** in the park, a folly larger than most houses and lined in fine wood panelling, was a retreat of the Empress Elizabeth. It is now a **photography museum**. In the resort itself is the **Trinkhalle**, the former pumproom on the *Aubockpl.* and tcshe riverside **Esplanade** once used by the salt refiners. The **Museum** is at number 10; *tel: (06132) 25476*, with material on the salt industry, and a useful leaflet in English.

Other attractions include the **Leharvilla**, *Traunkai; tel: (06132) 26992*, one-time home of the composer, and the entertaining **Haenel–Pancera Museum**, *Concordiastr. 3; tel: (06132) 64454*, an over-the-top 19th-century villa set in aspic. From the edge of Bad Ischl the **Katrin Alm** cable car takes visitors up to views and walking routes. From Bad Ischl itself are marked 'health resort' trails.

Since the rich discovered the pleasures based on the product of the nearby salt mines, the idea here is to take the brine-sulphur mud baths for your health. An **Operetta Festival**, inspired by one-time resident Lehar, runs mid July–beginning Sept. There is also a **Stadtfest** (Aug) with fireworks and music, a **Country Music Festival** (May). Just after New Year is the **Glöcklerlauf** of illuminated lanterns.

HALLSTATT

Station: on the opposite side of the lake, trains are met by a ferry, the last is at 1800. **Tourist Office: Kultur und Kongresshaus**, *Seestr. 169; tel: (06134) 8208.* Open Mon–Fri 0900–1800, Sat and Sun,

1000–1400, (July and Aug), 0900–1200, 1300–1700 (Sept–June) left from the ferry, offers an ÖS10 information booklet with map including ideas for walks. GC discounts on mountain lifts and sports in Hallstatt, Obertraun and Bad Goisern.

ACCOMMODATION AND FOOD

This is a pretty rather than elegant resort with mid-range options like **Frühstuck-pension Sarstein**, *Gosaumühlstr. 83; tel: (06134) 8217* (moderate), *Seehotel Zauner Seewirt, marktpl. 51; tel: (06134) 246* (moderate–expensive). A pleasant place to eat in summer is **Auberge Bräugasthof**, *Seestr. 120-1; tel: (06134) 8221* (moderate) with a terrace right on the lake. **TVN Naturfreundeherberge**, *Kirchenweg 36; tel: (06134) 8318*, acts as a hostel. The more central of the two **campsites** is **Klausner-Höll**, *Lahnstr. 6; tel: (06134) 8329*, near the public beach.

270

SIGHTSEEING

The annual **Corpus Christi** procession July/Aug takes place by boat on the lake. The 2000-odd graves excavated in the vicinity gave Hallstatt's name to an important prehistoric period. Most of the artefacts have gone but there remains the collection in the local **Museum** opposite the tourist office. The area's prosperity began with salt mining and the **Mines**; *tel: (06134) 8251*, at around 2500 years, the oldest in the world still being worked, can be visited April–Oct by a 10-min walk up a path behind the Pfarrkirche. The 15th-century **Pfarrkirche** has a fine early 16th-century altarpiece presented by a rich salt merchant. **St Michelskirche** is notable for the parish charnelhouse beneath, used since 1600 because cemetery land was so limited. Cable cars and lifts offer transport to mountain hikes and paths and in winter to skiing.

SIDE TRACKS FROM HALLSTATT

There are two **Stations**: the unmanned **Obertraun Koppenbrül-lerhöhle,** and **Obertraun Dachstein-höhlen** *tel: (06131) 352,* **Tourist Office** *tel: (06131) 351,* from where a cable car connects to caves open to visitors, *tel: (06131) 362* (May–mid-Oct). The impressive and near-freezing **Reiseneishöhle** are giant ice caves full of glaciers and 'ice chapels' and nearby are the **Mammuthöhle**, carved by giant underground waterways. These are reached after a 15-min walk from the middle station of the *Dachstein* cable car.

The **Koppenbrüllerhöhle** is actually a giant spring, though it is possible to enter the cave and see something of the underground water courses of the mountains here.

BAD AUSSEE

Station: *tel: (03622) 52130.*
Tourist Office: *z.H Bernhard Laimer, Kurhauspl.; tel: (03622) 52323,* 2 km into town, right from station on main road, hourly buses, Mon–Fri 0800–1900, Sat 0900–1400, Sun 1600–1300, offers free map with accommodation brochure.

ACCOMMODATION AND FOOD

Hotel-Pension Villa Kristina, *Altausee-str. 5; tel: (03622) 52017,* has been developed from the original hunters' inn. **Hotel Erzherzog Johann**, *Kurhauspl. 62; tel: (03622) 52507,* is very central. There are *Privatzimmer* available *Bahnhofstr. 210; tel: (03622) 553795.*

The youth hostel is 15 mins walk out of town at *Jugendherbergesstr. 148; tel: (03622) 52238* up the hill. **Gasthof Staud'nwirt**, *Grundlseestr. tel: (03662) 54565* (bus direction *Grundlsee*) offers camping.

ENTERTAINMENT AND SIGHTSEEING

A **spa** town, the local Glaubersalt spring reputedly useful if you want to lose weight. There are churches, most interestingly the 14th-century **Spitalkirche**. The **Pfarrkirche** was also Gothic but tarted up with baroque. There is an **Alpine Garden** *tel: (03662) 5251114* (April–Oct) and a few shops to entertain those taking the cure. There are suggested walking routes from the tourist office, or trips to the **Grundlsee**, for summer bathing.

SCHLADMING

Station: *tel: (03687) 22230-385.*
Tourist Office: *Hauptpl. 18; tel: (03687) 22268*, left out of station to cross river, then right up *Dachsteinstr.*, left and right to the corner of *Hauptpl.* Mon–Fri 0900–1830, Sat 0900–1200, 1600–1800 Sun 1000–1200 (June–Sept), Mon–Fri 0900–1830, Sat 0900–1200, 1400–1800, Sun 1000–1200, 1600–1800 (Oct–May) with plenty of information on outdoor options and runs a series of free walks and pay-for activities like mountain bike tours and glacier walking.

ACCOMMODATION AND FOOD

There are plenty of options, starting with right in the centre **Pension Mayer**, *Salzburgerstr. 26; tel: (03687) 22128* (moderate) or **Hotel-Restaurant Alte Post**, *Hauptpl. 10; tel: (03687) 22571* (expensive) in one of the town's older properties. The youth hostel is **HI:** *Coburgstr. 253; tel: (03687) 24531*, 2 km from the station. **Camping Rechte Ennsau**, *Zerngast; tel: (03687) 23195, is* approx 1 km out of the centre. A list of *Privatzimmer* is provided by the Tourist Office.

SIGHTSEEING

There is a programme of **classical con-**

certs (three a week July). The town is compact and attractive with surviving details like the **city gate, former miners' houses** and the **Museum** in a 17th-century house for sick miners, widows and orphans. **Blue Tomato**, *Salzburgerstr. 98; tel: (03687) 24223* organises a week's programme of events and will rent mountainbikes, roller skates and skateboards. There is summer skiing but the place really takes off in winter.

RADSTADT

Station: *tel: (06452) 4350*
Tourist Office: *tel: (06452) 4305* Mon–Fri 0800–1200, 1400–1800, Sat 0900–1200, 1600–1800, Sun 0900–1100 (Christmas–mid-April), Mon–Fri 0800–1200, 1400–1800, Sat 0900–1200 (June–Sept) Mon–Fri 0800–1200, 1400–1800 (May and Oct–Christmas) up the steps left of station and left at road, to main square.

ACCOMMODATION AND FOOD

The best hotel is the **Gut Weissenhof**, *Weissenhof 6; tel: (06452) 7001* (moderate–expensive). Closer to the station is the three-star **Stegerbräu**, *Schernbergstr. 14; tel: (06452) 4314*, or cheapest of all, rooms with **Familie Ellmer**, *Schernbergstr. 18; tel: (06452) 5400* (budget). There is also **Tauerncamping Lerchenhof**, *Schlossstr.; tel: (06452) 4215*, ½ km from station.

SIGHTSEEING

The town, built by a Salzburg Prince-Archbishop, still contains some handsome houses and has kept its **town walls**. **Schloss Lerchen** is now a folk museum and there is a 16th-century Gothic light tower by the church, the **Schusterturm**.

HALLEIN

See p. 131.

271

SALZBURG–KLAGENFURT

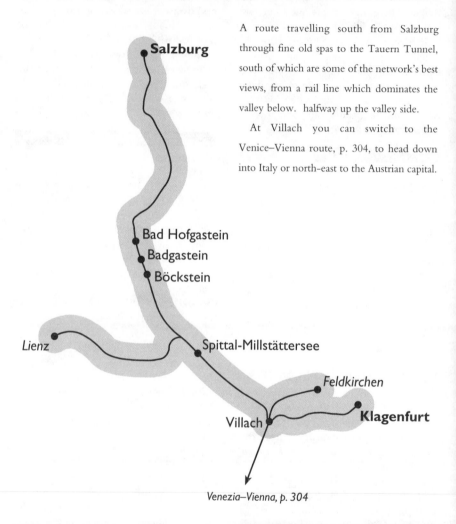

A route travelling south from Salzburg through fine old spas to the Tauern Tunnel, south of which are some of the network's best views, from a rail line which dominates the valley below. halfway up the valley side.

At Villach you can switch to the Venice–Vienna route, p. 304, to head down into Italy or north-east to the Austrian capital.

Salzburg

Bad Hofgastein
Badgastein
Böckstein

Lienz

Spittal-Millstättersee

Feldkirchen

Villach

Klagenfurt

Venezia–Vienna, p. 304

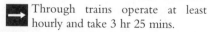

FASTEST JOURNEY: 3 HRS 25 MINS

TRAINS

ETT table: 820.

FAST TRACK

Through trains operate at least hourly and take 3 hr 25 mins.

ON TRACK

▶ Salzburg–Bad Hofgastein–Badgastein–Böckstein–Spittal-Millstättersee–Villach

The through trains call at all these stations. Salzburg to Bad Hofstein takes 1 hr 22 mins, Bad Hofstein to Badgastein 14 mins, Badgastein to Böckstein 5 mins, Böckstein to Spittal 45 mins and Spittal to Villach 30 mins.

Villach–Klagenfurt

A frequent service taking 15 mins.

GASTEIN VALLEY

The first major stop is **Bad Hofgastein, Station**: *tel: (06432) 6206*, 3 km from centre of town, buses hourly. **Tourist Office**: *Kongress-Zentrum, Tauernpl.; tel: (06432) 7110-0*, Mon–Fri 0800–1800, Sat 0900–1200, offers free map and accommodation list and activity pointers. Guest Card (GC) free city bus and ski bus,discounts on concerts, Langlauf (ski walking done on the flat) etc.

The smartest place to stay is the **Grand Park Hotel**, *Kurgartenstr. 26; tel: (06432) 6356* (expensive) in a modern chalet-style building. A cheaper alternative is **Kurhotel Germania**, *Kurpromenade 4; tel: (06432) 6232* (moderate) built around 1900 and full of period furniture. The restaurant to splash out in is **Lucullus**, *Hotel Kärnten, Dr-Zimmermannstr. 9.*

In addition to the radon-rich **waters**, reputed to stimulate the metabolism, available in a variety of centres and hotels, there is an open-air swimming pool and pleasant strolls around the village with turreted houses dating from the 16th century goldmining days. There is also access to winter skiing and treks, for example to Badgastein of about 2½ hours.

Badgastein, Station: *tel: (06434)*

2436390, rents bikes, **Tourist Office:** *Kaiser-Franz-Josefpl. 27; tel: (06434) 2531-0*, Mon–Fri 0800–1800, Sat 1000–1200, 1600–1800, Sun 1000–1200, offers a slightly vague pictorial map of the largely 19th-century resort, information on accommodation, will make bookings, organises free walks five times a week June–Sept.

The best hotel (in fact one of the best in Austria) is the **Hotel Grüner Baum**, *Kotschachtalstr. 25; tel: (06434) 2516-0* (very expensive) just out of town with regular minibus services, highly regarded food and multiple health treatments. Famous guests include Kaiser Wilhelm and the Shah of Iran. A cheaper option is the 19th-century **Hotel Mozart**, *Kaiser-FranzJosefstr. 25; tel: (06434) 26860* (oderate). Also central is **Gasthof Maier**, *Breitenberg 30, tel: (06434) 6220*, near the station (moderate). There are also various *Privatzimmer* or **HI: Jugendherberge Leonhard Lüftenegerhaus**, *Ederpl. 2; tel: (06434) 50688*, not far from the station, or **Kurcamping**, *Erlengrund, Erlengrundstr. 6; tel: (06434) 2790*, at the opposite side of town, 20 mins' walk.

The most revered place for pastries is **Dorn**, *Stubnerkogelstr. 42*. For meat snacks try the award-winning **Bayr**, with three shops.

The traditional occupation is taking the **waters** piped into several hotels. The same water, minus the radon gas, is used for hotel swimming pools which, because replenished almost daily, do not require chlorine. There is also a public **pool**, *Bahnhofpl.*, carved into a rock.

Attractions include a natural **waterfall** in the centre of town, the **Kaiser-Wilhelm Promenade**, a 4-km walk to the Grüner Baum, with views over the valley, and longer mountain routes. In winter with 54 lifts in the valley there are

273

plenty of **skiing** options plus horse riding, trekking, indoor tennis, curling, and ice skating.

⇄ SIDE TRACKS FROM BADGASTEIN

In **Bockstein**, a small village near Bad Hofgastein, the main attraction is a **natural sauna**, with temperatures of 38–41°C and humidity of 70–90%, reached by **underground train**. The site is in a one-time gold mine, taken over by the rich when they realised the miners never suffered rheumatism. Non-curetakers can visit Thurs, arriving by special bus or 20 mins on foot. **Alt Bockstein** is the old centre with a **Mountain Museum**; *tel: (06434) 4253.*

SPITTAL-MILLSTATTERSEE

Station: *tel: (04762) 39760*, rents bikes. **Spittal an der Drau**: *Tourist Office: Schloss Porcia, Burgpl. 1; tel: (04762) 3420*, Mon–Fri 0900–1900, Sat 0900–1200 (July and Aug) Mon–Fri 0900–1800, Sat 0900–1200 (Sept–June), from station up hill to park and diagonally to the far side of the castle, offers leaflets including on cycling routes for example along the old Roman road to pretty nearby Gmund. There is an electronic booking board at the park end of *Neuerpl.*

Millstatt am See, 20 mins by bus approx hourly from station, (on the lake divided from Spittal by a steep hill): **Tourist Office: Rathaus**, *Marktpl.; tel: (04766) 2022-0*, Mon–Fri 0900–1200, 1330–1800, Sat and Sun 1000–1200, 1600–1800, (June–Sept), Mon–Thurs 0800–1200, 1330–1700, Fri 0800–1230 (Oct–May).

From the stop continue in direction travelled to a path up the **Stift** outer courtyard to *Marktpl*. The office will check accommodation availability, GC discounts beach, bus, cable car, etc.

ACCOMMODATION AND FOOD

In Spittal one of the best hotels is the **Alte Post**, *Hauptpl. 13; tel: (04762) 2217* (expensive). **Haus Hübner**, *Schillerstr. 20; tel: (04762) 2112* (moderate) is a good, plain pension not far from the train station. The tourist office holds list of *Privatzimmer*. The **HI: Jugendherberge**, *Zur Seilbahn 2; tel: (04762) 3252*, is the most easily reached of the youth hostels, on the opposite side of the rail tracks. **Draufluss–Camping**; *tel: (04762) 2466*, is on the opposite bank of the river Drau.

In Millstatt am See **Hotel Postillion am See**, *Kaiser-Franz-Josefstr. 106; tel: (04766) 2552/2108* (expensive) is a four-star known for its fishing facilities, or there is **Familienhotel Post**, *Mirnockstr. 38; tel: (04766) 2108* (expensive). The Tourist Office also lists Privatzimmer. There is also a campsite at *Pesenthein* beyond the beach *tel: (04766) 2565* (bus no. 1 every 1½ hours).

The **Restaurant Zellot**, *Hauptpl. 12* in Spittal offers homemade Carinthian specialities. A good place for snacks is the **Café Konditorei** in *Schloss Porcia* on the park side of the castle and for pastries **Café Konditorei Moser**, *Jahnstr. 7*. The *Altdeutche Weinstube, Neuerpl. 17*, has an over the top 19th-century Teutonic interior. In Millstatt the *Stube* in the Hotel Post is one of the nicest options or there is **Buschenschenke Höfler**, half an hour's walk up the hill with home-produced food and a terrace overlooking the lake.

ENTERTAINMENT

A free **Calendar of Events** from the Spittal Tourist Office lists events held in the **Schloss** including, for a week in June every second year the **Salamancafest** reenacting the legend of the unhappy ghost of a certain Katharina von Salamanca.

At Millstatt there is a **Muskialischer Frühling** mid May–end June with three concerts a week in the *Stift* and **International Music Weeks** July and Aug with four concerts a week plus a **Musikalischer Herbst** Sept–mid-Oct. There is a **Country and Westernfest** mid-July.

SIGHTSEEING

Schloss Porcia in Spittal is a fine Renaissance castle around a pleasantly impressive arcaded courtyard. Inside is the award-winning **Museum für Volkskultur** *tel: (04762) 2890* of regional folk material. In Millstatt the main attraction in a resort developed for smart 19th century tourism is the **Stift**, founded in the 11th century and retaining an attractive Romanesque carved door. During Lent an impressive **Painted Altar Cloth** is on view. In the Italianate **courtyard** below is the entrance to the **Stift-museum** and a large **Linden tree**, used as a seat of local judgement, believed to have been introduced by the Slavs. There is bathing in the *Millstattersee*, including from a beach just below the bus station, ferries and boats for hire, plus a cable car up to Goldeck with possible walks.

SIDE TRACK FROM SPITTAL

MILLSTATTERSEE

LIENZ

Station: *tel: (04852) 66060*, rents bikes.

Tourist Office: *Europapl. 1; tel: (04852) 65265*, turn left out of station and at far side of modern square on right. Open Mon–Fri 0800–1900, Sat 0900–1200, 1700–1900, Sun 1000–1200 (end June–mid Sept, end

Dec–6 Jan) Mon–Fri 0800–1200, 1400–1800, Sat 0900–1200 (rest of year), it will make provisional accommodation bookings with options from an *Rk* or *BW* hotel to **HI** hostel, provides free map, free weekly guided town tours June–Sept Mon and Fri, Wed mid-July–mid-Sept, and organises mountain hikes in the Hohe Tauern Park. GC discounts at museums, swimming pools, country walks Weds and Thurs (ÖS140) etc.

Lienz (pronounced Lee-enz) is a charming small town beside the gleaming white rock of the Dolomites, backed by the greener heights of the Hohe Tauern Park. Sights include **Schloss Bruck** and **Osttiroler Heimatmuseum,** *Iseltalerstr. tel: (04852) 62580*, in the fortress of the counts who ruled before the 16th century saw the Habsburg takeover. It includes the medieval **Rittersaal** (Knights' Hall) plus local handicraft, dress etc. (April–Oct). Churches include **St Andrä**, *Patriasdorferstr.* considered the best Gothic architecture in the area, but at least as much of a draw is the baroque **Main Square**. There are buses to *Grossglockner* (see Zell am See, Innsbruck–Salzburg route, p.126).

275

VILLACH

Station: *tel: (04242) 1717*

Tourist Office: *Europapl. 2; tel: (04242) 24444*, ahead out of the station and left within sight of bridge, Mon–Fri 0800–1800, Sat 0900–1200, (July and Aug) Mon–Fri 0800–1230, 1330–1800, Sat 0900–1200 (Sept–June) offers free maps of the town including historical and sightseeing information in English, and maps of the area, plus a raft of extra information, and accommodation listings.

ACCOMMODATION AND FOOD

Goldenes Lamm, *Hauptpl. 1; tel: (04242) 24105* (expensive) is pleasant and central, or there is **Pension Eppinger Grete**, *Klagenfurterstr. 6; tel: (04242) 24389* (moderate). The **HI: Jugendgasthaus Villach**, *Dinzlweg 34; tel: (04242) 56368*, is also reasonably central. Hotel chains with property here are *BW* and *Rk*. Campsites are out of town, e.g. **Camping Gerli**, *St Georgenerstr. 140; tel: (04242) 57402* (buses to *St Georgen* from the station).

    Gasthof Bacchus, *Khevenhüllerg. 13; tel: (04242) 24192* (moderate) behind the Rathaus is good for traditional food and has rooms. **Kondotorei Bernholt**, *Nikolaipl. 2*, overlooking the river by the bridge, is a serious confectioners. The **Salatschüssl**, *Ankershofg. 3*, is a pleasant restaurant with bar and garden.

ENTERTAINMENT

The **Villach Kirchtag**, held the first Sat in Aug has been celebrating the city's birthday since 1225, while the **Annual Fair** takes place the week before combined with a **Folk Festival**. The **Thermal Springs** include the longest water chute in Europe as well as thermal and swimming pools in natural 29°C water. In this, the most Italian town in Austria, **Saturday night** is especially lively.

SIGHTSEEING

With a history going back to the Celts the **Altstadt** (Old Town) merits a stroll with sights including the **Pfarrkirche St Jakob**, originally Romanesque and currently mixing baroque and Gothic, and the usual **Trinity Column** commemorating escape from the Plague. The **Stadtmuseum**, *Widmanngasse 38; tel: (04242) 205383*, offers local prehistoric jewellery and knives, and medieval art. Five minutes out of the centre in the **Schillerpark** is the **Relief von Kärnten**, a giant relief model of the province of Carinthia. On the other side of the Drau river is the **Villacher Fahrzeugmuseum**, *Draupromenade 12; tel: (04242) 25530*, with several hundred antique 'people's' cars like the Fiat 500, VW Beetles, and Trabants.

> **SIDE TRACKS FROM VILLACH**
>
> Watersports are available on the warm **Faaker See**, reachable by train with a 10-min walk from Faak am See **station** *tel: (04254) 2149*. Rents bikes. Collect tourism material from Villach. The beaches are closest to the unmanned Fakersee Strand station but reedy parts of the lake are good birdwatching territory.
>
> On the **Ossiachersee**, on the opposite side of Villach, the unmanned Annenheim station is a good stop for watersports.
>
> Beyond, on the same line, is **Feldkirchen**, **station**: *tel: (04276) 1717* (rents bikes) turn left and fork left immediately up narrow *Bahnhofstr.* to T-junction in *Fussgangerzone* where you turn left through the *Hauptpl.* continuing to the **Tourist Office:** *Amthofg. 3; tel: (04276) 2176*. Open Mon–Fri 0800–1800, Sat 0900–1200, Sun 1000–1200 (mid-June–Aug) Mon–Thurs 0730–1230, 1330–1630, Fri 0730–1230 (Sept–mid-June), publishes accommodation and events lists and organises Weds walks in the area. The town itself, centring on the old *Hauptpl.* is attractive with plenty of Biedermeier façades though few specific attractions.

276

KLAGENFURT

Station: Hbf; *tel: (0463) 1717*
Tourist Office: *Rathaus, Neupl. 1; tel: (0463) 537223* Mon–Fri 0800–2000, Sat–Sun 1000–1700 (Nov–April) Mon–Fri 0800–1800, will book accommodation and offers a good free map showing suggested sights with background information in English, accommodation listings, useful leaflets and rents bikes. GC free city guide and discounts and cafés, museums etc.

ACCOMMODATION AND FOOD

The **Hotel Garni Blumenstockl**, *Oktoberstr. 11; tel: (0463) 57793* (expensive) has been around at least four centuries. Cheaper but pleasant is **Pension Zlami**, *Getreideg. 16; tel: (0463) 55416* (moderate). Hotel chains with property here are *BW* and *Rk*. **HI: Jugendgastehaus Kolping**, *Enzenbergerstr. 26; tel: (0463) 56965*, is the more central of the youth hostels. The nearest campsite is **Klagenfurt-Wörthersee Camping Strandbad**, *Mettnitzstrand 5; tel: (0463) 21169* (bus from station to *Heiligengeistpl.* then bus S to last stop).

Rathaustuberl, *Alterpl. 35*, by the *Pfarrkirche* offers Carinthian specialities or there's **Bistro Musil** in *Romantik Hotel Musil, Oktoberstr. 14*, where the owner was voted Middle Europe's best pastry chef. **A La Carte**, *Khevenhüllerstr. 2*, offers much lauded modernised local cooking. The seriously hungry might like the **Weinstube Kanzian**, *Kardinalpl. 2*, with gigantic *Wiener Schnitzel*.

ENTERTAINMENT

The Tourist Office lists concerts and exhibitions. **Carnival Processions** include the **Stadtrichter**, the town's guild of fools. There is a **Christkindlmarkt** in Advent. A **Disco Bus** from 2130–0200 collects and delivers passengers to discos and bars between Velden and back.

SIGHTSEEING

There are free guided tours 1000 Mon–Sat July and Aug from the *Rathaus*. If doing it yourself, start in the **Altstadt** which dates back 850 years combining Italian renaissance, baroque, *Jugendstil* (Art Nouveau) and Biedermeier, with 50-plus arcaded courtyards. Look for the 16th-century **Alterplatz** and **Landhaus**, originally an arsenal, now housing regional government offices. The **Wappensaal** (Hall of Coats of Arms) is open to the public April–Sept *tel: (0463) 577570*. The **Diozesanmuseum** (Diocesan Museum) *Lidmanskyg. 10/3; tel: (0463) 57770-84*; offers a collection of religious art in the area from the 12th to 18th centuries, while the **Bergbauhausmuseum** (Mining Museum) *Kinkstr. 6; tel: (0463) 537432* reached through the Botanical Gardens, is in a disused lead mine which gives a fair idea of the harsh working conditions up to the middle of this century. A boat plies the 400-year-old **Lend Canal** between Klagenfurt and the Wörthersee up to five times a day July–Sept.

277

⤴ SIDE TRACKS FROM KLAGENFURT

Maria Saal, (Tourist Office: *tel: (04223) 2214*), is renowned for its 2000-year-old **Pilgrimage Church**, built with walls against Magyars and Turks. The late gothic **Lantern of the Dead** and period tombstones are one attraction, the 1425 image of the **Virgin** is what draws the religious. The church is clearly visible from the train. A mile north is the **Herzogstuhl** – a Carinthian Ducal double throne of Roman stones and used for the granting of medieval fiefs. ⬚

SALZBURG–VIENNA

Dipping into the rugged heights south of the Danube, this loop passes well off the beaten

track – ideal for getting away from it all – before returning to the major tourist attraction of Melk. At Linz you can head off for Bavaria on the Munich–Linz route, p. 235.

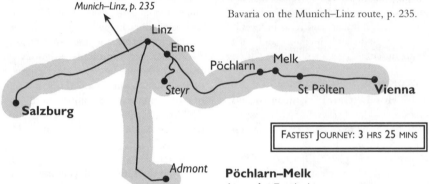

Munich–Linz, p. 235

Linz
Enns
Pöchlarn
Melk
Steyr
Salzburg
St Pölten
Vienna
Admont

FASTEST JOURNEY: 3 HRS 25 MINS

TRAINS

ETT Tables: 800, 825, 827, 826

FAST TRACK

 Through trains take 3 hr 25 mins and operate hourly, most with refreshment services.

ON TRACK

Salzburg–Linz
An hourly service taking 1 hr 21 mins.

Linz–Enns
A roughly hourly service taking around 15 mins.

Enns–Pöchlarn
A change of train is required at St Valentin with the through journey taking 1 hr 30 mins. Services are available every hour.

Pöchlarn–Melk
A regular 7-min journey.

Melk–St Pölten
A 25-min run, hourly throughout the day.

St Pölten–Vienna
At least 1 train every hour, often more. The journey takes 45 mins.

LINZ
(See Munich–Linz, p. 235)

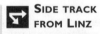 SIDE TRACK FROM LINZ

ADMONT

Station: *tel: (03613) 2230-0.* Rents bikes. 2½ hrs from Linz, changing at Selzthal.
Tourist Office: *Hauptstr.; tel: (03613) 2164.* 500 m from the station. Open Mon 0800–1200, Tues–Fri 0800–1200, 1400–1700, Sat 0800–1200 (June–Aug)

A market town which operates as a

walking base but also offers a fine **Stift** (monastery) in the centre of the town *tel: (03613) 2312-0*, with the world's biggest monastic library holding around 150,000 volumes, including 1400 manuscripts. Accommodation includes one of the country's more striking **Jugendherberge**, HI: **Schloss Röthelstein**, *Aigen 32; tel: (03613) 2432*, in a (renovated) 17th-century castle.

ENNS

Station: tel: (07223) 21330
Tourist Office: *Linzerstr. 1; tel: (07223) 3261*, Mon–Fri 0900–1200, 1300–1800, just off the central *Hauptpl.*, organises town tours ÖS30 May–mid-Sept daily and has a map and accommodation information. In the town centre is **Gasthof-Hotel Zum Goldenen Schiff**, *Hauptpl. 23; tel: (07223) 2327* (expensive). Between the station side and centre is **Hotel am Limes**, *Stadtg. 2b; tel: (07223) 6401* (moderate). The tourist office also lists private rooms.

Although claiming the title of oldest town in Austria, the style of Enns is predominantly Renaissance-baroque, though **towers** and **city walls** are reminders of earlier periods. The 13th-century **St Laurenz Basilika,** *Lauriacumstr. 4,* is based on a Roman temple and there is also the **Pfarrkirche St Marien,** *Wienerstr. 4,* also dating from the 13th century. The **Heimatmuseum** on the *Hauptpl.; tel: (07223) 2202,* houses a prehistoric and Roman collection from the area. The 16th-century **Schloss Ensegg** in *Wienerstr.* offers a glimpse of the Renaissance.

◄⊐ SIDE TRACK FROM ENNS

STEYR

Station: *tel: (07252) 595385.* Steyr is 40 mins from Enns, services running hourly.
Tourist Office: *Stadtpl. 27; tel: (07252) 53229,* right, then left along *Bahnhofstr.* to cross the bridge then left to *Stadtpl.* Open Mon–Fri 0830–1800, Sat 0900–1200, offers a free map and will book accommodation for the same day. A Walkman tour is ÖS40, walking maps ÖS70 or 198.

The best hotel is the **Mader**, *Stadtpl. 36; tel: (07252) 53358,* (moderate) a four-star property right in the centre with Renaissance courtyard. **Schechater Hof**, *Leopold Werndlstr. 1; tel: (07252) 53067* (moderate), next to the Pfarrkirche has its own beer garden and offers traditional regional food. **HI: Josef**, *Hafnerstr. 14; tel: (07252) 45580,* is the cheapest option.

Growing up around a 10th-century fortress, Steyr is largely a medieval town dating from its days of greatest trading success, preserving buildings like the fine Gothic **Bummerlhaus**, *Stadtpl. 32; tel: (07252) 53994-0.* Other attractions include a **Museum of the Working World**, *Wehrgrabeng. 7; tel: (07252) 67351,* on industrial heritage. The **Steyrtal-Museumsbahn** based at the local station, 15 mins west of the centre, *tel: (07252) 46569,* runs nostalgia rail trips Sat and Sun July–Sept. ◄⊐

PÖCHLARN

Station: *tel: (02757) 7301.* Rents bikes.
Tourist Office: *Stadtgemeinde Pöchlarn, Regensburgerstr. 11; tel: (02757) 2310,* broadly, left and ahead from the station in a courtyard where the office is on the left, Mon–Thurs 0800–1200, 1300–1530, Fri 0800–1200 offers free map with tourist information.

Accommodation includes **Hotel Moser**, *Bahnhofpl. 2; tel: (02757) 2448* (expensive) directly opposite the station, or among **Privatzimmer Hause Barbara**, *Wienerstr. 4; tel: (02575) 2321* (budget) offering free bike hire, useful for seeing the Danube cycle route.

This quiet town was the **birthplace** of artist Oskar Kokoschka, *Regensburgerstr. 29; tel: (02757) 7656* (May–Sept) containing some of his drawings.

MELK

Station: *tel: (02752) 2321.* Hires bikes.
Tourist Office: *Babenbergerstr. 1; tel: (02752) 230732,* from the station right at first junction then left, 0900–1900 (July and Aug), Mon–Fri 0900–1200, 1500–1800, Sat and Sun 1000–1400 (April–June). Offers free maps with historic pointers and accommodation list, area walking maps ÖS10, lockers (ÖS10) free bike racks and changes money. Will book accommodation for a ÖS100 deposit and has details of Abbey concerts.

Smartest accommodation is **Zur Post**, *Linzerstr. 1; tel: (02752) 2345* (moderate) with good restaurant. **Gasthof Wachauerhof**, *Wienerstr. 30; tel: (02752) 2235* (moderate) is a sensible central option, **Gasthof Goldener Stern**, *Sterng. 17; tel: (02752) 2214* (budget) offers food as well rooms. **HI: Jugendherberge**, *Abt-Karlstr. 42; tel: (02752) 2681* is close to the train tracks. The **campsite**, *Melker Fahrhaus; tel: (02752) 3291,* is approx 20 mins walk beyond the centre across the Melk river bridge. There are plenty of places to eat at in the *Fussgängerzone*.

SIGHTSEEING

The town is small though attractive as befits an important site since Roman times. However, the big attraction is **Melk Abbey**, *Dietmayerstr. 1; (02752) 2312.* The rocky promontory overlooking the river was eventually taken over by Benedictine monks who converted the property of the ruling Babenbergs into a fortified abbey. Renovated in 1702 it was turned into a baroque wonder. Highlights include a **pilastered hall** coated in red marble and rich allegorical images on the ceiling. The **library** is, if anything, even more impressive, with a fine ceiling and around 80,000 volumes. But the *pièce de resistance* is the **abbey church**, an overwhelming mass of baroque gold, marble and frescos.

Five km from Melk is **Schloss Schallaburg**; *tel: (02754) 6317,* reachable by bus from the station 1030 and 1510, departing from the castle 15 mins later. It can also be reached on foot. The architecture combines Romanesque, Gothic, Renaissance and mannerist, including a 1600-piece mosaic on the floor of main courtyard.

ST PÖLTEN

Station: *tel: (02742) 223-1717.*
Tourist Office: *Rathauspl. 1; tel: (02742) 353354,* Mon–Fri 0800–1800, ahead up *Kremserg.,* right at *Riemerpl.,* has an electronic booking board and offers a room list plus history leaflets in English. Places in the *Fussgängerzone* offer meals and snacks.

The **Landhauptstadt Fest** in July includes open air concerts and dancing. The **St Pöltner Festwoche** (end May) includes cultural events at theatres and museums. At the end of Sept is a free **Sacred Music Festival** in the churches.

Much of the town was destroyed during World War II but many baroque buildings have been restored. *Wienerstrasse* has been a thoroughfare since the Romans, whose remains are visible in the *Domplatz.* The **Dom**, austerely plain outside, is a riot of baroque inside.

A narrow-gauge railway operates 3-hr trips from Hbf to **Mariazell**.

ST MORITZ–ZERMATT

This is the route of Switzerland's most famous railway excursion, the Glacier Express. The full journey takes 7½ to 8½ hrs depending on the route selected though 'express' is just about the least appropriate description of the service as this particular Express ambles along at an average 22mph. You wouldn't want it to be any quicker, however, as the magnificent scenery deserves more than a mere glance.

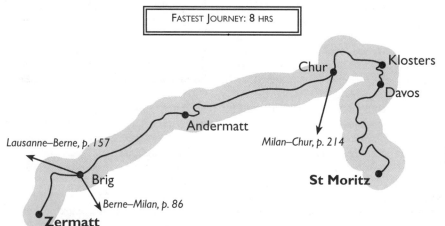

FASTEST JOURNEY: 8 HRS

Klosters

Chur

Davos

Andermatt

Lausanne–Berne, p. 157

Milan–Chur, p. 214

281

Brig

St Moritz

Berne–Milan, p. 86

Zermatt

TRAINS

ETT Tables: 330, 320, 327

FAST TRACK

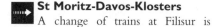 This scenic route is covered by one 'Glacier Express' during peak months. The journey takes 8 hrs. At other times change of train is neccesary at Reichenau, Disentis or Brig or all three!

ON TRACK

St Moritz-Davos-Klosters
A change of trains at Filisur is required. St Moritz to Davos takes 1 hr 34 mins, Davos to Klosters 30 mins.

Klosters-Chur
An hourly service changing trains at Landquart. Journey 1 hr.

Chur-Andermatt-Brig
A frequent service with a change of train at Disentis. Chur to Andermatt takes 3 hrs, Andermatt to Brig nearly 2 hrs.

Brig-Zermatt
A frequent service taking 1 hr 20 mins.

ST MORITZ

For details see p.216.

DAVOS

Stations: Davos Platz, **Davos Dorf**; *tel: 157 22 22 (both).*
Tourist Information: *Promenade 67, Davos Platz; tel: 081 45 21 21.*

Davos, the loftiest town in Europe at 1560 m, first achieved fame as a health resort, renowned for its high-altitude curative climate and sanatorium facilities. Nowadays it is the largest of all the Alpine resorts, a byword for quality skiing and high living, its spartan sanatoriums long-since converted to luxury hotels. The town divides into **Dorf** and **Platz** (the latter being the main centre of activity), and stretches for around 4 km along the railway line and river, linked by the main street of *Promenade/Dorfst.*

Davos enjoys some beautiful walking country and a favourite easy excursion is to take the funicular up to the **Alpine Garden** at Schatzalp, where 800 plant varieties flourish, then walk back down through the woods. Toboggans are also for hire at Schatzalp and there's a special summer toboggan run here. Another must is the cableway to **Jakobshorn** from where waymarked walks offer wonderful views. Davos offers three museums, the best of these being the **Kirchner Museum**, featuring the works of the German Expressionist painter, Ernst

Bridges and Tunnels

There are over 291 bridges, and 91 tunnels on the Glacier Express line. One of the great bridges to look out for is the **Wiesener Viaduct**, 204 m long and 87 m high, just after Filisur (heading towards Davos).

The Glacier Express

The journey described below goes via Davos, Klosters and Chur, but it is also possible to go via Tiefencastel and Thusis. This latter route section is also covered by the **Bernina Express** (see page 214). And of course you can also ride the Glacier Express in the other direction, from Zermatt to St Moritz.

The Glacier Express travels along ordinary scheduled service lines and so you may get on and get off at will. If you intend to ride the whole route in one go you must make a reservation at St Moritz (or Zermatt) and pay a small fare supplement.

Kirchner, who lived in Davos for 20 years. The **Heimat Museum** (Heritage Museum) and the **Wintersport Museum** deal with local matters. Note: Davos is so large that it never really shuts down but many of the lifts, gondolas and cable cars are closed from May–late June and Oct–Dec. Staying in the centre of Davos is expensive so look slightly out of town. **HI: Höhwald, Davos-Wolfgang;** *tel: 081 46 14 84*, is pleasantly sited near the Davoser See, a lake with a beach area. The **Gasthaus Parsennhütte**; *tel: 081 46 36 52*, is a mountain inn, 650 m above Davos Dorf (access by the Parsenn cableway), in magnificent mountain-walking country; double rooms cost around SFr.70 per night. If you must stay in the centre the charming **Alte Post**, *Berglistutz, Davos Platz; tel: 081 43 54 03*, is one of the best less-expensive options.

KLOSTERS

Station: *tel: 157 22 22*
Tourist Office: *Alte Bahnhofst.; tel: 081 69 18 77.*

Like neighbouring Davos, Klosters is world-famous as a ski-playground for the well-heeled (the Prince of Wales is a regular visitor).

Unlike Davos, however, Klosters has retained much of its traditional village architecture and atmosphere (though its main street is excessively busy) and is therefore even more exclusive. Being smaller means less to do in the evenings but by day it has access to marvellous ski-fields (including all the Davos runs) and wonderful walking countryside. Recently it has also gained a reputation as a mountain-biking centre.

A renovated 16th-century farmhouse is home to the local **museum**.

CHUR

Station: *tel: 157 22 22.*
Tourist Office: *Grabenstr. 5; tel: 081 22 18 18.*

Chur (pronounced Koohr) is the capital and business centre of the Grisons region. It's a thriving place, quite apparent as you walk from the station down lively *Bahnhofst.* into *Postpl.*, towards the old town. On *Postpl.* is the **Kunstmuseum** (Art Museum) with a fine collection of works, ranging from the 16th century to celebrated contemporary local artists such as Angelica Kaufmann (born in Chur), Augusto Giacometti and H R Giger, world-famous in sci-fi and film circles for his blood-curdlng creation, *Alien.*

Call at the tourist office and pick up the two town trail leaflets (one green, one red) which correspond with footprints painted on the streets around the old town and lead you to all the major places of interest. The office also distributes an excellent free 3-D map of the centre. For a quick circular tour start at the heart of the old town with the **Cathedral**, built between 1150 and 1272. Its superbly carved Gothic altar

---

Meals on Wheels

If you dine only on one railway carriage in Switzerland make it aboard the Glacier Express. The food is good, the atmosphere in the elegant old-world dining car is relaxed, and the wine glasses have stems which lean like the Tower of Pisa in order to compensate for the gradient as the train climbs slowly up over the **Oberalp Pass** (2033 m). Make reservations in advance; *tel: 081 22 14 25.*

---

is the finest of its kind in the country. Adjacent is the **Bischöflicher Hof** (Episcopal Court) a handsome fortified group of buildings with the Bishop's Palace at its heart. The present structure was renovated in the 18th-century but medieval remnants survive within.

Across the street is the old monastic **Church of St Luzi** (St Lucius) with a circular 8th-century Carolingian crypt. Walk back through *Hofpl.* to the **Rätisches Museum** (Raetian Museum). Raetia (or Rhaetia) is the old Roman name for the region and here you can trace the settlement's 5000-year-old history and find out why Chur is claimed to be the oldest town in Switzerland. Adjacent is the late 15th-century **Church of St Martin** with new windows by Giacometti (see above). Turn up Reichsgasse to find the 15th-century **Rathaus** (town hall) and several elegant houses dating from the 16th and 17th centuries.

The best of the cheaper hotels in the old town is the **Drei Könige**, *Reichsgasse 18; tel: 081 22 17 25,* costing around SFr.150 per double room. It also serves good food in its traditional *weinstube.* A cheaper option (SFr.100-120), also in the old town, is **The Franziskaner**, *Untere Gasse; tel: 081 23 16 88.*

283

ANDERMATT

Station: Bahnhof; *tel: 157 2222.*
Tourist Office: Verkehrsverein, *Gotthardstr. 2; tel: 044 6 74 54.*

Andermatt today is known principally as a ski resort but its location, at the crossroads of four major mountain roads (Furka, Oberalp, Reuss, St Gottard), gave it historical significance as a staging post. However, with the advent of the **St Gotthard Tunnel** in 1882, it was bypassed to north and south and lost most of its trading importance. The old part of the village features the fine baroque **Church of St Peter and St Paul** and a number of 17th- and 18th-century buildings.

BRIG

Station: *tel: 157 22 22.*
Tourist Office: *Bahnhofpl.; tel: 028 23 19 01.*

The small town of Brig has two claims to fame: it is an important railhead and it is the location of the **Stockalper Castle**. The castle is said to be both the largest palace and the largest private building in Switzerland, even though it now mostly houses Brig municipal offices. It's a very un-Swiss affair, built in Italian style between 1658 and 1668 by Kaspar Stockalper, an extremely wealthy merchant who controlled the flow of goods between France and Lombardy (Milan) and Switzerland and Lombardy and wielded tremendous political power. He called himself the Great Stockalper, and was dubbed the 'uncrowned king of the Valais'. The vast courtyard of the palace (40 m by 32 m) was conceived merely as a shelter for his goods. Around it are three tiers of arcades and on its three massive corner towers are enormous gilded onion domes. Guided tours of the castle will show you the **Knight's Hall** and four other rooms, though what stays in the

mind is the sheer bulk of the castle – which is exactly what the Great Stockalper intended. Walk a little further past the castle to find the town's 17th-century **Jesuit Church**.

> **SIDE TRACK FROM BRIG**
>
> The thermal springs of **Brigerbad** (25 mins by postbus from Brig Bhf) are a delightful complex of landscaped outdoor pools varying in temperature from 27°C–42°C. There's also a grotto pool and a river-style pool to enjoy. The adjacent camping site; *tel: 028 46 46 88*, is a good overnight option.

ZERMATT

Station: BVZ-Zermatt-Bahn; *tel: (028) 67 22 07.*
Tourist Office: *Bahnhofpl; tel: (028) 66 11 81.*

ACCOMMODATION AND FOOD

Although Zermatt can be an expensive place there are a reasonable number of cheap hotels. The friendly, family-run three-star **Hotel Bellrive Garni**; *tel: 028 67 13 13*, is in a peaceful position at the Matterhorn end of the village and enjoys a fine view of the Matterhorn. **HI:** *Winkelmatten; tel: 028 67 23 20*, also looks out to the mighty Matt. There's no shortage of pleasant tea rooms, pizzerias and fast-food places on and around *Hauptstr.* However for simple local food, or just a drink, in an authentic rustic setting try **Z'Alt Hischi**, *Hinterdorfgasse, tel: 028 67 42 62*. The **Café du Pont**, just beyond the parish church on *Hauptstr.* is another reasonably priced atmospheric rustic retreat with a comprehensive menu.

SIGHTSEEING

Zermatt is one of the classic Swiss resorts,

thanks in no small measure to the mighty mountain which sits on its doorstep – the world-famous **Matterhorn** (4478 m); its distinctive pyramidal peak is familiar even to couch potatoes as the logo of the Paramount film company. On a busy day as many as 200 brave souls may scale Mont Cervin (as it is known in French) but each year around a dozen are killed in the attempt. The cemetery in the centre of Zermatt is a sobering reminder of the dark side of the peak. The nearest that the average visitor gets to the top of the big one is Gornergrat (3100 m). The **Gornergrat-Bahn** provides a marvellous funicular ride and the 360-degree view from the top station (climb the small hill just behind the restaurant for maximum effect) is one of the great experiences Switzerland has to offer. In fact from here the Matterhorn is just one of many giants, with the tallest peak in the country, **Monte Rosa** (4634 m) also quite visible.

The most picturesque view of all, with the mountain reflected perfectly in a glassy blue lake, is not from the Gornergrat-Bahn however, but from the **Schwarzsee**, (accessible by cable car from Zermatt). From Gornergrat cableways fly onto three more peaks, the higest being Stockhorn at 3405 m.

Alongside the Matterhorn sits the **Klein Matterhorn** (3820 m), boasting the higest cable station in Europe. You can ski here all year round on Europe's highest slopes (it's worth taking the trip for the views alone) or you can choose from another 25 km of runs; Zermatt offers the most extensive summer skiing facilities in Switzerland. Trains and cableways also run to **Sunnegga** (2290 m) and the **Rothorn** (3103 m) and in all Zermatt claims to be the largest ski area in the Alps.

After such splendour high above, down below Zermatt may be something of an

Skiing the Matterhorn

Although Zermatt is one of the most famous names in Switzerland that doesn't mean the tourist board is happy to just rest on their laurels. Their most recent coup was to ship a huge block of ice from the Matterhorn to Tokyo. It was then chopped up and spread over the floor of a dry ski slope so happy customers could go home boasting they had skiied on the Matterhorn! The worth of this clever gimmick may be measured in the fact that Zermatt now attracts more visitors from Japan than it does from either France or Italy, even though the Italian border is a mere snowball's-throw away.

anti-climax. Like so many of its counterpart jet-set resorts it has mostly been built this century to accommodate tourism. However some old parts survive, most notably in the **Hinter Dorf** area (found between the *Hauptst.* and the river), where there is a ramshackle collection of rustic Valaisian houses and barns. The latter are often balanced on mushroom-shaped stone stilts to keep out of reach of vermin. There are more old houses to be found at the Matterhorn end of the village.

The only modern convenience that has no place in Zermatt is the motor car, and the only hazard on the streets is the hoteliers' little electric vehicles which meet guests at the station and whisk them to their accommodation. A peculiarity of Zermatt is the lack of street names so do pick up a street map from the tourist office, next to the station.

There's an interesting **Alpine Museum** to see and the **English Church**, with its sad mountaineering epitaphs, is also worth a visit.

TURIN (TORINO)

In the north, Turin is one of Italy's most opulent cities. A former royal capital, today it is famous for its associations with the car industry – in particular the Fiat. There are gilded *fin de siècle* cafés and a lovely baroque centre of ordered, elegant streets filled museums and galleries, churches and palaces. It is an aristocratic city, and was once the home base of the House of Savoy, which gave the unified Italy its first kings. In the shadow of the Alps, it straddles the River Po which rushes dramatically through its eastern quarters.

TOURIST INFORMATION

The **main tourist office** is at *Via Roma 226, tel: (011) 535181*, and is open Mon–Sat 0900–1930. Turin has another **tourist information office** at *Porta Nuova station; tel: (011) 531327*. Both offer a free 'room-finding' service. Ask here for listings information – concerts and so on – and remember to look in the national/local daily newspaper, *La Stampa*, for up-to-date listings information.

ARRIVING AND DEPARTING

Airports

Caselle Airport, 15 km north of the city, *tel: (011) 57781*, handles mainly domestic flights. There are only a few European services (London, Paris, Frankfurt). The airport bus is operated by **SADEM**, and runs from the main bus station at *Corso Inghilterra 1*.

Stations

Porta Nuova is Turin's main rail hub. It is right in the city centre – on the *Corso Vittorio Emanuele, tel: (011) 5613333*. There is another station at **Porta Susa** on the city's west side, and another, **Torino Ceres**, which is a regional line serving towns like Cirie, Lanzo and Ceres.

The main **bus station**, *tel: (011) 4332525*, is on *Corso Inghilterra*. From here, a very comprehensive bus service links the countryside and the ski resorts of the Valle d'Aosta with the city.

GETTING AROUND

Most sights are in the compact central zone and the best way to see them all is on foot. It is a bracing walk, however; it might be better to use the trams or buses, or to take a taxi.

Buses and Trams

Before using either trams or buses, you must be in possession of a valid ticket – buy them at tobacconists, in bars, or at the city tourist office at Porta Nuova station. Cancel them in the machine on boarding.

Taxis

Licensed taxis are not hard to find and not cheap. There are ranks by the train and bus stations and elsewhere – in the *piazze* and so on. Avoid unlicensed cabs, which are even more expensive. To call a cab, *tel: (011) 5730/5748*.

STAYING IN TURIN

Accommodation

Turin is not the busiest tourism city in

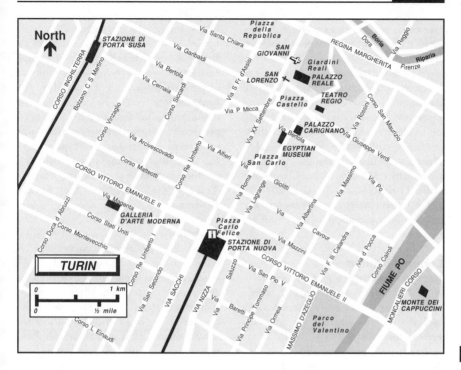

North ↑

STAZIONE DI PORTA SUSA
Via Santa Chiara
Piazza della Republica
Via Garibaldi
Via Bertola
Via Cernaia
Via S Fr d'Assisi
SAN GIOVANNI
SAN LORENZO
Giardini Reali
PALAZZO REALE
REGINA MARGHERITA
Dora
Via Reggio
Riparia
Firenze
CORSO INGHILTERRA
Bolzano C S Martino
Corso Vinzaglio
Corso Siccardi
Via P Micca
Piazza Castello
TEATRO REGIO
Via San Maurizio
Corso Rossini
Via XX Settembre
PALAZZO CARIGNANO
Via Bertola
EGYPTIAN MUSEUM
Via Giuseppe Verdi
Via Arcivescovado
Corso Matteotti
Corso Re Umberto I
Via Alfieri
Piazza San Carlo
Via Roma
Giolitti
Via Massimo
Via Po
CORSO VITTORIO EMANUELE II
Via Magenta
Corso Stati Uniti
GALLERIA D'ARTE MODERNA
Via Lagrange
Via
Via Albertina
Via
Cavour
Corso Duca d Abruzzi
Corso Montevecchio
Piazza Carlo Felice
STAZIONE DI PORTA NUOVA
Via Mazzini
Via F III Calandra
Via d Pocca
Corso Cairoli
FIUME PO

TURIN

0   1 km
0   ½ mile

Corso Re Umberto I
Via San Secondo
VIA SACCHI
VIA NIZZA
Via
Saluzzo
Via San Pio V
CORSO VITTORIO EMANUELE II
MASSIMO D'AZEGLIO
MONCALIERI CORSO
MONTE DEI CAPPUCCINI
Corso L Einaudi
Via Baretti
Via Principe Tommaso
Via Ormea
Parco del Valentino

Italy, though it is a major venue for trade fairs and for business travel. This is reflected in the range of accommodation – or rather, the lack of it – available. One or two are very opulent (the **Turin Palace**, *V. Sacchi 8; tel: 562 5511*, for example), while most others tend to cater for business travellers and are modern and rather featureless.

At the other end of the scale they tend to be very down-market indeed. The cheapest accommodation, not always the most salubrious, is to be found near to Porta Nuova station.

There is very little in between, but you could try the **Victoria**, *V. Nino 4; tel: 561 1909*, or the **Stazione e Genova**, *V. Sacchi 14; tel: 545323.*

Turin's **youth hostel** is at *Via Alby 1, tel: (011) 6602939,* open 0900–1800. Take bus no. 52 from the station.

Eating and Drinking

Some of the richest food in Italy comes from Turin. Much of it has a heavy, almost Germanic tone which is quite unlike what you will find even just a few miles further south. Upmarket restaurants are generally very sophisticated – and expensive. However, there are many moderate or reasonably priced places serving a variety of Torinese specialities as well as more popular and traditional Italian dishes. As always, you can cut costs by opting for fixed-price (*prezzo fisso*) meals which give you a choice of first courses, a choice of main courses, and fruit or cheese. Since one of the first course choices is always pasta, this makes a filling meal. An even cheaper option is the *tavola calda*, a buffet-style self-service restaurant where you can choose a single cooked dish or a full meal. These are found all over town and cover and service charges are included in the price displayed for each dish.

As in other Italian towns, drinks taken standing or sitting at the bar are a great deal cheaper than those drunk at a table, and restaurants outside the main sightseeing semicircle are usually cheaper than those catering to visitors close to the main sights. The cafés in Turin are famous. The classics are **Baratti e Milano**, *Piazza Castello*, and **Caffe Torino**, *Piazza San Carlo 204*. For picnic ingredients try an *alimentari* (grocery shop) – but remember that they shut for lunch.

Communications
The main **post office** is at *Via Alfieri 10, tel: (011) 546800.* You can buy stamps here or from a tobacconist. Attached is a telephone centre where you can make international calls.

To phone Turin from abroad: *tel: 39 (Italy) + 11 (Turin) + number;* to phone Turin from elsewhere in Italy: *tel: (011) + number.*

Money
Banks which change money usually display the sign *Cambio* (Exchange). There are also exchange kiosks at Porta Nuova station, the airport, and at numerous city centre locations. Eurocheques are also widely accepted, but credit cards are useful only in the more expensive shops and restaurants. There is a 24-hour cash machine at *Via Roma 224* (beside the main tourist office).

There is plenty to see and do in Turin. Not only is it a city burgeoning with museums and galleries – one or two of them of real international importance – but there is great architecture, theatre, bal-

let and music. The nightlife may not be as trendy as you might find it in Milan or Bologna, but there are still plenty of clubs and other venues. A particular time to come is during Turin's St John's Day (24 June) folklore festival. *Torino Giovanni* is a useful listings publication for young people, available from the tourist office. Turin is home to an internationally famous football club, Juventus, one of two of Italy's premier first-division clubs (the other is Torino). Both play at the **Stadio Comunale**.

Nightlife
A fairly lively, local youth culture is given a boost in the student area around *Via Po* where there are plenty of pubs and clubs, and venues for jazz and African rhythms, rock and reggae. There is often an admission fee for the larger discos and drinks are usually very expensive. Some venues allow one free drink with the admission fee.

Theatres, Cinemas and Concerts
Many recent US and UK releases come to major city-centre cinemas undubbed. The main theatre venue is the **Teatro Carignano**, while the **Teatro Regio** is used for opera and, from late autumn to late spring, ballet and symphony concerts. An arts festival, the **Punti Verdi** (plays, ballet, concerts) is held annually in July and August, while **Settembre Musica** is a Sept festival focusing on classical music. Venues for this include local churches, theatres and so on.

Turin is not noted as a particularly special shopping city any more than, say, Rome or Venice are. However, as it is situated in the wealthy northern region of Italy, there will be no shortage of opportunities for buying all the things that make Milan such an important shopping capital – clothes and accessories, designer equipment, luggage, stationery, textiles and so on. On Sat, an antique and flea market is held in *Piazza della Republica*. To bring home, you might consider buying foodstuffs from the delicatessen – dried sausage, cheese, oils, chocolates and biscuits.

SIGHTSEEING

It is very easy to find your way around Turin, the centre of which is laid out on a grid. Across its core, streets are lined with arcades which, in the rainy north, are practical and useful. The most fashionable street is *Via Roma* which links the *Piazza Carlo Felice*, in front of Porta Nuova Station, with the *Piazza Castello*.

Highlights of any trip to Turin should include the important **Egyptian Museum**, second only to the museum in Cairo for its wealth of ancient Egyptian exhibits, and the **Galleria Sabauda** which contains the magnificent art collections of the House of Savoy (works by, amongst others, Mantegna, Titian, Van Eyck, Rembrandt and Poussin). Both museums share the former **Palazzo dell'Accademia delle Scienze** just off *Piazza San Carlo*. The Egyptian Museum was the world's first, and was founded out of a small royal collection formed in the 17th century.

The **Palazzo Carignano**, nearby, is an important baroque building designed by Guarini. It contains in part the **Museo Nazionale del Risorgimento** (National Museum of the Unification of Italy).

A major highlight in a city which made its fortune in the car industry is the **Museo dell'Automobile Carlo Biscaretti di Ruffia** *(Corso Unita d'Italia 40)* which houses an important collection of classic Italian cars. The **Palazzo Reale**, just off

Piazza Castello, was the residence of the Princes of Savoy until 1865, and it is possible to go on a guided tour of its interior. One other very interesting museum is the **Museo Nazionale della Montagna Duca degli Abruzzi** (just by the Capuchin church on *Monte dei Cappuccini*). This houses a fascinating collections of artefacts illustrating life and folklore in, and the geography of, Italy's mountains. The **Galleria d'Arte Moderna** *(Via Magenta)* houses an excellent collection, reputed to be one of Italy's best, of modern art – including works by Klee, Chagall and Picasso.

Of the city's churches, **San Lorenzo** *(Piazza Castello)*, the former royal chapel, is the one you shouldn't miss. Its interior is by the baroque architect Guarini and it is characterised by an octagonal dome. The **Cathedral of San Giovanni**, *Via XX Settembre*, is famous for containing the **Turin Shroud**. Housed in a casket – under lock and key – on the altar of the **Cappella della Sacra Sindone** (designed by Guarini), this is one of the most controversial relics in Italy.

289

OUT OF TOWN

Two sights lie outside the city. One, the baroque **Basilica di Superga** (to the north-east), is the architect Juvarra's masterpiece. Quite apart from the architecture, the views from the summit of the hill on which it stands are stupendous. They stretch all the way to the Alps in the north. The other major sight outside Turin is the magnificent rococo former royal hunting lodge, the **Palazzina Mauriziana di Caccia Stupinigi** – 9 km south east of Turin. This too is the work of Juvarra. In reality it is a huge and stately country palace, and today it is run by the royal Mauritian Order as a furniture museum.

TURIN–MARTIGNY

Beyond Ivrea, the route, which darts in and out of tunnels, enters a picturesque corner of Italy where Europe's highest Alpine peaks – Mont Blanc, Monte Rosa and the Matterhorn – dwarf medieval castles perched on impenetrable crags. In this region, the skiing is the best there is, while in the spring the wild flowers are its greatest attraction. The route doesn't allow fast travel, and the Aosta–Martigny stretch has to be done by bus, but the views are worth the time the journey takes.

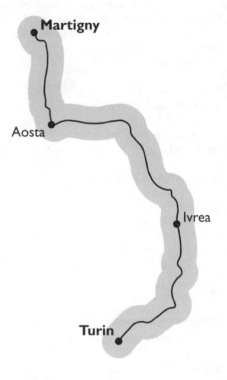

```
FASTEST JOURNEY: 5 HRS
```

TRAINS

ETT Tables; 353, 269

ON TRACK

Turin–Ivrea
A frequent service taking around 1 hr. A change of train at Chivasso is sometimes required.

Ivrea–Aosta
At least 1 train an hour taking 1 hr 30 mins.

Aosta–Martigny
Two bus services a day link these towns, crossing the Great St Bernard pass and taking 2 hrs in total.

IVREA

Tourist Office: *Corso Vercelli 1; tel: (0215) 49687.*

Ivrea is famous for typewriters; Olivetti was founded here in 1908 and office machinery is still the dominant industry. However, the **Castle of Ivrea** (built 1358) is still the town's most potent symbol. Once a prison, it has recently undergone extensive restoration.

In the older, labyrinthine upper town is the **Cathedral**, whose towers and crypt date from the 12th century. In *Piazza Castello* is the rambling **Bishop's Palace**, while the **Museo Civico** *(Piazza Carlo Alberto)* houses a wide range of items relating to the region's past - including an archaeological collection detailing Ivrea's role as ancient Rome's bulwark against the Gauls.

AOSTA

Station: *Piazza Manzetti.*
Tourist Office: *Place Chanoux 8, tel: (0165) 236 627.* Open daily, (June–Sept) 0900–1300 and 1500–2000. Mon–Sat 0900–1300 and 1500–2000, Sun 0900–1300 (Oct–May). Information on ski facilities and hiking routes. *Dove, Come, Quando* is the local listings magazine.

ACCOMMODATION

There is plenty of accommodation in Aosta. Inevitably, as the region's transport focus, it is busy during the winter, so prices are competitive. It provides good alternatives to neighbouring resort hotels and if you cannot afford top prices, and the cheaper alternatives are fully booked, an all year round **campsite** might be the answer: *Milleluci* at Roppoz, 1 km out of town.

SIGHTSEEING

Even if you cannot bear winter sports, Aosta has much to recommend it. To the Romans, Augusta Praetoria (later corrupted to Aosta) was an important city in the days when defence against the Gauls was essential. Nowadays the old core of the city, with its grid-like Roman street plan, stoically defends its identity against incursion from the suburbs and surrounding industrial estates.

The **Roman theatre** is one of Italy's best preserved and is the scene of theatrical performances during the summer. Nearby, straddling *Via Porta Pretoria*, the **Porta**

Pretoria is the city's original Roman gate. Going east, *Via Sant'Anselmo*, is named after the Archbishop of Canterbury, Sant'Anselmo, who was born here in 1033. It ends in *Piazza Arco di Augusto* in which is the well preserved **Arco di Augusto** – a triumphal arch (built 25BC) which honours Emperor Augustus and

---

The Road to Italy

Most of the traffic which crosses the Alps from France into Italy and vice versa does so these days by the 11.6 km Mont Blanc Tunnel, which on the Italian side feeds into the valley of the Dora Baltéa and on to Aosta. Our journey, however, takes a much more historic route, over the Great St Bernard Pass. The pass takes its name from St Bernard, 11th-century archdeacon of Aosta, who founded a hospice at Col du Grand St Bernard. It was here that the famous St Bernard breed of dog was first used to find and bring help to stricken travellers.

This pass for centuries served as one of the few transalpine connections between France and Italy, and as such was often used by invaders, generally going south. The Romans were seriously threatened by the descent of the Gauls into northern Italy in the last two centuries BC along this route, and much later it was used by Napoleon at the beginning of his Marengo campaign. Napoleon's invasion was nearly still-born; his army of 40,000 was held up by 300 Austrian troops defending Fort Bard, whose guns commanded the pass and prevented further movement. The narrowness of the path impeded all the French army's efforts to bring up artillery or even supplies, but eventually the fort surrendered.

291

celebrates the Romans' victory over the Gauls. Nearby, a **Roman bridge** spans dried-up River Buthier. In *Piazza Giovanni XX111* are the remains of the **Roman Forum**.

In the same square, the **Cathedral**, unprepossessing on the outside, is filled with treasures within. Chief amongst these are the stained glass windows (15th–16th century). The **Cathedral Museum** houses the cathedral treasury. **Collegiata dei Santi Pietro ed Orso** (10th century) has a series of interesting frescos contemporary with its construction, and a charming Romanesque **cloister**.

MARTIGNY

Station: *9 pl. de la Gare, tel: 26 22 21 21.* Open 0600–2200. Left luggage.
Tourist Office: pl. *Centrale, 1920 Martigny;* tel: 26 21 22 20; in the town centre about 8 min walk down *av. de la Gare* (opposite the station). Open Mon–Fri 0900–1200 and 1330–1800, Sat 0900–1200; also Sat 1330-1800 and Sun 1000–1200 and 1500–1800 July–Aug.

ACCOMMODATION AND FOOD

This small Swiss town has a reasonable choice of hotels, though prices can be high.

The region around Martigny – known as the California of Switzerland – is renowned for its wine, fruit and vegetables, especially asparagus, apricots and strawberries, so they feature strongly on menus.

SIGHTSEEING

Overlooked by ruins of a 13th-century fortress, the **Batiaz** tower, the town traces its origins back to Gallo-Roman times. The remains of an amphitheatre and temple discovered in 1976 now form part of an archaeological museum in the **Pierre**

Gianadda Cultural Foundation, *r. du Forum, tel: 26 22 39 78.* Concerts and art exhibitions are held there and modern sculptures, including works by Rodin, Miro and Moore, are displayed in the park outside. Open daily 1000–1800 (closed 1200–1330 in winter).

⤴ SIDE TRACK FROM MARTIGNY

VERBIER

Tourist office: pl. *Centrale; tel: 026 31 62 22.*

Verbier, one of Switzerland's famous celebrity winter-sports resorts and particularly popular with the Geneva weekend crowd, is a large chalet-style village enjoying a fine site on a south-facing natural terrace at 1500 m. Skiing is possible all year on the slopes of **Mont Fort** (3300 m) which is reached by Le Jumbo, the biggest cable car in the country, capable of transporting 150 skiers at a time. (Non-skiers should also go for the views). The resort also offers many other year-round sports facilities (but note that it effectively closes down from late Oct to early Dec and during May).

There's no authentic historical or architectural interest here, as Verbiers was purpose-built post-war, so to compensate a pleasant mock old-time **Hameau** (hamlet) has been built around a square. It includes a chapel (built using local materials from old ruins), a cultural centre, a rusticised restaurant and an Alpen Museum.

Neighbouring **Le Châble** is a car-free ski resort, offering powder-snow conditions ideal for cross-country skiing and heli-skiing, also with good summer facilities. ⤴

TURIN–MILAN

This route between the two commercial and cultural hubs of northern Italy, crossing the vineyards of Piedmont into the historic plain of Lombardy, takes in Asti, famous for its *spumante* wine and its horse-race, the *Palio,* and the ancient university city of Pavia, best-known for it Carthusian monastery, the Certosa.

FASTEST JOURNEY: 2 HRS

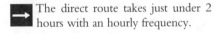

TRAINS

ETT Tables: 351, 360

FAST TRACK

The direct route takes just under 2 hours with an hourly frequency.

ON TRACK

Turin–Asti
A frequent but irregular service (study the timetable carefully for the gaps), taking around 45 mins.

Asti–Casale Monferrato
Nine trains a day taking 50 mins. No Sunday service.

Casale Monferrato–Pavia
Eight trains a day taking 30 mins. No Sunday service.

Pavia–Milan
A 30-min journey made at least once an hour.

ASTI

Tourist office: *Piazza Alfieri, tel: (0141) 60357.* Mon–Fri 0900–1230 and 1500–1800. Sat 0900–1230. The office provides information on Asti's main festival the **Palio** (annually, mid-Sept), and on the various regional wine festivals (Aug and Sept).

ACCOMMODATION

Accommodation in Asti ranges from the hugely expensive to the moderately priced – and all of it is subject to great competition during the Palio. Book early if you want to be there.

SIGHTSEEING

Asti is at the heart of scenic, hilly wine country and is one of the principal wine-growing centres of Piedmont. Come here in search of seasonal delicacies like *tartufi* (truffles) and other culinary delights often associated with the many festivals that take place in the area.

At the heart of town, the arcaded **Piazza Alfieri** is named after a local poet, one Vittorio Alfieri (1749-1803), who is famous chiefly for having absconded with the wife of Bonnie Prince Charlie. You can see Alfieri's bust in the **Palazzo Alfieri**, at *Corso Alfieri 375.* Just next to this is the 8th-century **Crypt of Sant'Anastasio** which has exceptionally fine capitals, and the **Museo Lapidario**.

The **Palio** is held in the big **Campo del Palio**, just near the *Piazza Alfieri.* This event is a fairly recent revival of a medieval tradition dating back to 1275. Various local town neighbourhoods compete in a bare-back horse race against a backdrop of hearty eating and drinking. Luckily it coincides with Asti's other main festival, the annual **wine fair** so that the process of intoxification simply continues unabated.

There is a good range of monuments to be seen in Asti. On the *Corso Alfieri* is the 15th-century church of **San Pietro in Consavia**. Its 12th-century **Baptistery** is now used as an exhibition space and, in a former hospice used by visiting pilgrims, is a little archaeological **museum.** Behind *Piazza Alfieri* is **Collegiata di San Secondo**, a late Romanesque-early Gothic church built on the site of the martyrdom of Asti's patron saint whose relics are kept here. The banners used during the Palio are housed here. See the polyptych by Gandolfino d'Asti, the town's one great Renaissance artist. There are further works by this master in the 14th-century **Cathedral**. Inside, there are some interesting holy water stoups made from converted Roman capitals in the 15th century.

Elsewhere in Asti is a range of medieval towers and Renaissance palaces. Of the former, there is the 13th-century **Torre Comentina** (in the *Corso*) and the finer **Torre Troyana**. Of the palaces, **Palazzo Malabaya** in *Via Mazzini* is the finest.

CASALE MONFERRATO

Tourist Office: Via L Marchino 2, tel: (0142) 70243.

Nestling in the hills of Monferrato on the south bank of the **River Po**, this town was once capital of the old Duchy of Monferrato.

Casale Monferrato is famous for three things: the cement works from which is derives contemporary renown; the Paleologno princes who held court here from 1319 to 1533; and a sumptuous synagogue.

Not much survives from the Paleologno period apart from one or two interesting buildings, most notably the **castello** and the Gothic church of **San Domenico** with its lovely Renaissance portal. The **Cathedral** dates from 1107.

However, it is the town's **Synagogue** (built 1595), and the **Jewish Museum,** which occupies the former womens' gallery of the synagogue, which are of greatest interest – *Via Saloman Olmer.* During the Renaissance period and the Counter-Reformation, it was a safe haven for those who fled persecution in Spain. There was a sizeable Jewish population here until the World War II.

PAVIA

Tourist Office: *Via Fabio Filzi 2, tel: (0382) 22156.* Mon–Sat 0930–1230 and 1430–1800.

ACCOMMODATION

There is very little inexpensive accommodation in Pavia – but try the **Aurora,** *Via Vittorio Emanuele 11 25,* or the **Splendid,** *Via XX Settembre 11.* There is a **campsite,** the **Ticino** at *Via Mascerpa 10.* Open May to September.

SIGHTSEEING

Pavia, close to Milan, was once one of the great cities of Lombardy. Situated on the Lombard Plain, a former capital of the ancient Lombards, it has long been a seat of learning – the **University of Pavia** is famous for law and medicine. Its medieval centre studded with Gothic and Romanesque churches, is well worth visit. A visit to the **Certosa di Pavia** is an essential excursion.

Pavia has two important main streets – the **Corso Cavour** and the **Strada Nuova.** Each follows the original Roman street pattern, the former having been the *cardum* and the latter the *decumanus.* Known to the Romans as Ticinum, Pavia was a frontier town whose greatest days came at the fall of the Roman Empire, when the barbarian Odoacer proclaimed it his capital and himself King of Italy.

Today people come to Pavia to potter in the medieval neighbourhoods divided into quarters by the two main streets. Here you stumble of ancient churches and hidden *piazze,* made all the more delightful because they are inevitably empty. The 15th-century **Duomo** (cathedral) backs onto the **Piazza della Vittoria.** This building, only completed in the 1930s, is the result of the work of many hands, Leonardo da Vinci and Bramante among them.

Next to it, not much remains of the 12th-century **Torre Civica,** which crumbled and collapsed in 1989 killing four people.

In *Via Cavallotti,* Romanesque **San Michele** has an interesting frieze of monsters and quasi-human figures carved onto its sandstone façade. Another Romanesque church to look out for (the top of the *Strada Nuova*) is **San Pietro in Ciel d'Oro** which, built in 1132, takes its name from the gilded ceiling which once graced its interior. Nearby, the **Castello Visconteo** (1330), built by the Visconti and the Sforzas, houses the **Museo Civico** with its archaeological collections detailing Pavia's ancient Roman and Lombard past.

Just outside Pavia, the **Certosa di Pavia** monastery (begun 1396 and completed over 200 years later) was intended as the mausoleum of the Visconti (accessible by either bus or train). In part Gothic, Renaissance and baroque, its ornate church houses the tombs of, amongst others, the medieval Duke of Milan, Lodovico il Moro, and his wife Beatrice d'Este. A great many artists and craftsmen had a hand in this magnificent building, none more prolifically than Giovanni Antonio Amadeo. Also worth seeing are the **Little Cloister,** the **Great Cloister** and the **Refectory**

VENICE

The island city of Venice, with its chequered history and magnificent works of art and architecture has captured the imagination of travellers for centuries. Once a powerful maritime republic and a city of enormous prosperity, these days it defies all the odds in an effort to remain upright, subject as it is to capricious tides, sinking mud and the tramp of nearly 10 million tourists' feet annually in the summer. Virtually unchanged over the centuries, the canals and alleys are still lined with curiously elaborate Gothic houses, Renaissance palaces and the baroque of the architect Longhena. The only modern additions to its urban landscape (apart from the railway station and the 19th-century causeway linking it to the mainland) are the *vaporetti* (the boat-buses) and the motor launches. The city's highlights include splendid secular buildings – civic and private palaces, galleries and museums – and a huge array of churches, many of which are adorned with the works of Venice's key painters, Vivarini, Bellini, Tintoretto and Tiepolo among them. Most extraordinary of all is its unique spider-web of canals which reach into every corner of the city. Some are deserted and moody, others are busy commercial waterways. Here, too, some of the finest food in Italy can be found and there is a singular array of articles to buy – the like of which are

296

found nowhere else in the country. Venice is a compact city and many of its highlights can be absorbed in two or three days, but it will certainly reward a longer stay.

TOURIST INFORMATION

The **Azienda Promozione Turistica (APT),** *Calle dell'Ascensione 71C, tel: (041) 522 6356 (off Piazza San Marco)* is open daily except Sun, 0830–1930 (Apr–Oct); 0830–1330 (Nov–Mar). APT also has offices at **Santa Lucia station**, *tel: (041) 719 078,* and at the *Lido, Gran Viale Santa Maria Elisabetta 6A, tel: (041) 526 5721.*

For youth information, contact the **Comune di Venezia Assessorato al Gioventù**, *San Marco 1529; tel: (041) 270 7650.* A **Carta Giovani** allows 14–29 year-olds cheap entry to museums, art galleries, theatres, cinemas and cultural events, maps, cut-price shopping guide and reductions on public transport. It is free from the APT offices – take a photograph and your passport. A **Biglietto Cumulativo** is available if you want to visit two out of five museums. Available to all ages, it certainly cuts the costs and is redeemable at Museo Correr, Palazzo ducale, Ca'Pesaro, Ca'Rezzonico and Mugello's Glass Museum. The total cost of the card is L16,000.

ARRIVING AND DEPARTING

Airport
Marco Polo International Airport is 13 km north-east of Venice; flight information; *tel: (041) 661 262.* The ATVO

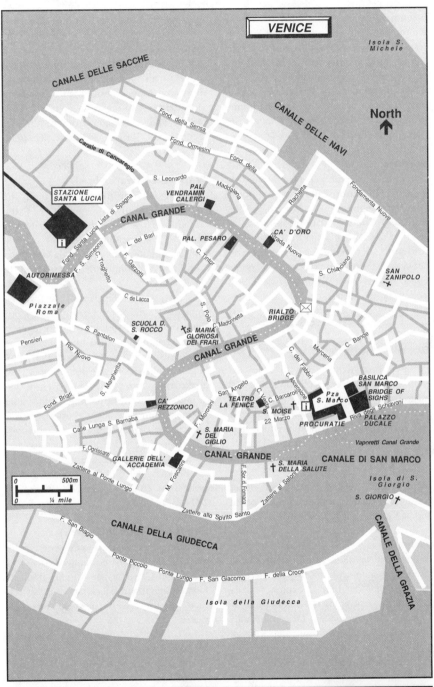

VENICE

Isola S. Michele

CANALE DELLE SACCHE

Fond. della Sensa

CANALE DELLE NAVI

North

Fond. Ormesini

Fond. della

Canale di Cannaregio

S. Leonardo

Maddalena

Racheta

Fondamenta Nuove

STAZIONE SANTA LUCIA

PAL. VENDRAMIN CALERGI

CANAL GRANDE

Fond. Santa Lucia Lista di Spagna

F. S. Simeone

C. Traghetto

L. dei Bari

PAL. PESARO

C. Tintor

F. Garzotti

CA' D'ORO

Strada Nuova

S. Chiacano

SAN ZANIPOLO

AUTORIMESSA

C. de Lacca

Piazzale Roma

S. Pantalon

S. Polo

C. Madonnetta

RIALTO BRIDGE

✉

Pensieri

Rio Nuovo

SCUOLA D. S. ROCCO

✝**S. MARIA GLORIOSA DEI FRARI**

CANAL GRANDE

C. dei Fabbri

C. Bande

Mercena

297

Fond. Briati

S. Margherita

CA' REZZONICO

F. Morosini

San Angelo

TEATRO LA FENICE

C. Vin

C. Barcaroli

C. Ascensione

C. dei Fabbri

BASILICA SAN MARCO

BRIDGE OF SIGHS

Pza S. Marco

S. MOISÈ

ℹ

Calle Lunga S. Barnaba

F. Ognissanti

GALLERIE DELL' ACCADEMIA

✝**S. MARIA DEL GIGLIO**

22 Marzo

Riva degli Schiavoni

PROCURATIE

PALAZZO DUCALE

M. Foscarini

CANAL GRANDE

F. Soc.d. Fornace

✝**S. MARIA DELLA SALUTE**

CANALE DI SAN MARCO

Vaporetti Canal Grande

Isola di S. Giorgio

Zattere al Ponte Lungo

Zattere al Salon

S. GIORGIO ✝

0 ────── 500m
0 ────── ¼ mile

Zattere allo Spirito Santo

CANALE DELLA GIUDECCA

F. San Biagio

Ponte Piccolo

Ponte Lungo

F. San Giacomo

F. della Croce

CANALE DELLA GRAZIA

Isola della Giudecca

bus no. 5 operates half-hourly (hourly in winter) between the airport and *Piazzale Romana*, where those travelling on into Venice must transfer to the city's water-borne public transport system (**ACTV**). The Co-operative San Marco ferry service operates from the airport (daylight hours, summer) via the Lido to the *Piazza San Marco* in the heart of Venice.

Stations

To get to Venice proper, take a train terminating at **Santa Lucia** station; some trains will deposit you at **Mestre**, on the mainland. The two stations are 10 mins apart by rail, and all Santa Lucia trains call at Mestre. A frequent local service operates between Mestre and Santa Lucia. Santa Lucia has its own *vaporetto* (water-bus) stop, right outside the station, at the northeast end of the Grand Canal. Santa Lucia enquiries, *tel: (041) 715555*.

GETTING AROUND

Europe's only roadless city is a joy to explore, with its great public buildings and magnificent palaces overlooking the grand canal or unexpectedly tucked away on the maze of smaller canals called *rii* which separate the city's 100-plus islands. Prepare yourself for plenty of walking, and don't be surprised when you get lost. A good map, with *vaporetto* routes and street names, is available from the tourist office and at Venice's many news-stands.

Tickets

A three-day *turisticche* (tourist ticket), cost L18000, enables you to use all *vaporetto* routes except the Line 2 express, and is ideal for those planning to explore some of Venice's outlying islands. Tickets are sold singly or in booklets of ten from kiosks at main stops, open 0600–2100, and must be validated in the machine provided at each

pier before boarding. The line 2 express costs approximately 50% more than normal services.

A **24-hour** pass is valid for unlimited travel on all lines – L9000. Anybody staying any longer should buy a **Carta Venezia** – valid for up to 3 years. It costs L8000 and is available from the ACTV central office, *Corte dell'Albero, tel: (041) 528 7886.*

Vaporetto (water-bus)

Other cities have the bus, the train, the tram or the metro. Venice has the *vaporetto*. These water-buses, operated by the **ACTV** transport authority, run at 10–20 minute intervals in daytime and approximately hourly from midnight to 0600.

The most useful lines are Line 1, which runs the length of the Grand Canal, stopping frequently, and Line 2, the express service connecting Santa Lucia station, the Rialto, *Piazza San Marco* and the Lido. *Vaporetto* piers bear the line number, but make sure you are heading the right way – it is easy to lose your bearings. Other lines connect central Venice with its island suburbs in the lagoon. Line 5 is a round-the-islands service taking in Murano and handy if you are staying at the youth hostel on Isola del Giudecca, which has its own stop. **ACTV**, *Piazzale Roma, tel: (041) 520 7555.*

Traghetto (gondola ferry)

The cheapest gondola ride in Venice is the *traghetto*. These two-gondolier boats cross the Grand Canal at many points along its length (signposted *Traghetto*) and cost less than half the price of a single water-bus ticket.

Water Taxi

Water taxis are very expensive. You could

take 40 trips on the Line 2 express for the cost of one taxi ride along the Grand Canal. The fare system is extremely complicated.

Gondola

Gondola rides are costly, but if you decide to treat yourself to a once-in-a-lifetime experience you should go in the evening, when the canals and the buildings overlooking them are at their most magical. Official rates, which are set according to time, not distance, are available from the APT, but make sure you agree a price with your gondolier before setting out.

STAYING IN VENICE

Accommodation

Don't come to Venice looking for cheap and cheerful accommodation. Space is at a premium, and although the city has some of Europe's grandest luxury hotels (such as the legendary **Cipriani**) there are slim pickings for those on a tight budget, especially in summer, when booking ahead is strongly advisable.

AVA (Venetian Hotel Association) has reservation desks at Santa Lucia station, *tel: (041) 715 016 or (041) 715 288,* open daily Apr–Oct 0800–2200; Nov–Mar, 0800–2130, and at Marco Polo International Airport. Hotel chains with property in the city include: *Ch, BW, Ra, Ex, Pu.*

The main HI **youth hostel** (Albergho per la Gioventù is on Isola del Giudecca (vaporetto: *line 5), tel: (041) 523 8211.* For further hostel information, contact the **Associazone Alberghi per la Gioventù**, *Palazzo della Civiltà del Lavoro, Quadrato della Concordia, 00144 Roma, tel: (06) 593 1702.* The nearest **campsite** is on the Lido, *Camping San Nicolò; tel: (041) 526 7415.*

Eating and Drinking

Like all Italian cities, Venice takes pride in its distinctive regional cuisine, and eating and drinking is a central part of the local way of life. As you would expect of a race of lagoon-dwellers and mariners, Venetian cooking leans heavily toward seafood.

In an expensive country for travellers, Venice is one of the more expensive cities, and the price of a meal or even a drink in one of the restaurants and cafés catering to tourists around the *Piazza San Marco* or *Rialto* will take your breath away. Drinks at a table cost up to three times as much as those taken at the bar. However, common sense will tell you that to eat in the centre is sheer craziness – you pay for the location.

Wander off the beaten track and see where the Venetians are eating. There you'll find the best food and considerably better – and more enticing – prices. You can save money and still eat well by choosing an *antipasto* followed by a plate of pasta or rosotto, omitting the traditional main course, which is always the most expensive.

Good news for budget travellers is the array of eat-as-you-go snacks available; buy a slice of *pizza* from a snack-bar, absorb an *espresso* standing at the bar of a back-street café, and you will save enough money to eat well in the evening at a small trattoria.

Look for places catering to ordinary Venetians rather than tourists. Though these are not always easy to find in a city so thoroughly devoted to tourism thereare discoveries to be amde once you forsake the tourist haunts of San Marco.

Good-value restaurants and *trattorie* include **L'Incontro** and **Riviera**, in the Dorsoduro quarter; **Nono Risorto**, in San Polo; **Alla Pergola**, in Cannaregio; and **Antica Besseta**, in Santa Croce – but

299

these are not the only ones by any means.

And why not have a picnic lunch? Buy the ingredients from a delicatessen, along with bottle of cold white wine which the vendor will be happy to open, and go and perch on the edge of a quiet canal.

Communications

Main **post office: Poste Centrali**, *Rialto, Fontego dei Tedeschi, tel: (041) 522 0606.*

To phone Venice from abroad: *tel: 39 (Italy) + 41 (Venice) + number*; to phone Venice from elsewhere in Italy: *tel: (041) + number.*

Consulates

UK: **Campo Santa Maria della Carità**, *1051, Dorsoduro, tel: (041) 522 7207.*

Money

All central banks will change your money, as will bureaux de change in the city centre, at the station and at the airport. Ask for a supply of small-denomination bills – every shop and café in Italy is perennially short of change.

Thomas Cook bureaux de change are located at *5126 Riva del Ferro (Rialto); tel: (041) 5287358* and *Piazza San Marco, 142; tel: (041) 5224751.*

ENTERTAINMENT

The entertainment calendar is busier in summer than in winter, with events like the annual **Venice film festival** (late Aug to early Sept). Music – opera, classical and choral – is prominent. The free *Guest in Venice* guide, available from the APT and at most hotel front desks, will tell you what's on.

The big event of the year is **Carnival**, ten days of masked balls, fancy dress parties and colourful street celebrations around Shrove Tuesday each year.

Nightlife

Venice has numerous bars and clubs offering live music, dancing and late-night drinking. As everywhere in Italy, nightlife only begins to warm up at midnight. The best guide to nightlife venues and events is *Notturno Veneziana*, from APT offices.

Theatres, Cinemas and Concerts

Venice is not a great theatrical city and Italian drama is a closed book to non-natives. **Opera**, with its gorgeous costumes and magnificent arias is, on the other hand, accessible to everybody and the works of Verdi, Puccini and others are in performance virtually year-round. The main venue, the **Teatro La Fenice**, has been gutted by fire, but plans are being made to restore it.

Free concerts are often held in the city's churches, especially in tandem with other summer cultural events; enquire at APT offices for details of these. Venice has fewer city centre cinemas than any other Italian city, but the *Palazzo del Cinema* on the Lido is the venue for the annual film festival and for frequent showings of international movies year-round.

SHOPPING

The Venetians' aptitude for commerce has been sharpened by more than 11 centuries of international trade and 200 years of tourism. Bargain buys are thin on the ground, and many people touring the neighbouring islands of the lagoon, such as Murano, are disappointed to find prices are much the same as in the city centre. **Venetian glass** is the big shopping deal, but much of what is sold is over-priced; try major vendors such as **Cenedese** or **Salviati**, both on *Piazza San Marco*. More affordable, and uniquely Venetian, are the painted papier-maché masks sold in many small stores.

The best time to visit the **Rialto open-air market** is early morning; it's closed on Sun and quiet on Mon. Otherwise, shopping in this city, which is full of merchandise treasures is much the same as you might find in Rome or Milan. You can always unearth a bit of old velvet from the antique shops, a gilded picture frame or a bit of coral jewellery.

SIGHTSEEING

The beauty of sightseeing in Venice is that the city is a living museum with (as yet) no admission charge, although there is talk of introducing one. This causes problems: during the summer months its heart – **Piazza San Marco** and the surrounding neighbourhood – is densely packed with tourists. There is, however, a steep entrance fee for almost all Venice's major sights. The biggest concentration of these is around the *Piazza San Marco*, making it the logical starting point for exploring the city. Almost all the rest – including the palaces of medieval Venice's great magnates – are strung out along the length of the S-shaped Grand Canal.

Piazza San Marco

Close to the mouth of the Grand Canal and overlooking the Canale di San Marco, the *Piazza* is Venice at its most striking – and, in summer, at its most crowded. Here there are four highlights. The **Basilica di San Marco** (St Mark's), consecrated in 1094, has a sumptuous façade, curious Oriental-style domes, elaborate mosaics (the best of which date from the 13th century), and a museum containing sculpture and carvings from all over the medieval Venetian empire. The basilica was built to house the bones of St Mark the Evangelist – swiped from their resting place in Alexandria in the 9th century. Within, its dark, sepulchral chapels, vaults and domes

ensure an appeal that is mysterious and otherwordly. There are ancient columns of rare, coloured marble, exquisite early pavements of inlaid marble, glass and porphyry and, best of all acres of ancient mosaic. See in particular the 13th-century originals in the atrium domes, the 11th-century image of the *Madonna and Saints* over the central door and the 14th-century scenes from the *Life of St John the Baptist* in the Baptistery.

One of the supreme prizes here are the legendary **Horses of St Mark** which adorn the external façade. Cast some time between the 3rd century BC and the 2nd century AD, and stolen from Byzantium by the Venetians in 1204, they are a powerful symbol of the Republic of Venice (they were originally taken from Chios by Constantine the Great to adorn to Hippodrome of Byzantium). The effects of pollution mean that the originals have had to be removed for safekeeping in the museum – those out in the *piazza* are recent copies.

Next to the basilica stands the **Palazzo Ducale** (the Doge's Palace) which was begun in 1309 then rebuilt in 1577. A sumptuous civic palace, built in an exotic, highly decorated Venetian Gothic style, it contains important Venetian works of art while providing an interesting view on the life and style of the Venetian rulers. There is lavish decoration by a range of artists (such as Tintoretto and Veronese) and architects (like Sansovino). The real business of state took place away from the grand rooms seen on a tour of the palace. On what is called the **Itinerari Segreti** (Secret Itinerary), you get to see into tiny, wood-panelled chambers, interesting, decorated meeting rooms, and the torture chamber where prisoners were strung up on ropes tied to their wrists.

The **Bridge of Sighs** next to the

palace leads to the **Palazzo delle Prigione**, the prison for petty offenders. Opposite the palace, the **Campanile di San Marco** completes the quartet of the square's most important buildings.

Canale Grande (Grand Canal): East Bank

Following the canal in its serpentine north-westward trend from *San Marco* you can stop off at the baroque church of **San Moise** and its neighbour **Santa Maria del Giglio**, and pass beneath the handsome **Ponte di Rialto**, built in 1592 at the geographic heart of the city, before stopping at the Gothic **Ca'd'Oro**, the most lavish of all the Venetian aristocratic palaces. Its best façade, adorned with intricately carved tracery, is best seen from the canal. Following a lengthy programme of restoration, it now houses the **Galleria Franchetti** in which is a magnificent collection of paintings (Mantegna, Guardi, for example), Renaissance bronzes and medallions. Last call is the Renaissance **Palazzo Vendramin Calergi** where Richard Wagner died in 1883.

Canale Grande: West Bank

On the west bank of the canal, heading north-west from its junction with the Canale di San Marco, stands the **Galleria dell'Accademia**. The is the best place in the world in which to make a study of Venetian art. Here there are canvasses, altarpieces and frescos taken from churches and palaces around the city, among them important works by Bellini, Veronese, Titian, Giorgione, Tintoretto, Carpaccio, Canaletto and Guardi. But it is not devoted exclusively to the Venetian school. There are also works by artists of the Florentine Renaissance – Piero della Francesca among them.

Nearby are two more splendid palaces.

The **Ca'Rezzonico** (designed by Longhena in 1667), is the place where Browning died. Now it is the **Museo del Settecento Veneziano**, the Museum of Venice in the Eighteenth Century, and home to rococo furniture and a collection of 18th-century art. From its windows there is a magnificent view out over the Grand Canal. The **Ca'Foscari**, the second of the two important palaces, was built in 1437 for the Doge Francesco Foscari.

Still on the Grand Canal, and not far from the Accademia, is the important **Peggy Guggenheim Museum** which contains a collection of 20th-century art, all of it put together by Peggy Guggenheim. Today this array of works by Bacon, Braque, De Chirico, Duchamp, Ernst, Giacometti, Picasso and Klee (just to name a few) is administered by New York's Solomon Guggenheim Foundation. From here it is only a short walk to the baroque church of **Santa Maria della Salute**, the masterpiece of the architect Longhena and built between 1631-81. Beyond, facing onto the Guidecca, is the church of **San Sebastiano** which contains astonishing illusionistic ceiling frescos by Veronese (c1555).

A short walk west of the canal, between the *Rio della Frescada* and the *Campo di San Paolo*, is the **Scuola di San Rocco,** once the headquarters of a charitable confraternity. Inside it houses a magnificent collection of canvases by Tintoretto. If you haven't time to see much in the city, then come here first. This is one of the finest cycles of painting in existence. In addition to these 54 panels, there are works by Titian and Giorgione.

Nearby is the medieval church of the **Frari**, principal church of the Franciscan order – and burial place of the painter Titian and of Monteverdi. Built 1330 –

1469, this huge, brick-built, barn-like church is a repository of art: it contains works by Donatello, Bellini and Titian, amongst others. In fact Titian is buried here (see the tomb Antonio Canova designed for him) – as is Monteverdi (once the choir director at St Mark's).

Other Sights

The **Fondazione Querini-Stampalia** (north-east of *Piazza San Marco*), housed in the 16th-century palace of the same name, is a good place in which to obtain an idea of the decor of an 18th-century Venetian residence. It is still decorated and furnished in contemporary patrician style and has the additional attractions of a variety of paintings by Pietro Longhi, Bellini and Tiepolo.

Not far away, the vast, brick-built Dominican church of **Santi Giovanni e Paolo** (begun 1246, rebuilt in 1333 and completed in 1430) is filled with the tombs of the Doges – there is a splendid array of Gothic and Renaissance sepulchral art. Outside is the equestrian statue of **Bartolomeo Colleoni**, the 15th-century condottieri who assisted the Venetians in establishing a realm beyond the watery confines of their city.

The Islands

The **Lido** is the most glamorous of Venice's islands. Here you come to swim, lounge in the sun and, for those unwise enough to try them, eat in one of a huge variety of vastly expensive restaurants. Made famous during the Belle Époque (and by Visconti – some of whose scenes from Thomas Mann's *Death in Venice* were filmed here), it still has a certain elegance, propped up by the sophistication of the bathing establishments which line the waterfront and for which you pay for the honour of having a swim. A free beach is at the island's north end.

Organised sightseeing tours of the outlying island **Murano** and its neighbours **Burano** and **Torcello** are little more than showcase trips for the glass factories. You can visit these and other islands just as easily – and much more cheaply – on an ordinary *vaporetto*. Worth it for the view, but the big sights are all in Venice itself.

Facing Piazza di San Marco from the other side of the Grand Canal is the church of **San Giorgio Maggiore**, situated on the little island of San Giorgio Maggiore. Its delicate Renaissance façade is quite at odds with the Oriental jumble of St Mark's and the Palazzo Ducale which it faces. Beside it, the monastery buildings were partly designed by Palladio. A little way to the west, situated on one of the eight islands of the Giudecca, is Palladio's church of the **Redentore** (completed in 1592). It is one of the architect's most important works and was built to commemorate the ending of a horrific bout of plague that killed nearly 50,000 people. The event is still commemorated today in the *Festa del Redentore* (July).

Views of Venice

The **Campanile di San Marco** on *Piazza di San Marco* is a 20th-century reconstruction of a thousand-year-old bell-tower which fell down in 1912. Take the lift to the top for a panoramic view of Venice and its lagoon. The view towards *Piazza di San Marco* from the island of San Giorgio Maggiore is also magnificent – particularly in the evening (if you go at dusk, make sure there is a way of getting back; San Giorgio Maggiore is an isolated island).

303

VENICE–VIENNA

Leaving coastal Trieste, and beyond the hills and valleys of western Slovenia, the more southerly alternative route passes Ljubljana and enters a green and fertile land, taking in Celje and Maribor, two interesting Slovenian towns. In Austria the route passes from the undulating hills of the south to the plains of the north. Along the northern route, the landscape is flat until Conegliano, from where it blossoms. The side track to Pieve di Cadore is dramatic as it ascends gradually, following the route of the River Piave, towards the peaks of the Dolomites.

FASTEST JOURNEY: 8 HRS

TRAINS

ETT tables: 88, 377, 830, 376, 930, 933.

FAST TRACK

Three trains a day make the journey between Venice and Vienna via the direct route through Villach. Two are day trains taking between 8 and 9 hrs. The other is an overnight sleeping car train taking 10 hrs.

ON TRACK

Venice (Venezia)–Trieste
A frequent service operates from Venezia Sta Lucia taking 2 hr.

Trieste–Ljubljana
Three trains cross the border between Italy and Slovenia The journey takes 3 hrs.

Ljubljana–Celje
A frequent but irregular service, the journey takes 1 hr 20 mins.

Celje–Maribor
The frequent journey takes around 1 hr.

Maribor–Graz
Two through trains link Maribor in Slovenia and Graz in Austria taking 1 hr. Two more services are available by changing at Spielfeld-Strass.

Graz–Vienna
A train every 2 hrs runs between Graz and Wien. The journey takes 2 hrs 40 mins.

Venice–Conegliano
A frequent service runs from Venezia Sta Lucia on this line taking around 1 hr.

Conegliano–Udine
Frequent trains taking just over 1 hr.

Udine–Villach
Just two trains a day taking 2 hrs.

Villach–Velden am Wörthersee–Pörtschach am Wörthersee–Klagenfurt
Frequent trains call at these stations, Villach to Velden takes 15 mins, Velden to Pörtschach 8 mins, Pörtschach to Klagenfurt 15 mins.

Klagenfurt–St Veit an der Glan–Friesach–Leoben
An hourly service links Klagenfurt and Leoben calling at these stations. Klagenfurt to St Veit takes 20 mins, St Veit to Friesach 30 mins, Friesach to Leoben 1 hr 30 mins.

Leoben–Vienna (Wien)
One train every hour taking 2 hr 20 mins.

TRIESTE
Station: **Stazione Centrale,** *Pza della Libertá 8, tel: (040) 418 207.*
Tourist Office: The central office is at *Via San Nicolo 20, tel: (040) 369 881,* and there is a second, smaller one in the station. The regional information office is at *Via Rossini 6, tel: (040) 363 952.*

SIGHTSEEING
Italy's easternmost city, once the chief port of the Austro-Hungarian Empire, is also the Istrian hinterland's window on the western world. Rebuilt in the 19th century, it is today a stately, solid place that relishes its role as a crossroads between east and west. At Trieste's centre, the **Borgo Teresiano** is a stately grid of regular streets which identify this city more with its central European counterparts than with anything Italian. Here, the *Corso Cavour* straddles the **Canal Grande,** an urban waterway where the locals moor their boats. Beside it, in *Pza Ponterosso,* is the daily **market**.

Trieste's civic heart lies in *Pza dell'Unitá d'Italia*: see the vast **Palazzo del Comune** facing the harbour and neo-classical **Palazzo del Governo** beside it, aglow with its mosaic ornamentation. Also in the piazza is one of Trieste's oldest cafés (1839), the **Caffé degli Specchi.** There is another, **Caffé San Marco,** on the other side of town – at *Via Cesare Battisti 18.*

The **Capitoline Hill** formed the heart of Roman and medieval Trieste, and it is here that its oldest surviving buildings are to be found. Apart from the surviving remains of the ancient **Forum** (ancient Trieste was called Tergeste), there is the 11th-century **Cathedral of San Giusto** (beside the Forum). Still on the Capitoline, the 15th-century Venetian-built **Castello** houses the **Museo Civico** in which can be seen a collection of weaponry and armour. Still close to the cathedral, the **Museo di Storia ed Arte** houses important Roman artefacts, as does the **Orto Lapidario.** In *Via Teatro Romano* are the ruins of a Roman theatre.

LJUBLJANA
Station: On *Trg Osvobodilne Fronte,* a 15-min walk north from the main street, *Slovenska Cesta.*
Tourist Office (TIC): *Slovenska Cesta*

305

35; tel: (061) 224 222. Open Mon–Fri 0800–2100, Sat and Sun 0800–1200 and 1700–2100 (April–Sept); Mon–Fri, 0800–1900, Sat and Sun 0800–1200 and 1600–1900 (Oct–March); **The Cultural Information Centre**, *Trg Francoske Revolucije 7,* offers free booklets about museums, and listings advice.

ACCOMMODATION

There is a good variety of **hotels** in the city, though none are in the 'luxury' category. **Private rooms** are available for rent: ask at the tourist information office. **Youth Hostels** are in very short supply. However, rooms can be rented in student hostels during the summer holidays only – ask at the tourist office for details. **Dijeski Dom Bezigrad** is at *Kardeljeva Ploscad 28, tel: (061) 342 864,* open July–Aug, and **Dijeski Dom Tabor** at *Vidovdanska*

Cesta 7, tel: (061) 321 067. **Camping** is the best cheap option and Ljubljana's site is located by the Sava River at the north end of *Dunajska Cesta –* **Camping Jezica**, *tel: (061) 371 383.*

SIGHTSEEING

A part of the former Yugoslavia, and now the capital of Slovenia, an independent state which has remained distinctly aloof from the Balkan conflict, Ljubljana is a metropolis where the West meets *Mittel Europa*. Dominated by a hilltop fortress, it is a lively city with an important historic core.

The River Ljubljanica divides the city into two parts that are joined by a triple bridge, the **Tromostovje**. This links the city's old heart, the *Presernov Trg*, on the west bank, with *Gallusovo Nabrezje*, the riverside thoroughfare flanked by medieval houses, skirting the eastern hill on which sits the mainly 16th-century **castle**.

On the east bank baroque **St Nikolas's Cathedral,** *Ciril-Metodov Trg,* abuts the **Bishop's Palace.** Beyond, on *Vodnikov Trg,* lies the weekly fruit and vegetable **market**. Going south from the cathedral, a baroque **fountain** by the Italian architect and sculptor Francesco Robba stands opposite the **Magistrat** (Town Hall) on *Mestni Trg,* which is the scene of the colourful annual (June) **Country Weddings** – a mass wedding ceremony conducted in peasant costume.

On the river's west bank, the 17th-century **Franciscan Church** dominates *Presernov Trg*. Within, the high altar is the work of Robba, as is the one inside the 18th-century **Ursulinska Cerkev**, an important baroque edifice on *Kongresni Trg*. The western flank of the city also contains most of the museums. The **National Museum**, *Trg Herojev 1*, houses important archaeological artefacts and a natural history section whose key exhibit is a complete mammoth skeleton. The **National Gallery**, *Cankarjeva 20*, is interesting if you are devoted to the Slovenian school of Impressionism. The **Modern Gallery,** *Cankarjeva 15,* provides an interesting view of 20th-century Slovenian art. The **Architectural Museum**, *Karunova 4,* highlights the work of architect Joze Plecnik, who altered much of the city before World War II, giving chunks of it a neo-classical style. In the **Tivoli Park**, the **Museum of Contemporary History** chronicles the changing history of this region.

CELJE

Tourist office: *Glavni trg 7, tel: 29 445.* Open 0800–1900 Mon–Fri and 0800–1300 Sat; July–Aug 0800–1300 and 1600–1900 Mon–Fri and 0800–1230 Sat.

Perhaps the best time to visit Celje is during September's **International Artisan Fair** – ask for details.

ACCOMMODATION

Accommodation is rather limited in Celje though none is particularly expensive. The best of what there is located around the railway station. Ask at the tourist office for information about private rooms which are very cheap indeed and of course the best way to learn about the people an their way of life. There are dormitory rooms available at the **Dijaski Dom** *at Ljubljanska cesta 21, tel: 28 013.*

SIGHTSEEING

Celje is a well known historic town that derives its fame from its former rulers, the Celje counts. Much of what there is to see here relates to this feudal dynasty and there is much to see.

The largest castle in Slovenia dominates Celje from the summit of a nearby hill. **Celje Castle**, built in the 13th century and much altered since, possesses a 35-m high tower, the **Frederick Tower**. There is also a **Lower Castle** (*Muzejski trg*) in Celje – the former residence of the Celje Counts who, before the advent of the Habsburgs, were one of Central Europe's most powerful feudal dynasties. Near it, *Muzejski trg 9,* is the **Narodni Dom** which, like the Lower Castle, is now an art gallery.

Much of the content of the **Celje Regional Museum**, housed in the 16th-century **Old County Palace** *(Muzejski trg)*, is devoted to documenting their rule, as is the Museum of Modern History, *Presernova ulica 17*. Opposite the museum is the **Minorite Church of Mary** where the counts were buried – although their bones were removed this century (there are some skulls in the Regional Museum).

Other interesting churches include, in *Slomskov trg* the **Abbey Church of St Daniel** (see in particular the 15th-century *Pietà* in the Chapel of the Sorrowful Mother), and 15th-century **St Maximilian** *(Askiceva ulica)*, named after a local bishop who was beheaded in the 3rd century.

MARIBOR

Station:
Tourist office: *Grajski trg 1, tel: 211 262.* Open Mon–Fri 0900–1800 and Sat 0900–1200. Ask for a city map and for the monthly listings calendar. Maribor has some excellent cultural festivals, of which the best are the June-July **International Baroque Music Festival** and a folkloric **Summer Festival**, and in early Oct the **grape harvest** ceremony.

ACCOMMODATION

Most of the hotels in the town cater exclusively to business travellers and are probably to be avoided. The best hotel accommodation will be found in the surrounding outlying districts of the *Maribor Pohorje*. Otherwise ask at the tourist office for private rooms or accommodation at one of the student hostels. **Camping**: take the no. 15 bus to the **Jezero campsite** (and a motel) near the village of Bresternica (7 km west of Maribor), *tel: (062) 621 640.*

SIGHTSEEING

Maribor is one of the most important cities in Slovenia and home to the country's only university. It has a lovely riverside historic centre and is located not far from the Mariborske and Slovenske Gorice wine-growing regions in the north and the east.

Slovenia's second largest city has a distinctly Austrian heritage. It straddles the **Drava River** and has an attractive **Old Town** with a pretty river front dotted with welcome cafés and bars. There's enough to see in Maribor to fill a day, though stay longer if visits to the surrounding countryside are planned.

There are two chief sights at Maribor. The first is the 15th-century **Maribor Castle** (*Grajska ulica 2*) which houses the **Maribor Regional Museum**. This is one of the best in the country. Apart from documenting Maribor's own history, there are important archaeological and ethnographic collections, Greek and Roman statuary and a military uniform that once belonged to Marshall Tito. Near the museum stands the 17th-century **St Florian Column**.

The other major sight is the **Cathedral of St John the Baptist** *(Slomskov trg)* which is adorned with virtually every architectural style from Romanesque to those of the present day. Its best asset is a lovely Gothic presbytery and a collection of intricately adorned choir stalls.

Maribor is an important wine-producing location. Pay a visit to the 160-year old **wine cellars** *(Trg Svobode 3)* whose 20,000 sq meters are capable of housing over 7 million litres of wine, and to the two little urban 'hills', **City Peak** and **Piramida**, which are covered in vines.

At the waterside are two interesting medieval landmarks – the 15th-century **Sodni Stolp** (the Judge's Tower), and the 16th-century **Vodni Stolp** (*Usnjarska ulica 10*), a water tower which today houses Slovenia's oldest *vinoteka*. This is the place to sample about 300 different Slovenian wines.

Elsewhere in town, in the medieval marketplace, there is an extraordinarily rich 17th-century **plague pillar** (*Glavni trg*) and, at *Zidovska ulica 4*, a 15th-century synagogue situated alongside the **Jewish**

Tower (the Zidovski Stolp), in what was the Jewish Quarter in the Middle Ages.

GRAZ

Station: *tel: (0316) 1717.* Rents bikes.
Tourist Office: *Hbf tel: (0316) 916837* Mon–Fri, 0900–1300, 1400–1800, Sat 0900–1200, 1300–1700, Suns and holidays 1000-1500. An office at *Herreng. 16; tel: (0316) 8352410;* trams 3 or 6 from the station to the *Hauptpl.* or approx 15-min walk, opens Mon–Fri 0900–1900, Sat 0900–1800, Sun 1000–1500 (May–Oct), Mon–Fri 0900–1800, Sat 1000-1500 Sun and holidays 1000-1500 (Nov–April). It offers give-away city map with a more detailed one for sale (ÖS25) plus regional information.

A 24-hour bus and tram ticket is ÖS40, for 10 trips ÖS140. There is a shuttle bus from the airport to hotels four times a day depending on flight times. The *Graz Total* booklet lists eating places and all cultural events.

ACCOMMODATION AND FOOD

The tourist office can book accommodation (ÖS30 per hotel). At the top end is **Grand Hotel Wiesler**, *Grieskai 4–8; tel: (0316) 90660* (very expensive) in a quayside property, or the **Hotel Erzherzog Johann**, *Sackstr. 3–5; tel: (0316) 811616* (expensive) with rooms on 19th-century scale. Alternatives are the two-star **Hotel Strasser**, *Eggenberger Gurtel 11; tel: (0316) 913977* (moderate) near the station. **HI: Jugendgastaus Graz**, *Idlhofg. 74; tel: (0316) 914876*, is 20 mins' walk from the station or bus no. 50. **Camping Central** is at *Martinhofstr. 3; tel: (0316) 281831*, south of the city close to the local *Strassgang* station. Chains with property here include *BW* and *Rk*.

Cheap eating places cater to Graz's 40,000 students while the area beside the *Hauptpl.*, centring on *Mehlpl.*, is alive with numerous cafés, notably **M1**, *Mehlpl. 1*, with great views. Most popular for food is probably **Gastwirtschaft**, *Harlbarthg. 4*. More expensive is the **Landhaus-Keller**, *Schmiedg. 9*, in the *Landhaus* itself. Or check out the Bauernmärkte, Mon–Sat 0700–1230, *Kaiser-Josefpl. and Lendpl.*; Mon–Sat 0500-2000, *Hauptpl.*; Mon–Fri 0700–1800, Sat 0700–1230 at *Jakominipl.*

ENTERTAINMENT

Music schools are big here, resulting in high quality **street performance**. The **Opera House** is the venue for major cultural events. July–Sept sees candlelit concerts at the **Eggenbergerschloss** and **open-air concert** July–mid-Aug in the **Generalihof** with jazz Thurs. **Styriarte**, June and July, is a classical music festival with a different theme each year. The **Steirischer Herbst** (Styrian autumn) international contemporary arts festival (Sept–Oct) includes anything from mime to jazz. There is also a **street art festival** Aug.

SHOPPING

Kastner & Öhler, a high tech department store in the heart of old *Altstadt* buildings is one of the smartest places to shop. For local cheeses try **Delikatessen F Nussbaumer**, *Paradeisg. 1*, There is a stylish local craftshop under **Café M1**. **Steirisches Heimatwerk**, *Herreng.* offers genuine *Trachten*.

SIGHTSEEING

The Tourist Office organises **2-hour tours** daily April–Oct ÖS75, Sat Nov–Mar. The **medieval centre** with small streets packed with shops and cafés, hinges round the **Hauptplatz** with nearby the delightful 16th century Italian-influenced **Landeshaus**. On the hill

309

above are the remains of the town's former castle – a **bell tower** of 1556, expensively ransomed from the French. But the most intriguing spot is the **Landeszeughaus**, *Herreng. 16; tel: (0316) 8017 4810* – in effect a supermarket for arms where local lords would equip their men. Built in the 17th century with 30,000 muskets, rifles, suits of armour and shields, it is still the world's largest armoury.

The **Mausoleum** erected next to the cathedral 1614-1638, was designed as Emperor Ferdinand II's tomb, impressive for its unabashed mannerist/baroque style. The **Dom** next door is decorated outside with the well worn **Scourges of God mural**, a reminder of the Black Death, Turkish invasion and plagues of locusts.

The **Neue Galerie,** *Sackstr. 16; tel: (0316) 829155* shows 19th- and 20th-century Austrian painting in the fine *Palais Herberstein*. The **Alte Galerie,** *Neutorg. 45; tel: (0316) 80174770,* has medieval through to baroque works. The **Kunstgewerbe,** *Neutorg. 45; tel: (0316) 80174780,* combines modern artists' works and ethnic and social history exhibits.

Slightly out of town (bus 1 from Hauptpl.) is the **Eggenbergerschloss,** *Eggenbergeralle 90; tel: (0316) 583264,* built in 1625 with, including false ones, a window for each day of the year.

⤴ SIDE TRACKS FROM GRAZ

The train to Stübing plus 20-min walk or bus from *Lendpl.* (three daily), leads to the **Stübing Open Air Museum** *tel: (03124) 54700* (April–Oct) with more than 80 historic country buildings.

Further up the line is **Bruck an der Mur**. **Station:** *tel: (03862) 515910,* **Tourist Office:** *Koloman-Wallischpl.,*

(in the middle) *tel: (03862) 54722,* Mon–Fri 0830–1800, Sat 0900–1200, which offers a town map and outline leaflets on accommodation and attractions including some historic buildings, notably the 15th-century **Kornmesserhaus** with its finely worked arcades.

Beyond is **Mürzzuschlag**. **Station:** *tel: (03852) 2530.* Rents bikes. **Tourist Office**: *Wiener Str. 4; tel: (03852) 4770,* Mon–Fri 0900–1200, 1330-1800, right out of station forking left to main square and left to *Wiener Str.,* then right. It offers free town map and information on the outlying region.

This is a sleepy little town, and the choice of accommodation and eating places is limited.

The **Brahms Museum,** *Wienerstr. 2; tel: (03852) 3434,* won European Museum of the year in 1994, backed in Sept by a **Brahms Festival,** based around the local music school. Other events take place in the **Kunsthaus,** *Wiener Str. 56, tel: (03852) 56200,* originally the ruined **Franziskanerkirche,** has been restored with glass and steel cladding. The **Heimatmuseum,** *Wiener Str. 79; tel: (03852) 3504,* looks at ski pioneers, Alpine skiing having started here. ⛷

CONEGLIANO

Tourist Office: *Viale Carducci 32, tel: (0438) 21 230.* Open Tues–Fri 0900–1200 and 1500–1800. Sun 0900–1200. Ask for details of the various wine routes in the area and, in particular, those beginning at Conegliano.

ACCOMMODATION

Accommodation is very limited in Conegliano, though the local hotels are very reasonably priced.

SIGHTSEEING

This small town sits on a hump in the midst of a sea of vineyards. It is famous for two things: Prosecco wine and a particularly important native, the painter Giambattista Cima.

Conegliano was the birthplace of an important Venetian painter, Giambattista Cima, otherwise known as **Cima da Conegliano**. The landscaped backdrops to his paintings seem faintly familiar: the cypress-crested hills, the warm light and the fortified hilltowns mirror the appearance of Conegliano itself. The only painting by the town's native master is to be found in the 14th-century **Duomo**, *Via XX Settembre*, the magnificent altarpiece, the *Madonna and Child with Saints and Angels* (1493). Cima's birthplace, the **Casa di Cima**, *Via Cima 24*, can be visited and there are prominent displays of his works there, all in reproduction.

Conegliano is a pleasant place to walk. *Via XX Settembre* is lined with Medieval and Renaissance palaces, and on the hill is the old **Castello** which, much restored, now houses the small **Museo Civico**. This houses a very eclectic display outlining the history of the locality, its art, people and key industry – **winemaking**. This area has a very gentle climate and some of the Veneto's finest wines come from the region between Lake Garda and Conegliano – around which is a DOC zone producing a delicious **Prosecco** which can be tasted in the town's bars. Conegliano has a wine-making school, and between the town and **Valdobbiadene** is the 42-km white wine route, the **Strada del Vino Bianco**.

◤ SIDE TRACK FROM CONEGLIANO

Pieve di Cadore's claim to fame is that is was the birthplace of the Venetian painter **Titian**, one of whose works, a *Madonna with Saints,* hangs in the parish church. The **Casa Natale di Tiziano**, the painter's birthplace can be visited. The 16th-century **Palazzo della Magnifica Comunita Cadorina** is the local historial and archaeological museum. The town is a pretty summer and winter **resort** (**tourist office:** *Via XX Settembre*) from which, in the region, there are endless possibilities for walking, hiking and skiing. Hanging over the town is the immense **Marmarole** peak of the jagged **Dolomites** – the mountains characterising the Cadore region which envelopes the upper valley of the River Piave. About 30 km away to the north west, **Cortina d'Ampezzo** is the most popular and sophisticated resort in the Eastern Dolomites. ◣

UDINE

Station: *Viale Europa Unita, tel: (0432) 503656.*

Tourist Office: *Piazza 1 Maggio 7, tel: (0432) 295972.* Mon–Fri 0830–1300 and 1430–1800, Sat 0830–1300.

Right at the heart of the city there is a variety of very good accommodation in all price categories.

Udine is a pretty little town through whose heart runs a series of canals. Birthplace of the Venetian painter Tiepolo, its chief attraction today is the fact that its old centre has survived largely intact.

The most famous sight in Udine is that of the town hall, the 15th-century **Palazzo Comunale** in *Piazza della Liberta*. Its pink-and-white facade is delightful, and mimics in part the Palazzo Ducale in Venice. Still in the square, the Romanesque **Duomo** (restored in the 18th century) houses altarpieces and frescos by **Tiepolo** – as does the adjacent **Oratorio della Purita** (you might have to ask the sacristan for the key). In the small **Cathedral Museum** is a fresco by Vitale da Bologna (1349 – *Funeral of St Nicholas).*

If art is what pleases you most, then you will be more than sufficiently satisfied. Udine, for a town of its size, contains more than its fair share. The **Palazzo Arcivescovile** *(Piazza Patriarcato)* contains interiors frescoed by Tiepolo while the **Galleria d'Arte Moderna** *(Piazza Diacono)* houses an important collection of 20th-century art – paintings by De Chirico, Lichtenstein, De Kooning, and so on. Even the town's **Castello**, situated on a mount approached through the **Arco Bollari** gateway designed by Palladio, houses, in its **Museo Civico,** an impressive array of ancient and modern art – including works by Bronzino and Caravaggio.

Piazza Matteotti is the scene of Udine's main daily market, held in the shadow of **San Giacomo**. This church has an outdoor altar so that the mass could be said without having to interrupt the all-important market activities.

VILLACH

See Salzburg to Klagenfurt p.272.

WÖRTHERSEE

This largest of the region's warm water lakes and warmest European Alpine lake, offers resorts easily reached by train. In winter the eastern bay is used for ice skating.

Velden am Wörthersee (Station *tel: (04274) 211539* rents bikes) is the most exclusive resort. **Tourist Office:** *Seecorso 2, tel: (04274) 2103,* walk downhill from station to main road, turning right to first major junction and Tourist Office at far side, Mon–Sat 0800–1900, Sun 0900–1200, 1500–1900, (July and Aug) Mon–Sat 0800–1200, 1400–1800 (Sept–June), offers free map and accommodation list and Tues free guided tours of the area. Walking maps are ÖS45.

The Tourist Office will check room availability though hotels with their own beaches such as **Seehotel Hubertushof**, *Europapl. 1; tel: (04274) 26760* (very expensive), or **Seehotel Engstler**, *Am Corso 21; tel: (04274) 26440* (very expensive) are booked well ahead. The **Hotel Alte Post-Wrann**, *Europapl. 4-6; tel: (04274) 2141* (moderate) is in the old post HQ. **Villa Brigitta**, *Koschatpromenade 5; tel: (04274) 2088* is easy walking distance from the station.

In a place well endowed with cafés, **Politzky**, *Am Corso 3,* is one of the best. For Carinthian food try **Schönblick**, *Augsdorferstr. 23.*

Events include a June **Carnival of Light** weekend, and **Veteran Car Rally** Sept. In July and Aug there are one or two **Concerts** a week and in Aug is the **Maria Himmelfahrt Schiff Prozession** (boat parade for the Assumption of the Virgin).

Watersports are the main draw with a season running from early May to end Oct and options including boating, windsurfing and waterskiing with regular competitions in summer. However, hanging out in cafés and smart hotels seems to be equally an attraction as is the Casino **Velden,** *Am Corso 17; tel: (04274) 2064.*

Portschach am Wörthersee (Station: *tel: (04272) 2304* rents bikes). **Tourist Office:** *Hauptstr. 153; tel: (04272) 2354,* Mon–Fri 0800–1800 (June–Sept) Mon–Fri 0800–1600 (Oct–May), walk out of the station down the hill to find on opposite left-hand corner at main road, offers a free map and accommodation listings.

Gasthof Joaninig, *Kochwirtpl. 4; tel: (04272) 2319* (moderate) a mile east of the town centre was built in 1911 as a country retreat. Alternatively there is **Gästehaus Ria**, *Koschatweg 2; tel: (04272) 2359* (moderate) or **Riviera**, *Moosburgerstr. 18; tel: (04272) 2691*. A hotel chain with property here is *BW*.

The lakeside promenade is the most obvious attraction at this resort patronised by the likes of the composer Brahms, plus the usual range of resort sports, particularly tennis with the first tournament staged here in 1896 only 10 years after the first Wimbledon.

KLAGENFURT

See Salzburg to Klagenfurt p. 272.

ST VEIT AN DER GLAN

Station: *tel: (04212) 3707*.
Tourist Office: *Hauptpl. 1; tel: (04212) 5555-13*, from the *Hbf* turning left along *Bahnhofstr.*, right at traffic lights and left into *Unterepl.* then *Hauptpl.* The Tourist Office is around halfway along on the right in the *Rathaus*, Mon–Fri 0700–1800, Sat & Sun 0900–1300, (July and Aug), Mon–Fri 0700–1700 (Sept–June). It offers a free map, restaurant and accommodation listings and guided town walks plus leaflet in English of the historical sights. Together with other local Tourist Offices it offers free hikes in the region every Wed end June–end Aug.

ACCOMMODATION AND FOOD

The best hotel is **Hotel Weisses Lamm**, *Unterepl. 4–5; tel: (04212) 2362* (moderate) or close to the station is **Gästehaus Steiner**, *Riesacherstr. 44; tel: (04212) 3206* (budget). The Tourist Office also has a list of *Privatzimmer*. Specialising in Carinthian food is **Restaurant Pukelsheim**, *Erlg. 11*, with an outdoor garden on the far side

of the *Hauptpl.* Otherwise look in the *Fussgangerzone.*

SIGHTSEEING

Capital of the region until 1518, specific sights include the 18th-century **Trinity Column** in the *Hauptpl.* marking the town's deliverance from Plague and a fountain called **Schusselbrunnel**, the bottom of which is said to come from Roman ruins. The **Rathaus** is baroque outside, charmingly 15th-century inside with an arcaded courtyard, *tel: (04212) 55513*. Tours of the great hall are offered. The **Herzogburg Museum** *tel: as for Rathaus*, originally the Duke's armoury, includes coins from the St Veit mint and a large collection of baroque shooting targets.

FRIESACH

Station: *tel: (04268) 2230*.
Tourist Office: *Hauptpl. 1; tel: (04268) 4300*, ahead out of the station and left on to the *Bahnhofstr.* curving round a supermarket, across the moat and on to the *Hauptpl.* where the Tourist Office is on the near lefthand corner, Weds 1000–1200 (Nov–mid April), Mon, Wed & Fri, 1000–1200, (mid–end April) Mon–Fri 0830–1200, 1500–1800, Sat 0830–1200, (May–early June) Mon–Fri 0830–1800, Sat 0830–1200, (mid June–early Sept) Mon–Fri 1000–1200, 1500–1800, Sat 1000–1200, (Sept) Mon–Fri 1000–1200, 1500–1700 (Oct), stocks a town map (ÖS25) with sites of interest marked plus some historical details, and a free general leaflet in English. A walking map of the area is ÖS45.

ACCOMMODATION AND FOOD

The Tourist Office will check availability but there is not a great deal on offer. Top of the range is **Landhotel**

Metniztalerhof, *Hauptpl. 11; tel: (04268) 25100* (moderate). Cheaper is **Zum Goldenen Anker**, *Bahnhofstr. 3; tel: (04268) 2313* (budget–moderate). There are also a few *Privatzimmer* outside the centre. The *Gasthofs* offer food, notably **Gasthof Weisser Wolf**, *Hauptpl. 8*, or there's *the Konditorei* next to the Tourist Office offering serious pastries. Sat mornings is a *Bauernmarkt*.

SIGHTSEEING

This is a town which feels unchanged since it grew up around the 11th-century **Schloss Petersberg**, *tel: (04268) 2600* and 13th-century **Schloss Lavant** (closed to public) which dominate it. The town is still protected by its small moat, as when Richard the Lionheart hid out here, there is still a **Working Monastery**, and there are almost no tourist shops. Schloss Petersberg contains a museum (May–Oct) containing attractive objects from a late gothic metal bowl to 17th-century jewellery. The other ruins and churches deserve a relaxed stroll. In June is the **Altstadtfest** when everyone appears in costume for three days of medieval-style entertainment and feasting. If you fancy some traditional clothes **Boos & Co.**, *Stadgrabeng. 5*, sells straight from the factory, round the back of the Dominican church.

LEOBEN

Station *tel: (03842) 42545*. Rents bikes. **Tourist Office:** *Hauptpl. 12; tel: (03842) 441018*, walk out of the station across the bridge turning right down *Franz-Josefstr.* to the *Hauptpl.* where the Tourist Office is halfway up on the right, Mon–Thurs 0700–1200, 1330–1700, Fri 0700–1300, offering a free town map and various brochures on the town and its history, plus local bus timetables. It will check room availability for same day.

ACCOMMODATION AND FOOD

The smartest option is **Kongress-Hotel**, *Hauptpl. 1; tel: (03842) 46800* (expensive). **Gasthof Altman**, *Südbahnstr. 32; tel: (03842) 42216* (budget–moderate) is alongside the railway. **Brauhaus Göss**, *Turng. 3; tel: (03842) 22100* (budget) is for those who don't want to stray too far from a supply of the local beer. *Kirchgasse,* alongside St Xavier Church, is a street with cheap pubs and restaurants.

ENTERTAINMENT AND SIGHTSEEING

The **Stadttheater**, *Karntnerstr. 224*, is the oldest working theatre in Austria, closed June–Sept when there is the **Leobener Kultursommer** of theatre, classical and rock concerts and more. Festivals include the **Gösser Church Fair** early Oct.

The town is on the so-called **Styrian Iron Road**, a traditional trade and transport route, and the *Hauptplatz* is lined with the houses of 17th-century 'Hammer Men', linked to the iron trade. The **Kirche Franz Xavier** just off the *Hauptpl.* was built during this prosperous period by Jesuits, who used a simple façade to hide a luxuriant interior.

There are also older buildings, notably the **Freimann Tower** on the *Glacis* south of the *Hauptplatz*, built 1480. The **Museum der Stadt Leoben**, *Kirchg. 6; tel: (03842) 43581* traces the town's history. The **Schwammerturm** or Mushroom Tower stands over the river and the **Kirche Maria am Waasen** has lovely 15th-century glass panels.

At the end of a 30-min walk south out of town lies the **Gösser Brewery**, *Brauhausg. 1; tel: (0842) 21566213*, where one of Austria's best-known beer is produced. Non-drinkable attractions include antique brewing machinery, and a beer museum, plus the adjacent **Stiftmuseum Göss**.

314

VIENNA (WIEN)

Of Central Europe's three greatest cities – Vienna, Prague and Budapest – the Austrian capital is the most modern, the most truly cosmopolitan, and culturally the most lively. Vienna's chief attractions are a rich store of architecture from the Gothic period to the present, numerous dramatic, musical and artistic events year round – and hundreds of atmospheric places to eat and drink.

TOURIST INFORMATION

The **Main Office** is *Kärntnerstr. 38; tel: (01) 513 88 92.* Open 0900–1900. There are also information and accommodation bureaux at **Westbahnhof**, 0615–2300; **Südbahnhof**, 0630–2200, (May–Oct) 0630–2100 (Nov–Apr); and **Schwechat Airport**, 0830–2300 (June–Sept); 0830–2200 (Oct–May). Written enquiries go to **Vienna Tourist Board**, *A-1025, Vienna, Obere Augartenstr. 140; fax: (01) 216 84 92.* The central enquiries number is *tel: (01) 211 140.* The Tourist Offices sells the **Vienna Card** (see p. 316) and has a free map plus a mass of information leaflets including *Vienna Scene*, highlighting special events. The youth information service, **Jugend Info**, has accommodation details in the *Bellaria underground passage, Dr Karl-Renner-Ring* (U2/3 *Volkstheater*) Mon–Fri 1200–1900, Sat and school holidays, 1000–1900; *tel: (01) 526 4637.*

ARRIVING AND DEPARTING

Airport
Schwechat International Airport is 19 km east of Vienna; flight information, *tel: (01) 711 10-2231/2*; tourist information, *tel: (01) 711 10-0.* Bus transfers (ÖS70) run to the **City Air Terminal** (Hilton Hotel building), *tel: (01) 5800-35404,* 24 hrs April–Oct, 0600–2430 Nov–Mar, and to *Westbahnhof,* via *Südbahnhof,* every hour 0640–2040. There is also a train service (ÖS30) to **Wien Mitte** station, *Landstr./Hauptstr.,* hourly 0730–2030. A taxi to the airport costs around ÖS450 which includes a fee for the return trip. The airport has telephone and postal facilities.

Stations
Vienna has three main stations. **Westbahnhof**, *Mariahilferstr./Europapl., tel: (1) 58 00-310 60,* serves Austrian destinations west, Germany, Switzerland and Hungary. **Südbahnhof**, *Wiener Gürtel/Arsenalstr.; tel: (01) 5800-310 50,* serves the south including Italy, former Yugoslavia, plus the Czech Republic and Hungary. **Franz-Josefs-Bahnhof,** *Julius-Tandler-Pl.; tel: (01) 5800-310 20,* serves the north plus Berlin and the Czech Republic. All three are 3–4 km outside the *Ringstr.* and are connected to the centre by metro or tram.

Travellers should check carefully to see which station their train uses. For general rail information, *tel: (01) 17 17*; for taped information on routes west and to Central Europe, *tel: (01) 1552*; for the south and south-east Europe, *tel: (01) 1553.*

You can buy all Austrian rail tickets centrally at branches of the **Österreiches Verkhersbüro** travel agency at the same price as at stations. Two central branches are *Friedrichstr. 7; tel: (01) 588 00 0,* and

315

Opernring 3–5; tel: (01) 588 62 8 opposite the opera house.

GETTING AROUND

The old city (*Innenstadt*) was enclosed by bastions until 1857 and is now encircled by the famous *Ringstrasse*. This makes sightseeing on foot relatively painless.

The tourist office offers a good free map with pictorial representation of the main sights. If you need a map with an index the Falk one is useful.

Tickets

Public transport is efficient, with U-Bahn, trams and buses all using the same tickets, on sale from all *Tabak/Trafik* (tobacconists and newsagents). Single tickets, sold in blocks of 5, and valid for one journey, are the most expensive option at ÖS17 each (ÖS20 on board). The 24-hr **Tageskarte Wien** is ÖS50 and the 72-hr **excursion ticket** ÖS130, an eight-day **Umwelt Streifnetzkarte** – a strip ticket punched each day used, ÖS265. A tourist option is the **Vienna Card** (ÖS180), available in hotels and Tourist Offices, valid for 72 hours' transport plus reduced entry to popular tourist sights, shopping discounts and more.

You must validate all tickets in the automatic puncher on the bus or tram or at the entrance to the U-Bahn. The fine for not doing so is ÖS520.

U-Bahn and Trams

The marvellously clean and modern **U-Bahn** (underground railway) was built in the 1960s and has been continuously extended ever since. It replaced, but in some areas still runs in tandem with, trams. There are currently five lines, operating 0500–2400. Vienna's **trams** run on 33 radial routes plus in both directions round the *Ringstr.*, 0500–2400. **Buses** fill gaps

not covered by trams during roughly the same hours, although there are some special all-night services on main routes (supplement payable), leaving *Schwedenpl.* on the canal edge of district 1.

A map of the transport network is included on the back of the free city map. **Information** on public transport is available at the offices in the underground stations of *Stephanspl., Karlspl. and Westbahnhof* 0630–1830 Mon–Fri, 0830–1600 Sat and Sun.

Taxis and Cycles

Taxis are not cheap, but extremely efficient and you may have to use them to get home late at night, *tel: (01) 40 100, (01) 31 300, (01) 60 160, (01) 81 400, (01) 91 091.* (They should arrive within 5 mins, almost anywhere in the city). Alternatively you can hail cabs with the *frei* sign lit or use one of the strategically placed ranks.

There are 500 km of **cycle** paths around Vienna and the Tourist Office lists bike-friendly accommodation. Train travellers get the best hire deals at the Westbahnhof 0400–2400, Wien Nord 0630–1930 and Südbahnhof 0600–2200. Hire is ÖS50 per day on production of a same-day ticket, otherwise ÖS90. For the cost of a half-price ticket, bikes are allowed on the U-Bahn (except U6) 0900–1500 and after 1830 Mon–Fri, after 0900 Sat and all day Sun. **Vienna Bike**, *Wasag. 28/2/5; tel: (01) 319 12 58*, offers daily tours by bike ÖS200 for two to three hours. Book two days ahead. Bike hire for the tour is ÖS60.

Rollerblades can be hired at **Schuh Ski** on *Donauinsel* (U1 *Donauinsel/Reichsbrücke)* ÖS70 per hour, ÖS350 a day. Inge Aupor-Labi is a licensed guide who organises rollerblade tours; *tel: (01) 319 12 58.*

A 20-min tour by horse-drawn **Fiaker**

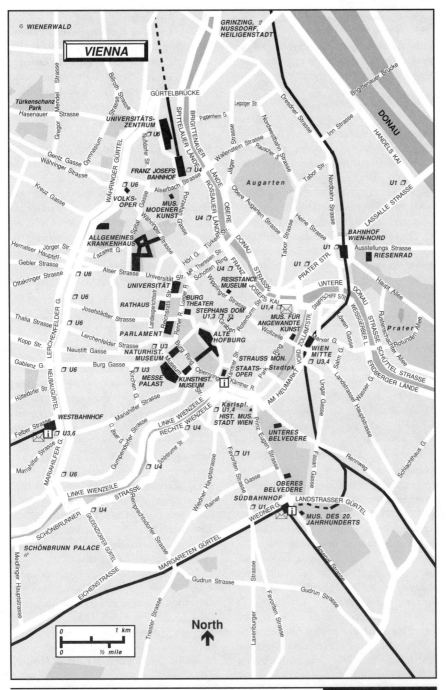

is ÖS400, 40 mins ÖS800 and per hour ÖS1000 plus 10% service tax. You will find fiakers next to Stephansdom, *Heldenpl.* in the Hofburg, and the Albertina behind the Opera.

STAYING IN VIENNA

Accommodation

There are lots of options but also lots of takers, so book well ahead May–Oct. However you might get a discount in midwinter. The Vienna Tourist Board issues lists of hotels, pensions and summer *saisonhotels* categorised according to quality. Don't expect much below ÖS500 per person a night. The Board also offers a leaflet on youth hostels and campsites, most of which only open in summer. Major hotel groups represented in Vienna include *BW, GT, Hd, Hn, Ib, IC, Ma, Mc, Nv, RC, Rd, Rn, Rk, SA, Sc, Sf, Sn, Tp.*

At the top of the hotel options are **Hotel Bristol**, *Kärtner-Ring, 1; tel: (01) 515 16* (very expensive) and **Hotel Imperial**, *Kärtner-Ring, 16; tel: (01) 50 110 0.* The **K&K Palais Hotel,** *Rudolfspl. 11; tel: (01) 533 13 53* (expensive), near the river, is the former home of the mistress of Emperor Franz Josef, and where they conducted their affair. **Hotel Kummer**, *Mariahilferstr. 71A; tel: (01) 588 95* (expensive), is near the *Westbahnhof.* **Pension Elite**, *Wipplingerstr. 32; tel: (01) 533 25 18 0* (moderate), is family-run and central near the university and cathedral. **Pension Sacher,** *Rotenturmstr. 1; tel: (01) 533 32 38* (moderate) on a central 7th floor right next to the cathedral, sees plenty of return business. **Hotel Goldene Spinne**, *Linke Bahng. 1A; tel: (01) 7124486* (budget) is out of the immediate centre but close to the City Air Terminal.

There are nine hostels, but the most central are the **HI: Jugendherberge Wien**, *Myrtheng. 7/Neustiftg. 85; tel: (01) 523 63160;* and **Kolpingfamilie Wien-Meidling**, *Bendlg. 10; tel: (01) 8135487,* or there's the smaller **Hostel Zöhrer,** *Skodag. 26; tel: (01) 430730.* Just across the Danube Canal is **Aktive Camping**, *Neue Donau am Kleehaüfel; tel: (01) 2209310,* mid May–mid-Sept.

Eating and Drinking

Vienna not only gave the world the *Wiener Schnitzel* and *Sachertorte*, but is *the* place to eat food from the former Austro-Hungarian empire. Typically Viennese are the moderately priced *Beis* or *Kellern*, atmospheric wine-bar/restaurants in baroque cellars, and *Konditoreien* – coffee houses which generally serve hot food as well as their pastry specialities and, like Viennese cafés, where people sit alone reading newspapers, are an institution for people watching.

Some of the best cafés, where are **Café Central**, *corner Herreng. and Stauchg.* in Palais Ferstel, a recently restored 19th-century Gothic institution; **Café Hawelka,** *Dorotheerg. 6,* which preserves its identity as an intellectual hang-out; **Café Sperl,** *Gumpendorfstr. 11,* a traditional coffeehouse dating back to 1880; and **Café Museum**, *Friedrichstr. 6,* a meeting place for everyone from lawyers to students. **Café Drechsler,** *Linke Wienzeile 22,* which opens at 0400, is the place to round off a late night. **Café Landtmann**, *Dr-Karl-Lueger-Ring 14,* near the *Burgtheater,* was Freud's favourite, and is still a traditional grand establishment.

Best *Konditoreien* include **Oberlaaer**, *Neuer Markt 15,* and *Favoritenstr. 90;* **Gerstner,** *Kärntnerstr. 11-15,* plus a café in the Kunsthistorisches Museum with evening buffet Thurs 1830–2100 when the museum opens late. If you really want to splash out, **Demel's Coffee House,**

Kohlmarkt 14, has achieved legendary status for both decor and baking.

Konditorei are not cheap at around ÖS60–120 for anything substantial. The university area (U2 or 4 near *Schottentor*) is better for cheap eats than the inner district with the following around ÖS200: **Fischerbrau,** *Billrothstr. 17,* offering homebrew and jazz; **D'Landsknecht,** *Porzellang. 13,* a plain bistro; or **Schweizerhaus,** *Strasse des 1 Mai,* a popular *biergarten.*

Best value for money though are the student canteens, open to non-students. Try the **New University,** *Universitätsstr. 7,* 0800–1700; **Academy of Applied Arts,** *Oskar Kokoschkapl. 2,* 0900–1800; or **Academy of Fine Arts,** *Schillerpl. 3,* 0830–1700.

In the centre with meals around ÖS300–500 are **Bukarest,** *Braunerstr. 7,* offering Balkan and Romanian food, **Gösser Bierklinik,** *Steindlg. 4,* offering beer and appropriately solid food, **Dubrovnik,** *Am Neumarkt, 5,* with a menu combining Croat, Balkan and Viennese cooking; and the **Glacisbeisl,** *Messepalast,* a first-floor establishment hidden in the trade fair centre off the *Ring* with a large outdoor terrace. **Alte Backstube,** *Langeg. 34,* offers Viennese and Hungarian food in an 18th-century bakery; **Figlmüller,** *Wollzelle 5,* is a *beisl* offering giant *Wiener Schnitzel* (and doggy bags) in a location patronised by the likes of Mozart.

Eating out in style costs anything from ÖS700 upwards. Options include **Zu Den Drei Husaren,** *Weihburgg. 4,* near *St Stephansdom,* with Viennese international food and gypsy music; and **Huswirth,** *Otto-Bauerg. 20,* with wood panelled interiors and gardens for summer. **Sachers,** *Philharmonikerstr. 4,* specialises in *Tafelspitz* and *rösti* potatoes – and,

naturally, sinfully calorific *Sachertorte.* However, it is both exceedingly expensive (ÖS1000) and very touristy.

In delightful villages such as **Grinzing, Nussdorf, Sievering, Neustift am Walde,** and **Stammersdorf,** are the famous *Heurigen* taverns where young local wine is served with traditional food, (around ÖS250 depending on the establishment) mid-afternoon–midnight.

Grinzing is the most touristy, Stammersdorf the cheapest. Options include **Altes Presshaus,** *Cobenzlg. 15, Grinzing,* the oldest in Grinzing, full of antique furniture. Beethoven lived in *Mayer, Am Pfarrpl. 2, Heiligenstadt* where the rose garden offers outdoor eating. One of the best known *Heurigen* is **Alter Klosterkeller im Passauerhof,** *Cobenzlg. 9, Grinzing,* with a menu dating to the last century and foundations to the 12th. **Buschenschank Helm,** *Stammersdorferstr. 21,* offers drier wine than average.

For the cheapest eating and fast food, try the counters in butchers' shops, *Würstelstände* (hot dog stalls), sandwich bars (the cognoscenti go to **Trzesniewski,** *Dorotheerg. 1*), and the fast food stalls at the *Naschmarkt* open air fruit and vegetable market *Linke/Rechte Wienzeile* (*Schwarzenbergplatz, Schottentor*).

Communications

The **Central Post Office** and poste restante is at *Fleischmarkt 19* (open 24 hrs). There are 24-hr post offices at Westbahnhof, Franz-Josefs-Bahnhof and Südbahnhof. Some phones in the centre (e.g. *Wallnerstr.* and *Goldschmiedg.*) accept credit cards and have instructions in English.

To phone Vienna from abroad: *tel: 43 (Austria) + 1 (Vienna) +* number; to phone Vienna from elsewhere in Austria generally: *tel: 01 + number;* however, older codes may apply eg 0222.

Money

Banks open Mon–Fri, 0800–1500 (–1730 Thurs in the centre); branch offices close for lunch, 1230–1330. There are exchange bureaux at Westbahnhof 0700–2200 and Südbahnhof 0630–2200 (May–Oct), 0630–2100 (Nov–Apr); the airport arrivals 0830–2330, departures 0600–2030, and the city air terminal Mon–Fri 0900–1900, Sat 0900–1800, Sun 0930–1630.

Credit cards, Eurocheques and travellers' cheques are all widely accepted. Foreign currency can also be exchanged into schillings at the *Fleischmarkt 9* post office. There are cash change machines at *Kärntnerstr. 7* and *Michaelerpl./Loos Haus.*

Embassies and Consulates

Australia: *Mattiellistr. 2-4; tel: (01) 512 85 800.*
Canada: *Laurenzerberg 1; tel: (01) 531 38 30 00.*
Republic of Ireland: *Landstr./Hauptstr. 2; tel: (01) 715 4246.*
New Zealand: *Sprinsiedelg. 28; tel: (01) 318 85 05.*
South Africa: *Sandg. 33; tel: (01) 32 64 93.*
UK: *Jauresg. 12: tel: (01) 713 15 75.*
USA: *Botzmanng. 16; tel: (01) 313 39.*

320

ENTERTAINMENT

Programm, an indispensable monthly listing of all entertainment but cinemas, is free from Tourist Information Offices. Cinemas (including those showing films in English) are listed in newspapers. Youth event and discount tickets are available from Jugend-Info (see under Tourist Information p. 315).

Trendy nightlife and focuses on the 'Bermuda Triangle', an area of lively bars, discos and pubs close to *Schwedenpl.*, but Vienna is better known as one of the world's great centres of classical music with everything from chamber concerts to grand opera on offer. Specific events include the May and June **Vienna Festival** of plays, concerts, opera and exhibition, the **Vienna Summer of Music** in July and Aug, **dance festivals** in Feb and July/Aug, and **Modern Vienna** in Nov and Dec of little performed classic modern works.

The **Staatsoper**, considered one of the world's leading opera houses, stages productions Sept–June. The **Volksoper** offers operettas and musicals. To avoid high agency commissions apply for tickets for both the Staatsoper and Volksoper in writing to **Österreichischer Bundestheaterverband/Bestellbüro**, *Hanuschg. 3, A-1010 Vienna; fax: (01) 514 44 ext 2969* (direct dial) at least three weeks ahead. Credit card sales, *tel: (01) 513 1 513*, are only offered seven days in advance, and standing room tickets sold only before the performance (be prepared to queue).

Mozart operas are performed at the **Marionette Theatre** at the *Schönbrunn*, though in July and Aug there are real opera performances at the palace as well. A cheaper substitute July and Aug is the free **Opera Film Festival** in the *Rathausplatz.*

The famous **Vienna Boys' Choir** performs at the *Hofburg Chapel* Sun 0915, Sept–Jun, ÖS60–250, standing room free. Write to *Hofmusik Kapelle, Hofburg, A-1010, Vienna,* and collect and pay for tickets on the Sun 0830–0900. The choir also performs Fri 1530, May, June, Sept and Oct at the **Konzerthaus**, ÖS370/470. For tickets contact **Reisebüro Mondial**, *Faulmanng. 4 A-1040 Vienna; fax: (01) 587 12 68*, well ahead.

Those visiting Nov–Mar might like to try one of the famous **Vienna Balls** The Tourist Office should have a programme by late autumn.

SHOPPING

Kärntnerstr. is Vienna's busiest shopping street and together with **Graben** the place to promenade. But the smartest addresses are now smaller parallel streets like *Kohlmarkt*. *Mariahilferstr.* is home to the large department stores. Ornamental objects with an Austrian flavour are found at **Österreichische Werkstätten,** *Kärntnerst. 26; tel: (01) 512 24 18.* A local speciality is **Augarten porcelain,** on sale at the factory in *Obere Augartenstr., tel: (01) 211 24,* 0900–1800 Mon–Fri with factory visits 0930, or more conveniently at *Stock im Eisenpl. 3,* near the Dom. Austrian-made **Riedal glasses** designed by a scientist to maximise the flavours of wines and spirits, can be found at **Rasper & Zöne,** *Graben 15,* where they will pack for transport. Alternatively buy duty free at the airport. A good outlet for **Loden,** the heavy Austrian winter coats, is **Loden Plankel,** *Michaelerpl. 6.* International fine art dealing is big business here but you might find something more affordable at the **Art and Antique market,** *Am Hofplatz,* Fri and Sat 1000–1900, Mar to Christmas. For **original artwork and prints** try the **Kunstverlag Wolfrum,** *Augustinerstr. 10.* **Arcardia Opera Shop**, *Wiener Staatsoper, Kärntnerstr. 40,* is considered one of the best classical record stores in the country and also stocks musical souvenirs (busts of Beethoven and the like).

SIGHTSEEING

The Centre

There are tours of the city in a 1929 tram daily May–Oct from *Karlspl.* Weds, Sats and Suns 1330, and Suns 1000. If you want special insights into Vienna, the Tourist Office runs themed walking tours (ÖS108), for example of Jewish Vienna. It's quite easy to see the basics yourself however, starting with the focal point of Vienna, the Romanesque and Gothic **Stephansdom** (St Stephen's Cathedral; U1: *Stephanspl.*) *tel: (01) 515 52 526,* with its jazzy green and gold roof. The loveliest parts are the Gothic **Albertine Choir** (1340) and the magnificent 14th-century 136.7 m South Tower (the '*Steffl*' – Steve – to locals), with 344 steps. Inside the cathedral, highlights include the pulpit (1510) and organ loft by Anton Pilgrim; a Gothic wing altar in the North Apse and the fabulous Renaissance tomb of Friedrich III in the South Apse. The embalmed entrails of Habsburg rulers repose in the Ducal Crypt (in the catacombs).

The **Hofburg** is the great Habsburg residence (*Michaelerpl. 1; tel: (01) 587 55 54*) occupying a vast area of central Vienna with 18 wings, 54 stairways and 2600 rooms. The main sights are the **Burgkapelle,** home of the Vienna Boys' Choir; the **Schatzkammer** (Treasury), containing the crown of the Holy Roman Empire; the **Imperial Apartments,** preserved as the penultimate emperor, Franz Josef, had them; and the richly baroque **National Library,** containing one of the world's best collections of manuscripts.

Also housed in the Hofburg is the **Winter Riding School**, where the famous *Lippizaner* horses perform except July and Aug. Tickets for the main performance should be booked well ahead (ÖS220 plus around 25% commission for the agency – eg *Amex, Kärntnerstr. 21-3; fax: (01) 515 4070).* If you can't get tickets queue at the door of the **Redoute**, *Josefsplatz,* to see 'morning training' Tues–Sat 1000–1200.

Galleries and Museums

Vienna's major museum is the **Kunsthistorisches Museum** (Museum of Art History), *Burgring 5; tel: (01) 54 770* (trams 1 and 2), based on the collection of the Habsburgs. The main museum contains classical and Egyptian antiquities, Palaeo-Christian art, decorative art and, above all, a picture gallery with a superb collection of Breughels as well as masterpieces by Rembrandt and Velazquez. Branches include the **Neue Burg** (part of the Hofburg) where musical instruments and armour are displayed plus the Ephesos Museum of classical material; and the **Palace of Schönbrunn** (coaches and carriages). The superb 18th-century baroque **Belvedere Palace**, *Prinz-Eugenstr. 27; tel: (01) 79 80 700* (tram D), built for Prince Eugene of Savoy, has two galleries and delightful gardens. The **Österreichische Galerie** (Austrian Gallery), *Oberes* (Upper) *Belvedere*, has important works by artists of the Biedermeier period (1814–1848), the Vienna Secession and Austrian Expressionism. The **Baroque Museum**, *Unteres* (Lower) *Belvedere*, at the *Rennweg* end of the park, contains works by leading baroque artists including Georg Raphael Donner. **Gemäldegalerie Akademie der Bildenden Künste** (Academy of Fine Arts), *Schillerpl. 2; tel: (01) 58 816* (U 1/2/4 *Karlspl.*), includes generous quantities of Flemish works by the likes of Bosch, Van Dyck and Rembrandt.

The **Museum für Angewandte Kunst** (Museum of Applied Art), *Stubenring 5; tel: (01) 711 36 0* (trams 1 and 2), is a recently up-dated cornucopia of Oriental, European and Austrian artefacts including pieces by Charles Rennie Mackintosh and early 20th-century Viennese design. The elegant café naturally draws designers and architects. Modern art enthusiasts will enjoy the **Museum des 20 Jahrhunderts** (Museum of the 20th Century), *Schweizer*

Garten; tel: (01) 78 25 50 (tram D) and the **Museum Moderner Kunst im Palas Liechstenstein** (Museum of Modern Art), *Fürsteng. 1; tel: (01) 317 69 00* (tram D), housed in a fine baroque building, with works by Austrian Expressionists and other leading European 20th-century artists such as Léger, Ernst and Magritte. The **Albertina**, *Augustinerstr.; tel: (01) 534 83* (U1/2/4 *Karlspl./Oper*), houses the world's greatest collection of drawings and prints. The delightful **Uhrenmuseum** (Clock Museum), *Schulhof 2;* tel: (01) 533 22 65 (U-Bahn: *Schottentor*) features 900 clocks of every conceivable type.

Rather different is the **Museum of Natural History,** *Burgring 7; tel: (01) 521 77 0 (U2/3* Volkstheater, trams 1/2) with the world's largest insect collection and 3 million fossils, plus the extremely rotund Stone Age *Venus of Willendorf* statue. If there are children in the party you could consider the **Puppen und Spielzeug Museum** (Doll and Toy Museum) *Schulhof 4, tel: (01) 535 68 60*, with dolls from the 1740s to 1930s, many from Germany.

Churches

Vienna abounds with intriguing churches. In the Gothic **Augustinerkirche**, *Augustinerstr. 3* (U-Bahn: *Karlspl./Oper,* trams 1, 2), the hearts of the Habsburgs are kept in silver urns. The **Kapuzinerkirche,** *Neuer Markt* (U-Bahn: *Karlspl./Oper*), is above the Capuchin crypt where Habsburg bodies were laid to rest in impressive baroque tombs. Other examples of Viennese Gothic include the **Church of Maria am Gestade,** *Am Gestade* (trams 1 and 2), the **Minoritenkirche,** *Minoritenpl. 2A*, and the **Michaelerkirche,** *Michaelerpl.* (both U3 *Herreng.*). There are also two superb baroque churches: the 1708 **Peterskirche**, *Peterspl.* (U2/3 *Stephanspl.*), and the 1713 **Karlskirche**, *Karlspl.* (U1/2/4 *Karlspl./Oper*, trams 1 and 2), the masterpiece of baroque experts von Erlach father and son, fronted by two vast Roman-style columns, with a great copper dome.

The **Museum im Schottenstift**, *Freyung 6; tel: (01) 534 98 600* (U2 *Schottentor*, U3 *Herreng.*, trams D/1/2) is in an abbey, founded in 1155 for the Irish, and has Gothic and baroque masterpieces.

Other Sights

The fine baroque former **Rathaus** *Wipplingerstr. 8* (trams 1 and 2) now holds the **Museum of the Austrian Resistance Movement** (against Nazism). On the curious art nouveau **Anker Clock**, *Hoher Markt 10/11* (U1/4 *Schwedenpl.*), figures from Austrian history move across the clock-face and parade together at 1200. For an idea of the architectural splendours of the **Ringstrasse** era, take trams 1 or 2 around the *Ring*, passing the neo-Gothic **Rathaus** (City Hall), the **Burgtheater**, the **Parliament** and the **Opera**. In deliberate contrast was Joseph Olbrich's exhibition hall for the painters of the **Viennese Secession**, *Friedrichstr. 12; tel: (01) 587 5307*, with plain cream walls and gold dome. Close by is the interesting **Historisches Museum der Stadt Wien** (Historical Museum of Vienna), *Karlspl. 4; tel: (01) 505 87 47*, opposite the famous **Musikverein** concert hall.

The **Pasqualati House**, *Mölker Bastei 8* (trams 1/2) is one of innumerable lodgings used by Beethoven, who also has a museum at the **Heiligenstadt Testament Haus**, *Probusg. 6; tel: (01) 37 54 08* (buses 37A/38A) in *Heiligenstadt*. Mozart's lodging, the so-called **Figaro House**, *Domg. 5; tel: (01) 513 62 94* (U1/3 *Stephanspl.*) has memorial rooms. The **Schubert Museum** is at the composer's birthplace, *Nussdorfterstr.; 54 tel:*

(01) 345 99 24 (trams 37/38). **Haydns Wohnhaus**, *Haydng. 19, tel: (01) 596 1307*, is where the composer taught Beethoven and composed his later oratorios.

The Sigmund **Freud Museum**, *Bergg. 19; tel: (01) 319 15 96*, in the psychoanalyst's old consulting rooms, gives some feeling of his work and its setting. An architecture leaflet from the tourist office highlights 20th-century buildings of interest. These range from the 1930s, with the 1 km long **Karl Marx public housing estate**, to the ecological and humanist playground of the **Hundertwasserhaus** (*Loweng./Kegelg.*) almost anarchic in its combination of colours and shapes. There's a matching small shopping centre beside it and Hundertwasser's **Kunst-HausWien**, *Untere Weissgerberstr. 13; tel: (01) 712 04 91* (trams N and O) is a nearby art museum in similar style.

OUT OF TOWN

Schloss Schönbrunn, *Schönbrunner Schlosstr. 13; tel: (01) 811 13 238* (U4 *Schönbrunn*, tram 58 from *Burgring*), is a grandiose rococo palace, the imperial summer home originally designed to leave Versailles looking silly, though the cost curtailed plans. There are tours of some of the 1500 rooms, including the frescoed **Great Gallery** and **Hall of Mirrors**

Prices in Vienna

A coffee in a coffee house ÖS15–40
A pastry in a coffee house ÖS15–50
A Coke in a café ÖS17–30
A glass of wine ÖS20–35
A sandwich ÖS20–50
A roll of 36-exposure film ÖS50–90
A half litre of beer ÖS30–45
A local phone call ÖS0.7 a minute

---

where Mozart played aged six. Around it is a superb park with **Butterfly House** and the oldest **Zoo** in the world.

The legendary **Prater** (U1 *Praterstern* trams O/5/21) is a vast park with a fun-fair and famous big wheel, originally opened to the public by Emperor Joseph II in 1766. Take care there after dark.

The **Wienerwald** (Vienna Woods) is a few thousand acres of wooded hills (tram 1 to *Schottentor* tram 38 to *Grinzing* and bus to *Kahlenberg*). **Kahlenberg** is the north-easternmost spur of the Alps and from there you can see to Hungary and Slovakia on a clear day.

**SIDE TRACKS
FROM VIENNA**

From Vienna Oper, **Badenerbahn** trams take an hour to reach **Baden bei Wien**. Local services from Südbahnhof take just 34 mins and continue to **Wiener Neustadt** (another 25 mins).

BADEN BEI WIEN

Station: (02252) 89362. Tourist Office: *Brusattipl. 3; tel: (02252) 4453159*, (broadly ahead and left from station) Mon–Sat 0900–1230, 1400–1800, Sun 0900–1230 (Easter–Nov), Mon–Fri 0900–1230, 1400–1700, (Nov–Easter), free town maps, Guest Card (GC) gives free entrance to trotting races, promenade concerts and guided walking tours plus reductions to baths and other attractions.

The smartest spot to stay is the **Grand Hotel Sauerhof zu Rauhenstein**, *Weilburgstr. 11; tel: (02252) 41251* (very expensive) south of the river in its own park. Visitors have included Beethoven and Salieri. Cheaper options, including *Privat-zimmer,* are listed by the Tourist Office. **Restaurant Ackerl**, *Gutenbrunnstr. 19,*

is an old-fashioned establishment serving coffee and meals. The Tourist Office offers **free guided tours** Mon and Thurs, May–Oct. The 33–36°C **springs** here were used by the Romans and they became fashionable again in the 19th century with the arrival of Peter the Great of Russia. Baden became the summer residence of the Habsburg Court and, in 1914–18, HQ of the Austro-Hungarian forces. Today the waters still draw crowds of frost tops who enjoy the **Kurpark** and bathing establishments, including the **Mineral-schwimmschule,** opened in 1847.

For culture there is the **Beethoven-haus,** *Rathausg. 10; tel: (02252) 86800,* commemorating the summers the composer spent here.

The **Doll and Toy Museum**, *Erzherzog-Rainer-Ring 23, tel: (02252) 41020* has items dating back to 1820 in a typical country villa of 1838.

WIENER NEUSTADT

Station: *tel: (02622) 23561.* **Tourist Office:** *Hauptpl. 3; tel: (02622) 23531 468,* (left and right up *Herzog Leopoldstr.* to the square), Mon–Fri, 0800–1200, 1300–1700, Sat 0800–1200. It has accommodation listings.

Despite the name, the town was founded in 1194 but over-run by Hungarians and destroyed by an 18th-century earthquake. Later Allied bombing was prompted by the presence of the **Military Academy** where Desert Fox Rommel was the first Nazi commandant. The Academy can be seen from outside in *Burgpl.* Other sights include **St Georgekirche**, *Burgpl. 1,* with remnants of early frescos, and the **Recturm**, *Babenberger-Ring* – a Gothic tower said to have been built with the ransom paid for Richard Lionheart.

ZURICH

Zurich, Switzerland's largest city, has something of a staid reputation. Perhaps it is because it is better known as Switzerland's business centre – the home of most banks, the world centre for gold trading and also the fourth most important stock exchange in the world. It also has a reputation for being expensive, but shop around and you'll find it no dearer than any of the country's major cities. In fact Zurich is scenically located at the northern tip of Lake Zurich (Zürichsee) and its waterside pleasures, its first-class museums and galleries, its medieval old town and a throbbing nightlife quarter all make it a place to enjoy life, not just do business.

TOURIST INFORMATION

Tourist Office: *Bahnhofpl. 15; tel: 211 40 00.* Daily 0830–2030/2130 (closes 1 hr earlier in winter). There is also an office at the airport, *terminal B; tel: 86 40 81.* Open daily 1000–1900.

ARRIVING AND DEPARTING

Airport: Zürich-Kloten airport is 11 km north of the centre and boasts all international airport facilities. Trains run every 10–15 mins and take just 10 mins to HB.
    Stations: Zurich Hauptbahnhof (HB); *tel: 211 50 10,* is north of the centre, on the west side of the River Limmat.

GETTING AROUND

Although it is Switzerland's largest city,

Zurich is quite small by European standards and easy to explore on foot. From the station *Bahnhofstr.* stretches for 1.4 km to the lake, running parallel to the River Limmat. The old town straddles the river with the majority of sights very close to the river bank. There is little of sightseeing interest west of *Bahnhofstr.* or east of *Hirschen Graben* which effectively encloses the old town. The tourist office sell a good street map for SFr.1.
    The public transport company is **VBZ Züri-Linie.** All buses and trams leave the terminal by HB every 12 mins (6 mins in peak time) 0530–2400. VBZ issue free route plans and tickets are available from machines at every stop.
    A scheduled boat service, the **Limmatschiffahrt,** runs along the river and out onto the lake. It goes from the Landesmuseum (behind HB) to Zürichhorn, on the east lake shore (Apr–Oct afternoons only). Swiss Pass is valid.
    The **S-Bahn** is Zurich's suburban railway network which actually stretches as far afield as Stein-am-Rhein. It meshes seamlessly into the national rail system.

325

STAYING IN ZURICH

Accommodation
Although many of Zurich's hotels are very expensive there's a reasonable choice of accommodation, so you have a good chance of finding something affordable.
    Hotel chains with property in the city include: *BW, Ch, EG, FE, Hn, IE, Mz, MO, Mv, Nv, Rn, RS, RC, Rn, Sh, Sh, SL, Sf, Sn, Sw, Tp, WS.*

Martahaus, *Zähringerstr. 36; tel: 251 45 50*, is a private hostel just off busy *Niederdorfstr.* Nearby, **The City Back-packer/Hotel Biber**, *Niederdorfstr. 5; tel: 251 90 15*, also offers dormitories and private rooms. There is plenty of other cheap accommodation in this area but it's likely to be noisy and some of the premises may not be entirely reputable. Slightly more upmarket in this same area are the **Leonhard**, *Limmatquai 136; tel: 251 30 80*, and the **Alexander Guesthouse**, *Niederdorfst.40; tel: 251 82 03*. Both are officially listed as two-star bed and breakfast hotels. Another fairly central option, though for men only, is the **Vereinshaus Glockenhof**, *Sihlstr. 33; tel: 221 36 73*, a YMCA establishment just 5-min. walk from the HB and the old town. **HI:** *Mutschellenstr. 114; tel: 482 35 44*, south of Zurich in Wollishofen (tram nos. 7/10: *Morgental*, then 15-mins walk). **Campsite:** *Seestr. 559, Wollishofen; tel: 482 16 12* (bus nos. 61/65 from *Bürklipl.*).

Eating and Drinking

You can sample the cooking of most of the world in Zurich, including Egyptian, Indonesian, Caribbean, Korean, Turkish and Hungarian restaurants. This type of restaurant, however, is mostly for the international business community, so prices are generally high.

The tourist office issue a restaurant listing guide called *Zürcher Gastro-Spezialitäten Führer* which, in spite of its grand name, includes many affordable places and indicates prices. There are many fast-food places and conventional restaurants around the huge station complex, including the **Rösti Bar**, *tel: 211 15 10*, which serves up to 18 different versions of the ubiquitous national potato-and-onion dish. A two-min walk away is the **Walliser Kanne**, *Lintheschergasse 21* (parallel to *Bahnhofstr.*); *tel: 211 31 33*, where fondues and Valaisian specialities are served in a dark woody setting. The largest selection of eating places is on *Niederdorfstr.*, a lively music-filled area with plenty of outdoor seating which is perfect for watching Zurich's young trendies. Fierce competition keeps prices at a reasonable level. One of the best value establishments along here for hearty local food (or jut a drink) is the **Rheinfelder Bierhalle**, at *no. 76; tel: 251 54 64*. Just off this street is the acclaimed **Le Dézaley**, *Römergasse 7; tel: 251 61 29*, more expensive but excellent for fondues. Another place where it's worth spending a little more is the **Kunsthaus Restaurant**, beside the Kunsthaus; *tel: 251 74 77*. Lunchtime is the best bet here, with Bohemian types taking a break from the Hodlers and the Picassos.

The best vegetarian food in town is claimed by **Hiltl Vegi**, *Sihlstr. 28; tel: 221 38 71*, which is also the oldest vegetarian restaurant in the country, established in 1898. It's not cheap however – the best value is the all-you-can-eat Indian buffet in the evenings. If you are a student (or look as though you are one), try one of the university *mensas* (refectories) on *Rämistr.* (tram no. 6 from *Bahnhofpl.* to *ETH Zentrum*). For meals on wheels, combining sightseeing and dining, board the **ChuChiChäschtli** tram which serves typical Swiss dishes on the move. It runs from May to Oct and covers a loop around both banks of the Limmat, starting at *Bellevuepl.*, which is where you should board if you wish to dine. This tram is part of the regular service network however, so you may just use it as a sightseeing vehicle – if there is room. Dining on the move is also offered on the lake where you can enjoy a 'Fondue party trip'; *tel: 482 10 33*, or enquire at the *Bürklipl.* office.

If you want to push the boat out in a

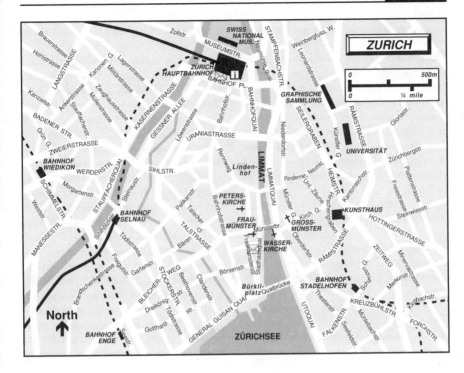

financial sense and try the very best of Zurich's own cooking, with many local speciality dishes on offer, dine at **Züri-Stube**, *Hotel Tiefenau, Steinwiesstr. 8; tel: 251 24 09* (tram nos. 3,5,8,9). In summer book a table in the garden.

For a picnic with a view try the **Lindenhof** (see Sightseeing) or, for sandwiches with culture, go to the park behind the Landesmuseum or the **Park Rietberg**.

The local speciality is veal in cream sauce, *kalbgeschnetzeltes*, though you may also find *schweingeschnetzeltes,* which is the cheaper pork version. Fish from the lake can be sampled at the two lakeside restaurants at Zürichhorn.

Communications

The main post office is the **Sihlpost**, *Kasernenstr. 95/7.* Open Mon–Fri 0630–2230, Sat 0630–2000, Sun 1100–2230.

There is a post office at HB, open Mon–Fri 0730–1830, Sat 0730–1100. The local area telephone code for Zurich is *01.*

Consulates

UK: *Dufourstr. 24; tel: 261 15 20.*
USA: *Zollikerstr. 141; tel:422 25 66.*

ENTERTAINMENT AND EVENTS

There is no shortage of bars on and around **Niederdorfstr.** There's also live music, street performers and street walkers – this is also the centre of Zurich's red-light zone (note the amazing and amusing window display in the **Condomerie** shop halfway along); stick to the main streets, however, and you will find this a safe area. In between the dodgy discos and flashy cocktail bars are a number of jazz venues. These really buzz each Nov during the city's acclaimed **International Jazz Festival**.

Zurich is also a centre for highbrow nightlife. The landmark **Opera House** on the east shore of the lake is home to an internationally acclaimed opera company, while world-class concerts are performed at the **Tonhalle** Concert Hall (both venues close late Aug–mid July). There are also a large number of small classical music concert venues. See *Zurich News* or *Zurich Next* (both in English) or the weekend supplements of the local papers for listings and reviews.

For a drink with a view the **Jules Verne** is the city's highest bar, some 48m directly above the town on top of the Urania Observatory (see Sightseeing). Entrance is via the **Lipp Brasserie** (good French food, though slightly expensive), at *Uraniastr. 9.*

Fasnacht is celebrated in carnival style (Feb, early Mar), as in all major Swiss towns, but Zurich's very own carnival, the **Züri Fäscht**, is held only once every three years, over a single weekend at the beginning of July. The old town becomes one huge fairground and the highlight is a spectacular firework display over the lake. The *Fäscht* will next occur in 1997, then 2000.

Another colourful event is the **Sechseläuten**, Zurich's spring festival, usually held on the third Mon in Apr. The city's guilds parade in their historic costumes and a 'snowman' (made of cotton wool) known as the *Böögg* is stuffed with fireworks and ceremonially sacrificed in order to drive out the spirit of winter. A children's parade is held the day before.

SIGHTSEEING

Walking tours of the old town are conducted daily (May–Oct, Mon–Fri 1430, Sat, Sun 1000 and 1430), taking 2 hrs and costing SFr.18. Among other things, they will show you where luminaries such as Lenin lived (*Spielgasse 11*). For a sea-level view of the city take one of the low, Amsterdam-style, glass-roofed cruisers which operate a scheduled service along the **River Limmat** and out onto **Lake Zurich** (see River Journeys below). A circular cruise takes 50 mins.

Immediately north of HB, the **Landesmuseum** (Swiss National Museum) is the country's largest history museum, housed in a 19th-century mock castle. Among the many exhibits are some fascinating examples of religious art, an impressive display of ancient weaponry and reconstructed rooms from all periods. Allow a couple of hours here.

To get to the old town stroll along **Bahnhofstr.**, a famous and very expensive shopping street, which is also home to many of the country's major banking head offices. Rest awhile at one of the many outdoor cafés along here and ponder that until the 19th century this prestigious thoroughfare was actually a moat as part of the city's defences. Today, they say, Zurich's gold reserves lie beneath.

A trip up to the **Urania Observatory** (48 m) will give you a fine view right down into the centre of town. Turn left into **Augustinergasse**, a beautiful narrow street featuring many colourful carved oriel windows. *Augustinergasse* ends at the 13th-century **Peterskirche,** (St Peter's Church) which features a medieval tower dominated by an enormous 16th-century clock, claimed to be the biggest in Europe, with a diameter of 8.7 m.

Step into the small alleyway just in front and to the left of the church, to admire the famous decorated façade of the **Weinstube Zur Grossen Rebläube**, where Goethe stayed in 1779.

A few yards from Peterskirche is **Lindenhof**, the highest point of the old city and a popular meeting square, where locals play giant chess and visitors enjoy the views over the river. This is also an historic site as the Romans founded Zurich (*Turicum*) as a customs post here in 15BC. Look for a Roman tombstone at the top of *Pfalzgasse*, which runs through the square.

Pfalzgasse is crossed by *Fortunagasse* and if you have children in tow, walk downhill a few yards to the **Zürcher Spielzeugmuseum** (Zurich Toy Museum), at *no. 15*, a small exhibition of playthings past, going back to the late 18th century (open afternoons only, closed Sun).

Walk back to Peterskirche and behind here, at the western end of *Münsterbrücke*, is the 13th-century **Fraumünster**, famous for its charming Chagall stained glass. Adjacent is the **Zunfthaus zur Meise**, the old wine merchants' guild, built in 1757 and considered the finest baroque building in the city. It now houses the porcelain collection of the Swiss National Museum. Closeby on *Münsterhof* is another guildhall, the **Zunfthaus zur Waag** (formerly the headquarters of the linen weavers and hat makers), built in 1637. Like many of the city's surviving guildhalls, it is now a restaurant. Across *Münsterbrücke* stands the landmark twin towers of **Grossmünster** cathedral. This was the starting point of the Swiss Reformation where the fiery Huldrych Zwingli (1484–1531) preached 'work and pray' (a statue in front of Wasserkirche, see below, honours him). The oldest parts of this imposing building date back to the 11th/early 12th century. Inside is stained glass by Augusto Giacometti (1933) while in the crypt stands an impressive weather-worn 15th-century statue of Charlemagne, who founded the church. Nearby, **Wasserkirche** (Water Church) on *Limmatquai*, along the eastern river bank is

a lovely late Gothic structure attached to the 18th-century **Helmhaus** (the old cloth market) where contemporary fine art exhibitions are staged.

Walk back along *Limmatquai* past the rather plain **Rathaus** (town hall) to see more of the city's old guild halls, then walk uphill crossing busy *Niederdorfstr.*, to *Rindermarkt*, which leads into **Neumarkt**. This is one of the least unspoiled streets in the old town and it's worth a saunter along its entire length.

The **Kunsthaus** (Fine Arts Museum) lies just outside the old town on *Heimplatz* and has a world-class selection of pictures ranging from medieval times to the 20th century. From HB take tram no. 3 or bus 31. There's something for everyone here, from the best of Hodler, to a whole room of Chagall, superb Impressionist works, plus important exmples of Expressionism, Surrealism and Dadaism (the latter school was actually born in Zurich in 1916). It also includes a definitive collection of the distinctive skeletal sculptures by the noted Swiss artist, Alberto Giacometti (1901–66).

Also in this eastern section of town, within the huge ETH (Federal College of Technology) building, is the **Graphische Sammlung** (Graphics Collection), *Rämistr. 101.* (entrance on *Karl-Schmid-str.*). It contains superb changing displays of woodcuts, etchings and engravings by such masters as Dürer, Rembrandt, Goya and Picasso. The quick way pf reaching this part of town is the **SBG–Polybahn**, a funicular which rushes from Central (across *Bahnhof Brücke*) to the Polyterrace in just three mins. From here there are fine views of the city.

For more superb works of art, primarily from French artists of the 19th and 20th centuries (including Cézanne, Monet, Manet, Renoir) catch tram no. 2 or 4 to

329

the **Foundation Emil G Bührle Collection**, *Zollikerstr. 172*. From *Monet's Garden at Giverney* just a short walk away is the **Zürich Botanischer Garten**, *Zollikerstr. 107*. There are over 1.5 million plants here including rarities from Africa and New Caledonia.

Lakeside

From the end of *Bahnhofstr*, close to *Quai Brücke*, where the lake meets the river, it's a pleasant 5-min walk to the lakeside **Arboretum**. From here it's another 10-min walk (along *Breitingerstr.*, then *Seestr.*) to Rieter Park, where you will find the outstanding **Museum Rietberg**, *Gablerstr. 15*, displaying non-European arts. Alternatively take tram no. 6/7 from HB direct to Rieter Park, or better still take the *Limmatschiffahrt* to the Seerestaurant landing stage, close to both the Arboretum and to Rieter Park. (Note: if you want to see both of the city lake shores in the same excursion on the *Limmatschiffahrt*, then do the west bank first, as the service only crosses from west to east). The permanent collection of the Museum Rietberg is housed in the **Wesendonck Villa**, featuring works from Asia, Africa, Oceania and the Americas. The villa is also famous as a former cultural hub of Zurich, and Wagner lived here for several months. The adjacent **Rieter Park Villa** houses select masterpiece paintings from India, China and Japan which rotate regularly.

Catch the *Limmatschiffahrt* to **Zürichhorn**, a charming pleasure garden area with two major artisitic features. Jean Tinguely's kinetic iron sculpture, *Eureka*, has been dividing opinions here for over 30 years while the lovely **China Garten** (Chinese Garden), a very recent addition, draws almost universal approval. A 5-min walk west is the **Museum Bellerive**, *Höschgasse 3*. This features changing exhibitions of crafts from the art nouveau era to the present day. It's a 10-min walk walk back along *Uto Quai* to *Quai Brücke*.

OUT OF TOWN

For an overview of Zurich you can't beat the **Uetliberg**, due east of the centre. The **Uetliberg Railway** (S-Bahn no. 10) ascends from HB to Uetliberg station. It's then a short 58-m hike to the summit, **Uto-Kulm** (871m). This is the city's best-known and highest vantage point, with an excellent view of the Alps. From here there is a panoramic 1½–2-hr **promenade** to Felsenegg (810 m). En route is a **Planetary Path**, which attempts to give you an idea of how far apart the planets are in the solar system by accurately spacing models of each one. All you then have to do is multiply the actual space by one billion! From Felsenegg you can take the cable car to **Adliswil**, then S-Bahn no. 4 back to the city.

Also east of town, the **Zürich Zoo** boasts some 2700 animals and 350 species from around the world. It is set in parkland atop the **Zürichberg** (600 m) and makes a pleasant jaunt, especially for children. Take the Zoo-Tram no. 6 from HB or no. 5 from Bellevue.

Although there are the usual lake boat trips (fondue cruise, dance cruise, etc.,) **Rapperswil** is the only worthwhile destination on Lake Zurich. It takes 1hr 50 mins by boat or 40 mins by train (S-Bahn no. 5 or 7). It's a small, pretty, lakeside town, famous for its roses, and it has a castle which is worth a visit for the views it offers. Children will doubtless enjoy the **Knie Kinderzoo**, behind the station, with elephant rides and performing dolphins. And if you can't get to Rapperswil then maybe the elephants will come to you – the **Knie Circus** is a travelling troupe which frequently visits Zurich.

ZURICH–INNSBRUCK

> FASTEST JOURNEY: 4 HRS

The first part of this route follows the line of the Zurich–Rorschach itinerary (see p. 338–340). After Bregenz this main line route passes through the busiest of the Tyrolean valleys with its historic towns but also offers the chance of side trips up into delightful mountain villages and small resorts.

Bregenz
Zürich
Feldkirch
Buchs
Schruns
Bludenz
Ötztal
St Anton am Arlberg
Oetz
Sölden
Obergurgl
Innsbruck

TRAINS

ETT tables: 86, 308, 800a, 800.

FAST TRACK

Two through trains with two more services available by changing at Feldkirch. Journey time 4 hrs. Buffet facilities available on trains.

ON TRACK

Zurich–Bregenz

Four trains link Zurich with Bregenz each day taking 1 hr 40 mins. Other services are available by changing at St Martgrethen.

Bregenz–Feldkirch–Bludenz–St Anton am Arlberg–Ötztal–Innsbruck

One train every 2 hrs runs along this route.

Bregenz to Feldkirch takes 30 mins, Feldkirch to Bludenz 14 mins, Bludenz to St Anton 38 mins, St Anton to Ötztal 48 mins and Ötztal to Innsbruck 26 mins.

BREGENZ

Station: *Bahnhofstr.*, 300 m south of the lake, 500 m south-west of the town centre. **Tourist Office:** *Anton-Schneider-Str. 4A; tel: (05574) 42 3940.*

An old Roman town at the east end of the Bodensee (Lake Constance), the lakeside is the place for promenaders. The pedestrian *Altstadt* (or Oberstadt) stands above, with its delightful medieval streets and the **Martinsturm** in *Graf-Wilkhelmstr.* In its base is St Martin's chapel, founded 1363, with 14th-century murals. The **Vorarlberger Landesmuseum**, *Korn-*

marktpl., has a good collection of regional items dating back to prehistoric times.

Bregenz Music Festival in July offers open-air and indoor concerts, as well as opera and operettas from a floating stage on the lake.

FELDKIRCH

Station: *tel: (05522) 1717.* Rents bikes.
Tourist Office: *Herreng. 12; tel: (05522) 73467* Mon–Fri 0800–1200, 1400–1800, Sat 0900–1200 (ahead from station, left along *Bahnhofstr.* through underpass and along *Hirschgraben.* Turn left at tower and left again). The office offers free maps and leaflet in English on historic attractions, and runs free hiking and cycling tours.

ACCOMMODATION AND FOOD

Hotel Alpenrose, *Roseng. 4-6; tel: (05522) 72175* (expensive) is in the *Altstadt.* **Gasthof Lingg**, *Am Marktpl.; tel: (05522) 72062* (moderate) serves traditional food on the main square and offers four rooms. A chain with property here is *BW.* **HI: Jugendherberge Altes Siechenhaus**, *Reichstr. 111; tel: (05522) 73181*, Jan–Oct, in a 12th-century building, is a 12-min walk towards Levis. **Waldcamping Feldkirch-Gisingen**; *tel: (05522) 74308* offers a pool and park (bus nos. 1, 2 or 5).

Café Zanona, *Monfortg. 3,* does good lunches. The **Schattenburg Castle** serves *Wiener Schnitzel* and *Apfelstrudel.*

SIGHTSEEING

A small, fortified town, there are still remains of original walls at the *Hirschgraben* – Stag's Ditch – with the **Chur Gate**. The main attraction is strolling the streets and arcaded marketplace with the **St Johannkirche**, responsible for guarding the way through the Arlberg. **St Nikolauskirche**, with its 15th-century double nave, contains a pulpit which is the most famous piece of Gothic wrought iron in the country. A steep walk above the town is the **Schattenburg Castle**; *tel: (05522) 71982*, which houses a museum of art and local artefacts and tools.

A **Wine Festival** is held the second weekend July. The **Schubertiade** celebrates the music of Schubert in late June, with some of the biggest international names. Tickets from **Schubertiade GmbH**, *Schubertpl. 1, A-6800, Feldkirch; fax: (05522) 38005.* First weekend in Aug sees a festival of **Travelling Entertainers** with jugglers, mimes and clowns.

> **SIDE TRACKS**
> **FROM FELDKIRCH**

BUCHS

Station: *tel: 081 756 01 31.*
Tourist Office: *Bahnhofstr. 16; tel: 081 756 65 65.*
Buchs (20 mins by train from Feldkirch) is best known as one of the two Swiss gateways to Liechtenstein but merits a visit in its own right. There's nothing of interest actually in Buchs but walk all the way along *Bahnhofst.,* bear to the right and after 10–15 mins in total you will come to the picture-postcard hamlet of **Werdenberg** (there is an infrequent bus service from Buchs Bhf). A beautiful small lake provides a perfect reflecting foreground for a cluster of picturesque houses. Behind these are more ancient dwellings, balanced on wooden stilts at precarious angles, lining narrow streets which spiral up the small hill to **Schloss Werdenberg** (Werdenberg Castle), housing the local museum. ◪

BLUDENZ

Station: *tel: (05552) 611.*

Tourist Office: *Werdenbergerstr. 42; tel: (05552) 62170* (right out of the station and left up *Bahnhofstr.*, the second left and head to the far side of the modern *Rathaus* at the level above pavement). Open Mon–Fri 0800–1200, 1400–1730, plus Sat 0900–1200 (July, Aug and Dec), offers free city map and list of hotels and *Privatzimmer* which it will book ahead. There is an electronic booking board in the station. Guest Card (GC) reductions on guided walking tours Thurs mid-June–mid-Sept (ÖS25) and bike tours Wed end May–mid Sept (ÖS30). Bikes are available at **Schlosshotel Döflinger** (see below) ÖS220 a day. There are also free maps and tips for walkers. In in summer there are more than 400 km of marked hiking trails; in winter these become 10 skiing areas.

ACCOMMODATION AND FOOD

Schlosshotel Döflinger, *Schlosspl. 5; tel: (05552) 63016* (expensive) is the best hotel: modern but with traditional style. Cheaper are *Privatzimmer* like **Gastezimmer Laterner**, *Obdorfweg 21; tel: (05552) 62519* (budget) or **Gastezimmer Sapper**, *Ausstr. 67b; tel: (05552) 63060*

Schokoladefest

Outside Bludenz station is a large sign – SUCHARD. Walk up the steps to the right of the building that bears it and on weekday afternoons there's a shop open. It sells the chocolate produced here by the kilo – premier quality plus slightly cheaper rejects. If you feel in need of more make sure you're around for the town's *Schokoladefest*, every year in mid-July. It's the largest chocolate festival in the world with more than 100 games around the old town's streets. The prizes in every case are chocolate. The overall winner wins their weight in the stuff.

(budget). **Camping Seeberger**, is at *Obdorfweg 9; tel: (05552) 62512.* Two possible restaurants are **Fohrenburg**, *Werdenbergerstr. 53*, behind the Suchard factory, or **Fuchs**, *Sturneng. 2* in the *Altstadt*. The *Fussgängerzone* offer cheap eats.

SIGHTSEEING

There are **open-air concerts** in the *Schlosspl.* Fri (July, Aug) and folklore evenings July. Cobbled streets offer medieval buildings like the 15th-century **St Laurentiuskirche**, the 18th century baroque **Schloss** (now government offices), and the **Heimatmuseum**, *Herreng/Oberes Tor; tel: (05552) 63621*, has archive material dating from the Middle Ages.

> **SIDE TRACK**
> **FROM BLUDENZ**

A private railway runs up the **Montafon Valley** from Bludenz station. The last stop is **Schruns (station:** *tel: (05556) 7238217)* where Hemingway came to write. It's known for skiing, hosting some World Cup races, but is open for summer too, with a big outdoor swimming complex. The **Tourist Office:** *Silverettastr. 6; tel: (05556) 721660* (turn right out of station, first left and first right). Mon–Fri, 0800–1200, 1400–1800, Sat 0900–1200, 1600–1800, Sun 1030–1200 (June–Sept), Mon–Fri 0800–1200, 1400–1800 (Oct–May), it will check availability of accommodation. The office has hiking information and organises free summer hikes Tues and Thur. Cable cars from the town reach spectacular heights. 🏔

ST ANTON AM ARLBERG

Station: *tel: (05446) 2402385.* Rents bikes.
Tourist Office: *Arlberghaus; tel: (05446)*

22690, (down the slope from station, right on main street, forking off the main road towards a modern building). Open Mon–Fri 0800–1200, 1400–1800 (May–June), Mon–Fri 0800–1200, 1400–1800, Sat and Sun 1000–1200 (July–mid-Sept), Mon–Fri 0800–1200, 1400–1800 (mid-Sept–mid-Dec), Mon–Fri 0830–1200, 1430–1830, Sat 0900–1200, 1300–1900, Sun 1000–1200, 1500–1800 (mid-Dec–April). GC reduction in ski passes, skating, tennis, museum admissions etc. July–mid-Sept free weekly village guided tours, easy treks, Alpine flower trail free. Twice weekly more serious hikes; ÖS100.

ACCOMMODATION AND FOOD

A 24-hr electronic board and computer outside the Tourist Office offers accommodation information. Top of the range is **Hotel Schwarzer Adler**; *tel: (05446) 22440* (expensive) built as an inn in 1570. Cheaper options are *Privatzimmer*. A hotel chain with property here is *BW*.

The *Fussgängerzone* has various food shops and eating places. The **Aquila Konditorei** is the smart place for coffee and pastries. Top of the restaurants is **Raffl-Stube** in the **Hotel St Antoner Hof** with six exclusive tables. Traditional food is offered by **Arlberger Dorfstub'n** and by **Die Einkehr** in an 18th-century farmhouse.

SIGHTSEEING

Another World Cup venue, in 1907 this is where tourists were first taught to **ski**. The original school remains one of Austria's best with a second recently opened. Alternative **winter sports** include curling, skating, tobogganing, sleigh rides and mountain tours. The **Ski und Heimat Museum**, *Kadaharhaus tel: (05446) 2475*, looks at skiing plus the history of regional tribal migrations.

ÖTZTAL

Station: Ötztal Bahnhof, *tel: (05266) 88225,* is the stop for visits to the Ötz valley where a number of villages are reached by bus approx hourly Dec–March, July and Aug, six a day rest of year.

⤵ **SIDE TRACKS FROM ÖTZTAL**

Oetz is 7 km up the valley. **Tourist Office**: *tel: (05252) 6669* Mon–Fri 0830–1200, 1400–1800, Sat 0830–1200. This is an old village but has modern additions, largely for visitors. **Café Restaurant Heiner**, *Hauptstr. 58*, is the place to try coffee and pastries or one of the 10 types of eggnog.

Sölden Post, is more of a mountain resort, almost entirely purpose-built, connected by cable car to 10,000 ft on the **Gaislachkogel**, the highest glacier in Austria. A tunnel connects to the summer resort of **Rettenbach** with **Tiefenbach glacier**, used for summer skiing. The **Tourist Office**: *tel: (05254) 2212 0,* Mon–Sat 0800–1200, 1400–1800, will book accommodation for visitors on the spot,

Obergurgl; Tourist Office: *tel: (05256) 258,* Mon–Fri 0800–1800, Sat 0800–1200, 1330–1530 (July and Aug), Mon–Fri 0800–1200, 1400–1800 (Mar–June, Sept–Dec) Mon–Fri 0900–1230, Sat 0930–1230 (Jan, Feb). Obergurgl is the second highest parish in Europe. The landscape is well above the tree line – ideal for hay fever sufferers – but in summer softened by Alpine flowers. Its main business is skiing but in summer it is a big draw for mountain bikers and there is a climbing school. The Tourist Office offers a free walking map GC reductions on cablecars, sports, folk evening, guided mountain tours and biking. ⤢

ZURICH–LUCERNE

This journey into Central Switzerland explores the heart and history of the country. Zug and Schwyz both provide small-town charm and historic heritage, while the ascent of Mt Rigi will provide quite literally a bird's-eye view of the region's impressive topography. The initial part of the journey is dull, but the shoreline of Lake Zug is worth waiting for and the most scenic route on from Arth-Goldau is very definitely across Lake Lucerne.

FASTEST JOURNEY: **49** MINS

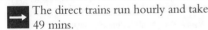

TRAINS

ETT tables: 295, 290.

FAST TRACK

The direct trains run hourly and take 49 mins.

ON TRACK

Zurich–Zug
Frequent service, around 30 mins.

Zug–Arth-Goldau
Hourly service, journey time 15 mins.

Arth-Goldau–Lucerne (Luzern)
Two trains an hour taking 29 mins.

ZUG

Station: *tel: 157 22 22.*
Tourist Office: City Reisebüro, *Bahnhofst. 23; tel: (042) 21 00 78.*

As you make the 10-min stroll along *Bahnhofstr.* towards the old centre of Zug the wealth of this small town is apparent in its prestigious office buildings. Favourable tax laws may have drawn investors to Zug but it is the delightful old town and lake front which attract more leisurely visitors.

The centre of Zug is **Kolinplatz**, marked by a colourful fountain statue of a knight and the blue-and-white tiled spire of the 16th-century **Zytturm** (Clock Tower). The entrance to the old town is beneath the tower but first explore the other side of *Kolinpl*. In very close proximity are **St Oswald's Church** (1478–1545), worth a look for its lovely sculptures; the **Afrika-Musem**, with a fine ethnographic collection and the **Museum in der Burg**. The 13th-century Burg (castle), an elevated half-timbered house with tower behind low battlemented walls, resembles more a fortified mansion than a conventional castle and contains some lively exhibits on the town's history. In the adjacent square are some very picturesque chalets and the **Kunsthaus** (Art Museum), with changing exhibitions of 20th-century art. Nearby are the 16th–17th-century **Kapuziner kloster, kirche** and **turm** (Capuchin cloister, church and tower).

The **Altstadt** (old town) is a little gem with many grand buildings dating from the 16th–18th centuries, a charming pastel-painted terrace of overhanging houses with delightful architectural detail. It opens onto the lake front where restaurants, cafés and a small aviary mark the start of the lovely promenade. This is a perfect spot to enjoy fish from the **Zugersee** (Lake Zug) and the famous Zug speciality, *Kirschtorte* (cherry tart), a deliciously moist almond pastry with a potent slug of cherry brandy.

HI: *Allmendstr. 8; tel: (042) 21 53 54*

SIDE TRACK
FROM ZUG

Take the Menzigen bus from the station for the 10-min journey to **Höllgrotte** (Hell's Grottos), one of the best stalactite and stalagmite caves in Switzerland, dramatically lit to live up to their fearsome name!

ARTH-GOLDAU

Arth-Goldau is the backdoor approach to the famous 'Queen of the Mountains' **Mt Rigi**. The view from here is rightly celebrated as one of the finest in the country, not for its height (a respectable 1798 m) but for its breadth and quality. Victor Hugo called it 'an incredible horizon'. Here, above a perfect vista of rolling high meadow, the Jura lies to one side, the Bernese Oberland to the other. Viewing the sunrise from the summit is a long-standing Rigi tradition but unless you plan to spend the night on the mountain it's easier to see it by sunset, then stay in Vitznau, Weggis or Lucerne (see p. 172).

It's a lovely 1-hr walk from the summit, **Rigi-Kulm**, to **Rigi-Scheidegg**, then back down to Arth-Goldau via Kräbel. Another popular alternative is to walk to **Rigi-Kaltbad** then descend to either **Weggis** or **Vitznau**, two of the lake's most charming resorts. The cable car goes down to Weggis ('the garden of Lucerne'), where there is a monument to Mark Twain, who stayed here. A venerable cog railway (the oldest in the world, built 1871) descends to Vitznau.

SIDE TRACK
FROM ARTH-GOLDAU

SCHWYZ

Station: Seewen; *tel: 157 22 22*, 2 km from centre of Schwyz (catch any bus marked Schwyz Post).
Tourist Office: in the Sparkasse Schwyz; *tel: (043) 22 19 91*.

Schwyz (pronounced Schweets) is

the birthplace of modern Switzerland, and has even given its name to the country. Here, in the **Bundesbrief-museum** (Swiss Federal Charters Archive Museum) – located between the station and the centre – you can see the original deeds of Union, signed by the cantons between 1291 and 1513, which led to the establishment of the Confederation of Switzerland.

The handsome cobbled main square, *Hauptplatz*, features the fresco-covered **Rathaus** and the beautiful baroque **Church of St Martin** (both built 1642). The latter is famous for its marvellous interior, considered to be one of the richest of any parish church in Switzerland. The town hall too is well worth a visit and features splendid panelling. Off *Hauptpl.* are many fine 17th- and 18th-century mansions. The best example of these, which is open to the public, is the **Ital-Redding Hofstat**, a short walk from the main square. The main house boasts some exquisitely panelled rooms while the attached **Bethlehem Haus**, built in 1297, is said to be the oldest wooden home in the country. Even more ancient is the **Turm zu Schwyz** (Schwyz Tower), dating from c.1200, just off *Hauptpl.*, which is also open to the public. Nearby the **Forum der Schweizergeschichte** (Museum of Swiss History) traces national and local history, and includes a number of interactive exhibits.

Opposite the station (cross under the subway) is the **Schaukäserei Schwyzerland** (Schwyz cheese dairy exhibition), a working dairy open to the public gaze. Its rustic restaurant, *tel: (043) 21 61 61,* is a very pleasant place to sample the local produce. ♿

337

ZURICH–RORSCHACH

The north east corner of Switzerland is one of the lower regions in the country so don't expect mountain vistas on this route. Winterthur, with its wealth of art museums, is probably best kept for a rainy day while St Gallen too has much to recommend indoors (though it would be a shame not to see its lovely architecture in bright sunlight). Appenzell on the other hand is very much outdoor country and an excursion into this region is literally a breath of fresh air from big-city life.

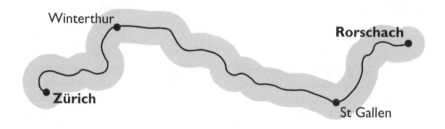

TRAINS

ETT tables: 308.

FASTEST JOURNEY: I HR 38 MINS

FAST TRACK

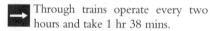 Through trains operate every two hours and take 1 hr 38 mins.

ON TRACK

 **Zurich–Winterthur**
Very frequent service taking 25 mins.

Winterthur–St Gallen
Frequent trains taking 43 mins.

St Gallen–Rorschach
Two trains every hour taking 15 mins.

WINTERTHUR

Station: *tel: 157 22 22.*
Tourist Office: *Bahnhofpl. 12; tel: (052) 212 00 88.*

The **HI** youth hostel is at *Schloss Hegi, Hegifeldstr. 125; tel: (52) 242 38 40.* A good place for reasonably priced food in the town centre is the **Café-Restaurant Obergasse**, *Obergasse/Schulgasse,* with pasta, salads and snacks.

Given Zurich's very fine collection of museums and galleries, it would ordinarily be difficult to justify a trip to a neighbouring town that had little to offer but more galleries – particularly when the main venue necessitates a bus ride from the station (no. 3 to *Spital* or no. 10 to *Haldengut*), plus a 10-min walk uphill! However, the **Oskar Reinhart Collection**, is no ordinary gallery, but an outstanding exhibition of 180 pictures, comprising many Old Masters and works by the great French painters and sculptors of the 19th century. Even non-art aficionados will recognise most of the artists' names and the quality of their work. Don't confuse this collection (based at art patron Reinhart's former home, 'Am Römerholz') with the **Oskar Reinhart Foundation**, in the centre of Winterthur. The latter comprises some 600 works by German, Swiss and Austrian artists, spanning the 18th and the 20th centuries and is a very fine collection, but lacks the star quality of the former.

Winterthur boasts several more museums within walking distance of the station. Ardent art lovers should complete their education at the **Kunstmuseum**, viewing an important collection of 19th- and 20th-century works from several famous names, and at the **Museum Jakob Briner**, which features some delightful works by 17th-century Dutch Masters. The latter is based in the **Rathaus** (town hall) alongside the **Uhrenmuseum** (Clock Museum).

ST GALLEN

Station: *tel: 157 22 22.*
Tourist Information: *Bahnhofpl. 1; tel: (071) 22 62 62.*

ACCOMMODATION AND FOOD

HI: *Jüchst. 25; tel: (071) 25 47 77*, a 20-min walk from Bhf; alternatively take bus no. 1 to *Singenberg* or the tram to

Schülerhaus, then it's a 7-min walk from either stop. Hotels are expensive and beds often scarce due to business conferences, particularly in April and Oct. Cheapest in the town centre are **Touring Garni**, *Engelgasse 8; tel: (071) 22 58 01*, and opposite, the **Weisses Kreuz**, *Engelgasse 9; tel: (071) 23 28 43.*

For a good choice of filling *rösti* dishes try the **Cafe-Restaurant Oberer Graben**, *Webergasse 8a; tel: (071) 22 48 44*, and don't forget to snack on the local speciality, *St Gallen bratwurst* (sausage), served with a warm bread roll.

SIGHTSEEING

St Gallen (or St Gall) is the seventh largest city in Switzerland and has been an important religious, commercial and cultural town for many centuries. It is famous for its landmark Kathedrale which dominates the charming pedestrianised old town which is full of architectural treats; colourful half-timbered turreted houses, carved balconies and ornate oriel windows are all very prominent. Look out in particular on *Galluspl.* and along *Gallusstr.*, *Schmiedgasse, Multergasse, Kugelgasse* and *Spisergasse.*

The **Kathedrale** was built between 1755 and 1768 and is a masterpiece – its interior is as huge and rich as any church in the country. The tour de force, however, is the adjacent **Stiftsbibliothek** (Collegiate Library). The manuscripts, of which around 500 alone date from the 8th to the 12th century, are impressive by any aesthtetic or historic yardstick, but it is the library itself which is breathtaking; built 1758–67 this flamboyant carved and gilded two-storey hall is the zenith of the rococo style in Switzerland.

To get a flavour of St Gallen's working past visit the excellent **Historisches Museum**, where you will learn, among

WINTERTHUR • ST GALLEN

other things, how it was once the world centre for embroidered textiles and about the lucrative 'white gold' linen trade (for more on this see the town's **Textilmuseum**, which is a lot more interesting than it sounds). The **Historisches Museum** also boasts an outstanding ethnographical collection, and adjacent is another museum complex housing the **Naturmuseum** and the **Kunstmuseum** (Art Museum).

↱ SIDE TRACK FROM ST GALLEN

From St Gallen it's possible to make a complete circuit of **Appenzellerland**, a verdant, hilly, pre-Alpine region wonderfully described by Herman Hesse as 'Sunday country'. The main settlement of the region, **Appenzell**, no more than a large village, is one of the country's most picturesque places

with many of its brightly-painted wooden houses dating back over 400 years. Nowadays it has become something of a tourist honeypot. One of the most photographed houses is the **Löwendrogerie** (chemist) on *Hauptgasse* though many visitors miss the charming parish church on the same street. There are two small museums here, one next to the tourist office, the other is in the **Blaues Haus**.

Appenzellerland is famous for its naive folk art paintings of classic Swiss pastoral landscapes and traditional scenes, usually featuring farmsteads, milkmaids and, of course, cows. You will see such paintings for sale (originals are extremely expensive), alongside other traditional arts and crafts items, in the many tourist and antique shops in the village. **Tourist information:** *Hauptgasse; tel: 071 87 96 41.*

Voting day

Landsgemeindeplatz, the oversize square in the centre of Appenzell, comes into its own once a year, on the last Sunday in April. This is voting day when the citizens of Appenzell turn out in their hundreds and raise their hands to decide *Landsgemeinde*, cantonal issues. Traditional dress is worn and the men carry swords or daggers, though not to influence the vote, it's an historical vestige of their proof of citizenship.

Such a show of democracy, however, belies how ultra-conservative the people of Appenzell really are. As recently as 1990, and only then after an appeal to the Swiss Supreme Court, were half the population finally allowed to raise their hands – and Appenzell thus became the last place in Europe to grant women the vote.

RORSCHACH

Stations: Rorschach Bahnhof, 2 km east of town, a 10–15-min walk from the centre. **Rorschach Hafen Bahnhof,** *tel: 157 22 22;* is right in the centre of town. **Tourist Office:** *Hauptstr. 63; tel: (071) 41 70 34.*

Rorschach isn't a particularly attractive place but its main sights all lie conveniently within a 5-min stroll of its quaint central (Rorschach Hafen) station. Directly opposite the station in the 18th-century **Kornhaus** (Corn Exchange building) is the town historical museum. Cross back over the tracks and a walk along the *Hauptstr.* will take you past a number of 16th–18th-century houses with fine oriel windows. Just off here, housed in the **Alten Garage** is a motor museum.

Try the relaxed modern **Café Mozart**, *Hafenzentrum; tel: (071) 41 06 32,* for light meals and cakes.

CONVERSION TABLES

DISTANCES (approx. conversions)
I kilometre (km) = 1000 metres (m) I metre = 100 centimetres (cm)

Metric	Imperial/US	Metric	Imperial/US	Metric	Imperial/US
I cm	3/8ths in.	10 m	33 ft (11 yd)	3 km	2 miles
50 cm	20 in.	20 m	66 ft (22 yd)	4 km	2½ miles
I m	3 ft 3 in.	50 m	164 ft (54 yd)	5 km	3 miles
2 m	6 ft 6 in.	100 m	330 ft (110 yd)	10 km	6 miles
3 m	10 ft	200 m	660 ft (220 yd)	20 km	12½ miles
4 m	13 ft	250 m	820 ft (275 yd)	25 km	15½ miles
5 m	16 ft 6 in.	300 m	984 ft (330 yd)	30 km	18½ miles
6 m	19 ft 6 in.	500 m	1640 ft (550 yd)	40 km	25 miles
7 m	23 ft	750 m	½ mile	50 km	31 miles
8 m	26 ft	I km	5/8ths mile	75 km	46 miles
9 m	29 ft (10 yd)	2 km	1½ miles	100 km	62 miles

24-HOUR CLOCK
(examples)

0000 = Midnight	1200 = Noon	1800 = 6 p.m.
0600 = 6 a.m.	1300 = 1 p.m.	2000 = 8 p.m.
0715 = 7.15 a.m.	1415 = 2.15 p.m.	2110 = 9.10 p.m.
0930 = 9.30 a.m.	1645 = 4.45 p.m.	2345 = 11.45 p.m.

TEMPERATURE
Conversion Formula: $°C \times 9 \div 5 + 32 = °F$

°C	°F	°C	°F	°C	°F	°C	°F
-20	-4	-5	23	10	50	25	77
-15	5	0	32	15	59	30	86
-10	14	5	41	20	68	35	95

WEIGHT
1kg = 1000g 100 g = 3½ oz

Kg	Pounds	Kg	Pounds	Kg	Pounds
I	2¼	5	11	25	55
2	4½	10	22	50	110
3	6½	15	33	75	165
4	9	20	45	100	220

FLUID MEASURES
I litre(l) = 0.88 Imperial quarts = 1.06 US quarts

Litres	Imp.gal.	US gal.	Litres	Imp.gal.	US gal.
5	1.1	1.3	30	6.6	7.8
10	2.2	2.6	35	7.7	9.1
15	3.3	3.9	40	8.8	10.4
20	4.4	5.2	45	9.9	11.7
25	5.5	6.5	50	11.0	13.0

MEN'S CLOTHES

UK	Europe	US
36	46	36
38	48	38
40	50	40
42	52	42
44	54	44
46	56	46

MENS' SHOES

UK	Europe	US
6	40	7
7	41	8
8	42	9
9	43	10
10	44	11
11	45	12

LADIES' CLOTHES

UK	France	Italy	Rest of Europe	US
10	36	38	34	8
12	38	40	36	10
14	40	42	38	12
16	42	44	40	14
18	44	46	42	16
20	46	48	44	18

MEN'S SHIRTS

UK	Europe	US
14	36	14
15	38	15
15½	39	15½
16	41	16
16½	42	16½
17	43	17

LADIES' SHOES

UK	Europe	US
3	36	4½
4	37	5½
5	38	6½
6	39	7½
7	40	8½
8	41	9½

HOTEL CODES
AND CENTRAL BOOKING NUMBERS

The following abbreviations have been used throughout the book to show which chains are represented in a particular town. Most chains have a centralised worldwide-reservations system in every country where they have hotels (occasionally these do not cover hotels within the country itself). Most telephone calls are either completely free (usually incorporating *800*) or charged at the rate for a local call (e.g. 0345 in the UK). (Aus= Australia, Can=Canada, Ger=Germany, Ire=Ireland, NZ=New Zealand, SA =South Africa, UK=United Kingdom, USA=United States of America, WW=Worldwide.)

Accor
This is a group name that encompasses Ibis, Mercure, Novotel and Sofitel, with central reservation numbers (handled by Resinter worldwide) that cover them all
Aus *(1 800) 642 244*
Can *(800) 221 4542*
UK *(0171) 724 1000*
USA *(800) 221 4542*

BW **Best Western**
Aus *(1 800) 222 422*
Can *(800) 528 1234*
Ire *(1 800) 709 101*
NZ *(09) 520 5418*
SA *(011) 339 4865*
UK *(0800) 393130*
USA *(800) 528 1234*

Ca **Campanile**
UK *(0181) 569 6969*
France *(1) 64 62 46 46*

Ch **Choice**
Aus *(008) 090 600*
Can *(800) 221 2222*
Ire *(1 800) 500 600*
NZ *(0800) 808 228*
UK *(0800) 444444*
USA:
(800) 228 5150
(Comfort)
(800) 228 5151
(Quality)

(800) CLARION (Clarion)
(800) 228 3323
(hearing impaired)
Cl **Comfort Inn**
see Choice
Ct **Climat de France**
Can *(514) 845 1236*
France *(05) 11 22 11*
UK *(0171) 287 3181*
USA *(800) 332 5332*
Do **Dorint**
WW: (0800) 960024
Ev **Exclusive**
See Forte (FE)
Ex **Excelsior**
UK *(0345) 40 40 40*
FE **Forte**
(Also covers Exclusive)
Aus *(008) 222 446*
Can *(800) 225 5843*
Ire *(01) 764 401*
NZ *(0800) 801 111*
SA *(011) 442 9201*
UK *(0345) 404040*
USA *(800) 225 5843*
Fm **Forum**
See Inter-Continental (IC)
GT **Golden Tulip**
Aus *(008) 221 176*
Can/USA *(800) 344 1212*
Ire *(01) 872 3300*
NZ *(0800) 656 666*
SA *(011) 331 2672*
UK *(0800) 951 000*
Hd **Holiday Inn**

Aus *(800) 221 066*
Can *(800) 465 4329*
Ire *(1 800) 553 155*
NZ *(0800) 442 222*
SA *(011) 482 3500*
UK *(0800) 897121*
USA *(800) 465 4329*
HI **Hostelling International**
UK *(0171) 248 6547*
Hn **Hilton**
Aus *(1 800) 222 255*
Can *(800) 445 8667*
NZ *(0800) 448 002*
SA *(011) 880 3108*
UK *(0345) 581595*
USA *(800) 445 8667*
Ib **Ibis**
See Accor
IC **Inter-Continental**
(Also covers Forum)
Aus *(008) 221 335*
Can/USA *(800) 327 0200*
NZ *(0800) 654 343*
SA *(011) 331 7422*
UK *(0345) 581444*
IH **Inter Hotel**
France: *(1) 42 06 46 46*
UK *(0171) 287 3231*
Ke **Kempinski**
Can *(800) 426 3135*
UK *(0800) 898588*
USA *(800) 426 3135*
(Also bookable through Lufthansa)

Ma **Marriott**
Aus *(1 800) 251 259*
Can *(800) 228 9290*
NZ *(0800) 441 035*
UK *(0800) 221222*
USA *(800) 228 9290*

Mc **Mercure**
Can *(800) MERCURE*
UK *(0181) 741 3100*
USA *(800) MERCURE*
(Also see Accor)

Mv **Mövenpick**
Switz *(01) 712 22 22*
UK *(0800) 898317*
USA *(800) 344 6835*

Nv **Novotel**
Can *(800) NOVOTEL*
UK *(0181) 748 3433*
USA *(800) NOVOTEL*
(See also Accor)

Pe **Penta**
UK *(0990) 300200*

Pu **Pullman Hotels**
see Accor

RC **Relais & Chateaux**
France *(1) 45 72 90 00*
Aus *(02) 957 4511*
UK *(0171) 287 0987*
USA *(212) 856 0115*

Rd **Radisson**
See SAS

Rk **Romantik**
Ger *(06188) 95020*
Aus *(02) 968 1783* or
(02) 957 0538
Can *(416) 695 1449*
Ire *(01) 661 9466*
NZ *(09) 799 716*
UK *(0181) 392 1589*
or *(0171) 408 0111*
USA – bookable
through all AAA travel
agencies

Rn **Renaissance**
see Ramada

Rm **Ramada**
Aus *(1 800) 222 431*
Can *(800) 854 7854*
Ire *(1 800) 252 627*

NZ *(0800) 441 111*
UK *(0800) 181737*
USA *(800) 854 7854*

RS **Relais du Silence**
France *(1) 45 66 53 53*

Rz **Ritz Carlton**
Aus *(1 800) 252 888*
NZ *(800) 443 030*
UK *(0800) 234000*

SA **SAS**
(Also covers Radisson)
Aus *(1 800) 333 333*
Can *(800) 333 3333*
Ire *(1 800) 557 474*
NZ *(0800) 443 333*
UK *(0800) 191991*
USA *(800) 333 3333*

Sc **Scandic (Crown)**
UK *(0800) 416 614*

Sf **Sofitel**
Can *(800) SOFITEL*
UK *(0181) 741 9699*
USA *(800) SOFITEL*
(See also Accor)

Sh **Sheraton**
Aus *(008) 073 535*
Can *(800) 325 3535* or
(800) 325 1717 (hear-ing impaired)
Ire *(1 800) 535 353*
NZ *(0800) 443 535*
UK *(0800) 353535*
USA *(800) 325 3535*
or *(800) 325 1717*
(hearing impaired)

SL **Small Luxury**
Aus *(008) 251 958*
Can *(800) 525 4800*
NZ *(0800) 441 098*
SA *(011) 331 2911*
UK *(0800) 282124*
USA *(800) 525 4800*

Sn **Supranational**
(Also covers
Concorde, Reso,
Sokos and Welcome
Swiss)
Can *(800) 843 3311*
UK *(0500) 303030*

Ire *(01) 660 5000*
SA *(0800) 119 000*
USA *(800) 843 3311*
USA *(800) 336 3542*

Sw **Swissôtel**
Switz *(01) 812 54 51*
Can *(800) 637 9477*
UK *(0800) 614145*
USA *(800) 637 9477*
(Also bookable
through Swissair)

Tp **Top**
Ger *(0211) 57 80 75*
Aus *(008) 221 176*
Ire *(01) 872 3953*
NZ *(09) 303 4526*
SA *(011) 312 672*
UK *(0171) 402 8182*
or *(0181) 446 0126*
or *(0990) 300 200*
USA *(800) 223 6764* or
(800) 44 UTELL
(Also bookable
through Lufthansa)

WS **Welcome Swiss**
See Supranational

343

Swiss Chains

The following abbreviations refer to hotel chains in Switzerland. The telephone numbers given are local, so include the dialling code for Switzerland if calling from outside that country.

AC Alpine Classics
(01) 482 19 81

EG E&G Hotels Schweiz
(036) 53 44 88

IE Inter-Europe-Hotels
(041) 40 22 44

MZ Manz Privacy Hotels
(01) 211 55 00

MO MinOtel Suisse
(021) 320 46 38

Ss Swiss Leading Hotels
(01) 383 96 96

THROUGH ROUTES

Some travellers will want to start their journey in Western Europe and join the Alpine routes in this book at the gateway cities of Basel, Lyon, Milan, Munich, Nice, Venice, Vienna and Zurich. The following table shows a selection of possible through routes, as an aid to journey planning, with approximate summer frequencies. All these through routes may also be taken in the reverse direction to that shown but the number of trains per day may differ. Some of the trains require payment of supplements and many involve overnight travel. Not all services are daily. Always consult the international section in the latest issue of the *Thomas Cook European Timetable* (ETT), which gives up-to-date schedules for these and many other international long-distance trains. Services shown from London include travel through the Channel Tunnel.

Through Route	ETT table no.	Approx journey time	Trains daily	Notes
Amsterdam–Munich	28	11 hrs	1	Overnight train
Amsterdam–Basel	73	8-11 hrs	3	1 overnight train
Amsterdam–Vienna	28	15 hrs	1	Overnight train
Barcelona–Milan	90	13 hrs	1	Overnight train
Barcelona–Zurich	81	13 hrs	1	Overnight train
Berlin–Vienna	60	10-11 hrs	2	1 overnight service
Berlin–Munich	770	8 hrs	7	1 overnight train
Berlin–Zurich	71	12 hrs	1	Overnight train
Brussels–Basel	40	7 hrs	4	1 overnight train
Brussels–Munich	21	11 hrs	1	Overnight train
Brussels–Vienna	21	14 hrs	1	Overnight train
Cologne–Zurich	73	6 hrs	1	Change at Basel for other services
Cologne–Munich	650	5½ hrs	11	Direct
Cologne–Vienna	66	10 hrs	6	2 overnight trains
Copenhagen–Basel	50	16 hrs	1	Overnight service
Copenhagen–Munich	50	15 hrs	1	Overnight service
London–Basel	40	12 hrs	3	Change at Brussels
London–Munich	21	16 hrs	1	Change at Brussels
London–Vienna	21	19 hrs	1	Change at Brussels
Paris–Zurich	41	6-8 hrs	3	1 overnight service
Paris–Lyon	150	2 hrs	20	Direct
Paris–Nice	164	7-10 hrs	5	3 overnight trains
Rome–Milan	370	4-8 hrs	19	1 overnight service
Rome–Venice	370	5-8 hrs	9	1 overnight train

345

346

ORDER FORM
European Rail Passes
Prices are U.S. $ Effective until December 31, 1996

AVAILABLE IN NORTH AMERICA ONLY

AUSTRIA RAILPASS
Any 4 Days in 10 Days   ❏ $165 1st Class
   ❏ $111 2nd Class

ITALIAN RAILPASS
Please add a $15 admin. fee to the cost of each Italian pass/non-refundable

	1st Class	2nd Class
8 Days	❏ $248	❏ $168
15 Days	❏ $312	❏ $208
21 Days	❏ $362	❏ $242
1 Month	❏ $436	❏ $290

ITALIAN FLEXI RAILCARD
Any 4 Days in 1 Month	❏ $194	❏ $132
Any 8 Days in 1 Month	❏ $284	❏ $184
Any 12 Days in 1 Month	❏ $356	❏ $238

ITALIAN KILOMETRIC TICKET
3,000 Kilometers in 20 Trips.
❏ $264 *1st Class*   ❏ $156 *2nd Class*

HUNGARIAN FLEXIPASS
Any 5 Days in 15   ❏ $55 *1st Class*
Any 10 Days in 1 Month   ❏ $69 *1st Class*

BULGARIAN FLEXIPASS
Any 3 Days in 1 Month   ❏ $70 *1st Class*

EUROPEAN EAST PASS
Any 5 Days in 15   ❏ $195 *1st Class*
Any 10 Days in 1 Month   ❏ $299 *1st Class*

SWISS PASS
Good on Swiss National Railroads, most private railroads, lake steamers, city transport, trams, etc.

	Adults		Couples/each	
	1st Cl.	2nd Cl.	1st Cl.	2nd Cl.
4 Days	❏ $264	❏ $176	❏ $198	❏ $132
8 Days	❏ $316	❏ $220	❏ $237	❏ $165
15 Days	❏ $368	❏ $256	❏ $276	❏ $192
1 Month	❏ $508	❏ $350	❏ $381	❏ $262⁵⁰

SWISS FLEXIPASS
Any 3   ❏ $264 ❏ $176 ❏ $198 ❏ $132
Days in 15 Days
(Couples Passes valid 5/1/96 - 10/31/96 only)

SWISS CARD
1 Month/1 Round Trip   ❏ $142   ❏ $116

GERMAN RAILPASS – Adult
Validity	1st Cl./Twin*	2nd Cl./Twin*
5 Days in 1 Mo.	❏ $260/$390	❏ $178/$267
10 Days in 1 Mo.	❏ $410/$615	❏ $286/$429
15 Days in 1 Mo.	❏ $530/$795	❏ $386/$579

*Twin: Total price valid for 2 people traveling together. Youth rates available.

PRAGUE EXCURSION PASS
From any Czech Republic border crossing to Prague and return First Class – within 7 days.
❏ $49 Adult   ❏ $39 Youth   ❏ $25 Child

CZECH FLEXIPASS
Any 5 Days in 15   ❏ $69 *1st Class*

ROMANIAN PASS
Any 3 Days in 15   ❏ $60 *1st Class*

347

SHIPPING There is a $9.50 handling and priority shipping charge for all US, APO/FPO orders using 2nd Day/AIR UPS. Rush service with overnight delivery is available for $25. We can not ship overseas. RAIL/DRIVE Programs are available for many countries. Call for rates and free brochures.

RAIL PASSES NOT SHOWN FOR: Spain, Benelux, France, Hungary, Portugal, Greece, Scandinavia, Finland and Norway. Call for rates and plans.

INDEX

READER SURVEY

If you enjoyed using this book, or even if you didn't, please help us improve future editions by taking part in our reader survey. Every returned form will be acknowledged, and to show our appreciation we will give you £1 off your next purchase of a Thomas Cook guidebook. Just take a few minutes to complete and return this form to us.

When did you buy this book? _____

Where did you buy it? (Please give town/city and if possible name of retailer)
_____

When did you/do you intend to travel in Alpine Europe?
_____

For how long (approx.)? _____
How many people in your party? _____

Which cities and other locations did you/do you intend mainly to visit?
_____
_____
_____

Did you/will you:
☐ Make all your travel arrangements independently?
☐ Travel on an Inter-Rail pass? ☐ Travel on a Eurail Pass?
☐ Use other passes or tickets, please give brief details: _____
_____

Did you/do you intend to use this book:
☐ For planning your trip?
☐ During the trip itself?
☐ Both?

Did you/do you intend also to purchase any of the following travel publications for your trip?
Thomas Cook European Timetable
Thomas Cook New Rail Map of Europe
Thomas Cook European Travellers Phrase Book
Other guidebooks or maps, please specify

Have you used any other Thomas Cook guidebooks in the past? If so, which?
_____
_____

Please rate the following features of On the Rails around The Alps for their value to you (Circle VU for 'very useful', U for 'useful', NU for 'little or no use'):

The 'Travel Essentials' section on pages 15–27	VU	U	NU
The 'Travelling by Train' section on pages 28–36	VU	U	NU
The 'Country by Country' section on pages 37–63	VU	U	NU
The recommended routes throughout the book	VU	U	NU
Information on towns and cities	VU	U	NU
The maps of towns and cities	VU	U	NU
The colour rail maps	VU	U	NU

Please use this space to tell us about any features that in your opinion could be changed, improved, or added in future editions of the book, or any other comments you would like to make concerning the book:

352

Your age category: ☐ 21-30 ☐ 31-40 ☐ 41–50 ☐ over 50

Your name: Mr/Mrs/Miss/Ms
(First name or initials)
(Last name)

Your full address: (Please include postal or zip code)

Your daytime telephone number:

Please detach this page and send it to: The Project Editor, On the Rails around The Alps, Thomas Cook Publishing, PO Box 227, Peterborough PE3 8BQ, United Kingdom.

We will be pleased to send you details of how to claim your discount upon receipt of this questionnaire.